Engineering America

Engineering America

The Life and Times of John A. Roebling

RICHARD HAW

OXFORD
UNIVERSITY PRESS

Oxford University Press is a department of the University of Oxford. It furthers
the University's objective of excellence in research, scholarship, and education
by publishing worldwide. Oxford is a registered trade mark of Oxford University
Press in the UK and certain other countries.

Published in the United States of America by Oxford University Press
198 Madison Avenue, New York, NY 10016, United States of America.

CIP data is on file at the Library of Congress
ISBN 978–0–19–066390–2

1 3 5 7 9 8 6 4 2

Printed by Sheridan Books, Inc., United States of America

For Ella, with all my love

Whenever necessity calls for new works of art, new expedients will be discovered, adapted to the occasion. It will no longer suit the spirit of the present age to pronounce an undertaking impracticable. Nothing is impracticable, which is within the scope of natural laws.

—John A. Roebling, 1852

CONTENTS

PART III   MASTER (1848–69)

ACKNOWLEDGMENTS

This is my first biography, and I'm really not sure how I would have gotten on without the assistance of dozens of local historians, archivists, and other enthusiasts. It also took me so long to write that I have no idea if any of these wonderfully helpful people are still where I first encountered them. Even so, in an effort to express my heartfelt thanks, I'll risk my ignorance. Many thanks to, in no particular order: Amy Rupert, Jenifer Monger, and Tammy Gobert at the Institute Archives and Special Collections, Rensselaer Polytechnic Institute; Fernanda Perrone, Helene van Rossum, David Kuzma, and Christine A. Lutz at Special Collections and University Archives, Rutgers University Libraries; Lisa Lazar, Mary Jones, and Tim Breslin at the John Heinz History Center / Historical Society of Western Pennsylvania; Lu Eisler at the Butler Public Library; Sara Jane at the Butler County Historical Society; Douglas Bosley from the National Park Service; Albert M. Tannler at the Pittsburgh History and Landmarks Foundation; Sarah Buffington at Old Economy Village; everyone in the Kentucky History Department at the Kenton County Public Library, Covington, and in the microfilm and local history departments at the Hamilton Public Library in Cincinnati; everyone at the Cincinnati Historical Society Library, especially M'Lissa Kesterman; the late David Shayt from the Smithsonian Institution; Anke Weisbrich at the Mühlhäuser Museen; Cynthia Van Ness at the Buffalo and Erie County Historical Society; Nancy Conod at the Minisink Valley Historical Society; Sarah Piccini and Mary Ann Moran-Savakinus at the Lackawanna Historical Society; Laura R. Brooks at the University of Pittsburgh; Sandy Marsh at the Ellenville Public Library and Museum; Carol Salomon and Katie Blumenkrantz at the Cooper Union Library; Andrew Porteus and Linda Reinumagi at the Niagara Falls Public Library; Aaron McWilliams at the Pennsylvania State Archives; Varissa McMickens Blair and Martha Moore at the Roebling Museum; Kaitlyn Pettengill at the Historical Society of Pennsylvania; Kathleen Dow and Kate Hutchens at the Special Collections Library, University of Michigan; all the members of the Lloyd Sealy Library at John Jay College of Criminal Justice, especially Karen Okamoto, who unfailingly delivered my interlibrary loan requests; and to everyone else who answered questions, pulled materials, found microfilms, or otherwise helped guide me around their archives and resources but whose names I embarrassingly failed to write down. Thank you all for your time, your goodwill, and your help.

In other capacities, Bob Kaltenhauser took time out to kindly show me around Saxonburg. Josiah Simon was an invaluable help with translation. Tonie Malone, Bernd Nebel, James Storrow, and Clifford Zink were all generous enough to reply to emails and send me materials. I have by now spent hours and hours talking over the project with David Nye and Erica Wagner, and their insights and input have enriched this book enormously. Betsy Gitter helped me think about Johanna. Jerry Markowitz read all the early chapters, offering excellent counsel and invaluable support. Several PSC-CUNY Research Awards, a grant from John Jay's Office for the Advancement of Research, and a CUNY Book Completion Award were all crucial in securing images and permissions and sponsoring research trips. At Oxford University Press, Dave McBride offered good advice and great friendship. Susan Ferber's enthusiasm was a real boon, while her editing was a marvel of skill, patience, and good grace, especially after my word count came in so extravagantly over budget. Thank you all.

I owe a huge debt to all who have written or thought about the Roeblings (and nineteenth-century suspension bridges) over the years: Dave Billington, Francis E. Griggs, Eda Kranakis, Emory Kemp, David McCullough, Tom F. Peters, and Henry Petroski especially. My understanding of John's life in Germany would be much the poorer—as would everyone else's—without the diligent and painstaking work of Nele Guentheroth, Andreas Kahlow, Eberhard Grunsky, and Christiane and Horst Vielhaber. The late Don Sayenga has long set the standard for researching and thinking about the Roeblings. He read every chapter with boundless enthusiasm and great warmth and heart. This book is much better for all his help, as was the experience of writing it. He was a wonderful person—kind, funny, generous—and I am immeasurably proud to have called him my friend and equally sad that he did not live to see this work published.

At John Jay, I have been lucky to find great friends in all sorts of places. For their excellent good cheer and for almost always knowing when I needed a drink, I would like to thank Priscila Acuna, Valerie Allen, Michael Blitz, Erica Burleigh, Alexa Capeloto, Susannah Crowder, Yasmin Dalisay, Katie Gentile, Amy Green, David Green, Devin Harner, Chris Head, Lila Kazemian, Nathan Lents, Pat Licklider, Christen Madrazo, John Matteson, Jean Mills, Paul Narkunas, Allison Pease, Adriana Pérez, Nina Rose Fischer, Dennis Sherman, Karen Terry, and Liza Yukins. Caroline Reitz especially has spent hours talking about John Roebling and the nineteenth century with me. She read the entire manuscript, offering all sorts of brilliant suggestions along the way. I will never be able to thank her enough for her love and support.

This book is dedicated to my daughter, Ella. She was born during the very early stages of writing the book and has shown great patience with her dada over the years since then. She is the light in my world and the laughter in my heart. While there's much less Harry Potter in this book than I suspect she'd prefer, I hope she eventually finds something to like about it anyway.

Engineering America

Introduction

"Fitting One's Self to the New World"

On May 23, 1831, the transatlantic packet boat *August Eduard* sailed up the Wesser River, edged past Bremerhaven, and glided out into the North Sea. On board were a random collection of German tradesmen: watchmakers, cobblers, farmers, tanners. Some were intellectuals, many were dreamers; all were bound for a new life in the New World. Most of the travelers belonged to the Mühlhausen Emigration Society and hoped to set up camp somewhere in the United States. Their leader was a twenty-four-year-old construction-site supervisor who failed to finish university, had been unemployed for almost three years, and had never previously traveled more than a couple of hundred miles from the town of his birth. His name was Johann August Röbling.

While skirting the length of the Frisian Islands, Johann busied himself finding his sea legs and helping to get everyone else settled. When he wasn't bent over the ship's railing dealing with a violent bout of seasickness or fussing around asking countless questions, he was busy recording his thoughts and impressions in his diary. Mostly he was curious and excited, but as the *August Eduard* left the English Channel and sailed out into the Atlantic, Johann's mood turned plaintive. "As we see the last of the shores of Europe vanish from our sight, we separate ourselves at a single stroke from the Old World," from all that is known and familiar. Fortunately, the long voyage across the great ocean provides "time and leisure enough to . . . prepare one's self mentally" for the rupture. Out on the ocean "everything moves more freely," and "the sight of the open, wide sea serves altogether to arouse the feeling of personal freedom and natural independence in every breast." "All impressions, which America will make upon us," Johann reasoned, "will in reality be new, no matter how familiar we may already have made ourselves with the new continent." Upon arrival, the colonists would discover an unfamiliar "national character" and an entirely new set of "political institutions." It would be easy to accept much that is good and honorable, but there would also be much that "will appear offensive to us, and there will be much which concerns the people, its disposition, and its character, which we cannot approve." Only the future can "teach us to what degree the picture we have sketched of the United States agrees with the reality," Johann reflected, but in the meantime they must prepare themselves: their most important effort would "consist in shaking off the old European prejudices and fitting one's self to the New World." After all, "every people demands of a foreigner . . . that he will assimilate himself to his environment as soon as possible."[1]

Johann's message was simple, both to himself and to his fellow emigrants: cast off the old and embrace the new. This was no idle cliché, but a heartfelt admonition he had struggled with his entire life. Johann's first twenty-four years were defined by a personal battle, a contest between the staid influence of place and the dynamic context of historical change. The place was Johann's hometown of Mühlhausen, a sleepy walled town—medieval in both look and feel—where his relatives were elder statesmen and where nothing much had happened in quite some time, which was how the townsfolk liked it. Established tradition ruled in Mühlhausen, and any change was viewed with skepticism at best, hostility almost always. Unfortunately for Mühlhausers, by the time the nineteenth century rolled around and Johann appeared on the scene, the forces of modernity— social, political, industrial—had been unleashed and were gathering steam. The Industrial Revolution recast how people understood their place in the landscape; the French Revolution reshaped how people understood their relation to each other and to their nations. Everything Johann experienced as a child and young adult flowed directly from one of these two events, despite the heavy, confining influence of Mühlhausen.

Johann spent his youth and early manhood in a world clinging desperately to the past while simultaneously hurtling pell-mell into an uncertain future. His burden was to choose: fidelity to family, home, and the past or to the coming world; to stay and settle or to jump into modernity's rising vortex? Johann leapt, committing himself to a lifelong act of creation and a new anglicized name: John Roebling. He would take his newfound "personal freedom" and "natural independence" and go looking. He would embrace new ideas, unearth new laws, and build new things. Investigation, invention, ambition, and growth became his watchwords and guiding principles, but they came with a deep-rooted contradiction: John's desire for freedom coexisted with a lifelong need for order and control. As a child of Napoleonic Europe, he longed for an end to discord and disarray. As a student in Berlin, he yearned to escape from the repressive crackdowns that followed in the Little Corporal's wake. As an engineer he dreamed of visionary new structures rooted in the minutiae of technical precision. As a new American he wished for the liberty of individualism amid the structure of a well-planned community. As a keen thinker and philosopher, he craved a precise understanding of the world that rejected religious traditions and embraced new ideas. Such were the constants—and the contradictions—in his life. John's mind and character were seldom in balance and at rest, even while he sought harmony above all things, which is what led him to the *August Eduard* and the great expanse of the Atlantic Ocean.

———

John's life in Prussia had been formative. After a youth spent amid the chaos and destruction of the Napoleonic Wars and the social control that followed in their wake, John earned a seat at the prestigious national Building Academy in Berlin, where he heard G. W. F. Hegel lecture on logic, experienced the rising might and the promise of the Industrial Revolution, and was introduced to the fledgling science of suspension bridges. He became enthralled by all three. After several years building roads in Westphalia and kicking about his hometown, he boarded the *August Eduard* hoping to establish a communal settlement in America along principles he had worked out (and published) with his friend and fellow technological visionary John Etzler. He succeeded only in establishing Saxonburg, Pennsylvania, a rather humdrum little village. Returning to engineering—the one thing he was good at—John worked on a variety of internal improvements projects: designing canals, surveying railroad routes, designing dams and locomotives. In 1841, he hit on the idea of making rope out of spiraled wire, a notion that made his fortune.

John worked furiously throughout the 1840s, bursting into the consciousness of the world's engineering community with a series of daring plans and proposals, even while his achievements were rather more modest: three suspension aqueducts and a single suspension bridge. During the same time, he also built up his wire rope works into a large national industry, so much so that by the end of the decade he was forced to move his entire operation east. He spent the next two decades only somewhat less furiously realizing all the plans and ideas he had proposed and establishing himself as America's preeminent bridge builder. He built the world's first functioning railroad suspension bridge (over the Niagara Falls gorge) and the first structure to link a Northern state with a Southern one after the Civil War (the Covington and Cincinnati Suspension Bridge). In 1867, he was awarded the contract to build a massive 1,600-foot span over the East River between the independent cities of New York and Brooklyn, a project he had actively lobbied for since 1857. On the verge of commencing his dream project, Roebling suffered a bizarre accident at the bridge site. He was soon diagnosed with tetanus, and he died in agony on July 22, 1869, several months before construction of his dream bridge had even begun.

Like his finest creations, John was held together by the delicate balance of countervailing forces. On the surface, he led an exemplary public life, and his accomplishments were legion. As an immigrant, community builder, manufacturer, and employer, he was admired and respected. As an inventor and engineer, his works profoundly altered the physical landscape of America. John believed in the moral application of science and technology, that great works of connection—bridges, railroads, the Atlantic cable—could help bring people together, erase divisions, heal wounds, and bring about a fairer and more equal society. He was deeply committed to the creation of a more perfect union, forged from the raw materials of the continent. He was a fervent abolitionist, a deep and voracious reader of philosophy, a proficient linguist, and an accomplished musician. Yet John's public persona—engaged, calm, rational, and specific—was offset by private mania. Behind closed doors he was intense, fierce, and often irrational. Oddly for a technical genius, John's understanding of the natural world bordered on the occult, and his opinions about medicine are best described as medieval. For a man of science and great self-certainty, he was also remarkably quick to seize on fads and foolish trends. He believed not just in science but also in the spirit world, in wrapping himself in a wet sheet at night, and in chewing charcoal on a daily basis. The two poles of Roebling's personality played out most poignantly in his relationship with his first and most burdened son. Washington Roebling was awed and inspired by his father; privately, he feared him and was haunted by their relationship. "Roebling was a great man," Washington once remarked, but "there was something of the tiger about him."[2]

John was a complex, deeply divided, yet undoubtedly influential figure—one of the foremost engineers in a century defined by engineering—and his biography illuminates not only his works but also the world of nineteenth-century America. Yet, while John's engineering feats are well known, the man himself is not, for alongside the drama of large-scale construction lies an equally rich drama of intellectual and social development and crisis, one that mirrored and reflected the great forces, trials, and failures of the American nineteenth century. Unfortunately, John has proved a hard man to know. Many of the details of John's life were invented or enhanced in the late nineteenth and early twentieth centuries by John's descendants in an effort to sanctify and sanitize his image, most of which has simply been repeated in books and articles over the years. Few people have gone to the archives to seek him out, ensuring that the story of John's story has remained thin. In 1972, while compiling the bibliography for *The Great Bridge*, David McCullough noted that there was "no first-rate biography" of John. Nothing in the intervening time has altered this fact.[3]

Engineering America is a book about one man's struggle to define himself: to learn, adapt, and change; to keep moving in new and unfamiliar directions; and to achieve independence, even as he clung to his own fixed ideas and opinions. It is about how Johann August Röbling, the third child of a provincial Prussian tobacconist, became John A. Roebling, CE, world-renowned American engineer and wealthy manufacturer. It is also the story of how a liberty-loving Democrat became first a corporate Whig and then an entrenched Republican. More broadly, this is a book about the nineteenth century: about Jacksonian and pre–Civil War America; about the market, transportation, and communications revolutions; about shifting notions of freedom and liberty, slavery and dependence; politics and philosophy; immigration and community; science and superstition; about a nation's passage from individualism to incorporation. And it is about one man's place within it all, as a witness, a participant, and a driving force.

John's life naturally breaks down into three parts, reflected in the structure of this book: "Novice (1806–31)," "Apprentice (1831–47)," and "Master (1848–69)." The years 1831 and 1846 were the two great linchpins in John's life, the years in which he stopped being an uncertain struggling young man striving to find an identity and a career, and started being an established engineer and manufacturer confident in his abilities and his place in the world. The year 1831 was one of profound decision and tremendous upheaval for John. The year 1846 was one of herculean effort, great vision, and creative achievement: he built his second, acclaimed suspension bridge; secured the long-term viability of his wire-rope business; toured New York for the first time; and drew up plans for several huge new bridges. Before the year was out, he had also conceived an audacious plan to build a massive Y-shaped bridge to stretch out from the point of Pittsburgh and branch off to either side of the Ohio River. In 1846-47, Roebling set the goals for much of the rest of his life, and he spent his remaining years fulfilling them. From 1832 until 1847, Roebling was a learner and an apprentice, a man in the making in an era and a country that were constantly making and remaking themselves. From 1848 through to his death in 1869, Roebling was a master, an acknowledged expert, and an unbending authority: a man in full.

PART ONE

NOVICE (1806–31)

In Napoleon's Shadow (1806–24)

All that is known about Johann Röbling's hometown of Mühlhausen before 967 is its name: *Mühle* (mill) *Hausen* (home), meaning place of watermills. Situated on the banks of the Unstrut River in Thuringia, in what is now the geographical center of Germany, Mühlhausen was granted free imperial city status in 1251 and subsequently became a major center for textile production, alongside tanning and dyeing, brewing, ironmongery, and other manufactures. By the end of the fifteenth century it was part of the commercially powerful Hanseatic League and boasted a population of almost ten thousand, making it one of the largest and most prosperous towns in the German-speaking world. Then its luck ran out. By the close of the late Middle Ages, Mühlhausen had declined into a backwater.[1]

Fueled by favorable legislation and royal patronage, the rise of nearby Leipzig as a major trading center helped erode Mühlhausen's influence, yet worse was to come. In 1524, the radical Christian reformer Thomas Müntzer arrived in Mühlhausen and in ten months managed to wreak havoc on the town, steering Mühlhausen into the teeth of the German Peasants' War. On May 15, 1525, Müntzer led eight thousand farmers into the Battle of Frankenhausen and was routed. Two days later, he was beheaded in Mühlhausen and his decapitated body displayed outside the town gates. Müntzer lived on as a Marxist icon, the hero of Friedrich Engels's *The Peasant War in Germany* (1850) and the face that graced the East German five-mark note. Mühlhausen fared less well. Forced into heavy reparation payments, it was stripped of its free imperial status and placed under the control of Saxony and Hesse.[2]

Mühlhausen regained its imperial status in 1548, but never its former trading might. It suffered terribly through the devastation and chaos of the Thirty Years War. Many of its leading residents left town for good, while others were conscripted, went to war, and never came back. By the close of the conflict, the town's population was half what it had been fifty years earlier. In the aftermath, Mühlhausen rolled on in relative peace: neither prosperous nor destitute. Johann Sebastian Bach brought some brief fame to town in 1707 when he took a job there as an organist, but a year later he left for a better-paying job—and much better choir—in Weimar.[3]

In 1670, the first Röbling—Hanns Jacobus—arrived in Mühlhausen from nearby Bad Tennstedt and did pretty well for himself. By 1756, his grandson Hermann Christian Röbling had made enough money to purchase a large house in the center of town and achieved sufficient local standing to get elected to the town council. Hermann's eldest son, Heinrich Wilhelm (born 1756), went into business as a wholesale merchant and accumulated a large fortune. Known as "the rich Röbling," he died in 1841. Hermann's second son, Ernst Adolph, became president of the Mühlhausen Clothmakers' and Sergemakers' Guild, and his third, Christoph Polycarpus (born 1770), contributed little of lasting importance to the world apart from fathering Johann.[4]

Polycarp Röbling was a popular figure in Mühlhausen. He owned a tobacco shop in the center of town and lived comfortably in the house bought by his father. He appears to have been a jovial, easygoing man with steady habits and an active imagination, yet with neither ambition nor a sense of adventure. According to his grandson, Polycarp spent much of his time telling tall tales of faraway places at his shop or the local pub, despite never having left the town of his birth. In 1798, he married Friederike Dorothea Müller, and together they had five children during the next eight years, four of whom survived into adulthood. Their first child, Hermann Christian, born in 1800, inherited Polycarp's tobacco business and sense of adventure: he never left Mühlhausen either and died in 1859. A daughter died in infancy in 1801, and another arrived the following year. Friederike Amalie—known as Malchen—married Karl August Meissner, a prominent local merchant, and eventually immigrated to the United States in 1852 after her husband's death. A second son, Friedrich Carl, was born in 1804. Carl also ended up traveling to America with his younger brother in 1831. The family was completed with the birth of Johann August on June 12, 1806.[5]

The town in which Johann was born was dominated by its defensive fortifications and by its religious devotion. In the twelfth century, Mühlhausen built a thick stone wall in an effort to keep out roving marauders and safeguard its growing prosperity. These new defenses created a sense of security, stability, and safety, as well as an insular feeling of encasement, as if the town had walled itself in, not others out. Rising up above the town's massive fortifications were the spires and steeples of Mühlhausen's numerous churches and chapels. Despite covering barely a square mile, Mühlhausen was home to over thirteen different houses of worship. The upper town (*Oberstadt*) was dominated by St. Mary's, Mühlhausen's largest house of worship, the preferred house of prayer of the town's civic leadership. The town's lower half (*Unterstadt*) was dominated by St. Blasius, the preferred church of the Röbling family, close by on Erfurterstraße.

Mühlhausen was also home to a modest Jewish population that appears to have existed since at least 1380 when the town's first synagogue was built.

The town hall (*Rathaus*) stood as a meeting place in the heart of the town's old quarter; farmers from the surrounding area assembled at the town market to sell their wares and blow off a little steam. The area was notoriously rowdy and, somewhat unfortunately, positioned directly opposite the town's main school, which Johann and his brothers attended. The market was also the town's main social and commercial hub, a bustling place from dawn to dusk, especially during the high summer harvest months.

While the churches were Gothic, most of the homes and houses were half-timbered or Baroque with steep, red-tiled gabled roofs and upper stories that overhung Mühlhausen's narrow, ramshackle streets. Built in 1587, Johann's family home was three stories, built of stone, with French dormer windows and a large, round-arch doorway. The Mühlhausen gymnasium was only a few hundred yards away, as was Polycarp's tobacco shop, meaning the family could live their entire lives without traveling more than a few blocks in any direction. The Röblings woke each morning to the peal of St. Blasius's huge church bells. The sound of the church's massive organ—the same one that Bach played a century before—filled the Röbling home with melodious sound. Unsurprisingly perhaps, Johann grew up with a great love of music; organized religion appealed to him much less, although like the rest of the family he dutifully attended St. Blasius's every Sunday.

Sealed off from the world behind its great stone walls, Mühlhausen stood as a bucolic, unchanging monument to the Middle Ages and the heavy, dead weight of history. Johann only managed to enjoy about four months of quiet and sleepy provinciality, however, before the gates to his city were forced open and his world overrun. By mid-October 1806, the Röblings were residents of an occupied town, and by the end of the month, subjects of a conquered country. Johann spent his first seven years in the middle of the largest and most destructive war the world had yet seen, all of which came as a great surprise to the residents of Mühlhausen.

———

Mühlhausen's first rude awakening occurred on April 17, 1803. In consequence of a war fought six years earlier and over 370 miles away—about which the Röblings knew absolutely nothing—Mühlhausen rather inexplicably lost its free imperial city status and passed into the hands of Prussia. The Peace of Campo Formio, signed on October 1797, acknowledged French victories over Austria in northern Italy and French acquisitions in the German Rhineland and, after six years of territorial bargaining, compensated Austria and Prussia for their losses in the west with gains in the east. Suddenly, the fate of Mühlhausen and the Röbling family was firmly and dangerously tied to that of Prussia.[6]

Since 1792, Prussia had been alternately at war with the French, at peace, or simply afraid to make a decision either way. Most often Prussia tried to preserve some neutrality, although as the philosopher Gottfried Leibniz once observed, Prussian neutrality "is rather like someone who lives in the middle of a house and is smoked out from below and drenched with urine from above." By trying to keep everyone happy, the Prussian leadership pleased no one. Worse yet, they vacillated, forming and then forsaking alliances with all the major powers. By the time Johann was born, Prussia had more or less run out of options: the Little Corporal was coming, ready or not.[7]

One can only imagine how the happy-go-lucky Polycarp felt in June 1806 as his final son entered the world. Mühlhausers were naturally inward-looking, somewhat complacent people, yet they must have caught an inkling of the changes underway all over Europe. Paris was a world away in late-eighteenth-century terms, but there was no ignoring the social and political ramifications of the French Revolution, especially once the internal struggle morphed into a series of external wars and the tremors of social revolution became the concrete rumblings of an advancing army.

Compared to Napoleon's Grande Armée, the Prussia military was laughably outmoded in tactics and materiel. Nevertheless, they mobilized secretly in August 1806 and sent an ultimatum to Napoleon. He mocked the Prussians, set his army on a course for Thuringia, and promptly destroyed the entire Prussian army in a single day at the battles of Jena and Auerstädt, only sixty miles from Mühlhausen. Any remaining Prussian troops scattered as the full might of the French Army crashed over Thuringia. Many of the fleeing Prussian troops passed through Mühlhausen during the general retreat, "dangerously wounded . . . their whole bodies covered in blood," according to one eyewitness. By the beginning of November, French troops marched through Mühlhausen, declaring that henceforth the town's inhabitants were Imperial French subjects. In barely three months, the once mighty Kingdom of Prussia had been brought to the edge of extinction, and the once free and proud town of Mühlhausen fell under the dominion of the French.[8]

The terms of Prussia's defeat were staggering and humiliating. With the Treaty of Tilsit (1807), the nation was stripped and dismembered. Mühlhausen itself became part of the Harz-Departement, a division of the newly created Kingdom of Westphalia under the hereditary monarchy of twenty-four-year-old Jérôme Bonaparte, Napoleon's loose-living younger brother. The kingdom was intended as a model state, complete with legal equality and religious freedom, designed to demonstrate to Germans the superiority of French ideals. "What people would want to return to arbitrary government," wrote Napoleon, "after they have tasted the benefits of a sage and liberal administration?" The gap between appearance and reality, however, was wide enough to march the Grande Armée through. In reality, the Kingdom of Westphalia existed as a vassal state of the new French Empire, was guided by absolutism, and was ruled by fiat. As Herbert Fisher notes, Napoleon "treat[ed] the Kingdom as a mere financial and military asset in his great game of politics."[9]

Mühlhausers paid the price of Napoleonic politics. Forced quartering turned family homes into boarding houses for a conquering army; conscription made a potential French soldier out of every adult male; a huge war indemnity, high levels of taxation, and forced requisitioning produced widespread poverty and hunger; disdain for local customs and practices by occupying soldiers and bureaucrats created resentment among the entire population. New rules and new realities disrupted natural rhythms. Likewise, law and order frequently broke down, as did traditional family discipline, so much so that the school principal was obliged to publicly remind parents to be more mindful of their children. By the time the Röblings were celebrating Johann's first birthday, all that remained of their previous life was the tolling of church bells, now the soundtrack to a barracked army on drill duty.[10]

For such men as Polycarp Röbling, a substantial town elder raised in imperial freedom and decidedly not inclined to change, the transformation must have seemed bewildering and terrifying. In three years, his town had lost its independ-ence, passed into the hands of Prussia, and become part of an odd new entity called the Kingdom of Westphalia, a client state controlled by an equally odd new entity called the First French Empire. His town was packed with strangers barking orders in a foreign tongue, and it was run by a king he had never heard of. For the first time in his life, Polycarp was brought under the yoke.

The burden of carrying the Röbling family fell to his wife, Friederike, a native of Osterode in the Harz Mountains. Little is known of Johann's mother, and what has been written is often less than flattering. Johann's son Washington came to believe that she "had the opposite characteristics from her husband and my father inherited many of her traits; she was of a very positive temperament"—Washington's preferred euphemism for strict and unbending—"had much executive capacity, made everybody work, managed her household, family, the business and her quarter of town besides." Most of Johann's biographers describe Friederike as cold, austere, and aggressively ambitious.[11] Her disdain for her neighbors is thought to have been as evident as her haughty, ruthless manner. This image seems unfair. With an ineffectual husband, four small children, and wartime conditions, Friederike would have been hard-pressed to maintain order. That she kept the family unit together and the family business running testifies to her wits and work ethic. It is also said that Johann was her favorite and that she channeled all her energy into his upbringing and education, at the expense of her other children. Friederike wanted Johann to become "a great man." While it seems certain that Friederike devoted much of her energy to her youngest son, it was for good reason. According to longstanding local tradition, the Röbling's eldest son stood to inherit the family business and the second son a small interest in it. The daughter of a prominent and somewhat wealthy local family could expect to marry the son of an equally prominent and somewhat wealthy family, which she did. This left Johann. With no guaranteed future, job, or position, he would need encouragement, drive, and ambition. That his mother provided this speaks to nothing more than her love and responsibility.[12]

As a child of a helpless and powerless town, Johann's earliest memories were dominated by the French subjugation of his family and neighbors. While he rarely mentioned his experiences, the prejudices that bloomed under the occupation lingered. As his son testified, even "late in life . . . my father hated the French and lost no opportunity to rail at Napoleon." Johann grew up with many quirks and obsessions, but none were as central and all-consuming as his intense lifelong hatred of chaos and confusion, out of which naturally flowed an overwhelming need for certainty, precision, and order.[13]

Not all German-speaking peoples held or developed such an abiding hatred for Napoleon. Among Germans eager for some *liberté, égalité,* and *fraternité* of their own, especially intellectuals, support for Napoleon was often strong. Immanuel Kant, Johann Gottfried Herder, Friedrich Schelling, Friedrich Schiller, Johann von Goethe, and Ludwig von Beethoven all cheered on the revolution. As a young man, Georg W. F. Hegel was positively giddy about the revolution, describing it as "a glorious sunrise." While working at the University of Jena, Hegel even glimpsed the emperor riding out of the city. "It is indeed a wonderful sensation to see such an individual, who, concentrated here at a single point, astride a horse, reaches out over the world and masters it." Remarkably, Hegel managed to retain his rosy impression despite the fact that Napoleon sacked Jena the very next day, leaving the philosopher destitute.[14]

———

Napoleon's conquest of Prussia took place close to Mühlhausen, as did his downfall. The Battle of Leipzig (October 16–19, 1813) was the largest battle of the Napoleonic Wars and left almost eighty-five thousand soldiers dead and many more maimed. "A more revolting and sickening spectacle I never beheld," reported George Jackson, "scarcely could one move forward a step without passing over the dead body of some poor fellow, gashed with wounds and clotted in the blood." With so many rotting bodies, diseases of all stripes soon took hold, increasing the death toll. By the end of the third day of fighting, the French were in full retreat, fleeing just south of Mühlhausen toward the safety of the French border, and the Cossack army had taken up residence in Johann's hometown. Their "campfires blazed all around," reported one observer, and "they were all over the streets." For all intents and purposes, the Napoleonic Wars were over. Having lived through more than twenty years of almost constant war and witnessed the radical breakdown—economic, ideological, civic—of an entire continent, the great powers of Europe had to find a way to rebuild.[15]

Prussian rule in Mühlhausen was restored in the aftermath of Leipzig, but a return to a pre-Napoleonic world was impossible. The war and occupation had scarred the town. Mühlhausen had sent men off to fight against the French, then for them, and then against them again, all in eight years. Their provincial world had been shattered by the continual presence of soldiers from a host of different nations. This sense of bewilderment continued long after the war ended when Mühlhausen was incorporated into the District of Erfurt (in the Province of Saxony), a rather diffuse collection of lands and places that contained eight different legal systems.[16] In a town split among burghers, artisans, and laborers, some Mühlhausers were radicalized by their experiences, further shaking the town's complacent unity. Young Johann, barely eight years old, had witnessed the advance, decimation, and full-scale retreat of two different large-scale armies and been subjected to a bewildering set of changes in authority and local control. His world was decidedly not that of his father. Polycarp would stay stuck in his idyllic eighteenth-century world, while Johann moved on to embrace the nineteenth. Johann would grow up as a new type of German, one defined by the events and tensions of the very recent past, not the traditions of bygone days.

The twin issues facing Europe after Napoleon's downfall were peace and political reform. The Great Powers wanted peace. So did most Europeans, although many, thanks to the rhetoric of revolutionary France, also had their sights set on a few personal rights of their own. Unfortunately, most of Europe's crowned heads and diplomats were quick to equate demands for democracy with revolutionary terror. They blamed the Napoleonic Wars not on the actions of a single demagogue but on the ideas fostered and promulgated by the French Revolution, and they sought to quell the rising sentiment for political reform. Their opening came in 1819 when Karl Sand, a Napoleonic War veteran and member of the Burschenschaft (a student organization devoted to ideas of democracy and pan-German nationalism), murdered August von Kotzebue, a reactionary playwright who had ridiculed the student movement and cheered on the political crackdowns. In the wake of Kotzebue's murder, the German Confederation passed the Carlsbad Decrees, a set of draconian social restrictions designed to halt all forms of protest. Student fraternities were banned while many professors were sacked or censored. Freedoms of the press were severely curtailed, and a new government agency—Zentralkommission zur Untersuchung hochverräterischer Umtriebe (Central Commission for the investigation of high treasonous activities)— was created to infiltrate clubs and associations, monitor all public activity, and deal ruthlessly with "revolutionary agitation." By the time Johann was ready to attend high school in nearby Erfurt, the crackdown by the Prussian state was complete.[17]

———

Napoleon's life and legacy forced Europe to move in two separate directions simultaneously. To preserve Europe's newfound fragile peace, the Great Powers rejected reform; to preserve themselves, they embraced it. While retrenchment helped quash calls for political inclusion, it could not address the structural flaws that plagued the continent. The Prussian military's abundant and often catastrophic failures during the Napoleonic Wars, for example, forced the state to focus on training and talent. Faced with the prospect of extinction, Prussia could no longer entrust its survival to aristocratic generals and hidebound traditions. It needed dynamic young leaders schooled in the arts of modern military warfare and civil servants capable of overseeing large-scale governmental operations. To survive, Prussia needed skill and aptitude in its leaders. To achieve this, it overhauled how the state trained its young men for the rigors of a new world. As with most of the rest of Europe, they rejected democracy with the same gusto with which they embraced meritocracy.[18]

If Prussia wanted to ensure its own survival, noted the king's chief minister, Baron Karl vom Stein, it had to focus its energies on "education and instruction." Thenceforth, talent and inclination alone should decide advancement and profession. Stein envisioned a "schooling revolution" designed to awaken and exploit the untapped potential of the Prussian people. The aristocracy alone could not win the battle for Prussian survival. Enlisting Wilhelm von Humboldt (elder brother of naturalist and explorer Alexander) and Privy Councilor Peter Beuth, Stein began to overhaul Prussia's education system. By the mid-nineteenth century, the Prussian educational model had spread across Europe and taken hold in the United States. The essence of Stein's system was twofold: first, teacher training to recruit and prepare a cadre of young educators in the goals and aspirations of the new system, and second, the implementation of a national curriculum stressing reason and lifelong patterns of humanistic learning. His goal was not to turn the sons of cobblers into cobblers but to create individuals capable of adapting to new realities and knowledge. Education became universal, standardized, and monitored, even in such backwaters as Mühlhausen, which hosted one of Stein's new teacher training seminaries.[19]

Johann reaped the benefits of the Prussian reform movement, which provided for his education and training as well as his vocation. The combination of reform and industrialization would ensure that Johann would play a part in the emerging new world.

———

Johann attended the Mühlhausen Gymnasium during the tenure of Rector Johan Georg Schollmeyer soon after the advent of Stein's reforms. Schollmeyer ran the gymnasium from 1799 to 1827 and was himself something of an educational reformer. He shifted the emphasis from Latin grammar to mathematics, physics, and technical training; he even hoped to institute a course on the "drawing of architectural layouts and buildings." Schollmeyer's pedagogical philosophy served young Johann well, reflecting as it did the direction in which Europe was rapidly moving. While Prussia had little interest in the ideals of the French Revolution (democratic), it plunged happily into the British Revolution (industrial), instituting an ambitious plan to upgrade and renovate its infrastructure, partly out of military necessity—the kingdom's roads and bridges were in an atrocious state—but mainly in the interests of economic growth. Post-Napoleonic Europe was a terrible place to agitate for civil rights but a great place to become a civil engineer, for just as the door to political reform was closing, entry into many vital occupations was being unlocked.[20]

The Mühlhausen Gymnasium, consisting of seven "bright and clean" classrooms housed in an old stone building at 10 Neue Straße, was only a five-minute walk from the Röbling home. The gymnasium was situated in the middle of town opposite the market, where produce carts blocked the road and farmers shouted, swore, told dirty jokes, and disturbed the peace. Such boorish behavior often made it difficult to conduct lessons, and Rector Schollmeyer worried that proximity to the market might pose a danger to the students' "health and good manners." This situation was exacerbated between classes when students were free to roam outside and by classroom overcrowding, which frequently stymied efforts to maintain discipline and order. The school's rules were rather outdated, which did not help either. Instead, the principal designed rules for specific classes which he then explained to the children.[21]

The gymnasium curriculum contained eight grades, none set by age or duration. Students simply moved up a grade once they had completed the necessary assignments or left after reaching an educational level adequate to their needs. Johann's two older brothers, for example, left the gymnasium before reaching the eighth grade to take up apprenticeships in their father's tobacco business. Myriad subjects were taught at the gymnasium: languages, science (physical and natural), history, religious instruction, philosophy, geography, declamation, music, and physical education, alongside the traditional disciplines of reading, writing, and arithmetic. The teaching load was spread broadly among the teachers, each

of whom provided instruction in "up to two languages" and in science according
to their expertise. Governance was overseen by the local superintendent and the
town magistrate, who visited the school "from time to time" to sit in on classes
and appraise the "prevailing school culture."[22]

Schollmeyer and the Mühlhausen Gymnasium sparked Johann's appetite for
practical learning and nurtured his impressive drawing skills. The school also
provided rigorous instruction in textual close reading, encouraged Johann's first
violin lessons, and got him started on the French language, a subject he would
continue at university. His learning was imbued with a broad humanistic and
philosophical foundation that would define much of his subsequent life and career. Certainly, Johann had already begun to wrestle with the idea of "thinking
for himself." At the same time, however, the school stopped short of providing
the vocational education Johann craved, specifically in the art and science of
architecture and engineering. By mission, the Prussian gymnasium provided a
general education orientated as much toward the humanities as the sciences.
To specialize and take advantage of the new climate of "careers open to talent,"
Johann had to move on: to Ephraim Salomon Unger's School of Mathematics in
nearby Erfurt.

Figure 1.1 Johann's first commercial lithograph, a view of his hometown printed by his
cousin E. W. Röbling. Johann Röbling, "Mühlhausen vom Stadtberge" (1825). Courtesy
of the Mühlhäuser Museen.

Like Schollmeyer, Unger was an advocate of the emerging *Realschule* movement. Created in response to the Enlightenment and the realities of contemporary industrialization, *Realschulen* were akin to polytechnics, promoting technical over classical education. A perfect candidate to open and lead such a school, Unger was an accomplished and respected mathematician who had previously held a professorship at the prestigious University of Erfurt and given private lessons to a host of young and aspiring engineers, including Friedrich August Stüler—also from Mühlhausen—who became the Prussian royal buildings inspector and Frederick William IV's royal architect.

Stüler was six years older than Johann, and they were probably not friends, although they may have known each other. More likely—given Mühlhausen's insular nature and relatively small population—their parents were acquainted and word of Unger's outstanding teaching reached Johann's parents. This, coupled with Johann's talent, need for a career, and early promise, persuaded Polycarp and Friederike Röbling to remove fifteen-year-old Johann from the Mühlhausen Gymnasium in 1821. This was no idle decision: at one hundred thalers per annum, Unger's school was expensive, and as Johann's sister, Malchen, reported the following year, the family "business is very bad right now."[23]

Unger's school was "designed for those who have committed themselves to architecture, mining, forestry and other enterprises, in which a thorough knowledge of theoretical and practical mathematics is necessary." The course of study was divided into two yearlong sections, the first devoted to "pure mathematics, practical geometry, and geometrical drawing," the second "concerned with higher and applied mathematics, in particular the art of construction including all its subfields, with mechanics, physics, and other branches." "In particular," read the official literature, "those who want to commit themselves exclusively to the science of construction will be adequately prepared for the state-approved exams as Baukondukteur [building director] in the Royal Prussian State Service."[24]

The school thrived, attracting students from all over Europe. Classes were held at Unger's house in the center of town, and it is likely Johann either boarded there or lived close by. Under Unger's tutelage, Johann became an excellent mathematician and an outstanding surveyor. He was also introduced to the science of geometry and the theory of catenary curves, which may well have sown the seeds of a latent interest in suspension bridges. Johann also developed great skill and artistry as a draughtsman and illustrator. In 1826, Johann found himself a published artist when one of his drawings was used to illustrate a history of nearby Eschwege. Admittedly this auspicious beginning came through the efforts of Ernst Wilhelm Röbling, a friendly cousin, who happened to own a publishing house, but this was no simple case of nepotism; Johann had talent. Several of his drawings from the time were also turned into lithographs and sold locally.[25]

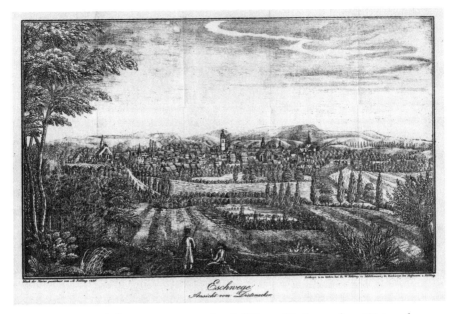

Figure 1.2 Johann's first appearance in a book. "View of Eschwege from Dietenacker, drawn from nature by A. Röbling, 1825," from Johann Charles Hochhuth, *Erinnerungen an die Vorzeit und Gegenwart der Stadt Eschwege in Thüringen* (1826).

Despite his pedagogical bent and intellectual expertise, Unger was no pure scientist. His interests stretched widely and often turned to philosophy. As a graduate student, Unger had studied not only the science of trigonometry but also the philosophy of Immanuel Kant, an enthusiasm for which he nurtured in young Johann. Röbling's first volume of philosophy—Hegel's *Encyclopedia of the Philosophical Sciences* (1817)—dates to his time in Erfurt, and his interest in Hegel, metaphysics, and questions of mind, matter, and spirit would last his entire life. More precisely, Unger was a philosopher-scientist, a label that could later be applied to Johann.[26]

Johann spent his time in Erfurt studiously and quietly. He returned home for holidays and during school breaks, while his mother and sister visited Erfurt during term time. By March 1823, Johann's classes and coursework were complete, and all that remained was word "from the government" as to the dates of his state building exams, so he returned to Mühlhausen for an extended visit and to meet Malchen's newborn son.[27]

Johann also wrote to his brother Carl. The earliest of Johann's surviving letters, it provides a glimpse into his character and temperament. He is polite beyond measure and affectionate, if somewhat formal. Most of the letter, however, sees seventeen-year-old Johann dispensing advice to his older brother with almost paternal warmth. On his upcoming trip back to Mühlhausen, Carl must "observe all the remarkable things and sights on your trip that opportunity affords" and "try to get as much recreation and pleasure on your journey as you possibly can, you will come to beautiful regions." He should "keep a thorough diary" and "drink a good wine" if it is "cheap." Practical matters—never far from Johann's thoughts—were also a concern: "Look around if you can see machines etc. about the tobacco business, and observe them carefully." As far as Carl's remaining time in Friedberg (near Frankfurt) where he was boarding with his employer, Johann cautioned his brother not to get "too angry." Anger, counseled Johann "is bad for you," ironic advice from someone who would gain a reputation for losing his temper almost hourly.[28]

Johann returned to Erfurt to take his state exams in May, taking his final examination in surveying before returning home to Mühlhausen. He was subsequently accepted into Berlin's Bauakademie (Building Academy), Prussia's top engineering school—a rather astounding feat for such a provincial teenager—but decided to postpone his studies. As he wrote Carl in March, his eldest brother, Hermann, "will probably have to join the militia at the end of May," and there was some doubt as to whether Carl would have to serve also. Clearly, Johann was needed at home and would have to wait patiently for the next stage in his education. By the following spring things were sufficiently under control for him to take his leave. On April 12, 1824, Johann packed up a bag, said goodbye to his family and friends, and headed off to the bright (gas)lights of Berlin.

Berlin and the Culture of Revolution (1824–25)

Johann August Röbling spent his youth in the shadow of one kind of revolution and his early manhood immersed in another. As the chaotic, war-torn energy of the French Revolution dissipated through the long years of European conflict, the dynamic energy of the Industrial Revolution took its place, sweeping across the continent, filling the vacuum. All across Europe, the fire and the fury of war became the smoke and noise of industrial activity, and nowhere in the German-speaking world was this more the case than Berlin.

Berlin was the center of Prussia's Industrial Revolution, and while the Iron Kingdom certainly lagged behind Britain in terms of trade and manufacturing, it was no less devoted to the cause. By the mid-nineteenth century, Berlin had emerged as one of Europe's largest centers of heavy industry. At the close of the Napoleonic Wars, Berlin's economy had long been dominated by the government and the military. In the postwar climate, however, Berlin's economic gaze shifted to industrial innovation. In 1816, gaslights were installed in the city, and Berliners were introduced to the wonders of steam power. Continental Europe's first steam-powered locomotive was manufactured in Berlin that same year, quickly followed by the production of steam engines, steamships, and steam-powered factories. In 1819, John Cockerill built a machine shop and a modern textile factory in the city. Two years later, F. A. J. Egells established an iron foundry and engineering works on Berlin's Chausseestraße. In 1824, he furnished the city with a hydraulic press.[1]

The city's rising industrial might led to the creation of a Ministry of Trade, a Technical Commission, and a Society for the Advancement of Industry. Berlin's Industrial Institute, effectively a two-year high school for civil engineering, opened in 1821. A year later the city hosted its first industrial exhibition, followed by a second in 1827. Berlin's economic energy was matched by a furious building boom directed by Royal Architect Karl Friedrich Schinkel, whose

Figure 2.1 Johann Röbling, student drawing: frieze design, griffins, and flowers (1825). Courtesy of the Special Collections and University Archives, Rutgers University Libraries.

grand buildings—royal palaces, museums, concert halls, and churches—helped turn Berlin into a Prussian Paris during the 1820s.[2]

Johann was likely a bit disorientated upon arrival in Berlin. After all, he had just left a rural walled town and journeyed two hundred miles to "the splendid . . . clean wide streets" of an outsized, thriving metropolis.[3] However, Johann took Berlin in his stride and dove into the Industrial Revolution head first. He arrived in town on April 18 and found himself some lodgings (at Kreutzgasse 15, just off the Spittelmarkt). He also found that classes at the Building Academy had begun three days earlier. Unfazed, Johann promptly paid his tuition and mapped his first semester of study, a program that followed heavily his talents in drawing and draftsmanship.

In his first semester, running from mid-April to late September, Johann took Architectural Drawing and Drawing and Ornamentation, where he spent most of his time copying Greek decorative motifs from the state's building magazine, *Vorbilder für Fabrikanten und Handwerker* (Examples for manufacturers and craftsmen). Not content with just two drawing courses, Johann also took a series of drawing lessons in architecture and perspective at the nearby Berlin Academy of Art. On the engineering side, Johann took General Architecture and Building Construction, the first half of an obligatory, yearlong foundational course in general architecture and engineering, along with Physics, Chemistry, and Mineralogy and Their Role in the Field of Construction. He also signed up for private French lessons.[4]

Figure 2.2 Johann Röbling, student drawing: urn (1824). Courtesy of the Special
Collections and University Archives, Rutgers University Libraries.

When he wasn't dutifully attending lectures, Johann was out on the streets
of Berlin examining modern building techniques and the new industrial reality
sweeping the city. Within a month of arrival, Johann had been granted permission
to visit many of the new construction sites that dotted the city, including those of
the great Schinkel, who was at work on his Greek-revival Altes Museum and the
neo-Gothic Friedrichswerdersche Church. Johann also visited Schinkel's grand
Berlin Schauspielhaus at the Gendarmenmarkt repeatedly, to study the building,
see plays, and people-watch. (In 1822, E. T. A. Hoffman likened the "colorful,
surging throng" at the Gendarmenmarkt to a "a large bed of tulips being blown
hither and thither by the wind.") Johann's encounter with Berlin—physically,
on the streets, and technically, as an engineer in training—served as a useful introduction to the emerging modern world, although his overall impression was
mixed. While he later described Berlin as "a city of poor, oppressed people," he
was transfixed by the building boom and intrigued by the elegance "lavished
upon a few public buildings."[5]

Regarding his intellectual development, Johann's most significant act was
to attend "Professor Hegel's lectures on Logic and Metaphysics [at Berlin

University], costing a Louis D'Or [French currency], and being held 5 times a week." Where Berlin was the site of the emerging modern world, Hegel provided the philosophical framework through which to understand it.[6]

———

Johann was already familiar with Hegel by this time, having read sections of the great man's *Encyclopedia of the Philosophical Sciences* (1817) at the Unger School. Yet young Johann—only a few days removed from Mühlhausen—must have been awed to find himself in the presence of such a great thinker and excited to hear him speak. Chances are he was a little disappointed with Hegel's performance, though. Hegel suffered from acute headaches and poor health during much of 1824 and was not a charismatic speaker at the best of times. His lectures, like his writing, were plodding and ponderous. According to Heinrich Hotho, who attended Hegel's classes at the same time as Johann: "His features hung pale and loose upon him as if he were already dead. . . . He sat there morosely with his head wearily bowed down in front of him, constantly leafing back and forth through his compendious notes, even as he continued to speak." Others noted Hegel's propensity for mumbling through laborious, long-winded monologues, only enlivened by some occasional sarcasm; still others remembered constant coughing and snuff-taking. What Hegel lacked in rhetorical skill, however, he made up for in the revolutionary power and originality of his ideas.[7]

Johann's deep interest in Hegel and his brief presence in his lecture hall have fueled a persistent legend that he was Hegel's favorite student, with whom he took long walks and engaged in complex metaphysical debates. Unfortunately, there is no evidence that Hegel was even aware of Johann's presence in his lecture hall, and Johann himself never made such a claim. Yet there can be no doubt that the great philosopher was a powerful thinker deeply involved in the form, substance, and implications of the newly modern world, nor that he exercised considerable influence over the diligent and receptive young man. Hegel did not counsel Röbling to move to the United States, as numerous historians have imagined, but his ideas certainly helped cultivate the intellectual maturity and confidence that allowed Johann to think boldly. Certainly, Johann was still thinking and writing about Hegel almost forty years later, and his son Washington ascribed many of his father's attitudes and beliefs to his time in Berlin and his contact with the great philosopher.[8]

Hegel spent the early 1820s lecturing on a variety of subjects, but it was his thoughts and theories about logic and reason that stood at the heart of his entire intellectual system. Painfully worked out over almost twenty years, Hegel's philosophy flourished in response to the events and the times he lived through. His aim was to comprehend, capture, and explain the bewildering sense of change that accompanied Europe's two revolutions.

Through the fire and terror of the last half century, something new had arisen, something untethered to previous norms and standards. How had this happened, Hegel wondered, and why? For starters, the era was marked by the emergence of what Hegel termed the "Absolute Idea," a concept that roughly equates to the idea of freedom. Yet what did Hegel mean by this? For Hegel, freedom was not some abstract notion of liberty and equality or a simple condition of existence but a rigorous mode of being that conjoined both intent and action. His system of logic was the deductive process by which one came to understand freedom as the presence of reason in history and then dedicate one's self to its "practical commitment."[9]

The first step was radical for an era still dominated by monarchs and ministries: submit to no external authority. The second was even more difficult: know yourself. People needed no bedrock on which to operate, no social conventions, customs, or dogmas, outside their own internal logic. To attain the "Absolute Idea" and thus become free, they had to reject the authority of others and embrace the authority of self. They must develop their own "practical commitments" and be able to understand them in relation to their ultimate ends and aims. These ends and aims had to be measured in relation to the overall "good" they provide. Conversely, in Hegel's system, people were unfree when they failed to develop their own logic, when they obeyed without question. The implications of such a message were clearly vast and radical. Old thinking and old modes of authority were out, and thinking for oneself was in. Needless to say, this was heady stuff for a young student from the provinces on the cusp of adulthood, not to mention an apprentice engineer on the cusp of the Industrial Revolution. Suddenly the possibilities were endless.[10]

The vast energies of the Industrial Revolution found their rationale in such sentiments as Hegel's. To create the world anew required a fundamental decoupling of action and habit. Hegel understood this just as well as the era's great engineers, industrialists, and political reformers. They were all, in some way or other, creating new tools to conquer the old world and shape the new. For Hegel, those tools existed in the mind. For an engineer, they existed in mathematics and in metallurgy. For Johann, ultimately, they existed in both. Steam power and suspension bridges were to architecture and engineering what Hegel's thought was to philosophy. They were the art of practical philosophy come into the concrete, self-determining world of things. They coupled new materials with new ideas and changed the way people thought about the world.

Hegel's philosophical pronouncements came with implications for all branches of knowledge. To buy into Hegel's revolutionary proposal was to fundamentally alter one's understanding of the world. Assuredly, the inexorable self-certainty Johann developed as an adult appears to flow directly from Hegel, as did his frustration with both the Prussian state and the world of professional engineering, which would ultimately fuel his decision to emigrate in 1831. The most obvious and immediate impact, however, was Johann's growing sense of doubt over spiritual and religious matters, along with his growing sense of the possibilities of technology.

By Johann's own admission, "As a boy and a young man I was devout and full of faith, then came doubts, vacillations, investigations," eventually leading to an intense distrust—bordering on hatred—of established religion, especially figures of religious authority. This transformation occurred during "his university life in Berlin," and the source was clearly his exposure to Hegel's ideas. While the philosopher went to great lengths to assert his own unswerving piety, his logic was a powerful call to free oneself from the shackles of established dogma. Moreover, Hegel's many frequent, and often very public, religious missteps failed to help his case. In 1822, for example, Hegel wisecracked that dogs ought to make the best Christians, given the purity and intensity of their devotion, and then followed it up by pondering what would happen if a mouse mistakenly ate a Eucharist wafer. Logically, of course, the mouse would contain the body of Christ, Hegel decided, though so, in turn, would the mouse's excrement. Needless to say, it was fine for a philosopher to pursue logic in such a tenacious manner but another thing altogether for a civil servant to find God in some mouse droppings.[11]

Hegel's religiosity has always been up for debate, but what seems indisputable is that many "devout" young men graduated from Hegel's lecture hall having foresaken their spiritual convictions. As the historian and jurist Friedrich Karl von Savigny complained in 1825: Hegel's "students are abandoning any relationship to religion."[12] Johann certainly fit this description, although more accurately, he swapped his faith in established religion for a life of science and self-governance. Some of that self-governance would lead John solidly back to belief, although it would never lead him back to church.

As an adult, Johann was by temperament a doer with an almost limitless sense of possibility. By profession, he lived by science and reason and abhorred what he understood as a submission to authority based purely on superstition. As he grew older, he developed a fundamental contempt for figures of religious authority—although not for God—a position he maintained throughout his life. As described by his son, Johann's "encounters with the poor clergy were harrowing spectacles—in a few minutes he would be worked up to a fever heat, the spit would fly, his arms gesticulated violently—the amazed opponent became terror stricken, finally seeking safety in flight."[13]

Much as Hegel believed that "Reason directs the World," so Johann would later write that "reason, when applied according to the laws of the mind, is *infallible*, and the only thing to which we can cling with assurance." This is not to say

Johann abandoned his spiritual yearnings altogether. While he no longer believed in established religion after his time in Berlin, he was never able to abandon his need for spiritual certainty. Instead, he did what any good inventor might do: unhappy with the established order, he cast about for suitable materials and made his own. In Johann's case, this turned out to be a rather odd mix of pseudoscience, spiritualism, transcendentalism, and abstract metaphysics, all of which he blended into something close to the sort of deism proclaimed by Thomas Paine: "I do not believe in the creed professed . . . by any church that I know of. My own mind is my own church."[14]

―――

While Hegel was exhorting a generation of young men to rethink the world and a cadre of engineers, architects, and latent capitalists were radically remaking the look and feel of Berlin, the Prussian state was working to stifle political change and keep cultural upheaval to a minimum. The provisions of the Carlsbad Decrees were ratcheted up during the 1820s as the state became obsessed with censorship and surveillance. Henry Dwight, who visited Berlin during Johann's second semester, described Berlin's public culture as a combination of "strict censorship" and widespread "government *espionage*," which together "prevent all . . . political discussion." Thomas Hodgskin grumbled that most hotel valets served as spies for the state, which felt "like hiring your servant to betray you." Johann himself later explained that "there are police officers [in Berlin] whose business is first to weigh most scrupulously every idea, every thought, which is to come through the press . . . and so to trim, distort, or entirely annihilate it, [so] that the public can not discover at all what the author really thinks!" Rather surprisingly, much of the nation seemed happy to comply with the crackdowns. Beginning in the 1820s, and lasting until the revolutions of 1848, Berlin and Germany settled into what became known as the Biedermeier era, or "the quiet years." As an artistic movement, Biedermeier was a reaction against the excesses of Romanticism and the trauma of Napoleonic Europe. As a culture it was staid, prudish, and above all apolitical.[15]

Most of the great figures of the Romantic movement abandoned Berlin during the 1820s, leaving the city an "intellectual wasteland," as Wilhelm von Humboldt described it. Music flourished, as did the theater, so long as it stayed clear of contemporary politics. Johann took advantage of this, visiting the Schauspielhaus to see plays by Friedrich Schiller: *Kabale und Liebe* and *Wallenstein's Todd*, both set in the suitably distant past. The popularity of Schiller's historical plays was part of a larger trend. Biedermeier culture studiously avoided dealing with its own contentious present. Instead, it gazed back at German history, idealizing the things it found there. For a new generation of writers, scholars, and everyday

Berliners, the medieval world was exalted as a time of German superiority: of ethnic unity, stability, and cultural greatness, all of which helped ensured that 1820s Berlin was more medieval than medieval Berlin itself.[16]

This retreat into a seemingly stable (although entirely mythic) past, where all was ordered and coherent, may have helped Johann adjust to life in the big city. He was, after all, from a medieval town with a very medieval sensibility. It may also have informed Johann's masterpiece, the Brooklyn Bridge, with its great Gothic towers and modern steel cables, which harks back to this cultural moment in numerous ways: a Janus-faced society retreating back into the cozy confines of an imagined past, while simultaneously flinging itself onward into the new industrial future. With this in mind, the Brooklyn Bridge emerges as a fitting tribute not just to Gilded Age and modernist America but to 1820s Berlin, a modernizing society struggling to stay rooted in a medieval past.

———

Despite Johann's fascination with the world of ideas, he was in Berlin to train as an engineer, not a philosopher. And in this he arrived at a fortuitous time, as the Building Academy had recently undergone reorganization. Wishing to focus more on the technical aspects of construction, Johann Albert Eytelwein, head of the Prussian Building Department, strengthened and updated the engineering curriculum and sent the more artistic elements off to the Berlin Academy of Art. The move reflected the need for a more up-to-date, state-of-the-art education— in 1822 the State Building Directorate complained that "a majority of candidates for the architect's exam . . . demonstrated incomplete knowledge of their subject"—but also the fact that the art of building was rapidly transforming itself into the science of engineering.[17]

The evolution of engineering from a somewhat amateur practice to an integrated scientific "system" helped drive the dynamics of the Industrial Revolution. Given the sheer scale of development (not to mention the associated costs), engineering in all its forms had to be organized along scientific lines, through the application of known principles. Engineering had to become a fully fledged discipline, with standardized rules, guidelines, and methods. Johann arrived in Berlin while this shift was in progress, just as the principles of engineering were being systematically discovered, fixed, and then taught.[18]

In reorganizing the academy, Eytelwein's most important move was to recruit a young engineer, Johann F. W. Dietlein, to devise a set of classes that addressed problems in contemporary engineering. Having worked for a number of years as a construction inspector in Merseburg, Dietlein was an accomplished practical engineer. Having just completed his PhD at the University of Wittenberg-Halle, he was also a blossoming academic attuned to issues in contemporary engineering, especially bridge building. In 1820, Dietlein translated a selection of writings by the noted French bridge engineer Jean-Rodolphe Perronet and four years later translated Claude-Louis Navier's influential *Mémoire Sur Les Ponts Suspendus* (1823), the first practical treatise on the construction of suspension bridges. In addition, Dietlein's own lectures on bridge building were highly regarded.[19]

Johann encountered Dietlein during his second semester, from October 1824 to March 1825, when Johann also took Urban Architecture and Analysis and Higher Geometry. His main focus was Dietlein's two courses: Statics and Hydraulics and Construction of Roads, Bridges, Locks, and Canals.[20] Statics and Hydraulics addressed the practical applications of steam power, the insurgent new force sweeping across Europe, causing a revolution in both transportation and power. The subject certainly had a great impact on Johann. He was "considered an authority on hydraulics" for much of his life, wrote a number of articles on the subject, and acted as a legal expert in the courts.[21] Yet despite this, and the fact that the steam engine was the great icon of the Industrial Revolution, Dietlein's other course—Construction of Roads, Bridges, Locks, and Canals—managed to have an even greater impact on the young engineer.

———

Most of Dietlein's course was standard fare, but it did include a brief introduction to the suspension bridge and Claude-Louis Navier's recent treatise on the subject. A professor at the École des Ponts et Chaussées (the French national school of bridges and roads) in Paris, Navier dedicated much of his early life to studying and promoting the fledging science of suspension bridges. His influence on the development of the new architectural form was large, yet he built only a single bridge, which almost slid into the Seine when the anchorages failed, a situation lampooned by Honoré de Balzac several years later: "All France knew of the disaster which happened in the heart of Paris to the first suspension bridge built by an engineer, a member of the Academy of Sciences; a melancholy collapse caused by blunders such as none of the ancient engineers . . . would have made; but our administration consoled its engineer for his blunder by making him a member of the Council-general."[22]

Nonetheless, Navier exercised significant influence on the profession and on Johann specifically. Without Navier's innovative work, Dietlein would likely never have addressed the subject of suspension bridges in his lectures, and, by extension, Johann would not have become so captivated by them. Navier's treatise was one of the first engineering books Johann ever bought. He kept it for the rest of his life.[23]

Navier's lasting influence was sustained by his *Mémoire*, a book that arose more from national interest than personal enthusiasm. With a pressing need to service the transportation needs of their own Industrial Revolution, France required cheap, stable, and reliable bridges. Timber bridges burned down often and quickly, while stone and metal arch bridges were very costly. France took note of a popular new bridging technique gaining traction in Britain: "bridges of suspension," as the eminent engineer Robert Stephenson described them. Louis Becquey, director general of the Corps des Ponts et Chaussées, sent Navier to investigate.[24]

Navier visited Britain in the fall of 1821 and again in the spring of 1823, to gather information, visit suspension bridges, and meet with engineers. His report opened with a brief summary followed by a section detailing the history and development of the suspension bridge from antiquity to the present. In the third section of the book, Navier brought the analytical approach of a mathematician to the study of bridge design. He believed that there was a theoretical solution for every engineering problem, and his analytical models solved numerous problems but failed to fully consider the effects of wind deflection or address the problem of stiffness or rigidity, two of the most crucial aspects of suspension bridge design.[25]

The book's final section laid out plans for two different suspension bridge projects. The first was a monumental structure to be erected over the Seine between the Champs Elysées and the Hôtel des Invalides, a project Navier lobbied for and that ultimately tarnished his reputation. The second was for a suspension aqueduct. Accorded just eight pages, this plan was included more as a whim than a serious proposal. It began with the proposition that if a suspension bridge could carry people and goods across wide bodies of water, so too, with the correct calculations, could it carry a canal. Navier's design ingeniously solved an old problem (carrying one body of water over another) with a new structural form (the modern suspension bridge), yet the idea went nowhere and was generally ignored, although not by Johann.[26]

As an apprentice engineer, Johann was captivated by the new architectural form and by Navier's ideas. His student notebooks are jammed with notes, hand-drawn diagrams and illustrations, and excited scribbling. Johann was clearly captivated by the history of suspension bridges and Navier's evocation of them. Amid all the theorizing, calculations, and pure science, Navier's *Memoire* contains the first great paean to the suspension bridge: "These structures will exhibit great elegance of form, invariably determined by the natural laws of equilibrium . . . contribute to the embellishment of capital cities, or, suspended across precipitous valleys, they could produce the most imposing of effects in the picturesque settings of mountainous areas. These edifices will present to the imagination a vision of the power of the human arts overcoming, for the public good, great obstacles set up by nature and long held to be invincible."[27]

———

It is doubtful Johann was even aware of the existence of suspension bridges before late 1824: they were rare and mainly confined to the United States and the United Kingdom. As a solution to spanning broad bodies of water, their potential was great. As an architectural structure, they were as yet completely unreliable. In their crudest form, as a rope or vine bridge, they had been around for centuries, and in a slightly more sophisticated form, with the use of iron chains, for almost eighteen hundred years in the Himalayas and the Central Andes. The concept was postulated by the Croatian nobleman and inventor Faustus Verantius in his *Machinae Novae* (1595), although it took a description of a real, functioning bridge for the idea to gain widespread credence. In 1667, Jesuit missionary Alhanasius Kircher described a two-hundred-foot, sixteen-hundred-year-old iron chain bridge he had encountered in China. Temporary suspension bridges—with the walkway resting directly on the cables—were common in the European military, and crude suspension bridges were erected occasionally in Britain in the eighteenth century, most famously the Winch Bridge over the River Tees in County Durham. However, the first recognizably modern suspension bridge—defined by the presence of a level roadway attached to the suspension cables by metal hangers—was built in an obscure corner of western Pennsylvania in 1801.[28]

The man responsible for combining all the basic elements of the modern suspension bridge was not an engineer but a justice of the peace; he was also a county commissioner, a judge in the Court of Common Pleas, a member of the Pennsylvania legislature, and an inveterate tinkerer. James Finley (1756–1828) was the antithesis of Navier. "Theorists may talk as large as they please, but the lessons of experience are more wholesome," Finley wrote. When his professional duties weren't enough to keep him busy, Finley studied the weight-bearing properties of chain links and investigated the quantitative relationship between sag/span, tension, and load. In 1801, Finley took six hundred dollars and built a seventy-foot-long, thirteen-foot-wide suspension bridge over Jacob's Creek "on the great road leading from Uniontown to Greensburg." The span was a simple affair, according to the local press: "two iron chains, extended over four piers, fourteen feet higher than the bridge, fastened in the ground at the ends," but the implications were immense.[29]

In 1808, Finley was granted America's first suspension bridge patent and shortly after began to publicize and license his invention. He distributed a pamphlet on the subject—complete with an elegant lithograph of the finished

Figure 2.3 The world's first modern suspension bridge, designed by James Finley in Fayette County, Pennsylvania. William Strickland, "View of the Chain Bridge invented by James Finley, Esq" (1810). Library of Congress.

structure—and published his plan in the *Port Folio*, a well-respected Philadelphia journal. By the time Johann sat down to listen to Dietlein in the fall of 1824, nineteen "Finley bridges" had been built in the United States, while a further two were being planned. Some had a single span, others had two; most were between 120 and 200 feet in length. Unfortunately, most of them were damaged by the elements—ice, floods, or snow—or they collapsed thanks to shoddy hardware. Only a couple of these bridges would survive into the twentieth century: Templeton's "famous chain bridge" (built 1810; replaced 1909) over the Merrimack River at Newburyport, Massachusetts, and Jacob Blumer's Lehigh Gap Bridge at Palmerton, Pennsylvania (built 1824; dismantled 1933).[30]

Finley's ingenious little bridge impressed the US secretary of the treasury, Albert Gallatin, who mentioned it in his influential *Report on Internal Improvements* (1808). "This new plan," wrote Gallatin, "derived from the tenacity of iron . . . deserves notice on account of the boldness of its construction and its comparative cheapness." Finley also received the endorsement of Benjamin Latrobe, America's foremost architect, who offered to help "overcome any inconvenience or objection which may exist in the general introduction of [Finley's] chain bridge." Yet his bridge received its greatest boost not from a supporter but from someone whose aim, ironically, was to ridicule the suspension bridge.[31]

Word of Finley's bridge spread across the Atlantic and was unwittingly popularized by an obscure inventor and landscape gardener named Thomas Pope in his *A Treatise on Bridge Architecture* (1811).[32] Pope pointed to five "notorious defects contained in the system," while promoting his own plan for his "Flying Pendent Lever Bridge," an 1,800-foot-long cantilevered wooden arch bridge. Nobody was fooled by his supposed expertise or bluff rhetoric.[33] They were, however, rather intrigued by the "description of the Patent Chain Bridge; invented by James Finley, Esq. of Fayette County, Pennsylvania" referred to on page 189. Thomas Telford had Pope's book "at hand" in 1818 as be began to plan his record-breaking Menai Straits Suspension Bridge (1819–26) and was certainly aware of Finley's bridges as early as 1814, when he wrote about the possibility of a thousand-foot-long suspension bridge crossing the River Mersey at Runcorn.[34]

Telford wasn't the only Briton with access to Pope's book or Finley's ideas. Robert Stephenson refers to both the book and the bridge in his article "Description of Bridges of Suspension," published in the *Edinburgh Philosophical Journal* (1821), the early nineteenth century's most widely read and influential account of suspension bridges. In addition, while Telford was searching for a good place to build a suspended structure, Samuel Brown, a retired naval officer, was experimenting with wrought iron at his London factory. Brown caught the suspension bridge bug in 1813, and by 1817 he had perfected and patented a new system of suspension cables and constructed a 105-foot prototype. Both Telford and John Rennie, Britain's second most famous engineer, came to visit and "drove a hackney-coach over" Brown's prototype to test it out. They pronounced themselves well satisfied with Brown's work, which helped immensely as he sought his first bridge contract.[35]

Brown built his first suspension bridge just outside Berwick-upon-Tweed in 1820. Reaching over the river Tweed from England to Scotland, Brown's Union Bridge set the tone and style for early-nineteenth-century British suspension bridges, while making use of Britain's thriving and comparatively cheap iron industry. Finley's American bridges were makeshift affairs, cheap to construct, easy to erect, and well suited to the "raise up and tear down" spirit that defined early-nineteenth-century US development. By contrast, Brown's bridges were big, hulking affairs; they were strong and felt permanent. The principles were similar to Finley's, but the scale was considerably larger, the effect decidedly more monumental. The length between towers on the Union Bridge was 437 feet, over six times the length of the Jacob's Creek Bridge. The towers themselves were made of block granite, where Finley had been content with a hardwood A-frame.[36]

The successful completion of Brown's Union Bridge attracted attention from all corners of Europe, including Johann's homeland. In 1823, Peter Beuth, head of the Prussian Technical Commission, traveled to the United Kingdom specifically to visit Brown's bridge and his factory in London. Impressed by what he saw, he had Stevenson's "Description of Bridges of Suspension" translated into German and published in the first volume of *Verhandlungen des Vereins zur Beförderung des Gewerbefleisses in Preussen* (Journal for the society for the promotion of industry in Prussia) in an effort to promote "hanging bridges" in Germany, which is where both Johann and Dietlein first read the essay.[37]

Pope's book was also popular in continental Europe, but word of Finley's bridges also reached France via Joseph Louis Etienne Cordier, whose American travelogue was published in 1820. Cordier described a number of Finley's bridges and also reported on an odd little footbridge in Philadelphia, strung from "one of the window mullions of [Hazard and White's] iron wire factory" over the Schuylkill River "to a great tree on the other" side. Built "to enable his workmen to go to & from their work," this "spider bridge," as it was described by Captain Joshua Watson, another visitor, was 407 feet long and could hold as many as thirty-four men at any one time. It was also America's—and maybe even the world's—first suspension "bridge of iron wire."[38]

Finley preferred chain links to iron wire because they could be forged by any blacksmith, while British engineers were vehemently opposed to wire cables. "A bridge of wires . . . is the most objectionable," claimed Brown, owing to their "lack of durability" and the potential for "rapid decay" among their "slender filaments."[39] Thanks to the efforts of Navier and a colleague, Louis Vicat, however, the French took to wire rope. Vicat especially believed it was not only significantly cheaper but also stronger and more durable, quicker to assemble, and far easier to hoist into place than massive and unwieldy iron chains. Visually, wire rope may look like a "slender filament," but physically it was as strong as any wrought-iron bar. Vicat's conviction was shared by Marc Seguin and Guillaume Dufour, both of whom successfully built wire cable suspension bridges in 1823 (the Pont de Annonay across the river Cance and the Pont de Saint Antoine in Geneva). Seguin and Dufour, along with Marc Brunel, helped the French catch suspension bridge fever: between 1823 and 1850 France built more suspension bridges than all other countries combined, using wire rope almost exclusively.[40]

Sown in the wilds of western Pennsylvania, the art and craft of raising a suspension bridge flowered in Britain and France before spreading to Russia, Prussia, Belgium, Hungary, and Switzerland, creating a worldwide, albeit small community of engineers and thinkers committed to the bold and beautiful new structure. For an apprentice engineer like Johann, it was an exciting time to be learning about this new architectural form, although an uncertain one too. Suspension bridges were still a fledgling form dependent on some rather shaky science. From iron chains to cables, from rickety structures on the American frontier to monuments of robust modernism in the capitals of Europe, the ultimate shape and composition of these bridges was still being worked out. While Johann sat in a lecture hall in Berlin, Thomas Telford was busy constructing the Menai Straits Bridge, and Navier was at the Seine. One bridge survived as "one of

Figure 2.4 The distinctive British chain-link—rather than wire—suspension system. View of Menai Suspension Bridge, ca. 1880. Getty Images.

the greatest undertakings ever executed"; the other was dismantled before it was even finished, its parts trashed, smashed, and dumped in the Seine. No trace of it exists. Such was the science of suspension bridges in the mid-1820s.[41]

Inspired by Hegel and the cultural climate of Berlin, Johann was clearly ready to embrace such fancy, newfangled ideas as the suspension bridge. Yet his schoolwork was severely challenging and relentlessly unremitting. Lectures were held every day, and each lecture had to be written out, and handed in for grading no later than eight days later. There was no slacking in class, and there was no skipping class. Some of the older students protested these rules, and Johann himself thought it a poor system—overly taxing and no substitute for good textbooks—but he persevered and by the end of his first year was one of only six (out of 126) students to receive a "book award."[42]

Yet not all was well at the end of Johann's first year of study. In September 1824, Eytelwein had told the students that "within one year a law would be introduced, that everyone wanting to do their second exam would have to engage in practical construction for at least a year with an architect already in royal service." Johann immediately sought such a job and such a man, but with no success. He stepped up his efforts the following year, writing to the state building director in Berlin and the chief construction officer in Düsseldorf, among others, and paying a visit to Baron Ludwig von Vincke, the visionary governor of Westphalia, "to be considered for future construction projects." Johann made a positive impact on Vincke, but by March 1, 1825—when Johann's classes ended—nothing had materialized. After three more weeks, with his funds dwindling, he decided to leave Berlin and return home to Mühlhausen.[43]

Luckily, just as Johann was packing, Dietlein's old boss from Merseburg, Chief Building Inspector Flachmann, contacted him. Johann had met and made a good impression on Flachmann a couple of months earlier, and the chief inspector—recently promoted to road and route inspector for the district of Arnsberg—needed construction site supervisors. Johann made an appointment to visit Flachmann at his home at Ammendorf bei Halle on his way to Mühlhausen, and so had reason to be somewhat hopeful as he prepared to leave Berlin after his first year of study.

On March 24, 1825, Johann shouldered his belongings, boarded a stagecoach, and headed south to Halle. The man who left Berlin was vastly altered from the youth who had arrived from the provinces the previous spring. That young man—so "full of faith"—was now a man of science and industry, a son of the Enlightenment, and an apprentice engineer. Unbeknownst to him, however, Johann would never return to the scene of his transformation or complete his studies at the Building Academy.

3

Building Roads, Designing Bridges (1825–29)

When the French invaded Prussia, the state's transportation system was in an abominable state; by the time they left, it was almost nonexistent. Poor upkeep and hard service during the Napoleonic Wars devastated Prussia's already inadequate roads. Then Prussia found it was unable to move sufficient men or materiel around to guard the borders of its diffuse new empire. What was bad for the military, of course, was terrible for Prussia's economic ambitions. Industrialization was as dependent on transportation as it was on fossil fuels. After all, why bother to mine or make things if you couldn't then move them to market? Clearly, if Prussia was to take the Industrial Revolution seriously—not to mention protect its own borders—it would have to start building roads. As the Prussian civil servant Christian Kunth reported in 1815, it was quicker to travel around much of the kingdom by foot than by wagon.[1]

Unlike the United Kingdom, Prussia's industrialization was primarily state-sponsored and state-driven. In an effort to spur development, Prussia built roads, railways, canals, and bridges; created technical and mining colleges; set up central banks; and established entire industries. Between 1824 and 1830, it spent 15.2 million thalers—or 20.3 percent of non-agricultural investment—on new roads, helping to reduce transportation costs by 17 percent while greatly expanding markets for both farmers and manufacturers. Coupled with major spending on canals and navigation, these investments made Prussia into an industrial power that drove the entire central European economy. Johann did not live to see his fatherland become the foremost economic power on the continent, but he did play a role helping to modernize Prussia's industrial heartland.[2]

———

Luckily for Johann, the road south from Berlin remained in decent working order, and he was able to make good time, arriving in Halle late the next evening.

His interview with Flachmann went well, but Johann emerged with no firm commitment. With nothing to detain him, he walked ninety miles home to Mühlhausen, where he tried to keep himself busy. He eventually received word from Flachmann on May 24 about "traveling [to Meschede] as soon as possible and starting work." Never one to dally, Johann packed a bag and a crateful of books—forty-eight technical reference books, one French grammar, and a single novel, *Der Kleine Telemachus*—which he shipped by coach to Arnsberg. On May 27, he set off through the thick rolling hills of the Thuringian Forest (where, as Heinrich Heine described it the very next year, "trees whisper like a thousand girls' tongues [and] strange mountain flowers gaze like a thousand girls' eyes") to Kassel, where he boarded a stagecoach to Meschede, arriving on May 30. "I began my work efficiently the same day," he wrote in his diary.[3]

With abundant coal seams, iron ore, and copper deposits, Westphalia was destined to become one of Prussia's most important industrial regions. As with much of Prussia, though, Westphalia's roads were in an atrocious state, "death traps for man and beast," as Friedrich Harkort described them. Luckily, the province was run by *Oberpräsident* Ludwig von Vincke, an energetic visionary under whose stewardship Westphalia was transformed from a collection of disparate lands and people—Voltaire's ideal of "perfect backwardness" in *Candide*—into a productive unified whole. Vincke achieved this in large part by building a network of roads to help bind the province together. By 1827, over 740 miles of roads had been built in Westphalia. An effective transportation system was "the best way to promote industrial development" and foster cultural cohesion, Vincke believed.[4]

As a *Baukonducteur* (construction site supervisor) in the Arnsberg district, Johann's primary responsibility was roads, specifically the new Rheinstrasse "stretching from Eslohe to Grevenbrück." Road construction was a multi-faceted process, involving not only surveying, "earthwork" (moving soil and rock), grading, and laying stone but also building drainage and ditch systems and small culverts, all skills Johann mastered quickly over the course of his time in Westphalia. In addition, Johann also built a number of toll booths and guardhouses along the course of the new road—small two-story affairs with a basement and a rear stall for horses—where supervisory personnel lived and worked, and where, for a fee, travelers could stop and feed their horses.[5]

Despite working full-time for the Province of Westphalia, Johann also freelanced in the local construction market. Encouraged by Governor Vincke, state engineers often found themselves employed in private construction. As an engineer and architect for hire, Johann designed all manner of different types of structures over the course of his time in Arnsberg. In 1826, he built a two-story house and stables for the local warden and tax collector. In November 1827, the Meschede district authority paid him 178 thalers to supervise a "police road project" running from Serkenrode to Kückelheim. That same year, Treasury Supervisor Gerlach paid the young *Baukondukteur* twenty thalers for the design of a new rectory building in Calle, and Postmaster Schulte paid him thirteen thalers to design a new post office in Eslohe. In August 1828, Johann was paid twelve thalers to plan a road from Freienohl to Olpe.[6]

While stationed in Arnsberg, Johann lodged with the mayor of Eslohe, Peter Vollmer, whose large, ornate three-story home also housed a "brandy tavern" run by his wife. Moreover, Johann became well integrated into the social life of the surrounding community. Roadwork, of course, took him to towns and villages all over the region, and his numerous outside commissions brought him into contact with employers and laborers alike. One of Johann's few expenses was new clothes so that he could attend the local folk festival. Another was joining the Elberfeld Newspaper Society as soon as he arrived in Arnsberg.[7]

Johann stayed in Westphalia much longer than he had originally planned, and much longer than was necessary. The Building Academy required "at least one year under a royal building official," yet for some unexplained reason, Johann stayed for three and a half, finally returning to Mühlhausen—not Berlin— in October 1828.[8] Johann, however, made excellent use of his time, receiving an education in both the processes—not to mention the whims, foibles, and idiosyncrasies—of the Prussian bureaucratic machine and the forms and functions of the construction practices that were coming to define the Industrial Revolution. He evolved into an excellent general contractor and engineer and received exactly the sort of hands-on apprenticeship he needed to complement his more theoretical university education. Just as importantly, he began to narrow his professional focus and build up a significant engineering library.

If Johann didn't arrive in Westphalia as a suspension bridge engineer, he did all he could to leave as one. He kept up a frequent and vigorous correspondence with Dietlein in Berlin, while voraciously consuming all the available literature: C. F. W. Berg's *Der Bau der Hängebrücken aus Eisendraht* (The construction of iron wire suspension bridges) (1824), Guillaume Henri Dufour's *Description du Pont Suspendu en Fil de Fer* (Description of an iron wire suspension bridge) (1824), and the *Magazin der Neuesten Entdeckungen und Erfindungen* (Magazine of the most recent discoveries and inventions), where in 1828 he read about William Tierney Clarke's newly completed Hammersmith Suspension Bridge (1827).[9] By 1827, Johann was ready to start planning and plotting. He flipped to the first empty page of the notebook he had used for Dietlein's lectures and wrote "Comments on the Subject of Bridge Construction." He then began to make comments in response to an article on chain bridges in the *Jahrbücher des Kaiserlichen Königlichen Polytechnischen Institutes in Wien* (Yearbook of the Vienna Polytechnic Association) and notes toward a correspondence with Karl Schottelius, designer and builder of the Malapane Bridge in Prussian Silesia, one of central Europe's first suspension bridges. The pages are crammed full of notes and drawings: plans for the construction of underwater bridge pillars, sketches of Thomas Telford's Conway Suspension Bridge (1822–26) and Clarke's Hammersmith Bridge (1827), and numerous thoughts on their design and construction. Also included are a number of experiments Johann carried out in Westphalia—comparing the weight and load-bearing capacity of iron bars wrought at different manufactories along the Lenne River, for example—and some important conceptual breakthroughs. Johann developed the idea of

Figure 3.1 Johann Röbling, sketch of the Hammersmith Bridge (1828). Courtesy of the Special Collections and University Archives, Rutgers University Libraries.

"stability through bracing" in the pages of his notebook and gave serious consideration to how suspension cables rest upon towers. The journal also includes a number of observations Johann made while touring the region's iron smelting and drawing plants.[10]

As 1828 dawned, Johann found himself in need of either gainful employment or a suitable subject for his senior thesis. He combined the two. In an effort to spur private development, Governor Vincke proposed that private joint-stock companies be allowed to build and administer new roads and canals. His offer caught the attention of Friedrich Harkort, who opened a successful "mechanical workshop" in 1819 on the outskirts of Dortmund and played a large role in the establishment of the Prussian railroad system.[11] Harkort was interested in forming a "stock association" to build a road between Witten and the Geitebrücke mining works at Hagen, so Vincke introduced the industrialist to Johann.

Unfortunately for Harkort, the Ruhr River stood between Witten and Hagen, which made Johann the perfect man to consult. Taking his leave from rural Eslohe, Johann traveled fifty miles to visit Harkort. As he later recounted to his son: "I stopped 3 weeks [from January 30 to February 27, 1828] at Wetter on the Ruhr River. . . . Mr. Camp was a young man of 18, who took me over the whole (Harkort) establishment. I made a survey on the Ruhr, for location of the Suspension Br[idge] which I had to plan as a Thesis for my second exam." Johann proposed a 450-foot chain bridge that met "the state's building requirements" and took "into account Europe's preferred building techniques for chain bridges." The project was put on hold through the spring, summer, and fall, and on November 4, 1828, the stock association submitted a request to the Prussian treasury for monies to construct "a chain bridge across the Ruhr River at Wetter." Sadly, the venture appears to have gone nowhere.[12]

Johann made sure to have other professional options. During the first half of 1828, Johann developed, wrote up, and submitted two fully fledged suspension bridge plans. One—dated April 9, 1828—still exists, while only the official response remains for the other. It would be logical to assume they were very similar. The first is a comprehensive eighty-nine-page proposal for "a single lane chain bridge over the upper Ruhr River at Freienohl" signed by the "Conducteur J. A. Röbling." The plan called for a rigid timber roadway 118 feet long (between towers) and 12 feet wide ("between railings"), stiffened by a wooden truss of cross braces. Positioned away from likely flood areas and a half foot "above the highest water level," the span would be supported using "46 wrought iron suspension rods" (twenty-three on each side) hanging on an inclined plane from four main cables of either linked iron chains or sheaves of bundled parallel wire. The main cables would pass over four separate, stand-alone towers, 19 feet 4 inches tall and built of "quarried limestone masonry," each with a rounded, domed iron cap to protect against weather damage and erosion. The anchorage chains were to be painted and then encased in earthenware pipes filled with charcoal. A step-by-step guide to assembly accompanied the proposal—as did a close accounting of each individual part and procedure—including alternative costing (and alternative assembly instructions) if one used chains instead of bundled wire. The effect is equal parts thorough professionalism and youthful desire to impress.[13]

Johann's proposal captures not only the young engineer's deep learning but also his mastery of a number of contentious engineering issues. How the main suspension cables passed over the tops of towers, for example, was a contested issue for a number of years. Navier, Marc Brunel, and others clamped the main suspension cables to the tops of their towers, which in turn led to diminished structural strength, since suspension cables move. They expand and contract in response to changes in the temperature, and they need time to find the equilibrium that comes with supporting so much weight. From the very beginning of his career, Johann understood that a more sensible solution lay in placing roller bearings on the top of the towers to allow the cables to move back and forth, thus preventing excessive stress that could cause structural failure. As he wrote: "Each chain will have to be able to move itself in the line of the curve without force and establish its own balance in and of itself [because if fixed to the towers] it will damage and prevent the stretched chain from quickly achieving its balance. This will result in chains breaking." Additionally, "any changes in the chain length that develop due to air temperature, in this case must disturb their balance [and] the effect of cold and heat will be equally expressed on each chain link."[14]

Another issue Johann appears to have understood instinctively was the need to achieve structural stability through stiffness and rigidity and not, as many believed, through sheer weight. A heavily weighted roadway could certainly provide sufficient deflection, but it was no defense against what Johann termed "horizontal flexibility." By contrast, a roadway stiffened by long timber girders, a rudimentary system of wooden trusses, and an integrated, reinforced railing would protect against high winds and the motion of crowds.[15]

That Johann could solve one of the more vexing issues in suspension bridge engineering in his very first plan is remarkable, yet not surprising. Structural rigidity—further stabilized and stiffened by the use of inclined cable stays—would help define all of his later American bridges, as would the use of non-perpendicular suspenders, reinforced railings to add structural strength, and roller bearings. To read the proposal is to understand Johann's instinctive feel for the relationship between structural stability and load variation, to glimpse a mind able to balance strength with weight while keeping them both in perfect harmony.

Undergirding the entire document is Johann's state-of-the-art knowledge and historical awareness. The proposal is littered with references to other engineers and other bridges. From the Winch Bridge in Teesside, the Dryburgh Abbey Bridge, and Brown's Union and Trinity Pier bridges through Marc Brunel's Isle de Bourbon bridges, Seguin's Tain-Tournon Bridge, the Malapane, and Navier's Pont des Invalides, to Telford's Menai Straits and Clarke's Hammersmith Bridge, just about every major suspension bridge is analyzed and evaluated in the text. Weak or inefficient ideas are weeded out. The result is a set of best practices, all of which are incorporated into Johann's design. By including the option to use parallel wires for the suspension cables (rather than chains), Johann took note of Seguin's and DuFour's experiences in France and Switzerland; his use of roller bearings was informed by Clarke's design for the Hammersmith Bridge; some of his ideas on structural rigidity were prompted by the design for the Dryburgh Abbey Bridge; and in fixing the hangers to the deck, he borrowed from Brown's design for the Union Bridge. Likewise, he was able to detect poor ideas amid larger, more successful projects, in effect cherry-picking from the era's finest engineering minds. Despite his admiration for the Union Bridge, for example, Johann refused to couple the suspension chains together as Brown had. "Each line of the [chains] should be able to move without external force and maintain its balance within itself," wrote Johann, so the chains wouldn't jam each other when temperatures fluctuated or a live load moved along the bridge, altering the strain. The effect is deeply impressive, especially considering that Johann was just twenty-two years old and had never actually seen a suspension bridge in person.[16]

Despite Johann's meticulous planning and the backing of Vincke, officials selected a different plan: a wooden bridge built by a workaday local contractor. That bridge lasted a scant ten years before being replaced by a suspension bridge, designed by the Count of Westphalia's building inspector and modeled in large part on Johann's plan.[17]

As soon as he'd submitted his plan for Freienohl, Johann got to work on another suspension bridge project, to span the Lenne River at Finnentrop. "From the end of April until June 1," he wrote in his journal, "I have 5 full weeks to design and estimate the cost of a chain and wire bridge over the Lenne River . . . to be submitted to government on June 1." No specifications or drawings exist for this bridge, but quite a lot can be deduced from the official response to it. As with his Freienhol plan, the Finnentrop Bridge employed four main suspension cables passing over four individual stone towers complete with iron saddles and roller bearings. Structural stability was again achieved through stiffening: the bridge's railings acted as an integral part of the superstructure.[18]

Johann submitted his plans on June 1. From there, the "government office at Arnsberg" sent Johann's plan—along with those of his only rival, another

Baukondukteur called Boese who submitted plans for a basic timber bridge—to the ministry for the interior at Berlin on July 8, 1828, which forwarded them to the Oberbaudeputation (Higher Council of Architecture). In the meantime, Johann returned to his roadwork and bided his time.[19]

Unable to wait any longer, Johann visited the Arnsberg government officer Regierungsrat Vahlenkamp on August 18 and asked for "any information from Berlin concerning the matter of the suspension bridge." Nothing had come in, reported Vahlenkamp. With his time in Westphalia running out, Johann left Arnsberg brooding and disappointed. He fretted over his plans and started to rework them. On September 28, he wrote to the government to say he had changed the location somewhat, now recommending a site a little farther upstream, where the span could be reduced from 210 to 180 feet. Johann may have hoped that by reducing the span, he could better persuade Berlin to take a chance on his bridge. It was his last act before leaving Westphalia. As soon as he mailed his letter, he packed his belongings and set off for Mühlhausen. It was October 1, 1828.[20]

As soon as he arrived back in Mühlhausen, Johann registered with the Erfurt government as a "surveyor, who was employed until autumn in the construction of roads in the county of Arnsberg," and who was also preparing "for the exam in construction and [was] very willing to improve his mastery of this discipline." There's no evidence Johann ever worked again in Europe, or even that he looked for any work. More likely he spent most of his time worrying about his Westphalian bridge projects or reading the latest technical journal rather than looking for gainful employment.[21] Johann knew as well as anyone how rapidly the science of suspension bridge construction was changing and how vital it was to stay on top of new developments. From Finley's seventy-foot-long prototype, erected in 1801 in an out-of-the-way corner of western Pennsylvania, had grown a mighty new arm of engineering. Within thirty years, Joseph Chaley was planning to throw a bridge almost nine hundred feet long over the Fribourg gorge in Switzerland.

Luckily, Johann could afford not to work. He had returned to Mühlhausen with 442 thalers saved, half of which he invested at 4 percent interest and the other half he deposited with his brother-in-law Karl Meissner. This allowed him to continue his studies in relative peace and to furnish himself with the latest literature. On December 6, 1828, he spent ninety-three thalers at Scheffler's Antiquarian Booksellers in Erfurt. Early the next year he bought a copy of Ignaz Edler von Mitis's recently published *Die Carls-Brücke; oder, Beschreibung der Ersten Stahl-Kettenbrücke in Wien* (The Charles Bridge, or a description of the first steel suspension bridge in Vienna; 1829), a full account and description of a new suspension bridge over the Danube at Vienna. Yet none of Johann's reading could lessen his frustration at how long it was taking the Oberbaudeputation to make a decision. Consequently, on November 28, 1828, Johann wrote again to Arnsberg to inquire about the status of his proposal. In addition, he asked that "the government in Berlin return his design plan and estimate . . . so that he might learn from the comments made by the royal highly praiseworthy Higher Council of Architecture."[22]

Unbeknownst to Johann, the council had rendered their verdict several months earlier. They had met on August 5 to study the proposals, written their verdict on August 22, and sent copies of their report to both Johann and the Arnsberg government on September 9.[23] Unfortunately, Johann's notification was lost and, with it, his chance to read the council's rather mixed review. "The project for this suspension bridge must be rejected," wrote the council, "because the chains . . . are surely too weak. As well, the non-perpendicular forms of the suspenders, the manner in which the roadway is suspended on two independent chains, the iron saddles, the intention of using railings to assist in the suspension, the wooden blocks on the columns under the chains, etc. do not have our full approval." It did end on a positive note, however: "Nevertheless, the industriousness with which the engineer Röbling has completed his suspension bridge project deserves our full recognition, and we wish to convey to him our encouragement."[24]

Johann spent most of the rest of his life railing against the inefficiency and unfairness of Prussia's bureaucracy. Yet Johann's accusations seem a little unfair, given that the Oberbaudeputation was able to study two different large-scale proposals, render a verdict, and write it up, all within a couple of months. More likely, there was a fair dose of sour grapes in Johann's response. The council's response is better described as timid or reactionary, rather than overbearing or inefficient.

In evaluating Johann's proposal, the council betrayed its basic objections to suspension bridges: "Chain bridges are only a good idea when large distances need to be bridged, and where neither a wooden structure, nor a stone arch provides an affordable solution." Ultimately, they believed that "a bridge with wooden beams and stone piers" was both more convenient and more desirable than "a chain or wire cable bridge." And this is exactly what they proposed. In their August 22 report, the council recommended that neither Boese's timber bridge nor Johann's suspension structure be built, but instead a bridge "with wooden beams and stone piers." With Johann no longer in Westphalia, the Arnsberg government gave Boese the order to draw up a new plan. He was to adhere to the council's advice in all things, and was further told: "In regard to the location where the bridge is to be built, Röbling is of the idea that the bridge ought to be laid more upstream. We are including [his] visuals dated September 28 that depict his idea. . . . You might find them useful." No wonder Johann's entire proposal is now lost.[25]

Johann was on the wrong side of an ideological battle over structural form. Arrayed against him was rooted conventional wisdom from some of the most influential engineers in all of Prussia, foremost among them August Ludwig Crelle, editor of the influential *Journals für Baukunst* (Architect's journal), who appears to have authorized Johann's rejection and written the response.[26] No fan of suspension bridges, Crelle penned a comprehensive article on the subject two years later in 1830.

In phrases that strongly echoed Johann's rejection letter, Crelle wrote: "Here and there a predilection for this form seems to have arisen . . . with the consequence that based on this prejudice, it is actually preferred to other kinds of bridges." Certainly, "in certain places suspension bridges are ingenious, appropriate and yes priceless aids, where, given excessive difficulties it is almost impossible to construct stable bridges." However, "in most cases and places suspension bridges are inferior to other bridge types." Crelle's reasons were sixfold: "Chain bridges are no more inexpensive than are *arched* bridges," "are more expensive to maintain than bridges with stone pillars and a wooden deck," "are more difficult to repair than stationary bridges," and "cannot last longer than a structure, whose parts *are still*." His "*main concern*" was that "a chain bridge is not any *safer*" and that "its strength is harder to guarantee than that of standing bridges." "Bridge safety"—and thus "the lives of the people who use it"—"depend[s] on a completely arbitrary *estimate*, for which there are no rules and it will be chance, if, to some degree, the master builder comes up with the correct calculations. . . . Any non-visible flaw in the iron can wreck the best calculations and as soon as an individual chain tears apart, the more weight the others have to carry, the stronger the tension, and the sooner they will rip." "It is recklessness to put human life in danger just for the sake of having construction that is venturous and requires clever algebraic calculations," he concluded. Crelle ended with a rather improbable appeal to the aesthetics of the thing: "If one is honest with himself, he will admit that suspension bridges are no more beautiful than standing bridges"; "minimal regard for safety [and] adventurous reckless building will never be more beautiful than a more stable, safe, and practical choice."[27]

Clearly, the council was leery of suspension bridges, and, to be fair, they had good reason to be. Despite the successes of Telford and Clark, suspension bridges were still unproven and risky.[28] After all, Navier's massive Ponts des Invalides almost slid lock, stock, and barrel into the Seine. If one of the structure's foremost theorists could fail, what of a twenty-two-year-old construction site supervisor with a single year of college and no final exam to his name? One couldn't just hand out suspension bridge commissions to any young Turk who came calling.

(For the State Building Directorate, it must have seemed like asking an infant to set economic policy.) Only a handful of suspension bridges had been built in Germany up to this point, each with wildly differing results. One of them, the Malapane (1825), survives to this day; another failed very publicly and spectacularly.[29]

———

In early 1825, while Johann was desperately casting about for construction work, Duke Ferdinand von Anhalt-Köthen sat down with his master builder, Christian Bandhauer, to discuss the need to span the Saale River at Nienburg. Bandhauer favored a suspension bridge, and Ferdinand consented. Construction began immediately. The span was completed by early August and opened on September 6, 1825. In between, tests were mounted and demonstrations staged—having ten horse carts lug eleven tons of cut stone over the bridge, for example—to assure everyone of the span's safety. Happily, the bridge held, and it was decided that a celebration was in order. The date was set for December 6, 1825. On that evening, the mayor of Nienburg welcomed Ferdinand with a short speech before someone in the crowd suggested they fire up some torches and march off to the bridge. By 8:30 p.m. over three hundred people, including a marching band, the assembled dignitaries, numerous torchbearers, and many villagers were on the bridge, although not equally: the marching band and assembled dignitaries had reached the middle and stopped; the villagers were lined up behind them. Within seconds of the standstill, a groan preceded a crack and a crash, and the bridge fell into the river below. Over forty bodies were pulled from the river that night; others were later found downstream. In total, the catastrophe amounted to fifty-five dead and over a hundred casualties.[30]

In reality, only half the Nienburg Bridge fell into the Saale River that night, not the entire structure. Bandhauer's span was less a genuine suspension bridge than a cable-stayed drawbridge. Made of two distinct halves, the bridge possessed no mechanism for distributing its live load over the entire structure. By the time the parade reached halfway across the span, the vibrations of the marching crowd had compromised the bridge's load-bearing capacity, while the live load was concentrated on one end of the bridge, not along the total length. Total structural collapse was only a matter of time—seconds probably—and the span duly complied.

The Nienburg Bridge was poorly and carelessly designed. It lacked even the most basic protection against vibration and had no hint of a stiffening system to help distribute the load or counteract the effects of high winds. Even without the marching crowd, the bridge could not have lasted much longer than the next big gale, but a commission was set up to investigate the disaster anyway.

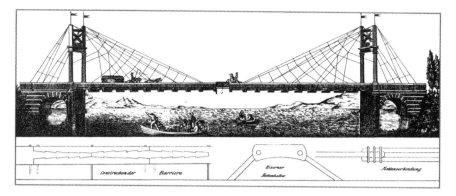

Figure 3.2 The Nienburg Bridge, from Gottfried Bandhauer, *Verhandlungen über die artistische Untersuchung des Baues der Hängebrücke über die Saale bei Mönchen-Nienburg* (1827). Courtesy of Bernd Nebel.

Remarkably, despite clear structural faults and some sharp outside criticism, the commission cleared Bandhauer of any wrongdoing and laid the blame for the collapse squarely on the form.[31] The engineer's incompetence became a matter of public record four years later when he was disbarred from his profession after a number of his other projects failed. But for the moment, by clearing Bandhauer of wrongdoing, the commission damned not the man or his methods but the structural type. This tallied with the ingrained prejudice of many engineers, not to mention the public's perception. People used to solid-looking arch or beam bridges saw suspension bridges as too flimsy, too incapable of supporting even a modest load. That which lent them their innate elegance also led to their undoing. The whole situation represented a failure of imagination, but a failure that nonetheless compromised the hard science of the situation and embittered Johann toward what he decided was an overly conservative state. Had Prussia been as amenable to suspension bridges as Britain or France, Johann might not have emigrated at all. Unfortunately, no state in Europe was going to allow someone like Johann to build a revolutionary new structure whose history was tilted more toward catastrophic failure than solid workable success.

———

In October 1828, just after returning to Mühlhausen, Johann confided to his journal that if his bridge proposals were not successful, he would return "to Berlin [in Spring 1829] to take my architectural exams." Yet Johann never returned to Berlin, nor did he take his final *Baumeisterexamen* (building exams). This is not to say that Johann did not plan or prepare for his exams. On the inside flyleaf of his *Euclid's Geometry* Johann wrote that he had "worked on my thesis & plans for examination." Additionally, the Roebling archive contains a plan for a five-arch stone bridge over the Ruhr River at Wetter dated August 1830; it is stamped by the State Building Directorate, implying it had, at some point, been submitted for examination. Johann's son thought it was his father's senior thesis, which seems like a reasonable conclusion, despite the fact that stamps normally signify receipt, not success. More revealing is the fact that Johann identified himself as *Baukondukteur* (construction site supervisor), not *Baumeister* (architectural engineer), on his emigration paperwork.[32]

That Johann tinkered with the idea of an arch bridge for his senior thesis is telling. It seems like an oddly safe choice, especially for a young man who had immersed himself so fully in the art and science of suspension bridge construction. Furthermore, he had already drawn up detailed plans for two different suspended spans. Certainly the failure of his Westphalia proposals might have given him pause and pushed him toward a concession. After all, if the state would not approve plans for a real suspension bridge, why would they approve plans for a theoretical one? Johann's heart was not in arch bridges, a structure with little innovation or excitement, nor in compromises. Most likely, Johann contemplated a concession before abandoning it.

Despite not completing his studies, Johann was a remarkably well-prepared engineer by the late 1820s, all official certifications excepted. He was already

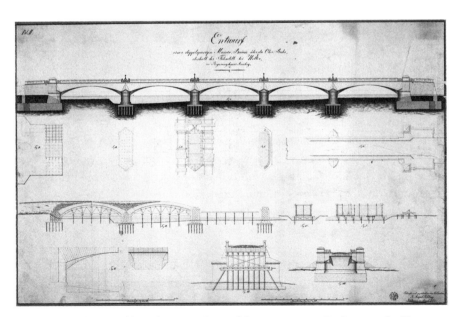

Figure 3.3 Johann Röbling, "Design of a Double Lane Massive Bridge over the Upper Ruhr" (1830). Courtesy of the Institute Archives and Special Collections, Rensselaer Polytechnic Institute.

an excellent mathematician by the time he arrived in Berlin. Subsequently, he studied at one of the finest technical colleges in Europe. In Westphalia, he gained practical experience working on all sorts of different projects, from surveying and contracting to building roads, bridges, and entire houses. As with his mentor Dietlein, Johann could legitimately claim to have conjoined theoretical savvy with practical excellence. Despite never taking his official building exams, Johann was, by the late 1820s, likely one of the best prepared and trained engineers in all of Prussia.

Unfortunately, Johann still had neither work nor opportunity, and for an ambitious, active young man it was hellish. He had made of himself a suspension bridge engineer, yet no one would let him build one. Correspondingly, Johann spent most of 1829 frustrated, blaming the entire state apparatus for their shortsighted ignorance and his lack of opportunity. As he complained in his diary: "Germans wonder" how the Erie Canal in New York "could have happened, without an army of government advisors, secretaries and other officials deliberating about it for 10 years." Nothing of any consequence could ever happen in such a bureaucratic nation, he concluded. But where the state was perhaps overly prudent, Johann was undoubtedly overly petulant, and he began to consider that Prussia might not be the place for him. In the spring of 1829, Johann started to take private English lessons. Whether this was in preparation for a move is unclear, although clearly the possibility had already occurred to him. It would take a chance meeting with a fellow Mühlhauser by the name of Johann Adolphus Etzler to help alleviate some of Johann's frustrations and crystallize some of his ideas.[33]

Johann Etzler and the Mühlhausen Emigration Society (1829–31)

Johann Adolphus Etzler was always on the move, always on the make. An odd mixture of Enlightenment economist, utopian dreamer, and idealist engineer, he was also, as one historian has written, "an anxious holy terror." The eldest of seven, Etzler was born in Mühlhausen on February 22, 1791, to Maria Christina Fröbe and David Christoph Etzler, a shoemaker. As a teenager, he apprenticed as a cobbler, eventually taking over the family business in 1808 after his father died. Etzler immediately began to display his precocious nature, promotional talent, and wide-eyed technological idealism. In 1809, the eighteen-year-old shoe-maker wrote to Mayor Stephan of Mühlhausen about his plans to invent, among other devices, "an underwater machine able to move in all directions" and "blast hostile ships into the air," adding audaciously that "his request be taken to the king [Jérôme of Westphalia]." Oddly, it worked. After his plans were reviewed by officials, Etzler received Jérôme's official stamp and a pension, which he used to pay for a private education. In December 1812, Etzler was ordered to present himself at the Artillery Academy in Kassel. There his trail ends until the late 1820s, when he returned to Mühlhausen, having spent the previous seven years in and around North America.[1]

Etzler wanted to establish a communal farming and manufacturing settlement somewhere in the United States and had returned to Mühlhausen explicitly to recruit able-bodied young Germans to accompany him back across the Atlantic. Johann was his first convert. The engineer met Etzler early in 1830, and the two became fast friends. The former cobbler took over Johann's English lessons, leaving them plenty of time to discuss their pasts and their hopes for the future. Physically, Etzler was "firmly knit" with a "muscular frame," a large "massy" head, and a look "more of the intellect than of the feelings." By temperament, he was a utopian visionary. He was going to harness America's abundant natural resources through the practical application of technology, a vision guaranteed to hook young Johann. Day after day, Etzler regaled Johann with tales of adventure and possibility in faraway America. Etzler, and the vision he represented, was exactly the tonic Johann needed.[2]

Etzler's vision tapped into several foundational American myths, while seeking to eliminate class and cultural conflict through universal abundance. Etzler believed that man could live fruitfully, happily, and with a bare minimum of effort, by harnessing the power of the sun, wind, and waves. In short, once the correct system had been devised and put in place, man could sit back and enjoy life. All of which sounded great, until he got around to the details. After a promising opening, Etzler's vision got strange and fantastical quite quickly. All of mankind's needs, he continued, could be achieved with a single, solitary device: Etzler's "Satellite," a multipurpose machine that would clear the land, cut trees, till and furrow the soil, plant seeds, and, in a pinch, also construct entire canal systems. The Satellite would be wind- and water-driven and would require only routine maintenance. It was all a bit like Einstein's unified field theory, but with agriculture and with a bunch of machines whirring and clanking away in the background. Much of this would be set out a few years later in Etzler's *The Paradise within the Reach of All Men* (1833), his most influential tract, but the form and substance were clearly on his mind as he chatted with Johann in Mühlhausen in early 1830.[3]

By the time he met Etzler, Johann had been cooped up in Mühlhausen for well over a year and was in need of either an adventure or a vacation. Just after the auspicious meeting, he decided to go on both, journeying south to the vulnerable old town of Bamberg, where Franz Joseph Schierlinger had just constructed a 210-foot-long suspension bridge over the Regnitz River. John set off at dawn on May 17, 1830, walking twenty-five miles to Gotha, where he boarded a mail coach to Coburg. After a "very scenic and enjoyable" journey, Johann trekked up to the fortress to see where Martin Luther had lived. "The rooms which he occupied have been restored," Johann reported, while "the sensational view in all directions is plenty of compensation for the effort it takes to make this difficult climb." At four o'clock the following morning, he boarded another coach, and, after a further ten hours traveling, through the "idyllic" Ilz Valley—"lot[s] of picturesque villages amid the green meadows"—he arrived in Bamberg. The journey had taken over two days, thirty-six hours of which he had spent on the rocky roads of Bavaria in a tiny mail coach. Enlivened by some sunshine and exercise, Johann spent the next two days roaming about the city and its seven hills, each of which was topped by a noted place of worship. His intense interest in art, architecture, and engineering led Johann to make detailed notes about all of these structures, including style, markings, materials, adornments, and even superstitions. At St. Getreu's, for example, "anyone who crawls through the vault under the graves and recites the Lord's Prayer three times is protected against colds." He was also compelled to record that Bamberg had "509 professional gardeners."[4]

Johann also found time to visit the Altenburg Castle and take a long stroll along the Regnitz River, "the banks of [which] are beautifully covered with trees, shrubs, and flowers," while the view from the castle was "magnificent . . . the whole landscape is gorgeous and offers a varied spectrum of view." Johann walked as far as the southern end of the city, where "the river offers a view of an enchanting forest and mountain," and spent some time chatting with a young Bavarian military officer. After the imperious contempt of the Prussian military, Johann was surprised to see the soldier get on so well with the local townsfolk. The young lad was much less "haughty" than his Prussian counterparts, although his uniform fitted poorly and his "pants look[ed] sloppy."[5]

Johann tried to see everything and talk to everyone during his trip, but his main focus was the city's brand-new suspension bridge, the first he had ever seen. Sanctioned by King Ludwig I of Bavaria on June 15, 1828, Schierlinger's Ludwigsbrücke was formally opened for traffic on December 31, 1829. In designing his bridge, Schierlinger visited and studied numerous chain bridges throughout Europe. The finished structure employed four isolated towers to carry the four main suspension chains across the river below.[6]

Johann managed to meet and talk with Schierlinger himself and conducted a detailed examination of the span. He measured the entire structure and inspected each and every nut, joint, and bolt. He calculated weights, pressure, load based on area, size, and the number of people who could reasonably fit on the bridge. His conclusions were myriad, the most serious of which concerned the main suspension chains—fixed, set and sealed to the towers and encased in stone and concrete—which he decided were gravely flawed. For starters, "the saddles . . . possess a rough surface on which the chains rest," causing an "extremely high" degree of friction. Furthermore, the design of the saddles failed to take account of expansion and contraction due to changes in temperature. Failure to provide for free movement could easily and quickly lead to cracked chains or fractured towers and, ultimately, structural failure. "During this year's spring, due to changes in temperatures, the chain expanded and all four pillars were slightly bent out of the proper direction," Johann reported, leading one to see "how necessary it is to guide the chains over the saddles using rollers which would allow the expansion or contraction of the chains without putting any pressure on the pillars." The saddle issue had also doomed Navier's Ponts des Invalides, and in response a flexible rolling saddle had been developed, most notably on the Menai and Hammersmith bridges. Johann did not solve the issue, but he was wise enough to weigh the implications of each system and correctly

Figure 4.1 The first suspension bridge Johann ever saw. Ludwig Lange, "Die Ludwigsbrücke in Bamberg" (1830).

decide between the two. Johann's conclusions were borne out shortly afterward when the towers of the Ludwigsbrücke developed fissures.[7]

"It is clear that major errors were made in constructing this bridge," Johann wrote, in addition to those surrounding the chains. The bridge's carrying rails were connected improperly; most of the couplings weren't watertight, and most of the wooden beams were not protected from water damage; the hanging rods didn't fit, weren't vertical, and weren't distributed equally; the handrails were not firmly mounted and were so open that "children could fall into the river"; the anchorages were built too close to the water's edge leading to the possibility of flooding during high water; the suspension chains were much stronger than the links connecting them; many of the bolt holes were significantly wider than the bolts they were meant to house; the ironwork "in general is not exact, clean or even." The "roadway was built in the winter when it was very cold [and] laid horizontally in summer when considerable heat occurred," he continued, meaning "the roadway sagged slightly below the horizontal in the middle due to the stretching of the chains." In Schierlinger's favor, Johann did concede that the "masonry work is excellent" and that the pillars were "quite elegant." "If you stand on the bridge or near the pillars, they look strong and secure. . . . The entire appearance of the bridge is enhanced by the pillars and the spaces between them give the structure a special 'look,'" he decided.[8]

The existence of Schierlinger's bridge irked Johann terribly, maybe even cementing his decision to leave for America. Schierlinger's bridge was fundamentally flawed, but nevertheless he had been allowed to build it. By contrast, Johann's bridges were state-of-the-art, neither flawed nor risky, but his chances of getting one approved seemed dim to desolate. At this point, sitting by the banks of the placid Regnitz, gazing up at the Ludwigsbrücke, Johann may have turned his thoughts to America, a place with seemingly little commercial interference and no regulatory bodies to deal with. In America, perhaps, he could be free of the frustrating, ultimately backward Prussian state; in America, maybe, he could build his bridges.

Johann left Bamberg on May 22 to travel by rented coach to Nuremberg. Stepping out of the cab twelve hours later, he was confronted with a bustling, commercial city of forty thousand inhabitants. Nuremberg was walled with 365 towers and eight gates, surrounded by a three-hundred foot-wide moat. Johann roamed, reviewed, sought out, and scrutinized. He inspected the city's seven stone bridges and its eight wooden spans. He took a morning to walk up the steep hill to Nuremberg Castle, built in the tenth century, which housed an impressive collection of Albrecht Dürer's etchings. He visited the great artist's grave, his house, his former house, and the town hall, which contained a gallery of his paintings, but recorded little about the artist or the art.[9]

As in Bamberg, Johann did a full tour of the town's places of worship and compiled a huge list of facts and figures. Nuremberg was home to twenty-seven mills, a prison, a workhouse, ten hospitals, and an orphanage, he reported, before going on to describe every type of business and public service in detail. No mere mathematician or pure scientist, Johann could appreciate the beauty of a finely wrought architectural detail or well-planned esplanade. Despite all his cataloging and calculating, he enjoyed Nuremberg most for its "pleasant walking paths, beautiful gardens and parks."[10]

Johann stayed in Nuremburg for three days before beginning the long journey home. On May 25, he took a coach back to Bamberg and then commenced to walk the rest of the way to Mühlhausen. The 110-mile journey took him five full days. He walked about eight hours a day and visited all the local sights on the way: the Schwarzburg, Ehrenburg, and Blankenburger castles, in addition to any mills, quarries, ironworks, or mines he could find. Johann arrived back home on May 30 weary but revitalized by what he had seen and thought about. His Bavarian diary shows him to be a compulsive recorder of facts and facades, a man intent on understanding by cataloging and remembering by describing. He is sociable and attentive, often noticing, for example, "a touch of Arabian art" in a column or an arch.[11] He is moved by beauty and absorbed by his interests. He loves an elegant, well-made building and a good view.

Johann continued to plot and plan bridges while journeying through Bavaria. His notebook contains numerous sketches and several partially formulated ideas. The most fully developed was "a project to build a 1,000ft long chain bridge over the Rh[ine]" at Cologne.[12] Johann based his plan in large measure on Thomas Telford's 1813 Runcorn Bridge proposal. His own plan called for a massive set of anchorages—fifty feet by fifty feet—and a rigid stiffened roadway.

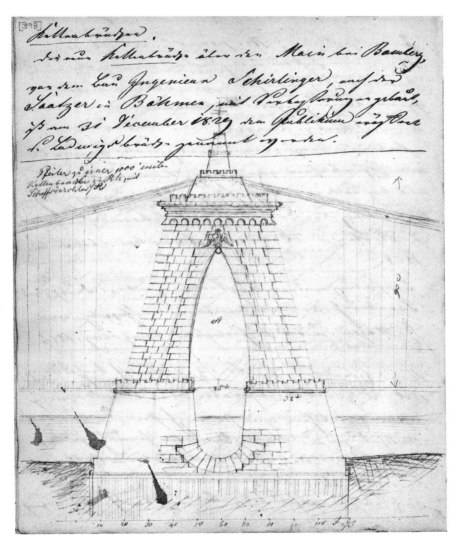

Figure 4.2 Johann Röbling, tower design for a one-thousand-foot-long suspension bridge to span the Rhine at Cologne to allow for the unobstructed passage of ships (1828). Courtesy of the Special Collections and University Archives, Rutgers University Libraries.

The project's most ingenious aspect was a central "two-part pillar" that allowed for the passage of ships without a draw or bascule element. Seen from an angle perpendicular to the roadway, the towers appear like a large arched gateway tall enough for the tallest commercial sailing ships to pass through. The overall design had unique visual appeal and a handsome outline but would have proved both expensive and difficult to construct. Cost, though, was irrelevant. Johann harbored no hopes that his Rhine bridge would be built. If his small, out-of-the-way Westphalian spans couldn't garner official approval, what chance did he have with a thousand-foot bridge over the Rhine? As Johann trudged back to the waiting Etzler, he pondered his present state and future prospects. By the time he returned to Mühlhausen, he was ready for the United States. Only one more event remained to speed things up.[13]

In Paris, on July 26, 1830, Charles X issued his Four Ordinances, and within hours the city was in an uproar and France, once again, in a state of revolution. Seen from Paris, the July Revolution was a brief affair, soon settled. Seen from the Röbling household, however, it was a rolling crisis that ebbed and flowed back and forth across Europe, lasting from 1829 well into 1833. While most of the era's main action occurred outside of central Europe, the implications reverberated around the German Confederation, which found itself dangerously surrounded by social turmoil and outright revolution. To the west, France, Belgium, and the Netherlands all experienced revolutions, as did Poland in the east; revolutions occurred in Switzerland and the Papal States, as well as Spain and Portugal to the south, just as they did in Sweden and Norway to the north.[14]

German-speaking Europe failed to host a full-scale, nationwide revolt, but the region saw its fair share of turmoil and violence. Riots occurred across the German Confederation, as did violent worker protests, calls for the establishment of representative parliament, and the burning of government buildings. All manner of riots had the Kingdom of Saxony in a state of almost total lawlessness for much of the autumn of 1830. In Göttingen, thirty-five miles from Mühlhausen, revolutionaries seized control of the town and held it for three days before they were ruthlessly crushed by the Prussian military. Protestors were more successful in Brunswick, where a citizens' militia deposed the much-reviled Duke Charles II, sent him into exile, and burned his castle. At the close of the year, at a Polish festival in Munich, soldiers wielding clubs and sabers rushed a crowd whose only crime was having just finished the first verse of "La Marseillaise."[15]

The year 1830 was neither an echo of 1789 nor a prelude to 1848, but a significant, continent-wide response to the unresolved tensions of 1815. By the late 1820s, Europe was in deep crisis, riven by myriad social, economic, ethnic, and political tensions. All it needed was a disturbance to turn this instability into chaos and set the continent ablaze again. And Charles X seemed happy to oblige.[16]

Democratic representation and national autonomy drove the revolutions of 1830, but the range of grievances and grudges was so broad as to make everything seem both bewildering and terrifying. From unemployment and inflation to police brutality, tariff reform, and fiscal policy, the people of Europe aired a laundry list of social problems. As soon as France first wavered, then fell, the continent tumbled into violent freefall, and for many the early promise of liberal reform slid inexorably into anarchy. Events in nearby Leipzig only confirmed this impression. On September 2 a group of local blacksmiths gathered to protest a colleague's arrest. Sensing the chance to express additional grievances, other groups joined the protests, and before long, respectable protestors had morphed into an angry mob, and the city was plunged into chaos. Barricades were thrown up all over the city, and the fury of random, undirected violence ruled the streets for weeks.[17]

Only a few score miles away, Johann must have wondered what was happening and what he had left to look forward to. Not the pride of continuing his father's tobacco business or the responsibility of erecting impressive new bridges. He knew that the last time this had happened, chaos had ruled Europe for over twenty years while national resources were funneled away from infrastructure and sunk into the military. As family friend Ferdinand Bähr wrote to Johann: "Everyone agrees that things will get worse here in Germany, despite the fact that war is not yet imminent. . . . It seems that entire nations have lost their senses: it can't get better! We should leave while there is still time and before everything is lost. There is no such thing as society any more. . . . What we have nowadays are schemers, cabals, and hypocrisy." A friend from Leipzig was more ambivalent, yet equally supportive: "You are quite right about going to America if you have a good offer there. We won't have peace here for a long time. . . . You should harvest the fruit of your labors. . . . With your brilliant mind you can easily adjust yourself to any science or art and, no doubt, you will in many ways be superior to the people with whom you will deal in America." Such feelings ran wild around the continent. Explaining his decision to leave Europe in 1831, Gustav Beaumont told his brother that he feared a coming catastrophe: "The present state of Europe seems to me like a volcano about to erupt."[18]

In Bamberg, Johann had seen a vision of what man could build and achieve. Throughout Europe, he subsequently saw the abject failure of political will and the collapse of social order. The time was ripe for new feats of engineering, he decided, but not in Europe, so he decided to get out while he still could, and many others agreed with him. As historian Mack Walker explains: emigrants of the early 1830s—the first great wave of German emigration to America—"had no faith in German's future, or at least no faith in their places in it." The grim realities of life in central Europe contrasted too sharply with the promise of life in the United States, one devoid of both financial taxes and personal duties and defined by its adherence to ideals of freedom and equality. The idea had great appeal for educated, reform-minded middle-class Germans. As fellow emigrant and intellectual Friedrich Muench later explained, "The conditions in Germany . . . were so horrible in my eyes, that I could no longer tolerate them. . . . The spy system made me sick." After 1830, he "could stand it no longer. The government, the nobility's relations with its people, and the dealings with the civil servants disgusted me. It drove me off, beyond and away." Muench set sail for the United States in 1833.[19]

———

Only a week or so after the Leipzig riots, Johann drew up a contract with his cousin Ernst Röbling to print six hundred copies of an emigration brochure. Co-authored with Etzler, Friedrich Christoph Dachröden, and Heinrich Harseim, the pamphlet served as the official manifesto of the Mühlhausen Emigration Society, formed by Johann and Etzler during the summer of 1830.[20] Its guiding principles and conceptual framework reflected Etzler's experiences and the two Mühlhausers' shared vision of a self-organized, communal US settlement. It also reflected Johann's latest new obsession.

After returning from Bamberg, Johann switched his reading from the latest technical journals to anything he could find about the United States. Luckily, German engagement with America had a long and substantial history, from religious emigrants to Pennsylvania in the seventeenth and eighteenth centuries to intellectual engagement with the terms of American independence and beyond. In 1793, Christoph Daniel Ebeling published the first volume of his mammoth *Erdbeschreibung und Geschichte von Amerika* (Geographic description and history of America, 7 vols., 1793–1816); two years later German-speaking Europe had an academic field (*Amerikakunde*) and a scholarly journal (*Amerikanisches Magazin*) devoted to the new country. The nation was uniquely situated— geographically and historically—to appeal to all factions. Enlightenment *philosophes* loved the idea of a nation founded on reason and democracy. Romantic dreamers were drawn to the idea of limitless nature, heroic action, and primitive authenticity, exemplified in the novels of James Fenimore Cooper. Radicals and liberals were excited by the political possibility embodied in a republic founded on personal freedom and individual rights. Karl Follen, a political refugee of the Carlsbad years and later professor of German at Harvard, went so far as to advocate the founding of a model Germanic state in the United States

as a home for Germany's political opposition, complete with formal representation in the US Congress and its own German-speaking university, a notion
others took up.[21]

Johann pored over laws and statistics, historical accounts and personal
narratives, trying to learn everything he could. He studied current and back
issues of Karl Nicolaus Röding's *Columbus: Amerikanische Miscellen*, a journal
published between 1825 and 1832 and the main source of information for
Germans thinking of emigrating. Johann took notes about individual states: their
size and population, projected growth, climate, number of lighthouses, transportation routes, agricultural prices, and whether any Indians lived there. He
scrutinized back issues of *Flint's Western Review*, the *Louisiana Advertiser*, and
the *Western Navigator* for information about the price of cheese in New York,
"fees paid by foreigners who wish to become naturalized citizens of the United
States," average temperatures, where Catholics lived, "vicious and bloodthirsty
mountain lions along the Missouri," Texas ("especially healthy for people with
lung sickness"), yellow fever ("seldom fatal if treated in the initial stages by
blood-letting"), and on all sorts of "crops farmed in the United States," especially
cotton, indigo, and sugarcane. He also made extensive notes on the Missouri
Compromise (1821) and the Indian Removal Act (1830). In several short
months, Johann collected a mass of information, applying the same tenacity of
purpose familiarizing himself with the United States as he had learning about
suspension bridges.[22]

Johann's understanding of the country was heavily influenced by two massively disparate figures: Ludwig Gall and Gottfried Duden. Gall, an idealistic
twenty-eight-year-old secretary of government in Tier, immigrated to the United
States in 1819 with the intention of founding a settlement for needy Germans
displaced and impoverished by the Napoleonic Wars. As with many Germans
of the period, Gall believed the new country to be the repository of all that was
good, fine, and noble in human affairs: "I went ashore [at New York] burning
with the desire to feel under my feet the pristine earth of freedom, to throw myself on the breast of the indisputable friend of the oppressed." He returned just
over a year later angry, penniless, and bitter.[23]

Gall's dreams of freedom and universal brotherhood lasted about as long as
it took him to disembark: "How fast the spell was broken! How quickly were
shattered my dreams of equality and freedom." Initially, he was charmed by the
fine crowd he found awaiting him on the quay—"I had never seen . . . such a large
number of people who looked so well-formed, joyful, and carefree . . . here was
no trace of misery or want"—but then the fleecing began. From the moment Gall
stepped off the boat he was suckered, swindled, and robbed. Everyone he met
in the land of freedom had their eyes on his wallet. Innkeepers blatantly charged
double or triple, and were brazenly upfront about it: "Are you really going to take

me to court over five or six dollars?" Even Gall's indentured servants learned to do as they pleased or demanded "a seat at [his] table and a suit of Sunday clothes as good as" his. Remarkably, Gall was even arrested for throwing an employee out of his house after the man refused to work. Gall emerged at the end of his journey as a veritable Candide, an innocent surrounded by money-grubbing thieves, his travelogue an absurd fable of epic farce.[24]

While Gall loathed Americans, he loved the geography, the natural landscape, and even the "astonishing work[s] of mechanical art" and architecture.[25] Exempting all the swindlers, one might find a happy home, especially in undeveloped western Pennsylvania: "The soil [there] is very fertile and on the whole superior. Springs gush forth often from hillsides, provide healthy drinking water, and feed creeks and streams partly navigable and everywhere suitable to drive mills. Besides having a healthy climate, this region is scarcely 200 miles from New York, Baltimore, and Philadelphia, and will therefore have the advantage, first among many others, of a three-part outlet to foreign markets when canals open it to international trade. . . . Pittsburgh, surrounded by inexhaustible deposits of iron ore and coal, and connected to all parts of the country by the Ohio and the Alleghany . . . seems determined by Nature itself to become a second Birmingham or Manchester."[26] Johann would echo Gall's sentiments almost word for word when he too reached Pittsburgh.

Gottfried Duden's *Report on a Journey to the Western States of North America* (1829) was by far the most popular book about the United States published in German in the nineteenth century. Gustav Körner, who emigrated in 1833, noted that "no other work has so strangely influenced particularly the educated class in Germany. . . . In many families it was read day by day on the eve of embarking for the New World."[27] It was also wildly exuberant, so much so that Duden was later criticized for his overly rosy depiction. By 1834, he was forced to issue a retraction and by 1837 was cautioning against emigration.[28]

Duden's travelogue is a masterpiece of promotional literature. America's climate is healthy and mild, her rivers cool and clear, her fish and wildlife abundant and strangely compliant ("Every evening I hear wolves howl, and yet sheep roam about without shepherds. Here, the farmer suffers as little from beasts of prey as from robbers and thieves"). Public culture is open and accepting. The land is easily cleared and quickly cultivated (although it helps if, like Duden, one owns slaves). The natural world not only supplies beauty and sustenance but helps create and maintain the nation's countless social and political benefits. Because the very stuff of life and happiness is so abundant, there is no crime, theft, want, avarice, or misery. "The great fertility of the soil, its vast expansion, the mild climate, splendid waterways, communication entirely unrestricted . . . and perfect security of person and property," Duden explains, "these are the main pillars of life in America." As for taxes, they "are so low that scarcely any thought is given to them."[29]

Alongside such romantic novelists as Charles Sealsfield and Friedrich Gerstäcker, Duden helped forge the Germanic myth of the American Eden, of the heroic individual living in prosperity and freedom on the American frontier. True, Duden never slaughtered an animal, cleared land, or raised a building, but that was hardly the point. Duden's America was an immigrant's fantasy, not the reality of hardscrabble pioneer life, which is not to say his book was entirely useless.[30] Amid all the celebratory rhetoric, Duden set out some helpful advice, much of which was adopted by the Mühlhausen Emigration Society. Germans wishing to start afresh there ought to pool their resources and talents, advised Duden, and try to establish German farming communities in the lands "over the Allegheny Mountains." They should take with them sufficient tools and equipment and bank on needing at about nine hundred thalers and about eighty acres of land to start with. Such terms were a fantasy for most Germans, but not for Johann and his group, who were able to blend Duden's excessive myth-making with Gall's cautionary, bitter experience into a relatively practical, plausible vision. All that was needed was a little more information on what a communal German farming settlement might actually look like. This they got from Duke Karl Bernhard's contrasting descriptions of Robert Owen's New Harmony and George Rapp's Economy.[31]

"Rapp's system is nearly the same as Owen's," reported Bernhard, a "community of goods, and all members of the society to work together for the common interest." Likewise, both, continued the duke, seemed very impressive on the surface: well-tended "fruit and vegetable gardens [with] sweet-smelling flowers," clean "broad streets" with "good brick houses." For entertainment, there were orchestras and regular dances; for work, both settlements housed a number of factories, along with animal, diary, and grain farming. Both New Harmony and Economy were bustling towns of people, work, and energy. The only trouble was that while Rapp's colony thrived—despite the ban on sexual relations—and continued to for the rest of the nineteenth century, Owen's New Harmony was dissolved before Johann even heard of it.[32]

For Bernhard, the principal cause of success or failure was leadership. "What is most striking . . . is that so plain a man as Rapp can so successfully bring and keep together a society of nearly seven hundred persons," reported Bernhard, while Owen's colony sank into "complete anarchy" the moment he left the compound. A vital part of such leadership, of course, was charisma and belief. Rapp led his colony through the force of his personality, wedded to an intensely religious worldview, which helped bind his colony together into a shared sense of mission and togetherness. Or, as another visitor described it, Rapp could take "his countrymen into a howling wilderness, and in five years . . . be flourishing 'like a green bay tree.'" By contrast, Owen was "an enemy to all sects. . . . He allows each person liberty to believe in what he may consider to be good," which generally led to no common beliefs or even shared expectation. Unity of purpose and outlook defined Economy's inhabitants, none of whom would have uttered a word against their esteemed leader. In New Harmony, however, the people seemed listless and unhappy. "Almost every member" of the colony with whom Bernhard talked allowed that Owen "had admitted too many members, without the requisite selection." A German lady complained "that the [colony's] highly vaunted equality was not altogether to her taste" and that "some of the society were too low." Rapp led his people. Always the committed egalitarian, Owen tried to let the people lead themselves, which proved disastrous. As his own son reported, Owen peopled his utopia with a "heterogeneous collection of radicals, enthusiastic devotees to principle, honest latitudinarians, and lazy theorists, with a sprinkling of unprincipled sharpers thrown in." He let almost anyone join with no thought as to what they could actually do, ending up with too many people and yet too little labor. Only 137 settlers (out of over eight hundred) had any experience or training in an actual profession, meaning, as historian Arthur Bestor points out, the residents more often "furrowed their brows rather than their fields." When things did not go according to plan, they rewrote the rules, rather than retraining the population. New Harmony went through almost ten structural reorganizations in its first two years. Eventually, without strong, decisive leadership, New Harmony sunk into blame, turmoil, and faction. Johann would be sure to avoid Owen's mistakes at all costs, even to the point of starting his colony with almost no one.[33]

———

Having listened to Etzler's stories and done his research, Johann composed a document entitled simply "Vereinigten Staaten" (United States). Whether intended as a recruitment speech or a set of personal notes, the short essay shows Johann's understanding of the country just prior to emigrating. In it, he wrote about the nation's historical development, specifically contrasting it with Prussia and explicitly criticizing the latter for its opposition to popular sovereignty. Overall, Johann's impression of the land he had never visited followed Friedrich Gerstäcker's dictum: "'To America,' exults the idealist, spurning the real world . . . hoping for a world over there across the ocean which matches the one produced in his own frantic brain."[34] There was no sense of social, racial, or ethnic strife, no sense of economic hardship or difficulty. Johann's America was a purely just society, working according to enlightened and rational principles, agreed to by all. As he wrote in the introduction: "The free country of North America is not yet sixty years old and it already . . . represents the ideal of a well-ordered, self-developed, civil nation, whose basis is the idea of a just contract, and whose life-force stems from reason and the greater collective will." It is "free of all those things which we attribute to the northern European countries, or to the savage conquest which initially brought it to life. It reveals a political life—both inside and out—unlike any seen before. It is a country with no typical authority, no nobility, no ruling church, no clergy (operating as a state within a state), no aristocratic privileges, no official army, no standing army, and no high and/or secret police."[35]

Shortly after composing "Vereinigten Staaten," Johann helped Etzler fire the first salvo of a promotional campaign that consumed the two Mühlhausers through the autumn and winter of 1830, co-authoring an article entitled "Was Für ein Land Sind die Vereinigten Staaten von Nord Amerika für Deutsche Auswanderer?" (What kind of country is the United States for German immigrants?) for Röding's *Columbus*. The article began with a problem: information about the United States was often biased or inaccurate. What was needed was a full and accurate accounting of conditions, which the authors were happy to supply. What then followed were "just a few of the many facts" about US life, some of which were objectively accurate—"Each foreigner can become a citizen and enjoy all of the rights that citizens enjoy"—others much more far-fetched: "If one man works two hours per day on average, he can cultivate enough land to provide an abundance of life's necessities for himself and his family." A direct comparison with life in Prussia was implicit. Of the twenty-four "facts," well over half were concerned with personal liberty: "In America, a citizen has no lord over him," for example, or, "Strict protection of individual property define the rights of the people;" there was "freedom to express one's views about anything (publicly, verbally and/or in writing)." Most of the rest concerned the country's plentiful natural resources or the certainty of making a very comfortable living. While Johann and Etzler's list was presented as "fact," it was also meant to sell an adventure, the details of which were published shortly afterward.[36]

Sometime during the late autumn of 1830, an anonymous pamphlet entitled *Allgemeine Ansicht der Vereinigten Staaten von Nord-Amerika für Auswanderer, nebst Plan zu einer gemeinschaftlichen Ansiedlung daselbst* (A general overview of the United States of North America for emigrants, with a plan toward a communal settlement there) began to appear in bookstores in and around Thuringia. The brochure was written for people who "had enough power and drive to acquire more happiness for themselves and for their loved ones by working independently, yet at the same time have little or no prospect of achieving this in their own country, and who turn their eyes with an inquisitive glance toward the great worldly continents of the earth." Locally, an advertisement appeared in the *Mühlhausen Wochenblatt* directing interested Mühlhausers to seek out the booklet (written by "a number of Germans, who are planning a settlement in

America and who are looking for others to join them") at the bookstores in the town center. Johann secured a short, positive review in Röding's *Columbus*. All "who cherish the thought of emigrating . . . and have the means to do so," wrote Röding, "should familiarize themselves" with this "very important booklet," one of the most "honest" in circulation. By the end of the year, thanks to Johann— the emigration society's distribution agent, publicist, and treasurer—the pamphlet could be purchased at bookstores in over thirty towns and cities. By the following February a second edition was published, this time explicitly naming Etzler, Röbling, Dachröden, and Harsheim as authors.[37]

The second, most complete edition of the *Allgemeine Ansicht* was made up of five sections: a preface, a general overview, a step-by-step guide to the "society's program," an addendum addressing the current state of the venture ("The society has now . . . grown so large that it can in all certainty carry out its undertaking within this year"), some of the lingering prejudices as regards a southern location ("yellow fever," "malaria," "mosquitoes," "snakes"), and a concluding summary.[38]

With "beautiful lands, a mild climate, rich nature in a free happy country . . . a magnificent future is blooming" in the United States, the pamphlet began. "Agriculture . . . beekeeping, orangeries, silk culture, fishing and hunting, commerce . . . the application of mechanics and chemistry etc., are all successfully united with enjoyment and pleasure [there]." The society itself is "made up of learned men . . . all of whom have the courage and power to found, beyond the ocean in abundant nature, a new and secure happy life [and will] execute every undertaking according to liberal principles of reciprocity, respecting the natural rights and free will of every person." "Not based on the harm and misery of others [but] solely on nature's rich productivity," continued the authors, "there will be no fights among our people, no arguments about what's mine and yours; rather only peaceful engagement for the good of man." "Only ignorance, arrogance and delusion force mankind together into clans, make the beautiful earth into a hell and its rational inhabitants into enemies against each other," claimed the authors, before posing a series of rhetorical questions: "What good does all that boasting about enlightenment do, when we don't apply science and don't know any other wisdom than to act like sheep?" "What good is the sailing of ships, when we only use them for the exchange of goods, while we cling like oysters to the place where we have been more or less thrown?" Clearly, all sensible readers should sign up for emigration.[39]

The principles and statutes according to which the society would act were summarized in thirty brief sections, ranging from the broad (it was the society's intention to settle in "one of the most advantageous and comfortable areas" of the United States during the summer of 1831) to the specific (disagreements would be decided by an impartial panel of three "referees," two of whom would be chosen by the parties in conflict, while the third would be chosen by the first two referees). Meetings were clearly an important way in which the society proposed to administer itself, with fully a third of all their rules devoted to how the settlement would call, run, record, chair, and otherwise proceed with these regular sessions. For those who refused to recognize the sanctity of the gatherings, the penalties would be severe: anyone "who disturbs the order of the meeting and does not follow the president's call 'to order,' so he shall without delay be expelled from the meeting and his name crossed out of the charter of the society."[40]

The society was careful to set out its general operating principle in the first statute: "It is the purpose of the union to give mutual help and support during the trip and within the settlement in all necessary cases, and to communally apply all available means that can make life comfortable; to carry out all undertakings communally [and] seek communal council in all opportunities." This was not to say that all members were created equal—established members, for example, would have the right to veto new members—or that all property was communally owned. After the settlement was established and its common buildings erected, "with mutual help from all, each family will look to build its own home on their piece of land . . . so that the settlement can be as orderly as possible. After this everyone begins their business on their own." For those unhappy with conditions, or presented with a better opportunity, "every member always has the right to separate themselves from the society."[41]

The longest statute dealt with the creation and administration of a great central warehouse. Designed to house everything the settlement made, harvested, or bought and guarded by two trustworthy people "especially hired for this purpose," the storehouse would serve as a funnel through which everything material passed. Settlers would deposit their goods there and receive a receipt. Likewise, a withdrawal would also be entered into the official log. At the end of every month a massive accounting would be held and declared at a public meeting. Each person's account would be determined and recorded in the stock book. Debt was to be paid off through "work or delivered products." Any surplus of goods "which remain in the warehouse after the needs of the society had been met" was to be taken to "nearest and best market" and sold or exchanged for "other things of need."[42]

The rationale for establishing such an arrangement was simple. Commercially, there is safety in numbers: "What is otherwise the business of many individuals, under disadvantageous conditions . . . is changed here into the business of one." Profits and buying power could be maximized by crafting an efficient, streamlined system that excluded the "greedy hands" of "profiteers" before reaching the consumer. Only by adopting what was effectively a producer cooperative could the society achieve "the greatest possible benefit to its members." If any prospective settlers needed proof of the value and workability of such a system, the authors concluded, they need only examine the German American settlements of Economy or Zoar, both of which prospered. Certainly, the "miracle" that was Rapp's colony was achieved "by combination," as one visitor observed.[43]

At the end of all these "principles and statutes," one might reasonably ask what this would cost. For the most fortunate, the answer was $3,000 (or 400 thalers), broken down into travel costs ($600), real estate ($1,000 for a square mile and "a very simple blockhouse"), provisions ($300), tools and supplies ($200), livestock ($400), and day labor for clearing and building ($500). For the less fortunate, there was always indenture.[44]

The authors concluded their pamphlet with a summary of what they meant by "communality," a word that crops up repeatedly in the text. Rather strangely, what the authors appear to have meant was libertarianism. "We hold it as the greatest tyranny to order any person around, and to tell them how and what to work and how to live. It should be left up to every person to pursue his life's happiness in such a way as he sees fit; to handle his property as he wishes. We understand *communality* only in the sense that every member may contribute as much or as little to every suggested communal undertaking *as he wishes*."[45]

That being said, the authors continued, an individual "is a helpless, poor being" but, in union with others, "endlessly more powerful." A collection of people "without a communal interest" will never work for a larger goal. If people never work together, only care about their own strict interests, and seek "gain only in the loss of others," then a whole can never be attained. There can be no society, only "a many-headed monster, where each head is trying to eat the other." Unless people combine their talents and resources, nothing ambitious can be attempted or achieved. There would be no factories, no ships, no foreign trade or interaction, and "everyone would have to live in deep ignorance." Such a collection of people would "stay in this poor, awkward, and ignorant condition as long as they hadn't learned to unite themselves in a rational manner and for a rational purpose."[46]

Clearly, the emigration society's vision was flavored with a healthy dose of what Roderick Long calls "libertarian socialism": a "*redistribution of power from the coercive state to voluntary associations of free individuals* [governed] via networks of decentralized, local, voluntary, participatory, cooperative associations."[47] And just as the society leaned left, it got all class-conscious. "There are of course many small and big capitalists amongst us; but they don't belong to our class, which make up at least 9/10 of the people. Capitalists have the ability to undertake big things, and to do this to their great advantage. But the mass of society languishes while the rich increase their riches; they keep themselves afraid of each other, hatefully, jealously, fearfully separated from one another; they keep doing business poorly, each on their own, as they are used to, and—help the rich get richer!" The people need to grasp the import and importance of "associa-tion" and "communality" before they can escape the "animalistic" grasp of "the marketplace." "What enormous undertakings they could carry out," the authors foretold, before abruptly switching ideological tack: "what enormous profits" they could accrue.

Quite broadly, the *Allgemeine Ansicht* reflects a change in the nature of German emigration to America: from seeking religious and political freedom in the late eighteenth century to economic opportunity in the early nineteenth. Yet at its core, the pamphlet reflects a time when such terms as communist, cap-italist, socialist, and liberal were still flexible. In some respects the Mühlhausen Emigration Society was a communist capitalist venture; in others, a libertarian socialist one. Much of what they proposed predates the modern cooperative movement by over ten years. Other aspects of their manifesto, however, read as if they were written by an arch, modern conservative: "Once again we repeat it, and we believe it cannot be repeated too often . . . the secure, indestructible ground on which our ideas rest is—one's own interest."[48] Clearly, the authors were attuned to such emerging concepts as capital, industry, profit, and class, but equally stuck in the past, envisioning a rather romantic, somewhat utopian community of like-minded artisans, all happily cooperating. While not afraid to engage with modern economic conditions, they did so by proposing to establish a premodern, cooperative society in the wilds of the New World.[49]

———

The Mühlhausen Emigration Society's plan didn't completely escape official at-tention. On February 17, 1831, Royal County Commissioner Karl von Hagen wrote to Theodor Gier, mayor of Mühlhausen, to ask if he could keep an eye on Etzler. Von Hagen worried that Etzler was "making a business out of mis-leading Mühlhausers" about the glories of emigration, taking their money with overblown tales of quick riches. "Even though each person has the right to find his own happiness any way they can," wrote von Hagen, "we cannot ap-prove of people roving about our country, systematically misleading those who are settled or well established, by over-exaggerating the benefits. . . . This is why I am mandating that the magistrate pay close attention to Etzler's con-duct and activities and that he be brought immediately to the police for a se-rious warning if my suspicions are confirmed." Von Hagen was neither paranoid nor overreacting in calling for Etzler to be monitored, but diligently responding to a local issue. Emigration agents—so-called *Seelenverkäufer* (soul sellers) or newlanders—were a serious problem at the time, roving the country defrauding unsuspecting greenhorns of what little cash they had. These greedy, unscrupu-lous hucksters peddled "seducing propaganda" rather than genuine, impartial information. Unfortunately, telling the swindler from the serious emigrant was often difficult.[50]

Grier wrote back to say that the "private tutor Etzler advocates emigration no more than any other," yet also that many of his ideas were indeed misleading, if not entirely farfetched: "How can 4 men in 8 days clear an acre of virgin forest without any machinery," wondered the mayor, especially when "eliminating the roots [of] a single wild pear tree can aggravate a planter/farmer for years?" Likewise, how could anyone "earn 900 dollars and acquire the requisite plants and animals [for successful farming] in 2 years" with only "a minimal invest-ment"? What was needed, the magistrate thought, was not police interven-tion but "an essay addressed to the public with corrections including, among other things, how the municipality was not obliged to take back impoverished emigrants."[51]

At this point Johann got involved, having heard that the mayor was thinking of issuing a "warning" to the public about their "settlement plan." "The publishers of this pamphlet had it printed solely for the purpose of informing the local public," he wrote, many of whom had requested "information about our ven-ture." As far as Johann was concerned, "nothing would contribute to the distri-bution of our ideas and spark public attention more than public debate, and for this reason we welcome it." The authors hadn't written anything that "they were not completely able to back up; *all of their information* is based on actual facts and experiences and other authentic sources." In fact, "many conditions are ac-tually better in the United States than those described in the book," he added. For this reason they didn't "fear any criticism of their ideas and they very much [wished] to avoid any pointless war of words." However, should their pamphlet be attacked, "the authors will mount a rigorous defense using all means at their disposal." "In short," Johann continued,

> I can assure you that convincing individuals to emigrate is not in our association's thinking; it would not serve our interests. That which can be said about the matter rightfully is being said; no more and no less. For those who make the decision to emigrate, who feel the need to change and the need to determine their lot in life and have good reasons to do so, we will not hold them back. It would be contrary to the spirit of the times. If you, sir, should have substantial doubts in regard to the facts found in the pamphlet, then I would be proud and happy to con-vince you of their accuracy.

"I am asking, Sir," he concluded, "that you not misinterpret this letter nor mis-judge my good intention, which is none other than to guard against inaccurate assessments, possibly caused by false reports and arguments, and I call on you to permit affirmation of my sincere deference, with which I will always be Your Most Loyal Servant, J. A. Röbling, Mühlhausen, Feb. 23, 1831."[52]

Gier wrote back promptly and with no small amount of warmth. Johann took the mayor's reply with him to America and kept it for the rest of his life. It read, in part: "In my opinion the calculations seem favorable . . . but you cannot become rich in America that quickly. . . . Your straightforward letter speaks to the integrity of the venture, which will help some people realize the happiness they seek in America. However, I am obligated by profession to pay attention to such occurrences, to monitor them, so that any damages to the city are averted. For this simple reason, I have concerns—which are surely reasonable—that no families or fathers capable of obtaining their livelihood here [in Mühlhausen] are misled by overly favorable descriptions."[53]

Given the popularity of the pamphlet and the number of emigration applications they received, the local authorities were uncertain and wrote to Berlin for clarification. On March 25, 1831, the Office of the Minister of the Interior and Police replied that, according to regulations, "where it poses no obstacle, the royal government cannot deny permission" to emigrate.[54] At this point, there was only the matter of Johann's building exams left to stop the group from departing, seemingly a moot point. Letters were sent, rounding up the emigrants and getting everyone prepared for the big day. From a distant relative in nearby Eschwege, Johann heard that emigration applicants were beating down his door: "O you Rulers of Germany, what would you say if you saw all this? Poor old Europe, what will become of you? You poor North German Lords will have no one left there but officers and beggars. The number of poor who would like to go is legion." And from old friends, he heard tribute and acclaim: "You have done well. Your names will be glorified by your children's children. You should be highly praised and honored for your brave hearts and the spirit of friendship you possess." Back in Mühlhausen, a Röbling family council was held, and Johann and Carl's "meager patrimony"—"amounting to about $3,000 each," apparently—"was scraped together and paid in advance," according to his son. Additionally, Johann borrowed money from Karl Meissner, his brother-in-law, and—one assumes—from his rich uncle Heinrich.[55] By the end of April, everyone was ready.

Almost half of the group hailed from Hesse-Darmstadt—a hotbed of emigration fever—while most of the rest came from Electoral Hesse, Mühlhausen, and the surrounding area. On April 24, 1831, Augustus Grabe, a "mechanic and workman" from "Kaysershagen near Mühlhausen," indentured himself and his wife to Johann and his brother Carl for three years "beginning with the day of landing in America." In return, the Grabes received passage to America, board, lodging, and medical attendance in case of sickness. At the end of their service, the Grabes were promised "a piece of land in lease on advantageous conditions."

In the meantime, August and the children were to work for Carl and Johann, receiving an "eighth part of the produce raised and prepared for sale" as wages. Frau Grabe was "to attend exclusively to the housekeeping business for said Röblings." During their service, the Röblings were to arrange an education—in both German and English—for the Grabe children. In addition, all the Grabes were to abstain from "strong spirits." Etzler signed as a witness. Intriguingly, the indenture papers state that the Röblings intended to establish "a settlement with a society of Germans in some of the southern parts of the United States of North America."[56] The *Allgemeine Ansicht* also supports the notion that the emigrants intended at this point to settle below the Mason-Dixon Line, with its detailed descriptions of growing cotton and indigo and strenuous efforts to rebuff the notion that the South's climate was all but poisonous. Johann would later explain that the institution of slavery was so odious that he wanted no part of any region that endorsed or supported it. The indenture document suggests no such scruples dogged him as he prepared to leave Europe.

The plan was for the Mühlhausen party to rendezvous with Dachröden, Harsheim, and the "Darmstadters" in Bremen sometime around the middle of May. To this end, Johann and his compatriots left Mühlhausen on May 11, 1831. They walked with friends and family as far as the Lengefelder Tower— about six miles northwest of Mühlhausen—before separating from the farewell party. By the end of the day, they had walked an additional fourteen miles and made it as far as Heilbad Heiligenstadt. There, twenty-four-year-old Johann took up a pen and paper and started a diary: "Farewell, all of you who think of us with sympathy! God keep you! We shall never forget you! Farewell, thou native plain, which hath fostered our childhood, and in which we have enjoyed so many happy moments. . . . It is not contempt for our Fatherland that causes us to leave it, but an inclination and an ardent desire that our circumstances may be bettered and that they may have a decidedly humane aspect. May Fate soon grant to Germany that which her educated populace can lay claim to with most well-founded right, and which has been so long unjustly withheld from her. You know what I mean. Farewell, my Fatherland!"[57]

Johann never saw his mother, father, elder brother, or the town of his birth and childhood again. Later that month, Mayor Gier wrote a short, simple note to von Hagen: "Etzler and the construction site supervisor Röbling . . . gone away to North America on May 12, 1831."[58]

Across the Atlantic (1831)

Johann left the rest of the party at Heilbad Heiligenstadt, after only twenty-two miles, in order to hurry ahead to Bremen and make arrangements. He arrived on May 13 after a journey that "offered nothing of interest for observation" and much to his surprise discovered that Dachröden and Harsheim, along with—rather astoundingly—230 other members of the Mühlhausen Emigration Society had set sail for Baltimore on the *Henry Barclay* two days before. Johann showed calm restraint in his diary, but he must have been troubled. Separate vessels were not part of the plan. Johann was always one to stick to a plan, and the Darmstadters' breach would have seemed like an affront. After all, they had spent over a year in thoughtful planning and only needed to wait a few more days for Johann to arrive. Instead, they left nothing but a forwarding address in Baltimore. Unfortunately, there was little Johann could do but make his own arrangements and wander around Bremen.[1]

Bremen was flourishing in 1831. Already a well-established port and trading center by 1820, the city embraced the business of emigration and by the end of the decade had the trade almost sewn up. Unlike most German states, Bremen—along with Hamburg—enacted favorable legislation and adopted a benevolent attitude to emigrants (*Auswanderers*: literally, those who wander out or away). By the early 1830s, it was well known that the voyage from these cities was less dangerous, much faster, and altogether more comfortable than from anywhere else. The emigration trade began to supplement more traditional merchant shipping, eventually becoming Bremen's major source of revenue. Between 1820 and 1830, 5,753 Germans immigrated to America. Over the next decade that number shot up to 124,726, almost all of them departing from Bremen or Hamburg.[2]

While waiting for his party to catch up, Johann reviewed the 230-ton *August Eduard*, the packet boat they were to sail out on; the terms and conditions of their passage; and the ship's captain, "a very just, straightforward and *sober* man." Every day he visited the massive Bremen Exchange, a "great hall so completely filled with merchants and business men . . . that an apple could scarcely fall to the earth." Johann estimated that over a thousand people assembled there daily. He also visited the Bremen Commercial Association's Union Club on Wall Street, which was "the most prominent place of social intercourse" with its "special reading room" featuring "all sorts of periodicals and newspapers, in various languages, relating both to business and to pleasure." The Union Club was to be found in the Ramparts neighborhood, with its "tasteful handsome dwellings" and earthen fortifications, upon which the city had built "a pleasant promenade [enclosed by] an avenue of young lindens, where one can drive, ride, or walk." Bremen itself was a town of two halves, with a somewhat ramshackle section on the east bank of the Wesser and a more formal "new town" of more "regular" streets on the west. Overall, "the city presents a lively appearance on account of the uniformly cheerful painting of the houses," Johann thought.[3]

Brother Carl and the rest of the party finally caught up with Johann on May 17, having taken six and half days to make the journey. The company numbered sixty to seventy heads, which when joined with the Darmstadters would make a final settlement "300 to 400 strong." Whether that was likely or not was an open question, as Johann and his group shipped their "effects" downriver to their waiting ship. Nevertheless, the colonists followed their belongings with excitement and good humor the next day.[4]

On May 20, they boarded the *August Eduard* and were settling in, when the "suspicious [Oldenburg] police force" paid them a visit. Everyone's papers were in order, and "a few bottles of wine for breakfast had the good effect of accelerating and lightening the business of inspection," Johann reported.[5]

The former mail-boat offered passage in the cabin for seventy-five thalers ("in gold") or in the steerage for thirty thalers, where passengers lay "four abreast" in "double berths . . . placed one above the other." Johann, Carl, and Etzler, along with two others, took accommodations in the cabin, which left "nothing to be desired in the matter of comfort." Eighty-six others traveled by steerage, which was much less salubrious. Johann took a very parental approach to his less fortunate companions, advocating on their behalf with the captain. He lobbied to have the side hatches opened at night to allow fresh air to circulate and helped to build an extra commode. The only privy supplied for the steerage passengers seemed to take the idea of an outhouse rather too literally, being a "sailor's seat outside the stem of the ship beside the bowsprit," which Johann feared would find "women and children and weak persons" needlessly "cast into the sea" on a regular basis. Johann also protested steerage passengers being roped into their own small enclosure on the main deck. Johann thought this not only curtailed their ability to exercise but also subjected them to an undue and unwarranted stigma. The experience taught Johann many things about managing large groups of people and legal contracts, most importantly to work out all the "smallest particulars" before starting out and leave "nothing unsettled." That said, Johann realized he could not control everything, "especially where there are families and little children, whose parents do not pay homage to cleanliness."[6]

The *August Eduard* sailed out into the North Sea, then headed south toward the English Channel. By May 25, "the beautiful English coast lay for the most part wrapped in fog" only a couple of miles distant. Dover, with its "old gray towers and its fortifications above the city, gave a fairly clear picture of a smoky English colliery town." "The interior," Johann decided, "must be very gloomy." On May 29, as they left the channel and "entrusted [them]selves to the ocean," all on board were full of good cheer, expecting the voyage to be easy and pleasant. Most of all they expected it to be brief. About six weeks would get them to "the North American Free States . . . in good time to celebrate the anniversary of the Declaration of Independence," a day on which "fourteen million free citizens of a state can thank for their present condition of freedom and well-being, and on which their brave ancestors, with the splendid and high-minded WASHINGTON at the head, cast off the servile fetters of the proud and over-bearing motherland," declared Johann. "We are all desirous of arriving in time to join in the celebration." Unfortunately, poor winds and poor sailing made for very slow going and an unusually long crossing. It took over ten weeks for the *August Eduard* to cross the Atlantic and enter the Delaware Bay, or about a week longer than it took Columbus to reach the Caribbean. It was another six full days before they could disembark—fed up, bored, and exasperated—in Philadelphia. Progress was so slow that at one point they were overtaken by a seal "snorting" merrily along.[7]

———

Johann was hardly the first German to lead a band of emigrants across the ocean to America in hopes of establishing a successful community, and he would not be the last. Since 1683, when Germantown was founded on the outskirts of Philadelphia, Germans had settled in Pennsylvania, New Jersey, New York, Virginia, Ohio, Kentucky, Maryland, and the Carolinas. A vast majority fled Europe wishing to established uniform societies of religious conformity. Others fled for political or material reasons. Thanks to the violent and bewildering scale of the French Revolution and its aftermath, many Europeans' time-honored ties to location, profession, and culture were broken. Then, to make matters worse, the crops failed. The harvest of 1816 was one of the worst in memory and proved disastrous after so many years of rising prices and forced requisitioning. Thanks to the violent eruption of Mount Tambora in Indonesia, much of the North Hemisphere endured what became known as the "year without summer." As volcanic ash littered the atmosphere, a cold rain fell, and when the downpours finally stopped, the frost set in. By the end of 1816, food prices were double those of 1810, and hunger and starvation, along with desperation and lawlessness, had spread throughout the continent. The situation became so fraught—absurd even—that early the following year Professor Johann Autenrieth of Tübingen University published "a thorough introduction to the preparation of bread out of wood."[8]

Faced with such turmoil and privation, many decided they had no choice but to escape. As the *Allgemeine Zeitung* reported in December 1816, even "in the richest and fairest parts of Europe there rules such discontent that whole families resolve to quit their fatherland. The spirit of restlessness and dissatisfaction is so general and so widespread that it must have a more profound cause than human foolishness."[9] For the first time, emigrants set their sights en masse on the United States. As reported by Jacob Strähle, a carpenter, the decision to emigrate with his family was not "an imprudent whim." On the contrary, "it was very hard for them." They "shed bitter tears that they had to turn their back on their Fatherland" and realized they could also be "approaching great perils, yes it could be that one would be in bondage in America, yet the oppression [that might await them] could not be greater than that which was certain" if they remained.[10] The choice of destination often boiled down to cheap passage, few entry restrictions, and distance from the strife and want that plagued Europe. Such was the scale of emigration that governments around the German-speaking world began to ask questions and commission reports. In April 1817, Friedrich List was commissioned by the government of Württemberg to investigate the issue. "Excessive taxes and dues and the suppression of all sorts of civil rights are the fundamental reason why these emigrants are not content with their lot," he wrote, while "the present great famine and the unemployment it has caused have made of this discontent a conviction that matters can no longer go on in this way; and that they hope on the other hand to be better off in America." Contrary to their hopes, the emigrants of 1816–17 fared no better than in Europe. Driven by poverty and hunger, many were forced to take passage as indentured servants. Broke and disappointed by their experiences, numerous emigrants opted to return home. Born of a crisis, the movement was a disaster, but it helped create an influential and far-reaching idea of mobility as an option, one embraced by Etzler and Johann.[11]

The emigrants of the 1830s went to found a "New Germany" in the wilds of North America, much as previous generations of Europeans had founded New England, New Sweden, New Netherlands, and Nova Scotia. Frustrated by the Biedermeier crackdowns, the failures of 1830, and what they understood as Germany's failure to live up to its own promises, the leaders of these ventures wanted to stay German, free from the yoke of want and strife. Their aim was to move their communities across the Atlantic to somewhere in America where they could perpetuate the language, customs, and culture of German civilization

and keep themselves ethnically distinct, culturally separate, and politically independent. Ultimately, these émigrés were so successful that in 1849 Kentucky
congressman Garrett Davis delivered a speech demanding greater restrictions
on German immigration: "In less than fifty years . . . they will be essentially a
distinct people, a nation within a nation, a new Germany," which, of course, was
the whole point.[12]

The "New Germany" movement helped settle huge German populations in
the states of Missouri, Illinois, Texas, and Wisconsin from 1830 to 1855. The
founding document of the movement was a pamphlet published by the Giessen
Emigration Society in 1833, which likely owed much to Johann and Etzler's own
emigration plan.[13] "We desire to establish a new Fatherland . . . a rejuvenated
Germany in North America," declared Friedrich Muench and Paul Follenius,
the pamphlet's authors. They believed that Germans "should settle as a group,
united as a whole . . . so that in this way the survival of German customs, language, etc., should be secured, so that a free and popular form of life could be
created." "This intention awoke in us," they continued, once they realized that
"conditions in Germany neither now nor in the future will satisfy the demands
that we as persons and citizens must make of life for ourselves or our children."
Johann and Etzler's pamphlet was a less overtly political document. Despite
Johann's antipathy toward bondage, his pamphlet never went so far as to explicitly forbid slavery or to preclude "any kind of aristocracy," as did Muench and
Follenius's. Still, the desire to found a communal agricultural settlement had
marked similarities, as did their specific plans (begin with a common building,
expand to individual lots, store all goods in a communal clearing house) and
the makeup and the inclination of the whole group. Crucially, the Mühlhausen
Emigration Society was a much less nationalistic venture, with a much less gran-
diose objective. As Follenius made clear in a speech he gave on the eve of departure, "We ought not to depart from here without first giving expression to
a national idea. The foundation of a new and free Germany in the great North
American republic can be laid by us, so we must take with us in our own migration as many as possible of the most worthy of our countrymen [so] we may
in at least one of the American territories create a state that is German from its
foundations up, in which all those to whom in future the situation here at home
may seem . . . intolerable can find refuge."[14] Johann and Etzler's vision was close
enough to New German thinking to be considered a fledgling moment in an
impending trend.

The first thing to happen to the Mühlhausen colonists once they were headed
to America was that almost everyone succumbed to seasickness. Feelings of

"dizziness" and "weakness in my chest and stomach" made even a sturdy young man like Johann feel "as if I had had a riotous time the night before" (in the process betraying a knowledge of nighttime carousing not often associated with the starchy young German). Of course, Johann's first compulsion was to study the phenomena. "Seasickness," he decided, "lies less in the rolling than in the pitching of the ship." He next attempted to conquer it. "For a time I sought to maintain mastery over the sickness but in vain. I had to surrender several times, but each time I felt well again after emptying my stomach," he observed. Finally, he went searching for a cure: I "kept myself briskly moving on the deck until 11 o'clock in the evening, to compel myself to become accustomed to the reeling of the ship." Finally he suggested: "If one has an inclination to vomit, but cannot do so, a glass of wine, or a swallow of gin, will often help." Booze of all descriptions was a surprisingly frequent feature of life onboard. Johann's advice was to bring plenty: "wine, beer, some rum, gin," which maybe helps explain why everyone was staggering around the deck feeling sick.[15]

Johann's mania for advice pervades his entire travelogue, as does his obsession with self-healing, especially as they relate to the bowels, a lifelong obsession. "For constipation a small dose of rhubarb is to be recommended, when it is very severe," he suggested. "On the other hand," he continued, "brisk motion on the deck, frequent use of prunes, beer and *Bierkaltschale* [a mixture of beer, grated bread, sugar, and fruit] commonly induce a good movement." As for diarrhea "it is not necessary to employ anything; it abates of itself," he observed, somewhat hopefully.[16]

When Johann was settled in America, he sent a copy of his diary back to Mühlhausen, along with some words of advice for future travelers, as a promotional tool to help solicit new converts. Later that year, at a meeting of the Mühlhausen Emigration Society, a motion calling for the publication of the diary was unanimously approved. The diary came out the following year in pamphlet form, although its influence appears to have been minimal. The booklet seems to have fallen out of sight until Johann's son Washington unwittingly discovered a dog-eared copy in a Mühlhausen bookstore almost forty years later. He was surprised to discover that his father had written such a thing.[17]

Johann's diary is undoubtedly one of the most revealing things he wrote. Its pages show the young Johann "in full": the science geek, the nature lover, the social animal, the intellectual omnivore, the natural philosopher, the strict organizer, the staunch champion of the steerage, and the comfortable member of the cabin. It is a starling portrait of Johann Röbling—as distinct from John Roebling, the famous manufacturer, inventor, and engineer—the excited, hopeful young emigrant unburdened by responsibility or experience. He would never again be so open about his thoughts and feelings. In equal measure he is a wondrous, wide-eyed adventurer and a diligent student. Johann enthuses at length about the most esoteric of subjects: transatlantic exchange rates; ocean currents and trade winds delineated by both degree and latitude ("this marvelous and magnificent phenomenon," he remarked). At one point, he spends page after page after page delineating the *August Eduard*'s rigging system item by item: differentiating a topmast from a fore-topmast and a mizzenmast from a mizzen-topgallant mast. By the time they reached the French coast, he had the entire arrangement committed to memory. Such deep immersive interest may stem from the boredom of a long voyage but is representative of Johann's compulsion to learn about and understand everything around him.[18]

Johann's diary is by no means all tedium and dry detail. A lively, colorful document, it provides ample evidence of Johann's ability to be amazed and transported by the natural world. "The sight of the clouds on the western horizon afforded me a pleasant diversion one evening, when the sun was setting beautifully and the calm seas permitted my gaze to follow its last rays," he wrote on June 1. "After these had disappeared, the glorious coloring of the still-illuminated clouds became more and more lovely, and from their fantastic forms the lively imagination created all the pictures, which only the sight of a beautiful shoreline can ever supply." This scene made him melancholy for his "native fields in Europe, and the scenes of [his] last farewell" but his "lively imagination [quickly] dreamed on and already seemed to see in the remarkable forms and nuances of color, which the light elusively painted before us, the shores of the new Western World, to which our gaze is ardently directed." Often, Johann would sit for hours on end watching "how the fore part of the ship . . . makes its way by main force through the onrushing billows." "Commonly the waves form long ridges like mountain ridges [that] in the twinkling of an eye . . . spread out opposite one another, or retreat still further back, apparently fleeing one another, and often create a valley twenty to forty feet deep. In another twinkling of an eye the valley has vanished and a mountain has arisen in its stead." Johann was so transfixed by the movement of the prow through the water, and for so long, that one wonders what else he packed away in his luggage along with all the beer, wine, rum, and gin.[19]

Johann's amazement wasn't confined to waves and sunsets. He marveled at the sight of flying fish ("surpassed by no others in beauty and in vivid gorgeousness of color") and the appearance of "meerleuchten" (ocean phosphorescence): "No artificial fireworks can furnish the eye with more beautiful examples of brilliancy." Just a week out he was lucky enough to catch sight of "a sea monster, a young whale, which was playing on the surface of the water," before "it swept its great tail entirely out of the water and shot down into the depths, whereupon we saw him no more." The most frequent event, however, was the arrival of high seas and vicious winds. "The violent buffeting of the waves and the howling of the wind has had no end," complained Johann on June 9. Under such circumstances progress was impossible, as were most of the usual onboard activities: "All objects have now been made fast in the cabin to prevent their being overturned. . . . If the reeling is very severe, one holds one's dish in one's hand, balances oneself on the stool, and eats, so to speak, like a gentleman. Often the meal is spiced with hearty laughter, when one passenger or another takes an awkward somersault, whereby the plate is also the loser." The tossing of the ship at least allowed Johann to exercise his imagination: "One easily becomes accustomed to the sight of the wild waves, which, like great wild animals, often seem to dance upon the deck, in order to devour the ship, but remain satisfied, however, with giving it such a cuff in the ribs."[20]

Storms made life on board the *August Eduard* unpredictable and difficult, but at night, if the weather was fine, a couple of flutes were brought out on deck and the men sang old German songs. Johann himself was never bored, of course. When he wasn't writing or ruminating on any one of a dozen different topics, he was diligently learning English and working his way through Alexander von Humboldt's *Personal Narrative of Travels to the Equinoctial Regions of the New Continent, 1799-1804.*

By June 12, the ship was stuck in the middle of the ocean, and Johann's frustration was beginning to show: "Still no good wind! In vain have we been hoping for a long time for the prevailing west wind to alter to our advantage. For several days the wind, on which everything depends here on this broad, unfathomable element, jeered at us. . . . We look with envy at several ships hastening toward the European coasts." Five days later, "the outlook" was still "gloomy," and Johann feared "there [was] little hope of celebrating the Fourth of July with the American patriots." He kept himself sanguine with some philosophy: "The loss of one is another's gain, and thus it is in all Nature, where from the downfall of the one is developed the material for the advance of the other." When "a good breeze got up and the ship started to shift," Johann quietly offered up a quick prayer: "God grant that Friend Aeolus, the keeper of the windbags, may remain propitious." He didn't.[21]

Instead of celebrating the Fourth of July in the New World, Johann and the rest of the passengers were stuck in the middle of the ocean engaged in an altogether more somber task: burying the body of "a one-year-old child in a box weighted down with iron . . . in perfect stillness in the cool, deep bosom of the Atlantic Ocean, mourned by the two parents who had brought the little being healthy and cheerful on board." The child had turned sickly soon after departure and had declined ever since. That it should die on such an auspicious day must have seemed a cruel irony, not to mention an alarming portent. Far from the crowds and the revelry in Philadelphia, the emigrants were instead adrift on the "great lonely ocean" with only death for a partner. All the emigrants had to look forward to was the occasional "sea monster" to enliven their day. On June 23, "a shipwreck" hove silently into view. Mostly intact, yet unmanned and missing all its rigging and the top of its mast, it presented "a mournful picture of destruction" as it glided eerily past. ("Such wandering corpses . . . dead ships bent upon mischief . . . are common enough in the North Atlantic," explained the author and sailor Joseph Conrad later in the century.) The wooden carcass would likely float on, a ghostly presence on the "open, wide ocean" for years, reasoned Johann, until it washed up on some shore or was hit by another vessel during a fog or at night. On July 10, an even more unsettling encounter occurred as a pirate ship glided by. Luckily, they did not attack—too many people on board and likely too little treasure, surmised the captain—but the passengers endured a tense, uneasy few minutes as they stared silently out across the bows at the passing marauders.[22]

When the passengers had been at sea for an interminable two months, there was still no sight of land. To make matters worse, on July 22 the captain revealed he was not entirely sure where they were. Lacking adequate navigation skills, the mariners were forced to rely on other senses and later in the day, they were rather improbably saved by a smell. "We had a pretty strong, westerly and warm wind [today]," reported Johann, "which bore a very noticeably aromatic odor of herbs to us from the vicinity of the American coast." Noses no doubt planted firmly in the air, they set off in hot pursuit. By July 25, they were sailing over Georges Bank and two days later passed the island of Nantucket. On July 28, they skirted the eastern tip of Long Island. "Opposite its western point lies that city of world trade, the city of New York."[23]

Over the next few days, they eased down the Jersey Shore and then spent a disheartening few days at the mouth of the Delaware Bay waiting for the right winds to take them inland. By August 2, they were able to edge into the bay, where they were met by a pilot boat whose captain scrambled aboard with some difficulty. The first American Johann ever met was "a fine-looking, very corpulent and well-fed figure." As for the rest of the passengers: "Everyone is rejoicing and longs to tread the solid earth." "For the first time we shall rest tonight within the boundaries of the United States. . . . If the wind remains favorable to us, we can drink coffee tomorrow afternoon in Philadelphia," declared Johann.[24]

"How am I to find adequate expression to communicate my feelings and my surprise . . . since we came up the Delaware Bay?" proclaimed Johann as the *August Eduard* traveled toward Philadelphia. "Handsome groves of trees and stretches of forest" line the banks of the river. "Three hundred years must have passed since the sheltered loneliness of these wild surroundings was interrupted by the all-disturbing European," Johann mused. "Then a few Indian tribes were living quietly on the property inherited from their ancestors. What changes have come about since that time! What life and activity now reign in these waters! Handsome steamers make their way up and down; countless sloops, schooners, ships, and flags of all nations cross one another's path." As for the riverside settlements: "Today we saw Delaware City on the right bank, a little, newly-built country town, with clean, substantial houses, amongst which one would seek in vain a ruinous dirty hovel, such as one sees in Germany in the vicinity of fine homes and affluence."[25]

The *August Eduard*'s cabin passengers were finally able to disembark on August 5, although not the steerage passengers, who remained agonizingly ship-bound. Even then they found themselves docked at New Castle, not Philadelphia. Nevertheless, Carl and Johann spent a pleasant afternoon and were treated with "much politeness and attention" by the town's residents. Johann spent his time inspecting the many steamboats that lined the docks and the recently constructed New Castle and Frenchtown Railroad. He also "had an opportunity to observe the condition of the slaves": "The few negroes that I noticed here were fairly well clad and did not seem to be in a very oppressive situation," Johann decided, although he would soon change his tune. By evening the cabin passengers were back on board and on the move. By the following morning, "the world-famous City of Brotherly Love" finally came into view. They docked at noon on August 6, 1831, after almost eighty days at sea. "The city affords no impressive sight from the river and seems to be only an irregular mass of houses," ventured Johann. Nonetheless, the Mühlhausen Emigration Society, or at least part of it, had finally arrived in America.[26]

———

Stretching for three miles on the western bank of the Delaware, the city Johann discovered upon stepping off the boat was about half the size of Berlin in terms of population but no less bustling or busy, especially around the docks that fronted the Delaware River. The wharves that welcomed Johann were thick with goods from all over the world. Boats from Montevideo, Brazil, Java, Germany, Ireland, Saint Croix, Jamaica, Santo Domingo, Bengal, Nicaragua, Sumatra, and Turkey—as well as up and down the US coast—crowded around the waterfront. Across town, on the wharves fronting the Schuylkill River, cargo was arriving daily on canal boats from the US interior. Coal was discovered throughout much of Pennsylvania during the early nineteenth century and was helping to fuel a steam power revolution that was transforming Philadelphia. "In twenty years," Peter Du Poncea declared in 1829, Philadelphia would be "the Manchester of America," and his prediction had already proved itself wildly accurate by the time Johann arrived. In 1831, Philadelphia was home to 104 textile mills and responsible for a quarter of the country's total steel production. By 1838 there were more steam engines in Pennsylvania than in any other state, all of them manufactured in Philadelphia. "There is no part of the world where, in proportion to its population, a greater number of ingenious mechanics can be found than in

Philadelphia," observed John Bristed, a reality guaranteed to make Johann feel very much at home.[27]

The first thing the Mühlhausen Emigration Society did in the New World was typical of even the best-organized emigrant groups. Sick of the sight of each other, they split up and headed off in separate directions. Long journeys in cramped quarters are rarely good for relationships, and the group's mood upon arrival in Philadelphia was toxic, especially after Johann discovered that a "new plan" had been secretly drafted and endorsed by almost everyone else, including Etzler. Moreover, its author "was not a member of our group." As Johann reported in his private correspondence, "social life aboard the ship" was at best "frustrating" and "disagreeable," and often just downright "intolerable." "Problems and arguments" were a constant feature of life on board, and by the end of the voyage Johann was convinced that "our existence would have been endangered" by sticking with the other colonists, most of whom he now regarded as "repulsive" dimwits. "Only disadvantage, not advantage, could result, both in pecuniary and social relations . . . from our longer association with these people," he concluded.[28]

A common problem experienced by many emigrant groups amid the long transatlantic voyage was the separation of members into classes, and the same may well have plagued the Mühlhausen Emigration Society. Life in the narrow confines of the steerage was revolting and humiliating, and made all the worse by the excessive length of their voyage. That they would disembark and gladly take direction from a man who had spent the entire voyage in a cabin seems unbelievable, especially for educated, middle-class professionals seeking liberty and equality. Johann's comfortable paternalism may well have seemed like the iron hand of Prussian authority to those whose reason for emigrating was that they wished to exist as leaderless freemen. Even Johann's decision to allow a little air into the steerage might have worked against him. According to Cornelius Schubert, who traveled over in 1834, life in the transatlantic steerage was miserable, especially when "waves forced their way into the steerage area . . . drown[ing] the whole floor such that any objects which had fallen to the floor during the night were absolutely soaking wet." A similar fate greeted the Giessen Emigration Society when they landed in the United States three years later. The Follenius family, having traveled over in the ship's cabin, were assailed and abandoned by the rest of the society when they finally arrived in New Orleans.[29]

Tensions between the visionary Etzler and the rational Johann were especially palpable and very public. This was hardly surprising. Johann learned over the course of their voyage that Etzler was not the kind of man to go into business with, and by the time they docked in Philadelphia, he had clearly had enough of Etzler's impractical ways. "Etzler . . . demanded only more sacrifices from our side after we had already sacrificed enough," Johann complained, "and what was even more annoying, he demanded that every man should subordinate himself to his views." Having Etzler around the settlement, he realized, would be like handing a child equal say in the running of a house. Such a concession—as others would later discover—would spell disaster and ruin for all involved.[30]

The depth of the breach was evident by the time Johann sat down to write to Dachröden and Harsheim a week after arriving in Philadelphia. In a curt and abrupt manner, he dismissed his former friend: "We have gotten rid of Dr. Kling" (whom Johann labeled "a stupid ass unacquainted with the world") "and Etzler's debts and want nothing more to do with them." Johann's tone would later soften, although not his assessment: "He has too *stubborn* a head, offends all the world, is not a businessman, not in the least and he does not know how to ingratiate himself with people or how to behave toward them." "I bear [him] no anger," Johann concluded; it's just "that I should not like to live with" him. Intriguingly, Etzler wrote Johann a farewell note "composed in a friendly but somewhat mystical tone," one that failed to "mention anything about his indebtedness to me," a copy of which has sadly not survived.[31]

Johann had intended to lead over three hundred settlers to a bright new future in the American West. Instead, he found himself stood on a reeking dockside in Philadelphia with a total posse of five and a family of indentured servants. Yet things improved after this fraught start. Johann and Carl checked into a local boarding house where for three dollars a week they got a bed and "coffee, tea, butter, maize, bread, meat, eggs, roast-meat, salad and the like" three times a day. The experience gave the Röblings their first up-close look at their new American friends. Johann was slightly perplexed by his landlady, who at mealtimes "simply gives the invitation 'Help yourself' and leaves," and by the dining habits of his fellow boarders. "Americans set to quickly, eat even more quickly, and leave the table without having said a single word," he wrote, echoing Charles Dickens's derisive description of Americans at table: "All the knives and forks were working away at a rate that was quite alarming; very few words were spoken; and everyone seemed to eat his utmost in self-defense, as if a famine were expected." Plates of cooked poultry "disappeared in desperation as if every bird had had the use of its wings, and had flown in desperation down a human throat." Luckily, Johann found the city itself slightly more congenial than he did his dining partners.[32]

The flurry of commercial activity that greeted Johann was mirrored in a building boom that transformed Philadelphia during the Jacksonian era. Thousands of new buildings had gone up across the city during the late 1820s, expanding Philadelphia's boundaries, both north and south. Where previously children had played on open ground south of town, suddenly there were streets, houses, and businesses, a rather amazed older resident observed. Nearly all of the new public and commercial buildings were fashioned in Greek Revival style, making Philadelphia a city of pillars and pediments. Johann himself was quite taken by all this. He admired the city's many "fine public edifices," especially William Strickland's Bank of the United States; John Haviland's looming, castle-like Eastern State Penitentiary; and the same architect's Philadelphia Arcade, along with its "very fine and artistically constructed" waterworks system. Philadelphia's streets, he observed, were "very roomy and in part planted with rows of trees." The "most animated" were Chestnut and Market. The former is "full of 'stores' and is the chief place of assembly of the elegant world." The latter "serves as the gathering point for all the city's meat and vegetable dealers." "Inasmuch as the houses are not ornamented or colored," maintained Johann, "the streets maintain a dead and monotonous aspect," a common complaint among visitors. "It is a handsome city, but distractingly regular," Dickens grumbled; "I would have given the world for a crooked street." Frances Trollope, who visited Philadelphia a year before Johann, agreed: "The city is built with extreme and almost wearisome regularity." Johann was more generous: "If the houses were ornamented and handsomely colored one might well assert that Philadelphia was the most beautiful city in the world."[33]

As for the people, "the impression the populace has made on me has turned out more favorably than I had expected," Johann remarked. "The outward de-meanor of the people . . . and their public conduct is more modest here and at the same time more free and unconstrained than . . . in Germany." "The removal of the hat and the frequent greetings," for example, "which are so burdensome in Germany, do not exist here. Even in the parlor the American keeps his hat on, which astonishes a foreigner and seems like a lack of politeness." As for their hon-esty: "I have not yet found that Americans seek to cheat more than inhabitants of the German commercial towns." In fact, Johann continued, Philadelphia seems "distinguished above other cities" by "its politeness." "I have spoken to no one yet, even when he seemed to be in a hurry, who has not fully replied to my ques-tion. Every American, even when he is poor and must serve others, feels his in-nate rights as a man. What a contrast to the oppressed German population!" As for "the negroes," they "are all free here and constitute the domestic class. They go cleanly and decently clad." About one out of twelve Philadelphians were black at the time, and the city was home to some of the country's most impor-tant black abolitionists. In June, just prior to Johann's arrival, a black "national convention" was held in the city, at which William Lloyd Garrison famously claimed, "I never rise to address a colored audience without being ashamed of my own color." Segregation was still very much the rule, but the city contained a growing black middle class who supported the Philadelphia Library Company of Colored Persons and the American Society for Free Persons of Color, along with numerous debating societies, literary clubs, and lyceums.[34]

Johann arrived "with the opinion that half of the population was never sober," but his experiences in Philadelphia helped change his mind, despite the fact that "the amount of spirituous liquor retailed here is considerable." "Actual drunkards are not more common here than in the great cities of Germany. I believe that such beastly results of drunkenness as free fights and the like do not occur often enough here to give public offense on the streets." The lack of overbearing rules and regulations was another seemingly less common aspect of American life: "The numerous hindrances, restrictions, and obstacles, which are set up by timid governments and countless hosts of functionaries against every endeavor in Germany, are not to be found here. The foreigner must be astounded at what the public spirit of these republicans has accomplished up to now and what it still accomplished every day." One need only notice, for example, the public hospital, the numerous poor houses, firehouses, and public academies. "In part, of course, this is the result of the natural and fortunate situation of the land and its manifold resources; but it is principally the result of unrestricted intercourse and the concerted action of an enlightened, self-governing people. Good, as well as evil, can spread here unhindered; the public is not guided by leading strings like a little child, but left to its own development."[35]

———

After getting acquainted with their surroundings, Johann's party got down to the complicated business of what they were going to do next. They discovered almost immediately upon arriving in Philadelphia that Dachröden, Harsheim, and the other Darmstadters had left again. Despite leaving only five days earlier than the *August Eduard*, the *Henry Barclay* arrived a whole five weeks ahead of it. The Darmstadters spent two weeks marking time in Baltimore waiting for word from Johann, before deciding to act according to the general principles agreed to back in Germany. Those who remained—as with the Mühlhausers, the Darmstadters split into numerous groups as soon as they landed—boarded a mail boat bound for Savannah. Provisionally, their plan was to lodge just north in South Carolina while formulating a more concrete plan. They promised to send word back to Johann once they arrived in the South, no doubt owing to the uncertainty of their intentions. After repeated attempts to contact them, Johann finally heard from Dachröden in early November: he was in Alabama with Christian Hupfeld (another member of the Emigration Society), while Harsheim had recently died of "bilious fever." Johann, it seems, never heard from any of them again.[36]

It did not take Johann long to realize that it was impossible for the entire Emigration Society to "act unitedly." "Time and delay are costly," he wrote, and "hence we must seek to know our purpose more intimately." When they left Germany, the entire group seemed fixed on eastern Florida as a likely destination, with other southern locations as second choices. Johan later remarked about how "strongly" he favored "the South, despite [his] brother-in-law's concern about health." Yet by the time they docked in Philadelphia, they had "altered [their] previous opinion regarding the Southern States and in general regarding the . . . States where slavery is still permitted." As regards climate, they had decided—"unwillingly, very unwillingly"—that it would prove especially difficult "to discover a healthful locality in the South," especially among the "many swamps and floods" of Florida. In addition, Johann was scared off by the idea of cultivating cotton: "Against the cultivation of cotton the objection is made that the cleaning of the cotton wool in the cotton gins is a very unhealthful business, on account of the pulverizing of the fibers, whereby the lungs of the workingmen are attacked and their lives thus shortened. A negro who is much engaged in cleaning cotton wool is said seldom to become over forty years of age."[37]

Primarily, the Emigration Society was "frightened away from the South by the universally prevailing system of slavery, which has too great an influence on all human relationships." "Earlier we believed that this circumstance would not injure us, in that we would tolerate no slavery," declared Johann, "but now we see already, after a few experiences, how hard it would be to accomplish anything with free German workers in a place where all the work is done by a despised race of men, namely the blacks. In time we would see ourselves compelled to hold slaves," he decided, "and this would have a highly injurious effect upon ourselves and upon the prosperity of the colony." "If the Society had been very large, entirely united and *heavily endowed*," Johann reasoned, then they might have made a go of it. "With our few tools and short wings we could undertake nothing significant," however. "No educated man can feel well there where he is surrounded by slaves; the slave states will never make progress in culture and in human education, never will factories or manufacture blossom there," he noted presciently, before concluding that "they will always remain barbarian states."[38]

The "injurious effect" of slavery and the wisdom of the society's decision were confirmed several days later when news hit Philadelphia of "a conspiracy and combination of the blacks recently discovered" in New Orleans. The enslaved population had secretly collected weapons and "had made a plan to massacre the whites, and thus attain their freedom by force." The example of Sainte-Domingue and the Haitian Revolution (1791–1804) —along with incidents in other US states where "many families of planters have been killed"—"is too great a provocation for the slaves." "Such scenes and horrors will and must occur as long as slavery continues to exist," Johann believed, and as long as whites "will not listen to reason." "The safety of the white people is constantly becoming more and more perilous, and under these conditions we would not feel happy there. . . . The whites are superior to the blacks, but the latter will revolt just as long as they are . . . suppressed and robbed of their human rights. I wish them

all luck." It took a mere five days for a smart and self-assured enslaved man by
the name of Nat Turner to make Johann look clairvoyant after he orchestrated a
slave revolt that killed over sixty white Americans.[39]

"It is neither lying nor dissembling, and in this all reasonable Americans agree,
to say that slavery is the greatest cancerous affliction from which the United
States are suffering," Johann summarized. "Slavery contrasts too greatly with the
rest of their political and civic institutions. The republic is branded by it and
the entire folk, with its *idealistic* and altogether purely *reasonable* Constitution,
stands branded by it before the eyes of the entire civilized world! Grounds
enough for us not to go into any slave-holding state, even if nature had created a
paradise there! It is hoped that, little by little, slavery will be entirely abolished,"
concluded Johann.[40]

Johann's assertion that blacks possessed "human rights," not to mention that
he "wish[ed] them all luck" in securing them, would have struck most Americans
as both dangerous and somewhat absurd.[41] It also marked him out as somewhat
unique in antislavery terms. A vast majority of abolitionists stated their principles in religious terms, not in terms of inherent, personal rights. But as a child
of European revolutions, schooled in the tenets of Martin Luther, Hegel, and
the Enlightenment, Johann understood and accepted the concept of universal
human rights. And since Prussians were banned from owning people, Johann
had no real experience with slavery. Being much less of a seagoing power than
Britian, Spain, or the Netherlands, for example, the German states had little or
nothing to do with the practice or expansion of slavery, leaving no lingering claim
on the public's loyalties or sense of nationalism. Johann was more cognizant of
oppression in terms of power and class. As he noted later that year, Prussian society was bound and defined by "compulsory rule and slavery." Despite his status
as a distinctly middle-class individual, Johann saw society—at least in 1831—
from the bottom up, putting him in the company of those who were also striving
to attain their basic "human rights."[42]

Needless to say, not all Prussian emigrants felt this way. Some actively
supported the institution and opposed abolition, especially German Lutherans
and Reformed Calvinists in Pennsylvania. Duden actively favored the practice,
buying into the idea that blacks were better off enslaved than as free men, being
so "primitive" and "dependent." Other groups, more in line with Johann, stood
opposed to the institution. The Giessen Emigration Society laid out the iron-
clad stipulations "that each [emigrant] renounces the introduction of slavery
forever." More accurately, German settlers before the 1848 revolution avoided
slavery and were against its expansion, but they were rarely abolitionists. They
were strongly opposed to the Kansas-Nebraska Act, mainly because it seemed
to prioritize the slaveholder over the immigrant in peopling new US territories. And this was often the key to the rhetoric behind German antislavery: it
represented unfair competition in the labor market.[43]

Johann's views were aberrant for an American but somewhat more main-stream for a reform-minded European. By chance, many travelers arrived in the United States in 1831, there tolook around, and pass judgment, especially on the inherent contradiction of a slaveholding nation founded on principles of freedom and liberty. Yet few were turned off by the idea of slavery itself, rather than by the physical treatment doled out to enslaved people. Godfrey Vigne spoke for many when he announced that "the slaves of the southern states are a very happy race" but generally rather "idle and careless." Others differed, and they were scathing in their criticism of America's peculiar institution. After witnessing a slave auction—"one of the most degrading and painful sights that can well be imagined"—Henry Tudor wrote, "Such a display, in a country declaring itself the *freest* in the world, presents an anomaly of the most startling character; and as long as so foul a stain shall tarnish the brightness of American freedom, this otherwise prosperous, powerful, and highly civilised country, must be content to forego its proud claims to superior advantages over the rest of mankind." Thomas Hamilton concurred: "Washington, the seat of government of a free people, is disgraced by slavery," he declared. Hamilton and Tudor came from Britain, which was about to seal its formal exit from the "odious commerce" of slavery with the Emancipation Act of 1833. But antislavery sentiment wasn't limited to the British. Sándor Bölöni Farkas, a Hungarian traveler who arrived in the United States in 1831, was equally repulsed. Reading a human sale notice posted on an inn door in Maryland, Farkas "felt as if an icy hand gripped my heart. I sighed in sorrow—we had arrived in the land of slavery!"[44]

Johann's most famous contemporary was Alexis de Tocqueville, the French nobleman who came to the United States in 1831 to inspect the country's prison system and went on—via his *Democracy in America*—to exert an immense influence on America. Like Johann, Tocqueville admitted "that the most formidable of all the ills that threaten the future of the Union arises from the presence of a black population upon its territory." Yet equally, Tocqueville was convinced that the "prejudice to which [slavery] has given birth is immoveable," especially in the free states of the North. Americans certainly wanted an end to slavery, but more importantly, an end to the presence of blacks in their country. To Tocqueville, there seemed little hope of coexistence *except* under the terms of slavery. "Slavery, now confined to a single tract of the civilized earth, attacked by Christianity as unjust and by political economy as prejudicial, and now contrasted with democratic liberty and the intelligence of the age, cannot survive," he concluded. "By the act of the master, or by the will of the slave, it will cease; and in either case great calamities may be expected to ensue," he wrote prophetically.[45]

Clearly, the South was out as a destination. But settling in the far west was also not appealing, given that the whole area was "cut off from all intercourse and all civilization" and patrolled by "bands of wild Indians."[46] Unfortunately, land prices along the eastern seaboard were too high for the purchase of sufficient acreage for the sizable settlement Johann had in mind. Setting the entrance to the far west at the Indiana-Ohio border, and with Kentucky and Virginia both entrenched slave states, left only Ohio and western Pennsylvania as reasonable options. As for Ohio, the signs looked good: its winters were "mild," its climate "healthful," and its soil "very rich." Most importantly, the state enjoyed good "communications with Cincinnati, Pittsburgh, and with New York." In researching the Buckeye State, Johann "availed [himself] of the judgment of a man . . . who settled six years ago in the State of Ohio and is now staying here. This man created an estate for himself by his own strength, is well-acquainted with the western lands, and has gone through with the work of settlement [with us] from beginning to end." Johann also met a man named Krumphaar who advised him "*not* to leave Pennsylvania," as it had, above all other states, the "most advantages."[47]

After ten days in Philadelphia, the last five members of the Mühlhausen Emigration Society decided on four principles that would guide them henceforth: "(1) To settle in a *slave-free* State in a locality, which has, where possible, good communication with the Eastern coast, with the principal centers of the American civilization, and at the same time communication with the principal markets of the West." "(2) In a locality, where culture, civilization, and trade have already attained significance, and where a German population is to be found." "(3) Where the soil affords every advantage to all for agriculture and keeping cattle, namely keeping *sheep*, and at the same time yet gives an opportunity for other undertakings in the future, such as factories, tanneries, mills, and the like. The latter purposes demand a locality where there are plenty of oak trees, waterfalls, coal beds, minerals, and the like." "(4) In a locality where we find the opportunity to purchase for our own beginning small 'farms' already under cultivation, with buildings and all, and where there are still sufficient uncleared lands for the rest of our friends and our posterity later on, and forest-lands which can be cleared when opportunity offers."[48]

With these priorities set, Johann's little group decided to move on. On August 20, Johann entrusted his diary to Captain Probst of the *August Eduard*, who was sailing back to Europe, and two days later set off "in a canal boat" with his associates. The plan was to go to Pittsburgh, which ironically was where Etzler along with about ten former members of the Mühlhausen Emigration Society had headed a few days earlier. On the way, Johann intended to "gather information about land in Indiana County in Pennsylvania," and "if we do not settle in

Indiana County, we shall travel to Pittsburgh, from whence we shall seek a place in the State of Ohio." "It is very likely we shall settle in the State of Ohio," Johann confided to his diary, before concluding somewhat optimistically that "we begin our journey with the conviction that our friends in South Carolina will follow us." They didn't. For all intents and purposes, Johann and his four followers were on their own, free to wander the wide-open spaces of America in search of a new home.[49]

PART TWO

APPRENTICE (1831–47)

And out to Western Pennsylvania (1831–32)

Despite appearances, Philadelphia's future was not as sunny as it may have seemed on the surface. Beneath the economic boom of the late 1820s lived an anxiety built on past glories and old achievements. Philadelphia's position as one of America's most prosperous and populous cities—at its height in the eighteenth century—had come under increasing pressure from a newly dominant New York to the north and an emerging Baltimore to the south. In 1825, New York had leapfrogged past Philadelphia in the race for economic dominance—via access to western goods and western markets—thanks to the Erie Canal, completed that year. And Baltimore was constructing its own western route in the form of a fast and reliable railroad running from Baltimore to the Ohio River.[1]

Pennsylvania's business leaders had already begun to fear the city's commercial decline. In 1824 they formed the Pennsylvania Society for the Promotion of Internal Improvements, declaring that "a large proportion of the western trade has been withdrawn from this city . . . and the present exertions are calculated not merely to regain what is lost. The struggle assumes a more serious aspect. It is to retain was is left."[2] Clearly, the Erie Canal had created a crisis in the Keystone State, and Pennsylvania needed to react. This they did two years later by commissioning a state-sponsored "main line" of internal improvements—railroads, canals, and a portage system—designed to cross the state, linking Philadelphia with Lake Erie in the north and the Ohio River in the west. Large sections had been finished by the time Johann arrived and helped transport his group to western Pennsylvania.[3]

———

Johann's small group of colonists departed Philadelphia on August 22, 1831, taking the Schuylkill Canal up to Reading, where they managed to make themselves even smaller. Only a few days out, Genss "became [so] feverishly ill" that he was unable to continue. He was forced to spend the next twenty days there with Manso as his nurse, after which they made their way to Pittsburgh by stagecoach. Having lost almost half their party after only sixty miles or so, the remnants of the Emigration Society took the Main Line Canal to Huntington, thus far its westernmost point. They completed the three-hundred-mile journey on September 19, having rented a "freight drayman" to take them to Pittsburgh.[4]

Life on the Pennsylvania Canal was "a microcosm that contains almost as many specimens of natural history as the Ark of Noah," avowed Philip Nicklin, who wrote extensively about canal travel in the Keystone State. Each craft was about eighty feet long and eleven feet wide. Sleeping berths were positioned in three tiers on either side, making the journey cramped and confined. "The number of berths, however, does not limit the number of passengers; for a packet is like Milton's Pandemonium," Nicklin explained, "and when it is brim full of imps, the inhabitants seem to grow smaller as to afford room for more poor devils to come in and be stewed." "The scene [is] a combination of the magnificence of nature in her grandest and wildest mood, and of the ingenuity of art in some of her greatest efforts," Nicklin gushed. Johann disagreed, as did Beaumont, who took the journey around the same time. It was "one of the most arduous [journeys] I have taken," he sniffed; the canal was "detestable," the accommodations "even worse." For Johann, the trip, which cost the Röbling brothers one hundred dollars, was "unpleasant, costly and boring." Large sections of the canal were "not in order" and, thanks to "the dry time of the year," "not sufficiently filled with water." Delays were an infuriating constant. Another problem—as Johann saw it—was the "influence" of "warm sun miasmas which cause fever to develop out of the stagnant water." Carl became "feverishly ill and so weak that [Johann] could transport him only in a hammock, which was strung up in a freight wagon."[5]

Johann was obsessed with climate and bodily health, and his journey across Pennsylvania only strengthened this fixation, as did Carl's sudden, lengthy illness. Even after they reached Pittsburgh, Carl remained bedridden for a further four weeks, no doubt due to the local "malaria cure": "strong doses of quinine" combined with mercury. Johann had read of the "famed climate of Pennsylvania" back in Mühlhausen yet failed to find "*one single* healthy face" while stationed in "Philadelphia with [its] 180,000 inhabitants." He expected to find "red cheeks" in the countryside, but there again: "nothing but pale suffering faces." Johann began to despair, until he reached Ebensburg high in the Allegheny Mountains, where he "found blossoming and healthy looking people . . . as in Mühlhausen." Immediately, Johann drew a quick, lasting conclusion: if "the most undeceptive proof of healthy air and healthy water is the blossoming *appearance* of the people," then the only "exceptions" to the sad fact that "the entire US was unhealthier than . . . Europe" were "the more northern and higher regions of Pennsylvania."

After all, if "*all* people in Philadelphia and in eastern Pennsylvania, almost *without* exception, had pale faces" but "here toward Pittsburgh the color of people in general became increasingly better," then one could only deduce that Johann had stumbled upon the most healthy place in the new nation.[6]

Rarely has anyone rhapsodized so forcefully about the climate of nineteenth-century Pittsburgh as Johann, albeit in letters back to Germany designed to solicit further emigrants. The city "is universally considered to be one of the most healthful places in America," he claimed. More accurately, French visitor Michel Chevalier described it as "the dirtiest town in the United States." Lying behind much of Johann's thinking was the fact that he was mortally afraid of malaria, and he seems to have intuited a link between mosquitoes and malaria, noting that Cincinnati "suffers each year from fever and the mosquitoes are said to be terrible." He might also have considered that any place inhospitable to mosquitoes might also prove somewhat rough going for human beings.[7]

———

The once mighty Mühlhausen Emigration Society limped into Pittsburgh with a total membership of seven, most of whom were indentured servants. The city they found was much smaller than Philadelphia but rapidly growing in both people and prestige. Its population more than doubled within ten years of Johann's arrival, and by the last quarter of the nineteenth century was undoubtedly one of the world's most important industrial centers. In 1831, however, it was a city in transition, from an isolated western military outpost to a eastern trading post and manufacturing center. As Edward Park Anderson observed, in the years after US independence Pittsburgh "deserted the Far West and gave its allegiance to the East."[8] Still, the seeds of Pittsburgh's commercial clout were evident by the time Johann first set foot there. Pittsburgh was already stacked with factories: iron mills, foundries, and boiler yards, along with metalsmiths, glass, brass and bell foundries, wheelwrights, wagon makers, saddlers, and tanners.[9]

Pittsburgh's rapid, unchecked industrialization was, however, fast remaking the city into an ugly netherworld of blackness and blight. The sight of it must have given Johann pause, despite his claims of the city's wholesome, healthful climate and his excitement at the city's position and prospects. Describing his first glimpse of Pittsburgh in 1829, Russell Errett wrote, "We reached Pittsburgh on a pleasant, clear day, so that we did not see it at its worst; but oh! The misery of that sight! . . . After traveling for two weeks through white, clean cheerful-looking villages and towns, to come all at once upon dirty streets and dark, filthy looking houses stretching away in rows continuously ahead and enveloped in an atmosphere of smoke and soot which blackened everything in sight . . . There

was enough [smog] to cover everything with a dingy pall and besmirch everything with soot."[10]

Johann never recorded his initial impressions upon reaching Pittsburgh, but
where others saw muck, he clearly saw brass. As he wrote home to Mühlhausen
with giddy excitement shortly after arriving: "Pittsburgh meets all [our] demands
more than *any other* [city] to the West of the Allegheny mountains. . . . It is the
first manufacturing city in America . . . and the key to the great western river region of the Mississippi. By virtue of its situation on the Ohio . . . Pittsburgh has
endless advantages, because nature here has done everything which is necessary
for the existence of factories." The region is "rich in . . . bituminous coal beds,"
"iron ores," "salt mines," and "wool markets." All of this spelled future prosperity.
As William Harris rhapsodized back in 1821, if the emigrant "asks, which is the
most flourishing town, or where he is the most likely to succeed, in almost any
branch he may mention, 'Pittsburgh' is the answer."[11]

Pittsburgh was a perfect place for a young immigrant to put down roots and
start anew. It was a small town about to burgeon and take off. It had direct access
to one of the nation's largest and most important commercial waterways, the
Ohio River, which connected it to the entire North, South, and West. To the
east, the soon-to-be finished Main Line Canal would make Pittsburgh competi-
tive with such other Western cities as Cincinnati or St. Louis. "Here in Pittsburgh
one can best observe the mobility of the Americans," wrote Johann; "life and activity here are astonishing. . . . It is the key to the West."[12]

Pittsburgh confirmed Johann's belief that Americans cared for business to
the exclusion of all else. Everyone "is a business man, everyone is after business
and after making money," Johann observed. And certainly Pittsburgh was one
of America's most business-minded cities. As Chevalier noted, Pittsburgh was
"one of the least amusing cities in the world"; he continued, "There is no interruption of business for six days in the week, except during the three meals, the
longest of which occupies hardly ten minutes." Yet there were signs that learning
and culture had started to penetrate the city's hard-headed commercial scene.
By the time Johann arrived, Pittsburgh was home to a university—the Western
University of Pennsylvania—in addition to a school for the deaf and dumb, a
public library, a subscription library, and an apprentice library; a mechanics'
institute; and the Pittsburgh Philosophical and Philological Society. There was
still no daily newspaper in 1831, but the city was home to numerous weeklies,
almanacs, and journals.[13]

In Pittsburgh, Johann and his brother lodged with the merchant Charles Volz
from Frankfurt, who was "interested in all his German countrymen." Volz lived in
the heart of Pittsburgh, on commercial Wood Street between Front and Second
Street, a block north of the Monongahela River, and he acted as the city's unof-
ficial welcome party for German immigrants. Through him Johann heard about

a certain "widow Collins" who had over twenty thousand acres of land for sale in Butler County, Pennsylvania, about twenty-five miles north of Pittsburgh.[14] Johann had already seen and inspected a number of different tracts of land to the north of the city—spending much time at Jacob Mechling's famous German Inn (Butler County's preferred destination for all fun-loving Germans looking for an authentic taste of home) in the process—and seems to have held out little hope for the widow's territory, despite hearing that she "had good lands and sold them *cheap.*" Never one to shrug off an opportunity, Johann went to Freeport to see Genss and Manso, who had split with Johann—amicably, it seems—and were both looking for land of their own. Neither could be found, however, and Johann later found out that "in a hurry . . . to settle down" they had already paid eight hundred dollars for two hundred acres of land lying between Freeport and Kittanning. "The land is *good,*" Johann thought, and "the vicinity is also pretty, however the location is lonely and closed away from the entire world." Jancke had also settled quickly, buying land much nearer to Pittsburgh for a vegetable farm he intended to run with some friends from Bremen.[15]

This left Johann alone with Carl and his indentured servants, the Grabes, who stayed for a few days after reaching Pittsburgh before moving on to establish themselves in Jefferson Township. Johann clearly tired of the Grabes very quickly after arriving in western Pennsylvania. "You cannot depend on the most honest person for whom you pay the [transatlantic] passage," Johann complained; "he will always believe that you are oppressing him." Grabe "is an honest fellow," he continued, "and yet he has his moods and in Philadelphia believed he had been cheated." By the time Johann wrote home to Mühlhausen at the beginning of 1832, he was adamantly against the idea of indentured servitude and actively advised against becoming so encumbered. The labor such people provided was never enough to justify the cost of passage across the Atlantic and the constant headache of managing them. After January 1832, Johann said nothing about the Grabes, although they ended up living in the town he founded.[16]

"Five miles from Freeport," traveling south from Butler Township, Johann "suddenly found [him]self in a region which has an entirely different character" from anything else he had seen. "The broken and torn terrain ceased, and I rode through a gently rolling continuous level area which fairly commands the surrounding territory. . . . I could see for many miles and everywhere had a free view toward beautiful sections of forest and the mountain in the distance. The soil along the road was good, and a farm through which I rode showed me land of such quality as I had not yet seen. The region conformed entirely to my wishes," he wrote, and over the next three days he "examined everything exactly." "On the western boundary," Johann discovered "a strong brook which has enough water and fall to drive machines," while he thought the soil was "the best to be found in Pennsylvania." "Nowhere . . . have I found such beautiful land in one piece," he scribbled in his notebook before hurrying off back to Butler to contact Mrs. Collins's representatives.[17]

In October, Johann returned to Pittsburgh to hire the smartest German lawyer he could find—Charles von Bonnhorst, a Pittsburgh alderman and good friend of George Rapp—and returned north. With von Bonnhorst in tow, he went searching through the records. Finding that all was in "good order," Johann sent the following official dispatch to Mrs. Collins in Pittsburgh: "My brother and I will take 1,600 acres *now immediately* at a price of 1½ dollars. . . . Further we offer for 2,000 acres (the tracts specified) the same price; and on 3,000 other acres (the other tracts) $1; but we reserve the right to make report to our friends in Europe and await their reply with regard to the latter 5,000 acres." John offered to pay $1,000, with the balance due "without interest" in a year's time. Collins counteroffered, essentially asking for $1.75 per acre and refusing to fix the price of the remaining five thousand acres; they agreed at $1.50 and postponed the issue of the additional five thousand acres. By the time the contract was signed and officially registered on October 28, 1831, the terms of the sale were for 1,582 acres at $1.39 with a thousand dollars down and the balance payable in two subsequent annual payments. "When this region is cultivated and especially when the low meadowlands have been cleared," it would be "a paradise," Johann proudly predicted. "Gently sloping cultivated fields [will] alternate with beautiful valleys [and] meadows, and on the higher spots the spared forests will form a beautiful interruption. . . . My description is not an exaggeration; it is the best which I have seen in America."[18]

Johann was clearly enamored by his purchase. With its "*healthy air*" and "*healthy water*," one "knows little about mosquitoes," "nothing of fever," and never sees "a *pale* face" in Butler County. Likewise, its relative proximity to Pittsburgh, a four-hour horse ride—not to mention the state's brand-new canal—meant that an honest farmer could sell his produce for cash, rather than relying on a barter system or selling to a "profiteer." "In no city in the interior of the United States," Johann proudly declared, "does as much *cash* money circulate" as in Pittsburgh. Still, Johann understood he could clearly learn a thing or two from some of his more successful neighbors, so he paid a visit to the most successful commercial operations in western Pennsylvania: Rapp's Harmony Society in the village of Economy, twenty-five miles west of Johann's new home.[19]

———

Born in Iptingen, in the Duchy of Württemberg, George Rapp was a Pietist, a separatist, and a charismatic religious visionary, which failed to jibe with the strict religious climate of late-eighteenth-century Germany. The clash was so pronounced that he decided to emigrate with his followers and establish an equally strict religious colony in the American interior. Like Johann, Rapp started out in Butler County, buying several thousand acres of land along the Connoquenessing River in 1804 and establishing the communal farming village of Harmony. Unfortunately—as Johann would discover—the farmland of Butler County was poor and difficult to work, and after ten years trying to make a go of it on the Connoquenessing, the Harmonites sold the land, to a group of Mennonites, at a huge profit, and moved to the banks of the Wabash in Indiana. The Rappites stayed on the Wabash for another ten years before once again selling out at a massive profit—this time to Robert Owen—and settling back in western Pennsylvania and establishing Economy.[20]

Rapp's final venture was a massive success, the "socio-economic showplace of America in the first half of the nineteenth century," according to his most assiduous biographer. "What is done here is clear and logical," declared the Hungarian Sándor Farkas, who visited the Harmonites the same week as Johann. Such "perfect equality," "bucolic domesticity," and "disregard of worldly luxury, balanced by full enjoyment of life's rich offerings," would seem like "dreams had we not seen it to be convinced of its existence." "As long as [the members] do not mix themselves into politics, and as long as the present Constitution of America continues to exist," Farkas predicted, "their society will last." Despite the Hungarian's political warnings, the Harmonites were committed voters and active political participants, albeit in a narrow sense. They were single-issue voters. They supported Henry Clay's "American System," a federal system of finance, protective tariffs, and internal improvements designed to promote and favor American manufacturing and national expansion, and they voted as a bloc. The Harmonites kept their religion private, but they wore their politics publicly. Just as Johann arrived in October 1831, in fact, the community was embroiled in a public argument over the Main Line Canal. As it was a public work likely to improve the commercial life of western Pennsylvania, the Harmonites were staunchly in favor of the project and in favor of raising taxes to pay for it, a controversial position to adopt in a region that had birthed the Whiskey Rebellion forty years earlier.[21]

What Johann found in Economy was the very model of a successfully planned, efficiently run communal settlement, complete with "beautiful, wide tree-lined streets," "uniformly built, new, two-story houses [and] a wonderful garden [with] a fountain [and] all kinds of flowers, orange, lemon and fig trees, all kinds of American plants, cotton, tobacco," and an assortment of beautiful vines and fruit trees. The inhabitants—750 strong, "all members of the society"—supported a "tailor shop, shoemaker's shop, cooper's shop, saddler, wheelwright's shop, tannery, hat-making establishment, apothecary and chemical laboratory, blacksmith shop, brickyard," and "a large threshing and blowing machine." The town was laid out in twelve squares "with broad streets intersecting each other at right angles." There were eighty dwelling houses, a large meeting house, a commodious hotel, a four-story cotton factory, a grist mill, a distillery (for which they became much admired, despite their strict abstinence), a tannery, and several other establishments "for prosecuting mechanical business." They also had a three-story brick building that served as a museum and a music and dining hall. At the town's east end there was a park with some deer, and "a large vineyard and orchard laid out in beautiful order." The villagers were "exceedingly attentive to strangers, receiving them always with a hearty welcome." "The authority of Mr. Rapp over his colonists and their affection for him are unbounded," wrote Farkas; "he is universally addressed by the title of *Father*, and as they have neither laws, nor courts, nor prisons, the whole authority, executive, legislative and judicial, is vested in him, from whom no appeal is ever made."[22]

Johann researched Rapp's colony in some detail before leaving Europe, and after visiting and meeting the patriarch, he was certainly of the impression that he was "one of the first and best informed land managers in America." "The factories in Economy are very efficiently arranged [while] everything [else] is purposefully arranged and shows contentment and prosperity," he decided. Yet for all his compliments, Johann seems to have misread much about life in Economy and the history of the settlement. As would become a persistent aspect of his character, Johann was very comfortable finding justification for his own actions in the actions of others, regardless of fact or circumstance. That Rapp moved back to Pennsylvania after a decade in Indiana, for example, was "clear proof of the correctness of my [Johann's] assertion" that Indiana's climate was unhealthy and its occupants sickly. In reality, Rapp left the banks of the Wabash for a number of reasons, none of which had anything to do with climate: poor communications, expensive and irregular transportation, unreliable mail service, scarcity of hard currency, and, most importantly, the fact that there were hardly any Germans in Indiana, which led to suspicion and xenophobia. Western Pennsylvania by contrast was awash in Germans.[23]

Despite the high esteem in which he held his host's "land management" skills, Johann was less complimentary toward Rapp's religious principles and social leadership, ultimately predicting a less than rosy future for the colony. "I have been there and saw everything," he confided to a friend. "Old Rapp has brought together a great deal of money, lets his farmers work, on Sunday preaches unreasonable stuff to them, keeps them in stupidity and does not allow them to marry. Because of this many young fellows and girls run away who do not care to live in celibacy. I heard him preach and, together with other incomprehensible chatter, he set up and defended the thesis that men can attain eternal bliss only if they suppress the needs of nature. . . . There is dissatisfaction among his personal body guard, because no one knows what he does with all the accumulated money, and a crisis threatens the entire unnatural Rappish establishment soon."[24] Oddly, Johann was right, but once again for the wrong reasons.

At the same time as Johann was establishing himself in western Pennsylvania and inspecting Rapp's colony, a man styling himself Archduke Maximilian von Este, Count of Leon, Anointed of God, stem of Judah of the root of David (the lion of Judah that opens the seven seals in the book of Revelation) appeared in Economy. Almost immediately, he mounted a serious challenge to Rapp's leadership, leading to "the Great Schism," a departure of several hundred members in April 1832, followed by a pitched battle a year later. "Many serious wounds were inflicted by both parties; and but for the timely arrival of the sheriff, lives would probably have been taken by the excited combatants," reported a local newspaper. Ironically, Count Leon attacked Rapp for his lack of millennial zeal, not for keeping the colony's funds or for his "unnatural" desire to "suppress the needs of nature," as Johann supposed. He was able to make headway with the faithful precisely because he was able to deploy as much "unreasonable . . . incomprehensible chatter" as Rapp.[25]

Frederick Muench of the Giessen Emigration Society noted sometime later: "A single Rapp could hold everyone together through religious delusion." By contrast, "our liberal ideas were not powerful enough against the individual interests and dogmatic nature of our fellow countrymen. . . . The societies based (solely) on liberal principles were the ones that dissolved the fastest," he argued. "German liberalism alone grants no [cohesion] of which one could rely on," which helps explain why so many emigration societies ruptured and broke apart upon arriving in the New World. German emigrants were often held together by their common hatred of Prussian absolutism and their shared hopes for more political and social freedom, not by their shared sense of communal interest, mission, or social cohesion. Once the former disappeared, the latter was abandoned.[26]

Rapp was more politically savvy and engaged than Johann suspected, and more than Johann would prove to be himself. In fact, Johann might have learned much from Rapp and his colony had he possessed a little more insight, a much more open mind, and a lot more patience. He returned to Economy several times over the next few years, and ironically each time was a testament to the Harmonites' success and also to Johann's own failures. One of Rapp's early successes was the development of silk culture. By 1831, Economy already led the country in efficient silk production and was "preparing to go extensively into the business." In 1834, Johann came shopping. On a subsequent trip, he bought thirty sheep and drove them back to Saxonburg. That he got them home at all can only be counted a minor miracle given the subsequent fiasco that was Johann's adventures in sheep-farming. In 1836, Johann wrote to Rapp to ask if he could buy three to ten bushels of rapeseed, depending on the price. The rapeseed seems to have gone the way of the sheep and the silkworms.[27]

———

On November 2, 1831, Johann wrote a 101-page letter to his friend Ferdinand Bähr back in Mühlhausen. It began: "My respected Friend! Good news follows bad, at least as far as we are concerned! My brother Carl and I, Manso and Genss have advanced so far in our undertaking that we can say: our future in America is *assured*," though they were all still in Pittsburgh. Yet this exuberant slice of rhetoric was typical of Johann on the verge of becoming a rather extensive land-owner. Bristling with plans and overcome with excitement, Johann could barely contain himself. Firing off ideas, Johann exploded with plans and schemes: "*oil manufacture*" ("*very profitable*"!), rapeseed production, sheep farming, "silk cul-ture" ("If these Swabians [Rappites] can do this, why should we not be able to do so?"). "Believe me, a great deal can be undertaken here," he enthused. Johann even contemplated sitting back and setting up a sharecropping scheme: "In the future we [can] set several poor families on the boundary of our land, who can work the land in return for 1/3 of the produce. . . . Each year many German families come here whose means are small and who would gladly enter upon such an arrangement."[28]

Johann's grand plans were most evident in the list of things he felt his new colony needed in order to flourish. When making the trip from Europe, Johann counseled, Bähr ought to bring over "a capable young shepherd"—"if possible with a wife"—along with "a *pair* of young shepherd dogs" and a "young cabinet maker." Additionally, he added, Bähr ought to bring over garden and field seed, field peas, hemp seed, lentil and vetch seed, rapeseed seed, poppy seed, mul-berry tree seed; books about silk culture; J. J. Prechtel's ten-volume *Technical Encyclopedia, or Alphabetical Handbook of Technical Chemistry and of Machinery*; all manner of tools for wood- and ironwork, "a good supply" of hoes, spades, shovels, axes (broad *and* carpenter), scythes, sickles, locks, window fittings, good saddles, hooks and hinges, hasps, padlocks, raps, picks, forks, tines, cooper's tools, drills, planes, chisels, saws (especially foxtail saws), flints, barbed wire, a supply of powder and shot, and some "percussion caps" ("hunting is *worse* here than around Mühlhausen," he explained), not to mention house-hold items: "all your cooking utensils," cooking pots, dishes, bed linen, glass and porcelain ware, paintings (!), "a *good* piano forte," a barometer, a thermometer, writing paper, "twined sulfur," sponges, and as many chests of drawers—"packed full of clothing"—as they could manage. On the subject of clothing, he advised him to look to "equip yourself for *many* years ahead" with shoes, boots, woolen and linen clothing, strong shirts (about "2 dozen"), linen trousers ("with a *low* waist"), stockings, and beaver coats from Europe. When working, one wears a dyed flannel shirt during the day before changing to a cotton one in the evening and hanging the flannel until the next morning, Johann informed his friend, despite having never worked a day in his American life. "In this way one can wear such a shirt 2 to 3 weeks and still keep the skin clean," he observed. (By contrast, Frederick Muench, who did work the fields, complained, "I often had to change my sweat-drenched clothes 2 or 3 times a day.") After reeling off the required inventory—"Noah's Ark would not hold it all," observed his son Washington— Johann eventually gave up and resorted to a brief: "Don't sell anything, bring everything with you," after which one wonders if Johann himself brought over anything at all.[29]

Johann was full of grand ambitions for his new settlement. Overall and most importantly, he advised, "Trust no one." "Americans do like to steal and cheat foreigners," he had discovered—likely through reading Gall—although "also each other," as if it was some national pastime. As for himself, Johann had carried his money "enclosed in heavy parchment," then "wrapped in a strong silk handkerchief" and encased in a band tied around his body just above the hips, since "here no one notices it, and it cannot be lost," he counseled. As for his colony, he was considering building a fifty- by thirty-two-foot simple two-story building where "all *decent* friends" can stay while they set their feet in the New World. After a while, of course, trades would be established, and more and more houses would be built; "later a *church* and a *school* will be built, a *concert hall* and a *theater*, to make the project complete. Factories may flourish in the future town. . . . Art and science can flourish, besides industry and the public bath; a German academy for the *sensible, well-rounded, harmonious* training and education of the body and soul will be the culmination and the main work of all."[30]

Ultimately, Johann chose Saxonburg—not Germania, his first choice—for the name of his settlement, perhaps hoping to lure some Saxons, a radicalized, often heavily disaffected population ripe for emigration, to the wilds of western Pennsylvania. He also hoped to lure the rest of his family. As he sat down to write to Bähr, Johann was undoubtedly under the impression that his elder brother Hermann would follow with his family once Johann was settled. "He will be very welcome to us and will be received with open arms," Johann wrote, before noting rather enigmatically, "I know his reasons and cannot condemn these." Johann also asked Bähr to see if his "cousin, the tanner and dyer, Röbling" would "come here and bring some funds with him"; likewise "my cousin, the printer," so as "to establish a German printing and lithographing business." The larger question was not his brother or the cousins, however, but "what should become of [Johann's] old parents." "Would it not be very ungrateful of us to leave father and mother all alone and to move into a strange part of the world?" Instead, Johann proposed a solution: Would Bähr ask their "parents, if they are still in good health, also to come over and to conclude their life among us . . . a quiet, peaceful, undisturbed and comfortable life, . . . carefree and *tax-free* [with the] enjoyment of free nature and in the company of their own and several other decent families"? "If our father has a comfortable room, a garden where he can plant tobacco, a beautiful region with an expansive view, where he can walk and in the evening have a few men about him for conversation, a pipe of tobacco and a glass of good beer, then I know he will be satisfied," Johann believed. Johann counseled Bähr not to put any pressure on his parents: "The decision must be of their own free will, and the condition of their health must be *good.*" If his parents were not interested, and if Hermann would not stay in Mühlhausen, then "Carl has decided to return and to remain with my parents so that they will not be left so alone." Clearly, Carl was not as enamored with life in the United States as Johann.[31]

In discussing his family's relocation, Johann did not mention his mother's needs even once. It may be that he already knew her thoughts on the matter, but his efforts were sadly already in vain. Unbeknownst to Johann, cholera had swept across much of Europe since his departure, claiming hundreds of thousands of lives. Among the dead were the famous (Johann's idol Hegel) and the noble (Carl von Clausewitz, the noted military theorist), alongside the anonymous and obscure. The full force of the pandemic fell on Mühlhausen in November just as Johann sat down to write to Bähr, and shortly afterward it claimed the life of Friederike Dorothea Röbling, Johann's mother. "I was her favorite and prior to her death she felt I had misled her," Johann revealed later, although what led to this judgment remains unknown. Friederike's death put an end to any plans for a Röbling family reunion in the New World.[32]

———

Johann spent much time comparing his new home with his old when writing to Bähr. He missed "German heartiness, German cheerfulness and German good nature" and worried that there was "little sense for art and science" in America. "Everyone [here] is after business," he declared, while "the real refined enjoyment of life, the spice of life, the refined joke, a refined and attractive conversation between the two sexes, more refined gallantry; all this one seeks in vain in America." That said, he could admit that "the American farmer lives a very happy life indeed, enviable in comparison with the German farmer; he raises all his necessities himself [and] has a surplus of the necessities of life." American farmers work "*half* as much" as a German farmer and "[live] like a prince" in comparison.[33]

Johann thought the descriptions and travelogues he had read before emigrating contained too much praise and too much criticism, and neither was especially accurate: "If a foreigner here makes his fortune and comes back, then he praises everything; if another has misfortune, then he makes everything bad and easily becomes unjust in his accusations." Despite all this, some important things remained "correct." Americans are "the most enterprising people on earth and in time will become the most powerful and the most wealthy. The geographic location secures the land against external wars." The political system was stable; the principles "are already too well inculcated in the 13 million strong population and have become to them a political guarantee that no potentate can establish himself here," he noted. "One type of human could become dangerous to the republic," he warned, "and that is the priests, who since the time of the creation of the world have always caused the most misfortune." Americans "are too bigoted and go to church too much," he worried, while Sunday's "fearful celebration" made life "uncomfortable" for the less than avid.[34]

Johann arrived during the high point of the Second Great Awakening, and in the fervor of worship he may have temporarily forgotten his own dire warnings about the effects of slavery on the new nation. His views on both religion and slavery, not to mention his views on the human condition, were wrapped up his concept of freedom (*Freiheit*), a word he used regularly and often. As he wrote to Bähr: "I can assure you in advance that you and Mr. Angelrodt will like it here in America, if you expect no more than a world with free people where everyone unhindered follows his interests as well as he can. Whether others will like it here I cannot say," he added; "not all are able to find their way and adapt themselves to such an extended freedom and equality as is here the rule throughout the country." Such warnings hint that Johann's confidence was beginning to be tempered by the reality of his situation. It also underscores his belief not only that freedom was the dominant feature of American life but that it came so hard and fast in the New World as to seem disorienting.[35]

What did Johann mean when he spoke of freedom? In Germany, freedom was a rather new term referring to the potential for emancipation through personal development, free from foreign or bureaucratic interference. Closely related, liberty (*Libertät*) was a much older and more established concept that stretched back to the Middle Ages. Evolving from the legal rights of German princes during the Holy Roman Empire to a more general concept of the "political rights" enjoyed by certain sections of society, liberty was a tangible expression of ownership and privilege. Oddly, this was somewhat similar to how American slaveholders in the southern states also understood the idea of liberty.[36]

Liberty was the rallying cry of the South, and freedom that of the North. In his famous dictionary, Noah Webster wrote, "*Liberty* has reference to previous restraint, *freedom* to the simple, spontaneous exercise of his powers. A slave is set at *liberty*; his master had always been in a state of *freedom*." Webster helped define and distinguish between these ideas, but he was only amplifying current usage. For Horace Greeley, Charles Sumner, Francis Lieber (a German intellectual immigrant and close contemporary of Johann's), and a host of other intellectuals, liberty—enshrined as a set of legal protections, property rights, and civil privileges—stood increasingly opposed to freedom, which came to rely on ideas of economic and educational improvement, exemption from personal control, and—as Johann and other new immigrants understood almost instinctively—access to land. In both Germany and the United States, freedom was for the aspirant, liberty for the entrenched.[37]

In his understanding of freedom, Johann fit his new nation: "As far as the advantages of the country, its institutions and arrangements are concerned, one cannot praise them too much in comparison to Europe. I can honestly tell you that I have not been disappointed *in the least* as far as the main points are concerned. Freedom and equality are at home here to such a high degree, and yet everyone lives peaceably side by side. . . . All this is here done without kings and emperors, without standing and devouring armies of soldier dolls, bureaucracy and *tax servants*, without the splendor of court or courtiers, without *police officials* and hangman's slaves. Of all these European instruments of suppression and spoilers of the people, who like vampires suck the blood from the veins of the farmers, one here knows nothing." In the United States, government officials "are servants of the people, not masters and suppressors"; "here everything strides forward while in Europe everything moves backwards."[38]

Johann's final piece of advice to Bähr was wrapped around an admonition: "I warn you . . . be careful about people with whom you get into contract. You cannot expect that even the most righteous and well-meaning man will always remain *sensible* and keep his head *clear* in the execution of such an undertaking as you are planning." As for whom Bähr ought to bring: "Do not encourage [just] anyone to come to America; many come here who do not fit in here and who are then tremendously disappointed. Farmers fit in here best, who are used to cultivating the fields, who in Germany are oppressed and who here live as free as kings and can have abundance in everything." Unfortunately, many "finely educated and fiery young men who shine in good society in Germany . . . do not have the courage and resignation to exchange the book for the plow and the pencil for the clearing hoe, in order to live here as *free* men, independent and quiet in the enjoyment of free nature," and they will not fit in. It was ironic advice from a well-educated young man who had never worked a field before. Out of the hundreds of people who signed up for the Mühlhausen Emigration Society and journeyed to the United States in the summer of 1831, only one ended up settling with Johann in western Pennsylvania, and that was his brother. This says much about the disorganized and restless state of German emigration, but also about Johann himself, who could be autocratic, unyielding, and hard to fathom. As he concluded in his letter to Bähr: "What do several weeks of discomfort [on a transatlantic voyage] mean incidentally to the entire remaining life? Think of that philosophic truth which Etzler proves very beautifully. An eternal determination rules, everything has its causes, and the first causes go back to the endless beginning. This is the fate of the ancients. Man depends less on his will than on circumstances; circumstances have also brought me to America." What he meant by this is anyone's guess.[39]

———

Johann was full of optimism as he wrote home to Mühlhausen at the end of 1831, but all was by no means well in his adoptive new country. As Johann discovered within days of his arrival, the cancer of slavery was corroding America's reputation as the Land of the Free. Nat Turner's Rebellion marked a new era of sectional crisis, with savage reprisals in the South and moral repugnance in the North. The arena of national politics was just as fraught as the issue of slavery. The year 1831 saw the rise of the Anti-Masons as a political force (especially in western Pennsylvania), the reentry of Henry Clay into the US Senate (the trigger for the creation of the American Whig Party), the escalation of the Nullification Crisis, deep and complex battles over the issue of internal improvements, hard questions over the need for a federal protective tariff, and, most divisive and bitter of all, the beginning of the Bank Wars, which would dominate political discourse for the next several years. No less seismic were changes in the way people lived, worked, and understood their relation to themselves, their land, and their nation. In the summer of 1831, Cyrus McCormick exhibited his "mechanical reaper," and by the end of the year the country was beginning to catch "rail-road mania" as America's first steam locomotive made its maiden trip. Ralph Waldo Emerson quit the Unitarian ministry amid the "dim confusion" of 1831 and took up the call of transcendental philosophy, forever altering American intellectual history. All these issues and events may have seemed far removed from rural, isolated western Pennsylvania and the life of a recent immigrant, but they all exercised considerable power over the young Johann and touched his life in profound and important ways—once, that is, he could get himself and his brother settled in Butler County and through their first American winter.[40]

Establishing Saxonburg (1832–37)

Johann's timing was often impeccable, but not in the case of his move to Butler County. Rather than waiting until spring, Johann and Carl moved to their new rural home in mid-November, just as the days were shortening, the frosts setting in, and the snow beginning to fall. While Johann was told that the weather did not normally get bad until New Year's, he wrote, "This year it snowed a month and a half earlier than usual," or, more precisely, almost as soon as he arrived. Despite Johann's assertion that western Pennsylvania winters were more pleasant than those back in Mühlhausen, in reality they were long and bitter. Washington later testified that his father's first winter was very "severe," while Beaumont complained bitterly of the "perpetual tornado of snow" that greeted him and Tocqueville when they arrived in the region. Determined to put a positive spin on the situation, Johann declared that "raw snowstorms" were a rarity and that "the cold is most intense [only] because of the sharp wind," as if this somehow excused the numb fingers, frozen eyebrows, and red-raw face. The sun "shines as warm here as over there in May," he concluded, in what was clearly an outright lie.[1]

Luckily, the Röblings owned three hundred acres of woodland—along with five hundred acres of meadow and "fifteen acres of cleared and fenced-in land"— which could be quickly turned into firewood and used to warm the small blockhouse where they were forced to spend the winter. To help with this labor, the brothers bought a couple of horses, along with a cow, all of which proved useless once snow covered all the available grazing. Instead of having the animals roam and feed themselves, the Röblings were forced to spend valuable cash reserves to feed their beasts. Johann was undeterred: "In the spring we will buy another cow, several calves, sheep, pigs, and some fowl."[2]

Johann and Carl's rural paradise was not only cold and rugged but also isolated. Besides the bustling village of Butler to the north and the canal town of Freeport to the south, there were only a couple of nearby settlements, neither of which has survived. In between there was nothing but "a primeval forest where wild pigeons would not even alight" and a couple of makeshift roads. Both Butler and Freeport were only ten miles away, and Pittsburgh a further fifteen, but between snowdrifts, lakes of mud, and exhausted horses, the journey often took two days. Even the main Pittsburgh Road—by far the most well maintained in Butler County—was a hazard. Once winter descended on Saxonburg, you were effectively on your own. Even decades later, residents described Saxonburg as "a terribly desolate place," and the pastor of Saxonburg's largest church wrote: "It is [still] debatable if the choice of this area was practical. Many are in doubt." An apocryphal story has it that John's new neighbors "clapped their hands over their heads as they saw the foreign newcomers and realized their intentions. They cried out: 'What are you doing here, where the rabbits can hardly make a living?'"[3]

At least there were no wolves or bears around, crowed Johann, and "not a single big snake," although "it is said you can still find [rattlesnakes] almost all over but they are becoming less common all the time because hogs are after them." This was not strictly true; the scarcity of sharp-toothed predators was likely due to hibernation rather than actual absence. Johann's friend Jacob Mechling inaugurated an annual wolf hunt in 1828, an event that regularly brought an impressive haul of wolves, bears, and panthers. To keep everyone focused, "no spirituous liquors were allowed" during the hunt. Oddly, neither were firearms. Still, wild creatures continued to roam the area. During a blizzard in the early 1830s, a panther attacked the Hofman family home just outside Saxonburg. Johann's son Washington remembered a black bear strolling down Main Street as late as 1845.[4]

Despite all the challenges of his new environment, Johann wrote back home in mid-December: "We now live as *free* men in a land whose reasonable and humane Constitution assures every inhabitant his natural rights; where no unnatural compulsory rule robs a person of that which he acquired by his own efforts; where no laws exist that hinder human endeavor; but where everyone can go his free and unchecked way as long as he keeps peace with his fellow men." What more could we want? he asked of his German correspondent. "Nothing more than some honest, cultured German countrymen, who are capable of forming a happy, free, and sociable community. . . . Then we will live a contented, *undisturbed* life, in a German manner, and will never long to be back in our unfortunate Fatherland in the realm of compulsory rule and slavery."[5]

Johann was happy to report he was "red [of] cheek," "much healthier," and "more corpulent" than ever.[6] Of his brother, he mentions almost nothing. Carl remains a shadowy, silent figure throughout Johann's correspondence, always in the background of the action and the decision-making, often ill, and happy to return home, if need be.[7] Their only troubles, according to Johann, were money. By the end of 1831, the Röbling brothers found themselves with "more expenses than our present funds permit." They had bought a wagon and two horses ($80), two plows ($14), and a cow ($12), and had $50 reserved for the purchase of a pair of oxen once spring arrived. In addition, they needed to buy provisions to get them and their beasts through the winter, all of which left them $480, $300 of which was deposited in the Bank of Pittsburgh, and obligations totaling almost $1,200, albeit due in two payments over the next two years. "We doubt that father is inclined to make an additional allowance," Johann wrote to Bähr, "and we could not expect him to make a further sacrifice," but if he could "aid us with five hundred dollars" to meet the next year's mortgage payment, the brothers could devote themselves to developing their rural utopia. Why Johann didn't write to his father directly is a mystery.[8]

Johann's long, fact-filled reports home from late 1831 and early 1832 balanced hard truth and promotional rhetoric; they were oftentimes exuberant and sometimes candid. Johann didn't want to lie and thus end up living with a crowd of disaffected and disappointed emigrants, nor did he want to scare anyone off from buying land. He needed to be reasonably honest while still advertising easy and plentiful employment, fine climate, prime location, and absolute freedom. Whether he knew it or not, Johann was also battling a rising tide of anti-emigration sentiment in Mühlhausen. For much of 1831–32, the *Gemeinnützigen Unterhaltungsblatt* and the *Mühlhausen Wochenblatt*, the town's two main newspapers, had made a trade of printing such articles as "Ist die Auswanderung nach fernen Zonen nothwendig?" ("Is emigration to distant lands necessary?") that drew attention to the profound disappointment and anger suffered by many immigrants and questioned the wisdom of the emigration movement.[9]

Unfortunately, life in western Pennsylvania was very different from that described by the emigration society back in Germany. Unless he wanted to deal with a boatload of furious new neighbors, Johann had to address this in his letters home, and luckily he had a scapegoat. "The difficulties which are associated with emigration, especially for someone who is taking his first steps at it, have not been emphasized enough," Johann wrote before blaming "Etzler's recklessness and bold unfounded claims." Had Johann known what he knew now, he would never have published their "short write-up." "Not at any price would I want to entice anyone to come here" under false pretenses. "We do not want to mislead anyone. We just wish very much to see our countrymen around us"— fine words for a man who had just spent the previous fifty pages imploring his correspondent to bring all his friends and most of Johann's family over.[10]

Despite the work and the weather, Johann was happy with his situation—"In the main part I have found all that I sought"—but he was more cautious and concerned by the expectations and experiences of others. He was disappointed by those like Jancke—or any number of Darmstadters from the *Henry Barclay* who periodically drifted into Saxonburg—who "came over with exaggerated and romantic ideas . . . and now feel themselves deceived and wish to be back." "He who is for freedom and equal rights . . . and depends on his own strength and ability . . . he may come here with ease [and] find opportunity for a livelihood. The slave-free states of North America offer advantages that Europe *never* had and never can have."[11]

Johann continued to ponder the implications of freedom and slavery over the winter of 1831. "If this region is built up by industrious Germans, then it can become an earthly paradise," he believed. Not only were they "in one of the most *advantageous* sections of America," they were also "in the vicinity of a good market . . . where we can dispose of all products for *cash*, with little trouble," he declared, marking himself as an early and active believer in what Charles Sellers dubbed America's "market revolution." Conversely, he was overjoyed that he had not followed Etzler's advice and settled in the South, where "freedom and equality are in bitter contradiction on account of the detestable slavery of the black race. . . . These unfortunate negroes will use their natural rights and will revolt anew each year—will murder their oppressors, guilty or innocent—to secure final freedom for themselves; the slave owners will then continually become more and more tyrannical, and despair will force the Africans to risk all and commit horror and crime." "To take poor Germans there to work was a laughable idea of Etzler's," John realized. "How could an educated German feel happy under such conditions . . . if he must regard every negro as a natural enemy, where even the law *strictly forbids* him to treat the negro humanely, to educate him, to draw closer to him with kindness, or even to set him free?" "How would we small planters be scorned there if we tilled our land ourselves!" he concluded, not that he ever did much tilling.[12]

———

Johann's thoughts on his new homeland bear comparison with those of Alexis de Tocqueville, who arrived in the country the same year. Both Europeans found and valued many of the same things in America. Like Johann, Tocqueville understood the nation in terms of freedom and equality (Johann almost never used the word "freedom" without adding "and equality"). "The entire society," Tocqueville explained, "is founded on a single fact, and everything follows from [that] single principle," by which he meant "the ideal of social equality," which functioned like "a great river toward which every surrounding stream seems to flow." John likewise thought that "every American, even when he is poor and must serve others, feels his innate rights as a man" and cherishes that "reasonable and humane Constitution assures every inhabitant his natural rights."[13]

For Tocqueville, equality was born in the absence of aristocracy. It was the leading idea of democracy and the guarantor of individual liberty. Accordingly, the American was "accustomed to subjecting his movements to no rule other than his personal impulses." Americans "owe nothing to anyone," Tocqueville continued, "and in a sense they expect nothing from anyone," which Johann rejoiced in. Getting out from under the stifling constraints of "overbearing rules and regulations" and "unnatural compulsory rule" were a driving force of his emigration. Yet this acute sense of individualism led not to narrow ambition but to a burgeoning "associational culture." This impressed and delighted both Tocqueville and Johann, especially since his own country forbade open assembling without official state authorization. Johann thought that associations encouraged and fostered the "reasonable natural relationship of the people toward each other." Tocqueville believed that free assembly was the visible expression of democracy and proof that democracy was as much a mindset as it was a political system. In this he agreed with the influential German expatriate and intellectual Francis Lieber, that democracy "is everywhere in the streets as much as in Congress. . . . The people have the republic in the marrow of their bones."[14]

Johann likewise felt "astounded at what the public spirit of these republicans has accomplished up to now and what it still accomplished every day," most of which was undertaken through "the concerted action of an enlightened, self-governing people." Altogether, one could not but laud the "reasonable natural relationship of the people toward each other," and mainly because it was achieved through self-interest. Again, this linked Johann's reading of US social relations with Tocqueville's. The Frenchman believed the doctrine of "self-interest properly understood . . . lies at the root of all action" in America. "It does not inspire self-sacrifice on a grand scale, but it does prompt small sacrifices every day. By itself it is incapable of making a man virtuous, but it does create a multitude of citizens who are disciplined, temperate, moderate, prudent, and self-controlled. And if it does not lead men directly to virtue by way of will, it gradually draws them to it by way of their habits." For Tocqueville, "self-interest properly understood" had come, in the United States, to replace virtue as the moral foundation of society, the idea or trait that guaranteed community and the common good, providing tangible benefits for all. "Men [in the United States] are united only by interests and not by ideas," he announced.[15]

John championed "freedom and equality" with glee. Tocqueville was more measured, and his enthusiasm came with a small warning. Equality was a fine thing, but it came with profound risks and potential dangers. As a member of a prominent aristocratic family that had lost its lands and its fortune during the French Revolution, he understood that despotism came in many forms. It belonged to groups and assemblies as much as to powerful individuals. He called this new social reality the "tyranny of the majority." It was created by democracy but for some it led down the opposite path. "If I refuse to grant to any one of my fellow men the power to do whatever he likes, I will never grant that same power to some number of my fellow men," he declared, before making the case for balance and minority rights. "Liberty [in any form] is imperiled if that power meets with no obstacle capable of slowing its advance and giving it time to moderate itself." Tocqueville believed that "omnipotence in itself [is] a bad and dangerous thing," and that "nothing should rule without impediment." All things need "oversight," he concluded, even freedom.

No such worries dogged Johann's scrutiny, but this was telling. Johann could patiently work through a technical or engineering problem, but he rarely showed as much intellectual flexibility with any other kind of endeavor. As would become a hallmark of the rigid German, he found what he wanted to find. He rarely approached anything with the open mind that Tocqueville brought with him from Europe.[16]

———

While Johann was desperately trying to interest German immigrants in the drafty experience that was Saxonburg and decidedly *not* farming anything, Etzler was scouting for a place to land. After parting with Johann, Etzler and his motley band of followers "rushed through Pennsylvania like a steer . . . just following a blind instinct which guided him to the West," arriving in Pittsburgh several weeks later. From there, he boarded a steamboat and made his way to Cincinnati. Along the way, he met up with a Mr. Kleber who found himself in Johann's company several months later and told him Etzler was heading out to Ohio to scout out potential sites for the establishment of a German communal settlement.[17]

Etzler never got farther than Cincinnati, which was a perfect place for him to land. It was full of German immigrants and kindred spirits: utopian technologists and philosophical futurists. Etzler also managed to find himself indebted to George Rapp. How is not known, but on September 3, 1832, Etzler wrote to Rapp apologizing for raising the uncouth issue of money and urging him to continue to extend Etzler's line of credit, presumably negotiated sometime previously. He also counseled Rapp to ignore any "malicious slander" he may have heard about him. He had suffered the "most awful treatment" lately at the hands of gossips and connivers, he complained. He was not a rogue or a swindler, as his detractors would have it, and to prove it he gave Rapp "the full power to declare openly that I am a liar without honor, if not everything that I assert is found literally true." Rapp believed Etzler but did not allow him to cloud his financial judgment. Etzler ended his begging letter with a cryptic message: "I must forfeit an important invention at a great damage to me . . . and return to Pittsburgh," he wrote, if Rapp was unable to help him. By the end of the year, Etzler was indeed back in Pittsburgh.[18]

Despite Rapp's failure to renew Etzler's line of credit, the relationship never soured. In May 1833, von Bonnhorst recruited Etzler to work as Rapp's interpreter and translator in the legal battle that followed the Great Schism. After this, he became editor of *Der Pittsburgher Beobachter* with his friend Reinhold, who had been a major source of the friction on board the *August Eduard*.[19] By the middle of 1833, while Johann was toiling away in his backwater, Etzler was a publisher and newspaper editor, and he was getting to meet some rather outsized figures, including John Greenleaf Whittier—one of America's most eminent men of letters—who wrote of the "small, dusky-browed German"—his "whole mental atmosphere thronged with spectral enginery"—and his "plans of hugest mechanism": "Brobdingnagian steam engines; Niagaras of water power; windmills with 'sailbroad vans' like those of Satan in chaos . . . the ocean itself covered with artificial islands."[20] Etzler wrote up his vision in the summer of 1832 and published it the following February as *The Paradise within the Reach of all Men, without Labor, by Powers of Nature and Machinery*, the work that would secure his legacy.

Etzler began his treatise with no small sense of enthusiasm or ambition: "FELLOW-MEN!, I promise to show the means for creating a paradise within ten years, where every thing desirable for human life may be had for every man in superabundance, without labor, without pay; where the whole face of nature is changed into the most beautiful form of which it be capable; where man may live in the most magnificent palaces, in all imaginable refinements of luxury, in the most delightful gardens; where he may accomplish, without his labor, in one year more than hitherto could be done in thousands of years."[21] Henry David Thoreau critiqued the book for aiming to "secure the greatest degree of gross comfort and pleasure merely." Thoreau saw in Etzler's book "transcendentalism in mechanics," but he shuddered at the prospect of a world where all man's work could be done with "a short turn of some crank." Work had intrinsic value for Thoreau, and he worried about the momentous implications of Etzler's vision, for what it would do to men. For others, however, that was exactly the point.[22]

As Thoreau understood it, Etzler's main aim was to eliminate work altogether, which may help explain his decided failure in a country where the Protestant work ethic was already firmly entrenched. More significantly, Etzler's utopian vision was about technology and class. As he states at the beginning of his book: "The basis of my proposals is that there are powers in nature at the disposal of man, million times greater than all men on earth could effect," namely, winds, tides, and "sun-shine." Such statements have earned Etzler the title of "the first green-technology futurist." His aim, however, was not so much ecological as political. By creating alternative forms of energy, Etzler thought the links between people, land, and power could be severed. With people no longer dependent on traditional systems of ownership (i.e., of land) but on abundant, commonly held resources, established hierarchies would crumble, leaving a more equal society. In Etzler's scheme, the very means of existence—food, shelter, clothing—would be free and available to all.[23]

Thoreau called Etzler a "bold schemer" and a "resolute dreamer" whose "success is in theory and not in practice." As things turned out, the theory wasn't far wide of the mark; the tools that could successfully harness them, unfortunately, were. What he needed was Johann, who was just better at science than Etzler was. Etzler certainly understood the age, but Johann had the aptitude.[24]

After publishing his book Etzler wandered around the Midwest promoting his ideas, usually unsuccessfully. In 1834, he arranged a meeting with a dozen or so of Cincinnati's most prominent German intellectuals to discuss his plans and enlist support. Carl Rümelin wrote an account of Etzler's plans, which consisted of three proposals: "First, an artificial movable island with a circumference of one mile, built in front of a seaport, with a hotel on top of which trees, vegetables and other plants would grow. The island could be moved to any healthful part of the sea during summertime. It should be moved by the weight of the waves combined with steam power." Rümelin remembered how well calculated all the details were and how the audience was in awe when he concluded with the prophecy, "The world has no idea yet of the size of vehicles which, soon, will cross the ocean without sails. . . . My island, which has you flabbergasted now, will not seem all that big anymore in twenty years," which seemed perfectly prescient after Isambard Brunel launched the SS *Great Eastern* in 1858. His second proposal was to dig a series of artificial lakes ten feet deep that would collect "summer heat" through use of mirrors and slowly release it during the winter. Etzler's third proposal was his infamous Satellite, to which one of Rümelin's pals rejoined: "The world is all wind, hooray!" Despite being generally mocked, Etzler managed to establish a school of mathematics in Cincinnati, if only for a few days. "Five students were at the first lesson, three at the second, one at the third (the writer of these words) and the fourth never took place." Etzler left town shortly afterward, "furious over [Cincinnati's] materialism."[25]

No one knows if Johann ever read Etzler's *Paradise within the Reach of all Men*, nor whether the two ever met or spoke again after they parted in Philadelphia, although history has them linked indelibly. It is certainly possible that Johann and Etzler accidentally met in Pittsburgh, where they both spent time in the early 1830s. Undoubtedly, Etzler was often in and around the region, even as late as 1843, when he conducted a demonstration of his Satellite for Andreas Smolnikar, who was starting a millennialist farming community just outside Limestone in Warren County, western Pennsylvania. Smolnikar was "confident" Etzler's Satellite would "work wonders," although that's not how things worked out. According to one source, "The first experiment . . . failed, in consequence of using wood in some parts . . . where iron was needed." According to Smolnikar,

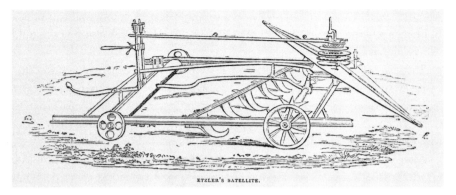

ETZLER'S SATELLITE.

Figure 7.1 Etzler's Satellite, from *The Artizan: A Monthly Journal of the Operative Arts* (1845). Library of Congress.

the spiritual mystic, however, the failure was a natural test of religious fidelity and had in fact "been foreseen and foretold" by a "seeress" who belonged to the group. Smolnikar then went on to declare that "in the next night would be revealed to one of [his flock] how the machines made by Etzler should be corrected and the machine should be put in operation." By the following morning one George Karle had received the requisite vision and been put in charge of Etzler's "Iron Servant." Unfortunately, before he could get started on the repairs, Karle "was brought into the Allegheny River and drowned by the instrumentality of the departed Mormon Prophet Joe Smith . . . indirectly by the instrumentality of a cow." Rümelin also witnessed one of Etzler's demonstrations, and it ended almost as badly. A company of Germans set out to see the Satellite in action; "however, they were all quiet when they returned."[26]

John was aware of these goings-on, writing to his brother the following year, "Etzler is now staying in a new settlement of Germans in a county on the Allegheny River north of here, and is making a new attempt to get his machines completed. However, he will probably not realize his plans in this life; the man has marvelous ideas; he is a liberal-minded keen thinker, but an extremely impractical fellow. . . . Many of his plans will be carried out in due course of time, but by other hands," Johann concluded presciently. Etzler did get the chance, as it happens, although with predictable results. In 1845, he escorted hundreds of members of the Tropical Emigration Society on a mission to Venezuela to establish a communitarian farming colony. The endeavor was a total disaster. Etzler abandoned the few settlers who remained in the summer of 1846, boarded a boat at La Guaira, and set sail for Curaçao. He was never heard from again.[27]

After the bleak winter months of early 1832, the Röbling brothers could relax a little and start to prepare for the summer. Initially, they had planned to spend their time building a communal blockhouse. Yet at some point during the spring of 1832, their intentions shifted. No doubt harried by fear of debt, Johann decided against a communal settlement and chose as an alternative a massive sell-off. By the time the next wave of Germans arrived "to find a new home in the wild and strange solitude," Johann had much of his acreage surveyed, parceled up, and ready for sale.[28]

The new group was headed by Johann's faithful correspondent and good friend Bähr, who had left Bremen with his wife, Anne, and a young son, Leonhard, who had tragically died en route. The Bährs had no further children, and they became very attached to Johann's first son, Washington. Bähr "was a kind hearted man, versatile and well informed in many branches," according to Washington, "but he came over too late in life." In fact, why he should "leave a good business at home and dry rot the rest of his life in Saxonburg" was a total mystery to Washington. "He must have had the emigration fever bad," he concluded. Bähr built a large house opposite Johann's on Main Street and painted it pink. He also established a spinning and carding mill with his wife's brother, a man called Eisenhardt whose "chief accomplishment was drinking schnapps," and regaling young Washington with accounts of his daring service at Waterloo. When Bähr passed away in 1844, his greatest regret was "that he should die without having seen a steam engine."[29]

Washington later claimed, "The people my father hoped would come there, came not," but many families did. The Tolleys (the wife "was an unmitigated termagant, with the vilest tongue, to escape which [her husband] spent his whole time in Pittsburgh, coming home only once a year, and getting away again as fast as possible") and the Stübgens (a "skilful mechanic" and locksmith) both came from Philadelphia in 1832, having emigrated from Leipzig six years before. Also arriving during that crucial first year were the Graffs (farmers who settled on Thorn Creek and earned themselves the nickname, in Washington's rendering, of "Sic-dich-fur" [look out for yourself]); the Muders ("excellent carpenters and house builders"), Adam Ohl ("a staunch Lutheran" who "became old and tired of living, like some others in Saxonburg"); F. A. Kunze ("a skilful weaver"); the Koenigs ("machinists"); the Bernigaus ("one of [Johann's] cronies—a quaint genius of many attainments who wasted his sweetness on the desert air of Saxonburg . . . a wit, a philosopher and scholar"); and Ernest Herting, a tailor who arrived with a wife and three daughters.[30]

Herman Miller also arrived in late summer of 1832 with his wife, who after a few weeks became Saxonburg's first death. A couple of weeks afterward, Frederick Lamb—born to Christian ("a jovial, genial citizen, our best butcher") and Wilhelminia Lamb—became the fledgling community's first birth. Some, of course, arrived and quickly moved on. Ernest Charles Angelrodt—a member of Saxony's radical Provisional Assembly—joined the Mühlhausen Emigration Society and fled Europe for explicitly political reasons, traveling over to Pennsylvania with Bähr. Unlike his friend, however, Angelrodt was appalled by what he found. He wrote home to Mühlhausen to say that Johann was "a swindler" and that the place picked out was not fit for civilized human beings. He then headed off to find himself a patch of land to farm in Missouri. Despite striking out on his own, Angelrodt ended up becoming one of the most accomplished Mühlhausen emigrants. Tired of farming life, he soon moved to St. Louis and quickly became one of the city's leading citizens. By 1840, he was the millionaire owner of a large wholesale firm, and by 1845 he was serving as the first Prussian consul in St. Louis.[31]

While many came, others did not. Johann's sister, Amelia, abandoned the idea of moving sometime during 1832, dashing her brother's hopes for a family reunion. "In order to enjoy your much-praised freedom we would have to give up our own servants, a thing which we would not like at all, now that we are accustomed to have them," she wrote with no trace of irony. "We prefer our comfortable living here to being our own servants there," she continued, before asking her brother: "Would you not rather live here in our circumstances than stay there and do your own rough work?" One can only guess what Johann's reaction was.[32]

At the close of their first year in western Pennsylvania, Johann and Carl had every reason to be cautiously optimistic. There was as yet no doctor in Saxonburg and no proper brewer—"Monongahela rye whiskey [was] the staff of life"—yet their fledgling community was filling up, and trades and businesses were being established. More were to come the following year. The Maurhoffs and the Schwieterings (who "had a beautiful daughter who became a leading lady in a circus troupe") both arrived in 1833, and soon after joined up to open a general store, which operated continuously until 1989. The Aderholds also arrived in 1833 and opened up the village's first hotel: the Saxonburg Exchange. They inaugurated the village's first festival—the Schützenfest —a sharpshooting competition that lasted for three days and drew large crowds. Gottfried Helmhold arrived with his family in an elegant coach pulled by four fine horses and brought a piano all the way from Thuringia. Johann would stop by to play the piano every once in a while, while the coach saw out its useful days as a chicken coop. Later, Saxonburg developed a robust cultural scene. Regular and well-attended theatrical performances were held in the summer. There was even a village band, with Johann on the flute or the clavier.[33]

By 1840, there were upward of sixty families living in and around Saxonburg; by 1850, there were 133. There was nothing haphazard about the community. Johann diligently worked out his plan during the quiet, undisturbed months of spring and early summer 1832. By the time everyone arrived on August 4, everything was finalized. The spine of the settlement was to be Main Street, which ran directly east and west, on a ridge 1,500 feet above sea level that marked the natural dividing line between the watersheds of the Allegheny and Ohio Rivers. Johann surveyed the land north and south of Main Street, dividing it into lots somewhere between one hundred and two hundred feet wide and around 1,500 feet deep, running downhill on the north side to Water Street. Isabella and Rebecca Streets—both named for distant relatives—ran north from Main Street directly adjacent to the land Johann marked out for himself.[34]

As described by a later historian, "The district retains much of the historic street plan which founder John Roebling laid out. . . . He planted a grid of streets and spacious building lots, long and narrow in dimension, allowing for homes and shops to be erected at the front of the lots—most of which faced Main Street. The rear of the lots was intended for agricultural use (stables, barns, farming)." Johann's vision was a balancing act of autonomy, community, and social class. Having so much room out back allowed every family enough space and freedom to exercise their own trade. At the same time, Main Street pulled the whole endeavor together, creating a village feel that was noticeably communal (rather than dispersed) in character. The depth of the lots also allowed for autonomy. In other words, while the width made for community—exiting by the back door led to one's own private world—walking out the front door brought one to the communal world of Main Street. For those who couldn't afford to live on Main Street, Johann also built a taxonomy of class into his village plan. "Poor people lived on Water Street," Washington once remarked, the sort Johann hoped would sharecrop his land for him. Or, as a more recent resident describes it, "Main Street still keeps its original haughty distance from the lower, quieter Water Street."[35]

The look and feel of Saxonburg were preserved in July 1835 by a painter named T. Gosewisch, who settled in Saxonburg before moving swiftly on "to where people could afford to pay for artistic work." Entitled "Sachsenburg: Colonie von Thüringern und Sachsen bei Pittsburg" and drawn from nature from the perspective of Horne's Heights just south of Saxonburg, the image shows the line of homes on Main Street, from the large homes of Röbling and Bähr on the right to the more modest log cabins of Bernigau, Tolley, and Muder on the left. Down below, at the bottom of the hill, lies the modest home of Ernest Herting. The overall feel is somewhat gloomy and slightly threadbare, but things seem functional. Farmers are pictured in honest labor, hoeing the earth and clearing the land; horses and sheep graze peacefully; cabins have been built, some of the land enclosed, and

Figure 7.2 Johann's fledging community of Saxonburg. T. Gosewisch, "Sachsenburg" (1835), printed by Johann's cousin E. W. Röbling in Mühlhausen, from Hamilton Schuyler, *The Roeblings* (1931).

a nice broad road opened up; the homes are set out in a neat line, while smoke pours from Herting's chimney, signaling that the hearth is working and the home is warm. Johann sent Gosewisch's drawing to his cousin in Eschwege, who printed up several lithographic copies for distribution around Thuringia.[36]

"Many of the buildings erected in the 1830s and 1840s by the first German settlers are of heavy timber construction," reads the nomination document for the Saxonburg Historical District, "many with brick and straw inserted into the cavities between the framing," including Johann's house. The house was built by Andrew Emerick, a well-respected local carpenter, along with Johann, who mixed clay to coat the whole thing, made the bricks to fill the open framework, and hammered wood pins and tree nails into frames, crossbeams, and rafters. Roebling believed that "the eyes must have a clear, free view all around," and in his house they did. It was built on the village's highest point; from the second story "the chestnut ridge of the Alleghenies" was visible far off to the east. Entering through the front door on Main Street, one found oneself in a large, sparsely furnished central hallway. A platform stairway leading up to the second story stood opposite. To the left, a square room of fifteen feet by fifteen feet served as Johann's office and drawing room. A similar room on the east side served as a bedroom and sitting room. Upstairs was a hallway, a children's room, and a spare room "which served as a haven of refuge for some of the numerous unfortunate Germans who were stranded periodically in Saxonburg." A single-story kitchen, with a dining room and pantry, stood out back.[37]

Day-to-day life in Saxonburg was difficult. Most dry goods were a nine-mile wagon ride away in Freeport. Grain had to be laboriously ground on hand mills and water lugged from distant springs and streams. The back-breaking labor of clearing land, building homes, and setting up shop could last years and claim the best years of one's life. Still, almost everyone made a go of it, except Johann. Despite all his assertions to the contrary, Saxonburg was a poor farming area. The soil was "stiff" and full of clay, the drainage was poor, and the frosts came early and stayed late. What good farmland there was in western Pennsylvania had been snatched up years ago by its earliest white settlers. Worse, Johann had no real knowledge or experience of agriculture. His father was a shopkeeper from a small town. He had been raised in a townhouse, not on a farm. For all his myriad opinions about raising cattle and breeding horses and the pages upon pages of findings and judgments he sent back to Germany on the subject, Johann had neither the skill nor the temperament for agriculture. If a farmer "must be content to wait patiently upon events," as Hamilton Schuyler believed, then Johann was congenitally unsuited for such a job.[38]

"I know that my father had a hard time learning to farm, and realized before long that he was not fitted for that kind of work," explained Washington, "but he gave it a faithful trial." He bought some sheep and a German shepherd; unfortunately, he couldn't keep either in line, or even in the meadow. The sheep gamboled off into the woods at the first opportunity, and the dog refused to follow, leaving Johann to drag the poor beasts back home. On the rare occasion he got them in the same field, the sheep openly defied both dog and shepherd, sending Johann into fits. One is left with the impression of a crazed German screaming and shouting and chasing over hill and dale after a pack of heedless sheep, his faithful dog gazing on with bored indifference. What must have seemed easy on the surface—breeding a bunch of pliant ruminants—turned into Johann's worst nightmare: waging a constant, losing battle against creatures with neither reason nor sense of authority.[39]

Johann tried all sorts of bizarre schemes to avoid farming, most of which he knew even less about. Taken by the success of Economy's silk production, he bought a number of mulberry bushes and tried to raise silkworms, but with dismal results. The work was tiresome, tedious, and unprofitable. After a solid week's work, he often found himself with only "a pound or two" to sell. Another idea he got from Rapp was the cultivation of rapeseed, which seems to have gone the same way as the silkworms. A further story has "a jolly rogue" named Miller arriving in Saxonburg with the idea to raise canaries. Thousands could be made, he promised Johann, and soon they were buying birds and food and creating a heated room, all at Johann's expense. Once everything was ready, however, Miller ran off, taking many of the birds with him, not to mention his ability to distinguish between males and females. Johann tried to mate the remaining birds, all to no avail. He then turned the whole thing over to Herting, "who had only one tenth the brains but ten times the patience," and soon worked things out, turning the birds into a profitable little enterprise. Johann also built a dye house at the behest of another itinerant genius before realizing that "Saxonburg did not want to be dyed."[40]

Johann did much better as a landowner and real estate developer. After quitting the life of the soil, he leased most of his land to a German named Gerstner ("a splendid woodchopper, good sausagemaker, cow midwife and hay mower"), who prospered. The rest of his land he sold off slowly by private mortgage during the 1830s, with individuals and families working off the interest and principal. All this making contracts and drawing up deeds made Johann an expert in legal matters and a thoroughly shrewd practitioner. It also brought him into contact with some important people. He became "warm friends" with the Honorable Samuel Anderson Purviance, for example, a prominent lawyer and Whig activist from Butler, who went on to serve in the US Congress and help found the Republican Party. Such connections heavily influenced Johann's political development, from a committed Democrat in the 1830s to a Clay Whig in the 1840s, and finally in the 1850s into a staunch Republican.[41]

"I presume my father was happy for a short time" in Saxonburg, enjoying the freedom, the adventure, and the challenge, wrote Washington, and certainly Johann once believed that stumbling upon Saxonburg was "the greatest piece of luck." "Later on," however, "he did not think so," and he grew to despise the place. Saxonburg was the scene of Johann's greatest indignities, although also the scene of some of his most impressive efforts and achievements. Saxonburg was Johann's village. He bought it, surveyed it, planned it, and brought it to life. In it, he watched others succeed where he had failed. The entire experience must have been humiliating, and it is no wonder he came to hate the place. It confirmed that Johann's life was way off track. The few real successes he had enjoyed had occurred almost ten years earlier and well over four thousand miles away. Increasingly he took himself off to Pittsburgh during the mid- to late 1830s in an effort to improve his lot and get back into engineering. In Pittsburgh he was free to make business contacts and read up on the latest theories and inventions. If anyone needed engineers, he reasoned quite accurately, it was the Iron City with its rising industrial base. At home he took out his notebooks and began to tinker with some new ideas. Thinking he might eke out a living from patent rights, he designed a series of tubular boilers, a steam plow, and a traction engine. Slowly, Johann started moving on.[42]

Casting about for a useful occupation to keep him busy, Johann helped design and build many of his neighbor's houses during Saxonburg's first decade. He also drew up a design for an elegant church and, in an effort to raise money to fund its construction, had an announcement printed up and handed out all over Butler County: "The citizens of the newly developed small town of Saxonburg, in Butler County," it began, "have the highest desire to erect a German Evangelical Christian church, and turn therefore, to all noble-minded citizens with the request to aid this undertaking. . . . We want to reach it through our own power; and we speak therefore, to the Christian charity of our esteemed fellow citizens to give only that, which we would under better circumstances, willingly give ourselves." Donations proved meager, and accordingly Johann was forced to shelve his initial plan and design a small, plain church. "Like a simple house," Johann explained.[43]

The contract for construction of Johann's revised design was signed on January 9, 1836, the same year the congregation began to adopt binding rules and regulations. A full church constitution was adopted in 1841, and it included such stalwart decrees as "As long as there remains one member in later years who doesn't agree to change, it is not permitted under any circumstances to change to a pure English church." Johann's friend Christian Rudert, with whom he had lodged after first arriving in Butler County, donated the stone and hauled it to Saxonburg, and the church was dedicated in the fall of 1837.[44]

Saxonburg had a religious congregation almost from the moment it came into existence. The church's first historian describes its members as "intelligent, educated persons with liberal and sensible philosophy, whose minds could not be enslaved with unworthy and blind party or dogmatic belief." The Reverend William Fuhrmann began preaching in and around Saxonburg in late 1832, although he lasted only a few years. The Reverend Joseph Schuely was the next to stay any appreciable length of time. He performed ninety-seven baptisms and nine marriages, and moved on in 1841. He was succeeded by Robert Clemen, a graduate of the University of Giessen who ended up committing suicide after his wife's death. Life for a Saxonburg preacher was tough, worse even than it was for a pioneer. "Even the poor Vicar of Wakefield could be envied compared to the preachers of Saxonburg," wrote one church historian. The congregation was both "poor and meager," and they had little to spare in terms of goods, produce, or cash. Baptisms and marriages were paid for in bags of flour and other likely tender, none of which were ever as heavy as promised. Preachers were housed wherever anyone had room, which when combined with the nonexistent pay ("too much for dying, too little for living," as one preacher described it) might have contributed to some early problems. Little is mentioned officially, except that some early preachers suffered from "religious licentiousness and unrestrained moral looseness," which in turn led to "many very unpleasant experiences." One can only guess at what this alluded to.[45]

———

On April 1, 1836, Johann and Carl donated an acre of land to the German Evangelical Church for the erection of a school and the laying out of a cemetery. A month later, Johann had further business with the church, this time of a more romantic nature. In May 1836, Johann married Johanna, the eldest daughter of Ernest Herting, the tailor who lived down the hill. Writing to his family back in Germany the following year, Johann described his new wife in terms of rank, not beauty: "The only mistake, which my wife could have in the eyes of those from Mühlhausen, is that she is the daughter of a tailor, . . . which does not bother me in the least, because here in this country people never ask about class and because there is only one class. Respectfully and finely clothed I along with my wife have access into the best of American Society."[46] Washington was warmer in describing her. Johanna, he wrote, was "a handsome young woman of 18 or 19 [at the time of her wedding], of an amiable and gentle disposition, entirely too good for him."[47]

What Johann's father-in-law thought of his new son-in-law is anyone's guess. Herting was, by all accounts, a kind and gentle man, who loved his garden and a good joke. Besides tailoring and taking over Johann's failed canary business, Herting grew his own flowers, fruits, and vegetables, alongside hops when the village finally attracted a brewer. Despite his rather humble beginning, Herting did very well for himself, socially, financially, and politically. In 1846, he was elected as a councilman in the newly formed Borough of Saxonburg's first-ever election, although only nine votes were cast in total.[48]

Johann's romantic adventures appear to have begun almost as soon as he landed in the United States. In a cryptically worded letter from 1832, Johann's sister, Amelia, asked, "How are things with you and Anthonia, dear August? Have you lost all confidence in me, because you never write about it any more?"[49] Exactly who Anthonia was and what happened to her has never been answered: a secret sweetheart from the Emigration Society, perhaps, or a recent acquaintance from the New World? Sadly, neither of the ships' manifests nor any of Johann's correspondence provide any clues. A more persistent rumor concerning Johann's love life—repeated by many of his biographers—has the testy young German meeting and falling in love with a beautiful young woman named Helena Giesy soon after arriving in Butler County. They became engaged, it was said, and the wedding dress was made. Unfortunately, she then came under the spell of one William Keil, a local religious leader who was gathering up converts and recruits to head west and form a new religious colony. Helena entreated

Johann to come away with her (and Keil); he hesitated and stayed. Eventually, she forsook Johann and went out west, where she "led a helpful and saintly life . . . lavishing great love upon her people" and never married.[50]

This rumor seems to have begun in the pages of a small farming newspaper in Oregon in the 1920s. A couple of booster articles imagine what might have happened had Johann first followed his supposed sweetheart out to Bethel, Missouri (where the colony first settled), continued out to Oregon (where they settled next), taken over leadership of the religious colony, and finally "made an industrial colony there, instead of an agricultural" one, despite the geographic isolation. "What a future Aurora might have had with the full development of the linen and lace industries there, under the leadership of such a master as John A. Roebling!" the paper editorialized. The story was expanded upon with endless small details ("Sadly but firmly Helena Giesy turned her tearful face westward") by Robert Hendricks—who professed to have known Helena in his youth—in his *Bethel and Aurora: An Experiment in Communism as Practical Christianity* (1933).[51]

The mind boggles at the thought that Johann, under different circumstances, might have devoted his life to the manufacture of lace. Yet he did know of Keil and his plans to "move to the Oregon Territory" with "a number of Germans." He may also have met the "Witchdoctor," as Keil was locally known, in Pittsburgh, where he operated an apothecary and carried out "mystical cures," a practice Johann was strongly drawn to. Whether Johann knew Helena is unclear. He never mentioned her in any of his correspondence, and the dates don't make sense either. Keil and his crew set off west in 1844, not 1834, by which time Johann was married with three young children and fantastically busy at work. These facts alone make the story highly unlikely.[52]

———

Johann's life changed suddenly and irrevocably shortly after his marriage. In early August, Johann received an unexpected letter from Edward Thierry, an old friend from the Unger Institute. Within days Johann had packed a bag, said goodbye to his new bride, and headed off to a spot on the Ohio River twenty-eight miles below Pittsburgh. By August 20, Johann was working as an engineer for the first time in eight years.

Thierry immigrated in 1834, independently of Johann, hoping to start a school on the Unger model. This idea, it seems, went nowhere, and Thierry ended up working on the Main Line Canal. Thierry's letter inquired if Johann might be interested in engineering work and if he might like to join his old friend down in Beaver County. Johann leaped at the chance. He was thoroughly disillusioned with farming and the rural life by this point, and he had Johanna to look after the homestead, a task she was well cut out for. Saxonburg held few charms for its founder: his village was established, and there was little left for him to do there. By 1836, Johann had no income, little in the way of produce, and still owed Meissner a tidy sum. Paid work of any description was more than welcome.[53]

Johann worked on the Beaver Division of the Main Line Canal from August 20 until September 26, earning two dollars per day for a total paycheck of seventy-four dollars. Most of the work was repairing rather than building. Many of the locks and dams had been damaged or destroyed during the harsh winter of 1835–36 and the spring floods of 1836. At the end of his first stint, Johann immediately signed up for an additional twenty-two days.[54]

The terms of Johann's employment show the precarious nature of employment at the time, with even engineers hired on a piecemeal basis with little or no job security. Nevertheless, it got him off the farm and out of Saxonburg and reunited him with work he loved. His experience working on one of the largest and most ambitious canal projects in the country provided entrée into the professional world of internal improvements. It brought him to the attention of more influential engineers, as well as bureaucrats in Harrisburg looking to hire competent technicians and surveyors.

Thanks to his stint on the Main Line Canal, Johann worked early the following year as a "sub assistant engineer" building locks and dams on the Eastern Division of the Sandy and Beaver Canal. His boss was an Irish-born chief engineer by the name of Edward Hall Gill, one of the nation's foremost canal engineers. The Sandy and Beaver was a private venture and as such was subject to almost constant financial uncertainty. It was charted in Ohio in 1828, but it took the shareholders six years to raise sufficient capital to start digging. Work proceeded for about two and a half years before being halted again. The canal was finally completed in 1848, only to be made obsolete within a matter of years as railroads spread out over the country.[55]

———

As the spring thaws of 1837 wreaked havoc on the locks and dams of the Sandy and Beaver, the speculative bubble that had dominated the last years of Andrew Jackson's presidency collided with falling cotton prices in the South and rising food prices in Britain. The results were disastrous. By March, businesses were beginning to fail in New Orleans, and within a few weeks the effects were being felt all over the North. By the following month few people were accepting paper money of any description. Even in Pittsburgh "money . . . vanished, silver was hoarded and bank-notes were of uncertain value. . . . The whole community was set back upon the first principle of commercial intercourse—barter." On May 9, over $650,000 of specie was withdrawn from banks in New York, and the following day a full-fledged national panic was on. Businesses from all over the country went bankrupt, states immediately cut back their expenditures, and almost all internal improvement projects were shut down. By the end of May, the New York and Erie Railroad had discharged its entire corps of engineers, while Indiana cut the number of engineers on the state payroll from forty-five to three. Such drastic measures left hundreds of thousands of Americans newly out of work. By May 22, 1837, less than two weeks after the onset of the panic, Ralph Waldo Emerson took up his journal and wrote, "The land stinks with suicide." Four days later, the recently laid-off Johann became a father for the first time.[56]

Washington August Roebling was born in his father's house on May 26, 1837. The new father's thoughts on the birth of his first child went unrecorded. The son's thoughts on his father would be written out painfully over many years, despite his growing up to become his father's right-hand man and most trusted lieutenant. It would seem natural to presume he was named after America's first president, and certainly Johann seems to have had some reverence for the founding father. Washington had "always understood," however, that he was named for Edward Gill's younger brother, Washington Gill, who worked on the Sandy and Beaver with Johann. This would seem to make some sense. Johann seems to have felt both personal affection and gratitude toward the Gills, especially Washington, with whom he worked many times, including for many months in 1839 surveying a potential southern route for a railroad from Harrisburg to Pittsburgh. Johann also favored naming his children for close friends and relatives rather than public figures. He named his second son Ferdinand after his close friend Bähr.[57]

Johann used his experience working on the Main Line and Sandy and Beaver Canals to inform two of his first US publications—"An Essay on the Obstruction of Streams by Dams" and "A Treatise on Reservoire [sic] Locks"—both of which appeared the following year in the prestigious *American Railroad Journal*.[58] He also tried to use his newfound contacts to secure some paid employment during the worst days of the panic. Whether in financial need or because he was less than keen to stay home, Johann wrote to Edward Gill from Saxonburg on June 28, 1837, hoping to be reengaged on the Sandy and Beaver. He had inquired about work elsewhere, but the depression was hard and the job market flat, especially in the realm of internal improvements. "Although in possession of a fine library and my time being principally occupied by interesting studies, I cannot reconcile myself to be altogether destitute of practical occupation and I shall embrace the first opportunity which offers itself to me to enter service again," he wrote, signaling the end of his attempts to make a living from his land. "But I should decline any offer, if I could entertain the hope of being reengaged by you," he continued. "It is always with pleasure that I recollect the time of my service on the S&B and the kind treatment and confidence with which you have favored me."[59]

Johann was also hoping to tap Gill's ingenuity and expertise. During his "present leisure" he had developed "some new plans," which he wanted to submit "to your judgment, before I apply for any patent." The first was an entirely "new plan [for] dams and locks to improve the navigation of large rivers." "These dams and locks will render the shallowest water navigable during the dry season, without being an obstruction to rafting . . . and without swelling the water much in time of a flood above the former river." Another plan involved opening up the "mouth of the Mississippi R[iver] below New Orleans." "The channels of this noble river are filling up every year more and more," he explained, "and the city of N.O. after some time will cease to be the port of entrance for the large kind of sea vessels, unless they adopt a better and more effective plan, suitable . . . to keep its channel open and deep." Finally, Johann had been thinking of railroads. "Another improvement of mine regards a simple contrivance in the construction of railroads to make switches and movable rails in turnouts and passings altogether dispensable." Nothing was too insignificant to escape his attention: "I have also computed a number of tables, being useful in tracing railroad curves in the field. Any engineer, familiar with the use of these tables, will find them preferable to any other tables, calculated for that purpose and which I know of." All his plans, he was careful to stress, with one eye on their commercial potential, could be achieved at little or no added expense.[60]

The summer of 1837 arrived with a birth and ended with a death. In the late summer, Johann's brother Carl passed away, the result of sunstroke contracted while out in the fields all day reaping wheat. He left a wife—Wilhelmina—and two young children, Amelia and Charles. Carl was buried in the land he and Johann had donated for that exact purpose just a year before. His children were for some reason entrusted to a guardian who lived in Butler, much to Johann's annoyance. Wilhelminia quickly remarried, but her new husband ran off, leaving Carl's widow with another boy. Wilhelminia, it seems, found happiness in her third marriage, to Christian Warneck, a wood turner who lived just outside Saxonburg. Christian "occupied for a proper length of time the retreat of impecunious philosophers in our second story," Washington remembered: "My father helped him all his life—the poor devil was epileptic."[61]

Carl's death marked the end of Johann's agricultural career. Carl had always been the more diligent and enthusiastic farmer, and after his passing Johann gave up the pretense and quit the practice for good. Being recently bereaved and a new father and facing a massive national depression might have helped clarify things, but his recent experiences had rekindled his enthusiasm for engineering.

———

On September 30, 1837, Johann August Röbling passed away, and John A. Roebling came into being. The change was effected at the Butler County Court of Common Pleas, where Johann went "praying to be admitted a citizen of the United States of America." "And having, to the satisfaction of the Court, made the proofs and complied with the requisitions prescribed by law, was allowed to take the usual oaths, and make the requisite renunciations," after which he was granted US citizenship. Whether Johann thought the change in status would help his chances of securing more state work, or whether he believed his new family needed the stability of US citizenship, or even if his brother's death had brought a need for greater security and definition, the move was significant and symbolic. The subtle shift in name marked a larger shift in personality. Increasingly, Johann was redefining himself in specifically American terms. The Johann Röbling who had arrived so enthusiastically in Philadelphia over six years earlier was fading away to make room for a newer model. But who was this new man, this John A. Roebling?[62]

Johann was a Democrat—more precisely an "Improvement Democrat" of the sort found all over canal-conscious Pennsylvania. Like a majority of German immigrants of the time, this was as much a question of temperament and inclination as a question of policy. Put simply, Johann wanted to be a Jacksonian Democrat, whether he knew it or not, a farmer living free on the frontier, cut loose from the bonds of banks and bailiffs, far from social pressures or conventions. That he had failed to make a go of it was neither here nor there. The Jeffersonian ideal of the stout yeoman farmer resonated strongly with Johann and fed his dreams of personal independence and improvement. By contrast, the Whigs seemed like the party of entrenched wealth and power—the party of bankers and business owners and stuffy old European conservatism—to most German immigrants of the 1830s, especially Johann.[63]

All this would change over the next ten years as Johann slowly morphed into John. By the close of the Jacksonian era in 1848, John had forsaken the Democratic Party and pledged his allegiance to the Whigs and Henry Clay's "American System," a combination of a national bank, protective tariffs, and internal improvements designed to nurture and grow American industry. The reasons were simple: like most Germans of his era, Johann quit the Democrats in the late 1830s and 1840s just as the Democrats were reorienting themselves southward and ossifying into the party of states' rights and slave power. Just as political parties changed, so did Johann/John. One of the most significant aspects of Jacksonian America was the battle between whether one was able to exercise individual choice and self-government or whether one was subject to arbitrary rule by an external authority. This balancing act—between individual liberty and group power—describes the conundrum at the heart of Johann's transformation into John. John hated to fall under anyone's heel, and when faced with the choice to boss or be bossed around, John chose the former. If Johann Röbling championed liberty, so John Roebling practiced power, at least in the world of work. Much of this transformation was still ahead of John as he walked out of the Butler County courtroom, but he knew that he was at an important crossroads: he had ceased to be one thing but had yet to become another.[64]

———

One of the first things John Roebling did as a new American was to give a speech about being a new American. On October 18, 1837, a huge "German convention" was held in Pittsburgh. Delegates arrived from around the country. "The object of the convention," according to Gustav Körner, the delegate from St. Clair, Illinois, "was to devise means to maintain the German language, to sustain the German press, to establish a central Normal School for the education of German teachers, and to protest and counteract the efforts of the nativistic American societies." The point of the meeting was not, however, "to create a separate German party. Far from it, the Germans were admonished to become naturalized, to familiarize themselves with the language, the constitution, and the laws of the country, to retain what was good in the German character and to adopt cheerfully what was good in the American." Some of this last effort fell to John.[65]

John attended as a representative of Butler County and took to the occasion with characteristic confidence and vigor. Wilhelm Schmoele—who met John at the convention and later helped found the Penn Medical University—described his demeanor as that of a "striving philosophy student." John's subject was how to maintain the German language, establish a German press, and secure a German education in concert with established American norms and institutions. To maintain their heritage, he argued, Germans needed to engage, not separate. "Have not many of us come over here inspired by the desire and with the idea not to bury ourselves politically," he argued, "but to assume an active role in the national life of this large republic and according to each of our abilities contribute to it, such that this large bastion of freedom, this sanctuary for the politically persecuted might establish an ever stronger base?" The best way to achieve this was to bridge "the communication gap" that existed between "the German immigrant and the natural born American citizen," an activity John had diligently and wholeheartedly thrown himself into over the past six years.[66]

John believed that proficiency in the English language was the key to his own early successes and vital for the future prospects of all German immigrants. English was the language of American "history," of "law and politics and of business," and in consequence, "any German, who speaks proper German and proper English well, will have a considerable advantage in this country." For those who failed to make the effort, disaster surely awaited. "If a German is involved in a civil dispute and if he has put his just cause in the hands of one of the magistrates or advocates, who has no knowledge of German," John hypothesized, "then woe is him, if he falls into the hands of scoundrels and bad interpreters. This is an injustice," John continued, "a liquid manure . . . thrown on our countrymen in great abundance; one which will never dry up under the present circumstances." The language issue was also important on a group level, beyond the fate of any one individual. German immigrants would only gain recognition—and thus respect—in their adoptive new country to the degree that they could participate in local and national discussions, a vast majority of which were conducted in English. If they were to be taken seriously as a national group, John counseled, they needed to speak the language of national affairs.[67]

John did not believe in forgetting one's German, however. He demanded that in overwhelmingly German neighborhoods residents, and especially elected officials, ought to speak both English and German. Much of the "disdain" dished out to recent German immigrants was "clearly a consequence of their unfamiliarity with our language and literature." "The majority of the Americans and the English are of the opinion that Germans lack education," John declared, which was absurd. "From its inception Germany has been the cradle of human culture, a hub for the arts and sciences and a place where high quality fine poetry has been written. In no other country has philosophy been dealt with in such volumes and with such free intellect, as it has been in our fatherland."[68]

John's proposed solution to this problem was the creation and "ongoing support" for a "German-English language newspaper." Such a publication "will advance the intelligence of everyone; the Americans, the Germans and the English and promote favorable and friendlier communication between German and English speaking citizens," he believed. Everything in the paper ought to "appear in English and German in a select and worthy style." "In regard to politics . . . any squabbling and/or partiality shown to political parties must always be banned from the newspaper as material unworthy of its higher purpose." In addition, "select literary pieces from German and English, poetry, and information about the advancement of the arts and sciences, about commerce and about trade in regard to the US" should be included. Such a newspaper would help Americans "more easily learn German" and help foster respect for German Americans, while "introduc[ing] our fellow American citizens [to] our ideas," alongside "the good works of our soul-filled writers" and the worth and value of "German invention." "The newspaper should never concern itself with anything religious," John counseled, but it should remain open to printing what he termed "outlawed philosophical ideology, the rationale and evidence of which is simply derived from nature and from facts." Such ideas seemed rare to John, "in this country of dark religions and bigotry," but their dissemination seemed vital and sure to have "a most beneficial impact on the enlightenment of all Americans."[69]

German-language newspapers had existed for just over a century by the time John rose to make his speech, and many major cities already had a well-established German press. Yet, as Herman Ridder, publisher of the *New Yorker Staats-Zeitung*, noted later in the century, there existed no solidly bilingual, bi-national papers along the lines suggested by John: "The daily papers published in the German language are not German papers, but American papers printed in the German language. They represent American interests as completely as the papers printed in the English language. They educate the Germans which come to this country to become good and loyal American citizens."[70] John's speech was a clear statement of hyphenated Americanism, and a wholly positive one at that. After delivering it, he packed up, returned to Saxonburg, and set about being American.

Internal Improvements (1838–41)

The year 1838 was a pivotal one for John in a number of ways. He met the man who would become his most important early mentor, saw his name in print for the first time, and was reintroduced to the subject of suspension bridges. The year did not begin with any evident promise, however. John's fortunes continued to stall with the faltering economy, and he found himself with nothing to do but stay home during the winter and spring. By May 1838, little had changed for John in almost a year, except his name, along with the loss of a brother and the addition of a son. Luckily, his adopted home state was just as desperate as he was. Having poured millions of dollars into its internal improvements plan, Pennsylvania was anxious to start making it pay, and in May a huge improvements bill was pushed through the state legislature. By early June the financial spigot of the state coffers was reopened, and John was rehired.[1]

From the confines of Mühlhausen, John had marveled at the state of US public works projects. "Germans wonder how [the Erie Canal] could have happened," John wrote, "without an army of government advisors, secretaries and other officials deliberating about it for 10 years, without sending out thousands of letters, and without bankruptcy." It didn't take ten years to get started on the Erie Canal, but it did take nine—from concluding the initial surveys to sticking the first spade in the ground—and the Erie enjoyed numerous advantages not shared by any other US project. In many respects, the United States was little different from Prussia with regard to its internal improvements.[2]

The term "internal improvement" was coined in the 1780s to describe a loose collection of undertakings designed to secure public prosperity—roads, lighting, education, sewer and water works, and so on—but increasingly it described the creation of a comprehensive internal navigation and transportation network. As Prussia realized several decades later, economic prosperity depended as much on moving as on mobilizing. Despite their recent union, the country in the late eighteenth century was a rather diverse collection of isolated lands and disparate people. Linking them all was the key, which was not in itself controversial. When George Washington looked down at a map of North America, he saw an immense, seemingly providential system of waterways that spread out across the entire right side of the continent, as if "nature [had] designed the interior region expressly for improvement by the new United States." A short road or canal here, some improved navigation there, and the whole could be united into a comprehensive national system. Washington believed that "inland navigation" was "the cement of interest" that could bind the United States into "one indivisible band." Internal improvement was more than just clearing riverbeds and constructing roads and canals, it was the work of building a nation: fostering harmony across communities, promoting economic development, and sustaining the Union. As the southern firebrand John C. Calhoun urged somewhat later: "Let us bind the republic together with a perfect system of roads and canals. Let us conquer space."[3]

Unfortunately, not everyone agreed—not even Calhoun eventually. The dilemma of internal improvement became wholly contentious, helping to define presidencies and political parties, from Washington, Adams, and Jefferson to Jackson, Clay, and Calhoun. The main sticking point was somewhat simple: natural geographic boundaries failed to jibe with political boundaries; rivers would insist on crossing state or county lines or otherwise failing to respect the boundaries the United States had set up for their own governance. Pennsylvania was an excellent example of this. The state was best described as a series of micro-regions, all of which loosely belong to three or four larger regions, which themselves made up the state of Pennsylvania, itself split down the middle by a three-thousand-foot-high mountain range. The state's waterways were even worse. In the west, the waters flow toward the Ohio River; in the east toward the Delaware. In the south they flow toward the Potomac while in the middle of the state toward the Susquehanna. Clearly internal improvement needed a federal solution if it was to effectively improve anything. Predictably, this was an impossible feat in a country paranoid about federal overreach.[4]

The issue was not helped by the development of a deeply partisan politics predicated less on national development than on competing visions of government (and regional) activity. Politicians—and those who voted for them—feared the extension of federal power: the rise of a massive new arm of government, fed by new taxes and run by unelected individuals making decisions about local matters from far away. The issue became divisive yet clear: Did the federal government have the authority to enact such a widespread program? This impasse threw the issue back to the states themselves, which was fine for New York, which had the Hudson River and the flat Mohawk Valley within its jurisdiction, but less so for anyone else. Most state-sponsored internal improvement projects failed, or at least failed to pay for themselves. They did, however, help train America's first great wave of professional engineers.[5]

From June 11 to June 30, 1838, John was employed by the Pennsylvania Canal Board at a rate of two dollars per day. He found himself working as a surveyor this time, a task he had mastered over fifteen years earlier at the Unger School. More specifically, he was charged with surveying a route for the planned Sinnemahoning extension of the West Branch Canal to the Allegheny at Kittanning. He took up the task with great energy, efficiency, and skill, despite the fact that it entailed as much exploring as it did surveying. Setting off from the recently established village of Lock Haven, John had to battle his way through the thick mountain forests for about eighty miles before ambling down the side of the Allegheny Plateau and meeting up with the Redbank Creek, which snaked its way to the Allegheny just north of Kittanning. Still, John completed the job in only twenty days, surveying an impressive average of about seven to eight miles a day.[6]

Back in Butler County, John was immediately offered further work by the canal board, this time as a sub-assistant engineer on a new feeder canal. He began the very next day, despite having just trudged 150 miles over the Alleghenies, all while helping to lug a trunk full of surveying equipment. Designed to take water from Kittanning to the Main Line Canal at Freeport, the Allegheny Feeder Canal was a short-lived project, a part of the frenetic, scattershot world of nineteenth-century canal construction. It enjoyed momentary favor and support before losing the interest of the Canal Commissioners in Harrisburg. Even its chief engineer regarded it as "*useful* [but] not *necessary*," a sentiment shared by John. Although he worked on the project for several months, John started looking for a new job after only two weeks on the job.[7]

The Allegheny Feeder did place John close to Principal Engineer Charles L. Schlatter and close to home, not that he seems to have taken much advantage of this. John began work on the feeder system the day after returning from his Sinnemahoning expedition, and he proceeded to work 184 days straight, from July 1 to December 31. Such eager and ceaseless commitment showed John's mania for employment and professional advancement, especially during a national economic depression, but also, one suspects, a lack of concern for his young family. Freeport certainly was a mere twelve miles from Saxonburg, but this was a good day's journey in 1838, and instead he worked every day. John's preference for industry over the company of his family would continue for much of his life.[8]

John's capacity for work was immense, and a regular workday was rarely enough to keep him busy. His son couldn't remember seeing John "idle. . . . He never took a rest or a vacation." Despite working every day for six straight months, John still found time to write and published several articles and submitted a slew of different applications—"a new and improved mode of constructing steamboilers," a steam plow he'd been tinkering with for years, a "new and useful

Self-Acting Gauge," and a rather vaguely described "propeller"—to the US Patent Office. He also wrote to Charles Ellet, chief engineer of the James River and Kanawha Canal Company, asking for work.[9]

As expected, construction of the Allegheny Feeder barely lasted past the New Year. Work ground to a halt in February before it was officially suspended by the legislature. John still managed to get paid for eighty-six days' work, though it was unclear what the state had spent their money on. Despite having been up and running for over eight months, "very little work [was] done upon the principal portion of it," according to the superintendent's final report. Whatever John had done had impressed his boss, however, and a week after the legislature abandoned the feeder canal, they "appointed [Schlatter] to take charge of the surveys for a continuous railroad from Harrisburg to Pittsburgh." Evidently well-impressed by the hard-working, tireless, and tenacious German, Schlatter brought John with him.[10]

The source of Schlatter and John's mutual admiration remains a mystery. Described by friend and fellow engineer James Worrall, "Charley [was] a lady killer . . . with a perfect whisker and an Apollonic leg—knacky at many things, his highest talent being artistic," a description that could never have applied to John.[11] Despite his evident ability and expertise, John was doing little more than piecemeal engineering and surveying work before linking up with Schlatter. Certainly, he was held in high regard, but so were dozens of other young engineers working around the nation. Schlatter picked John out, advised him, challenged him, and believed in him. Schlatter was a true mentor, who was admired both in the profession and in Harrisburg, where all the money came from.

As a member of the state canal board in the early 1840s, Schlatter was instrumental in helping John establish a reputation and a market for his wire ropes, especially on the Main Line Canal's Portage Railroad. It is doubtful John would have gotten an opportunity to construct his first suspension bridge without the sound reputation—fostered and sustained by Schlatter—he enjoyed in Harrisburg. Without Schlatter's patronage, John may never have had a chance to test his wire ropes or to build a suspension bridge. In turn, John never forgot Schlatter and always spoke of him with the highest respect, "not a common thing for [John] to do," his son added.[12]

———

Around the time it was thinking about shutting down work on the Allegheny Feeder, the Pennsylvania legislature began to think that a Main Line railroad might be even better than a Main Line Canal. The first order of business was to survey the land, for which Schlatter was selected. Appointed principal engineer on July 15, 1839, Schlatter took office on August 1. His first official act was to appoint three of his most trusted lieutenants—S. Moylan Fox, J. C. Stocker, and John A. Roebling—as principal assistants at a wage of four dollars per day, double their previous salaries. Unknown and unemployed just three years earlier, John was slowly being enveloped by the vast network of public works projects that were gradually binding the massive state together, being incorporated as a still small but useful cog into the larger system of public planning at work in Harrisburg. And, ironically, John owed his start much less to his formal schooling at one of Europe's foremost technical colleges than to his practical training as a surveyor in out-of-the-way Erfurt. John's opening came courtesy of his surveying skills, not his engineering acumen, which in many respects fitted the US model. US engineers in the first half of the nineteenth century rarely had any formal schooling. Instead, they usually began young, working as lowly rodmen on large-scale public works projects, and worked their way up. As such, and unlike the strong-willed and independent-minded John, they were most often "creatures of the organizations in which they worked."[13]

John was beginning to play a limited but crucial role in the project that carved up the country, laying lines upon the land for communication, transportation, and property. As a result, Schlatter was "highly sensible of the vast importance of the work entrusted to [his] charge, not only to the state of Pennsylvania, but to the United States at large." The canal board had surveyed a northern, middle, and southern route for the Main Line Canal in 1825–26, and they undertook—under Schlatter's direction—a similar set of surveys for a railroad. To Stocker fell the job of surveying the northern route, while John shouldered with the southern route, designed to run from Pittsburgh to Chambersburg. All the surveys "were prosecuted with vigor, until the parties were obliged, by the inclemency of the season, to close their field of operations early in the month of November."[14]

Between assignments, John paid a quick visit home to Saxonburg, hired a few needy Saxonburgers, and spent some time with his pregnant wife (their second daughter, Laura, was born early the following year; their first had died in infancy two years before) and set off for Pittsburgh. There he secured some tents from the Pittsburgh Arsenal, an experienced "waggoner"—John Clarke, who "understands the mountains and the business"—and got to work immediately. "The position of a depot, and the entrance of a railroad" into Pittsburgh being of "so much importance," several different lines and routes were surveyed down to the mouth of Turtle Creek. A route following the banks of the Monongahela was ruled out thanks to the "numerous slips" that dotted the river, impeding a roadbed. The most promising route ran east from Liberty Street in Pittsburgh to the village of Wilkinsburg, before heading south to the Monongahela. Not only was the ground clear and level, but it was ripe for development. If adopted, John thought, "the beautiful valley of East Liberty, would soon become one of the

suburbs of Pittsburgh, and be a most convenient outlet to the growing population of that thriving city."[15]

From the Monongahela, John's party took a sharp left turn at Braddock's Field
and headed off along Turtle Creek Valley to its meeting with Brush Creek. Thus
far John encountered nothing but "favorable ground," but the land was about to
start rising. From the Little Branch of Brush Creek up to Barclay's Summit at an
altitude of 525 feet, the grade was forty-five feet per mile, the maximum gradient
allowed for a railroad at the time. The route then descended at a similar gradient
to the town of Greensburg. "Long embankments or viaducts" would be needed
to cross the Sewickley River on the way back down, John reported, although he
also thought the gradient could be reduced "by tunneling Barclay's Summit," a
solution John found easy to endorse: "A town of that importance appears to be
entitled to the benefits of such an improvement, even if it should connect with a
considerable extra expense."[16]

John expended "much time and labor . . . examining the country about
Greensburg," running many "experimental lines" through the hills in an effort
"to obtain the best route which the difficult feature of the ground will admit."
"No feasible summit has been left unexplored," Schlatter later informed the
canal commissioners. The main problem was surmounting the mountainous
spine that cut through Westmoreland County, separating Greensburg from its
neighbors to the east. "An accurate knowledge of it was of the greatest importance to us," John explained, before detailing the two routes he had decided
were the most feasible. The first ran from Greensburg to Youngstown before
heading out over "light grades, and over ground particularly adapted to the economical construction of the road bed," to Laughlinstown at the base of Laurel
Hill. Another ran to Loyalhanna and on to Bernhard's Summit. This was "a few
stations longer," John explained, "but the least expensive . . . the most level and
easiest made."[17]

The whole distance from Pittsburgh to Laughlinstown, John calculated, was
fifty-three miles, while the elevation gained was 540 feet. His "reconnoisances
[sic] embraced every point where there was a possibility of discovering more favorable routes," and they had left him at the western base of Laurel Hill—a "wild
and almost inaccessible region"—at the onset of winter. Laurel Hill was generally considered the most formidable barrier in the way of the southern route.
"Its topographical features are not so generally known," John reported, "owing to
[its] wild character." "It is not so often visited by the inhabitants of the adjoining
valleys for the purpose of hunting as other parts of the Allegheny mountains
are," John continued, "and some of its dark recesses and laurel thickets, which
offer a fine abode to the deer and the bear, will, as they present no inducement
to settlers, probably remain for ages to come, in the primitive state in which they
are found now."[18]

To get a better sense of the terrain, John visited Paul Stiffler's farm on Chestnut Ridge in early November. Commanding "an extensive bird's eye view of the western slope of Laurel Hill" for twenty miles in either direction, Stiffler's farm was a perfect place to study the mountain's rugged silhouette. With winter slowly settling over Westmoreland, there was no time to walk a wild and uncharted mountainside. Thankfully, John was an excellent surveyor, and he quickly found a tributary of the Loyalhanna River that cut a break in "the western slope of that difficult mountain" at an elevation of 1,930 feet.[19]

John thanked his staff and wrapped up field operations on November 9, 1839, after three months living in a tent in increasingly isolated and difficult conditions. Surveying was hard and dangerous work. Surveyors lived almost constantly with accidents, injuries, and scarcity, and they put up with great discomfort, awful weather, and instruments that barely worked. "There is, perhaps, no class of men who endure so many hardships and privations—whose fortitude and energy, whose intellectual powers, are taxed to a greater extent than the Government surveyor in the wild forests of the . . . Western portions of the United States," wrote W. L. Perry a few years later. Not the settler but the surveyor shoulders the burdens of westward expansion, Perry believed, for "when the heavens open and the rains descend, the settler enters his log cabin . . . secure from the beating storm [while] the surveyor has no alternative but to lay his troubled head on a *soft lightwood knot*, his body on the wet ground, and *let it rain*, thanking his stars it isn't a hailstorm instead of rain." The wind in the Alleghenies was described by one surveyor as "so high as to blow heavy pieces of bark from the bodies of dead hemlock trees." Still, despite the strains and hardships, John was a natural surveyor. He was hardy and energetic by nature; precise, detailed, and exacting by inclination; and he loved clarity in all things. If surveying is the mathematical mind in action, then John was a natural.[20]

John ended his report to Schlatter with a plea for the southern route. The region was "hardly surpassed by any in the state [as] an agricultural district," John counseled, while its "mineral wealth is truly astonishing." John was convinced the region was poised for an industrial boom, one that would sustain the business end of the new railroad. Powered by "the never failing waters" of the Loyalhanna, the region promised "an immense business to the [rail] road" that alone would be "sufficient to pay for its expense," John concluded. Like the Rhineland of John's younger days, all Westmoreland needed to blossom was a reliable transportation system.[21]

Everyone went home after the end of the expedition except for John, who went off east to Harrisburg. He had his report to write for Schlatter, the latest technical journals to catch up on, and as much glad-handing as he could manage. He also worked on several mechanical problems, most notably on the theoretical mechanics of the crank system ("Is the change of a straight motion into a rotary motion, attended with any loss of useful power or not?" he wondered), ultimately publishing a number of articles on the subject in the *Railroad Journal* and getting into a series of heated exchanges with a number of other "crank theorists." "Whoever will take the trouble to examine my communication with attention, will see that no such error has been committed, which indeed would be too palpable to escape the notice of anyone who is at all versed in mathematics," John sniffed at one correspondent. Another he accused of outright "mathematical plunder." John was even so brash as to start an argument with Benjamin Aycrigg, his old boss on the Sinnemahoning project and a canal engineer of no small repute. Aycrigg charged John with attempting to "annihilate the whole theory of mechanics." John, in turn, "confess[ed] to be at a loss to understand how [such errors] could be admitted by the mathematical talent of the distinguished writer," succinctly showcasing a burgeoning talent for what might best be described as flattering to insult.[22]

Just as importantly as articulating and defending his theory of the crank, John had some drawing to do over the winter months. He could happily wander around the "wild and almost inaccessible region[s]" of Pennsylvania at Schlatter's behest like some kind of nomadic pathfinder, but he could also sit patiently at a desk in Harrisburg for weeks on end translating what had been seen, measured, and classified into a series of meticulously crafted maps. The results received wide praise. None bore John's name, although they all revealed his handwriting, his craft, and his dedication. They testify to John's penchant for detail, precision, and exactness, yet somehow wonderfully turn those dutiful skills into a beautifully textured, marvelously evocative vision of both pioneering progress and American futurity. They blend the findings of the mathematical mind with the talent of an artist and the myth of the wilderness, creating a powerful vision of the western imagination. A large map of all three routes, drawn by John "as they were *then* surveyed"—three different visions of the future—was exhibited in the halls of the Pennsylvania legislature in 1840 and again the following year. Impressed by the work of his new protégé, Schlatter "believed [John's map] furnish[ed] more correct geographical information than any map which has been made of that portion of the State."[23]

———

As the spring arrived, John headed back into the field with the rest of Schlatter's team, this time to Moylan's middle route. With state appropriations still pending, Schlatter was unsure if the legislature would come up with sufficient funds for full surveys of all three routes, so he pooled his resources. Determined to have at least one continuous, fully realized line from Pittsburgh to Harrisburg to show the canal board, Schlatter sent all three engineering corps to the middle route, the shortest of the three. To John fell the work of surveying a route from the western slope of the Alleghenies near Ebensburg, through "the forks of the Black Lick," over the Conemaugh and Loyalhanna Rivers, and on to Pittsburgh. "No portion of the country to be traversed . . . required more judicious examination and surveying, than that" undertaken by John, Schlatter later informed the canal board. "I cannot refrain from noticing," he continued, "the skill, patience and industry exercised by my principal assistant, Mr. Roebling, in developing the route through this most intricate country." The principal problem, as Schlatter saw it, was the "general character of the country . . . one irregularly formed mass of hills, crowded together promiscuously and without any apparent system or order." Charles Dickens was a little more generous a couple of years later: "The wet ground reeked and smoked, after the heavy fall of rain; and the croaking of frogs . . . sounded as though a million of fairy teams with bells were travelling through the air. . . . It was wild and grand." Philip Hone agreed, calling the mountains "astonishingly grand [and] wild beyond description."[24]

John had to create some order out of the "wild and grand" Pennsylvania landscape, and he did so by devising a complex system of cuts, tunnels, viaducts, and embankments, along with an eight-hundred-foot "reverse curve" thrown in for good measure. The landscape confounded all of John's reasonable hopes for compliance: where the summits were lowest, the rivers were widest; where the valleys were straightest, the streams were invariably ridiculously crooked. It was hazardous surveying the deep wooded forests, replete with an untold number of rattlesnakes and huge swarms of gnats and mosquitoes. Many surveyors "greased [their] entire faces to keep the insects from biting." John looked everywhere for the best route, scaling "high bluffs" and making his way through dense timberland. "Nothing has been neglected," Schlatter confirmed, before detailing John's elaborate plan to cut a route through the undulating landscape from Blairsville to Murrysville and on to Pittsburgh. Several tunnels, including a 450-foot tunnel through McCartney's Hill, would be required, along with numerous viaducts, three of which would exceed a thousand feet in length.[25]

Schlatter could not have been happier with the work done on the middle route and reported his "entire satisfaction . . . in the manner in which" the surveys were conducted generally by his three principal assistants. "Living almost entirely in tents, and traversing for the greater part of the time occupied by the survey the wildest portions of our State, they pursued their laborious occupation with a steadiness and perseverance which overcame every obstacle," he announced. John's reputation for competence, diligence, and reliability was beginning to spread in Harrisburg. In 1840 he served as an official delegate to the Pennsylvania Railroad Convention in Pittsburgh, an event that gave him a good excuse to make his way home to Saxonburg to meet Laura, born June 24, 1840. Unfortunately, the family reunion did not last long (although long enough for Johanna to find herself pregnant again shortly afterward). The Pennsylvania legislature soon after granted Schlatter the money he needed to complete all three surveys, and John had to return to his southern route and the mountains of Westmoreland County.[26]

———

Frigid and unforgiving in winter, Westmoreland County teemed with life and color in the summer. Great forests of maple, chestnut, and oak grew thick and plentiful, providing shelter and sustenance for elk, deer, bears, and all manner of small game. Wild fruits grew with such vigor that one could travel for hundreds of miles through southern Pennsylvania, it was said, without carrying any food. Such provisions and scenery accompanied John and his crew as they retraced his steps from the previous fall, filling in and systematizing the various structures and improvements that would be needed to traverse the southern route. The entire surveyed route from Pittsburgh to Laughlinstown was fifty-two miles, which was only about a quarter of the way to Harrisburg, leaving progress on the southern route way behind that of the other routes. Oddly, Schlatter then had John work on something entirely different.[27]

Schlatter ended his first report to the Canal Commission with a plea for a macadamized road from Laughlinstown to Chambersburg, and then gave the work to his most trusted lieutenant when the job was approved. "The great importance attached to this road induced [Schlatter] to direct Mr. Roebling" to conduct the surveys, establishing a regular system of gradients not to exceed 2.5 degrees, or 235 feet per mile. An old turnpike had served the needs of southern Pennsylvania since 1818, replacing the Old State Road laid out in 1791. Unfortunately, its gradient was too steep, and it was in great disrepair. "Travelers frequently found it more comfortable to walk than to ride," reports one historian, while Philip Nicklin, who traveled the road in 1835, described it as "hard, and rough, and jolty . . . profitable to blacksmiths and wheelwrights," meaning it was likely a very fair representation of American roads at the time. Travelers "rated American natural roads as the worst in the world [apparently] and American turnpikes little better." John's charge was to find the "best and most direct" route within the parameters, without "any reference" to the towns and villages that dotted the old road. Schlatter freely admitted that local interests might change the direction of the road to serve their needs, but he asked John not to take such concerns into account when surveying.[28]

By late summer, John was exactly where he had been a year before, atop Laurel Hill staring down the eastern slope. His team was more or less the same, although his surroundings must have struck him as wildly different. The previous year, John had battled the shortening days, the dropping temperatures, and the onset of winter, whereas the bright glory of early fall offered stunning views in all directions. The days were still warm, long, and fragrant, the views still remarkably verdant. For a man so used to slogging through dense, thick underbrush, this must have seemed like bliss.

Abandoning the heights of the ridge, John and his team marked out a route running southeast from the crest of Laurel Hill to Stoystown and on through Clear Run Valley to the Alleghenies, a slow climb never exceeding the maximum grade. They crossed the Alleghenies a mile and a half south of the old turnpike before descending steadily to Cove Mountain, the greatest obstacle on the whole route. John needed to summon all his talents as a surveyor to plot an accessible route—all twists, turns, and complex reverses—down the eastern slope to the base of Cove Mountain and on to Fort Loudon. The total distance from Laughlinstown to Loudon was ninety-eight miles, eleven miles more than the old turnpike, although with a major reduction in the overall incline. Such a significant decrease in gradient, Schlatter explained, would lead to "a *virtual* saving of distance in the new line" of one-third for heavy wagoning and one-fifth to one-fourth for light conveyances. The reason for this, Schlatter continued, was that where the old turnpike took thirty hours, the new line would take only twenty. More significant, however, was haulage. With significantly lower gradients, "a load of one half more *at least*" could be managed along the road, at least according to the "intelligent wagoners" Schlatter had talked with.[29]

John finished his surveying work in October, took the Cumberland Valley Railroad from Chambersburg to Harrisburg, and settled in the state capital to write his report and get started on all the maps, profiles, and estimates he had to draw. Schlatter intended to furnish the Canal Commission with a single map containing all three routes, and he again turned to John as his draftsman. Schlatter, of course, was busy writing his own report, which he delivered on January 9, 1841. With all the surveys more or less complete, Schlatter's "Second Report" held great importance for the state. It was well known that where the railroad went, so went trade and prosperity. And Schlatter clearly understood this, which may explain his reluctance to come out with a preferred route in print. "Local advantages and local interests do not, in my opinion, properly pertain to the department of an Engineer," he was at pains to stress, in the process acknowledging the long and often very public history of surveyors and boards disagreeing. Such incidents, of course, rarely ended well for the chief engineer. "Holding this opinion," he continued, "I have endeavored, as far as lay in my power, to discover the nearest, cheapest and best route for a railroad *between Harrisburg and Pittsburgh*. It remains with your Board to decide which route would prove most *beneficial to the interests of the State*, as it is by no means certain that the shortest road would prove most profitable."[30] Schlatter was perhaps being coy here; "nearest, cheapest and best" routes are usually the most attractive, even for the most contentious politician. Even so, a cursory reading of Schlatter's report led to the rather obvious conclusions that the northern route (at 320½ miles) was just too long to take seriously, despite crossing the Alleghenies at a much lower altitude to the other routes; that the southern route (clocking in at 291½ miles) wasn't much better; and that the middle route (a paltry 229½ miles) was both the shortest and the cheapest.[31]

It's tough to argue against the shortest and the cheapest, but John did. In "The Great Central Railroad from Philadelphia to St. Louis," a speech he delivered several years later at the Odeon Theater in Pittsburgh, John argued (incorrectly) that the southern route was shorter, encountered a much more moderate gradient (true in essence, although the overall altitude was much higher), passed through rich agricultural country and extensive coalfields, and entered Pittsburgh from the south, where all docks and trade were concentrated. John had an ally in the town of Greensburg, which had been lobbying for a southern line since April 19, 1836. Unfortunately, the citizens of Greensburg had about as much pull as John.[32]

John was deeply interested in the engineering of railroads in the early 1840s. His notebooks from the period are packed full of notes on almost all every aspect of railroad building and railroad development. He took copious notes on the Baltimore and Ohio Railroad, as well as on the Boston and Providence, the Philadelphia and Columbia, the New York and Erie, the Carbondale, and a host of other railroads. He copied down huge sections of official railroad reports and wrote up plans and drew diagrams for various different railroad superstructures. He designed tunnels and bridges for railroads, assessed the costs of locomotive construction, and compared potential routes for a railroad from Pittsburgh to Cleveland. He even drew up a plan for a railroad from Philadelphia to Pittsburgh, with estimated length, construction costs, and usage, designed so as "not [to] allow companies to enrich themselves at the expense of the community at large."[33]

After all the surveys were completed, the reports submitted, and the maps dutifully drawn and exhibited, the project ground to a halt. The state had spent millions of dollars on a canal system that now seemed outdated and outmoded. No one, it seems, was interested in starting all over again on a similar project, albeit this time with rails and sleepers instead of ditches and towpaths. The Pennsylvania Railroad was eventually incorporated on April 13, 1846, and work was commenced on the middle route the following year. Back in Harrisburg in the winter of 1841, however, John was bursting with ideas, writing articles, submitting patents, planning a wire rope factory, and lobbying the state legislature, some of which activity found him embroiled in a controversy, one whose origins stretched back initially to 1838 but whose gestation had begun seventeen years before in a lecture hall in Berlin. For, shortly after completing his maps and report, John's mind was once again firmly set on building himself a suspension bridge.[34]

———

In 1813, a massive 340-foot clear span wooden arch bridge, stretching across the Schuylkill River between Powelton Village and Philadelphia's astounding new Fairmount Water Works, was opened. Designed and built by Louis Wernwag—America's most accomplished wooden bridge builder—the span was a marvel of engineering skill. Quickly dubbed "the Colossus," the span became a major tourist attraction, noted for the grace of its form and the beauty of its setting. It provided stout and secure service for almost a quarter of a century before meeting the fate of almost all wooden bridges. At about nine o'clock on the evening of September 1, 1838, someone put a torch to the structure's west end, and within twenty minutes the bridge's western abutment had "burned off," after which the once mighty Colossus collapsed into the Schuylkill River.[35]

The incident caught the attention of two young engineers, one at either end of Pennsylvania, and initiated a long-lasting rivalry. The enmity between the two would last fifteen years and end with the establishment of the suspension bridge as the preeminent structural form for spanning wide waters in the United States. One of the engineers was John. The other was Charles Ellet, a man John had recently written to asking for work.

Born four years after John in 1810 near Philadelphia, Charles Ellet was a brilliant, self-educated maverick with a propensity for shooting himself in the foot. Standing over six feet tall with a large pointy nose, a prominent forehead, and an unruly great mop of hair, Ellet had the dramatic flair of a showman, the energy of a dervish, the intolerance of a genius, and the humor of a Puritan. Edwin Stanton, Lincoln's secretary of war, thought Ellet had "more ingenuity, more personal courage, and more enterprise than anybody else I have ever seen. . . . If I had a proposition that I desired to work out to some definite result, I do not know of any one to whom I would intrust it so soon as Ellet." Others were more measured: "He was a mercurial genius who was his own best advertisement and worst enemy."[36] Ellet was hired as chief engineer on the James River and Kanawha Canal in 1836, not because of his engineering ability but because he excelled at "the politics of internal improvement" (otherwise known as promotion and public relations). He was summarily fired two years later for his "sarcasm" and "dictatorial manner," and for insisting on his own independence in all technical matters. Over the course of his career Ellet's mind ranged over a host of different topics: canals, railroads, dams and reservoirs, flood control, the navigation of internal waterways, economic theory, physical geography, harbor and

Figure 8.1 John's great rival: Charles Ellet. Photograph by Rehn and Hurn, Philadelphia ca. 1860–61. Courtesy of the Transportation History Collection, University of Michigan Library (Special Collections Library).

coastal defenses, and ultimately naval rams. Ellet's first real love, however, like John, was the suspension bridge, which he discovered in France.[37]

Ellet got his start working on canals, including on the North Branch of the Main Line Canal, where he worked eighteen- and nineteen-hour days walking the entire 365-mile route, eventually coming to the attention of Canvas White, inventor of water-resistant cement, and Benjamin Wright, "the father of American civil engineering," two of America's foremost canal engineers. Wright took Ellet with him to the Chesapeake and Ohio Canal after he was appointed chief engineer, and Ellet stayed for two years, long enough for him to learn enough French and borrow enough money to get him across the Atlantic.[38]

Ellet had just turned twenty when he departed for Europe. With every engineer in America trying to make a name for himself in the field, Ellet forsook the field for the classroom. Continental engineers were held in some regard in the United States, as was continental engineering itself, but not as high as those who had mucked around on American soil solving problems and setting up systems.

Fancy degrees were not apt to sway a canal board when they had the option of an engineer with "defined experience" on some large-scale US public works project. Yet Ellet's decision paid off. He returned after two years in Europe with something no American engineer possessed, except perhaps John. Ellet arrived in Paris in May 1830 and set about studying as strenuously as he was able, with the occasional trip to visit General Lafayette, hero of the American War of Independence, to whom he had secured a letter of introduction. Ellet enjoyed Lafayette immensely, and the general returned the affection, helping the young engineer gain his prize: admittance to the prestigious École Nationale des Ponts et Chaussées in Paris. Ellet was accepted in late July, yet almost immediately the Revolution of 1830 broke out.[39]

With his well-laid plans in jeopardy and all his money committed, Ellet was in crisis. Luckily, the École Nationale resumed its normal operations in the autumn. Ellet studied hard and dutifully from November through to the spring of 1831, when he decided to get a close-up look at some of the things he had been learning about. For the next six weeks, Ellet toured through France and Switzerland, inspecting railroads, canals, and dams. He visited the Languedoc Canal, the Saint-Ferriol Dam, and the Canal du Midi. Increasingly, however, his attention was drawn to a beautiful and strange new engineering marvel called the suspension bridge. He scrutinized every inch and detail of suspension bridges on the Rhône, the Loire, the Garonne, and the Seine, becoming—like John—entranced. Growing up near Philadelphia, Ellet may have seen White and Hazard's wire

Figure 8.2 The bridge that captured Ellet's imagination. Marc Seguin's Remoulins Suspension Bridge, built in 1830.

footbridge over the Schuylkill or one of Finley's chain bridges. Equally, Ellet almost certainly heard Louis Joseph Vicat's lectures on the subject delivered at the École Nationale shortly after Ellet arrived. Either way, he had come to Europe to learn the theory and had fallen in love with the real thing. A letter written to his sister May from the south of France reveals the depth of his affection: "Though it was raining still and 12 o'clock at night when we arrived [in Remoulins], my curiosity drew me at that hour to go examine a suspended bridge across the Gardon [built by Seguin the year before] rather than wait till morning. The people in the house looked upon me as upon a crazy man [but] I slept soundly [that night] in a scented apartment and dreamed of Suspended Bridges."[40]

———

Ellet returned to Paris in April 1831, a couple of weeks before John set out for America, to finish his studies before returning home in early 1832. By chance the US Treasury Department decided they needed a bridge built over the Potomac between Washington and Alexandria just as Ellet was recrossing the Atlantic, a fact Ellet noticed "in the Philadelphia papers" upon his return. He set to work, requesting soundings, tidal information, and a profile of the river bottom, among numerous other details. On October 6, 1832, he submitted a plan for a wire suspension bridge forty-six-feet high (to allow for masts and funnels) with a span of 582 feet between the towers. The total cost would be $518,528. Ellet was at great pains to stress the durability, strength, and stability of the structural type, along with its widespread approval and adoption throughout Europe. His proposal was overseen by Roger B. Taney (later, author of the infamous Dred Scott decision) during his brief and tumultuous tenure as Secretary of the Treasury and it went nowhere, despite Ellet's repeated attempt to force a decision and then just to get his drawings back.[41]

By the time of the Colossus fire, Ellet had grown impatient with the US government, but not with the idea of suspension bridges. The destruction of one of his hometown's most important thoroughfares rekindled his ambition. Ever the salesmen, he had an impeccable plan. On January 13, 1839, Ellet visited Harrisburg to lobby for the immediate replacement of Wernwag's Colossus, this time with a more permanent, less flammable structure. His work in the state capital done, Ellet scurried home to start writing. On March 16, the Pennsylvania state legislature passed "an act to authorize the erection of free bridges over the Schuylkill at or near Philadelphia." Known as the Free Bridge Act, the legislation called for the spans to function as extensions of the city's street system, not as separate conveyances, making them a public, not private, undertaking, unusual for the time. The designs, engineer, and general contractor were to be decided upon by the county commissioners. The cost was not to exceed $80,000.[42]

Bridge proposals flooded into the county commissioners' office as soon as the governor signed the Free Bridge Act. Two plans came from William Strickland: one for a stone arch bridge, the other for a wire suspension bridge. Strickland had already designed many of the city's most famous landmarks: Eastern State Penitentiary, the Merchants' Exchange, and the Second Bank of the United States. As an engineer, Strickland had also helped lay out the state's Main Line Canal and subsequently played a hugely important role helping to introduce and promote the locomotive in the United States. More intriguingly, Strickland—a commercial artist before he was an architect—was also the engraver of the marvelous images of James Finley's suspension bridge that appeared in the *Port Folio* in 1810. Another proposal for a suspension bridge came from Professor Walter Johnson, a Harvard graduate, ex-faculty member at the Franklin Institute, and current professor of chemistry and natural philosophy at the Philadelphia College of Medicine. Johnson was a renowned expert on the structural strength of iron and steel, although where his interest in suspension bridges came from is anyone's guess. Yet another suspension plan came—rather surprisingly—from John's friend Edward Gill, who had gone to work with Ellet on the James River and Kanawha Canal in Virginia right after leaving John on the Sandy and Beaver. It might be considered odd that Gill came up with his plan after having spent so much time with John and Ellet, and the latter certainly thought so, but it may also be that the idea of suspension bridges was in the air. Historians often think of Ellet and Roebling pushing their ideas against the accumulated weight of established knowledge. Yet clearly the idea had currency, although whether anyone had the capability outside of Ellet and Roebling is another matter. Certainly no one had built a suspension bridge in America for well over a dozen years and never of sufficient length to span such a river as the Schuylkill.[43]

Despite the number of proposals and the weight of the reputations behind them, Ellet was way ahead of the pack. Displaying a talent for recognizing and grasping his opportunities, Ellet had a public campaign ready. It wasn't enough to furnish a credible design. He also had to convince everyone that he was the man for the job. To this end, he wrote a deceptively short yet profoundly influential little pamphlet as his opening salvo. Published on April 15, 1839, thirty days after Pennsylvania passed the Free Bridge Act, Ellet's *A Popular Notice of Wire Suspension Bridges* is one of the most important documents in the history of suspension bridge engineering. The pamphlet's significance was recognized by the *American Railroad Journal and Mechanics' Magazine*, which endorsed and reprinted it almost immediately. The effect of the twelve-page pamphlet was almost instantaneous: within weeks Ellet was recognized as the country's foremost expert on suspension bridges.[44]

Ellet's pamphlet starts with a simple claim: suspension bridges have been around in one form or another for thousands of years. They were a tried-and-true system, albeit one that needed adapting to modern needs, methods, and materials. All that was needed for the form to blossom over the last forty years was the application of modern mathematics, which had happened first on native ground, not in Europe, Asia, or South America. Finley's successes in western Pennsylvania in 1801 had blazed the trail. His efforts had inspired "the design of [Thomas Telford's] famous bridge across the Straights [*sic*] of Menai," which successfully spanned almost one thousand feet while also providing forty-eight feet of clearance, thus ensuring "no obstruction to the ships navigating the channel." Once Telford's mighty structure was carrying traffic across the Menai, France sent Navier across the English Channel to study it, Ellet continued, mixing up his history, although it was beside his point. Telford's success was noted throughout the civilized world and it inspired them to action. Unfortunately, in America, Finley's ideas had "fallen into neglect, if not disrepute." A nation built on shipping and with broad, often colossal rivers needed to establish an effective bridging capacity that did not interfere with navigation. Ellet's lesson was simple: the British faced the same problems as the Americans, and they solved it with a suspension bridge, as did the French. America would have to be next.[45]

Ellet went on to describe the fundamental elements of a suspension bridge, before making his departure from Telford. Telford's bridge used iron chains, but Ellet wanted to propose a somewhat different plan, one he had seen over the Rhône at Tournon. As the title of his pamphlet made plain, he was interested in *wire*—not chain link—suspension bridges, specifically the type developed and championed by Marc Seguin, whose short volume *Des Ponts en Fil de Fer* (1824) "sustained the merit of his plans by many cogent and irresistible arguments." Seguin's suspended system had "spread with extraordinary rapidity" across the continent, where wire suspension bridges were making ferries redundant. The secret was cost and strength. Manufacturing wire was significantly cheaper than casting and transporting massive chain bars. Additionally, the manufacturing process for iron wire imparted great "tenacity" and "an extraordinary increase of strength and toughness" to the wire. As Sequin proved, drawn wire cable exceeded the strength of iron chains by 100 percent.[46]

While stone arch or wooden bridges were perfectly reasonable and worthy structures for the right locations, for broad, fast-moving waters, Ellet counseled, a suspended structure would be nothing less than essential. One location generally discussed was the Schuylkill at Philadelphia, where the population had some experience with wooden bridges. Any replacement for the Fairmount Bridge would have to take into account the Schuylkill's winter ice floes and spring freshets. A suspension bridge, needing no piers in the river, would alleviate such problems while providing easy clearance for any vessel likely to find

Les deux Ponts sur le Rhône à Tain (Drôme).

Figure 8.3 Marc Seguin's two bridges over the Rhône at Tain. In the foreground, the world's first long-span wire suspension bridge, erected in 1825. To the rear, Seguin's 1849 span, erected after his earlier bridge was converted to foot traffic only.

itself passing downstream, Ellet wrote with—seemingly—all the objective disinterest of a professional expert. Cheaper than a stone bridge, more permanent than a wooden bridge, suspension bridges were a perfect solution to a distinctly American problem, Ellet affirmed. In addition, "as a contribution to the architecture of the city, and an ornament to the Schuylkill [a suspended span] would be unsurpassed."[47]

Ellet's pamphlet was short on detail. As described, his bridge was simply strands of wire ("about the diameter of a common writing quill"), coated in varnish, and laid parallel on a curve between masonry towers, supporting a roadway. The specifics came later, but the point was not to describe a suspension bridge so much as to link in people's minds the name Charles Ellet with the idea of a suspension bridge. Ellet's pamphlet wasn't a plan but a promotion: a suspension bridge "never parts with its beauty, [while] the lightness, grace and beauty of these structures, when tastefully designed and judiciously applied, can be only adequately appreciated when witnessed in place." Many of these structures "constructed in Europe . . . are regarded as among the most remarkable of the victories of modern art." Who wouldn't trust such a man to build a suspension bridge?[48]

A Popular Notice of Wire Suspension Bridges had a profound impact on the Schuylkill Bridge debate, as it did on John Roebling. Within days of Ellet submitting his plan, the Philadelphia papers were all "quoting from [his] pamphlet and talking about [his] plan," to the exclusion of all others. Ellet himself was unsure of his chances—"There is no chance for the bridge," he wrote on May 6, with no good reason, but soon got good news from Frederick Graff, one of the bridge commissioners. "As you have been the first to offer a plan *new in this country* I feel anxious that if such a structure should be erected that you should have preference," Graff wrote, including a number of suggestions in his letter, alongside some rather handsome drawings to illustrate his points. Not content with Graff's word on the matter, Ellet sent his uncle to visit the commissioners' office to ask around. The uncle wrote back that Ellet's plan "*as yet* appears the favorite of the Commissioners" but that they were worried about safety, especially given "the heavy loads of marble from the quarries that must pass over." Any fears over the plan's structural integrity soon dissipated. At the end of July, Ellet heard that he had been awarded the contract, in no small measure thanks to Graff's influence.[49]

Flush with his Schuylkill victory, Ellet immediately wrote to William Car Lane, mayor of St. Louis, outlining a plan to build a "permanent bridge" over the Mississippi for "a sum not to exceed $600,000." Remarkably, it worked. On September 23, 1839, the city's board of aldermen instructed Ellet to take soundings, survey the area, and prepare a report. In his *Report and Plan for a Wire Suspension Bridge Proposed to Be Constructed across the Mississippi River at St. Louis*, Ellet called for a central 1,200-foot span flanked by side spans of nine hundred feet, at a time when the longest suspended span was Chaley's 889-foot-long Freiburg Bridge. The deck was to be twenty-seven feet wide, with a nineteen-foot-wide carriageway and a four-foot-wide walkway on either side. At $737,566 the total cost was a little more than promised. Ellet was "entitled at least to the credit of great courage," quipped one historian.[50]

The St. Louis City Council "stood aghast" at Ellet's report, believing the plan to be "extravagantly wild and unsafe." A 1,200-foot-long span suspended upon towers both squarely in the middle of "the great and violent Mississippi" (to use Ellet's own words) seemed like a death trap, if Ellet could even get his towers built in the first place. As he explained: "The bed of the Mississippi [was] unstable and composed of a material which readily shifts from place to place with changes in the regimen of the river." A rapid scour and the bridge would likely be down in a matter of minutes. The mayor concluded that "the time is inauspicious for the commencement of an enterprise involving such an *enormous* expenditure of money." The city cut Ellet a check for one thousand dollars, and he soon left town.[51]

———

There was no such squeamishness in Philadelphia, where events seemed to be moving along seamlessly. By the end of the year, Ellet had the bridge contract in hand and changed financial circumstance. On November 20, 1839, Ellet's father-in-law—Judge William Daniel of Lynchburg, Virginia—died, leaving Ellet and his wife independently wealthy. A life of leisure, however, was not in Ellet's plans, and he continued to worry about almost everything. His main fear was that he would end up serving as both engineer and contractor, since there were so "few who really know anything about [suspension bridges]." Oddly enough, he was about to get a letter from someone who did.[52]

Being out in the field for most of 1839, John had no idea what was happening in Philadelphia or in the pages of the *Railroad Journal*. Ensconced in the state library at Harrisburg in January 1840, however, he happened upon Ellet's *Popular Notice*. Suddenly, John was transported back to Dietlein's lecture hall, to Bamberg in the spring of 1830, and to the banks of the Schuylkill, which he had visited during his first few days in America. Ellet's pamphlet, along with the news that he had secured contracts in Philadelphia and St. Louis, returned John's long-dormant dreams to the forefront of his thoughts. Ellet brought John back into the suspension bridge game, and John immediately fired off a letter to the younger engineer.[53]

John feared that his "communication . . . [would] appear inopportune and [was] an uncalled for obtrusion upon [Ellet's] time," and he pleaded to be forgiven because of his "great interest [in] the subject." "The study of Suspension Bridges," he continued, "formed for the last few year of my residence in Europe, my favorite occupation." Finding the issue "little cared for by the engineers of this country," the subject slipped from his mind, until he chanced upon Ellet's article. John was overjoyed by the news and offered hearty congratulations. "Let but one single bridge of the kind be put up in Ph[iladelphia], exhibiting all the beautiful forms of the system to the best advantage, and it will need no prophesy to foretell the effect which the novel and useful features of this new construction will produce upon the intelligent minds of the Americans." "You will certainly occupy a very enviable position, in being the first engineer, who aided by nothing but the resources of his own mind and a close investigation, succeeds to introduce a new mode of construction, which will find more useful application in the U[nited] States, than in any other country."[54]

No mere fan letter, it was designed to demonstrate his own expertise. After his effusive opening page, John went on to request "the favor of some data respecting your plans" and to suggest "an improvement in the construction in the kind of saddles applied by Mr. Telford on the Menai Bridge." John clearly understood Ellet's veneration for Telford's bridge and suspected that Ellet would be impressed with John's keen insight and technical mastery. If he should ever require an assistant engineer "who is competent for the task and who at the same time would [do] with pleasure all the necessary drawing, please bear me in mind," John signed off, requesting that Ellet "look upon this communication as a professional homage due to you." John clearly thought he was writing to a much older engineer, not someone four years his junior.[55]

Ellet's reply was pleasant but somewhat perfunctory, amounting to a reassurance ("Your communications on any professional subject will always be received with sentiments of satisfaction"), a broad general agreement with most of what John had written ("You correctly estimate the character of the American people, in supposing that they will not fail to recognize the merits of these structures when furnished with one respectable specimen"), and a pointed silence on the issue of Telford's saddles or John's advice. Nevertheless, John sent Ellet a diagram and a full description of the saddle he'd "planned and proposed . . . to the Prussian Engineer Department about 9 years ago" from Harrisburg on February 24. "The merits of this construction will be intelligible without further comments," John explained, before going on to describe "the partial failure of a suspension bridge [presumably Bamberg], constructed by an acquaintance of mine . . . where no provision was made for contraction and expansion." "The piers rented considerably," he revealed. Despite his cool reserve, Ellet ended his February 8 letter on a hopeful note: "Should the system prevail . . . I hope to have the pleasure of engaging the services of one who is familiar with the subject." He named no names, and he never contacted John when his contract was approved. Their nascent relationship was already in ruins by the time Ellet finally got to build his first suspension bridge.[56]

Ellet's Fairmount plan was published early in 1840, but with the state coffers still depleted from recession and the state's infrastructure plans still uncertain, he spent much of the first half of 1840 frustrated. Financing for his bridge seemed about as certain as for Schlatter's railroad survey. By spring, the Schuylkill Bridge project had been postponed and delayed innumerable times and for innumerable small reasons, so Ellet went traveling. In May, he was in Cincinnati discussing the possibility of a suspension bridge over the Ohio. Things were progressing nicely until Ellet fell seriously ill in the middle of the talks and the project was abandoned. Even worse, the county commissioners suddenly wanted Ellet back in Philadelphia to discuss his surveys and estimates. As he was too sick to travel, his Schuylkill bridge project began to unravel. On June 23, 1840, Ellet's mother wrote that the low bidder for the contract to build Ellet's bridge was a man called Andrew Young, who had somehow earned himself the great enmity of Jonathan Johnson, one of Ellet's biggest boosters on the county commission. Johnson hated Young and paid repeated visits to Ellet's mother in an effort to find out where the engineer was and when he expected to return.[57]

With Ellet nowhere to be found, the county board passed a resolution on June 29 directing the county commissioners to make a contract with Young to build a bridge across the Schuylkill "according to the plan of Charles Ellet, Jr." for $65,000. No contract was forthcoming—the board was waiting for word

from the commissioners that financing had been secured—but Young publicly affirmed that he would happily build Ellet's bridge for $45,000 (the other
$20,000 being reserved to purchase the bridge site). Advertisements appeared
on the streets and in the press stating that Young had received the contract and
would build the bridge. Johnson called on Ellet's mother incessantly while trying
to delay the final verdict and demanded that no contract be awarded until Ellet
returned.[58]

John was back in touch with Ellet at the end of the year, this time to ask an
explicit favor. He needed Ellet's help selling an idea he had had to replace the
hemp ropes on inclined planes of the Allegheny Portage Railroad—used to haul
railroad cars up steep mountainside—with wire cable, which John himself was
hoping to manufacture. Ellet wrote back several days later. In acknowledging
Ellet's quick response, John thanked him for the "free and open communication
of your opinion" on a subject "so new to all Engineers who hear of it, that no one
will venture to have a decided opinion at all, and all are afraid of recommending
it." John happily adopted a couple of Ellet's suggestions and proceeded with his
plan.[59]

All this talk of inclined planes and wire rope might have led Ellet to conclude
that John was no longer interested in suspension bridges. Nothing was further
from the truth. John learned few things more acutely from Ellet's *Popular Notice
of Wire Suspension Bridges* than the need to mount his own public relations campaign. On March 15, 1841, he did so, publishing the first section of a two-part
essay on suspension bridges in the *American Railroad Journal*. Suspended spans
were much in the minds of the public and the profession at present, John began,
but it would only be through the "successful erection of some good specimens"
that their standing would be secured. "Ocular demonstration . . . will advance
this cause more than all treatises," he believed.[60]

The trouble with John, however, was that he wasn't Ellet. Where Ellet might
have set out a vision or grabbed his readers' attention early in the essay, John
went straight into technical details, describing at great length the discrepancy
between the elasticity and structural strength of iron chains and those of wire
rope.[61] "The superiority of wire cables over chains cannot be contested for a moment," he affirmed after much citing of studies and tests. "Wire cables in place of
chains [have] prevailed over the whole continent," and it was, to John, "truly a
matter of astonishment why the English Engineers still cling to the old system."
The strength of wire cable is two-thirds greater than chains; they are cheaper
to manufacture, much more reliable, better protected against the elements, and
more uniform in quality. Crucially, wire rope was also a much better and safer
option for suspenders, the vertical connectors by which the roadway was attached to the main cables. In order to clarify and solidify his point, John quoted
at length from Colonel Pasley's description of the destruction of the Montrose

Suspension Bridge from the *Transactions of the Institute of Civil Engineers* (1839). The problem was longitudinal movement, not lateral, a problem that could be solved by using more flexible suspender cables and an "inflexible line of longitudinal trussing from pier to pier."[62]

With his essay, John established himself as a man of knowledge and reflection, although a rather boring one. The second part of John's essay helped establish his problem-solving acumen, and he began with the topic of storms, "unquestionably the greatest enemies of suspension bridges." The play of wind on a structure specifically designed to shift and move was a huge issue. It doesn't take much to put a suspension bridge in motion, and once they have begun—because they are hung vertically—the suspended portion "will follow the laws of the pendulum." Railings and a vertical truss system help only when combined with "a stiff and well-constructed floor." Unfortunately, the floors of most suspension bridges were "entirely too light." The main danger occurred "when the force which sets a pendulum in motion [wind] is continued . . . at regular intervals [that] correspond with the oscillations and their direction." If this were to occur, the oscillations would increase, finally rending the bridge apart. This was a danger, not a certainty. When set in motion by "high winds," two possible outcomes are possible. The bridge could be buffeted by "irregular gusts," the most likely and positive outcome, or a bridge could be "oscillating to a great extent" and be hit by "another furious stream of air . . . just at the time it is moving in the same direction." The effect "cannot fail to be destructive." Suspension bridges that survived major gales normally did so through pure chance. A similar difficulty is encountered when soldiers march in unison over a suspended span, John continued. The oscillations are amplified by the steady rhythm of the march. Conversely, "a crowd of people, moving promiscuously, will not produce a strain so severe as the momentum of a much smaller body of men, the united weight of which is rising and falling at regular intervals."[63]

Unlike Ellet, John only dipped into the history of suspension bridges to highlight successes and failures, examples that were useful for the contemporary engineer. "Telford displayed the power of his genius by the erection of the noble Menai," John declared, but he made no provision for oscillations or vertical motion. Marc Brunel, however, when designing his Isle de Bourdon bridges (1823)—"where hurricanes are of frequent occurrence"—fixed chains to the underside of the bridge to provide extra stability.[64]

Ellet's *Popular Notice* was a celebration; John's "Some Remarks" was more sober. "The superiority of these structures . . . needs no argument of mine," he maintained, but some caution was necessary. "To insure the successful introduction of cable bridges into the United States," their construction should be trusted to "the most eminent Engineers, whose practical judgment was aided by a rich store of scientific knowledge." Under no circumstances should the building of suspension bridges be "left to mere mechanics." These were "beautiful and noble structures" but they were dangerous and difficult to get right. Ellet's *Popular Notice* and John's "Some Remarks on Suspension Bridges" were in many respects perfect reflections of their authors: Ellet's pamphlet was bold and broad, John's deliberate and specific. Ellet could sell anything. John could likely build anything and felt he had to establish his credentials. By the close of his essay, John had established the superiority of wire cables over iron chains and the need for a heavy, stiff roadway, two of the fundamental principles of a modern suspension bridge. With neither flash nor fanfare, John had moved the technical discussion forward immensely. Whether anyone was paying close attention was another matter.[65]

On March 17, two days after John's essay appeared, Ellet's wife, Ellie, wrote hurriedly to her husband, who was in Albany lobbying for a contract to build a suspension bridge over the Hudson, that "Young has applied to Roebling [implying that John's name was already familiar throughout the Ellet household] to be his engineer as if he were certain of attaining his contract; and that he declared he will have it [even] if he loses $20,000. And Mr. L[yons, of the county commissioners] thinks he will not scruple to use *any means whatever* to gain his end." Whether Ellet was aware of John's essay—which made no mention of Ellet or the Schuylkill bridge project—or not, he must have been worried. By the end of the month, Ellet was back in Philadelphia, and on March 27 he finally replied to John's various letters over the previous few months. His reply was cordial but brief. He gave some vague and perfunctory advice about the wrapping of cables, which John had asked about in a previous letter, before signing off with a somewhat nonchalant remark: "I leave it for your ingenuity to make what it can of [my] suggestion." Ellet was aware of John's essay when he wrote and would likely have begun to suspect a genuine rival, an idea buttressed by John's connection with Young. Clearly this was no neophyte but a man capable of building his own suspension bridge. Ellet's letter of March 27 was the last he addressed to John, although John had one last letter for Ellet.[66]

On April 2, John wrote with great openness and honesty to Ellet: "A Mr. A. Young, it appears, has got the contract for the building of the Suspension bridge at Fairmount. He has again requested me to assist him in the construction. I was in Ph[iladelphia] during the month of February and anxious to consult you in this matter. I could however not find your place of residence for all inquiries I made, and understood afterwards, that you had left the city. I have as yet made no definite arrangement with Mr. Young, and before I do so, I should like to be informed, if any relation is pending between you and him with respects to the bridge. I understood that you had refused to go into partnership with him. . . . Although I am very desirous of superintending the building of the Fairmount Bridge, I shall abstain from all dishonorable interference." Ellet never replied.[67]

On May 3, Young wrote to inform John that there were no new developments and that he hoped to start work June 1, so as to finish the bridge "this season." He also asked John "to inform as many of the Members [of the board] as you will have an opportunity of seeing, that you have entered into an engagement with me in assisting to execute the work." Young also wrote to Schlatter to ask him to vouch for John before the county board. Schlatter was more than happy to give John "the highest testimonial in my power respecting his qualifications to plan and superintend such a structure." He and Roebling had worked closely together over the past two years. He possessed unparalleled "professional skill" along with a "gentlemanly and correct deportment." Back in the summer of 1840, Ellet's friend Johnson had warned that Young "knows nothing about the business" and it appears he was right. Young was pinning all his hopes on Roebling.[68]

Ellet was pinning his hopes on inside access. While Young was plotting to retain his contract, Ellet was plotting to take it away. John, by contrast, was off minding his own business, doing some additional surveying work for Schlatter and seemingly oblivious to the scheming going on around him. Ellet's influence was apparent during a meeting of the County Board on June 9, when a man named Penneman introduced a resolution repealing the board's decision to make a contract with Young. The motion passed twelve votes to seven. The board then adopted a motion to award the contract to Ellet. Young was furious: "I have been most shamefully cheated out of the Contract for the Bridge—by the influence of Johnston the County Commissioner and the course that Ellet pursued," he wrote John. Ellet "went underhandly and offered to take from the men that subscribed, Lots as payment for work done. . . . It is considered one of the foulest acts that has ever been committed in the City of Philadelphia," he explained. "It has degraded Ellet in the eyes of every man of his professional line," Young added as a postscript, strong words for an era where bribery and corruption were as good as the law of the land when it came to public contracts.[69]

Young penned a final letter to John on June 21, 1841, in an attempt to explain how he had lost the contract. "I assure you that it is really as great a mystery to me as to yourself," he wrote, before going on to explain how it wasn't much of a mystery at all. From the moment Young had received the bridge contract, "Ellet and his partisan were secretly at work undermining and endeavoring to supplant" him. Young's great mistake had been to underestimate the level of corruption on the board—"They resorted to every underhand measure to effect their purpose"—and he called on John to "oppose him [Ellet] in every honourable [sic] way we can." Only through a concerted public campaign would they have "a chance of letting the publick see that [Ellet] is not the only man that can build those Bridges." Young felt sure more suspension bridges would be built and hoped Roebling would "enter into partnership" with him to see to it that they were. "I will go with you hand & hand," he concluded. Young was right, but he played no part. John learned his lesson from the Schuylkill fiasco. From June 1841 on, he acted as an individual in all things. He never swapped information or tried to ingratiate himself with any other engineer, and he never once discussed or even considered going into partnership with anyone again. The whole thing left a sour taste in his mouth, much like his Saxonburg experiment.[70]

———

Ellet began construction of the Fairmount Bridge in early July and was finished by the end of the year. Remarkably, this included a two-month delay caused by "the loss of some vessels freighted with granite for the columns." The finished structure was handsome and impressive, "the most remarkable structure of this kind in the United States," according to the *Railroad Journal*. The central span was a whopping 357 feet flanked by two hundred-foot stone abutments. "Firmly secured at their extremities," ten iron wire suspension cables (five on each side) "hang in festoons sweeping from the summits of the granite columns on one side to the corresponding columns on the other side of the river, and descend, at the centre, nearly to the level of the [twenty-six-foot-wide] road-way." The design was French in almost every aspect: the deck, main cables, and suspenders all hewed closely to Seguin's ideas. Its towers, four granite obelisks each 30 feet high and 8¼ feet square at the base and quarried from Hallowell, Maine, were copied almost exactly from Navier's *Memoire sur les Ponts Suspendus*, a book Ellet described as "a complete and beautiful analysis of this whole subject." Curiously, Ellet ignored Vicat's preference for on-site cable spinning. Instead, the main cables were spun elsewhere and dragged to the bridge site and affixed. John felt this was the bridge's biggest flaw. Wires not woven under tension are likely to become loose and saggy, which is exactly what happened.[71]

Ever the showman, Ellet opened his bridge with a spectacular display of strength. On New Year's Day 1842, Ellet loaded the bridge—"from end to end . . . as compactly as they could be crowded upon it"—with fifty-nine teams of horse and cart each loaded with as much stone and rubble as they could bear (approximately two tons each). In addition, between one hundred and two hundred spectators crowded onto the bridge's walkways, giving Ellet "the satisfaction of seeing some of the parties who had vociferated most loudly against the adoption of his plan, forcing their way through the thousands of spectators, in order to be permitted to stand on the flooring." Everyone agreed: Ellet's bridge was a triumph. The editor of the *United States Gazette* called it "an exceedingly graceful and imposing structure, and particularly adapted to the picturesque

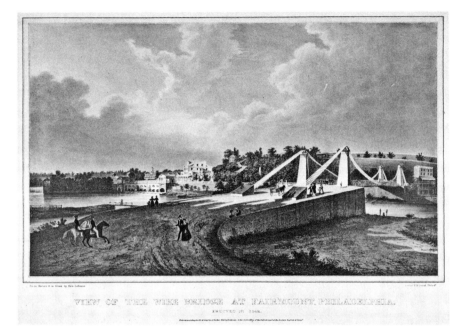

Figure 8.4 Ellet's suspension bridge over the Schuylkill River in Philadelphia. George Lehman, "View of the Wire Bridge at Fairmount, Philadelphia" (1843). Courtesy of the HSP large graphics collection [V65], call number: Bc7 W798, Historical Society of Pennsylvania.

scenery in which it is situated." A team of official inspectors sent by the city reported "the highest degree of satisfaction." The only dissenting voice appeared a couple of years later in a letter to the *Railroad Journal* concerning another suspension bridge recently erected in Pittsburgh: "The Fairmount Bridge is well known here, and is in disrepute, on account of the vibrations to which it is liable." This assessment—most likely penned by John himself—was confirmed by Colonel Samuel M. Wickersham, the noted Pittsburgh ironmonger, who declared that Ellet's bridge "was very graceful and pretty to the eye, but very unsteady to the feet."[72]

John's and Ellet's careers crisscrossed repeatedly over the next fifteen years. They would clash over projects in Wheeling, Cincinnati, and, most famously, Niagara. While John won out eventually, Ellet was crucial to the establishment of the suspension bridge in America. His Fairmount Bridge was the first long-span suspension bridge on the continent, and its success marked the beginning of an era. His publications were vital in promoting, explaining, guiding, and coaxing people toward the idea. In numerous proposals and reports, he set out the history of suspension bridges and the principles that undergirded their construction, their potential, and their efficiency. Ellet turned people's attention to suspension bridges, and by creating a functioning structure, he cemented their reputation. Without Ellet—and Finley before him—John might never have gotten the chance to build a suspension bridge. In this, he owed at least some gratitude to the charismatic, slightly reckless Ellet. Undoubtedly, John built better bridges, but Ellet was a more skillful promoter with a more savvy and sophisticated understanding of public opinion. Ellet won the first battle—and the second, if truth be told—but Roebling, the lowly surveyor and canal engineer, won the final battle, the battle for history. If Ellet was the first, Roebling ended up as the most famous.

Making Wire Rope and the Wire Rope Industry (1840–48)

John's first great career success was not, however, as a suspension bridge engineer but as a manufacturer of wire rope. By the winter of 1840, he had been tinkering with the idea for several months and, suddenly finding himself with both time and motivation, decided to devote his full attention to the issue. After working as a surveyor for Schlatter and as an engineer against Ellet, he realized the need to get ahead and make something for himself. Surveying and engineering were nice work, but what he really needed was a commercial endeavor. Ellet had for now won the battle of the suspension bridges, but John hoped to win the war of wire ropes.

—

Ropes are one of humanity's most basic and longstanding tools. As a means of transferring power across distance, they are unequaled for efficiency and simplicity. For millennia, their manufacture was equally straightforward: fibrous vegetable matter braided or twisted together into strands. But with the coming of the Industrial Revolution their character changed dramatically. Flexible fiber cordage gave way to massive wire ropes capable of immense strength and great durability.

Wire ropes had their origins in Europe, but they flourished in the United States, much like John. Beginning in the 1820s, Wilhelm August Julius Albert, a royal engineer from the mining districts of Hanover, started experimenting with iron wire. Albert was searching for a more dependable and efficient means of hoisting coal from the deep mines of the Upper Harz. Traditional hemp ropes were both expensive and weak. He experimented with iron chains but found them dangerous and unpredictable. Before long it occurred to him that "iron wire might be plaited or twisted together so as to form a whim rope." Within months, he had worked out most of the details and successfully tested a number of ropes. "In regard to durability and economy" he could give few hard facts, since none of his new ropes had yet "worn out." Albert published his findings in Berlin in 1835 in an effort to "render some service to practical science," then in London, and his idea quickly took hold throughout Europe. Traditional cordage firms began to churn out wire rope, government agencies and institutes began to study Albert's findings, and his ropes were adopted extensively in the French, Swedish, and British mining industries, along with the German one.[1]

Where Hanover had mines, Britain had a large navy, and it required a lot of rigging. Traditional rigging, made of fiber ropes, was almost constantly damp and liable to rot and decay. In an effort to provide a more dependable, long-lasting substitute, a London inventor named Andrew Smith began to experiment with wire ropes in 1828. By the close of the 1830s, his ropes adorned some of the Royal Navy's most prestigious vessels, and Smith had been granted several important patents, one for a parallel wire rope in 1835 and another for a "stranded" (or spiral) rope in 1839. Smith's ropes were made of much finer wires than Albert's and thus were more flexible and versatile. Eventually they were used for a variety of purposes all over Britain, most famously on the London and Blackwell Railway.[2]

Wire rope arrived in the United States in the late 1830s. Albert's treatise was translated and published by the Franklin Institute in 1837. Shortly afterward, steamboat engineer Isaac McCord developed "a new and Improved Mode of Manufacturing Round Flexible Wire Rope," receiving US patent no. 1219 on July 6, 1839. Much like the ropes manufactured in London, McCord's ropes were more versatile than Albert's but were primarily used to meet a new and urgent demand in the steamboat industry. In 1832, Congress passed a law requiring all tiller ropes to be "metallic."[3] McCord died soon after receiving his patent, and he was not the first man in America to patent a wire rope. In December 1831, Aaron Bull, a farmer from Caroline, New York, was awarded the country's first ever patent for a combination wire and cordage rope, but all that remains of his work is a somewhat risible assessment in the *Journal of the Franklin Institute.* John himself had broached the question of wire ropes back in 1828 when he considered using bundled wire rope instead of chains on the bridges he designed for Freienohl and Finnentrop. His revitalized interest in wire ropes came as a result of some reading he had done a year or so before.[4]

———

John hit upon the idea of using wire cables to replace hemp ropes on the Allegheny Portage Railroad, the section of the Main Line Canal that scaled the Allegheny Mountains, in Harrisburg during the winter of 1840. John had studied the canal commissioners' reports from 1839 and 1840 and knew how inefficient and expensive hemp ropes were. He also knew from his study of French suspension bridges how strong and reliable wire cables could be. Whether John was aware of Albert's article or not, he forged ahead with the idea. Back home in Saxonburg, John ordered a consignment of iron wire from his friend Robert Townsend in Pittsburgh and started tinkering and testing. At some point in 1840, he wrote to the canal commissioners to ask about installing "an experimental cable upon a plane of the Portage Rail Road." The board considered John's proposal and was, apparently, "aware of the important savings which may be affected to the State, if Wire Cables could successfully be substituted in place of Hemp Cables." The trouble was, as John explained to Ellet, whom he wrote to on the subject, that "the application of wire cables . . . is so new a matter in this country" that the board was leery. One of the board members—a Mr. Packer—"has examined your publications on Suspension bridges, and knows you by reputation," John told Ellet. "In order to throw more light on the matter, and to be enabled to lay before the Board the opinion of a distinguished Engineer, who is not immediately interested in the scheme," John took "the liberty to communicate to [Ellet] details of my plan, sufficiently to enable you to form a correct idea of it; and I request you to favor me with your opinion upon the main points, and to allow me to lay your statement before the Canal Board."[5]

The details of John's plan were relatively simple. His wire rope would be made "precisely in the manner in which the cables of Suspension bridges in France & Germany are usually made; and I shall take care, that all the wires will be uniformly stretched during the manufacture, so as to afford the greatest strength when united." All the wires that constituted the cable would be "coated with the best varnish," "stretched by a weight of 50–60 lbs," and passed "through a number of gauge plates, in order to secure their even position throughout the whole length of the cable." Once all the wires were "placed in their proper position and united into a round cable by bands tied around at intervals," the wrapping would be applied. John intended "2 coats of wrapping. The first will be made of annealed wire 1/20 inch thick while the second would be 1/16 inch thick, . . . also annealed." He had made two experimental cables using this method, John explained, and was more than satisfied with the results.[6]

John figured that a cable composed of parallel wires wrapped under tension with annealed wire would last longer and resist abrasions better than hemp rope. He also figured it would pass smoothly around a sheave and coil nicely around a drum. Ellet disagreed—"The wrapping will necessarily have to be dispensed with," he counseled—as did the other engineers John turned to for advice. The day after writing to Ellet, John wrote to William E. Morris, the principal engineer on the Allegheny Portage Railroad, whom he had gotten to know while surveying. Like John, Morris believed "the heavy annual expenses of ropes upon inclined planes" needed to "be reduced" and the "advantages" of using "iron instead of hemp . . . if found practicable" seemed equally "many & obvious." The strength of wire rope would likely be "amply sufficient," he concluded; the "flexibility" along with the "difficulty of securely attaching the cars to so small a cable" much less so.[7]

The main problem, as Morris saw it, was the system already in place on the Portage Railroad. John spent page after page detailing the changes he would need to make to the on-site machinery, including replacing the sheaves and adding "good firm *sole leather*" to the grooves to improve "adhesion." The trouble was that John was selling his ropes on the idea that they would save the state thousands of dollars, but a plan that requires the wholesale replacement of much of the machinery hardly qualifies as a cost-saving measure. If John could not fit his ropes to the existent machines, his plan would go nowhere. Morris did not think he could. As Morris explained it, when a rope passed around an eight-foot wheel, it is four inches longer on the outside than on the inside. Hemp "stretches" and can adapt to this; a wrapped wire cable, unfortunately, cannot. "In passing around the sheaves & geared wheels," he continued, "the strands of wrapping would either be separated on the outer side of the cable, or flatted & crushed together on the inner side," leading to "the ultimate destruction of the cable." A similar process would likely dog the "hitching" rope that linked the cable to the cars, Morris imagined. The stress placed on the rope would crack the outer varnish and crush the covering. Wire rope was the solution, everyone seemed to agree, but not wrapped and varnished.[8]

John replied to his correspondents with profuse thanks, but little in the way of change. He decided to alter his splicing technique, as per Ellet's suggestion, but stuck by his varnish, his wrapping, and his parallel wires. Ellet had suggested "twisting or platting" the wires in much the same way as traditional cordage ropes were made. This method very soon became the industry standard, but John—stubborn as ever—wanted an endorsement, not suggestions. With nothing definitive to show the canal board, he wrote up a lengthy patent application and engaged a patent agent. In this respect, his judgment proved excellent.[9]

John enlisted Dr. Thomas Jones, former head of the US Patent Office and founding editor of the *Journal of the Franklin Institute*, as his agent. Jones had served as McCord's patent agent, and he knew about as much as anyone alive about "existing English, French and American technology."[10] After agreeing to act on John's behalf, Jones wrote with several reservations and some sound advice. "Your plan has not any resemblance to Mr. McCord's," Jones counseled, "nor am I aware that wire rope has been made in the manner proposed by you." His "main fear in the plan," however, was the wrapping, which he thought would "break, uncoil, and produce trouble." Like Morris, Jones was also worried about the effect of running John's rope around a sheave or a drum. Such motion, if more or less constant, would put serious stress on the wrapping and coating, leading to unraveling and failure. Without platting or otherwise weaving the wires, the only thing keeping a rope made of parallel-laid wire together was the wrapping. Jones's most important piece of advice was eminently practical: Why not ensure the wire rope works before spending time and money finalizing the design and applying for intellectual protection? If John was so eager to get his ropes on the Portage Railroad, Jones figured, "would it not be well for you to defer taking a patent until this essay has been made?" It would indeed take several experiments, and some significant failures, for John to perfect his ropes. Within a year he had disavowed almost all of his initial, unfiled patent application and revised his plans entirely.[11]

———

John was back on the Allegheny Mountains during the summer of 1841, doing some more surveying for Schlatter, although he also found time to mount an effective campaign on behalf of his ropes. Morris sent a report "to the Board on the subject of Wire Cables," which he believed would "coincide nearly with your wishes." By the end of the summer, Schlatter had also agreed to "speak to the Commissioners of your rope," while cryptically admitting, "I have heard nothing about Ellet." More importantly, John managed to hunt down a place to test his ropes and a person willing to do so. As John wrote to Schlatter in early fall, "I am just now largely engaged in the manufacture of a wire cable . . . for Capt Young in Johnstown, calculated to draw the boats from the basin to the R[ail]R[oad]." John expected to be finished in a week and hoped "to be able to demonstrate its practicality before I return to Harrisburg."[12]

Captain Thomas Young owned and operated a small inclined plane on the north end of the Johnstown Canal Basin at the western terminus of the Allegheny Portage Railroad, where the Portage Railroad system met up again with the Main Line Canal. Section boats were hauled out of the Main Line Canal at Hollidaysburg, sent over the mountains on the Portage Railroad, and lowered back into the canal at Johnstown, all using hemp ropes. This last section was Young's responsibility and was a perfect place to test one of John's ropes. The stress of hauling section boats in and out of water put the hemp ropes through more wear and tear than normal, and they rarely lasted more than a few months. Being constantly in and out of water, they deteriorated quickly.[13]

Supremely self-assured, John wrote up his patent application before subjecting his ropes to even the most modest trial. He clearly thought finding a willing taker for his ropes meant success. In his campaign to get his ropes adopted on the Portage Railroad proper, he wrote to the canal board, "The experience of Wrapped Rope at Johnstown, and the Unwrapped Rope on the other inclines will soon exhibit the comparative merits of the two methods and decide in favor of one or the other to be adopted in the manufacture of the Rope for the Portage." And so it did, but not to John's satisfaction.[14]

Handmade on the meadow behind his home in Saxonburg, John's first rope was approximately 656 feet long and three-quarters of an inch thick. It was composed of parallel wires laid together uniformly under tension and wrapped tightly in annealed iron wire, and it didn't last much longer than it took to make. As his son Washington reported later, "The rope went to pieces as soon as the [wrapping] wore out."[15] The problem was conceptual as much as anything else. John had gotten the idea from thinking about suspension bridge cables. And the rope he made would have been excellent for such a purpose, where tension and strength are paramount. On an inclined plane, however, you need something that will hew to a sheave and run smoothly around a pulley wheel—something flexible and malleable, something much like a traditional cordage rope, but stronger and more durable. In short: exactly what Ellet, Morris, and Jones had counseled.[16]

The whole affair was a dispiriting experience for John, and even more so for Young, who found himself out of business by the end of the season. John rarely listened to anyone, but he was forced to respond to his own direct experience of failure, and for one of the few times in his life, John was forced to do something entirely out of character: change his mind, although without having to admit he was wrong. In an article on the subject of wire ropes published a couple of years later, John indulged in some rather flagrant revisionism, disavowing wrapped parallel wire ropes as an inferior English invention ("A collection of parallel wires, bound together by wrappings in the manner of a suspension cable, is no rope and not fit for running") and annealing, as well as some outright lying. "The first rope of my make," he wrote in November 1843, two whole years after his Johnstown debacle, "has now been in successful operation two seasons, hauling section boats from the basin."[17]

Back in Saxonburg, John devoted himself to a renewed effort to make some ropes fit to be deployed on the Portage Railroad. In remarkably short order, John had a new rope and a new patent application. It was much less radical in many regards, but much more workable. As John noted, it was in essence a hemp rope made of iron wire, with two new "improvements." "The novelty" of his new rope "chiefly consists in the spiral laying of the wires around a common axis *without twisting the fibres,* and secondly in subjecting the individual wires while thus laying to a uniform and forcible tension under all circumstances." By this method, John could achieve great strength and "a high degree of pliability."[18]

The secret to John's rope were weights, a wooden frame, and some swivels and pulleys. Each wire was attached to a swivel, which itself was attached to a short length of hemp rope. Each length of rope was draped over a pulley mounted in a wooden frame and attached to a heavy weight. Six wires were stretched out on

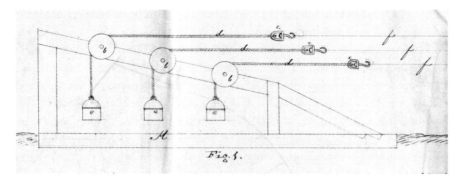

Figure 9.1 Diagram of John's weighted frame for ensuring uniform tension during rope making (1842). Courtesy of the Institute Archives and Special Collections, Rensselaer Polytechnic Institute.

the ropewalk and spun around a central seventh to form a helical strand. The weights maintained uniform tension as the rope was spun; the swivels allowed the individual wires to move freely and twist as the torsion increased. The process was then repeated twice more, with the finished rope acting as the central core rope around which a further six wires were spun. The end result was a cable composed of nineteen individual wires. Seven such cables were made and then finally spun into the final product, a 7 × 19 rope, John's trademark. The process of making a single rope was slow and tedious, taking between one and two very long days and requiring great exactitude. Eight men were needed to spin the smaller ropes, while twice as many were used for the final, larger rope. John oversaw every aspect of the process with care and attention.[19]

John was a confident man, but it is unlikely he fully understood what he was doing with his makeshift ropewalk or that he dreamed or envisioned where it would all lead. But laboring away in the meadow behind his home with a rather motley collection of unskilled friends and neighbors, John was creating not a business venture nor a single factory but an entire industry: the American wire rope industry. Over the next one hundred years wire ropes would transform the landscape of America. Wire ropes would haul elevators up and down new tall buildings, making possible thousand-foot-high skyscrapers in New York and Chicago; pull funiculars up the steep hills of Pittsburgh and Los Angeles; power rigs, derricks, and cranes all over the country; hold up suspension bridges of prodigious length from the Hudson River to the Golden Gate; and power mass-transit cable car systems in thousands of towns and cities nationwide. All of this and more flowed from the industry John created in his back garden in the 1840s.

With a new rope developed and a new patent application submitted, John again wrote to the Pennsylvania Canal Board. By this point, he had written them numerous times and been ignored at almost every try. More usefully, he had enlisted a number of influential supporters. Morris and Schlatter were on board, as was James Clarke, a member of the Board of Canal Commissioners. Known as the Father of the Main Line Canal, Clarke was "favourable to the project," he informed John, and had been "ever since you first communicated to me your design." To this end Clarke had just written to his "friend Major Reynolds on the subject." Clarke also admired John: "You must have unlimited confidence in its success to warrant you in making the State such a favourable offer" (John had offered to supply wire ropes for the Portage Railroad "at my *own risk entirely*"). Clarke's endorsement was followed by a favorable political reshuffle. (Like every other public body in the nineteenth century, membership was as much a question of political patronage as professional skill and acumen.) By February 1842, John had the right ropes; a new, potentially friendly canal board; and a perversely friendly financial climate, which is to say the state was almost bankrupt and desperately trying to save money.[20]

John's letter of February 1842 was more detailed, more explicit, and much more direct than any of his previous communications. He proposed installing a 3,400-foot-long wire rope on Plane no. 3, the shortest of the ten main inclines. It would cost the state a dollar a running foot, and he would install it at his own risk. It would prove superior in strength, durability, and cost to hemp rope, he asserted. Befitting a man who had diligently done his research, John sounded like an expert. He waxed lyrical about the excellent uses wire rope was being put to in Europe: down the mines of Lower Saxony, on the rigging of the British Royal Navy, and on the London and Blackwell Railway, where in its first eight months of use one cable "traveled a distance of 25,000 miles, equal to the circumference of the earth, without showing the least mark of weakness." John also asked to be appointed principal assistant engineer on Plane no. 3 for the duration of the testing period. If he was going to manufacture, transport, and install the ropes, he ought to be put in charge of using them too, or so he thought.[21]

On March 14, 1842, the canal board accepted John's proposal, drawing up a resolution to the effect that John should be allowed to put his ropes into service on Plane no. 3 and that if it should "be found to answer the purpose as well as good hemp rope," then John should be paid at his requested rate. If the cable should break while "in usual and regular operation by reason of its unfitness in plan or structure," John was required to remove it and would be compensated what it would have cost to use a regular hemp rope for the same amount of time—that is, what it would have cost them anyway. As for aid and elbow room, John was allowed sufficient room to stretch and splice his ropes and enough "hands to assist the contractor in putting it on tracks and in operation." The board also agreed to replace the four-foot-diameter sheaves with a ten-foot sheave to account for the less flexible wire ropes. As historian Hubertus Cummings explains, "Beyond that the Canal Commissioners hazarded nothing," and they never even addressed John's request for an official position of employment. Regardless, he was elated.[22]

———

The Allegheny Portage Railroad was the first mountain railroad in the United States and as such was something of an engineering marvel. Admittedly, it was also expensive and inefficient, and its usefulness only lasted about fifteen years.[23] But in an age when canals were king, portage railroads and the inclined planes they depended on were the only means to scale the mountainous heights that separated most of the Eastern Seaboard from the expanding inland west. Before the Portage Railroad, goods from the Midwest were floated down the Mississippi to New Orleans, sent around Florida, and then sent up the Eastern Seaboard to awaiting markets in the Northeast. Remarkably, it was easier, cheaper, and quicker to ship goods from Pittsburgh to Philadelphia via the Deep South than to send them three hundred miles across the state. As Charles Trcziyulny reported in 1824, "Here nature has refused to make her usual kind advances to aid the exertions of man; mountains are thrown together, as if to defy human ingenuity, and baffle the skill of the engineer."[24]

David Stevenson, the eminent British engineer, called the Allegheny Portage Railroad "a work of so difficult and vast a nature, and so peculiar, both as regards its situation and details, that it cannot fail to be interesting to every engineer."[25] Others were equally exuberant, if a little more jingoistic: "The whole of this stupendous labor was . . . a monument to the intelligence, enterprise and public spirit of Pennsylvania, more honorable than the temples and pyramids of Egypt, or the triumphant arches and columns of Rome," wrote the *Boston Atlas*. "These magnificent works are intended to . . . encourage the arts of peace, to advance the prosperity and happiness of the whole people of the United States—to strengthen the bonds of Union—induce a more universal and ardent patriotism—give stability to our political institutions—excite a veneration for the Constitution, and extend the glory of this vast Republic."[26]

In its details, the Portage Railroad was a system of short interconnected railroads and inclined planes that ran thirty-six miles over the Allegheny Mountains from Hollidaysburg on the eastern base to Johnstown on the western base. The distance from Hollidaysburg to the mountain's summit—2,326 feet above sea level—was about ten miles, and the height scaled was 1,398 feet. The distance from the summit down to Johnstown was about twenty-six miles with a descent of 1,173 feet. None of the inclines were especially steep, with gradients ranged from 7.25 percent to 10.25 percent. As described by one of its most famous riders, Charles Dickens, who passed over them on March 27, 1842, "There are ten inclined planes; five *a*scending, and five *de*scending; the carriages are dragged up the former, and let slowly down the latter, by means of stationary engines; the comparatively level spaces between, being traversed, sometimes by horse, and sometimes by engine power, as the case demands. Occasionally, the rails are laid upon the extreme verge of a giddy precipice; and looking from the carriage window, the traveler gazes sheer down, without a stone or a scrap of fence between, into the mountain depths below."[27]

Each inclined plane housed a double track of rails upon which cars, carriages, and section boats were drawn up (and simultaneously lowered down) by means of a huge hemp rope. Mounted on rollers running between the railroad tracks, the ropes extended in a huge endless loop anchored at either end of the inclined plane by small pulley wheels turned by a steam engine. Locomotives pulled cars and carriages between the various inclined planes. Traffic up and down the planes was rather slow. Stevenson reported that the thirty-six-mile journey took about seven hours, including an hour for lunch, at an average of six miles an hour.[28]

For some, the journey up the mountain was a novel but frightful experience. For Nicklin, the "refreshing and invigorating" ride up the mountains was "succeeded by the fear of the steep descent which lies before you; and as the car rolls along this giddy height, the thought trembles in your mind, that it may slip [and] rush down the frightful steep, and be dashed into a thousand pieces at its foot." Dickens reported to his friend John Forster that the locals "have terrible legends of its danger," but otherwise he had a fine time on the mountain: "It was very pretty travelling thus, at a rapid pace . . . in a keen wind, to look down into a valley full of light and softness; catching glimpses, through the tree-tops, of scattered cabins. . . . It was amusing, too . . . having no other moving power than the weight of the carriages themselves, to see the engine released, long after us, come buzzing down alone, like a great insect, its back of green and gold so shining in the sun, that if it had spread a pair of wings and soared away, no one would have had occasion, as I fancied, for the least surprise. But it stopped short of us in a very business-like manner when we reached the canal; and, before we left the wharf, went panting up this hill again, with the passengers who had waited our arrival for the means of traversing the road by which we had come."[29]

Despite complaints about speed, bottlenecks, and vertigo, the railroad's most significant problem was the maintenance and replacement of its ten long hemp ropes. The ropes were the system's single largest expense, and they didn't last very long. The pulley system caused nicks and abrasions, which severely weakened the ropes, rendering them liable to break or disintegrate. During the offseason, when they weren't in use, they were left open to the elements to suffer the floods and frosts of a harsh Pennsylvania winter. By the time spring arrived, rot had set in on most ropes, leaving most of them unfit for service. Given the manner of their treatment and storage, it's surprising any of the ropes lasted a season, but most of them did, if not much more.[30]

To increase the life of the ropes and reduce costs, John Snodgrass, superintendent of motive power on the railroad, started coating the ropes in tar to keep water out and project them from deterioration. This innovation was somewhat successful, extending the lives of most ropes to about sixteen months. Snodgrass even considered building a series of roofs to cover all of the inclines, claiming they would pay for themselves "in less than five years." Unfortunately, the railroad's precarious financial state prevented long-term planning and certainly did not allow for the sort that involved immediate capital investment (with savings to come), which made John's offer at least worth a try.[31]

John had come to know the Alleghenies intimately during the long months he had spent surveying. By the time his offer to install wire rope on Plane no. 3 was accepted, he had traveled on the Portage Railroad dozens of times, even making an in-depth study of the system in 1841. Like everyone who worked on the railroad, he knew the ropes were the weak link in the system and that most of them could fail at any moment. Stories were told of ropes suddenly snapping, leaving cars to career down the mountainside and smash at the bottom. It is often written that John's inspiration for developing wire rope came as a result of witnessing two men die in such a terrible calamity, but this is pure fantasy. Certainly there were plenty of fatalities on the Portage Railroad, approximately thirty-four or so between 1841 and 1854, many of them gruesome. In 1844, a young man rushed onto the tracks to retrieve a letter he had dropped and was struck by a descending train "knocking him directly onto the track, the wheel . . . passing lengthwise over the body disclosing all the internal parts." Boiler explosions also occurred, "rending the cars into a thousand atoms." Safety cars were introduced in 1835, however, and they solved the problem of snapped ropes and runaway cars. Ropes broke frequently, but cars rarely lost control, and passenger cars never. More likely, John saw a great inefficiency and a huge outlay for a small return, not a terrible accident.[32]

Not only had John seen how inadequate hemp ropes were, but he had read all the reports and knew how worried and exasperated everyone on the canal board already was. As reported in 1840, two years before even a single wire rope was introduced on the inclines: "The very inferior quality of the ropes . . . has been a source of continued vexation and difficulty." New ropes had been installed on three of the ten planes within the previous three months, while five others had been ordered. The remaining two would need to be ordered in early spring, and the average cost of a new rope was three thousand dollars. Thinking about the problems of hemp ropes and coming up with wire rope as a solution was logical for a man obsessed with suspension bridges.[33]

If John managed to catch a glimpse of Dickens on Plane no. 3 at the end of March 1842, he never mentioned it, although he was certainly nearby. By April 10, less than two weeks after Dickens rode, John wrote to Schlatter to proclaim victory. "Allow me to congratulate you for your success," Schlatter replied, "although I have entertained not the least doubt with regard to the success of your experiment. It would have afforded me great pleasure to have witnessed the *first* experiment, but I must content myself with waiting for the [next] trial." Unfortunately, despite his early enthusiasm, John's next trial would not take place for several months.[34]

John held a rather simplistic view of the problems he was likely to face installing his ropes. He presumed that wire rope would function exactly like hemp rope, except that it wouldn't rot and break. Unfortunately, wire doesn't flatten down upon and grip a pulley wheel like a traditional fiber rope, which is exactly what John discovered. Despite him changing to a much larger wheel, John's cables were too slick to provide sufficient traction to drive the mechanism, so the ropes just spun. Changing to a "double-wrap sheave" solved the problem, but did not engender confidence. Superintendent Snodgrass had been worried that John's ropes would snap under pressure. Now the problem seemed more basic: Would they even move enough to take the weight in the first place? To this was added the problem of splicing. The cable for Plane no. 3 was made in three parts and spliced together close by the incline. All objects are only as strong as their weakest point, and splicing naturally provides such a point. Unsurprisingly, the results of John's first efforts were poor. Shortly after testing resumed in the summer of 1842, a splice unraveled. The incident so alarmed Superintendent Snodgrass that he immediately cut short the trial and refitted the hemp ropes, much to John's concern.[35]

Despite all the problems installing and employing his ropes, John received his first patent (no. 2720, "Method of and Machine for Manufacturing Wire Ropes") on July 16, 1842. The award was rather fortuitous, given the timing of Snodgrass removing John's ropes. But there was still very little wrong with John's "method." The problems were the mismatch between materials and mechanism, as well as the difficulties of devising an effective splicing technique.[36]

Further good news followed in the autumn when Schlatter—who "continue[d] to be on excellent terms with the Canal Commission"—was able to hire John as an assistant engineer on the Portage Railroad. John started work in September and quickly became Schlatter's right-hand man, vetting proposals and suggestions, and empowered to make changes and alterations on much of the machinery and motive power. Schlatter encouraged the young engineer to make any "change[s] which you may see proper to make," which he did. John was able to rebuild the incline machinery on Plane no. 3 to his exact specifications, installing wooden idler wheels (instead of iron, which wore into John's wire ropes) and clamps and supervising their installation. By the opening of the 1843 season, he had transformed the whole operation to suit his ropes. In time, the results transformed every facet of the railroad system and cemented John's reputation as the country's foremost manufacturer of wire rope.[37]

He also worked on getting his ropes adopted elsewhere and even had time to invent a "spark extinguisher," which he sent to Thomas Jones (along with ten dollars) to patent. By the end of the year, John was supplying all the wire ropes for the boat slips at Hollidaysburg and Johnstown and was deep in correspondence with Schlatter about getting his wire ropes installed on the Philadelphia and Columbia Railroad (P&C), which ran eighty-two miles from its terminus in Philadelphia to the Susquehanna River, where it met up with the Main Line Canal. By December 1842, Schlatter was "happy [to write that the road] is now *entirely* under the control of one man [and] that man [is] under me." By the spring, orders had been filled, and John's ropes were on all of the P&C's inclines. "The wire rope arrived here this morning, and is indeed a perfect specimen of neat and compact workmanship," Schlatter informed his protégé.[38]

John had his mentor to thank for his successes that winter. Notwithstanding all the setbacks that afflicted his efforts to establish his ropes on the Portage Railroad, the canal board was clearly convinced of the plan. Snodgrass continued to counsel cautious reservation, believing John's wires were only a moment away from failure. After all, John had so far failed to establish a working rope on a single one of the Portage Railroad's inclined planes, despite almost ten months of effort. With this in mind, the canal board set about flirting with another player. Unbeknownst to John, they sent an enquiry to Andrew Smith in London to ask if he might be interested in supplying wire ropes for the Portage Railroad. Schlatter intercepted the Englishman's reply and sent a copy to John.[39]

Smith's letter outlined the price, suitability, and quality of the wire rope he could supply "relative to the Phila & other inclined planes in the state," along with testaments as to its strength, durability, and application. Smith's ropes on the London and Blackwell Railway were two years old, he crowed, and had "not yet worn through." So impressed was the British establishment that Smith's ropes were used extensively on the *Penelope*, the largest steamship in the British Navy, and he was currently under contract to supply the standing rigging for Ismbard Kingdom Brunel's massive new "Iron Steamer, the 48,000 ton SS *Great Britain*, currently under construction in Bristol." Despite these impressive credentials, Schlatter feared the English rope would be inferior and "hate[d] the idea of sending to England for anything we can manufacture here." In the face of British competition, Schlatter advised John to adjust his prices and specifications accordingly. "Put the price as low as you can without your losing anything and to make a fair profit," he counseled, which turned out to be tricky. Neither Schlatter nor John had any idea how to decipher the British system of weights, measures, and costs. Working out whether the English ropes were cheaper or not was more a matter of guesswork than analysis: "'60/' I suppose means shillings. '50' for duty per lb—means 5 cts & 114 per cwt means—I know not what—I cannot understand it," Schlatter conceded rather comically, before counseling a somewhat different tack. In the absence of concrete facts about weights and cost, perhaps John should threaten the board with copyright infringement. Oddly enough, this worked. Almost immediately, the board backed down.[40]

The bidding war averted, John spent the remainder of 1843 devoted to the proper installation of his ropes and the successful running of the inclined plane. As industry historian Donald Sayenga notes, John lavished about as much care and attention on this first rope as he did anything else in his life. It repaid his fidelity and dedication with great service, eventually lasting five full seasons on the incline, a marked increase on the service usually provided by hemp ropes. Ironically, John's first spun rope was likely the best, most substantial rope he ever made. It made his reputation, and its own. From this point on, John's living was secured, as was the primacy of wire rope. Sadly, his friend and mentor fared less well that year. "The legislature has driven me out of the State by their penurious laws," Schlatter informed him in the spring; "my salary is reduced to $1,000 and I am obliged to travel all over the State at my own expense." Unable to make a living, Schlatter secured a permanent job as United States Superintendent of the Harbor at Chicago, but his sadness was palpable. "My regret at leaving my native State I cannot attempt to describe," Schlatter confided to John, "but the Legislature of Penna will eventually drive every man out of the State *who acts honestly*, by actually starving them." "I rejoice indeed to know that your energy and perseverance have at last conquered the prejudices of ignorance and envy and that your rope has been pronounced successfully OK," he concluded, kindheartedly reserving the final words of his farewell for his friend's new found success.[41]

———

By the close of the 1843 season, John had worked 161 straight days on the Portage Railroad and won over both Snodgrass and the canal board. "The [hemp] ropes for the inclined planes and ferries on the line of our improvements, have hitherto been an enormous annual expense to the State," the board bemoaned, "requiring an aggregate yearly expenditure of $35,000.00 merely for cordage."

They had hoped to reduce "this heavy expense, if at all practicable." "For that purpose," they declared in their annual report, they ordered one of John's wire ropes, which they "used a considerable portion of last season, and the whole of the present year, and which seems to have been but little injured by use during that period." Wire ropes, but "of a lighter size," had been also used for hauling out section boats at Johnstown, Hollidaysburg, and Columbia. "So far as these wire ropes have been tested, they bid fair to answer the purpose; and, if the experiment shall ultimately prove successful, a large annual saving will be made to the Commonwealth, by their substitution for hempen ropes." John's ropes could also be used in all weathers and all conditions.[42]

Snodgrass, long the most wary member of the team, was even more effusive: "The wire rope, on plane No. 3, has been running, successfully, during the whole of the season, and has given entire satisfaction. The difficulties which attended the experiment last year, and which chiefly arose from the want of adhesion and the rupture of some part of the machinery, were entirely removed by a thorough repair of the latter. . . . The wire rope was capable of pulling the heaviest loads in frosty and wet weather; when, on the other planes, the loads had to be limited for the want of adhesion, or delayed until they could be balanced." "The wire rope, thus far, has realized all expectations," he concluded.[43]

John used the occasion to push for further adoption of his wire ropes on the Portage Railroad. "The superior performance, and successful operation of the wire rope on Plane no. 3 during the [last] season; the greater safety it has accorded; its present condition which shows little wear" along with the "greatly reduced expense," John reasoned, all recommended implementation elsewhere. Plus, there were "no such fearful accidents [on Plane no. 3] as took place at No. 6," he noted cryptically. Still, Snodgrass was a congenital worrier: "As there exists a possibility of the wires becoming brittle, and breaking suddenly, it would be well to test the rope still farther, before coming to the determination of introducing them on all the planes." To this end, the canal commissioners continued to use hemp on a majority of the planes, but they did order two more of John's wire ropes. By the opening of the 1844 season, John had ropes on three of the ten planes. Finally, after dozens of letters, trials, and trips, and months of worry, effort, and doubt, he was on his way.[44]

Or such was the public record, set down in the official state reports. Beneath the official record lies a shadowy tale of politics and power. As superintendent of motive power, Snodgrass was a key man on the mountain, in charge of almost all aspects of transit: appointments, contracts, technical decisions, and budget. He was also a deeply divisive and controversial figure. Schlatter loathed him, as did John B. Butler, president of the canal board, and a number of local residents, many of whom felt compelled to write to the local newspaper on the topic.[45] His relationship with John is much more difficult to distinguish. In the summer of

1842, while John was feverishly trying to get his ropes to work, Snodgrass wrote to Butler as president of the canal board to say he "had every confidence in Mr. Robling [*sic*]." Later, during the crucial summer months of 1843, Snodgrass's assistant John W. Geary wrote to John to say that his boss "was decidedly in favor of wire ropes." Yet Schlatter's letters paint another, altogether different picture. "Snodgrass's sun has set. . . . He is fairly discovered," he wrote John in May 1843, "and I have returned to him with interest the poisoned chalise [*sic*] he held so long to my lips. It is the first time in my life that I have retaliated upon anyone but this man has used such mean, sneaking ways of injuring me for the last four years." Clearly, Snodgrass had played some important part in Schlatter's leaving the state's employ, and, of course, he would have known of John's close relationship to Schlatter. "Not the least cause of my indignation was his double dealing, and mean conduct towards yourself," Schlatter wrote to John, indicating some deep deviance on the superintendent's part.[46]

The seeds of Schlatter's retaliation bore fruit later in the year. On November 20, 1843, after a brief meeting of the canal board, Snodgrass was removed from office for reasons made plain in a searing letter of indictment written by Butler. The president of the board had listened to Schlatter's warnings (and those of others) all year, eventually deciding to visit the portage and make his own inspection. "Inquiry and observation have confirmed the worst fears and predictions as to the numerous charges and complaints made to us against Mr. Snodgrass," Butler began. "The operations upon [the Portage Railroad] are most bunglingly and tardily conducted," he declared; the whole system was in "disorder." Worse, Snodgrass was a "tyrannical" boss: "incompetent," "negligent," and "inattentive to an extent that is almost incredible." He used the road for his own private business, abused the financial discretion entrusted to him, and treated his workers terribly, insisting, for example, they buy provisions from him at usurious rates while simultaneously paying them late. He was running the public conveyance as his own private fiefdom and making a fortune.[47]

Quite remarkably, Snodgrass was reelected superintendent of motive power on January 15, 1844, by a new canal board, presided over by John's old supporter James Clarke. Unsurprisingly, the news infuriated Schlatter: "How such a man can possibly be allowed to go on gulling the public is to me a mystery, for he has no talent, save that of making money out of the State works, and that most probably by the advice of men more cunning than himself." "He is as treacherous as he is cowardly, and would no more meet you upon fair, open, free ground, than he would meet the 'Hyrcanean Lion in his den,'" he continued, before turning his attention to John's dealings with this "sneaking creature": "The details of your business with Snodgrass were interesting to me, as they showed the man precisely in the same light in which I always viewed him. He never was friendly either to you or myself, and the Board pursued a suicidal policy in not cutting off his head as soon as they discovered his character and incompetency." John's letter outlining his business with Snodgrass hasn't survived, but what remains clear are the twin facts that Schlatter was clearly right about Snodgrass and that John managed to do business with him anyway. Not only were none of John's ropes removed from the portage, but they were validated by Snodgrass in his official reports, and John's share of the business was increased.[48]

John most likely did not like Snodgrass, but he certainly understood that he had to deal with him. That John managed to navigate this tangled situation and get his ropes adopted and approved speaks to his political savvy and pragmatism. It also speaks to his relationship with those on the portage. Luckily for John, he was remarkably well liked by the engineers on the mountain, those who actually operated his ropes. John O'Neill, assistant engineer on Plane no. 3, informed John in the spring of 1844 that Snodgrass—"universally disliked here"—had tried to question John's ropes on a recent visit and found himself arrayed against the entire crew. In contrast, O'Neill signed off by writing, "I shall always [be] glad to give you any information in my power and whenever you come this way will be always delighted to see you." Earlier in the year, ex–Snodgrass assistant John Geary sent word to John that, amid all the Snodgrass men, he still had "one friend . . . here yet remaining." More would follow. James Bowstead labored "untiringly" (according to a local newspaper) all through the winter of 1843–44 fitting John's ropes on Plane no. 10, only to find himself out of work soon after, thanks to Snodgrass, who seemed angry "that the wire rope was doing to [sic] well [and] the cars were coming up the plane to [sic] fast they did not like to see it." Bowstead "determined to do you all the justice that lay in my power," meaning "the next day my discharge was sent up." He had worked on the Portage Railroad since it had opened in 1834, "discharg[ing] his duties to the entire satisfaction of all parties." His dismissal "smacks of petty tyranny such as no officer of the commonwealth should be allowed to visit upon any individual," wrote the *Beacon Light*. Happily for all concerned, Snodgrass left the Portage Railroad to run the mails shortly afterward, and to no one's surprise he prospered. By the opening of the Civil War, Snodgrass was the largest landowner in Westmoreland County.[49]

———

John topped off his most successful year to date by writing an article on his recent endeavors for the *American Railroad Journal*. He began with the difficulties faced (most ropes are "failures") and the reasons for this (mainly "English manufacturers"), carefully omitting his own initial misconceptions and all the British successes. He also described his efforts to establish his ropes on the Portage Railroad, the problems with traction and adhesion, and the successes that followed a suitable solution: "When in unfavorable weather there is delay and slipping on the other planes the wire rope can at all times pull as heavy a load *without* a balance, as the engine is capable of hauling." "From my present experience," he concluded, "I may safely assert that *wire rope* deserves the preference over *hemp rope* in all situations . . . where great strength and durability is required."[50]

The tone of the article was decidedly commercial. Despite titling the essay "American Manufacture of Wire Rope for Inclined Planes, Standing Rigging, Mines, Tillers, etc," the true subject was obviously Roebling's manufacture of wire rope. His principles differed markedly from those of "English manufacturers," he asserted, and were wholly "original," although it was difficult to see how exactly. "By my process of manufacture" (one of the most oft-repeated phrases), John boasted, the humble wire rope offered "pliability," longevity, "flexure," and strength. By way of argument, John made the same claims he had been making to the Pennsylvania Canal Board for a couple of years: wire rope was sturdier, stronger, and lighter than hemp rope, and altogether less dangerous "in time of action." He cited naval captain Basil Hall that wire rope would substitute well as standing rigging and likely be significantly better than the usual hemp. As for concerns about rust, nothing rusts when in use, and, even when idle, the only affected areas would be those exposed to the elements. Luckily, John's method of manufacture laid the wires into the "closest contact" and with such "mathematical precision" that they were "no more subjected to rusting than the link of a chain." John's wire ropes needed "no other protection but oiling or tarring once or twice a season" to present "a most elegant appearance and be exempt from all rusting."[51]

John's article was a hit. "American Manufacture of Wire Rope" helped cement John's reputation as the oracle to which all commercial enquiries should be sent. His reputation was furthered by D. K. Minor, the editor of the *Railroad Journal*, who happily sent out copies of John's article to prominent industrialists. One of the men Minor approached was Peter Cooper, a leading industrialist, who owned glue factories, iron mills, and real estate of all descriptions. Cooper designed the first American-built steam locomotive and later pioneered the metallurgic practice of "puddling," which enabled the production of a much higher grade of iron. Cooper did not know of anyone looking for wire rope at the time but expressed his belief that it would eventually "become an important branch of manufactur[ing]" and promised to keep his eye out for interested parties. Cooper also told Minor he would "gladly receive any communication [John] might feel disposed to make." Eventually the two became friends and associates, with much in common.[52]

By 1844, the Commonwealth of Pennsylvania's finances were in an atrocious state. The state had spent lavishly on a series of ambitious internal improvements projects, none of which had come close to servicing their debt, let alone paying off the principal. The Main Line Canal was great for business but bad for the state's finances. Governor David R. Porter tried to balance the budget by raising taxes and cutting costs, but his measures failed to check the ever-ballooning debt. With the state sliding further toward bankruptcy, Porter turned to the state's internal improvements projects. In the spring of 1844, Porter cut many of them, including much of the work on the Portage Railroad (including maintenance), slashed salaries, and laid off hundreds more, including both John and Schlatter. The situation left John without a salary but ultimately created his first big break. After the state's maintenance budget was slashed, the wooden aqueduct that carried the Main Line Canal into Pittsburgh began to deteriorate, and in 1844 it fell into the Allegheny River. John won the contract to rebuild it.[53]

The year 1844 was a trying time for John as a manufacturer. The state's enthusiasm for his ropes was tempered by its lack of funds, so despite having the right product for the right job, he had no ready market. In January 1844, John wrote to the canal board with a somewhat daring proposition: he would supply wire rope for every plane on the Portage Railroad for a flat annual rate of seventeen thousand dollars (compared to annual expenditures of thirty-five thousand dollars for hemp ropes) for a fixed period of five years. The board responded on April 27, 1844, saying, "It is inexpedient for them to enter into any engagements, such as you propose at present." In a further effort to tempt the state, John offered to furnish a three-strand rope. "Such a rope can be made cheaper than a 7 strand rope and is easier spliced," he argued. He even wrote, "If the receipts of the Portage R.R. in the coming season should not prove ample enough to pay for the wire rope, I will wait 'til next year, provided the money now due will be paid to me in the course of this season."[54]

John was clearly confident in his ropes, and he had every reason to be: they were well made and gave excellent service. Everyone seemed to concur: "The result of the trial of the wire ropes at Plane 2," wrote the *Beacon Light* in an editorial endorsement, "has furnished abundant evidence that the introduction of wire ropes on all the planes will tend not only greatly to facilitate the business of the road, and add security of the transit of both freight and passengers, but be productive of a great saving to the commonwealth." In addition to Plane no. 2, John's ropes were on Planes no. 3 and 10 for the entirety of the 1844 season, along with the boat slips at Johnstown and Hollidaysburg, and on the P&C. In September, Ellet briefly mounted a campaign to displace John, writing to James Clarke with a proposal to replace John's ropes on the inclined planes of the P&C with an "atmospheric rail road," the sort that "was rapidly coming into favour, both in France and England." But nothing seems to have shaken the faith in

John's wires. By 1847, he had wire ropes on all the planes of the Portage Railroad and kept them there until 1853, when Erskine Hazard, an old business acquaintance, began supplying wire rope on Planes no. 5, 9, and 10. Hazard's gain was by no means John's loss, however. The Portage Railroad was more or less out of service by 1853 and supplying its wire rope needs was only a fraction of John's business. Outside of Pennsylvania, owners of inclines in less cash-strapped regions began to send in enquiries and orders, as did mine owners and even the builders of the USS *Michigan*, who wrote to see if John could supply tiller ropes. Schlatter believed John was "lost in [his] present seclusion." Should "you to be long enough at Washington to become known to the proper persons . . . your success [would] be certain, whilst your reputation and fame [would] spread as I know it deserves to spread."[55]

———

While John didn't invent wire rope, he did manage almost singlehandedly to establish the American wire rope industry in his backyard. All of the wire ropes made by John A. Roebling and Sons between 1842 and 1848 were laid out in the five-hundred-foot-long meadow behind John's house. They were all handmade, all pulled, laid out, spun, and bound out in the open. Luckily, Saxonburg was blessed with a good range of artisans and experienced craftsmen by the time John was ready to start his manufactory in earnest, as well as a reliable pool of laborers and farmers. During a rope making, most of Saxonburg could be found on John's meadow, and during busy periods people were summoned from all over the surrounding countryside to help with the work. John paid well and he fed well. His son Washington acted as "the little messenger who did all the running." His arrival at neighboring houses and farms portended a good day's pay in a place of privation and an era of uncertain rewards.[56]

Rope work started at sunrise and finished at sunset. John's wife Johanna prepared and served three meals per day "with a snack of bread and butter in between—including whiskey" at mid-morning and mid-afternoon. "My poor mother was ground to the dust in trying to cook for so many on a primitive stone hearth, with a wood fire and one pot hook and iron kettle," Washington lamented. The rope work was more strenuous than skilled, involving much walking and carrying and turning of cranks. Precision was the key to accurate and efficient rope making, and John was a stickler for rigor. Laying out individual strands was the work of about eight strong men; rope making (combing the finished strands) took at least twice as many. Two of the workers carried an iron "top" (a conical device that separates the various strands and regulates the spinning of the rope) on a crossbar down the meadow, at the end of which was a simple twisting machine operated by another two men. Behind the men, the individual wires, attached at one end to their swivels and weights and draped over John's wooden frame, passed through the top and laid themselves into a strand. As the twisting shortened the wires, the weights rose and had to be lowered by hand. Once the strands were finished, the ends were severed, looped, and placed around big strong pegs driven into the ground. Seven strands were used to make a rope. Ropes were spliced and finished in a small building at the very bottom of the meadow.[57]

Once the rope was spun, oiled, and set, the most pressing challenge of lugging the wires to their destinations began. The only affordable and reliable means of transporting the wires to market was the Main Line Canal, a route that closed for the winter months. To be ready to start shipping when spring arrived, John and his team often had to work long winter hours in the cold, mud, rain, and snow. "Rope hauling was wretched business in muddy weather," Washington recalled, since wheels would spin and refuse traction. The massive drums were both heavy and unwieldy, and transporting them by horse was a lengthy and dangerous business. Getting his ropes even as far as Freeport, where they were loaded onto the canal, was a trial. Extra-strong and ultra-reliable wagons and a small army of laborers were needed to load them. Then all the bridges along the road had to be maintained, strengthened, and reinforced. Once in Freeport, the great reels of wire had to be entrusted to "frail" canal boats. As John's clients increased and his business expanded, so did the range of his shipping. Wires headed to the Delaware and Hudson Canal endured a prodigious journey of several weeks. Manhandled onto massive wagons at Saxonburg and hauled by a stout team of horses to Freeport, they were then loaded onto canal boats, sent over the Main Line Canal to Philadelphia, floated down the Delaware to Bordentown, rerouted to the Delaware and Raritan Canal, shipped to New York, run up the Hudson to Kingston, and finally put back on canal boats for the final leg to Carbondale, Pennsylvania. John soon found himself spending more time on the problems of hauling than the process of production. It quickly became obvious to everyone that western Pennsylvania was no place to run a thriving and successful business whose main markets were all in the east.[58]

John's ropewalk kept Saxonburg afloat, and the little hamlet continued to grow, creating a culture and set of traditions, if not a self-sustaining economy. "It was nice to live in Saxonburg," noted Francis Laube, "but we were all too poor to stay there all the time. So it had always been since they started it. The head of the family always had to go to the city to make money to keep his family." Still, life was lively in Saxonburg, and the cost of living was low. The village suffered a blow in 1844 when John's great friend Bähr passed away shortly after the birth of John's second daughter and fourth child, Elvira, on May 22. Ironically, one of Bähr's final acts was to recommend John move his business east and build himself an indoor ropewalk, advice John ignored at the time. Bähr's place in the hearts and minds of the Roebling family, especially Washington, was taken up by one of Saxonburg's great characters: Julius Riedel, a "short stout man" with a "huge pair of spectacles" who arrived in Saxonburg in 1843. Riedel was born in Tilsit, the son of a Lithuanian baron who was cousin to Field Marshall Blucher, the commander of the Prussian Army in the battles of Leipzig (1813) and Waterloo (1815). As an adult, possessing neither trade nor occupation, Riedel was put to work teaching Washington Roebling his "three R's." He also served as a popular preacher, before the Pittsburgh Lutheran Synod demanded his removal. Riedel had attended neither a theological seminary nor all that many actual church services. Riedel then married John's sister-in-law and moved to Columbus, but he was soon back in Saxonburg, living in John's house.[59]

It was clear that John needed to energetically cultivate some new customers to sustain his business. From his new home in the port of Chicago, Schlatter helped spread the gospel of wire rope by placing orders with John for dredging machines, pile drivers, and tillers ("I do assure you we all here . . . have the wire rope fever") and by writing a letter of introduction to James Madison Porter, the secretary of war. But John's main focus was still slips and inclined planes. On October 14, 1843, John wrote to the canal board proposing to install wire rope on the Millersburg Ferry. The same year he began a three-year campaign to get his wire ropes on the Belmont plane of the P&C. In 1847, he finally got word that his ropes would be used on the Schuylkill Plane as well. Despite gaining significant traction within Pennsylvania's Main Line system, John needed to find his next big market and his next big customer. Thanks to a little word of mouth and the attention generated by his wire rope article, they found him instead.[60]

On August 5, 1842, L. Chamberlin, secretary of the Beaver Meadows Railroad and Coal Company, wrote to John that he had heard of his successes with "iron wire rope" on the "inclined plane on the State road at Hollidaysburg" and had it "in contemplation to try the use of one on our road." Before placing an order, however, the secretary had a few questions. John replied promptly, explaining his method and differentiating it from those of "Smith of London." "My claims are secured by patent. . . . I am the only person in the US who has made essential improvements in the construction of Wire Rope and Wire Rigging," and he could deliver a rope according to Chamberlin's specifications in about two months. Such a rope, he concluded, "would on your road last almost forever, if treated properly."[61]

Chartered in 1830, the Beaver Meadows Railroad and Coal Company was a small player in a booming industry: excavating and transporting coal from the anthracite fields of eastern Pennsylvania to waiting markets in Philadelphia and

New York. Their "road" was a series of inclined planes and rail tracks that ran from a mine just outside Beaver Meadows to waiting canal barges on the Lehigh River. It was about twelve miles long and needed many different ropes, especially on the planes that got the railroad up and down the hills above Weatherly. Chamberlin replied that John's information was "highly satisfactory and much more favourable with the exemption of price than I expected." He needed delivery much faster than two months. One of the hemp ropes they were relying upon to get their cars up and down the 2,200-foot inclined plane was about to give way when the secretary first wrote to John and had broken when he wrote again three weeks later. "I believe we can get an English wire rope at far less cost than you propose," Chamberlin informed John, and in much less time, which is exactly what they did. Nonetheless, Chamberlin wrote to John from time to time badgering him to reduce his prices and speed up delivery times. He was still haggling to see if he would match the price of "English ropes" two years later. The English ropes were certainly cheaper but not necessarily better. In 1847, Roebling wire ropes were installed on the Spring Vale Railroad. A local paper reported, "This is the first experiment of the wire rope in the region since the Beaver Meadow Company tried one on their planes a few years ago. [That rope] failed to answer good purpose through some fault in its manufacture."[62]

John's experience with Chamberlin and the Beaver Meadows Railroad helped draw him away from his roots as a western Democrat and into the realm of the business Whigs. As a farmer (by aspiration at least, if not necessarily in practice) and recent immigrant, John believed in a life free from the clutching hands of authority, in individuality, small government, and self-reliance. As a businessman, he believed in the protection of American manufacturing and supported Clay's American System, with its central bank, state-supported system of internal improvements, and protective tariffs. This last issue was especially important if John was to survive as a manufacturer. How could his business survive if it was cheaper to buy a wire cable from England than from the other end of Pennsylvania? His dealings with Beaver Meadows and other coal-mining concerns lured him away from belief in individual liberty and into the realm of manufacturing power. His subsequent relationships with powerhouse coal and transportation companies only cemented this change, further expanding John's business, reputation, and influence and drawing him into the protectionist camp. "I think they are right in their arguments and facts," John concluded, if American industry and American labor were to grow and prosper.[63]

There were two major players in the eastern Pennsylvania coalfields, neither of which, thankfully, were the Beaver Meadows Railroad, and in the wake of John's essay in the *Railroad Gazette* both of them got in touch. On February 16, 1844, James Archbald, the chief engineer of the Delaware and Hudson Canal Company (D&H), wrote to John to enquire about his wire ropes. Horace Hollister, who knew Archbald well, described him as "a man of few words, open, honest and sincere, esteemed for the accuracy of his judgment and the vigor of his intellect, and for his friendship for the industrious workmen."[64] The D&H was one of the country's largest companies at the time, with a number of illustrious alumni. Their first chief engineer was Benjamin Wright, chief engineer of the Erie Canal, followed by John B. Jervis, who went on to design the Croton Aqueduct, and then Archbald. The D&H built and operated the world's largest gravity railroad—fifty-five miles long—which ran from Carbondale to the company's canal terminus at Honesdale, Pennsylvania. There coal was loaded onto barges and sent south to the Lackawanna River and then east to the Delaware. Unable to scale the Kittatinny Mountains and the Shawangunk Ridge, the canal took a sharp left at Port Jervis and headed up to Kingston. From there the coal was floated down the Hudson River to New York.[65] Washington Irving rode the length of the D&H in 1841 and left this description: "The canal is laid a great part of the way along romantic valleys. . . . For many miles it is built up along the face of perpendicular precipices, rising into stupendous cliffs with overhanging forests, or strutting out into vast promontories; while on the other side you look down upon the Delaware, foaming and roaring below. . . . Altogether it is one of the most daring undertakings I have ever witnessed, to carry an artificial river over rocky mountains, and up the most savage and almost impracticable defiles."[66]

By 1844, the D&H operated more inclined planes than anyone else in the world, but it planned to expand its capacity by 500 percent. With so much at stake, it needed to be cautious and certain. Archbald ordered three large wire ropes from John in the spring of 1844 and put them to work. John was "a little apprehensive" about the splices holding up running around the D&H's tiny three-foot sheaves, but they succeeded, at least for a while. After about a year of limited and generally positive tests, a rope failed. With no small sense of panic, John wrote to Archbald in the autumn of 1845: "It being reported in Philadelphia that the wire ropes . . . have given no satisfaction, and are considered a failure, I would ask as a favor to be informed as early as convenient of . . . the causes of the failure." Fortunately, the problem was less with the product than with the system, which was set up for hemp ropes, not wire. As Archbald wrote to Russel Lord, head of the D&H's canal division, the problem could only be alleviated by "an entire change of machinery." Sensing that the future belonged to wire, the D&H got to work overhauling their roads. By the beginning of 1848, John had his next big customer.[67]

John's relationship with the D&H helped boost his fortunes and career in other crucial ways. In lieu of payment, John often took stock in the D&H, which turned out to be one of his more lucrative investments. More substantially, when the company went looking for someone to build a few aqueducts, they naturally turned to John. Between February 1847 and 1851, John built four separate suspension aqueducts for the D&H. They were the third, fourth, fifth, and sixth suspension bridges of John's career. One—stretching over the Delaware between Minisink, New York, and Lackawaxen, Pennsylvania—still stands, the nation's oldest suspension bridge.[68]

John's business dealings with the D&H were helped along immeasurably by his warm relationship with Archbald. Their confidence in each other and their mutual respect were almost instantaneous. As two technically minded engineers devoted to issues of transport and technology, they shared ideas and debated details. Archbald's feedback helped John refine his ropes, as well as his future projects. When John was "contemplating the establishment of another Rope Walk, East of the Allegheny Mountains," it was Archbald he wrote to for "candid" and "unreserved" advice. With no one else did he have such a close professional and intellectual relationship. If Charlie Schlatter was John's first great comrade and colleague, then James Archbald was his second and his most enduring.[69]

Everyone in the anthracite industry waited while the D&H decided on John's ropes, but when they did, the orders came rolling in. The D&H's main competitor for the lucrative New York City market—and the other great eastern

Figure 9.2 John's friend James Archbald, ca. 1860s. Courtesy of the Lackawanna Historical Society.

Pennsylvania mining concern—was the Lehigh Coal & Navigation Company (LC&N). The LC&N shipped their coal along the Lehigh River from Mauch Chunk to Easton, where it was loaded onto the Morris Canal and floated down through the Lehigh Valley to New York. The LC&N's chief engineer, Edwin Douglas, was thoroughly tired of hemp rope's costs and inadequacies and the unpredictability and the accidents that accompanied iron chains. "We had another smash this afternoon on the Mount Pisgah plane. . . . Do you know anything about wire rope?" he wrote on April 20, 1846, to Erskine Hazard, co-owner of the LC&N, just before getting in touch with John. Douglas had taken note of John's successes on the Portage Railroad portage and Archbald's initial trials on the D&H, and he decided to act. In November, he visited John's ropewalk in Saxonburg and the planes of the Portage Railroad that used Roebling wire rope.[70]

Impressed, Douglas immediately ordered an eight-hundred-foot trial rope for the coal chutes at Mauch Chunk—a complex system that emptied coal from railroad trucks directly onto canal boats before returning them to the mine shaft—and one for the Morris Canal. He was dazzled by the results. He quickly ordered six more ropes for a series of inclines the company was building and started to get a few ideas of his own. Hazard, it turns out, was also captivated by John's ropes and beguiled by the possibilities, so much so that together they began to plot and plan the LC&N's own wire rope concern. Douglas and Hazard dreamed of an indoor, mechanized ropewalk that could operate all year round and manufacture ropes of all sizes. They wasted no time. Hazard designed it, Douglas built it, and, remarkably, the Mauch Chunk wire rope factory was up and running by 1848 and supplying wire rope all along the Lehigh navigation. "On Monday Evening, the third of July, at 12 o'clock, the new wire rope machine of this place was completed and set in operation," reported the *Carbon County Gazette and Mauch Chunk Courier*. "We have our machine in place and it works well," Douglas wrote, adding, "I do not think it will cost over two cents per pound to make them including oil. My opinion they will be cheaper than hemp if they do not last longer. I have no doubt however but they will last twice as long." With this, Hazard and Douglas created the first modern wire rope factory.[71]

The Mauch Chunk wire rope factory was a major blow to John, although not immediately to his business. Because the LC&N's ropes were used internally and were not for sale, they did not infringe on John's patent rights. So while he lost a substantial client, he did not gain a business rival. More worrying was the speed with which they were able to decide upon, design, and build their factory and get it operational, not to mention the prospect that John's other clients might well decide to make their own ropes. Oddly, John and Douglas maintained a friendly relationship throughout the whole process and beyond, although John found Hazard and Douglas's machinery "very defective indeed," as he confided to his notebook. But this was entirely beside the point. The LC&N's ropeworks was water-powered and used high-speed indoor machinery, meaning it could produce rope at a cost far below anything John could achieve in his back garden. If the LC&N's ropes weren't up to John's standards, they at least had the virtue of costing less and being quicker to manufacture, and should one fail, all they had to do was make another. Forced to respond, and never one to fall behind, John moved his entire operation east, indoors, and into the world of the new mechanized factory, all within a year.[72]

———

John's first rope was an experimental six-hundred-foot parallel-wire wrapped rope made with very little real technical knowledge in the fall of 1841. The last ropes John made in Saxonburg were three 2,300-foot helical strand ropes in the second week of August 1849, after which silence descended on John's noisy back garden; the ropewalk was packed up and the land sold off. In between, John established an industry that would help transform the hauling capacity of a young nation that was increasingly on the move and a business that would sustain him, his ever-increasing family, and their descendants. Between March 20 and November 11, 1847, for example, John and his helpers made over forty-two thousand feet of rope by hand, aided by a special "grooved cone"—developed and eventually patented by John—that allowed them to spin all nineteen wires in one operation. He supplied new ropes for all of the inclines on the Portage Railroad (over twenty thousand feet), along with all the wire rope requirements of the Delaware and Hudson Canal Company, the Lehigh Coal and Navigation Company, and a host of other smaller industries. After eight years, John not only had a successful business, but he had established himself—finally—as one of the most reliable, respected, and innovative suspension bridge engineers in the country. He got his start right as he was furiously trying to establish his wire rope business: "We send you by mail this day a paper with a proposal from the Aqueduct Committee [in Pittsburgh]," wrote his friend Robert Townsend, "offering a premium . . . for the best plan for a wooden or suspension aqueduct [to carry the Main Line Canal over the Allegheny River and into Pittsburgh]. Now is the time for you to strike, it is at present impassable." Despite desperately trying to drum up new business and get his wires adopted all over the Portage Railroad, John got to work immediately.[73]

Private Life, Public Works (1844–45)

Rebuilding the Allegheny Aqueduct was John's big break as a bridge builder. That there was ever an aqueduct to fail in the first place was both fortunate and somewhat unlikely. The Pennsylvania Main Line Canal was built to link Philadelphia with the Ohio River. But the fact that the canal ended in Pittsburgh at all was a matter of luck, coupled with some cold hard politics, as much as anything else. The canal approached the mouth of the Ohio from the northeast, on the north side of the Allegheny River, across from Pittsburgh. Where it would terminate remained undecided. As with the building of much of America's infrastructure, the logical choice was not always the final choice. Nathan Roberts was charged with surveying both sides of the Allegheny for a possible Western terminal. The Pittsburgh side would prove "almost impractical" (thanks to flood-related problems and "hill slips"), he reported, and certainly "very expensive"; a canal ending at the Allegheny on the north shore opposite Pittsburgh would be less than half the cost and significantly easier to plan and execute. "The contrast presented between the two sides of the river, could have left no doubt which to select," read the official report.[1]

The problem for Pittsburghers was that the opposite shore was in the independent municipality of Allegheny City.[2] Pittsburgh's town elders were not looking to have goods float all the way from Philadelphia only to then be delivered to a rival city across the river. They argued that legally the canal had to terminate at Pittsburgh, that a terminal on the opposite side of the Allegheny "would be a serious blow to the welfare of their city," and that the problems of construction could be alleviated by building an aqueduct to carry the canal across the Allegheny. And remarkably they got their way. Although the engineering and fiscal arguments supported Allegheny City, Pittsburgh's influence trumped the engineers' expertise. The Main Line would travel north of the river, take a sharp left before reaching Allegheny City, flow over the river on a massive new wooden aqueduct, and terminate in Pittsburgh. Scrupulously honest in almost all things, John nevertheless owed his big break to some local dealings and some shady politics.[3]

Sylvanus Lothrop and William LeBaron built the original Allegheny Aqueduct for $104,000, back when the state of Pennsylvania thought large and spent lavishly on its internal improvements. Lothrop and LeBaron's bridge had seven spans, each consisting of four parallel wooden arches (two on each side of the trunk). The huge water-filled wooden trunk—thirty-four feet wide— was affixed to and suspended from the arches by a series of iron hanger rods. The total length was almost one thousand feet, and it was likely the strongest wooden bridge ever built, supporting upwards of two thousand tons of water. Abolitionist Elizur Wright visited the construction site and marveled at "huge stone piers rising from the surface, some of them already 30 feet above it." During the highest freshet of the 1830s, the waters of the Allegheny "rose to about the floor line of the canal trunk; the weather boarding of the outside formed a kind of dam, against which tress, barns, houses, &c., accumulated, until they formed a wide field of drift on its upper side. A large concourse of people stood on the banks of the river, expecting to see the whole structure lifted off from its piers and float away; but it stood perfectly firm, and . . . sustained no injury whatever."[4]

When the aqueduct was opened on November 10, 1829, the awaiting crowds "were in fine spirits" and continued cheeringly through noon the next day when the canal was filled and "three packet boats crossed in fine style, hailed by ten thousand spectators, and under a salute of 105 guns from the artillery." "We distinctly remember that nearly the whole city was congregated on it at one point of the day," wrote the editor of the *Gazette and Advertiser*. In fact, so many people tried to jump on the canal boats as they passed and get themselves a ride into Pittsburgh on the smart new aqueduct that the local "Volunteers" had to "flash their weapons about at a great rate." Dickens called it a "dreamy place" that nevertheless led to the "ugly confusion" that was Pittsburgh's canal basin. Such opinions were nice, but the reality was that the city was asking an eighteenth-century structure to do the work of the nineteenth century, and Pittsburgh's poor aqueduct was soon overmatched.[5]

Despite its enormous size and strength, the aqueduct rested on inadequate foundations. Lothrop and LeBaron underestimated the weight of the water in the aqueduct's flume during their initial calculations—a mistake that doomed the span—and, to make matters worse, laid the structure on a series of piers that were ill-equipped to handle the extra, uncalculated weight. A more durable or robust material would have done a better job, but the piers were built of medium-grade sandstone, more typically used for facing, not supporting, and they began to crumble under the massive strain. Leaks, breaks, and strains were almost constant, as were repairs and patch jobs. This approach sufficed to carry the span through a decade or more of work, but by the early 1840s, it was in a deplorable state and in need of extensive help.[6]

The aqueduct's structural crisis coincided with Governor Potter's efforts at reform, and with the state's support withdrawn, the aqueduct fell into disrepair and began to fail. Boats were frequently banned from traversing the "rickety old concern" (as the *Gazette and Advertiser* dubbed it), and increasingly traffic was shut down for long periods.[7] This state of affairs was a disaster for Pennsylvania, which had poured millions of dollars into their Main Line Canal, but even worse for Pittsburgh, which had staked much of its commercial future on the canal. John, among thousands of others, had moved to the area because of the canal and the opportunities it heralded. The state's massive public works project snaked its way through several hundred miles of dense forest and steep mountainsides, all the way up to Pittsburgh's doorstep, before effectively stopping. If the aqueduct collapsed, so would Pittsburgh's main connection to markets in the east. The fate of the city was left to depend on an overburdened, leaky wooden bridge on the point of collapse.

In 1842, John Trautwine, a respected local engineer, conducted a comprehensive examination of the structure. After measuring and testing the span, Trautwine concluded that the trunk was brilliantly designed ("Viewed as a whole, this aqueduct . . . reflects the highest credit on Mr. Lothrop, for boldness and mechanical skill") and constructed ("I look upon the arrangement of the timbers as the best yet devised for large spans"), but that the piers were terribly designed ("such immense weight and so soft a stone"), which spelled disaster. As all good engineers know, nothing can overcome a poor foundation. Things were so bad, in fact, that "one of the spans, at the time [the engineer] saw the Aqueduct was in imminent danger of falling."[8]

The aqueduct limped on in limited use until August 1843, when one of the piers started to give way. The span was immediately declared unsafe for boat traffic and drained. Pittsburgh was cut off from the canal, and all the goods and trade flowing from the east were delivered to Allegheny City. Repairs were attempted, but to no avail. In September, J. and A. C. Beck were paid four thousand dollars for straightening and fixing the arches and laying a new floor, but the job was more serious than had been imagined. Shortly after, the toll collector John Fleming reported that four king posts had broken, along with a number of other supporting limbs, and that the aqueduct would not last a week if the water wasn't immediately withdrawn. It was subsequently reported—"upon good authority"—that water would be let back into the aqueduct by the end of September and that "the repairs had been done in such a manner that the bridge may stand for years," but this was pure fiction. As reported by the canal commissioners at the end of the year: the aqueduct was "examined by competent and practical men, and was condemned as being no longer safe, or worth repairing." Plans to rebuild the span were solicited, but with no money available, the project stalled. Having been built on eight inches of soft sand(stone), Pittsburgh's prosperity seemed about to sink into the waters from which it had risen.[9]

———

The issue was unlikely to fade away with so much at stake, and on January 13, 1844, the citizens of Indiana and Westmoreland Counties—located immediately east of Pittsburgh—petitioned the state "praying for immediate provision for repairing the aqueduct over the Allegheny River, at Pittsburgh." The plan was swiftly and vociferously objected to in the state legislature on January 17 by representatives from Allegheny City. The city was loath to give up its newfound commercial clout, so representatives tried to block the repairs with jurisdiction, claiming that Allegheny City's rights extended halfway across the Allegheny River. Pittsburgh had no right to build anything in another city's territory or collect tolls on land within Allegheny City's jurisdiction. The legislature disagreed; they ruled that the canal belonged to the commonwealth. Rebuilding the aqueduct was "optional," but the law was "just and expedient."[10]

On January 19, 1844, the Pennsylvania state legislature voted to allow Pittsburgh to make repairs or rebuild the aqueduct at its own expense, and later that day the governor signed the bill into law. Although the city could rebuild its much needed aqueduct and collect tolls, it could only do so to recover the costs of construction. After that, the revenue would revert back to the state. The risk was all Pittsburgh's, but the city happily accepted it. On January 29, the city passed an ordinance that put William B. Foster, Jr., a toll collector and canal engineer, in charge of the Aqueduct Committee, accepted the state's "provisions and conditions," and set out a plan of action. Because the city had raised an extensive infrastructure to accommodate the trade on the canal, it had "every reason to believe that" the state would "protect the pledge . . . that the terminus [in Pittsburgh] should be preserved." The canal must be maintained despite the "peculiar and unfortunate condition" of the state's finances.[11]

The city found itself in a quandary. To rebuild immediately was to risk the entire summer trade. Proposals would need to be solicited, evaluated, and amended, putting the most likely start date no earlier than late spring. Construction itself would take at least three to four months, meaning the new aqueduct would open just as the season was closing. With this in mind, the city went for "a temporary repair that will secure the Aqueduct for the business of the coming season," in the process guaranteeing that construction would be as difficult as possible. Winter ice floes had helped bring down the old aqueduct, and whoever received the contract to rebuild would be forced to do so during the frigid western Pennsylvanian winter. The city set aside six thousand dollars "to keep up the structure, so as to accommodate the business until the 30th day of November 1844." While it spent the money, it did not get the repairs. At the end of January, it was reported that the city "intend[ed] to repair it so as to last the coming season, then to rebuild it permanently," the first in a relatively long line of repair attempts. On May 27, the day after Townsend wrote to John about the aqueduct competition, James McClellan, who would himself try for the contract to rebuild the span, recorded in his diary that the "Aqueduct [had] given way." A month later "water [was] drawn off the *aqueduct* for the purpose of repairs—3rd time." By the close of June, the *Philadelphia Inquirer* reported that "the Aqueduct has given way again—it is to be hoped forever."[12]

The ordinance required Pittsburgh to invite proposals for rebuilding the aqueduct "until the first day of April," but for some reason the call was delayed until late May. "To Engineers: A premium of One Hundred Dollars will be paid for the best plan and complete specification of an aqueduct with wood or iron trunk, either suspended or supported, to be constructed on the piers now standing in the Allegheny River opposite the city, provided the same be handed to the Mayor of the city on or before the 20th of June," read the announcement.[13]

———

While Pittsburghers were trying to keep their decrepit aqueduct working and mulling over what to do next, John took time out from his fledgling wire rope business—not to mention circling warily around the malign Snodgrass—to write a letter to his father. Washington later called it "a long drawn out confession of Faith," many facets of which he maintained throughout his life. The letter is certainly one of the most revealing that John ever wrote, showing as it does the private individual who coexisted with the public figure. It is also one of the few times when John tried to explain his personal beliefs to another person. John spent many hundreds of hours in the 1860s committing his philosophical beliefs to paper, yet none of the essays were as intimate or as candid as the letter he wrote his father on March 30, 1844. It helps remind us that public faces obscure private people. For while John was certainly a man of science and reason, he was also a spiritual mystic, inclined to the hard lines of the Enlightenment as well as the soft textures of Romanticism. In fact, he alternated between them at a rather bewildering pace. John believed in physics and metaphysics, science and spirit, the promise of technology and transcendentalism. He was a man of parts and compartments: while much was on display (his engineering genius), other facets remained hidden.[14]

Often cold and businesslike in his correspondence, even with friends, John in his letter to his father was warm and personal. He admitted that his "interests are merging more and more with those of this country," yet nevertheless his memories of "homeland and family connections remained vivid" and loving. "If my affairs here permitted it in any way," he wrote, "I would not deny myself the pleasure of paying you a visit and seeing you and talking to you once again, before death separates us." Despite the fact that his father was seventy-six years old and had recently had to give up his daily walk, John's work and family commitments were too numerous to permit him the luxury of a foreign trip. This was sad, but not to be worried over. "Death and life, these are two very strange, inexplicable, apparently totally opposite conditions in the economy of nature, whose ultimate purpose we cannot comprehend!" declared John, not that this was going to stop him from comprehending and then explaining them to his aged father. "Priests, the rulers of the earth and religious fanatics, have always used the theme of death, of future reward and punishment, as a means to their ends, and have attributed to the Creator of the world things and arrangements which cause sensible people to shudder." Death was not "destruction" but "only a change" from one thing into another. John was vague about what exactly that might be, but he did have some rather well-developed ideas about what governed existence, not to mention being human.[15]

The essence of John's worldview was simple: there are no religions, only a single guiding "spirit" that "animates all of creation." One could call it "God" or "the Great Spirit of the Indians," but one should acknowledge that there were no competing "spirits." "The existence of an evil spirit or a so-called devil is *nonsense*," he informed his father. John's "world spirit" operated through the "spiritual functions that have their seat in the brain," and so long as "our brain and the remaining human organism" continue "their natural activity," we receive "the impulse of the world spirit." Once the brain is destroyed, we are released. "We should not imagine that we have a soul that burns within us like a little lamp!" John continued; "there is only one soul, and this is the soul of the whole world, whose nature we cannot measure. . . . Just as gravity affects all objects, so the world spirit acts upon your brain and also upon mine." "Thence the natural sympathy between human beings," John reasoned, "which is based upon the common spiritual being."[16]

What exactly was the "impulse of the world spirit"? John's father might well have asked himself. Thankfully the answer was rather pleasant: "Man was created for no other purpose than to be happy, and calm reflection, the application of reason, observation of human nature, are for us an undeniable proof that the whole organization of man is calculated to make us happy. . . . Life here is a system in itself, *independent of a world to come*," but we must remember that we are part of the world spirit and need to be "responsible beings with regard to the whole." John's philosophical boundaries were literally universal. There exists a "spiritual coherence which extends beyond our globe and beyond our earthly existence. . . . We are responsible in what we do . . . to the whole universe."[17]

John's "world spirit" was underpinned by his philosophical key words: reason and nature. "Whoever . . . does not let himself be guided by reason does not deserve the name of a human being," he declared. "Reason, when applied according to the laws of the mind, is *infallible*, and the only thing to which we can cling with assurance," he advised his father. We have reason so we can understand ourselves and our surroundings and "cling to nature," John explained, quoting Romantic philosopher Johann Gottfried Herder. "There is no *special* providence." Instead, that "which governs the world governs all through very simple but universal and eternally unchanging laws, with regard to the moral as well as the physical": "Entrust your feelings to the bosom of nature which deceives no one, but is a kindly mother to all," he explained, before finally getting to his main point. "While the priests of the various denominations keep on quarreling and fighting over articles of faith . . . the sun calmly continues to shine, for the good as well as the bad." "Jews, Christians, heathen and Baptists will in the end, when universal culture and civilization have made one single great family out of all mankind which is now rent asunder, finally come back to that" one simple fact: that "*there is only one true religion, and that is in nature.*"[18]

John's worldview owed much to Hegel's all-controlling *Weltgeist* ("world spirit")—the guiding force of historical development, the animating crackle and hiss of subconscious intellectual movement—but also to Ralph Waldo Emerson's ideas on nature and the soul. John read widely in Emerson's works, and his notebooks of the period mention buying several of the philosopher's books. Emerson, in turn, believed nature was the essence and manifestation of the world's divinity. To understand the world, one needed to become one with the natural world. John was unlikely to go quite that far, not after his disastrous time as a farmer in Saxonburg, but he also found a totalizing image of power and potential in the natural world and would have wholeheartedly agreed that the real value of life could be more clearly found in nature than in churches, books, or laws. John might have extended nature to include some of the works of man—great feats of architecture and engineering—demarcating him from Emerson, but often with a similar aim: to bind men together in a spirit of connection. The phrase "*There is only one true religion, and that is in nature*" does not appear in Emerson's "Nature" nor in Thoreau's *Walden*, but in a letter John Roebling wrote to his aged father in 1844.[19]

John read Emerson's famous essay "The Over-Soul" (1841), in which the philosopher complained that humanity lived "in division, in parts, in particles. Meantime within man is the soul of the whole; the wise silence; the universal beauty, to which every part and particle is equally related, the eternal ONE." Unlike John, Emerson believed in the individual soul, but also that all souls were connected, much like John. "The Supreme Critic . . . is that great nature in which we rest . . . that Unity, that Over-soul, within which every man's particular being

is contained and made one with all other," wrote Emerson, which bears comparison with John's belief that "the natural sympathy between human beings" was
based on a "common spiritual being." Emerson, Hegel, and John were all striving
toward the belief that we are all connected somehow, by nature and a common
soul in Emerson, by the *Weltgeist* in Hegel, and by a combination of them in
John.[20]

"You are perhaps surprised at the course and the content of my letter," John
commented at the conclusion of his dispatch; "at this moment I am surprised
at myself as I reflect to whom I am writing." But, he continued, "I am a grown
man who has learned to think independently." John's aim was merely to help set
his father's mind at rest. He often spoke with his neighbor Bähr (an "enlightened, clear-sighted man") on the subject and found him "calmly awaiting death,
whenever it may come." John "curse[d] every cleric who depicts Hell and punishment to a dying person, and embitters the last few hours of his existence."
The established church had "so distorted" the "simple original teachings" of the
New Testament so as to make of it "a scarecrow with which to frighten children
and feeble-minded people." What Polycarp Roebling made of John's philosophical musings or the attempts of a man in the prime of life to counsel a seventy-
six-year-old how to approach death can only be guessed at. Perhaps he thought
his youngest son had become a crackpot out in the American sun. Perhaps he
was more indulgent, thinking John a wise philosopher and a dear son. Certainly,
he must have been touched by the last words he received from a son he hadn't
seen in thirteen years: "Do not fear death! It signifies nothing bad—finish your
few remaining days in calmness and peace with yourself and the whole world—
universal love is the great law of nature."[21]

Along with this letter, John also sent a friendly note to his brother Christel.
A sense of lazy familiarity and congenial good cheer—entirely absent from anything else he wrote at the time—pervades John's writing in both letters. He
seems interested and warm, like a father and a brother, not a manufacturer or
an engineer, or even a pioneer trying to lure settlers to his remote corner of the
world. John thanked his father for paying the five hundred florins he'd owed to
Meissner since 1831 and reported that his "present business . . . is going pretty
well, but is only in its early stages." He asked after his four nephews and nieces—
"Carl must have become a fine young lad, and Emma . . . a budding maiden"—
and passed on news of his own growing family. Washington was a "well-built,
sturdy, quiet boy," while Ferdinand was turning into "a promising lad with good
prospects." Laura "has been suffering a great deal for two years from a protracted
illness," but seemed on the mend. Carl's widow Wilhelmina was back living on
John's land in Saxonburg, he was pleased to report, after another sad marriage
and very quick separation. Thankfully, her children remained "well-educated
and well-bred."[22]

John signed off his letter to his brother with a prescient vision of America's future: "In a few years the American population will spread out along the Pacific Ocean," from which they would likely establish trade with China, the East Indies, and the Sandwich Islands. "A connection will soon be established between the East and the West by means of railroads over the Rocky Mountains," and John wouldn't be surprised to see people "working on the canal through the Isthmus of Panama."[23]

The warmth of John's letters to his family hide a troubling personal darkness, at least according to Washington. Even with a growing circle of influential friends and colleagues and the rapid success of many of his endeavors, John's private behavior was increasingly erratic. Put simply: John Roebling may have been a very violent man, at least behind closed doors. Our only authority for this is Washington, who enjoyed a complex relationship with his father, at once fearful and admiring. Perhaps crucially, he set down his impressions and recollections almost fifty years after the events he described. "His domestic life can be summed up in a few words," wrote Washington, in the candid but also flawed and sometimes unreliable biography he wrote of his father late in life: "domineering tyranny only varied by outbursts of uncontrollable ferocity—His wife and children stood in constant fear of him and trembled in his presence," Washington disclosed. "To fell my mother with a blow of the fist was nothing uncommon. My good old grandmother once saved my life by knocking him down with a fence rail as I lay writhing on the floor in my last agonies—It was a fortunate thing that his engineering engagements kept him away for prolonged periods, otherwise his children would have all died young—a huge cowhide always hung by the clock, ready to come down without warning—all our ingenuities were bent to one purpose, to keep out of sight—The result was that he brought up a set of sneaks."[24]

If Washington's graphic descriptions are reliable, the effects on John's family could only have been traumatic and profound. "The table was a gloomy feast," he writes; "not a word was spoken or sound heard. The cravings of hunger satisfied, each poor wretch would slink away, fearing to hear some harsh reproof before he escaped from the room." Moments of discipline were frequent and dreaded: "When anyone was sent for to his room, it was with fear and trembling, as it was a grave question whether he would return alive from the execution chamber." The overall effect "could only humble the pride and crush all manly independence in his children—His 4 sons and daughter now living are simple examples of warped—misanthropic cranks, peculiar, odd and unhappy."[25]

What accounts for John's appalling behavior—if such it was—is unknown. He may well have suffered from some violent impulse control disorder. Or maybe an angry son was bitter at the end of a life dedicated to his father's works. John was certainly capable of great kindness to his children, in addition to the extreme cruelty alleged by his son. His notebooks contain numerous references to little presents he would buy his children on his trips around the country, perhaps indicating the sort of remorse alluded to by Washington: "As he grew older he realized what he had done and tried to control himself, but it was impossible." And his violent fury was clearly not limited to his family. John "preferred to trample a rattlesnake to death rather than waste powder and shot on it," wrote his son, while "a disobedient dog or horse had the alternative of life or death presented to it at once." In addition, Washington alludes to a horse dying "under suspicious circumstances" and his father's practice of making recalcitrant animals move by "driving nails" into their backsides.[26]

John's fundamental, ironclad sense of his own infallibility had him following numerous fads and fashions long after they were discredited. It also fueled both his engineering and manufacturing brilliance and many of his personal failings, helping foster a level of intolerance that may have spilled over into violent dysregulation. He was capable of warmth, kindness, and good humor, but also—potentially—of great anger and rage. His professional genius may have hidden a destructive series of odious personal failings. While John's reputation was growing and soaring and his public works were admired and lauded, his private life was perhaps spiraling off into the realm of the deeply unpleasant.

———

John deployed all of his genius, his contacts, and his indefatigable energy once he had heard about the competition to replace the Allegheny Aqueduct. The effort was massive—especially considering how time-consuming his wire rope business was—and the results were impressive. Washington called it "in many respects the greatest feat of his life," mainly because it was accomplished in such a short time frame during a severe winter and because John had to overcome so many problems, not the least of which was the "violent opposition, raised by the press, by rival contractors, engineers, canal men, merchants, etc." Washington was right about the size of problems but overstates the strength of the opposition. By this point, John was a well-liked and well-respected local inventor and manufacturer. He was known by some of the state's most influential engineers, and they knew that he did excellent work. In many respects he was the natural choice. In fact, it took barely a month from the competition's announcement for John to win over the city. By early July, John was writing to the Board of

Canal Commissioners in Harrisburg to see when he could visit "for the purpose of having the plans approved for the new Aquaduct [*sic*] over the Allegheny River." The work "needs to be commenced immediately," he added. A couple of days later, John's victory was common knowledge: "Captain Young informed me today that your plan had been adopted, and that you would in all probability get the contract for rebuilding the Aqueduct," John Linton, a local cement dealer, wrote John.[27]

By the middle of July, John was busy soliciting endorsements from prominent industrialists and engineers. He sent his initial calculations and plans to D. K. Minor in New York and to others, most notably Edwin F. Johnson (one of America's "ablest and most scientific" men, according to the *New York Times*), W. R. Casey (a prolific author and expert on all aspects of railroad and locomotive construction), and James Archbald, all of whom wrote back at length. Johnson and Casey thought the acceptance of John's suspension plan was an excellent portent that "public judgment in such matters is improving." They answered some of John's technical questions and spoke of the applicability of the suspension principle to an aqueduct. Both engineers thought it much more applicable to an aqueduct than a highway bridge, actually. Live loads are more uniformly distributed on an aqueduct than on a road bridge, they reasoned, therefore providing less opportunity for "vibration or undulating movement." As for John's cables, they seemed "abundantly sufficient to support" the aqueduct. John sent the same list of questions to Archbald, requesting that his friend "please answer these questions *simply*" while supposing "the features of the plan are good without exception." Clearly at this point John was looking for endorsements, not advice.[28]

By the end of July, John had prepared a detailed report on his plan, which he submitted to the office of the canal commissioners. He planned to use the old piers, which still appeared "good," although much of the old masonry would need repairing, grouting, and pointing. Icebreakers at the head of the piers would also be built. John planned to build up the piers with three courses of granite blocks, which "will conform with the sides of the trunk." The new towpath would sit at the same height as the old towpath, while the "upper courses of the new masonry" would be about eight feet above "the heads of the present piers." Upon these courses, John would build a series of "pyramids" that would carry and support the suspension cables. The pyramids would consist of two stones, "hard and durable" and 6½ feet by 4 at the bottom and 5 by 3 feet at the top, with a total height of 4 feet 5 inches. Cast iron saddles would sit atop each pyramid, making the total height six feet above the towpath. The pressure on each pyramid would be twelve tons per square foot, John observed, before concluding that "it would require ten times this pressure to affect at all the stone" he intended to use.[29]

The cables themselves would each be composed of 2,200 wires and would "extend *below* the beams" by one foot six inches, in order to "*decrease* the elevation of the pyramids and increase the deflection of the cables." In addition, they would be "braced against the beams" with wrought iron straps and fastened to each side of the river in huge, enclosed underground anchorages. As for the aqueduct's trunk, "the bottom as well as the sides" would be composed of a double layer of lumber, laid diagonally at an angle of forty-five degrees, the two courses crossing each other at right angles. The trunk would sit on a series of beams grouped in pairs four feet apart. Each beam would be twenty-seven feet long, sixteen inches deep, and six inches wide. The sides of the trunk would be supported by posts, which would also support the towpath railing.[30]

John's conclusion addressed the novelty of suspended spans, although somewhat obliquely. An empty "suspension structure will not weigh more than one half of what a wooden one would," John asserted, and "the weight exerted by such a structure, is a . . . vertical pressure, exerting no other force whatever against the piers." "The argument that wooden arches serve as braces for the piers, and preserves their stability is ridiculous," he declared. "Wooden arches brace against each other and will balance each other as long as they are in good condition and in line." Yet "when one arch gives way, the next one will soon be affected, as can now clearly be seen in the old work." "If it was true that the piers are not strong enough for the support of a Suspension Aquaduct, it would be *still more true* that they are not strong enough for the support of a Wooden Structure." In comparison, John's plan for the support and construction of the trunk would form a very solid connection between the piers, without having any tendency to "overthrow them." John's plan and explication exuded great skill and confidence, even though he would rework and amend his plan several times before construction begun.[31]

Before the contract had even been officially announced, a war of words exploded in the press. John's plan was publicized in Pittsburgh toward the end of July 1844, and it aroused the ire of numerous locals. Someone calling himself "Taxpayer" objected vociferously to anything that would add to the public debt. "Another Pittsburgher" also worried about costs. John had offered to build the aqueduct for $63,000, while "other persons of equal responsibility" offered to build it for $40,000. Surely John's plan would lead to higher tolls, they reasoned, which would "assuredly drive a considerable portion of the business to Allegheny." "A Native" worried about the bidding process too. A bid four thousand dollars lower than John's "from one of our own citizens, well known for his mechanical qualifications," had been rejected for "lack of confidence," which seemed suspicious. "If the temptation to make money should prove stronger than the ambition to obtain a name from the erection of a stable and durable work," worried the Native, "the city may in the end be the sufferer; it has now no competent functionary to stand between it and harm." The ill-fated history of Pennsylvania's public works "should have taught Councils a useful lesson on the subject."[32]

"Pittsburgher" set out a list of objections and sent them to the *Pittsburgh Daily Gazette and Advertiser*. Most of his fears centered on the suspension principle: that suspended structures suffered more through deflection than wooden structures, that they held up less well to sustained vibration, that John's plans for rebuilding the piers were entirely inadequate, and that suspended spans were still in their infancy, leaving too many questions and too many unknowns. Despite several notable successes, suspension bridges still fell down more often than they stayed up, and either way they just looked too flimsy.[33]

John responded almost immediately to the outpouring of objections, writing a long letter to the *Gazette and Advertiser* on July 27. He began by effectively accusing all his critics of cowardice for failing to use their real names. Throughout most of his life, John treated almost all opposition as pure stupidity, and it was no different here. To be fair, Taxpayer's assertion that it would cost fifty thousand dollars just to repair the piers was laughable; John not only repaired the piers but also built a whole new aqueduct for only a few thousand dollars more. The claim that the cables could not cope with the transient weight of moving water appeared to John "so supremely ridiculous and so utterly void of all reason and common sense, that I acknowledge that I am at a loss how to meet a man who can advance such a proposition." Still, John took pains to defend the suspension principle and assert that "no system of bridge building has been carried to a higher degree of perfection." John extolled the strength and durability of the Menai and Fryburgh bridges as evidence of this, and even defended Ellet's Schuylkill Bridge, albeit faintly. The Philadelphia bridge was "not remarkable for its stiffness," but the vibrations were significantly less than on any wooden bridge, and after all, "there is no necessity for a high degree of stiffness." In short, Ellet's span might not be a great suspension bridge, but it was still a suspension bridge and thus far superior to any other kind of span. John's final judgment was simple: "It is much easier to doubt and quibble than to understand and prove."[34]

John also kept up a less public correspondence with William Galway, chairman of the Aqueduct Committee, making sure to address any complaint he heard in the press. "Among other objections raised against the practicality of my plan," John had heard "that the *swell* of water in *advance* of a boat would cause such an unequal load upon the two adjourning spans, as to effect the equilibrium in a serious manner." According to John's calculations—"which [he] made in strict conformity with the laws of *statics*"—this was untrue. All the spans could

"support an *extra weight* of 100 ton without endangering the safety of the structure," he explained.[35]

Among the grumblers and nitpickers was someone calling themselves "Aqua,"
who wanted to test the city's ambition. Canals were nice, but harbors were a more
natural and expansive improvement. If the city built a lock on the Allegheny
side, it could pass boats along the sides of any of the bridges already stretching
between Pittsburgh and its sister city to the north, down to the waiting harbor.
John's rivals for the contract also raised their voices in the pages of the press.[36]
Mr. Jacob Guiser, having deposited a scale model of his plan at the mayor's office two weeks earlier, entered into "the controversy" in the pages of the *Gazette*.
Guiser had spoken with "some of our best Merchants" and decided that an aqueduct made of Butler iron stiffened with timber could be placed on the existent piers quite safely and for the low price of forty thousand dollars. Such a
structure would be stiffer "than the complicated wood frame work proposed by
Mr. Roebling, hung upon elastic wire cables." Guiser's correspondence elicited
no reply. Perhaps John was too busy preparing for a meeting in Harrisburg, or
maybe he instinctively knew not to argue with fools in public, especially after
Guiser tried to school John on the difference between iron chains and suspension cables, all of which was a little like telling a carpenter how to saw wood.[37]

Thomas Weston Glisby submitted a plan that called for the suspension of
the floor only, while John's called for suspending the floor and the sides. What
this would look like, Glisby failed to say. "I only mention it as a curious circumstance that he should have hit upon the same idea [as me] in re-modeling his
original design," he remarked. Glisby's most compelling qualification was his
having been "professionally engaged" during the erection of Captain Samuel
Brown's Brighton Chain Pier in 1823. Glisby regularly visited the pier during
storms and was often "obliged to cling to the railing in order to save [himself]
from being prostrated on the platform of the pier, which would rise and fall like
a ship in a troubled sea." Had the pier's suspension system been made of iron
wires, asked Glisby, what "would have been the result"? Immediate destruction,
as soon as one of those storms arrived, which may have been one of the reasons
Glisby failed to secure the contract. Wire cables looked light and delicate, but
they could easily do the work of the iron chains used by Brown. Plus, as every
serious engineer knew, the Brighton Chain Pier had fallen down in a gale, not
once but twice.[38]

———

On August 12, 1844, James Clarke, John's recent supporter in the cause of wire
ropes, convened the Canal Board in Harrisburg. Clark presented a communication from William Galloway, along with John's twenty-eight-page plan and

a scale model he had built in Saxonburg to illustrate the principles behind his design. The board examined the plan and the model. They listened to John's "explanations in relation thereto" and asked questions, after which the matter was referred to William Foster. Foster recommended that the board approve the plan—with modifications, mainly concerning the rebuilding of the piers—and proceed with construction as soon as possible. The board unanimously resolved to adopt Foster's findings. The job was to be completed by April 1, 1845. Sixteen years after designing his first suspension bridge, John was finally given the go-ahead to build one.[39]

John's bid for the Allegheny Aqueduct was the lowest, but his proposal was also the most impressive and precise. It was obvious to everyone that John knew exactly what he was talking about. As described by Herbertus Cummings, in its "exactitude of statement" and "complete coverage of every problem," "a fine simplicity of eloquence inheres in" John's proposal. He "was convinced; he wrote convincingly," Cummings adds; "words and tables, every one a prelude to the other, converged all to one purpose. His design was revolutionary [yet] his precision and his candor were the attributes of a genuine conservative mind." John also promised to have the aqueduct functioning by the beginning of the canal season, which was vital. Time was of the essence, the stakes were high, and the problems many, but thirty-eight-year-old John had prepared for this his entire adult life. He knew bridges: he knew wooden bridges, cable bridges, stone piers, abutments; he knew metal and wire; he knew load-bearing capacity and displacement theory. He was more than ready and resolutely self-confident.[40]

John's plan was in many respects a mirror image of the original structure: a huge wooden trunk hung from suspension cables—rather than large wooden arches—which was an adroit way to present it. In essence, John sold a revolutionary new form as a mere upgrade. In its details, John's plan called for the removal of the old wooden structure, the rebuilding of the old piers, the erection of the stone pyramids upon those piers (over which the two great suspension cables would snake), the digging and setting of the huge anchorages that would receive and anchor the cables, the in-situ spinning of two huge suspension cables, the mounting of iron saddles on the tops of the pyramids that cradled the cables, the fixing of double-rod suspenders that would rest on the cables and receive the weight of the water in the massive trunk, and the construction of a huge wooden trunk designed to hold two thousand tons of water, with its understructure of beams, struts, and stringers.[41]

The weight of the structure was borne from beneath and above. The rebuilt piers would sustain the weight of the massive wooden trunk; the cables would carry the weight of the water. The great trunk itself was to be made of two courses of 2½-inch white pine, laid to form a tight lattice. "The stiffness of the trunk will be sufficient to prevent vibration, even in the most violent storms,"

John asserted, in contrast to Ellet's Schuylkill Bridge, which did shake the ankles somewhat. The span was designed to be self-supporting when empty, meaning it would solve a serious problem: excess weight on the piers, leading to the slow disintegration of the foundations on which the trunk sat. The use of suspension cables would, in short, allow for a much lighter wooden structure. The trunk had only to be watertight and to carry its own weight. In addition, the inclusion of canal boats to this balancing act would have no effect on the structure. The weight of the boat would never equal the weight of the water displaced, thus keeping the whole structure in equilibrium. Plus, as would become John's trademark, the overall load-bearing capacity of his span massively exceeded what was required. This meant that the aqueduct wasn't a true suspension bridge but more of a wooden truss/suspension hybrid. The cables didn't support the roadway, which was self-supporting; they supported the water. In the winter, when the flume was drained, the cables performed no function.[42]

John designed and built four more aqueducts over the next eight years, all of them based largely on his Allegheny design. His underlying principles seemed to emerge fully formed in the details of his first creation, which is hardly surprising considering that John had been thinking about suspension bridges for almost twenty years. That said, his design was tweaked during development and planning, going through four distinct phases. In the first phase of design, John confronted the span's main problem: accounting for the massive weight of water concentrated in the center of the trunk when the means of carrying that weight were isolated at the edges. Added to this was the problem of achieving sufficient strength and rigidity in a structure made primarily of wood, not the strongest or stiffest material. John initially designed thick beams—forty inches deep—to undergird the trunk and transfer the huge weight of the water to the suspension points at the edge of the trunk. In the next incarnation, the beams were lengthened while diagonal struts were added to better transfer weight from the middle to the outer portion of the span. By the time John got to his third round of revisions, he had added Egyptian Revival towers and reworked the struts as a double bowstring, which increased the overall strength but reduced stiffness. John's final design, accepted "as part of the agreement of 28 August 1844," was altogether different from its predecessors, as if John fiddled then scrapped the whole thing and started again. Having failed to find an acceptable, foolproof manner of transferring weight across such a distance, he made the eminently sensible decision to just reduce the distance. Or, if he couldn't bring the weight to the cables, he'd bring the cables to the weight. He discarded the idea of fixing the suspension points to the outer ends of the floor beams—outside the towpath, at the very edge of the aqueduct—and instead fastened them snugly to the sides of the trunk, inside the towpath. This reduced the length of the supporting beams from twenty-eight to eighteen feet and increased the structure's load-bearing capacity by 250 percent. Opposing diagonal bracing struts, cantilevering out in a V shape, further helped transfer weight to the suspension points, from both the water in the trunk and the towpaths. The flume's metal plating and the Egyptian motif were lost to thrift.[43]

John's plan was "a combination [of] *great strength, stiffness, safety, durability* and *economy*," he reported in the press shortly after his final plan was finalized. The whole enterprise would not prove overly costly. "I have estimated, and I am willing to undertake a thorough repair of the piers and abutments for $7,000," which "adding to . . . the expense of the new structure, of $56,000" left the city with a bill of only $63,000. This, John argued, was "a very small sum indeed for a work of such magnitude . . . the first of the kind ever attempted." John was also at pains to stress the degree to which the bridge would be "a permanent work." "All the wooden parts, the trunk and the beams can at any time be substituted by iron ones, so as to render the whole structure imperishable."[44]

"Mr. Roebling . . . appears to have thoroughly investigated everything likely to have any bearing on the success of this new and—as we think—great improvement on the ordinary wooden aqueducts of this country," editorialized the *Railroad Journal*, whose only regret was that the older and more established

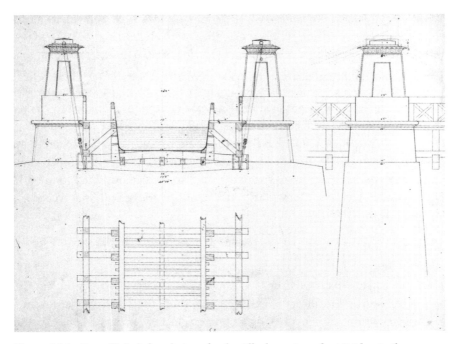

Figure 10.1 One of John's first designs for the Allegheny Aqueduct Bridge, in the Egyptian style (1844). Courtesy of the Institute Archives and Special Collections, Rensselaer Polytechnic Institute.

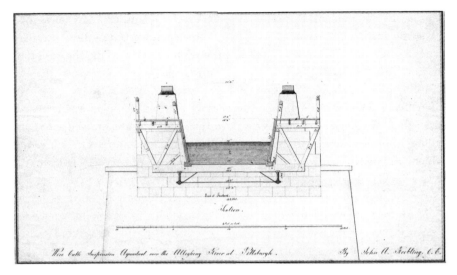

Figure 10.2 John's final design for the Allegheny Aqueduct Bridge, with the towpaths moved outside of the cables (1844). Courtesy of the Institute Archives and Special Collections, Rensselaer Polytechnic Institute.

Jervis hadn't considered a similar structure for traversing the Harlem River—a tidal strait, despite its name—when designing the Croton Aqueduct. Jervis went with a massive stone arch bridge—the iconic High Bridge (1837–48)—in the process spending a somewhat staggering $836,613 and taking almost twelve years for construction. Of course, the High Bridge was a much longer, more complex structure than John's Allegheny Aqueduct, but the comparison is instructive. Roebling's suspension plan belonged to the future, while Jervis's stone arch bridge belonged to the past. Still, Jervis wanted permanence—fearing fire, rot, high winds, and salt-water corrosion—and he achieved it. Despite his retrograde plans, and perhaps because he lavished so much time and money on his span, Jervis's massive masonry bridge outlasted John's first effort by many decades. Remarkably, eleven of the bridge's original arches are still in place today.[45]

John returned to Pittsburgh from Harrisburg to find a city defined by fire, smoke, work, and noise. Pittsburgh "is without question the blackest place which I ever saw," wrote Anthony Trollope a few years later. Journalist James Parton concurred: "Every street appears to end in a huge black cloud"; the whole city seemed like "Hell with the lid taken off." Alexander Mackay complained that "the dingy and sickly character of the vegetation in the immediate vicinity; the fresh green leaf and the delicate flower" were thoroughly "begrimed . . . by the smoke and soot with which the whole atmosphere is impregnated." The Reverend B. F. Tefft, writing just after John completed the Allegheny Aqueduct, believed that "Pittsburgh . . . is a sort of United States smokehouse, large enough to accommodate the government . . . and all the people, from the Rio Grande to Eastport." All citizens of the city look "sallow and baconish," he added.[46]

Pittsburgh's population had doubled to almost forty thousand since John arrived in the region, but little else had improved, especially its appearance. The "helter-skelter architecture of the place" looked like "an individual with a brick in his hat," while "the animal life of Pittsburgh's streets was a never ending source of wonder." The streets themselves were "seas of polluted mud where hogs and dogs ran wild." Even this "animal life" was thought to resent the amount of mud in the "humorously termed streets . . . where they stick fast [and] squeal like other irate citizens." Subsequently, the city enacted legislation banning wild pigs in the streets after a number of vicious attacks on children. True to John's predictions, Pittsburgh was a burgeoning boom town. All the abundance and the raw materials of western Pennsylvania flowed relentlessly into Pittsburgh to be shaped, honed, molded, and then released in a cascade of goods and waste, seemingly in equal amounts.[47]

Needless to say, Pittsburghers took their work very seriously. Everyone, it seemed, realized their opportunities and the potential price of failure. "Joking among men of business, especially in business hours, was well nigh as irreverent as would have been the singing of 'Yankee Doodle' in the First Presbyterian Church on Sunday." The city was celebrated as the "Birmingham of America," which came with myriad problems, most of which would have been obvious to anyone who had actually visited Birmingham. For one, the city was growing too quickly for its infrastructure to keep up. There were few paved roads, no gas lamps, and almost no sewage systems or fresh water, which was a huge problem in the early spring when the snow thawed, the rains came, and the city was suddenly flooded with all manner of nasty effluents. Along with waste in the streets came sickness and disease. The city experienced frequent outbreaks of cholera and typhus, which did not seem to halt the city's massive population growth. Pittsburgh had dirt, disease, and child-eating pigs, but it also had a diversified economy and jobs.[48]

John was the perfect engineer for the job, but he was also in the perfect place: Pittsburgh was just about the best place in the United States to build a modern bridge. The region could supply raw materials in abundance: lumber of all shapes and sizes, iron and alloys of all grades and compounds, and enough coal to keep John's "smithy fires" burning for two hundred days straight. The city and its surrounding regions were home to dozens of ironworks that churned out screws, rivets, wire, nails, rods, and tools by the thousands. Most importantly, the city was packed with an excess of skilled workers and day laborers. It was a city primed for—and adaptable to—industrial innovation: original structures built by ingenious engineers out of new materials. John knew perfectly well how to build his aqueduct, but he was successful because he had easy access to the right things and the right people.

———

John arrived in Pittsburgh at the end of August 1844. Over the next several days, he directed the slow marshalling of forces: the assembling of craftsmen, carpenters, stonemasons, and day laborers; of horses, derricks, carts, workstations, smithies, wood, and splicing shops. One imagines him staring out at the Allegheny: at the broken and ruined old aqueduct, hanging and sagging over the wide river; at the weight of the water straining against the locks, waiting for the work to be done and its energy let loose; at the desperate need to connect the two arms of the canal reaching out to the river, a quarter of a mile apart, then halted; about to unleash a stack of men and machines upon the riverside. Behind him was the bustle of Pittsburgh and the Canal Basin, now silent but formerly a watery town square, choked with canal boats delivering a host of goods and foodstuffs. The streets fronting and surrounding the basin were normally a chaos of noise and activity. Over 120 boats trafficked between Pittsburgh and Johnstown, employing between eight hundred and nine hundred men. "About the docks of these odiferous havens of bilge water," reports one historian, "gathered the offices and warehouses of those whose business was the handling of goods that traveled by the 'raging canawl,'" around which proliferated a multitude of hotels, rooming houses, and laboring men's homes. During the spring of 1839, fourteen hundred canal boats arrived at the Canal Basin carrying a total freight of twenty-five thousand tons.[49]

John woke each morning before dawn, just as the noisy drama of life in Pittsburgh was beginning. By six o'clock, as John strode off to the riverfront, the roar of the city was rising. Factories were open and in operation. Shops and markets were unshuttered and stocked. People and produce poured into the city from the surrounding countryside, arriving at the Monongahela Wharf, a buzzing storehouse of all the city's saleable goods and unruly energies. On a normal day, "boxes, bales, barrels, and other freight were piled six feet high on the bank and in front of the stores on Water Street, sometimes for the greater part of the mile from Try Street to the Point. The low two-wheeled, one horse drays then in use clattered over the cobblestones, and long cues of negro 'mudsills' droned their minor refrains while they carried boxes and barrels to or from the waiting steamboats." It was nothing for thirty different steamboats to arrive at the wharf in a single day.[50]

Work started in earnest on September 2 with the delivery of two huge wooden logs. This was soon followed by a delivery of spades, picks, and a massive block and tackle. On September 8 followed more raw lumber, along with cement, posts, anchor chains, 1,040 feet of cut oak timber, crane masts, nails, assorted tools, and equipment of all descriptions. The area soon began to resemble the great city just to the south, as if all the energy of Pittsburgh had expanded north, bringing with it all the noise and bustle of industrial activity. As Sam Wickersham was at pains to remind readers of *Scientific American* many years later: all the "work in the shop [during the construction of John's first span] was done principally by hand. The slide rest was a novelty, and the straight edge and steady eye and hand turned out the piston rod. Screws were still cut in the lathe by hand. The whip saw was used to cut the floor beams of the aqueduct in 1844. The trip hammer was still doing its noisy work, afterwards so effectively silenced by the squeezer. The canal boat controlled the freight traffic between West and East, and steel was almost among the precious metals."[51]

John's first task was to plant the anchorages. So while all the tools, tackle, and materials for the rest of the job were being delivered to the worksite, an assortment of laborers started to dig. They dug four massive holes, two on either side of the shore, and by the end of September the anchorages were finished and ready to receive their cargo. At the bottom of each hole was placed a massive six-foot-square, two-inch-thick, cast iron anchor plate, with six openings to accommodate the first links in the six anchor chains. The plate was fixed in position and covered in timber and cement. As more links were added to the anchor chains, cement and stone were added, and as the masonry in the holes built up, more chains were added to form a slow curve reaching up from the anchor plate to the surface, where they met the suspension cables. The anchorages were filled with stone and cement so as to completely "exclude air and moisture effectually."[52]

John's main concerns were rust and corrosion. Both would be impossible to detect once the anchorages were sealed, yet either could bring the whole structure down. To this end, John "executed with scrupulous care" the filling of the anchorages. John mixed "lime mortar" into the rubble that bound the plate and chains to the bottom of the anchorages to stop any moisture finding its way beneath ground and to "add another calcareous coating to the iron." He even made sure that the only wood to come into contact with the anchor chains was pine. John worried that the tannic acid present in oak might cause corrosion. All together "700 perches of masonry" (approximately 17,500 cubic feet)—all tightly compacted and kept in place by John's mortar—was jammed into the anchorages, or roughly twice the resistance needed to counter the cables (110 tons), the trunk (97 tons), and the water (2,100 tons).[53]

Meanwhile, another gang was out in the river removing the broken old span and rebuilding the piers. John elected to use Laurel Hill sandstone—"the hardest and best sandstone which can be had"—for the repairs and for constructing the "pyramids" that would sit upon the piers and carry the cables. The stone was quarried, cut, and delivered by Andrew Smith of Allegheny between October 7 and December 14, 1844. The pyramids themselves comprised three separate sandstone blocks of decreasing size, all fixed and grouted using a mixture of equal parts Johnstown cement and lime. The total height was 4 feet 5 inches, with base area of 6½ feet by 4 feet rising to a narrower 5 feet by 3 feet. The sloping inner wall was designed to fit snuggly against the outer wall of the flume. On top of each pyramid was fixed a grooved iron saddle that would guide and carry the cables. Once finished, the pressure on the piers would be twelve tons per square foot, and "it would require ten times this pressure to affect at all a Laurel Hill stone," John confidently predicted.[54]

The effort to haul the stones off the delivery carts, ship them out to the middle of the river, and hoist them up to the waiting piers was immense. Capstans and derricks—both operated by hand—were used to drag the massive stones up to the waiting stonemasons, which was a slow and tedious operation, especially in winter. Strained muscles, bruised hands, broken bones, and the occasional disfigured digit were the norm, as were subzero temperatures, glacial winds, and driving sleet. The task took months. Having begun at the beginning of October, John and his crew were still at it in December as the days were shortening and the temperatures dropping. As he wrote to Archbald, "I will be done with the stone work by the middle of next month and then commence with the formation of the Wire Cable which will be a very considerable job as it will require about 165 ton of wire." John still hoped to have the aqueduct "ready for navigation by next April."[55]

There was little respite for John's crew once the piers were finished. Not only were the working conditions extremely difficult, but the project also involved numerous operations that were new to everyone. To this was added the problem that the Allegheny Aqueduct was not John's only responsibility. He was simultaneously keeping the Portage Railroad supplied with wire ropes. Orders for two new portage ropes arrived in early January just as John was waist-deep in his first span and about to start spinning the suspension cables. John replied that he couldn't possibly get these new ropes made and shipped to the mountain before the middle of March, which turned out to be a problem. The ropes currently in place weren't fit to raise a single car, and the portage was hoping to open for business on March 10 at the latest. Like a blown bulb on a set of Christmas lights, a single shuttered portage plane would short the entire Main Line circuit, depriving the state of much-needed toll revenue and delaying all trans-state traffic. "Do the best you can for us but for God's sake don't keep us back," pleaded the official. John, of course, understood the absolute urgency of the appeal, and he didn't, managing to fulfill the request before the portage opened.[56]

John's success was of his own design, but the burden was shouldered by a small army of laborers, craftsmen, supervisors, and assistants. Without a skilled, adaptable crew, John's genius might never have emerged, nor might his first bridge have been realized. Despite the verdicts of his son and of history, that John was ferocious and intractable in all things, he seems to have treated his crew with respect and goodwill. It would be hard to imagine any success at the Allegheny without a large measure of trust and confidence between the chief engineer and his team. John was extremely lucky to have a fleet of helpers used to working with wire rope, having brought many of his Saxonburg people to help spin, splice, and bind the suspension cables. Their skill and experience, as much as John's inventive genius, lay behind the successful completion of John's first bridge.[57]

Needless to say, there were exceptions to John's seemingly nurturing leadership. John chose Jonathan Rhule, one of the state's foremost master carpenters, as one of his principal assistants, and they did not get on. Rhule was "a man of rather positive character—too much for my father," Washington wrote, and they argued frequently, often publicly, which didn't stop John from rehiring Rhule two years later on a different project, although it did not work out any better. By 1849, John was writing to his principal assistant, "If Jonathan Rhule should come" looking for work, "I wish you to say as little to him as you can in relation to me & the works. He is already an *Ellet man* and I do not want any news carried between myself & Mr. Ellet. Ellet has promised Rhule work for no other reason but because I discharged him." On subsequent projects, John employed Jonathan's "gentle," meeker brother David. John's disastrous association with Jonathan Rhule, however, led him to one of the master carpenter's own assistants, "a bright black haired rosy cheeked chap named Charles Swan." Swan "distinguished himself [in John's eyes] by his daring, his handiness, adaptability to all kinds of work, and the good natured honesty which characterizes the German," and John singled him out. Swan was soon dispatched to Saxonburg to oversee the manufacture of John's portage ropes and by the 1850s was established as John's right-hand man, in charge of his entire rope-making enterprise. "The mutual respect and esteem and the implicit confidence and trust which my father reposed in him grew with age," wrote John's son, "and only ended with his life."[58]

Thirty-five men made up John's cable-making crew, and they began work in early January, just as John's portage orders were coming in. One hundred and sixty gallons of linseed oil were delivered on January 3, closely followed by several huge coils of iron wire. Wickersham delivered 104,000 lbs. of no. 10 wire and 6,725½ lbs. of no. 14 wire over the next two months, while Robert Townsend delivered 100,246½ lbs. of no. 10 wire and 3,440 lbs. of no. 14. All this wire and oil fed John's cable making, piece by piece and splice by splice.[59]

The secret to successful suspension cables is creating and maintaining uniform tension, which is where John secured his first great innovation. Unlike the system used by Ellet on the Schuylkill Bridge, which used pre-spun, preassembled cables hauled to the bridge site, hoisted into position, hung over the towers, and anchored at ground level, John elected to lay out his cables in situ, spinning his cables up over the river between the two great anchorages. The process was much more difficult and much more dangerous, but it made for a significantly stronger and more secure structure. To run out his cables, John made a two-thousand-foot stranded rope in Saxonburg and spliced it to form a huge continuous loop, so it could function as a traveler rope. The great wire

Figure 10.3 John's right-hand man for the last twenty-five years of his life: Charles Swan (n.d.), from Hamilton Schuyler, *The Roeblings* (1931).

loop was then mounted on a pair of horizontal grooved wheels, one on either side of the river. The wheels were themselves placed on nine-foot-high poles, to which was hitched a horse. As the horse walked in a circle around the pole, the system rotated, moving the traveler wire around the horizontal wheels. At opposing points on the traveler rope were mounted wooden traveling wheels, their "rims furnished with a large groove made of sheet tin" that ran out wire over the piers. At the end of a run over the river, the wire was looped through the anchor chains—themselves attached to the massive anchor plate at the very bottom of the anchorage—and sent back over the river, moving back and forth across the river laying out wire to form a mighty cable, anchored firmly on either side of the river. This system maintained uniform tension in the wires. The traveler went back and forth almost a thousand times before sufficient wire was in place to form the two cables.[60]

Needless to say, manufacturing a single length of wire sufficiently long to run over the river and back a thousand times was impossible. To this end, wires were made in sections of around 620 feet and spliced together at the riverside. John had experimented with wire splices on the Portage Railroad and, after several initial missteps, had a good sense of what he was doing. He first experimented with a "pressure weld,'" annealing the wire for about three to six inches on each side of the intended splice, "twisting them around each other in a spiral manner, while held in a vise, and then squeezing the joint straight and round," but seems to have found it less than satisfactory. He then ditched twisting the wires themselves and added an external wrapping. As described by a reporter for the *Pittsburgh Morning Chronicle*, "The splices of the wire are made by [filing the two ends to increase friction], placing the two ends together," and winding fine annealed wire around them. "It is done so strongly, that sufficient force will break the wire, but will not affect the splice."[61]

The wires then had to be gathered, ordered, and wrapped into a single cable. For this part of the process, John used the cable wrapping device featured in his 1842 patent. At the center of John's invention was a cast iron tube, or sheath. It enclosed the cluster of individual strands and moved along the entire length of the cable by means of a winding mechanism operated by hand. As the wires entered the sheath, they were compressed and ordered into a tight cylinder. As the wires emerged at the rear of the sheath, they were tightly wrapped in a continuous covering of soft annealed wire. As the wrapping device was turned around the cable, it fed wires in one end and wrapped them at the other, all in proportion. The wrapping was then painted to create a hermetically sealed, weather-resistant cover. As with John's method of running out wires, this process was a great innovation with a tremendous shelf life.[62]

On January 23, 1845, the *Morning Post* reported that John had been engaged in spinning the cables "for some days" and that all was proceeding well. The

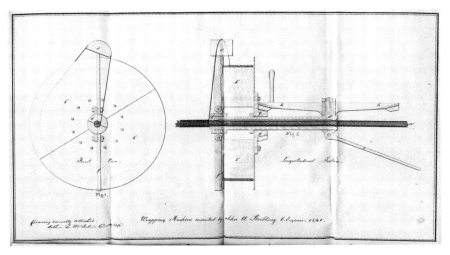

Figure 10.4 John's cable wrapping device, invented in 1842. Courtesy of the Institute Archives and Special Collections, Rensselaer Polytechnic Institute.

woodwork for the trunk was "nearly all framed and ready for putting together," and John was hoping to be finished by March 1, a full month ahead of schedule. "The new aqueduct will be a great work," they continued, "creditable to the ingenious builder, and of the utmost importance to the prosperity of Pittsburgh. Its completion will be hailed as a memorable and joyful event, by all who wish our city well." The trunk was still not in place by the end of February when a staff writer for the *Pittsburgh Chronicle* visited the worksite. The writer's report was subsequently picked up by a number of publications, hinting at the significant interest shown in John's work, not just by the residents of Pittsburgh but by the engineering community too. The initial reaction was positive, at least according to the *Chronicle*'s reporter. John had "labored with the utmost perseverance, day and night," for the whole winter in an effort to get the structure finished by April 1. Admittedly, he was not likely to get it done, but "the contractor" had clearly "done everything in his power to have the Aqueduct finished" on time. As of February 25, almost half of the wire strands had been stretched over the river, and another was due to be finished that very day, after which the cables would be wrapped and painted and made "impervious to water and . . . not liable to be weakened or impaired by the weather." The trunk—so "independent, strong and immovable [a] structure" that "the aqueduct will not be . . . moved either from the swell of water or the effect of storms"—would then be laid out and fixed in position. John's "labor and energy," the reporter concluded, were "impressive."[63]

John finished spinning the cables in early March, and the results were huge and impressive. The Allegheny Aqueduct had seven suspended spans, which were held up by two cables, one on each side. Each cable was composed of 1,900 wires, spliced together and run continuously between the anchorages, varnished to prevent oxidation, gathered tightly together, and wrapped "in the most perfect manner" with no. 14 annealed wire to form large round cables. The result was 1,175 feet long (from anchorage to anchorage), weighed two hundred thousand pounds, and was seven inches in diameter. The cable spinning went well and proceeded on time, although John later discussed how difficult this was, especially the effort to achieve uniform "parallelism": "The wires composing the cables are laid parallel to each other, so that each single wire will occupy the same relative position throughout the whole length. . . . If the wires cross each other, or are tight at one place and slack at the other, their tension will not be uniform. . . . Simple as are the principles involved in this process, its practice is by no means so simple. To produce a uniform tension throughout, means to make every wire do its allotted duty. Any attempt at the manufacture of a 12 inch cable in one process," for example, "no matter what its length, would result in a complete failure. It is simply impossible to do."[64]

With the anchorages dug and secured, the piers stabilized and rebuilt, and the wires spun and hung, all that remained was to construct and position the trunk. Physically, the flume was essentially a large, open-ended wooden box, 1,140 feet long, 8½ feet deep, and 16½ feet wide at the top, or wide enough to allow one boat to pass, meaning there would be one-way traffic in and out of Pittsburgh. All three sides were made with two layers of 2½-inch-thick white pine planking, positioned in a diagonal lattice formation and held together by side posts and a frame so as to make the structure self-supporting. Huge inverted U-shaped suspension rods were mounted on cast iron saddles, hung over the cables, and run down to the understructure. Pairs of twenty-seven-foot-long timber beams were bolted to these rods to form a secure foundation. The trunk lay on these beams, and the result would have looked much like a series of plank and rope swings running the length of the span. John was at great pains to design and build a structure that would avoid the problems of its predecessor, namely, that a fault in one span would compromise any other spans. "The stiffness and rigidity of the structure is so great, that no doubt is entertained, that each of the several [spans] would sustain *itself*, in case the woodwork of the next one adjoining should be consumed by fire. The woodwork in any of the arches separately may be removed and substituted by new material, without effecting [*sic*] the equilibrium of the next one," John confidently predicted. Seven-foot-wide towpaths were constructed on either side of the finished trunk, and the entire thing was caulked with oakum to prevent leaks.[65]

As with every other aspect of the work, the business of construction was laborious and difficult. It was begun in February with the delivery of 3,200 pounds of caulking thread and 1,070 screw bolts and nuts, followed by twenty-four barrels of pitch and seventy pounds of coal tar, not to mention thousands of feet of lumber. Much of the work was done on the banks of the Allegheny: the lumber sized and cut, the suspension rods turned and molded into shape by a smith. The metalwork was demanding, but at least those laborers had the comfort of working by the heat of the forge. No such warmth greeted those working out over the river hoisting and manhandling long planks and huge twenty-seven-foot beams into place, undertaking precise tasks with small screws and nails—all with frostbitten hands—or balancing on constantly moving boats pushed and tugged by the fast-flowing Allegheny or cast about mercilessly by ice floes and spring freshets. The river work was arduous and onerous, but it was dangerous too, and capricious. Often, it seemed, a fatal accident was only a step or two away. In early March, two German brothers who were employed in the wood shops, "drove to the Allegheny at the foot of Wayne Street, with a load of shavings. They went further into the water than they should have done, when the horses lost their footing, and the wagon broke in pieces. One brother was riding one of the horses, but he got off in order to attempt to save the other." Both were swept away and their bodies discovered several days later downstream. All in all, according to Washington, "seven persons lost their lives that winter, mostly from accidental drowning, some of them Saxonburgers."[66]

———

As spring arrived, the snow and sleet gradually petered out and the rains refused to come. A long drought gripped Pittsburgh through the early weeks of the spring, drying the city out and depleting its reservoir. While the precipitation ceased, the awful winds of winter were less subdued. Gusty winds blew around Pittsburgh through March and into April, wreaking havoc with John's work. Screws, nails, and tacks rolled around the worksite, while wooden planks flapped and flew. John woke on the morning of April 10 to find little changed. The day was as dry as a bone and still blowing a gale, but it was warmer than it had been and pleasant, just such a day "as occasionally is sandwiched between the rough days which in general mark [the Pittsburgh] spring." John spent the morning on the Pittsburgh side of the Allegheny, directing the construction of the trunk. All was proceeding well until just after noon, when a cry suddenly rang out from the Canal Basin. A massive fire had broken out across town and, fanned by the high winds, was spreading rapidly, "like a vast flood," according to one witness. Within moments came screams and panic and strife. The city was ablaze. Life in Pittsburgh would never be the same, and neither would John's career.[67]

Rebuilding Pittsburgh (1845–46)

The Great Fire of 1845 started around noon on the southeast corner of Second and Ferry Streets. Accounts differ on what was actually burning—an icehouse, a large pile of wood shavings, or an old shed—but it soon got out of hand. After weeks of high winds and drought, Pittsburgh, a town made primarily of wood, was as dry as a bone while its reservoirs were dangerously low. William Johnson ran out from his office upon first hearing the alarm and followed the fire trucks. He watched the firemen get in position "within a few feet of the burning shanty," and stood aghast as "a weak sickly stream of muddy water, powerless against the mad flames" trickled out. Robert McKnight—who began his diary entry for the day with the wonderfully pithy "GREAT FIRE!!!! CONFLAGRATION!!!!!!!!!"—also "heard alarm bells ring for fire" at noon and "followed the crowd." "A pretty strong wind was blowing from the West," he reported, "and some alarm existed as to the spread of the flames." The presence of the fire crews calmed the crowds, until "the supply of water failed" and "the destroying element raged towards Market Street." A city surrounded by rivers found itself in the rather embarrassing position of not having enough water with which to fight a fire, at which point they feared "the city was doomed to destruction."[1]

Pittsburgh could have quelled the fire had it had sufficient water, but no: aided by gale-force winds, the flames jumped across the street to Captain Wood's Globe Cotton Factory, which went up like a bonfire. From Wood's factory, the flames "danced from roof to roof . . . hissing across as if eager for their prey." In the blink of an eye, much of the area from Third Street to the river was "a sea of flame," reported the *Gazette*. By two o'clock "the fire had become ungovernable," sweeping across much of the southern and eastern part of the city, while "the arm of man was impotent."[2] The fire and the wind were perfectly placed to produce a wholesale catastrophe. Kindled near the head of the city's point, the conflagration was blown by strong easterly winds back toward the fan of the triangle, leaping from building to building and street to street in what seemed like a headlong gallop to the rear of the city. The fire spread so "fearfully rapid" that many residents had no time to remove their goods from their homes. Others managed to remove their goods only to see the flames come along, seize them on the street, and burn them up before their eyes. The city even dynamited entire rows of houses in an effort to isolate and hopefully stop the conflagration. This stemmed the tide somewhat but didn't halt it. The city's gasworks went up in flames, ensuring the city would lie in darkness once the flames died down. More symbolically, the Monongahela House, one of America's great hotels, "defended by high walls and covered with an iron roof, fell before the flames like a reed."[3]

"People were running in all directions wild with excitement," Johnson wrote that night in his diary, while "cinders and burning shingles were falling every-where, setting fire to everything combustible." William Brackenridge, a resi-dent of the Monongahela House at the time, fled north to Allegheny City and watched the destruction. The flames were "like a blow torch driving a sheet of flame three hundred yards wide," he remarked. Others hid, climbed, or just ran. Thomas Mellon watched as the fire "surged like a vast flood" over Pittsburgh. "People were running in all directions wild with excitement," he recalled. From the height of the courthouse he watched the Smithfield Street Bridge burn down, "the flames running and crackling along it with railroad speed." Watching "one span speedily falling into the river after another like a rope on fire . . . was a grand and imposing sight," he concluded with no small amount of awe.[4]

The fire raged on at its height from about two to four o'clock, sweeping east and northeast across the city. After gobbling up the Monongahela House, the conflagration leaped over the Pennsylvania Canal and descended on Pipetown, a working-class neighborhood that would be almost entirely destroyed. A shift in the wind direction arrived fortuitously about 5:00 p.m., pushing the blaze back on itself. By six o'clock, "fire engines [were] still playing vigorously in Wood Street," according to the *Morning Post*. At the same time, across town, one of the *Gazette*'s senior writers "sat down at their desk with a sad heart to record the most fearful calamity that ever befell any city the size of Pittsburgh." "While we now write an awful fire is raging," he lamented, "consuming the fairest portions of our city, and no human being can tell where it will stay its ravages." The city was in the grip of "fearful ruin," but an hour later, the winds calmed down, and the fire finally fell under the control of the city. The boundaries of the "burnt dis-trict" ran from Water Street up to Diamond Alley and from Ferry Street near the Point to Pipetown at the city's eastern edge. Twenty blocks of the most valuable part of the city, representing two-thirds of its wealth and covering fifty-six acres, were destroyed, while two thousand families were left homeless. Fortuitously, the fire stayed on the Monongahela side of the city, far removed from John, his crew, and his aqueduct.[5]

People wondered in the days afterward how Pittsburgh would ever recover and how such a colossal loss of goods and property could mean anything but ruin and disaster. "TREMENDOUS CONFLAGRATION—Twenty Squares of the

City in Ruins! From 1000 to 1200 Houses Destroyed! Loss Estimated at TEN MILLIONS!" proclaimed the *Morning Post* the next morning. "No description can reach the reality," wrote another newspaper, while Robert McKnight wrote of "the sad spectacle of the fairest portion of our city 'a heap of ruins.'" "It is impossible for any one . . . to give more than a faint idea of the terrible, the overwhelming calamity which then befell our city, destroying in a few hours the labor of many years, and blasting suddenly the cherished hopes of . . . thousands of our citizens," wrote one observer.[6]

Reverend E. P. Swift of Allegheny's First Presbyterian Church was not so sure. He thought that God had "doubtless . . . been greatly displeased with our unthankfulness for His mercies" and visited a fiery plague upon the town.[7] Others were more prosaic in their analysis: Pittsburgh needed to rebuild if it was to avoid falling into permant ruin. The city needed investment. Thankfully, aid poured in from the state legislature and from around the country. All state and mercantile taxes were refunded for that year and abated for a further three years. What had made Pittsburgh great before could easily make it great again. In the following months, massive stores of energy and dedication were devoted to the city and Pittsburgh began anew. "The traces of our disaster are now disappearing before the magic wand of industry and enterprise," wrote Heron Foster later that year. "The blow was stunning," added Sam Wickersham, owner of one of Pittsburgh's largest iron mills, "and for a time it seemed that it would be fatal to our prosperity. But soon, the native energy asserted itself, and the work of restoration commenced." From April 11 onward "the city entered upon a remarkable era of

Figure 11.1 John built his first true suspension bridge on the ruins of the old Monongahela Bridge, after the great fire of 1845. William Coventry Wall and James Fuller Queen, "Great Conflagration at Pittsburgh. View of the Ruins of the City of Pittsburgh from Near Birmingham" (1845), lithography by Wagner & McGuigan Philadelphia. Library of Congress.

development." New businesses quickly replaced old; rickety wooden structures were replaced by more permanent brick buildings. Two hundred new buildings were erected in the burned district in the months that followed the Great Fire, as was a brand-new suspension bridge, designed and built by John.[8]

———

The loss of the Monongahela Bridge was a huge blow to Pittsburgh. Suddenly, the city found itself cut off from its neighbors to the south and, with John's aqueduct still unfinished, cut off from the east too. To make matters worse, the whole city, including the company that owned the bridge, was effectively bankrupt. Still, it didn't take long for the city and the bridge company to make up their mind. On April 20, Andrew B. Stevenson confided to his diary, "I have this day been informed that the Monongahela Bridge is to be rebuilt immediately." Two days later, the rumors were confirmed. Advertisements appeared in all the local papers calling for plans for rebuilding the Monongahela Bridge to be submitted to John Thaw, treasurer of the Bridge Company, by 3:00 p.m. on May 1, 1845. A meeting of the stockholders was also called for April 24 "to take such measures as shall be deemed necessary for the re-building."[9]

How many people could realistically have worked up a solid plan and submitted it within ten days, especially as a large proportion of the city was homeless and lacking such essentials as a desk, paper, or instruments? Luckily, there was a man across town finishing up a similar project who happened to command a whole team of experienced laborers and bridge builders and possess all the requisite equipment. John grasped the opportunity and the urgency and set to work finishing one bridge and planning another. In this, of course, he had numerous allies. Washington believed that "the rebuilding of [the Monongahela Bridge] came to [his father] almost without an effort, most of the directors being his personal friends."[10] This may have been true, but John also was experienced, established, and on site. Plus, he had some help from the press.

The *Morning Post* weighed in on the bridge debate on May 1, the last day for formal submissions, running a long editorial on the subject. "A bridge across the Monongahela is almost indispensible," they declared. It should be "on the most improved and modern plan of construction—one that will combine durability and usefulness, and at the same time be an ornament to the city." The *Post* hoped the span would be both strong and good-looking so as to impress visitors: "Although the bridges which now span our rivers are, without doubt, substantial and excellent of their kind, still it cannot be denied that they present a clumsy and graceless appearance to the observer."[11]

The *Post* was advocating not just a specific approach but a specific person: "We understand that Mr ROEBLING, the skilful constructor of the new Aqueduct . . . will submit a plan. The industry and skill of Mr. ROEBLING, as manifested in the building of the Aqueduct, give him an exalted rank among the most scientific and useful men of our country," they affirmed. "Under the most discouraging circumstances, he has pushed the great public work he is now completing, and has produced a superstructure which, in the opinion of men best able to judge, will establish his fame as an engineer." "The great success of Mr ROEBLING in building the Aqueduct," they continued, "should give him a strong claim on the support of the people of this city, and of those who take pride in its advancement." "The fact that he has his machinery, hands and his tools all on the spot will greatly facilitate his operations," they concluded.[12]

John Thaw, treasurer of the Monongahela Bridge Company, recieved numerous bridge proposals on May 1, including a long one from John.[13] "Sir: I hereby propose to construct a 'Wire Cable Suspension Bridge' on the piers of the old Monongahela bridge and on the accompanying plans and specifications for the sum of $53,500," wrote John, all business. "The bridge, when completed, to be subjected to any test the Company may think proper, for instance a drove of 100 head of cattle on one span without any balance on the adjoining spans, or as many loaded coal trains as can be placed." The bridge, he guaranteed, would be "as stiff as any of the wooden structures on the Allegheny River" and be "completed before the 1st of January 1846." After all, "no other structure can be put up in so short a time."[14]

On May 7, less than a month after the Great Fire and only two and a half weeks after announcing the competition, the directors of the Monongahela Bridge announced they had decided to rebuild the span "on the Wire suspension plan" and award the contract to the man "who has given such general satisfaction in his construction of the Wire Suspension Aqueduct," namely, John A. Roebling. The *Post* approved, of course: "This Bridge, when finished in the style designed by Mr. R., will be an ornament to our city." So did the *Chronicle*: "The old bridge was an unsightly, disagreeable affair, which everybody shunned as much as possible." By contrast, John's new bridge—no doubt "a light, graceful structure, a great benefit to the public"—"will not only be used for crossing the river, but we believe, as a fashionable promenade." The decision was made official at a meeting held at the Allegheny Bridge tollhouse on May 13, 1845, where it was unanimously resolved that the Monongahela Bridge Committee be "directed to conclude the contract with John A. Roebling, agreeably to the terms of his specifications."[15]

In many respects, John's plan and proposal were similar to that he had issued for the aqueduct project: the erection of a multi-span wire suspension bridge—"forming 8 spans of an aggregate length of 1500 feet"—using the piers of a previous structure, in an effort to minimize costs. He also proposed to use "the same plan of repairs which has been applied to the piers of the Aquaduct [*sic*] with the best success" and to construct the entire anchorage on the same plan. In other respects, the plan diverged, starting with the cable structure. Instead of running out a continuous cable from shore to shore, passing over each of the piers, and anchored on either side of the river, John elected for something different: short individual lengths of cable running from pier to pier, attached to and held in place by a pendulum hung from a cast iron tower. The cables of the first and last span were to be "balanced by the load chains, which extend under ground and are anchored to heavy metal plates" in the anchorage. "This arrangement which has been applied by Brunel in several instances successfully," John wrote, "will preserve the stability of the spans in all cases, no matter if any of them are overloaded or not. The equilibrium between adjoining spans will by this means . . . always regulate itself without ever endangering the stability of the cast iron columns, or of the piers. No danger would arise from the burning of the timber in one span, while the next span was loaded," for example.[16] With each span independently supported, the bridge would be easy to repair and difficult to bring down, both prime considerations after the city's recent traumas.[17]

The Brunel John had in mind when writing his proposal was Marc, not his more famous son Isambard. Marc had used this pendulum process to anchor each of the main chains in both of the bridges he designed for the Isle de Bourbon in 1823, allowing them to "play a little lengthwise, to allow of expansion and contraction."[18] As with Brunel's bridges—all the parts of which were made in Sheffield and assembled at the bridge site—John's plan involved significantly more prefabrication than his aqueduct plan. With the frigid, painstaking work of the previous winter still fresh in his mind, John opted to have his cables "made on shore, ready wrapped, put on board boats and raised into their places." The cast iron towers that housed the pendulum system were also manufactured elsewhere. Each cable would contain six hundred wires, and the tension and load-bearing capacity were worked out to easily accommodate "100 head of cattle large and small moving promiscuously" along the span. "It is evident that the Cables as proposed would possess an abundance of strength, and that they would last an unlimited period of time," John declared.[19]

John's other major change would prove more of a lasting innovation than his new cable system. "The greater rigidity and stiffness of the structure will be insured by the application of strong *lattice railings*," he announced, "and by a system of iron stays running in diagonal position from different points on the floor to the cast iron columns and to the pier below the floor." Made of solid iron rods and forming a triangle between themselves, the floor, and the columns, the stays created rigidity and added to the stiffness, triangles being the strongest and most stable geometric shape in engineering. John's stays were attached to the cast iron columns above the road and to the piers below. John never used his new cable system on another bridge, but he used stays on almost every other bridge he built, albeit cable stays rather than solid rod stays. The combination of a strong horizontal truss and diagonal stays would become a hallmark of John's bridges, the stays creating the distinctive web-pattern celebrated by artists and poets.[20]

The most crucial element in John's proposal was the piers. Without a useable base, the project was going nowhere. After all, the bridge company could only just scrape together enough money to get John started and, in fact, were forced to mortgage much future toll revenue in an effort to pay for the project, even with such a scant bid. If they had had to pay for a whole new set of piers, the city would have found itself cut off from the south for the foreseeable future. With this in mind, John took precious time off from his aqueduct to survey the blasted scene and conduct a thorough investigation. The fire damage on the northern piers was noticeable, he concluded, but "not sufficient to impair the solidity of the masonry." The "top masonry on some of the piers and on the Pittsburgh abutment has been injured and partly thrown down by the falling of the burning timbers," he discovered, while the foundations of the piers were all good, as were the icebreakers. In John's opinion, "The old piers and abutments will answer for the support of a suspension bridge." That said, John was at pains to caution that additional repairs might be needed. Who knew what they would find beneath all the "loose material on top of the piers"?[21]

John signed off his proposal with reference to the aesthetics of his project. "In deciding upon a plan of construction some regard should be had to appearance," he insisted. "The basin of the Monongahela at Pittsburgh, one of the most beautiful and most visited spots in North America, should not be disgraced by the unsightly and clumsy appearance of a long wooden box, which obstructs the view of the river above and below, and which induces nobody to walk over for the sake of pleasure. How different will be the effect of a graceful suspension bridge, which would be looked upon as an interesting and novel feature in the scenery. The toll would be enhanced from the fact that many citizens would take an evening stroll on the suspension bridge as a pleasure walk." One might quibble with the idea that the Monongahela wharf was either one of the most beautiful or one of the most visited spots in North America, but not with the rationale for an open, graceful structure, nor with the city's need for a new, airy promenade. Aesthetic appeals played an increasing role in John's evolving ideas on bridge design, as did his sense that bridges were just as important for foot traffic and leisure as they were for trade and commercial traffic.[22]

John supplied a few additional details in a short report written two weeks later and submitted on May 16, 1845, primarily in regard to the cast iron towers and the cables. The towers were to be seventeen feet high and consist of four "pilasters" cast one inch thick, connected by lattice work, the whole resting on a 7½-feet-square casing bolted to the piers. Each column was to be topped by a "frame" for the support of the pendulums and connected to its opposite neighbor on the other side of the bridge by a "beam 16 inches square . . . covered with a coating of pitch, tar and sand and . . . painted in keeping with the columns." Such a beam should last "a great number of years" but could also be replaced "at any time by a new one." Their job was to "insure the lateral stability of the columns," while the cables were "strongly inclined towards each other to brace the bridge horizontally." The cables themselves were to be made from six hundred individual wires, wrapped and finished in a like manner to those used on the aqueduct. They were to be made onshore and hauled to the bridge. The suspenders, like the stays, were made from rigid "round iron" rods, one inch thick and positioned four feet apart.[23]

John was to have the bridge "finished and completed . . . in every way (except painting)" by January 1, 1846, and if it was not finished by then, "the said Roebling shall and will forfeit and pay to said Bridge Company" the sum of $150 per week. For all this, except the painting, John was to receive $47,500, plus the costs of the masonry needed to rebuild the bridge, although not the labor costs. The payment scheme was as complex as the city's post-fire finances and as convoluted as the Bridge Company's economic position. Out of the total, $23,500 was to be paid out in eight semi-annual installments after the "completing and delivery of the Bridge." The rest would be paid by the following method: $2,011 paid for the iron and timber saved from the old bridge; $12,000 paid in the form

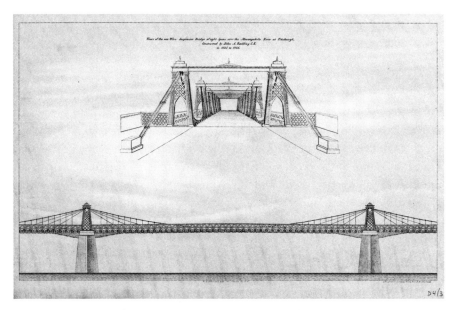

Figure 11.2 "Views of the New Wire Suspension Bridge of Eight Spans over the Monongahela River at Pittsburgh, Constructed by John A. Roebling C.E. in 1845 and 1846." Courtesy of the Institute Archives and Special Collections, Rensselaer Polytechnic Institute.

of 240 shares of stock in the Bank of Pittsburgh, with each share valued at $50; $2,500 paid with fifty shares of Exchange Bank Stock (again valued at $50); and $10,989 in cash. The terms were threadbare and the construction would be exacting, but John was happy for the work and more than grateful for the contract.[24]

———

The Monongahela contract was a major stride forward in John's career and a much-deserved endorsement by the city. Yet John still had to finish his first bridge, and he wasted no time. He and his crew were back at work on April 11, the day after the Great Fire, "putting up the timbers on this indispensable work with great activity," while the city was still shrouded in despair. John's single-minded sense of purpose drove the project forward. He knew the city needed his aqueduct if it was to rebuild quickly. As Washington once remarked, his father "conquered everything with that wonderful personal force, a power that only fed on opposition and knew no defeat."[25] And the city singled John out for praise amid all the ruin and devastation: "All who observe the progress of the work speak warmly in praise of . . . Mr. ROEBLING. His science, skill, and energy are daily made more apparent, and the work will be one of the most remarkable structures ever constructed in the country. . . . Its utility . . . will mark a new era in the construction of aqueducts and bridges"—fine words for a man who was furiously trying to finish one bridge while simultaneously trying to get a contract for another.[26]

On April 23, 1845, the editor of the *Gazette* stopped by to check on the progress. He was "agreeably surprised by the appearance of things." The floor had been laid out as far as the second pier, and everything seemed "ship-shape." Most of Pittsburgh had been so absorbed by the fire, he feared they had "forgotten" about John's aqueduct.[27] The city was in desperate need of goods and raw materials, and it had precious few ways to bring them into the city other than on the canal. Unfortunately, while John and the city were in full agreement on the need for haste and completion, they were also in competition for its small army of laborers. The only major tasks remaining to John were laying and coating the aqueduct's flume, which required a great deal of work but not a great deal of actual skill. Increasingly John found it hard to hire suitable laborers, especially for the more mundane tasks of pitching, caulking, and hauling, which led to delays and frustrations.

By the beginning of May, dozens of Saxonburg residents were in Pittsburgh helping to haul up, hammer down, and otherwise finish John's first bridge. Slowly, the timbers were bound together and the bridge's flume was extended across the Allegheny. The *Morning Post* visited at the end of April and enthused, "This job, when finished, will reflect lasting honor on Mr. ROEBLING . . . and will

settle, not only the practicability of, but the great superiority of the wire suspension Bridge over every other plan." "A large number of our citizens did not believe it practicable, and were strongly averse to the city entering upon what they
considered a very doubtful experiment," they continued, yet "now all are warm
in their admiration of the success that has attended the labors of the enterprising
builder." When completed, the bridge was sure to stand as "a proud monument
of the expansive views of our city authorities and the skill of our architects, mechanics and workmen," not to mention a "source of pride" to Pittsburghers "to
remember that their city was the first to grant . . . encouragement to this system."
They only hoped that "Mr. Roebling may have abundant opportunities to employ his talents [elsewhere] as successfully as he has in the construction of the
Pittsburgh Aqueduct."[28]

The *Gazette* added its own endorsement a few days later: "No one can examine
[John's bridge] without admitting the simplicity of the design, its immense
strength, the completeness of the workmanship, and its perfect adaptedness for
the object designed." The cables were "specimens of the highest perfection"; the
timber work was appropriately "simple" and thankfully lacking "that clumsy appearance which aqueducts supported by wooden arches present." The towpath,
meanwhile, afforded "a delightful promenade, with an unobstructed view up
and down the river." The *Gazette* also spoke to John, who told the paper he was
hoping to let water into the span in eleven days but was having trouble finding
sufficient caulkers to finish the job. Still, amid all the shortages and delays, John's
reputation was booming: "Mr. ROEBLING deserves great credit, both for the
manner in which he has executed his work, and the expedition with which he
has pressed towards completion."[29] By the time the bridge was finally opened,
John was beloved across the city as a problem-solver and facilitator.

The city wanted to mount a public celebration—including a large public
dinner to honor John at the United States Hotel—to open the bridge, but amid
all the upheaval and frenetic rebuilding, fixing the date with any advance notice was almost impossible. The city had to make sure the aqueduct held water
and that boats could float safely across, as well as fend off arsonists. Pittsburgh,
it seems, got a little fire crazy after the great conflagration and found itself
"infested with a gang of incendiaries who are bent on reducing it to ashes," as
the *Baltimore Daily Clipper* described it. A huge blaze broke out across the river
in Allegheny City on May 17, about a month after the Great Fire, wherein "a
vast deal of valuable merchandize, household furniture, mechanics' tolls and machinery were destroyed." The *Indiana State Sentinel* blamed the whole thing on
that "vile set of wretches" the Millerites, a prominent millennial cult believed
that Christ would return to earth in 1843 andthat had just endured the aptly
named "Great Disappointment" when he had failed to show. Others thought
it "undoubtedly the work of an incendiary," and the very next day, a man was

arrested at a building on the corner of Washington Street and Coal Lane trying to set light to a warehouse. Several hours later, "a daring attempt" was made to "fire the Aqueduct at the abutments." Some shavings and a little wood had been collected and placed beneath some of the timbers at the base of the abutment, then set on fire by "some fiend in human shape." Had the "fire been discovered a few moments later, it would have undoubtedly got under such headway as to have rendered it impossible to save the noble structure." A man named Love from Allegheny City was arrested, then bailed and released, oddly enough. One presumes he was watched for a while in case he tried again.[30]

John spent his days running around frantically trying to get everything in working order, all while a full musical band stood by in case they were needed. A certain number of small leaks were to be expected while the wood was thoroughly soaked and allowed to expand, making it difficult to detect what was settling and what was a structural fault, especially at night. John let water into his span at 3:00 p.m. on Friday, May 23, and "a large number of people" showed up in anticipation of something to cheer about, but a breach was discovered at the Pittsburgh end of the abutment. Robert McKnight was in attendance and described the scene: "Water had been passed over & the structure seemed to answer admirably being of a light & pretty finish, airy looking & scarcely leaking a drop—but the abutments on each side leaked copiously." In an effort to resolve the problem, John determined to extend the trunk beyond the abutment on either side. Unfortunately, this would likely take another week, although the aqueduct itself seemed fine, fully watertight, and came "up to the most sanguine expectations of all."[31]

On Monday, June 2, 1845, "the rejoicing up-town was universal" as "about a dozen freight boats belonging to the different lines came over" the aqueduct. A writer for the *Gazette* hopped on a canal boat as it passed by and rode over "Mr. Roebling's noble structure" into Pittsburgh. He was "highly gratified with the compact and solid appearance of the structure"; "it evidences the head and hand of a master of his profession." John was the first to cross over on a packet boat, accompanied by "a band of music." The barge's "appearance on the Pittsburgh side was hailed with cheers from a large concourse of spectators that had assembled to witness the interesting event." After all the hoopla, John, his workmen, and members of the council were invited into the United States Hotel by the owner "to partake of an entertainment which he had prepared for them." Before the evening was out, a committee had been appointed to organize "a more general celebration of the accomplishment of this great work," although nothing further came of it. Pittsburgh was a place of business and repair, not much inclined to celebrating.[32]

Still, no one who witnessed the crossing could doubt that the council made the right choice in picking Roebling for the job. "It is a matter of just pride to

Pittsburgh that, despite all the endeavors of the prejudiced, all the efforts of the interested, and all the fears of the nervous enemies of innovation, she boldly ventured to patronize a man of science and genius, in his efforts to introduce an improvement of immense utility," editorialized the *Morning Post*. "To all but Mr. Roebling, the scheme of a Wire Aqueduct, seemed more or less experimental, while many of those who laid claim to superior scientific knowledge . . . discountenanced the plan, and predicted its entire failure. Under all these circumstances of doubt and discouragement, we repeat, it is a matter of unaffected pride to Pittsburghers, that they stood forth and assisted Mr. Roebling to test his new and wonderful invention." Praise rolled in from across the country and the profession. "All but Charles Ellet Jr. his great rival" acknowledged John's achievement, wrote Washington, although to be fair, Ellet was in Europe at the time and might not have known of John's triumph. Dennis Mahan, a professor of military engineering at the US Military Academy, was so impressed that he included a section on the aqueduct in his new edition of *An Elementary Course in Civil Engineering* (1838), the principal textbook for the Army Corps of Engineers students at West Point. Washington first saw the aqueduct in May 1845. "Although I was only eight years of age, I remember its appearance very well and shall never forget the disagreeable smell left on my country nose by the coal tar with which everything was drenched," he wrote, unwittingly letting slip one of John's few poor decisions. The acid in untreated bituminous coal tar quickly destroys wood.[33]

John's description of his aqueduct in the *Railroad Journal* was almost immediately reprinted all over the engineering world. Even historians were impressed, despite the bridge having accrued little actual history. Dr. Upfold included the span in a list of "the inventions of the age" in a lecture on "The Last Hundred Years" of human progress at the Western University of Pennsylvania's Philomathean Literary Institute. The public was also impressed. As predicted, the aqueduct became a popular place to take a stroll; the *Chronicle* even proposed installing gaslights on the bridge so people could safely walk over after dark. The bridge became a favorite walk for Robert McKnight, who often took himself to the "airy" span for an evening walk, even before it was formally opened. "It had just been so far completed as to admit of pedestrian crossing and a great crowd availed themselves of the privilege," he wrote on May 4. "It is apparently a substantial well-finished work & does great credit to the city & the architect Mr. Roebling." Hundreds of others took McKnight's lead and helped make the bridge not just an economic blessing but a social good: an escape from the heat and the rising fumes of an increasingly smoky city.[34]

The aqueduct's total cost was $58,297, leaving John with only a sliver of the compensation he had expected from the project, especially as he had served as both contractor and engineer. Washington reckoned his father made $3,500 from the job, although it was more like $1,700. Unfortunately, John deposited this money with a Pittsburgh bank, which promptly failed. Yet the scene was far from bleak. John's wire rope business was blossoming, as were his prospects as a bridge builder. "We hear it said that he has made little or nothing by the contract; however this may be, he has erected a work which will secure him a high reputation and eventually an ample return in a pecuniary sense," wrote the *Gazette*.[35]

John built his bridge to last and even bragged that any one of its spans could be replaced without affecting the others should rot set in, but ultimately the span scarcely lasted any longer than its impressive predecessor. Within a year the Pennsylvania Railroad was charted by the state, and by 1852 its iron tracks had reached Pittsburgh. This put the railroad in direct competition with the Main Line Canal, a battle the latter could never win. In 1854, the Pittsburgh City Council granted permission to the railroad to "lay a track across either of the bridges or the aqueduct from Allegheny to Pittsburgh as well as the right of way down Liberty street" in an effort to stave off the inevitable. It didn't work. The state sold the entire Main Line Canal to the railroad at a bargain-basement price in 1857. The railroad continued to use the canal's Western Division but refused to spend money on upkeep, leading to serious deterioration. By 1860, one of the spans was leaking and sagging dangerously, creating a major clearance problem for boats plying the Allegheny.

The last recorded toll was collected in February 1861, when a group of pedestrians walked over the dry trunk. Two months later, in an article called "Sinking of the Pittsburgh Aqueduct," the *Gazette* informed its readers that the aqueduct had recently "sunk some twelve or fifteen feet between the second and third piers" on the Allegheny side. It had been "sagging" at this point for several months and proved itself "utterly useless" at holding water. A couple of months later, Thomas Wierman wrote to John to tell him that his bridge "has fallen down." John's first span was demolished by the end of the year, and the entire Main Line system was abandoned in 1864. Ironically, Jonathan Rhule, who had fought so frequently with John during the aqueduct's construction, got the contract to dismantle the bridge. John went out to examine his handiwork before it was torn down for good. "The wire in the cables was perfectly well preserved," he decided. "The . . . half oil and half coal tar . . . mixture had become brittle [but] the splices looked well." There was also some rust at one abutment "where the rain was allowed to run inside of the wrapping next to the saddle." Afterward, the cables were "sold for telegraph wire." No trace of the structure is visible today.[36]

Many Pittsburghers were overjoyed by their new bridge, by their new celebrity bridge builder, and by the plans to quickly rebuild the Monongahela crossing.

But not everyone in western Pennsylania was so happy. As soon as some of the city's more disadvanatged and less prosperous neighbors caught whiff of the plan to rebuild the old Monongahela Bridge, they spoke up angrily. The result was a classic case of cutthroat commercial rivalry meeting the economics of disaster and the politics of internal improvements. On May 24, the day after John signed the contract for his second bridge, the *Brownsville Herald* ran an editorial denouncing the decision. Their complaint was not so much the bridge itself but the specifics of its reconstruction. "It is with feelings of great regret and not a little indignation," wrote the *Herald*, "that we learn that the managers of this bridge have contracted for its rebuilding upon the old piers and at its former height, for the purpose and with the *fixed* and *avowed* determination, of obstructing the navigation of the Monongahela River for all time to come." The old bridge had vexed those living along the Monongahela Valley below Pittsburgh for years. Anyone wishing to travel downriver to the confluence of the Ohio and on to western markets had to get past the bridge. Boats were forced to lower their chimneys or worse, "take off their pilot houses," to pass beneath. Even this was impossible "when the river was moderately swollen." So great was the inconvenience "that complaints were loud and increasing," wrote the *Herald*. In fact, the issue had so irked the surrounding counties that the question of how to effect the bridge's removal had been "gravely considered" for years. After the Great Fire, the people of the Monongahela Valley had looked forward to a replacement that would allow free, unobstructed passage up and down the river.[37]

The *Herald* was incensed by the decision to deliberately build a low bridge over navigable waters for the express purpose of obstructing traffic. The "*outrage* . . . must be proclaimed far and wide," they declared, the people must "rally to the rescue—the aid of the legislature, as well as the courts, must be invoked, and we predict that this corporation, whose arrogance is unprecedented, and subversive of all law and justice, will repent in 'sackcloth and in ashes' the recklessness and inequity of the act." Others joined the fight in an equally strident and visceral manner. The *Genius of Liberty* thought the idea was "as extraordinary as it is ridiculous." "It scarcely seems possible that the bridge company can be in earnest," they concluded. The *Waynesburg Messenger* was "sorry to think the company could be guilty of so ungenerous and *dangerous* an act, as to build it as *low* as it was before, and for the contemptible and iniquitous purpose of preventing the passage of boats on the Monongahela." Will such "a dirty act . . . as this be tolerated by free and enlightened people?" they asked.[38]

In a style common to nineteenth-century journalism, the Pittsburgh press heaped scorn on the criticisms emanating from the Monongahela Valley. The *Gazette* "had nothing to reply but ridicule." The *Herald*'s claims were "so full of wind and fury" as to lay the paper "open to be laughed at." "The people of

Pittsburgh need no such advantageous means to promote their interests or secure their prosperity," they continued. "To read our important neighbor at the head of the 'Slackwater,' one would suppose that he had serious expectations of that thriving little place rivaling Pittsburgh!" "From her size and wealth, her geographical position, her situation at the terminus of the Pennsylvania canal, and as the converging point of roads and trade, and means of intercourse with a wide extent of the country," Pittsburgh "is eminently a point of commencing and closing voyages. . . . How preposterous, then, to suppose that the raising or lowering of a Bridge is going to affect her trade!"[39]

Writing in the *Post*, a correspondent calling themselves "Commerce" joined the debate on the side of the *Herald*, or at least those fighting rampant, unobstructed private enterprise. The problem, as Commerce saw it, was that "the bridge is the property of, and is managed by a corporation," meaning "the citizens and councils have no authority or power." The law, it is true, "*should* control the company," he continued, "but submission and toleration, like precedent and custom, *become* law," leading the public "to acquiescence under all kinds of impositions and aggressions." "In this age of charters, monopolies and incorporations," he continued, who has not "felt the force of this new law"? The *Herald* ought "not appeal to the magnanimity of the citizens and councils of Pittsburgh,—nor to the majesty of the written law for justice and redress," Commerce concluded, "but he should appeal to the *mercy* of the 'Monongahela Bridge Company.' " Amid all the claims and counterclaims for and against malice or obstruction, Commerce was also skeptical about the Bridge Company's claims of poverty. The sheer amount of river traffic in and around Pittsburgh "renders it indispensible" that the bridge's height be increased, he thought. Yet the Bridge Company was claiming they simply couldn't afford the extra height. Surely, the future prosperity of the city, stretching out into the coming century, depended on a free and clear navigation in all directions. The *Herald* agreed. The "expenditure [necessary to build a higher bridge] would be trifling and inconsiderable when compared to a permanent obstruction of the navigation."[40]

Commerce was right to proclaim that the key to the growth of the western states was trade and that the main agents of this were its great rivers. Pittsburgh of course stood at the head of the Ohio River, but in a world of shifting political loyalties and ever-evolving systems of transport, this location guaranteed nothing. It was a geographic advantage but not a commercial fact, at least not unless they secured ease of movement.[41] Yet Commerce was also clearly not aware of how desperate the bridge company was for money. In fact, John and the Bridge Company did correspond about raising the height of the bridge. John's initial proposal, submitted on May 1, "proposed to raise the Pittsburgh abutment and the 3 first piers 6 feet for the purpose of elevating the floor of the bridge to the level of Smithfield Street and allowing a greater height for the passage of steamboats." The bridge managers wrote back almost immediately asking John to detail the additional cost.[42]

John responded quickly, calculating the cost of the materials needed to raise the bridge "6 feet above the present height" at about four thousand dollars. Realistically, all he needed was the cut stone, some grout, and a fleet of masonry workers, but it would take time and require a significant amount of manpower. Neither John nor the Bridge Company mentioned the issue again, and nothing was set out in John's final plan, dated eleven days after this correspondence. One key to the eventual decision was the cost of labor, which, according to the final contract, was to be borne entirely by John (while the costs of the masonry, eventually over eight thousand dollars, were born by the Bridge Company). It is certainly possible that John abandoned the plan to raise the bridge himself for financial reasons. His budget and his time frame were both about as tight as could be. Failure to finish on schedule would also result in fines, meaning the more work John did, the less he would be paid for it. Eventually, each of the piers was raised by three feet, although that was more a case of repairing than allowing for greater clearance. In addition, John's cable system helped rivermen. Thanks to the pendulum system that regulated the suspension cables, each span could operate as something of an independent body, capable of vertical movement. A section of the bridge could be raised slightly by placing extra weight on the two contiguous spans, which would depress the side spans and lift the center, often enough to allow boats to pass underneath without waiting for the river to fall. On one occasion, a man named William Robinson was able to raise one of the spans fourteen inches by this method, which allowed several boats to clear the span and pass beneath.[43]

Issues of commercial power and local rivalry were also factors in the Bridge Company's decision. As historian Richard Wade has noted, "Struggles for regional primacy characterized the urban growth of the entire West." "Before a city could hope to enter the urban sweepstakes for the largest prize, it had to eliminate whatever rivals arose in its own area," which for Pittsburgh meant cities and towns not just in western Pennsylvania but also in eastern Ohio and western Virginia.[44] In this, the upriver press was certainly onto something significant when they asked Pittsburgh to cast their eyes downriver, toward Virginia, Ohio, and Kentucky. "If the head of navigation is to be made at any point by *building a bridge*," wrote the editor of the *Waynesburg Messenger*, "we would advise the citizens of Wheeling to build a bridge at that place, and make their dilapidated city the head of navigation, when it will soon become a thronged, vigorous and thriving place. Pittsburgh could not certainly complain of this if she is willing to do a similar act in relation to the towns and villages along the Monongahela," they claimed sarcastically. The *Herald* agreed. "No people have been more sensitive on the subject of obstructing the navigation *below* Pittsburgh, than the citizens of that place," they declared before getting to the main point: "What is *wrong* and *injurious* to the public *below* Pittsburgh, cannot be *right* and *beneficial* to the public *above* Pittsburgh."[45]

Only when the talk turned to a Wheeling Bridge did the Pittsburgh press really get into the fight. The two towns had been locked in a commercial battle for years. The rivalry was sparked in 1811, when Wheeling was named the terminal of the National Road, the nation's first highway and one of its largest internal improvements projects, although Pittsburgh was far larger at that point. "A miserable Virginia country town, which can never be more than two hundred yards wide, having the mere advantage of a free turnpike road and a warehouse or two, to become rivals of this *Emporium* of the West!" huffed the editor of the Pittsburgh *Statesmen*. "Strange that a 'miserable Virginia Country Town,' a 'mere village,' should have attracted so much attention as the 'emporium of the West,' " shot back the *Northwestern Gazette*.[46]

Few things were secure in the world of early-nineteenth-century western development. Fortunes could change as quickly as the towns and villages that appeared and disappeared all over the country. Pittsburgh was certainly flourishing, but should Wheeling capture the National Road and commercial headship on the Ohio, then Pittsburgh's fortunes could potentially decline. If Wheeling built a low bridge, and if Pittsburgh's steam packets couldn't get by, then Pittsburgh would cede the crucial Ohio River trade. To some, this made sense. Wheeling enjoyed unimpeded navigation down the Ohio all year round, which was not the case in Pittsburgh. Shoals, shallows, and large boulders downriver hindered river traffic during the summer when the river was low. In fact, clear sailing downriver from Wheeling—and rocky, unpredictable sailing going upriver—had long made the Virginia town the preferred embarkation point between June and October. No wonder some Pittsburghers worried about living in a "deserted village." Of course, the National Road wasn't up to the work of a canal, and a canal wasn't up to the work of a steamboat, and neither would compete with the railroads once they branched out over the country. But for now, Pittsburgh depended on the Ohio, and the issue of a Wheeling Bridge constantly threatened to eclipse their advantage.[47]

———

After finishing up the aqueduct, John headed home to Saxonburg to get some rest. By the time his first span was finally opened, John was utterly drained. As reported by Washington, "Whatever a man gets he has to pay for in some shape— [My father's] ambition was satisfied at the expense of health—The strain had been too great, the pace too fast for human nature to stand it—He worked hard all day out in the winter weather, losing a meal now and then—At nightfall, in place of resting he had to work at his plans until midnight or later, attend to his books, lay out work for the morrow, make bargains and purchase supplies— When tired nature would succumb, stimulants were resorted to, smoking and strong coffee," none of which could ward off the relentless fatigue that had come to define John's daily life.[48]

Unfortunately, John was neither suited for nor enjoyed rest and relaxation. Gaps in time always needed to be filled with productive work. Spare afternoons or barren evenings were answered by diving into a conundrum. Later, during the American Civil War, when John endured a prolonged period of inactivity, he wrote hundreds of pages on a multitude of subjects, almost all of which went unpublished, and a huge philosophical treatise he called "The Truth of Nature." John's favorite way to relax was working hard on a new problem, and in June 1845 John's problem was his body. It had begun to fail him, and it needed to be fixed. But John harbored an abiding distrust of doctors and a general hatred of the medical profession. "There were two professions which were the subject of [John's] especial animosity," wrote his son, "namely a respectable intelligent physician and a theologian." John's children were "brought up to look upon hospitals as the abode of the devil and upon a doctor as a criminal. . . . The average kindly family physician was held up to his children as a monster in human form."[49]

Part of John's phobia was cultural and part was personal. The medical profession had only just reached its infancy in 1845, and even then only in the centers of civilization, not in the wilds of western Pennsylvania. There was little generally accepted medical knowledge and few established practices, just numerous systems ranging from the vaguely plausible to the truly bizarre. Bloodletting, blistering, emetics, sweating, and purging were all still common, while mercury was universally applied for all sorts of ailments. Even if John could somehow bring himself to submit to a doctor, he would never have deferred to another person's expertise. After the nonstop exertions of the previous nine months, John returned to Saxonburg exhausted and tried to cure himself by wholeheartedly adopting one of the "endless list of *pathies*" that defined medicine in the 1840s.[50]

John's chosen "pathy" was hydropathy, also known as the water cure. "Like everything else he did," wrote Washington, "he practiced it to the extreme limit of an iron constitution." In many respects the move reflected John's longstanding commitment to homeopathy, in addition to his penchant for all things "German." Both systems were developed and popularized close to where John grew up. Samuel Christian Friedrich Hahnmann, a lecturer at the University of Leipzig, developed the modern approach to homeopathy, publishing his *Organon of Homeopathic Medicine* in 1810, while the origins of the water cure originated a little further down the economic ladder. In 1816, Vincenz Priessnitz, a peasant from the village of Gräfenberg, Silesia, cured himself of broken ribs by wrapping himself in wet bandages, breathing in deeply, and apparently pressing himself with great force against a chair. He was up and about in ten days, after which he discovered he was something of a local celebrity.[51]

Water cures achieved great renown and garnered numerous disciples in the early eighteenth century, especially in England. But Priessnitz took matters further, turning a treatment into a whole system. He opened a sanitarium in the mountains of Silesia in 1826, affectionately known as "Water University." He had forty-five patients in 1829 and over 1,600 by 1840, including princes, princesses, archdukes, and barons. Priessnitz believed that all ailments could be cured by the correct application of water. His main contribution to the practice was the wet sheet, although he also created a system for sweating, developed the douche shower, and devised specific baths for specific parts of the body. With the correct preparation and application, he insisted believed, impure water in the blood could pass through the skin and into the water of the wet bandages. Conversely, the pure water of the bandages passed into the blood, with the cloth performing a transfusion of sorts, extracting the bad water and dispersing the good. Priessnitz maintained a strict environment at Gräfenberg. There was no reading, writing, or "immoral excitement"; no cotton or flannel garments were allowed (they weakened the skin); regular strenuous exercise was a daily requirement, as was cold, coarse, heavy food and twenty to thirty glasses of water a day. No other drinks were allowed. Robert Graham, a staunch critic of Priessnitz and the cure, thought Gräfenberg required "the courage of the lion, the strength of the bull and the stomach of the hog," but the truth was less painful. Any cure that removed its "patients" from the stress and turmoil of their daily lives, avoided the mercury that often laced allopathic treatments, and introduced a nutritious, balanced diet and plenty of exercise might have succeeded anywhere and without all the dunking and douching. Ultimately, the lifestyle choices likely helped more people at the Water University than the water cure itself.[52]

As word of Priessnitz's clinic reverberated around Europe, hundreds of experts and dozens of sanitariums appeared. Many differed in their particulars, but most agreed that illness flowed from one of three conditions: lack of vital life energy, "the presence of morbid matter in the system," or the violation of laws of hygiene. To deal with each of these, experts developed a seemingly endless stream of immersions and applications. Baths were the favored treatment, and a bewildering array of them were promoted: the wet towel bath, sponge bath, affusion bath, sitting bath, sweating bath, and plunge bath, along with a separate bath for almost every part of the body: half head, nasal, mouth, hip, leg, hand, foot. All were meant to cure a specific ailment. A sitz bath, for example, drew down "humors from the head and chest," while foot baths counteract "morbific agents operating on the upper part of the body." Often, patients were prescribed an entire regiment of treatments: "3 minute cold bed at 4am; folded in a large blanket and packed with bedding and allowed to sweat for an hour; then wrapped in a blanket and given another bath; dressed, walked about; breakfast; 10am douche for 4 mins, then a sitz then a foot bath each 15 mins; lunch at 1pm; at 4pm, douche, sitz, foot bath; at 9:30 wrapped up in a wet sheet and put to bed." One can only imagine what the patient looked like at the end of the day.[53]

Word of the Silesian miracle arrived in America via Joel Shew and R. T. Trall, who opened a sanitarium in New York City in 1843. A year later the *Water-Cure Journal* ran its inaugural issue. By 1852, it had over fifty-five thousand subscribers. Graham's exposé of the "Water Daemon of Graefenberg," published in 1845, caused a stir, but the practice remained popular, if controversial. Harriet Beecher Stowe, Horace Greeley, and Julia Ward Howe all visited water cure establishments, while Walt Whitman celebrated the water cure in his poetry. Likewise, most doctors approved of regular bathing, vigorous exercise, good food, avoidance of alcohol, and all the other treatments that often came with hydrotherapy. Few, however, felt water was an aid to anything but a healthy life, and many openly cautioned against an overreliance on the practice. A cold-water compress applied to a burn, for example, worked very well, within certain constraints, but not as a cure for cancer or as a remedy against infection. It offered a plan for healthy living, not fighting disease.[54]

The 1840s were a time of fads and follies. Magnetism, mesmerism, and phrenology all enjoyed a level of vogue, along with a whole host of other cures: the curd cure (eating only curdled milk, occasionally soaking in it), the wine cure (patients were sweated between dry blankets for hours and fed on a diminishing scale until just about starved), and the straw cure (drinking straw tea and sleeping naked inside rough straw beds until the flesh was raw). John took to many of them at various points in his life, although as his son later explained, "With all my father's preaching and practicing I have never heard him acknowledge that he had cured himself, on the contrary his troubles became confirmed chronic ailments with advancing age." As most doctors and physicians agreed, and Washington admitted, "No doubt there is some merit in the judicious practice of water cure, but to apply it to the exclusion of all other treatments is simple murder," no better than bloodletting or mercury cures.[55]

John took to the water cure much longer than almost anyone else involved in the practice. Hydropathy itself was simply the application of cold water, but it was often accompanied by various other lifestyle choices: vegetarianism, exercise, fresh air, "dress reform," and other modes of personal behavior, including abolitionism.[56] It offered an all-inclusive set of answers to life's problems and uncertainties. It was applicable to all things and (seemingly) all manner of ailments, from ringworm, scrofula, and smallpox to lethargy, gout, and "bilious fever." Quite simply, water was a purifier. It cleansed and removed, and it promised individual autonomy. As Susan Cayleff notes, the "water cure as a system and as a world view promoted a sense of meaning, ordering, power, and control," all things John craved throughout his life. As an idea and a practice, hydrotherapy's "single central vision" united self-reliance, habit, morality, philosophy, and self-determination, along with the hope of perfectibility. It was a comprehensive approach to life. John's commitment to the water cure was a direct reflection of his need to establish systems and order. But it was also infinitely malleable and adaptable. Hydropathy was a project John could work on and perfect over his whole life, without submitting to anyone's authority or losing control. Unsurprisingly, John practiced hydropathy for the rest of his life and read dozens of books on the subject, but he never once visited a water cure establishment.[57]

Once back in Saxonburg, John fitted the old dye house on his meadow with a "douche, plunge & sprays. . . . A sweating bed and pack were added later." He delegated most of the subsequent work to Johanna. Initially, John's "idol" was Priessnitz—he knew the peasant's "little book by heart"—but he soon moved on, finding the farmer "too simple." He devoured S. W. Avery's *The Dyspeptic's Monitor* (1830) and J. H. Rausse's *Miscellanies of the Gräefenberg Water-Cure and Errors of Physicians and Others in the Practice of the Water-Cure* (1849), before moving on to the same author's rather optimistic *The Water-Cure, Applied to Every Known Disease* (1852). John maintained a standing order with a German bookseller to send any new volume on the subject, and each new book was championed, "denounced and succeeded by another, embraced with fresh zeal, and denounced in its turn." One of John's lasting favorites was James Manby Gully's *The Water-Cure in Chronic Diseases* (1846), as it was of Charles Darwin, who spent several months at Gully's clinic in Malvern, England. Darwin dallied with the water cure for several years, finding it improved his health and helped with relaxation but little else. By the 1850s, Darwin, like many others, broke with the practice. Likewise, graduates of the University of Pennsylvania medical college were being warned against "false systems, which hang like hideous parasites upon the regular practice of medicine [and] which are the constant reliance of an easily deluded and superstitious people."[58]

Much of the burden of John's passion, as always, fell on his family. Once he had decided on a method, he was sure to enforce it. In consequence, "when one of his children fell ill, the first impulse was to conceal it from him, because the torture of his water treatment was worse than death," wrote Washington. Any unfortunate soul unlucky enough to find themselves even mildly ill beneath John's roof was "packed and douched and steamed, plunged into cold water and hauled out by the heals a la Achilles, sitzbathed, hip bathed, Sprayed, water bagged, fomented and revulsed and God knows what else." John took it as a personal insult if the patient did not respond.[59]

Despite Washington's complaints, John was often his own first test subject. Whenever he found himself with a spare moment, John was out in the dye house plunging, bathing, douching, or wrapping himself up in a wet sheet. John especially loved the wet-sheet-wrap treatment—which, according to a contemporary source, "cools febrile action, excites the action of the skin, equalizes the circulation, removes obstructions, brings out eruptive diseases, controls spasms, and relieves pain like a charm." "This morning took another wet-sheet, felt relieved, but I was again awake half the night, this requires more wet sheet," he confided to his diary. In fact, John was so taken with the practice that he often slept encased in one, which was hardly surprising. Mental institutions used the practice well into the twentieth century to induce sleep in their patients. John was always certain about his methods, but the correct application seemed to elude him. In early 1852, John conducted a month-long series of water cure experiments upon himself, with less than impressive results. After seven years of self-doctoring, and with little if any improvement, he was determined to solve the puzzle. Each day involved a new regiment of treatments. All month, John tested and tinkered to find the right balance, the right order, and the right length of time to devote to each treatment. On one day he would wrap a wet sheet around his neck, take a sitz bath, shower, and finish with a cold plunge. On another he would soak in a "full bath" for an hour, sweat himself for longer, and then wrap up in a wet sheet. At the end of every day, he would record his findings, his conclusions, and his bowel movements for the day.[60]

Many of John's determinations were rather hopeful: "Wet bandage around the neck every night, for years, will help much to strengthen the body and prevent colds." Others were bewildering: "Sweating is to be avoided whenever there is active irritation of the viscera or feverish symptoms of the skin, gullet, mouth." He was particularly worried about "excess sweating": "As the process is continued, the sweat from clear affluent, devoid of smell, becomes colored, viscous, glutinous, fetid." An entry from March 5, 1852, is somewhat typical in its baffling logic: "Sweating in blanket, one face bath and sitzbath, had been continued for the past week, but a change has taken place. Lassitude, heaviness in lower limbs, laziness, want of reaction after bathing and want of warmth all day were decided symptoms. Irritation, sleeplessness at night, excitement, all this indicates that sweating must be stopped & be replaced by the wet-sheet packing. . . . Accordingly last night had the sheet well-wrung out in *tepid* water and remained over 2 hours & got out before sweating commenced, washed off in tepid water, and took a walk in a snow storm. Reaction was perfect all over, warm feet felt greatly relieved & very well, much better than for the last 10 days."[61] And this from a man who could wrestle two hundred tons of wire, wood, and iron across a broad river, creating a sublime object of strength and beauty, a man revered and admired for his scientific brilliance.

THE ASCENDING DOUCHE.
"Now Sir, please to take a seat here."

THE FOOT BATH.
Doing penance in the Stocks, for past transgressions.

Costume of the Establish!
Doing Penance in the Wet Sheet.

Preparing for the packing
"Why my nearest and dearest friends
wouldn't know me. I'm a perfect mummy."

Figure 11.3 John's chosen "pathy": hydropathy, or the water cure. Images from Thomas Onwhyn's satirical *Pleasures of the Water Cure, by A Patient Well-Drenched and Restored* (1857).

Much of John's experimentation seemed designed to unblock himself. Washington notes that constipation was a "lifelong ailment," and John's notebooks are peppered with personal descriptions ("Since the copious water drinking my stool's diminished, bowels did not act once in 3 days") and dubious discoveries ("Constipation in full-blooded person . . . cold shallowbath in the morning, douche at noon, sitzbath in the afternoon, must be used daily and for a considerable length of time to remove obstruction"). His month-long regiment seems to have done nothing but aggravate the problem. He began with a "light stool" and ended with "dry black." A better, more balanced diet would have helped tremendously. Unfortunately, he took to the question of nourishment and nutrition with the same energy and absurdity that he did to water. A notebook entry from 1856 provides a list of foods and drinks John had decided should be "forbidden": "all condiments, except salt; Fish; Shellfish, Oysters; Dry beans and Peas; Beets; Carrots, Cabbage, Radish; Cucumbers, Celery, Lettuce; Cherries, Apples; Plumbs, Melons; Hard Apples (bad); Coffee & Tea; Chocolate; Cider; Coffee *immediately* after dinner; Malt Liquors except small beer; Wines and all liquors; Green Peas, Parsnips; asparagus when young; Orange, Melon, Peach; Ripe Grapes, not dried." Above this rather extensive list is written the rather brief and austere "oatmeal gruel—nourishing." One hardly wonders why John's body gave him so many problems.[62]

John's commitment to self-doctoring and hydropathy reflects a key aspect of Jacksonian America. New breakthroughs in science had unleashed a revolution in how people worked, thought, traveled, communicated, and otherwise experienced the world. They had spurred a boundless faith in material progress "extending civilization, republicanism and Christianity," declared the *New York Herald*. "The age is remarkable for scientific research into the heavens, the earth, and what is beneath the earth," extolled Daniel Webster; "the progress of the age has almost outstripped human belief." John played his part in this, but also contributed—albeit in a small way—to what David Reynolds calls science's "tremendous failure" in the arena of "human health" during the second quarter of the nineteenth century.[63] As an engineer, inventor, and manufacturer, John was a genius and a visionary. As his own doctor, he was a dangerous and deluded quack.

Pittsburghers greatly admired John Roebling as a local manufacturer and engineer, but there was a private individual evolving alongside this public figure and he was very different. He was a real crackpot, not just potentially violent, but often deeply strange as well. He was smart enough to solve some of the most fundamental problems in bridge engineering, but he also believed that clean fresh water applied to the skin could suck bad liquid out of the body through some form of osmosis. His understanding of physics and mathematics was astonishing, but he failed to grasp even the rudiments of biology.[64] And he was gullible enough to be taken in by hydrotherapy, even when all the evidence, and even his own experience, went against it. "How often was my father taken in," wrote Washington. "One rascal would come after the other [and] bleed him to his heart's content (of money not blood) and then run off."[65] Time and again, John's judgment was either excellent or awful, and he lacked the self-reflection to question himself. He spent his entire life searching for order and certainty, convinced he would find answers. In the service of his profession—engineering—it served him remarkably well. In the service of his health and his family, it was ruinous.

Work on the new Monongahela Bridge commenced in mid-June, a fact noted by a correspondent from the *New York Herald*, who arrived in Pittsburgh on June 21 "expecting to see a field of ruins." "Nothing met [his] astonished eyes," however, "but . . . long rows of fine warehouses . . . some finished, others being roofed, and some just rising out of the ground, as it were from their graves; and all swarming with workmen as busy as bees." "True, there stood the piers of the Monongahela bridge, like monuments of the past," he lamented, "but upon my nearer approach, I perceived they were covered with workmen busily engaged in tearing them down, preparatory to rebuilding the bridge on the suspension principle."[66] Much of the initial summer work involved preparing the charred and crippled piers. John's stock in the local press remained high. "We notice in late foreign papers objections to Suspension Bridges because of their motion," sniffed the *Gazette and Advertiser*, before asserting: "We have sufficient confidence in . . . Mr. R's improvements . . . or rather in his genius—to believe they will be successful."[67]

With the old piers rebuilt, fixed, and grouted, large stone pedestals, nine feet by three feet, were constructed on the tops of each pier, there to receive the cast iron towers. As described by Gustav Lindenthal, who dismantled John's bridge in 1883, "The towers had the appearance of square truncated pyramids, 7½ feet square at the base and 4 feet at the top, and 16 feet high." Cast iron lattice frames "filled the entire space on the road and river sides" of the towers, while "openings were left for the sidewalks, which led through the towers" on the other two sides. A "massive cast-iron top-piece" sat on top of each tower "in which the pendulums for the cables were hung." The towers were "connected at the top with a horizontal wooden brace, which prevented the towers from being pulled towards each other by the cradled cables."[68]

The towers were much shorter than would have ordinarily been required, but they were as tall as the narrow piers would allow. To compensate, John designed a pendulum system. Each of John's pendulums was attached to adjacent cables and hung from the apex of each tower. The device was a novel solution to the problem of countervailing forces, providing balance to competing, oppositional forces pulling in different directions. The pendulums were able to counterbalance inequalities in load on adjacent spans and more equally distribute weight concentrated on one span over the entire length of the bridge. The system was "so sensitive that a load at one end would be felt at the other, each set of pendulums swinging a little less and less."[69]

The "beautiful cast iron" towers were in place by the end of October, and by the middle of November all the cables on the east side of the bridge were up and attached. With "the work progressing rapidly," it was hoped that the rest of the "wire fixtures [would] be completed in about ten days," wrote the *Morning Post*.[70] The cables themselves were composed of 750 individual wires, laid parallel and closely wrapped in annealed wire. The resultant cable was 4½ inches in diameter and rather unwieldy. The cables were prefabricated on land—"stretched between posts under tension and wrapped"—and then hauled to the bridge. "The attempt to move them however came near proving disastrous," wrote Washington, "and it could only be accomplished by putting each one in a long closed wooden box, then skidding that down to the flat boat on which 2 were placed and floated over in the span where they were hoisted in place by a tackle worked by a capstan." The work proceeded from anchorage to anchorage. "To prevent the towers from canting over they were guyed by wire ropes to the next pier which had a hole for an anchorbolt drilled clear through it."[71]

The cable system was something of a backward step for John. It meant abandoning the elaborate and laborious endless rope system he had used on the aqueduct for the inferior French system used by Ellet and explicitly criticized at the time by John. John also used inclined stays for the first time on the Monongahela Bridge, and he never abandoned them, despite opposition and cynicism in some quarters of the engineering profession. Not only did the stays provide something of a failsafe against main cable malfunction, but the diagonal braces beneath the floor acted "as cantilevers, giving some rigidity to the suspended platform near the towers."[72]

Slowly, the bridge was coming together. Whenever "it was possible, especially on Saturdays," Washington "would run away from [his] German teacher [in Bayardstown, two miles away] and go to the Sligo side across the Monongahela River—here were the workshops and a row of shanties where my father boarded most of his men most of whom were old friends from Saxonburg." John had brought Washington from Saxonburg to attend a more rigorous and formal school in Pittsburgh. It was a terrible wrench for Washington to leave Saxonburg, where "the people were jovial and contented." "To me as a child it was the finest place in the world," he reminisced. Rather unsurprisingly, Washington's "father was always a crank on the subject of education—He could orate by the hour on the merits of the systems of [Johann] Pestalozzi, of [Joachim] Campe, [Johann] Richter and others, as respects the bringing up of children." "Worse than that," John "believed that a mother was not the proper person to bring up children, and so I was torn away from a happy home, a little strippling, and sent away among strangers, to be educated some more—I have always looked upon this act as a crime and the evil consequences of it have affected my whole life." Still, Washington learned the rudiments and practices of large-scale engineering at his father's side, not to mention how to handle a crew, deal with suppliers, and improvise in the face of difficulty, which would prove vitally important lessons. "I really think that this work was a pleasure to my father," Washington wrote, "and not a source of anxiety and hard work like the aqueduct."[73]

None of which is to claim that the building of John's second bridge was free of incident. On November 13, 1845, Thomas Huddling was "taken with a fit" while working on one of the piers on the east side of the bridge. He fell backward off the bridge, struck one of the stone piers on the way down, and was killed instantly. Huddling had a wife and family and was thought to be "an honest, sober, worthy man." John had given him work in the shop on account of his "infirmity"—which may have been epilepsy—but he had been "unwilling to acknowledge that he was subject to fits and persisted in exposing himself" to more dangerous work over the river. According to the coroner's inquest, this was the second time this sort of thing had happened on the bridge site. A few weeks earlier, a mason named Jackson had also "fallen off the pier and died."[74] On a lighter note, on December 17, an unnamed Irishman scampered over the as yet unfinished Monongahela span "for a small wager." The feat was much harder than it might seem, given that the roadway had yet to be built. The skilled adventurer had to leap from support timber to support timber, each placed six feet apart. A single misstep would have landed him in the river forty feet below. Luckily, he succeeded in crossing and pocketed his winnings.[75]

In contrast to the frigid winter weather that accompanied the construction of John's aqueduct, the weather a year later was much milder, which brought its own problems. On January 30, 1846, "the Monongahela burst her winter fetters, and poured out a mighty volume of ice, covering the turbid surface of the stream from bank to bank with a growling and roaring crowd of *cakes* a foot thick and running from the size of your hat to the sweep of a town lot," as the *Railroad Journal* described it. "Of course there was an active elbowing for the soft places among the river craft. It was sneak here and dodge there, among the flats, keels and even the saucy steam packets," they continued, before declaring the whole affair "a pretty how d'ye do; for it was market day and thousands of country folks caught on this side by the outbreak of the river, could only drive to the wharves and look helplessly and mutely on, thinking how nice it would be were they at home, with a fresh log on the kitchen fire, toasting their feet." "No boat could navigate in that tumbling and twisting mass of ice," while "the upper line of the wharves was packed with wagons and horses from Liberty Street to Smithfield."[76]

With the entire city in gridlock, John voluntarily threw his unfinished bridge open to traffic the following day. "The few remaining planks which remained to be put down" were "hastily placed in their proper order, and the entire passage for vehicles [was] completed!" Soon, the "immense assemblage" of coal and country wagons that "had blocked up Smithfield Street" were rumbling over the bridge, with as many as seventeen carts on a single 150-foot span at one point. The worried Bridge Company secretary John Thaw paced the bridge the whole time, but everything got over. "We venture to say that an equal degree of pressure will not soon again be felt upon this structure," wrote the *Railroad Journal*. "All doubts of the practicability" of John's bridge had been "forever silenced." For the *Gazette*, the great "over-laden" wagons had caused "little vibration," proving the bridge was as "*stiff* as promised." Building a suspension bridge, they continued, was thought to be "rather a hazardous undertaking," but clearly the results have proved "amply, completely successful." The whole affair was "a glorious triumph for Mr. Roebling, and a joyous relief for our belated market folk," they concluded.[77]

That same month, D. K. Minor paid a visit to Pittsburgh and was happy to see the city "rapidly restoring those useful and necessary structures" destroyed by the Great Fire. "She has indeed passed through a fiery ordeal," he wrote, "but we venture to say that she will be not only purified but also greatly *beautified* by it." Minor was a friend of John's and was overjoyed to hear all the talk in the city of the need for "*more* suspension bridges," a view echoed in the press. "Erect a neat, elegant, and beautiful suspension bridge that will do one's eyes good to gaze upon," wrote the *Chronicle*. Minor earnestly hoped the city would eventually earn the nickname "*the city of suspension bridges*," with the honor belonging entirely to the credit of one "*John A. Roebling*." The *Post* agreed. As soon as the Monongahela span was finished, "the citizens of Pittsburgh should, in some manner, express their high respect for him as an Architect—he has no superior in America."[78]

John finished his second bridge during the second week of February, and it was opened immediately. There were no official celebrations, just thousands of happy users. "The Monongahela Suspension Bridge was opened today for wagons, and was literally covered with teams from one end to the other, without showing any signs of the *fever and ague. . . .* It proves *more* steady and firm than a wooden bridge," John wrote in a letter to the *Ohio Union*.[79] The editor of the *Gazette and Advertiser* took a stroll over the span on the day it was flung open and found it "alive with foot passengers and wagons, going to and fro. . . . Indeed we scarcely know a more pleasant promenade about the city. It affords the passenger a view of the three rivers . . . as well as the picturesque hills near at hand and at a distance." "What a contrast to the dark, gloomy, unsightly structure, destroyed by the fire, which people avoided as much as possible," the *Gazette* continued. John's bridge, by contrast, "is like an open street, suspended on wire cables. . . . There is no roof to it, and the passenger is not annoyed with the dust and disagreeable effluvia of such closed structures." "We predict that this will be one of our most popular and profitable bridges," they concluded.[80] Others believed that "the bridge *surpasses* the expectations even of her friends." "The stiffness promised . . . has been fully attained"; "it *shakes* less than the old wooden arch bridge," and it was also well used, with most of the iron, coal, and other goods arriving in the city over the bridge.[81]

The *Morning Post* was overjoyed at the two bridges that "grace the rivers on either side of our smoky city. It is a matter of just pride to Pittsburgh that, despite all the endeavors of the prejudiced, all the efforts of the interested, and all the fears of the nervous enemies of innovation, she boldly ventured to patronize a man of science and genius, in his efforts to introduce an improvement of immense utility," they continued. "While many of those who laid claim to superior scientific knowledge, and the would-be wise in all departments, discountenanced the plan, and predicted its entire failure," John persevered—"under circumstances of doubt and discouragement"—and "made his way against impediments of the most formidable character." "We congratulate him on his deserved success, and would hope that his science, skill and energy, will bring him such a recompense as they deserve."[82]

———

John's bridge gave sterling service under very trying conditions for dozens of years. It was a genuine commercial workhorse. For over thirty-four years, it carried "the heaviest kind of street traffic, steam rollers, and eight horse trams

Figure 11.4 John's Monongahela Suspension Bridge after several years of service. "Smithfield Street Bridge over the Monongahela River" (1880). From the Pittsburgh City Photographer Collection, 1901–2002, AIS.1971.05. Courtesy of the Archives and Special Collections Department of the University of Pittsburgh.

pulling heavy trucks loaded with iron and machinery," yet by 1880 it was "undulating up and down about 3 feet in each span" and had become "very shaky and loose." The principal problem was the relationship between the cable structure and the continuous longitudinal truss system that gave the bridge its rigidity. One was designed to move up and down, and the other was fixed along the entire length, meaning they worked in opposition. As civil engineer Gustav Lindenthal explained, after inspecting the bridge, "Every passing load would deflect the wooden floor beams and raise their ends, the suspender from the cable acting as a fulcrum. At the ends of the floor beam was the Howe truss, which in this way was lifted up for a certain length." The effect was twofold. The action of this fulcrum distributed the bridge's live load to the end truss, not to the cables. This placed the suspender rods under enormous pressure and "subject to alternating bending strain from the vibratory motion of the floor at and near the middle of the span." By 1880, suspender rods broke every day, while the fulcrum placed additional strains on the truss, lifting it at certain points while simultaneously lowering it at others. By the time Lindenthal arrived, the warning signs were audible. A carriage's approach was accompanied by "the grinding noise of the moving pendulums" as they rose to meet the oncoming load. "The movement in the floor," he wrote, "seemed to the eye like an advancing wave."[83]

After dismantling John's bridge, Lindenthal conducted a full set of tests. He found that all the pendulum pins were bent, broken, and almost useless. "How the bridge ever stood up with such pins I can't say, unless it was by sheer force of habit," he quipped. Conversely, he found the lumber to be in "excellent condition" thirty-seven years later and that much of the ironwork, although "highly strained for a long number of years," had not "deteriorated in quality." The most impressive results were reserved for the cables, which had "lost little if anything of their original strength." "There was still life" in them, despite being daily subjected to almost a half of the cable's "ultimate strength." In fact, after separating the "wires from the cable some of them would coil up, presumably to the curve they originally had on the wire drum."[84]

Lindenthal not only dismantled John's bridge; he also built another above and around it so as not to interrupt traffic, in the process finally raising the clearance height for upriver craft. Even more remarkably, Lindenthal managed to keep John's bridge standing and in operation while he was building the new span, even after removing the old suspension cables. He simply suspended the old bridge using cables attached to the new. Lindenthal's bridge—a distinctive Pauli or lenticular truss bridge—survives to this day, although in a somewhat modified form.[85]

———

In January 1846, just a couple of weeks before the Monongahela Bridge was opened, the Philadelphia *Saturday Courier* sent a journalist to look at the work John had undertaken. Having examined "the now well-known and beautiful Suspension Aqueduct Bridge over the Allegheny," the journalist, styling himself Aristides, was "struck with the simplicity and unity of design, and the compact and solid appearance of skillful and workman-like execution." Likewise, the "New Monongahela Suspension Bridge . . . when entirely completed, will present a most magnificent appearance. It will truly be an ornament to the city and a noble triumph of art, for which the contractor justly feels, and should be proud." John's bridges, Aristides continued, were beautiful but also built with the twin virtues of great strength and "great economy." During the last season, for example, the aqueduct had borne "one-fourth more water in the trunk" than it had been designed for without the least show of strain "or the slightest deflexure of the wooden trunk." In terms of cost, John had built both bridges for under $120,000, or just over half what it had cost Pittsburgh to build the two structures John's bridges had replaced.[86]

Aristides's article was intended to praise John for his work and Pittsburgh for trusting him, but it was also written with one eye set firmly on the future. The United States was growing, but there were obstacles to expansion. The Mississippi River was the largest of these, but there were others: the Ohio, the Hudson, the Missouri, and the Susquehanna. Bridges were essential to national growth, and only suspension bridges—built by knowledgeable, competent engineers, of which the country had very few—would be able to surmount the natural barriers that stood in the way. For Aristides, suspension bridges were the ultimate solution to a fundamental American problem.[87]

Aristides oddly made no mention of Ellet in the piece, but the comparison with John was implicit. The journalist hoped his piece would "lead to enquiry, and a close inspection [of John's] bridges, with others of similar construction," which was almost inevitable. Within a few months, the two engineers found themselves in competition again, on the project that lay at the heart of Aristides's piece: one of the most daring engineering feats of the century, "the proposed construction of a suspension bridge at the Falls of Niagara." John would get around to the Niagara project, but not before working up complete designs for two other, much larger spans. By the time he finally made his way up to Niagara, John was widely acknowledged as one of the most competent and creative suspension bridge engineers in the world.[88]

Setting the Future (1846–47)

John's accomplishments in Pittsburgh raised the profile of suspension bridges across the country, bolstered the reputation of wire ropes as a dependable structural unit, and helped reconnect the city with its surroundings during a vital time of rebuilding. They also proved that John was an engineer in the fullest sense of the term. Not only could he design an impressive set of structures, but he could build them too, employing all the skills of the craft: planning, managing, making, calculating, contracting, adjusting, and carrying through and executing the entire enterprise, from the drawing board to the finished structure. Each stage of the job encompassed myriad skills and apitudes, each of which had to be mastered and effectively deployed. John's accomplishments also proved his energy and ambition. Even before his triumphal completions of the Allegheny and Monongahela bridges, John had his eyes on bigger rivers and larger projects.

On February 10, 1846, the editor of the *Ohio Union* wrote that he had recently seen a letter "addressed to a highly respectable citizen here from John A. Roebling, Esq the architect of the new Monongahela suspension bridge." The letter made the following rather bold claim: "A Wire Suspension Bridge can be constructed at Cincinnati, which would span the Ohio, in *one single arch*, leave the river entirely unobstructed, form a perfectly safe communication with the Kentucky side at all seasons of the year, prove the best paying stock, and the same time, a great ornament to the city, and one of the most remarkable works of modern engineering. A span of 1200 feet . . . is perfectly practicable, and *far* within safe limits," John continued, although "if economy were a great object, two piers might be resorted, for the support of a centre span, of six to seven hundred feet, and two end spans of lesser dimensions." Ever the aesthete, John counseled not to "obstruct 'La belle riviere' there is but one in the world." This was no blind speculation; John was serious. As reported in the press, he left Pittsburgh for Cincinnati just a few days after his Monongahela Bridge was opened "for the purpose of making an examination and estimate of the cost of a wire suspension bridge over the Ohio."[1]

———

Bridging the Ohio was an idea that had been around for decades. In 1815, Daniel Drake, known locally as the "Western Ben Franklin," wrote that "some enthusiastic persons still speak of a bridge across the Ohio at Cincinnati; but the period at which this great project can be executed, is certainly remote." Less than five years later, the authors of the *Cincinnati Directory* wrote: "Many have ridiculed" the idea of a bridge across the Ohio "as an hypothesis, at once absurd and visionary, whilst others have viewed it in a more serious light," but "it is now satisfactorily ascertained that a bridge may be permanently constructed, and at an expense vastly inferior to what has generally been supposed." Consequently, there seemed to be "little doubt that very few years will elapse before a splendid bridge will unite Cincinnati with Newport and Covington." By the 1820s, a bridge was inevitable. The city had forged links with inland trade via improved roads and new canals, and it dominated trade on the Ohio itself, fast eclipsing both Pittsburgh and Louisville. A bridge would have brought northern Kentucky more reliably into the commercial fold, except for a few key factors. No part of the river was actually in Ohio. Kentucky's borders were inherited from Virginia, whose state boundary extended not to the Ohio River, nor to the middle of it, but to its northern edge. Additionally, Cincinnati was first and foremost a port city, and the implications of a bridge for shipping were enormous. Any span to cross the Ohio would need to plant a leg or two in the middle of the river, maybe even more. Piers in the river would impede river traffic, affect currents, and serve to collect river debris, further restricting shipping in and out of the harbor.[2] Creating an integrated system of land and river traffic was a complex dance, but for now the interests of the river were uppermost, leading some to propose fantastic new hybrid solutions. "The feasibility of throwing a permanent bridge over the Ohio . . . at an expense which would secure a handsome interest . . . is generally admitted," wrote one enterprising young engineer in 1826, before proposing to erect a massive stone masonry bridge across "La Belle Riviere." Composed of eight or nine large heavy piers, the bridge would stretch out south into the Ohio, two hundred feet from the Kentucky shore, from which "branches should be carried to Newport and Covington, thus uniting those two villages with each other, and both with Cincinnati." At the northern end of the river's main channel, near the Ohio shore, a draw could be constructed to admit the passage of steam boats. The total cost would about $150,000. The plan was bold, and it owed much to Zanesville's famous "Y" bridge, built twelve years before. John himself had already designed something similar, but much bigger, a fact that would very soon become known in Pittsburgh.[3]

The idea gained credence, and the impetus—perhaps naturally—came from the Bluegrass, not the Buckeye State. In March 1839, a meeting of the citizens of Covington urged the legislature to approve a charter for an Ohio bridge. Three years later, Sylvanus Lothrop proposed to build a wooden bridge sixty-five feet above the low-water mark with a "draw or swing opening of seventy feet [on the Covington side] constructed as to be opened or closed in about one minute." Ellet's suggestion that he could bridge the Ohio for $150,000 made a comeback in 1843 after a sixty-foot wire bridge "with a very light graceful appearance" was thrown over the Miami Canal at Race Street in Cincinnati. The idea was quickly dismissed, however, by a local engineer named Drake. "Suspension bridges can never be considered serviceable," he wrote. Suspended spans possessed neither "solidity" nor "durability." It is a fact, he declared, "that one out of every ten of these bridges falls."[4]

Opinion remained divided. The Pittsburgh press thought it would "all end in talk," while the *Kentucky Intelligencer* disagreed. "We think [the region] will lose but little for the present, and gain much in the end." By January 1846, a petition was before the Ohio legislature, while a bill was before the Kentucky House. "This great measure [is] within our grasp," wrote the *Licking Valley Register*, before setting out the facts of the case: "Such a work would be the 'making' of Covington. The trade between the two cities is now immense; but it is greatly retarded by the want of such rapid and regular facilities of intercourse as a bridge would afford." The only real questions were whether the stock would be taken and whether such a span could realistically be built across the Ohio. This last issue seems to have been resolved by "the architect of the wire bridge, now in course of erection" at Pittsburgh, "a man of deserved celebrity [who] we understand is willing to construct it for $100,000."[5] There is no evidence that John was in cahoots with the *Register*, but he clearly got wind of their sentiment and reacted. John's offer to construct an Ohio bridge was written two months after he was referred to in the *Register*, and it appeared in the Cincinnati press on February 10, 1846, three days before the Kentucky legislature passed a bill chartering the Covington and Cincinnati Bridge Company. Reactions in Ohio were mixed.[6]

The *Morning Atlas* considered "the whole [bridge] scheme a moonshine affair," which was a far cry from how Cincinnati officials saw it.[7] On the same day that the Kentucky legislature passed their bridge bill, the city council of Cincinnati passed a "very extraordinary" resolution asking the Ohio legislature not to charter a bridge company. Their reasoning was controversial but simple. A bridge across the Ohio would make Covington, Cincinnati, and Newport into "one city." The effect of this consolidation "would injure the *real estate* in

Cincinnati," transferring "part [of Cincinnati's] wealth and population . . . to the opposite side of the river."[8] The *Enquirer* didn't believe one should legislate against proximity. Covington and Newport were already suburbs of Cincinnati, bound up in the fate of the Queen City, not in the commercial fortunes of Lexington or Louisville. Treating them as foreign bodies would cripple growth in Cincinnati, not sustain it, just when the region was experiencing rapid expansion.[9] The *Chronicle* heaped scorn on the city council. "People who really, in good faith, hold such ideas as [those of the city council], ought to have a Province in the Empire of China assigned them, and the great wall of Tartary built round it, to keep them from those parts of the earth, infected with the notion that Railroads and Bridges are useful things." The question was not one of redistribution, with the wealth and population of southern Ohio flowing into northern Kentucky, but of mutual growth. A bridge was a commercial necessity for the entire region.[10]

Unfortunately, many jealousies and fears existed between the two states— Ohio farmers feared competition from over the river, while laborers, even those opposed to slavery, feared competition from African Americans—yet everyone knew the main issue was one of shared concern, namely, the Ohio River. Few members of the council believed one could erect a bridge across the Ohio without interfering with navigation, nor did the local press. The *Morning Atlas* thought piers in the river would "ever be a serious obstruction to navigation." Others wondered if a "*Draw* [could] be inserted in a suspension bridge without piers." Everyone agreed that the charter specifically forbade any bridge from interfering with navigation, but how could one tell if it would until one had sunk tens of thousands of dollars into the project and the bridge was built? The *Register*, among others, thought the answer was simple: interfering with navigation was commercial suicide. Luckily, "the ablest and best informed engineers in the country . . . have declared that a Bridge can be built over the Ohio, without impeding navigation or injuring the 'harbor' of Cincinnati."[11] To this, some of the press wondered "what *might* be done before it can be prevented."[12]

The main difference between the two states was their predominant labor systems, a fact pointed out and analyzed by almost every visitor to the region from Alexis de Tocqueville to Abraham Lincoln. "The Ohio," wrote Tocqueville in 1831, "forms the boundary between two vast states [that] differ in only one respect: Kentucky allows slaves, whereas Ohio has expelled them from its midst." "On the left bank of the river . . . society seems to slumber. Man appears idle, whereas nature is the very image of activity and life." "By contrast, the confused hum emanating from the right bank proclaims from afar the presence of industry. . . . Prosperity is apparent everywhere. Man seems rich and content: he is at work." Few things had changed by the time British visitor Alexander Mackay traveled downriver just a few months after John wrote to the *Ohio Union*. "The

Ohio, for almost its entire course, separates from each other the realms of freedom and slavery," he wrote; "whilst the one side presented every appearance of industry, enterprise, and activity, sleepy languor seemed to pervade the other." For Alexander Lakier, the Ohio's "desolate" southern banks seemed to suggest that Kentuckians had "purposely moved away from the shore so as not to see the other side and get any ideas about freedom's happy consequences."[13]

These "real and palpable" differences were in turn controversially written into the heart of Kentucky's bridge legislation. Section 10, which outlined the Bridge Company's primary responsibilities and liabilities, included the following: "It shall be unlawful for said company, their agents or officers, to suffer or permit any slave or slaves to pass over said bridge without written request of the owner" or unless they were in the company of their owners. As in most other southern states, the movement of enslaved people was strictly regulated in Kentucky in an effort to keep them from straying too far from home. Much more significant was what came next: "And said company shall be liable to pay to said owner or owners, for every slave or slaves so permitted to pass contrary to the provisions of this act, the full value of said slave or slaves, to be ascertained by the verdict of jury, together with a penalty of ten per cent. thereon, to be assessed by the judgment of the courts." This was explosive stuff. Cincinnati was one of the best organized and most active stops on the Underground Railroad. Building a bridge over the Ohio would make this work much easier but would directly implicate the Bridge Company, effectively saddling it with the costs of runaways.[14]

The slave clause combined a genuine fear that a bridge would simply ease the flight of those enslaved to freedom in Ohio with a rather diffuse commercial and ideological opposition to the bridge. "The Bridge Bill has triumphed," wrote the *Licking Valley Register* about the bill's fate in the Kentucky legislature, although it "passed through a fiery ordeal." The bill's opponents tried "to kill the measure by tacking to it odious and restrictive amendments and thus render the law a solemn farce." The bridge's supporters thought the amendment "objectionable" but "not of a character thought to seriously injure the bill." "Progress," a correspondent of the Cincinnati *Enquirer*, certainly believed that "Louisville, when finding it could not kill the bill, put the slave clause in" knowing it would likely scuttle the bill up in Ohio.[15]

The reaction in Cincinnati was instantaneous. The *Atlas* complained, "We do not see how the members of our Legislature, can consistently with their oaths, vote for a law treating human beings as *chattels* . . . and making the citizens of Ohio *responsible* for their escape." Much of the city's abolitionist sentiment was expressed by the *Herald and Philanthropist*. "No Ohio man in his senses would subscribe for any of the [bridge] stock," they insisted, if it required the tacit endorsement of human bondage. Kentucky was asking "the good people of Cincinnati to station themselves as sentinels over runaway slaves, and pay for the birds when they have flown off in spite of their watchfulness. Just think of it—the net profits of the bridge . . . to go to a few of our beloved brethren across the river, for certain slaves who walked off in the night season over the timbers! That would be one way of colonizing Slavery."[16]

A notable exception to the outrage was the commercially minded *Chronicle*. To oppose the measure out of some vague sense of social injustice was to ignore the great economic interests at stake. "Will Cincinnati be injured by the competition of towns in a slave State, when she is in a great, fertile, rapidly increasing free State?" they wondered. "No one can dream such a thing without distrusting the superiority of free labor." The *Chronicle* believed free Ohio had nothing to fear from slaveholding Kentucky, which did not address the financial obligations embedded in the Kentucky legislation. Free states might well have had little to fear from slave states, but that wouldn't help the Bridge Company when it found itself having to underwrite the emancipation of much of the Kentucky slave population after it had fled to freedom over their bridge.[17]

The implications of erecting a bridge across the Ohio were significant. Few spots in the United States were more emblematic of the contradictions and realities that defined pre–Civil War America than "La Belle Riviere." The Ohio was an important commercial artery, but also a fraught boundary, a metaphorical River Jordan, which linked and bound a nation just as much as it divided it. For black Americans, it embodied the promise of freedom caught in the teeth of slavery, and it bore a dark symbolism. Unlike Huck Finn's Mississippi, the Ohio was a dangerous obstacle to be strenuously overcome and decidedly left behind, not a route to freedom. As Harriet Beecher Stowe would show so dramatically six years later, with her depiction of Eliza's "desperate retreat across the river . . . impossible to anything but madness and despair," getting across the Ohio could be a high-wire act of desperation and luck. "With wild cries and desperate energy she leaped to another and still another cake [of ice]; stumbling—leaping—slipping—springing upwards again! Her shoes are gone—her stockings cut from her feet—while blood marked every step," until she reached the Ohio side. As historian Keith Griffler notes, "The northern bank of the Ohio River [was] the front line of African Americans' struggle to become free, remain free, and help others attain their freedom."[18]

Cincinnati was a prominent battleground on the "Frontier of Freedom," as prominent abolitionist John O. Wattles termed it, a hotbed of racial struggle, a vibrant center of black American life, and a leading training ground for those looking to undermine slavery. The city was home to slave catchers and to prominent abolitionists in equal measure. Levi Coffin (self-proclaimed father of the Underground Railroad), Salmon P. Chase (influential abolitionist lawyer and ultimately Lincoln's treasury secretary), Calvin Fairbank (who served a total of nineteen years in prison for aiding fugitive slaves), Gamaliel Bailey (firebrand editor), and John Fairfield (who regularly rowed fugitive slaves across the Ohio to Cincinnati) all lived in the Queen City in 1846. Just as importantly, Cincinnati was a hectic port city with plenty of opportunities to bolt and vanish. Black intellectual William Wells Brown escaped from slavery in 1834 by slipping from a steamboat as it docked in Cincinnati. In addition, it boasted a large free black population that was vocal and active. To enslaved peoples living below the Ohio, Cincinnati was a beacon of hope, the Promised Land over the Jordan. To slaveholders, it was a taunt and a tangible threat.[19]

Ohio's "black laws" placed limits on all sorts of legal rights. Yet by the 1840s, blacks had successfully established their presence in the city after much struggle. This was reflected, and compounded, in 1841 by the Ohio Supreme Court decision *State v. Farr*, which automatically freed enslaved men and women brought into the state with their owners' consent. "If a master brings his slave into the state of Ohio he loses all power over him," wrote the Ohio justices. "The relation of master and slave is strictly territorial. If the master takes his slave beyond the influence of the law which creates that relation, it fails—there is nothing to support it, and they stand as man and man." The ruling did not extend to those fleeing, "since the Constitution and the act of Congress, under which alone the state of slavery subsists in Ohio applies to *fugitives* only."[20] Still, the decision was a huge victory for abolitionists and a serious blow to relations between the two states, a fact that was registered in the Kentucky bridge legislation.

Slavery across the Ohio was something of an anomaly. With little or no cotton, rice, or sugar production and no culture of forced bondage in the state's mountainous east, slavery was more tenuous in Kentucky than anywhere else but it still held some economic importance. Slave trading was an important part of the state's economy, and Kentucky protected it. Movement was tightly controlled, strict rules of assembly existed, and "slave patrols" roamed throughout the state, especially on the "Ohio shore." The absence of bridges at any point along the Ohio maintained the cultural difference. John's proposal, however, threatened it. Getting across was difficult in the best of weather and the most fortunate of circumstances. A bridge between Covington and Cincinnati would forever alter that fact, providing a safe passage for all the Elizas and Uncle Toms in Kentucky. Strictly speaking, John was proposing a commercial route between neighboring towns, but also a potential national highway from slavery to freedom. According to Levi Coffin, "The Ohio River was the principal barrier between them [slaves] and freedom." John's plan would remove it.[21]

The slave clause, the Cincinnati city council's resolution, and the question of navigation were enough to postpone Ohio's decision. By the end of February, the state legislature had decided to put off the vote to the following winter.[22] Two weeks was hardly sufficient time to consider the implications of a bridge, especially without a team in place or a fully developed plan. None of this stopped the chatter in the press, of course. Nor did it stop John, who quickly made plans to revisit the city in the summer to conduct surveys and meet local bigwigs. He had timed his letter to accompany Kentucky's legislation as an opening salvo. Next would come the plan, then the plotting and promotion, hopefully followed by legislation and financing.

———

John's Ohio bridge proposal wasn't the largest project he developed in 1846. It wasn't even the largest bridge project he developed that month. Almost the day that the Kentucky legislature passed their bridge charter, a storm broke out in the Pittsburgh press about an audacious proposal to construct a gigantic Y-shaped tripartite bridge at the Point. The plan was John's, and over the next couple of months a violent reaction, a strenuous defense, or an angry letter were near daily occurrences. Back in October 1845, Sam Wickersham wrote to John asking about "the Point Bridge." The idea was "very much agitated" right now, he explained. "I hope you will soon be ready with a rough plan."[23] By February 1846, despite the sapping effort of erecting bridges over the Allegheny and Monongahela and his work in Ohio, he was indeed ready. And it was stupendous, involving five different suspended spans and encompassing a combined 2,550 feet of roadway. The bridge would start at the very tip of the Point and stretch out into the Ohio with two spans of three hundred and six hundred feet to a center pier built on a "gravel bar." From this midpoint, the two upper branches of the Y diverged. One span, of 750 feet, swept over to the Monongahela shore. The other branch stretched in two spans of six hundred and three hundred feet across the Allegheny River to an abutment on a small island and on to the main shore via a short truss bridge. The total cost was estimated at between $250,000 and $300,000.[24]

The *Morning Post* took it "as a settled matter that Mr. R. can carry out any thing in bridge building that he says he can do." The paper's only worry was the shareholders who controlled Pittsburgh's other bridges. Trouble might yet await the project if they decided to mount a campaign against the span. But the city was enjoying rapid growth, and "there will be enough for all the bridges to do." As for the broader issue of transit, "The idea . . . that, in these days of advance-ment, the people . . . must be content with ferries, is preposterous [and] will not be tolerated in this era of wire suspension bridges," they concluded. The *Chronicle* thought the span would be "a noble one" and a fitting next project for the creator of the Allegheny and Monongahela bridges, "two works which cannot be equaled in the world." Pittsburgh's Common Council agreed. They thought John's bridge would "materially conduce to the prosperity of our city" while having no effect on navigation. On February 16, 1846, they endorsed

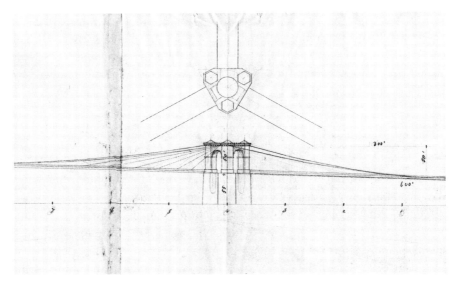

Figure 12.1 Sketch of John's plan for a tripartite bridge (1846). Courtesy of the Institute Archives and Special Collections, Rensselaer Polytechnic Institute.

the plan and sent their recommendation to the state legislature. The Common Council's vote was "an indication of the general feeling of the public," reported the *Gazette*, which reasoned that there would "be some individual interests affected by it" and "some opposition," but that "the mass of the population will view the project with favor when it is rightly understood."[25]

The opposition to the plan was confined to the *Daily Commercial Journal*, which ran a series of hostile op-eds. Much of the resistance mirrored the arguments that had dogged John's Monongahela Bridge and were defining the Ohio debate. "We should preserve the navigation of our river free," wrote one correspondent, and guard against "the secret efforts of a few persons to procure the incorporation" of a bridge company. Another wondered "whether a limit should not be put to this system of walling in the port of Pittsburgh with the abutments of numberless bridges—which already bristle around us like the buttresses of a fortified city." Must we further "decorate ourselves [with] more of these structures and on a more stupendous scale?" they asked. "A Citizen of Pittsburgh" thought "all the credit [belonged] to Mr. Roebling for the skill and perseverance he has manifested in the construction of the suspension aqueduct and bridge" yet also thought that his new plan was "fraught with too serious consequences to be rightly adopted by our citizens." The city was actively trying to attract the B&O Railroad, and cutting itself off from the Ohio would only hurt that effort. The issue of rivalries and precedents animated others. Pittsburgh had long resisted efforts to bridge the Ohio at Wheeling and at

Cincinnati. "With what face, with what show of constancy, can we resist these grants of privileges to Cincinnati and Wheeling, while we ask the same for Pittsburgh?" asked the *Journal* before reprinting an editorial from the *Wheeling Argos*. "A wonderful change of opinion seems to have suddenly taken pace up at the Forks," wrote the *Argos*. "We suppose that our citizens may now, without opposition, renew the project of erecting a bridge at this place." The *Journal's* solution to the bridge problem was simple enough. Erecting "a splendid structure across the Allegheny, near its mouth," would "accomplish nearly all that the liberal projectors of the Tri-Partite Bridge seek to obtain," without setting a bad precedent or interfering with navigation. Another correspondent agreed: "We must drop the *Ohio* part . . . and put a handsome wire suspension bridge across the Allegheny [only], employing Mr. Roebling's elegant genius, upon a bi-partite structure."[26]

On February 19, a writer styling himself Civis appeared on the scene. He brought an easy expertise to the subject, displaying an uncanny grasp of all aspects of the proposal and genuine understanding of the issues at stake. He stood out so much, in fact, that the author could only have been John. What persuaded John to take up his pen seems to have been the naive belief that by setting the record straight he could satisfy the opposition and let the project "stand or fall by its own merits." He was "pained" to see the *Journal* take such a stand against the bridge and hoped "to convince them" their "fears were ground-less." As far as he could tell, the *Journal's* objections seemed to be twofold: that the bridge would "obstruct the free navigation of our rivers" and that it would create a "precedent for those who wish to erect Bridges across the Ohio." John spent much of his letter refuting the first, quoting facts and figures and citing the heights of myriad local steamboats, all of which could easily pass beneath the eighty feet of clearance the bridge provided. As to the second, if the cities below Pittsburgh wanted to erect bridges that "do not interfere in any way with navigation, what possible objection can we have?" "Will they not add to the beauty of our rivers," he asked, while providing sure and steady transit across the nation's broad waterways? "Properly guarded, I should not object to see a bridge at every large city from here to New Orleans," he admitted.[27]

The *Gazette* was more than happy for either Wheeling or Cincinnati to build a bridge over the Ohio, as was the *Chronicle*. "If bridges can be built across the Ohio at Wheeling, Cincinnati, and Louisville, without piers and above the reach of the tallest steamboat chimneys, no objection ought to be raised," they thought.[28] Such sentiments reflected the shifting implications of technology and transit that defined the era. People had been conditioned to think of bridges as intrinsic impediments, but that was before suspension bridges brought with them the capacity to vault over rivers in a single leap, providing plenty of clearance. While still in their infancy, suspension bridges were enabling people to have both free navigation and cross-river transit. They were changing the way people thought about their world and how they moved around it.

The debate in Pittsburgh was as much about modern urban planning as it was about boats and bridges. "The triangular piece of ground on which Pittsburgh is built, is too limited to hold the population of the mighty metropolis of which this beautiful valley is to be the site," wrote the *Chronicle*, "but the largest portion of this ground is cut off from access to the city, except by circuitous route." Metropolitan Pittsburgh was growing beyond its city limits to include Allegheny City, Coal Hill, Monongahela Village, Manchester, and Temperanceville. To form an effective urban environment, all these places needed to be linked together. Someone doing business at the Point, for example, but living in Manchester would have to travel miles out of his way, complained the *Chronicle*. This "can be remedied only by a bridge at or near the Point." Everyone knew that ferries were time-consuming and inconvenient. Instead, Pittsburgh needed bridges. The tripartite bridge would give people "a safe and certain means of crossing from one to the other, without delay and without travelling far out of their direct way." Friends and neighbors would be "brought nearer to us," they editorialized; "the effects would be invigorating."[29]

Cities needed effective transit routes, but they also needed healthy outlets, an idea John would adopt and point out in almost all his subsequent bridge proposals. Whether he got it from the *Pittsburgh Gazette* or whether they got it from him is unclear. "As an ornament to the city [John's bridge] would be both her pride and glory, the greatest attraction to strangers," declared the *Gazette*, but just as importantly, "in pleasant weather, a public promenade unsurpassed in the country. This in itself is an object of the utmost importance to Pittsburgh, hemmed in as we are, without any public ground, or any means of escaping from the dust and heat, for an hour's walk in warm weather. The Tripartite Bridge . . . give[s] us one of the most airy and picturesque promenades the country affords, entirely out of the smoke and dust."[30]

The tripartite bridge debate was dogged by questions of public good and private interest. Could the public good best be served by spanning the rivers or keeping them clear of any interference? The bridge was an intrinsic public good, argued some, while others contended that it was just financial speculation. We only "raise our voice against a scheme which is well calculated to enrich a few at the expense of the common prosperity," argued the *Journal*, as did the *Chronicle*, albeit in the other direction. "Nine out of ten citizens . . . are in favor of the construction," it announced. "The opposition comes almost entirely from those interested in the ferry at the foot of Liberty Street, and those holding stock in other bridges, or owning property in the upper part of the city." The paper was sorry that "those individuals [must] suffer loss, but private interest must ever yield to public good. The welfare of the many must ever be consulted rather than that of the few." Others worried about placing the future of a public resource in private hands. "The right of obstructing the Ohio river, of limiting, if not destroying, the greatest of all the advantages of our natural position, is about to be granted to a company whose privileges are to endure forever," complained one correspondent. John's contribution to the debate was all frustration and sarcasm: "And really it is lamentable, is it not? That a great public work of this kind, beneficial to a whole district, should be permitted to interfere with a [ferry] corporation consisting of about a dozen members, all told, which has for years been paying a dividend of fifteen percent." To which the *Journal* responded with its own brand of insult. "It is not impossible for the Ass to attempt the stately stride of a nobler animal, and it is very common for a stupid blockhead to attempt sarcasm where he is unable to controvert successfully the arguments of an opponent. It is not difficult to imagine 'C[ivis]' in precisely such a category," it retorted.[31]

The *Journal* continued to hurl abuse and complaints against what it dubbed the "tripod affair." It took delight in deriding the "three-legged bridge" and its supporters, which helped bring John back into print. Still in the role of Civis and still clinging to his composure, John tried to address each and every point leveled against the bridge by the *Journal*. His reply was long—marshalling facts, figures, and other technical details—but measured and logical, betraying none of the angry petulance of his earlier forays into public debate. He identified three main objections to the project and then set about demolishing each of them. First, that the project was nothing but "a scheme of speculation and as such deserves no favor from the public." John thought both sides had "interested motives," but that proponents would likely come out better than the opponents when comparing "purity of the motives." After all, "this project must be judged by its own merits and by its influence for good or evil upon the community." Second, that the bridge was the continuation of a system designed to "destroy our harbor and take away the facilities of our distant trade." John disagreed. The current bridges "are undoubtedly obnoxious," but this bridge would be something new, something higher and bigger, built to satisfy "builders and owners of steamboats and commercial men of intelligence." Third, John quoted the *Journal* directly: "It is calculated to draw away our capital and population, and to build up rival villages at the expense of the prosperity of the eastern parts of our city, and perhaps finally transfer our harbor to some point on the Ohio." This seemed like pure fantasy to John. To accuse anyone of favoring Manchester and Temperanceville at the expense of Pittsburgh was nothing more than "a dry joke."[32]

The final Tripartite Bridge Bill passed the state house and senate in early April and was signed by the governor.[33] The *Journal* was apoplectic but moved on swiftly to critique the financing. The legislation called for the company to offer five hundred shares at five hundred dollars per share, with sales to start on July 13. No one seemed to have any doubt that the shares would sell quickly. The

Gazette seemed to think that "$225,000 can be obtained at once." From far-off New York, the *Tribune* thought "the requisite stock will be subscribed in due time, and the work be put under contract for construction." In a private diary, John wrote, "Mr. Chest on the Monongahela side, owns coalmines & offers to subscribe 15000 for the Point Br."[34] The *Journal* perceived that the tides of public opinion were changing around public utilities, however. A recent increase in the tolls on the Allegheny and Monongahela bridges had caused a storm of "angry indignation [serving] most effectually to open the eyes of capitalists to the utter insecurity of this sort of investment. Why, the managers of bridges dare hardly call their souls their own," they complained. "Progressive democracy has taken them in hand, and bridges, and managers, and toll collectors, and assessors are grown suddenly odious." Was this the sort of climate into which investors wished to pour thousands of dollars? they asked. "Free bridges are the talk and topic of the day," they argued. "There *ought* to be free bridges spanning both our rivers—there *will* be within a very few years," and who then "is going to invest his thousands in the Tripartite Bridge Stock? Who is bold enough to cast his *tens of thousands* into the forlorn hope for a six or ten per cent return?" This was an inspired attack, and it worked brilliantly. "We believe as firmly that the *stock will not be subscribed nor the work begun*," they concluded. The stock went on sale as planned in July, and not a single share was bought.[35]

John wasn't in Pittsburgh when shares in the tripartite bridge went on sale. The years 1846 and 1847 were two of the most active and involved ones in his life. If he wasn't in Pittsburgh or Cincinnati writing, campaigning, and surveying, he was elsewhere drumming up business, meeting customers, or at some large body of water thinking of how best to throw a suspension bridge across it. John was rarely in one place for long from the beginning of 1846 to the middle of 1847. As soon as the tripartite-bridge legislation passed, he set off on a "tour east." His main object was to visit the people and places of eastern Pennsylvania's burgeoning anthracite mining region, where his wire ropes were already being used to haul coal and then transport it along inclined planes and gravity railroads to waiting canal barges and on to market in New York. His itinerary took him from Saxonburg to "Harrisburg, Philadelphia, Pottsville & region, Mauch Chunk, Canal RR, Wilkesbarre planes, Wilkesbarre, Carbondale, Honesdale, Middle town, New York, Easton, Morris Canal, Philadelphia," and back home. Along the way he toured factories, met with other engineers and experts, and made notes on "Cornwall engines," "the Dauphin and Susquehanna RR," "refining pig iron," "the trade of New Orleans," "the Reading Rail Road," "the Erie Canal," and dozens of other subjects, including notes on Charles Ellet's formula for calculating the cost of "freight over and above the repairs and maintenance of the road."[36]

His main interests, of course, were wire rope and coal. He toured John Stewart's rolling mill in Easton, Pennsylvania, which had recently started producing iron wire. John also made extensive notes on the coal industry: where it was mined, where it was taken, what it cost to move it, and who the main players in the industry were. He met with officials and toured facilities at the Delaware and Hudson (D&H)—who were already customers—and the Lehigh Coal and Navigation Company (LC&N) and the Morris Canal, both of whom were about to be. Edwin Douglas, superintendent of the LC&N, returned the favor later that year, visiting the Saxonburg ropewalk, along with Planes no. 3 and 10 on the Portage Railroad, in November. Suitably impressed, Douglas began ordering Roebling ropes almost immediately. John also filled a number of trial orders, including some in New York for ship rigging, and by the end of the year was offering a whole range of new ropes: different gauges, diameters, and lengths, all "seasoned and varnished." John's rope-spinning team worked furiously from April until the middle of November making 42,650 feet of rope by hand. By the end of the following year, that number would rise again to an astonishing 61,921 feet.[37]

John's "tour" of the mining and manufacturing regions of eastern Pennsylvania helped secure the future of his wire rope business and ultimately his personal fortune. Just as importantly, it brought him to New York, where he met one of the few people he could call a genuine personal friend and where he glimpsed the East River for the very first time. It is uncertain exactly how John met Frederick Overman—the "worthy and accomplished man of science," as John called him, and author of *The Manufacture of Iron* (1850), *Practical Mineralogy* (1851), and *A Treatise on Metallurgy* (1852), to which John supplied a touching introduction—but the two quickly became close. The depth of their friendship in many respects mirrors the similarity of their backgrounds and beliefs. Not only were they both technologists, intimately concerned with metallurgy, but the two also shared an uncannily similar life path. Both were born to "modest parents" and grew up in provincial Prussia before attending university in Berlin, where they studied under some of the same professors. Like John, Overman worked as a mechanic on various construction projects in and around East Prussia and the Upper Rhine Valley. Neither enjoyed the idea of "a permanent situation as a government official"; both emigrated to America—Overman much later than John—with "a love of freedom and unfettered action" after "various disappointments and dissatisfactions." John must have seen something of himself in Overman and perhaps enjoyed a rare moment of nostalgia for his family and his homeland, and the lost, carefree days of his youth. In terms of personality and temperament, the two seem cut from the same cloth, despite Washington's claim that

Overman's "placid disposition was the reverse of my father's." Both were indefatigable thinkers, researchers, and doers. John thought Overman was "endowed by nature with a vast cerebral organization." Many thought the same about John.[38]

John's record of this "tour east" contains numerous references to Overman, as well as the final feature that sealed their friendship. Overman, like John, was an active homeopath and a committed self-medicator, although his mania was charcoal, not water. "Overman's Great Remedy" was "Charcoal of Hard Wood, Hickory, reduced to small grains, *no dust*, one spoonful of Charcoal and one spoonful of sugar in one tumbler full of water, drink in the morning, and if inclined, several more tumblers full during the day," and he applied it for everything. "Charcoal acts mechanically upon all the mucous membranes," Overman explained to John, "clears the whole system and acts as an antidote against most poisons, and regulates the stool. But sugar should always be taken with the Charcoal. . . . This is very important. Physicians will order charcoal powder, which will lodge in the membranes and stick there, until it is removed forcibly by a laxative. . . . Charcoal in the stomach acts very beneficially by absorbing all acid and indigested slime. . . . It then passes into the large bowel and will clean them & facilitate the formation of foeces [sic]." Much as John's water cure mania had some basis in fact, so Overman's belief in the medicinal properties of charcoal had merit. Charcoal has long been used as a means of removing certain toxins, especially in cases of poisoning. However, the method doesn't extend to every unwanted substance in one's system, as Overman seemed to believe, especially in relation to iron: "If there is too much iron in the system free, too much oxydation [sic] going, too much heat making (inside) there will be *fever*. To reduce the quantity of free iron in the system is the object of Charcoal, which absorbs the iron & carries it out of the system." While charcoal has no effect on iron in the system, it does affect digestion if taken orally in the sort of quantities recommended by Overman. In large doses, it can jam the gastrointestinal tract; in smaller doses, it leads to black stools and constipation, both long-standing complaints of John's.[39]

The trust John placed in Overman is apparent from the fact that he was allowed to diagnose and treat John: "O[verman] thinks that the vitality & nervous system is too active in me, and wants to be reduced, so that fat can be formed to give strength & tone to the muscles, which is necessary for a good digestion, assimilation and secretion." Unsurprisingly, he counseled the use of charcoal, but also "salmiac," or ammonium chloride. "The use of Charcoal may be carried to a great extent beneficially and continued on," wrote John, "until the coating of the stomach and of the bowels are perfectly cleaned, its muscles lubricated & fattened by the use of sugar, and then the system will have regained enough strength to help itself & remain in good order. . . . Salmiac will open the pores of the skin, cause a great secretion, therefore caution is necessary, else one will take cold, when using it in large quantities. Several ounces a day, with cor-responding quantities of Charcoal and Sugar may be necessary in severe cases." Needless to say, John's health continued to decline over the next several years, despite his ability to keep up a furious work rate.[40]

John's friendship with Overman has left little in the way of a written record, although it does provide confirmation of Washington's claim that "regarding personal friendships there was nothing lukewarm in my father's character—his friendships were of the warmest type and his animosities correspondingly bitter." Overman died unexpectedly on January 7, 1852, from the effects of arseniuretted hydrogen inhaled while engaged in a chemical experiment. The inhalation occurred on Christmas Day 1851, after which Overman "treated himself, dieting and using charcoal" until New Year's, when, according to John, he "yielded to the solicitations of some people at the Allegheny House [where Overman was staying] and took medicine." "This made him worse, he began to be delirious and in consequence became very careless in his diet, ate pie & this no doubt deranged his digestion very much, he got the *typhoid fever*," John wrote in what may have been his strangest diagnosis.[41] The incident would haunt John until his death, which transpired in remarkably similar circumstances, and may even have fueled John's own intransigence in the face of a deadly infection.

John's grief at his friend's passing was palpable: "A great genius is gone! My best friend is no more!! Did not see him alife [*sic*], came too late, on Thursday and attended to his burial—but I hope to see him in the next Sphere of existence, and shall no doubt admire the advance of his Glorious Spirit and have the ben-efit of his wise counsel! Peace to your soul my dear departed friend!" "Poor hu-manity," John continued, "so long as thy best desires and impulses are constantly suppressed and outraged by our defective social relations, so long whilst thine suffer and the [*sic*] best children will be sacrificed to the brutal passions and corrupt usages of this sublunary world! Adieu my dear Overman, Thine Spirit remember me and be ready to meet mine own when one day freed of its present body!!!" John's official, published tribute was less cryptic and mystical: "Those who have been intimate with the deceased, appreciated his exquisite taste and mature judgment in all that is ennobling and beautiful. In his mind there was a rare union of the ideal with the useful, the practical and the rational. But the most prominent trait in his character was an exalted love of truth and moral freedom, those two features essential to form the basis of a really great man." Subsequent to Overman's demise, John supported his friend's family—a wife, a daughter, and two sons—and left them a "handsome legacy" after his death.[42]

John met his best friend only a day or so before he first encounterd the strip of water between New York and Long Island known as the East River. Back home in Saxonburg, he pondered the waterway over the next several months, ulti-mately developing a plan to span the East River in October 1847. His "Bridge over the East River across Blackwell's Island" was designed to carry water from Manhattan to Long Island beneath a twenty-three-foot-wide roadway. In its particulars, it was remarkably similar to the span erected by Gustav Lindenthal in 1909, although both plans owe more to the convenient presence of Blackwell's Island (now known as Roosevelt Island) in the middle of the river than engineering inspiration. A central span of four hundred feet, with a pier planted on either side of Blackwell's Island, linked two 1,600-foot side spans. The cables in the former "will require anchoring, to balance the large spans, so that the small span will serve as fixed anchorage for the large spans." Movable rollers would carry the main suspension cables, while "stays will add to the stability of the centre span." Seven-foot-high wooden stiffening trusses linked with vertical iron rods to carry three two-foot-wide cast iron water pipes located beneath the upper deck.[43]

John's initial East River bridge showed ambition. Its two 1,600-foot spans were far longer than any bridge in existence or even proposed at that point. However, it is unlikely that the plan enjoyed any official standing or any relationship to John Jervis's massive Croton Aqueduct project, then being finished. Still the project and the idea behind it were novel and impressive. Jervis's plan brought water from the Croton River, in Westchester County, down through the Bronx, across the High Bridge over the Harlem River, down the east side of Manhattan and into a receiving reservoir at Yorkhill (now part of Central Park's Great Lawn). There was no plan to extend the aqueduct's benefits to any of the surrounding regions, nor was it Jervis's mandate to do so. John's plan did, however, propose to ship fresh, clean water across the East River from the receiving reservoir in New York to both Queens Village and the thriving independent city of Brooklyn. Equally novel was a very patchy alternative plan John worked up to accommodate trolley lines or railroads on the bridge. As if not entirely satisfied by covering so many bases, John then added: "By adding outside cables and widening sidewalks the plan will answer for the East River Bridge Aqueduct."[44]

John returned to the idea of bridging the East River at Blackwell's Island in 1855–57, drawing up several plans and designs, before eventually settling on a location farther south, closer to the population centers that would use the bridge.[45] Such a development illustrates both the mundane, workaday nature of engineering—not to mention waiting for the right climate and financing, or a change in public opinion—and the poor ratio of bridges designed to bridges built in a career, even for an engineer as successful as John. He designed dozens of bridges in his lifetime, sometimes tweaking and revising them multiple times. Some designs were vague and abstract—little more than doodles—while others were fully formed. Rarely a year passed without John tinkering with an idea. In March 1846, for example, John received a letter from one James Taylor stating, "The citizens of Pendleton Co. wish to construct a bridge across the Licking at Falmouth—& they think that a wire suspension bridge on your plan a good one—they wish me to write you on the subject." John replied that he would happily build them a two-hundred-foot span for $16,000, after which he heard nothing more. The following year, John drew up plans for a five-hundred-foot-long suspension footbridge over the Delaware River at Barryville, New York. Again, money was the sticking point, and the project went nowhere.[46]

More significantly, John communicated with A. G. Morton of the St. Lawrence and Atlantic Railroad about the feasibility of constructing a bridge over the St. Lawrence River at Montreal, just north of La Prairie Bay, "for the passage of R.R. trains and common track." It would be massive, wrote John, "a vast undertaking, [although] if properly accomplished [also] a great national work, and the

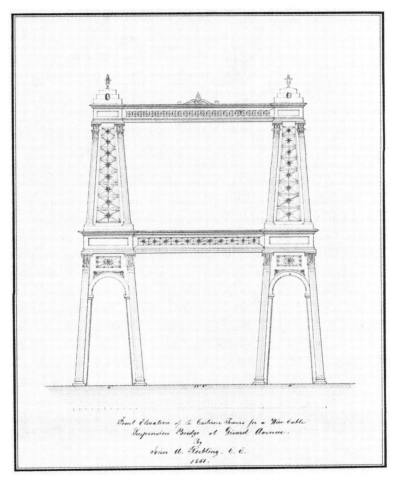

Figure 12.2 John Roebling, "Front Elevation of the Cast Iron Towers, Suspension Bridge at Girard Ave" (1851). Courtesy of the Institute Archives and Special Collections, Rensselaer Polytechnic Institute.

largest and most remarkable bridge on the globe." It would also require "great caution and foresight . . . to overcome the great difficulties of construction," of course. John had "frequently noticed the action of the ice on the Susquehanna, Allegheny and Ohio [rivers], but this [was] but child's play when compared to [the] ice gorges" of the St. Lawrence, "where large masses of ice, when checked in their course, are so suddenly piled up by the force of the current, until the accumulation of the pressure becomes so great that everything must give way before it." A wooden bridge would of course "be carried off the first winter," while a series of suspended spans—four hundred feet apart so as not to interfere with navigation—would prove extremely costly and difficult. Still, John worked up some partial designs, including a set of elegant towers, designed to support two massive suspension cables and a set of eleven cable stays radiating out from the towers across the roadway.[47]

The St. Lawrence bridge project was fantastical given the likely costs and the state of the art of bridge building at the time, and the idea was soon dropped. Other projects loomed, more aligned with price, needs, and practice. On January 20, 1846, J. Brady of the Merchants Bank invited John "to come to Wheeling on the subject of Susp. Br.—they have a Charter," John wrote in a notebook.[48] Already preoccupied with multiple jobs and schemes—finishing the Monongahela Bridge, planning his tripartite span, closely following the debate in Kentucky, about to reveal his controversial Ohio claim, planning his "tour east" to test the market for his wire ropes and drum up new business, and his visit to Cincinnati—John deferred, although not indefinitely. By late 1846, he had produced a detailed initial plan and by the early months of the following year was in correspondence with members of the newly established Wheeling and Belmont Bridge Company. In April, John was invited to submit a formal proposal. He visited Wheeling in June 1847—after a whistle-stop trip to Niagara Falls, where another group was looking for someone to build them a bridge—and by the end of the month had produced a comprehensive plan. Unfortunately, the bridge company also invited Charles Ellet to visit Wheeling and submit a proposal, which turned out poorly for John. Much to John's incensed disbelief, the Wheeling and Belmont Bridge Company awarded Ellet the contract on July 14, 1847, after which, in Washington's arch commentary, "their troubles commenced."[49]

John tried to disguise his public defeat in a letter to Hamilton Merritt, one of the promoters behind the Niagara Falls bridge, two weeks later. "I have been negotiating with the people of Wheeling for the contract of a bridge over the Ohio R. but have withdrawn disgusted with the treatment I have experienced," he lied.[50] He lost out to Ellet in large part due to his own timidity and to Ellet's more aggressive vision. John's plan called for a central pier in the middle of the Ohio flanked by two side spans (531 and 384 feet), while Ellet proposed a single, soaring leap of 1,010 feet from shore to shore. John's bridge provided more clearance, Ellet's less immediate obstruction. The ramifications of the decision were initially huge. In large part due to the Wheeling contract, Ellet was also able to secure the contract to bridge the Niagara Gorge between the United States and Canada, a project that had attracted John's interest since January 1846 and on which he worked assiduously for over a year and a half. As at Wheeling, both John and Ellet submitted formal proposals in the spring of 1847, as did Samuel Keefer and Edward Serrell. Remarkably, all four engineers would end up throwing bridges across the Niagara Gorge at one point or another, but again Ellet prevailed. He was awarded the contract on November 9, 1847, at which point the Niagara International Bridge Company's troubles also began—as did Ellet's.[51]

———

John returned to Cincinnati in late May just as the city was rapidly remaking itself from wretched, rancid "Porkopolis," so wonderfully ridiculed by Fanny Trollope in *Domestic Manners of the Americans* (1832), to a "Queen City," the Athens of the West.[52] Cincinnati had established itself as the steamboat capital of the Ohio Valley by 1825 and by mid-century was "the economic colossus of the entire West." Its economy was "enormous and diversified." It was the nation's largest producer of beer and liquor, the West's biggest furniture maker, and the biggest American book publisher outside of New York, Philadelphia, and Boston. It had almost cornered the market in stoves, while myriad thriving foundries, boat works, packing houses, clothing mills, soap plants, and lard-oil and stearin works spewed forth an array of products. The city was still by far the country's largest producer of pork—butchering upward of seventy thousand beasts a year—an industry that fueled much of Cincinnati's expansion. As Frenchman J. J. Ampere explained, "It is the hogs that have made it all possible!"[53]

The Miami and Erie Canal was completed in 1845, making Cincinnati the central western hub linking the Great Lakes with the Mississippi, further cementing the city's commercial standing. Furthermore, a railroad linking the Queen City to Dayton and Columbus was also in the works. Cincinnati's population—24,831 in 1830—was 46,338 by 1840, twice that of Pittsburgh and three times the size of St. Louis. By 1850, it was the sixth-largest city in the United States, with a population of 115,435, almost half of whom were foreign born. John Quincy Adams called Cincinnati the "Herculean City" in 1844. Harriet Martineau thought she would "prefer Cincinnati as a residence to any other large city of the United States." According to diarist Frank Blackwell, "Progress and prosperity are everywhere evident, and the long lines of steamboats and piles of merchandise on the levee, the bustle of the passing crowds, the whizz and whirr of factories, and the elegant stores and bank buildings give token of a brilliant future to the 'Queen City of the West,'" a future not entirely confined to commerce. To add to its economic vibrancy, Cincinnati was "also a seat of education and culture, a Boston of the West," as one visitor described it. Its streets were "pleasant [and] cheerful with the green of trees and almost always ending brightly with a view of the river or of the hills." It was much shabbier around the river, with saloons and "windowless shacks," where John spent much of his time, but very "orderly" otherwise.[54]

Across the river, Covington was "moving at a rapid rate, in the march of improvement. A walk over the City will convince the observer that she is destined to become one of the most flourishing cities in the West." The town's "commercial business has more than doubled itself within the last twelve-month" while Newport, its neighbor across the Licking River, was "rising rapidly" too. "To go on with [these] gigantic strides" required only two more things, reported the *Chronicle* in September 1846: a bridge over the Licking between Covington and Newport and one over the Ohio between Covington and Cincinnati.[55]

John took all this in as he gazed out across the Ohio. He saw the scale of trade and the mass of activity. He experienced the chaotic public landing, the overburdened river, the conflicts between those crossing over and those passing down the river. Crossing the Ohio with livestock—the very source of Cincinnati's wealth—was especially perilous. Even in the best of conditions, spooked animals could upset the stoutest vessel. In fact, several boatloads of swine were lost to the Ohio that year. The seasons also complicated crossings. The weather had been so bad during the last few winters that communication across the river had been cut off for long stretches, leaving goods and livestock stranded for days. As the movement of goods in the region increased, making Cincinnati a large-scale commercial market, so did the need for reliability and dependability.[56]

John's guides in the Queen City were R. H. Rickey, a local surveyor and mapmaker, Captain R. L. Browning of the US Navy, and a local businessman named Withers. John spent most of his time along the waterfront, measuring, noting, calculating, and thinking. He met with local business leaders to assess the scale of the commitment and the depth of their pockets. He also met prominent riverboat captains and steamship owners to hear their thoughts and concerns. After an exhausting couple of weeks, he had all he needed and took a steamboat back to Pittsburgh to work on his plan.[57]

———

In mid-October, a man calling himself "Enterprise" wrote to Cincinnati's *Daily Chronicle* to say that he had "seen the plan and report of Mr. Roebling, a practical and scientific engineer," for bridging the Ohio and that it would soon be published for general consideration. "The plan is beautiful," he avowed. "Such a bridge as Mr. Roebling proposes, will be an honor to the West—the admiration of every stranger, and a monument of fame to the Queen City," he concluded; "she ought to be the first to span the Ohio, and the last to say it can't be done." There is no evidence about who Enterprise was or how he got a look at John's proposal. He may have been one of those to whom it was addressed, but he clearly intended to prime the pump for the coming discussion. "Let not our views be limited by the opposite shore," he cautioned, "nor our minds contracted by jealousy; these hills [must some day] encircle one great city, united by several bridges, and by all the ties of interest, consanguinity and friendship." Predictably, John's report followed quickly after.[58]

John's *Report and Plan for a Wire Suspension Bridge, Proposed to Be Erected over the Ohio River at Cincinnati* (1846) was his first fully fledged and fully realized written proposal, a form at which he would eventually become a master. His style was clear and simple but evocative and wholly persuasive. According to Washington, "Every part of the project is treated in a clear and concise style, with short telling sentences—The language is plain but forcible, and everyone can understand what is meant. There is nothing ambiguous, and no essentials are left unsaid." He improved each time, refining ideas and replicating themes that seemed to resonate. For some, John's written reports—as much as his finished bridges—were the reason he was able to win so many important contracts.[59]

John began his pamphlet with some rhetoric, a little history, and a short introduction to the state of the art of modern engineering. "As one of the great thoroughfares of the country, and spanning one of the great rivers of the West, this bridge, when constructed, will possess great claims as a national monument," he declared. "As a splendid work of art and as a remarkable specimen of modern engineering," he continued, "it will stand unrivalled upon this continent. Its gigantic features will speak loudly in favor of the energy, enterprize and wealth of the community which will boast of its possession." John employed an almost identical opening in his *Report to the President and Directors of the New York Bridge Company* (1867), and he coupled it with a plain statement of intent. John's aim was simply to present the plan to the public for discussion and debate. Any action taken "in opposition to public opinion . . . must turn out a fatal enterprise, and cannot succeed," he affirmed.[60]

John's first move was to admit the primacy of the navigation argument. All those voices clamoring for an unimpeded river were right, of course, as "a general proposition," although they also missed something crucial to their future prosperity. "It appears but justice," John argued, "that the state should be allowed the right of forming communications across the river, accessible at all seasons, for the promotion of commerce and intercourse, provided such communications do not impede the navigation." After all, "the time is not very distant, when millions of people will crowd both shores of the Ohio, and when the question of *bridging* will become highly important to the *landsmen* as well as to the *riverman*," a prescient remark given the spreading influence of railroads. All of this raised a question: How to have free navigation and cross-river communication? Fortunately, modern engineering had solved "the problem of crossing large and deep rivers" by inventing and perfecting suspension bridges. "Spans of 1,500 feet or more" were perfectly feasible for any "competent builder," John explained. The only real issue facing the profession at this point was expense versus need. The longer the bridge, of course, the more expensive the construction costs would be. Engineers would happily build bridges, so long as the money was there to pay for their expertise. At this time, William Tierney Clark was hard at work on a thousand-foot-long bridge over the Danube at Budapest, John wrote, before getting back to his pitch: "It is on the great rivers of the *new world*, where this system of bridge-building will, in course of time, be fully applied and perfected."[61]

John also dutifully addressed the issue of clearance. "I should not countenance a scheme which was calculated to bring about results so disastrous" as interfering with navigation, he avowed. The bridge he was proposing, however, did not. It possessed an elevation of ninety feet "above *low water*" rising to 121 feet near the middle of the river, which was more than sufficient for any of the packet boats currently plying the Ohio. Certainly, a flood the likes of which Cincinnati hadn't seen since 1832 would make life tricky, but all boats plying the central channel would still be able to pass beneath the bridge. Much more likely than clearance troubles would be a general reduction in the height of steamboats. The prevailing wisdom on the Ohio suggested that powerful boats needed high chimneys, but boatmen on "our eastern waters, and in ocean navigation" had already learned this was not true.[62]

After successfully touching on the main points of likely opposition, John got to the details of the proposal. His bridge would be 1,576 feet long from abutment to abutment and 2,070 feet long including the approaches. It wouldn't necessarily look like most other modern suspension bridges, with two piers supporting a central, graceful parabolic arc. Instead, John proposed to plant a single "gigantic stone pier"—two hundred feet tall and forty-five feet wide—right in the middle of the Ohio. Two side spans, each 788 feet long, would flank the middle tower and "sweep across the river in a curved line, which will improve the graceful appearance of the work." The central pier was designed as a somewhat plain affair, with little or no adornment. In appearance it resembled a large, relatively stolid A, reinforced by buttresses. Two much smaller, shorter towers—thirty feet high—would be built on each abutment. The main suspension cables would run from the anchorages, snake over the short abutment towers, and stretch up and over the massive main tower, before sloping back down to the opposite shore and on to the antipodal anchorage. The main cables would support the side spans and rest on cast iron rollers on the smaller side towers to allow for free movement but be clamped and fixed to the main tower. "The uniformity and symmetry of the two ends will add much to the splendid appearance which this great structure will present to the eye of the traveler who approaches the city by the river," John claimed.[63]

John's two-span, single-tower suspension bridge would be thirty-four feet wide, with a 20½-foot-wide carriageway and two six-foot-wide sidewalks. The carriageway would be supported by two suspension cables (eleven inches in diameter), spun in position and inclined inward slightly, toward the roadway. Each cable would be made of 5,500 individual wires, wrapped and spun using the method he had used on the Allegheny Aqueduct. In addition, each wire would be manufactured to bear more than "four times the greatest tension to which it can ever be subjected." A system of inclined stays would radiate out from the main tower and help to protect against vibration, aid support, and "counteract the effects which heavy loads may have upon one span, while no load is on the other." The stays were designed to act "entirely *independent*" of the cables. Each pair of stays, occupying a corresponding position on each side of the tower, was to be made of a "single *wire rope*" so that when one side was overloaded, that side's stay would yield, while the other would tighten. In common with the main suspension cables, the stays would also help transfer pressure from the live loads on the bridge to the massive central tower. Needless to say, John also believed the stays would add greatly to the bridge's appearance.[64]

Regarding his controversial single tower, John had a little explaining to do. Although he had initially been in favor of two towers and a single span, his new plan achieved the same end while allowing other important advantages. A single, clear span "would appear to be more independent of the river," but the public need have "no fear" about a two-span, single-tower bridge, he counseled. A two-span bridge was cheaper. It would also allow for better, more integrated and convenient approaches; impinge much less on the overall harbor area; and make it easier to attain the required clearance at mid-river. In short, John's two-span bridge provided adequate clearance and helped maintain the integrity of the harbor.[65]

"If properly constructed," John's bridge would also survive "the effects of a hurricane," which have so often "proved destructive to suspension bridges." This is normally due to insufficient strength, John explained, along with "the undulations of a very flexible floor, the rise and fall of which produced a succession of shocks." The "yielding nature" of John's bridge would save it from such a fate, provided its stiffness was "great enough to check undulatory vibrations." Likewise, "the allowance for the strength of the cables, might indeed be considered extravagant. But we have to remember that this bridge will have to accommodate an immense traffic," he advised, before getting more than a little carried away: "and that it will stand foremost in the rank of such works, from its location as well as its magnificent proportions. As it is calculated to last for ages, it will, in the course of time, become the greatest thoroughfare of the world, not even the London bridges excepted," he announced. The success of the bridge would depend on all these things to some degree but most importantly "on the intelligent observation of the workmen who have charge of it," John wrote. He estimated that it would take three years to complete, although completing it in that time frame would "require . . . energetic and systematic management." The total cost would be $374,460, with the cables alone costing almost a third of that. The precise location had yet to be determined. John had surveyed from Wharf and Main Streets in Cincinnati to Garrard and Wharf in Covington but was at pains to stress that "the bridge is perfectly practicable at any point in the city."[66]

Befitting the nature of the proposal and its intended audience, John ended with some promotional rhetoric: "Less than one hundred years ago the greater part of this Union of states was one vast unbroken wilderness," he began, "traversed by none but prowling savages and beasts of prey. . . . Where now can be witnessed at each hour of the day, scenes of great commercial activity, the bustle of the arrival and departure of hundreds of travelers, there reigned, fifty years ago, the unbroken solitude of a dense forest. Where now the bosom of the Ohio is ploughed up and down by hundreds of swiftly moving steamers, conveying thousands of intelligent beings, transporting the products of industry and of the soil, and distributing the necessaries, comforts, and luxuries of life in all directions." "You have all witnessed these great and wonderful changes," he continued, hoping to flatter and persuade; "they astonish you less since you have participated yourselves, in this great move of civilization! Where, fifty years ago, the Indian trader hardly dared to penetrate, there your city stands now— a new city, emphatically—boasting the proud name of the *Queen of the West*, the commercial emporium of three of the richest states in the Union!" Clearly, John's rhetoric had caught up with his technical knowledge. As if to underline his newfound confidence and station, John signed off as "John A. Roebling, C.E. [Civil Engineer]," a piece of professional affectation. Despite all his successes John possessed no official honors or qualifications. He did, however, know how to make an impression.[67]

John's proposal was not the only plan under discussion in 1846. The eight-month gap between discussion and submission allowed time for others to get into the race. In a private notebook, John made reference to a plan by a Dr. Orr for an 1,800-foot-long bridge—"2 spans of 600 feet each with a center pier"— costing $175,000. Orr was a distinguished physician from Cincinnati, and his bridge was "a modification of the wire suspension bridge . . . composed entirely of iron, except the floor." "I have seen no work of Art, of this species, that comprises so much neatness, and at the same time so much adequate strength," reported someone called Shawk, "an eminent mechanic of Cincinnati." Other proposals included a hundred-foot-wide stone arch railroad bridge, flanked by fifty-foot-wide streets submitted by a Mr. Willard. The "scheme has its advantages," wrote the *Enquirer*, but "serious objections" persist. Believing John's project was "impractical," the *Enquirer* favored a plan by someone named Lane, which called for a single span of 1,300 feet "perfectly level" and involved ascending roundabouts at each abutment to gain the necessary clearance. The *Enquirer* felt Lane's "strong, elegant and light structure [would] resist and sustain every possible pressure."[68]

———

Most of the press had a copy of John's proposal by December 1. The *Chronicle* found it "prepared with great labor and care." It clearly "establishes, beyond all doubt or cavil, the practicability of the work," they concluded. The *Daily Commercial* agreed. John's report "meets boldly every objection ever brought forward by the opposition to this gigantic project and completely overthrows them all." "The gigantic features of this work, spreading over the mighty Ohio, will speak loudly in favor of the enterprise and wealth of our citizens," they concluded. "It is practicable! It will be incalculably useful! *It should be built*." The *Railroad Journal* believed that "Mr. R. is fully equal to [an] undertaking of [such] vast magnitude."[69] It wasn't popular with everyone, however. "Single Span" mocked John's plan in the *Gazette*: should this scheme come off, the Queen City would become the most "*thrillingly* interesting" city "for wrecks and drowning," he proclaimed. "Cincinnatus," writing in the same paper a couple of days later, was sympathetic to the plight of those who might lose out in the deal but— echoing a theme that seemed to stretch down the entire Ohio, from Pittsburgh to Cincinnati—also believed wholeheartedly that "private interests must bend to public necessities; the bridge is indispensible." Another of the *Gazette's* correspondents—"A"—was more to the point: the bridge was a "public utility" and thus beyond the scope of property owners and rivermen who could not be trusted to give a disinterested view. The only valid response was the following questions: Would the piers be a nuisance, and would it cost more than its value? Thankfully, both of these questions were answered in John's plan, the work of "an engineer of talents and experience, which have gained for him so high a reputation" that he deserved the public's "attention."[70]

The most sustained attack on John's proposal came from a small, privately published pamphlet that appeared early the following year. "The consequences of erecting such a structure, as is now proposed, across the Ohio River at Cincinnati, are too important and extensive, either for good or evil, to be slightly considered, or entirely shut out from view, by those who are engaged in its navigation, or who reside upon or near it," declared the anonymous pamphleteer, launching into a rather tortuous argument about jurisdiction and decision-making. Certainly, Kentucky and Ohio needed to sign off on the bridge, he wrote, but the matter was more complex than that. At the time of the Northwest Ordinance (when the free navigation of all US rivers was declared), Kentucky was a part of Virginia, so logically Virginia would also need to sign off too. Even if Kentucky, Ohio, and Virginia all approved the bridge, "it must be remembered that Congress was a party to it also," so their "express assent" must also be secured. Congress of course acts for the entire United States, and not as a single entity but as a series of "*sovereign*" states, all of whom "hold navigable rights, which are substantive, definite and legal." In case anyone was confused, the writer gave an equally tortuous summary: the legislation could not pass with the support of "Kentucky alone, nor Kentucky and Ohio together, nor Kentucky, Ohio and Virginia, nor the Congress . . . alone, nor yet in conjunction with these three, nor yet with them and with all the other States on the river or between its mouth and the seas, nor [even] by the unanimous concurrence of all the States of the present confederacy." In passing the Northwest Ordinance, Congress had intended to put free navigation "beyond the reach and grasp of change . . . *Forever!*"[71]

The argument could well have stopped there, with the permanent sealing of the nation's riverbanks, but the author objected on still broader grounds. Despite the title of his pamphlet—*Remarks upon Mr. Roebling's "Plan & Report, of the Proposed at Cincinnati"*—the author opposed all plans. John's bridge would impede navigation, but so would "*any other plan.*" Any addition to the Ohio would make it difficult for boats to dock, turn, and otherwise maneuver around and about the river. It would also significantly affect current, creating eddies, sandbars, and shoals, and "even islands," in ways that would be both destructive and difficult to predict. Any changes made to the Ohio would lead to "apprehension and terror" among boatmen and would likely result in boats "grounded, sunk and wrecked." To reinforce his point, the author presented a long letter from the former port warden Joseph Pierce, who recalled the horrific winter of 1832 when "the river was gorged with ice." At thawing, when fresh water came down the Licking River, loosening the floes, "the whole came down with such rapidity and forces as to destroy almost everything that came into contact with it." Two steamers "were totally destroyed," and another "was cut through." No bridge piers in the world could possibly withstand such an onslaught, Pierce insisted.[72]

In conclusion, Pierce wrote, "Destruction, great loss of property and life, must inevitably be the consequence, if a pier to support a bridge is suffered to be erected in the Ohio river." As for the ever-present danger of the Ohio bursting its banks, "be it remembered [that] mighty floods bear upon their bosom trees, wrecks, houses, barns and every imaginably object, all of which must, at this bridge, stop, sink or jump it, [exposing the city] to dangers too appalling to be hazarded." "Posterity will find no satisfaction, and but little justification in this, for the accumulation of injury which . . . must result to Cincinnati, to Ohio, to the Union, from any such work that is now proposed. For good or evil, the subject is too momentous to be acted upon without a patient and, if necessary, long investigation of all its multiplied bearings," he concluded.[73]

"Let the actions of our Legislature, then, be governed by a keen anxiety to consult the just interests of all classes and by the purest principles of practical republicanism," wrote the *Sunday News*, ahead of the legislative session of 1847. "Go for the good of the whole—of the mass," they advised, "and if our Legislature will look at the subject with open eyes," they would understand the benefits to be "incalculable" while the "evil effects so trifling." The Ohio legislature returned to the bridge bill during the winter of 1847, adding measures about lighting, liens, congressional approval, and timeline, ultimately voting the measure down by twenty-five votes to eight. There was clear discontent with the Ohio pier. John had promised a clear span and delivered a "gigantic" two-hundred-foot obstruction. No amount of calculations and explanations could fully convince people otherwise. The legislature clearly equated free, unimpeded navigation with a clear river, from side to side, although there were other significant factors that played into the decision. The weather, for one, didn't help. John's proposal had made light of excessive flooding, which didn't help much on December 10, 1846, when the Ohio burst its banks, raising water levels to heights not seen in decades. Similar floods visited the region again, in early January 1847, further eroding some of John's credibility. By the time the legislature voted, Cincinnati had experienced what many of John's opponents had warned of twice in a six-week period, hardly a happy omen.[74]

The fate of the legislation, as State Senator Charles Reemelin saw it, came down to two factors, one technical, the other political. Reemelin was "tense" about the proposal because, he explained, "I realized that, with my lack of knowledge about mechanics . . . I could not support Röbling's projects skillfully enough before the senate." John did his best instructing the state senator, but Reemelin was still nervous. "Then, I thought of inviting Mr. Röbling for a Sunday promenade when I would take him to the former Hessian artillery captain Jäger leading both to discuss the issue of the bridge in order to listen to their controversy, it was my intention to confront Röbling with an expert who would be able to face any of his claims with expertise." Luckily, the two "forgot everything else around them, once they were discussing the subject, and they threw themselves intensely at the diverse technical matters. I listened carefully and with the utmost interest learning about what I needed to know. Röbling proved himself to be competent in all respects to build the bridge proposed; and all my doubts were gone."[75]

The political problems resulted from the slave clause. Reemelin thought the bridge charter more important, and he "managed to push through the draft proposal; yet, I could not prevent a clause from being added which declared void the stipulation of the Kentucky charter about slaves; because political prejudices withstand all reason." At this point—whether it was reason or race, riverboats or rivalry—the legislation died. John failed to record his thoughts on the controversy. Reemelin happily recorded his thoughts on John: "Röbling lives on in my memory as the hardworking technician who had the boldest skills of conception with the greatest knowledge. No order of the eagle covered his chest and, yet, so much of an eagle was inside him. He let his eyes wander through the field of technology, but he also looked at details with the greatest precision."[76]

———

The years 1846 and 1847 were the two most significant in John's life. He finished his second suspension bridge to national acclaim, traveled the country in search of clients and projects, and drew up complete plans for four massive new bridges, at Cincinnati, Niagara, Pittsburgh, and Wheeling, all of which would have ranked easily as the longest spans and the biggest bridges in the country. The energy and scope of his ideas were breathtaking, while the physical effort was massive. His diary for the second half of May 1847 gives some sense of his life at this point: "May 12 leave Sax for Pitt; May 14 leave Pitt for Erie; May 16 arrive at Erie; May 17 leave for Buffalo; May 24 remain about Falls; May 25 return to Saxon; May 28 arrive at Sax; May 30 to Pitts; 31 to Wheeling," while his notebooks—crammed full of the names of almost everyone associated with an active improvement project, along with thousands of thoughts, tests, calculations, and ideas—tell an equally frenzied story. By the close of 1846, he had written the first in a series of brilliant bridge proposals, and his wire rope business was established as a fully fledged concern. In addition, John prepared and gave a lengthy address on the future of railroads at the Pittsburgh Board of Trade and wrote, submitted, and was granted two separate US patents.[77] Against all odds, he also met his best friend.

The man who emerged from these experiences was a fascinating combination of absolutes and opposites. He was capable and professional, but also impassioned and unpredictable. He was strict but inventive, learned but intuitive, a sophisticated modern engineer and yet something of a Renaissance man. He was a technical genius and a medical quack, capable of great friendship and great anger. He was inexhaustible. He "conquered everything with that wonderful personal force, a power that only fed on opposition and knew no defeat."[78] John was also changing, much as the country around him was changing too. The Jacksonian period, whose market, transportation, and communications revolutions and battles over individual liberty and corporate and governmental power, was coming to a close. In its place would rise a bitter, more sectional union, one in which John would thrive. The years 1846–47 also marked the end of a particular type of German American experience. In 1848, legions of radical political refugees would pour into the country in the wake of a new European revolution, changing the nature of German American life, opening it up in ways that John would encourage and support: a greater sense of assimilation and Americanization, and huge shifts in political affiliation. John's generation of German immigrants were natural Democrats in thrall to ideas of individual liberty and freedom. The Forty-Eighters, as the new wave came to be called, were Whigs like John, opposed to slavery and nativism and eventually the cornerstone of the new Republican Party.

Although John conceived, planned, wrote up, and submitted designs for four huge suspension bridges from 1846 to 1847, what he got was the commission to build two (ultimately four) small aqueducts, the longest of which was only 535 feet long from end to end, significantly shorter than either of his Pittsburgh bridges. Even worse, he lost two of the contracts—both crushing blows—to Charles Ellet, his biggest rival. Despite these setbacks, it was a period of great success. From June 1847 on to his death, John spent his time and energy fulfilling the terms he had set for himself over the previous fifteen months. He, not Ellet, would bridge the Ohio at Cincinnati and throw the world's first railroad suspension bridge over the Niagara Gorge. He, not Ellet, would go down as the nineteenth century's most accomplished suspension bridge engineer. Certainly, Ellet earned tremendous acclaim for building the Wheeling Bridge, but the glory was short-lived. Opened in 1849, it fell down in a gale five years later.

PART THREE

MASTER (1848–69)

Economies of Scale (1848–51)

After the explosion of creative energy that marked 1846–47 and the myriad disappointments that followed in its wake came the hard work of keeping going. With Ellet in ascendance, John had to swallow his rejections and move on, which he did with remarkable alacrity. He may have doubted others, but he never doubted himself. Consequently, the following two years "were perhaps busier years with him and more fraught with successful results than any two previous years," wrote Washington.[1] John set about dealing with his diminished ambition through the hard work of meticulous planning and by grappling with a few major decisions. It would all culminate in a great prize, one of the greatest in the realm of global engineering. First, however, came the drudgery of small steps. John's next job wasn't spanning the broad, majestic Ohio or throwing a mighty web across the yawning, abyssal gorge at Niagara; it was working for a regional canal company, albeit one of the nation's most successful.

In 1820, William and Maurice Wurts, dry goods merchants from Philadelphia, decided to diversify their business. They realized there was a large potential market for anthracite coal and an abundant supply in the hills around northeastern Pennsylvania. They also realized that traditional transportation costs were prohibitively high. All that stood between them and a flourishing business, they thought, was reliable and affordable transportation. Embracing the nation's emerging love affair with canals, the Wurts brothers decided to build themselves a waterway so they could float their coal to market. They hired Benjamin Wright to survey a route, and they were soon digging, not south to Philadelphia but north to the Hudson River. The Philadelphia market was already oversaturated by the 1820s, so the Wurts brothers set their sights on New York City, which as yet had no direct coal supply.[2]

The Delaware and Hudson Canal Company was formally organized in 1825, with famed diarist and future New York mayor Philip Hone as company president. The canal itself was finished in 1828 at a total cost of $1,875,000. The route began with a series of gravity railroads, seventeen miles long, running from Carbondale to Honesdale. At Honesdale, the coal was loaded onto barges and sent down the new canal, which ran alongside the Lackawaxen River to its confluence with the Delaware River. Barges were poled and pulled across the Delaware, where they reconnected with the canal, which then ran up the Neversink and Rondout valleys to the Hudson tidewater near Kingston. The coal was then sent down the Hudson River to New York. The canal was 106 miles long and employed over a hundred locks. The *Albany Argus* called it "an improvement of incalculable importance." John Johnson, (1819-1911) who grew up alongside the canal in Barryville, New York and become a much respected lawyer and citizen in the region, described it as the lifeblood of the region, "not only to the corporate owners; but to the horde of men, women, boys and girls to whom, in various capacities, it furnished employment." All along the line, Johnson declared, the canal "was monarch."[3]

The use of coal for smelting, generating power, and heating took off once a steady supply could be guaranteed. And once the supply was there, the need increased. During its first decade or so, the canal and the company were remarkably busy and wildly profitable. But like all such ventures, it had to continually adapt and innovate. The canal reached something approaching its carrying capacity in 1841, after which Russel F. Lord, the canal's chief engineer, instituted a series of improvements and enlargements—dredging the trench and building up the embankments to allow for larger and more capacious boats—but these were largely inadequate. A major overhaul was needed if the D&H were to stay ahead of its rivals.

The construction of the New York and Erie Railroad in the mid-1840s brought competition to the New York coal market. And with the addition of the Erie, absolute economy in transportation became crucial for the D&H. The canal had to be enlarged and not just in bits, but significantly. It was widened to forty-eight feet and its depth dug to six feet (its initial dimension had been thirty feet by four). The effort was calculated to cost over a million dollars but also to double the annual carrying capacity. A larger canal also allowed for larger and more robust barges, ones that could be sent to all destinations on the Hudson, along the Erie to the Great Lakes, or even along the Long Island Sound to faraway New England. The effort to widen the canal would necessitate the replacement of the canal's two aqueducts—one over the Rondout Creek at High Falls, New York, the other at Cuddebackville, New York, over the Neversink River—but the D&H's most pressing need was farther south.

The Delaware crossing had been troublesome from the beginning. It was an expensive operation and a natural bottleneck. Barges approached the Delaware just to the north of its confluence with the Lackawaxen and came

Figure 13.1 Russel F. Lord, chief engineer of the Delaware and Hudson Canal Company, ca. 1855. Courtesy of the Minisink Valley Historical Society.

to a full stop at a guard lock on the Pennsylvania side. The barges themselves were then "poled or floated" across the river to the lock on the New York side, where they rejoined the canal. Their crossing was aided by a slack-water dam, about two hundred feet downstream from the confluence of the two rivers, that created a pool of calm, slow-moving water so canal boats could cross the river in relative safety. Positioned a few dozen feet farther up the river, a scow connected to a stout rope stretched across the Delaware was used to ferry horses, tow men, and anything else across the river. "The demands were so many that the scow was kept in constant motion during the day and a por-tion of the night," reports Johnson. If all went well, barges and scows arrived simultaneously on the other side of the river. Needless to say, it was always a small miracle when they did. Not only did the two parts of the crossing travel under distinctly different conditions, but they depended on animals staying docile while being dragged across the river. Horses bolted frequently, leaving barges without their horsepower and sending canal hands off into the surrounding countryside in search of their beasts, all while the horse's barge stood motionless, holding up traffic.[4]

The "slow tedious process of pulling [boats] across by a rope," as Johnson described it, "requiring the strength of 3, 4 and 5 men," was at best wildly inefficient and time-consuming. Water in a canal can be controlled, but the process is much harder in a free-floating river. The dam created a level of calm, but this equilibrium could be dashed by drought, floods, or ice. A severe and extensive drought in 1845, for example, halted navigation intermittently for fifty-three days. On most days, there was simply not enough water in the river for boats to float across. In other years, melting snow and heavy rains swelled the river to the point where crossing was dangerous or impossible. The implications for the entire canal were huge. With coal barges stranded in Pennsylvania, nothing was moving up through New York, and the canal's business was at an absolute standstill.[5]

Not only was the Delaware crossing tremendously expensive and wholly inefficient, but it was also a cause of real tension—and great antagonism—with members of the surrounding community, who were clannish, insular, and quick to take offense and raise their fists. "Nothing [was] known nor comprehended . . . of the forces then being gradually set in motion," wrote Johnson, which put the community on a collision course with the company. Locals were confused by "the appearance of a company of ten or twelve men in a body, designated by the unheard of title of engineers, with their cabalistic instruments, of which none could conjecture the use." They treated anyone representing the D&H with great suspicion.[6]

The greatest bone of contention was the dam, which the locals loathed. In April 1829, after it became "impossible for a raft to pass without being more or less wrecked," over a hundred "hardy pioneers of the forest" took matters into their own hands. "Heavy blasts of powder were exploded, axes and saws were freely used," until about eighty feet of the dam had been "tore away," enough to allow passage down the river. The men who made their living on the Delaware resented the interference and the presumption. "Wedded to their course of life by every tie which nature and reverent custom could bind," Johnson explained, "many of the old settlers . . . carried in their hearts an embittered hatred towards the canal." The D&H fixed the dam, but maintaining the structure was constant and expensive work. "Rocks and stones enough to build a second Chinese wall" were required, while the D&H's annual reports are constantly littered with "great violence," "disastrous injury," and "unusually heavy repairs," all of which cost money and hampered movement. The crossing limped on in use, but as competition encroached, the need to fix the Delaware gained greater urgency.[7]

That an aqueduct would be needed at the Delaware was understood from the beginning, even if the company couldn't as yet procure the necessary funds. John Wurts, president of the D&H, asked Lord to research the topic in early 1841, and the idea was again raised four years later when the New York and Erie Railroad threatened to intrude on company territory. This time Wurts was more willing to open the company coffers. There was no fighting the railroads by 1845, which is not to say there weren't ways to coexist. "It is in the interest of both companies to cultivate good feelings, and strive to get along in harmony," Wurts wrote to Lord, before adding, "We must keep a vigilant eye to the location and construction of their work . . . and we must hold them strictly to . . . every particular affecting our works or interest." One of the ways to accommodate their new neighbors was to lay claim to the crossing and get their bridge built first, forcing the Erie to work around them. "I think it would be well for us to do something there *immediately* to demonstrate our intention to build an aqueduct," Wurts wrote Lord. The other was to enlarge and streamline the entire operation, from mine to market. The bottleneck at the Delaware, not to mention myriad other problems up and down the canal, would sink the company if it was placed in direct competition with the railroad.[8]

———

John's involvement in the project was a natural offshoot of his relationship with the D&H. He was on excellent terms with Archbald thanks to his wire ropes, and with Lord, with whom he corresponded about his work in Pittsburgh.[9] "Mr. Douglas, the Engineer on the Lehigh works went with me to Pittsburgh to examine the Aquaduct," John wrote Lord in November 1846. "He is very well pleased with it. The works stands firm and remains perfectly tight."[10] Not that this guaranteed John anything. The D&H was a deft and accomplished concern, and its president was fastidious and thoughtful. Wurts was impressed by John's "honest integrity" and "struck by his ability," but, writing to Lord in December 1846, he worried that he didn't have enough "information . . . to make a comparison between [John's] plan" and a wooden aqueduct proposed by Solan Chapin. The wooden bridge would cost $38,000, while John's would cost $60,000. This was a significant extra expense, yet it was also offset somewhat by the fact that Chapin's bridge would require repairs in twelve years, while John's would require repairs in seventeen years, and that those repairs would be $17,000 cheaper than Chapin's. The answer was in the numbers: compound interest on the $22,000 initially saved with the wooden span laid against the $17,000 saved on repairs with John's bridge, together with the five years' interest compounded on the whole amount. In such a minute and meticulous manner were decisions made at the D&H.[11]

The board met on January 6, 1847, to discuss the two proposals. John's plan seemed to suggest savings of about $55,000 over sixty years, provided "the wire is imperishable, never to be replaced." Admittedly, the board was skeptical about this but decided to "submit to the opinions of those who have examined the subject more fully," which was prescient. Remarkably, John's cables are still at work today, holding up the Delaware crossing at Lackawaxen. But if the details seemed murky, the bigger picture was clearer. There was genuine agreement among the board members that John's plan had broad, inherent benefits not found in a traditional wooden aqueduct. It required no falsework, provided greater clearance, and called for fewer piers in the river, which meant fewer problems with ice floes, freshets, debris, or river craft generally. At the close of the meeting, the board voted unanimously in favor of John's plan, but with the proviso that Lord travel to Pittsburgh to inspect John's handiwork.[12]

Lord landed in Pittsburgh at the end of the month and spent five days with John examining his bridges and discussing a potential contract. Lord was "well pleased with the Aqua & bridge" and even had a chance to sit in on John's public lecture "The Great Central Railroad from Philadelphia to St. Louis" at the Pittsburgh Odeon. For his part, John seems to have handled the scheduling conflict with suitable efficiency and style, winning Lord over. Lord left Pittsburgh with a copy of John's official proposal on February 2, promising to write to John "as soon as the Contract was confirmed."[13]

Running to only three pages, John's proposal was little more than a promise wrapped around a reputation. He would build a four-span aqueduct over the Delaware and a two-span structure over the Lackawaxen, both "works to be constructed exactly alike" except the width of the cables and the size of the anchor chains, and both spans to be almost exact replicas of his Allegheny Aqueduct. The Delaware cables were to be 8½ inches in diameter, while the Lackawaxen's would be 7 inches, all well-varnished, bound and wrapped, and painted. The cables would rest on cast iron saddles atop stone piers. Those closest to the abutment were to be mounted on rollers to account for expansion and contraction. Solid U-shaped suspenders, four feet apart and held in place by a small iron saddle, would loop over the cables and run down to the huge support beams beneath the trunk and be bolted in place. The beams—30 feet long, 6 inches high, and 1½ feet wide—would carry half of the weight of the water, with the suspenders carrying the other half. As with the Pittsburgh aqueduct, the trunk would be self-supporting. It would be nine feet deep and nineteen feet wide at the top. It would be made of a double course of 2½-inch white pine planks laid diagonally to each other, well-caulked and pitched "to render them tight," forming a sort of solid lattice truss. Six-foot-wide towpaths would be constructed on either side and held in place by diagonal brace struts. "I agree to put up the whole superstructure of the Delaware and Lackawaxen Aquaducts . . . for the sum of *Sixty Thousand and Four Hundred Dollars* for the works together," John explained, "the company to do all the masonry of the piers and abutments, also the excavation and masonry for the Anchorage, and to furnish all the hydraulic cement required for the work." The price—approximately eighty dollars per foot—was a major increase on the forty-eight dollars per foot the Allegheny Aqueduct had cost. The price hike represented the costs of doing construction in upstate New York, far from the conveniences of industrial Pittsburgh, but also to John's improved stature. He had been desperate for the Allegheny contract, and he worked for almost nothing. He was bolder and more self-assured three years later. This time he would be paid for his work. In fact, when all was said and done, John made $8,600 on the deal. Not an extravagant amount, but a handsome 14.5 percent return nevertheless.[14]

Wurts wrote to John to offer him the contract on February 12, explaining that "the needful work [ought] to be commenced as soon as the masonry . . . is completed." This was absolutely fine with John. He sent a bill of particulars, a set of flyers soliciting bids for the required lumber ("free of shakes, rents and black knots"), a series of diagrams, and a lot of questions to Lord, who was wasting no time himself. Even before the board had made their final decision, Lord had a team in place constructing the abutments. "The work for the construction of the Delaware Aqueduct is progressing as was contemplated," wrote Thomas Tracey to Lord in early February; "the stone [is] cut and dressed ready for a vigorous commencement of the masonry soon as the weather will permit."[15]

One of John's first moves was to reach out to Jonathan Rhule, despite their epic falling-out in Pittsburgh. "If I fare well in the contract and am ably assisted by you, and you look to my interests—it will then give me much pleasure to reward you accordingly," he wrote. The decision to hire Rhule made perfect sense; the decision to offer him a ride in a rented freight boat all the way from western Pennsylvania did not. The two couldn't stand the sight of each other, although they had clearly found a way to work together. John was a brilliant engineer, and Rhule was one of the foremost carpenters in the state. Their work on the Allegheny crossing was outstanding, even if their relations with each other were not. For John, bridge-building was about building on successes, and he knew that if he wanted to make a success of his Delaware venture, he ought to repeat his successes in Pittsburgh as closely as possible, which meant availing himself of the best available craftsmen. The decision had mixed results, exactly as it had before. Again, he quickly fell out with the master carpenter but he also erected two brilliantly conceived and executed structures.[16]

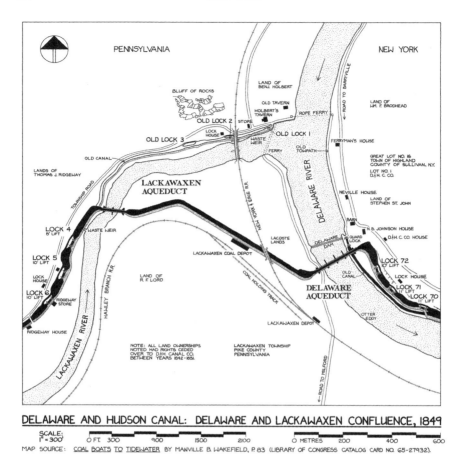

DELAWARE AND HUDSON CANAL: DELAWARE AND LACKAWAXEN CONFLUENCE, 1849

SCALE:
I" = 300'

MAP SOURCE: COAL BOATS TO TIDEWATER BY MANVILLE B. WAKEFIELD, P. 83 (LIBRARY OF CONGRESS CATALOG CARD NO. 65-27932).

Figure 13.2 "Delaware and Hudson Canal: Delaware and Lackawaxen Confluence, 1849," part of the Historic American Engineering Record (HAER), PA-1. Library of Congress.

John spent the next few months at home in Saxonburg, calculating, sketching, revising, planning, and ordering for his new aqueducts. In the meantime, a small army of laborers descended on the Delaware, most of whom were veterans of the Croton Aqueduct project. John wanted William Skew to act as superintendent. He expected to be paid three dollars per day, John wrote, and "he is worth it fully." Lord was unable to oblige. "I have no doubt but that he is a good and desirable man for our work; But there are considerations which render it difficult for us to engage him as a Superintendent," namely, that he had already given the job to Jervis's friend Watson (at Jervis's insistence). "If we put on another superintendent," Lord explained, "it would create a distrust and be attended with unpleasant circumstances, all around." Unfortunately, Watson tuned out to be a disaster.[17]

All hands set to work on the abutments and anchorages for the Delaware Aqueduct in the bitter cold of February. By March, the D&H had already spent $23,932.74 but could report that "considerable progress" had been made. As Robert Vogel notes, "That excavation and masonry work could be carried on during that period, at that season, in that notoriously cruel climate, was something of a small miracle, and a sure reflection of the company's anxiety to capitalize on the improvement." Lord hoped to have the piers finished and the anchorages ready to receive the anchors by July 1 so that John could "commence the superstructure" in the fall "and pursue it during the winter." Progress on the Lackawaxan span ran a little behind that of the Delaware. Lord hoped to have the pier and one of the abutments done by the fall, while the other abutment would need to wait until the winter.[18]

On May 10, John wrote Archbald asking if he had a spare lathe. Archbald ignored the lathe request and instead offered John a job as an assistant railroad engineer. John's reaction to the offer was cagey, not to mention overly optimistic, offering a revealing glimpse into his state of mind at the time. "To your question whether I would prefer to be in regular business at a salary equal to my present receipt, I can hardly answer," John wrote; "this would depend upon the kind of employment offered, and whether it would occupy all my time or not." He clearly was not opposed to offers, but he had a clear plan. "My prospects in bridge building are *very good*," he continued, and "I have no doubt I will undertake the Niagara Br, the Wheeling, Cincinnati and several large works, which are in contemplation at Pittsburgh. For the next 10 years I will, to judge from present appearances, have enough to do. My Wire Rope business is also extending so much that I must put up new machinery next year to supply the demand. . . . As to bridge building, I must say, that I have a great taste for it and should not like to give it up. So far it has not been very profitable, but it is only the commencement, and I have no doubt, I will fare better with the works I shall undertake hereafter."[19]

———

While John was at the Delaware, Ellet was in Wheeling, once again stealing a march on his rival. Or at least James Dickinson, Ellet's antisocial chief assistant, was. Ellet was in Philadelphia, directing the Wheeling operation by mail and planning yet another coup up at Niagara, all to John's great annoyance. Losing the Wheeling contract was the biggest disappointment John ever experienced, as he was so certain he would get it. "A bridge over the Ohio at Wheeling is to be forthwith commenced. Ellet & myself are competitors, I expect to get it," he wrote Archbald in early 1847. To be fair to Ellet, he had drawn up and submitted a plan for a castellated single span as early as 1836, and he had a track record. He was the engineer who had built the Fairmount Suspension Bridge. To be fair to John, he had been approached by several interested parties over the previous few years and been misled by James Wharton, editor of the *Wheeling Gazette*, into thinking the commission was there for John's taking. "I sincerely hope that your engagements will not be much as to prevent your taking the contract," he wrote John in 1847. John certainly knew that Ellet was involved in the discussions, but he had good reason to also think he had the inside track.[20]

Amid all the chatter and rumor, Henry Moore wrote to both John and Ellet on April 14, 1847, to inform them that the Wheeling and Belmont Bridge Company had been formed and intended to "erect a wire suspension bridge across the eastern branch of the Ohio opposite the city of Wheeling." "I have been directed by my associates," he continued, "to apprise you of these facts and to invite your early attention to the subject." John wrote back immediately asking if he could visit Wheeling on May 15. He was planning to be up at Niagara Falls by the end of the month and could pass by Wheeling on the way. If all went well, maybe they could start quarrying for granite blocks before the end of the month. John was working with information gleaned from the unreliable Wharton: that the company was in a hurry and hoping to sign a contract by the middle of May. Moore wrote back coolly to John's offer of haste, suggesting June 1 instead as a date for the visit, despite knowing that John would be up at Niagara only a few days before.[21]

John jumped at Moore's invitation. Ellet was coy. Although he wanted the contract, he wrote, he had been burned in open contests before and had made up his mind never again to compete for a public work. "On such a struggle men are brought into conflict with a class of speculators who can always underbid a fair proposal," he explained, with the uncertain battle for the Schuylkill Bridge no doubt in mind. That said, if the company didn't find what they were looking for, he would happily furnish a proposal.[22] Ellet may have been playing hard to get, but much was happening behind the scenes. Moore sent Ellet "a very rough + I fear imperfect statement of the measurements of a survey made by Mr. Roebling of the proposed site for the bridge" on June 3, only a few days after John's visit. Earlier, James Baker, one of the company managers, and William Fleming, a stockholder, had visited Ellet in Philadelphia to solicit his participation.[23]

The day of the decision was set for July 13. John dutifully turned up with three different plans, "none of which however were satisfactory," according to Baker, despite the fact that the board asked him to adjust his plans and estimates several times. By July 14, John had reduced the width of the roadway from 26 to 24 feet (saving $3,000), lowered the Wheeling abutment 10 feet (saving $2,100), raised the island abutment 10 feet (costing $2,700), and raised the central pier (costing $450). At the request of the committee, John also calculated the costs for an eight-hundred-foot-long single-span bridge. Such a plan would save the costs of a pier, John noted, but add substantially to the costs of the towers, abutments, and cables, making it $53,500 more expensive than his initial plan. The board remained unconvinced. After they dismissed John, Ellet—who had yet to submit a plan—was chosen with only "one dissenting voice."[24]

The board wrote to Ellet that night to inform him that he had been selected as "engineer to superintend the construction of a wire suspension Bridge over the Ohio" and invited him to Wheeling at his earliest convenience "to aid . . . in forming some plan which will at once meet the views of the Board and the means of the Company."[25] Ellet wrote back that he was "exceedingly gratified at this manifestation of confidence." "It is a great work," he continued, "and one on which an Engineer may found hope of wide reputation. . . . I have from the first regarded the pecuniary gain in this case with comparative indifference—my great object being to associate my name honorably with the edifice."[26] Others were gratified too. Charles B. Stuart, a distinguished engineer who knew both Ellet and John, wrote to congratulate him after seeing "the appointment notices in the papers . . . but could scarcely credit it, as Mr. Roebling had informed me, when at the Falls last July, that *he* had just concluded a contract for the *Wheeling bridge* and must hasten back to begin the work. I can now see the object of the story, which proves to be as *true* as the one about the Niagara Bridge," he concluded with great mystery; "I have a history of this matter to tell you when we meet, that will astonish you."[27]

Posterity has failed to record what Stuart knew about John, although it managed to preserve some evidence of what happened to John and what he thought about it. It seems a resolution favoring John's third plan was adopted by the board on July 13, then rescinded thanks to Baker's influence. Evidence also exists that the board had started to act on John's plan much earlier, ordering lumber to fit John's specifications on June 2, right after his first visit. No contract had been signed, but clearly John was receiving mixed messages, and he wasted no time in writing to disparage the board over their handling of the contract. They had "repeatedly asserted that one single span was beyond the means of the Company and that the locality did not favor such a plan," John wrote to Henry Moore and the board on July 20, 1847, yet they were now actively courting Ellet and his single-span plan. "I owe it to myself to explain and hope to show conclusively that I am right," John continued, which hardly mattered. The board concluded a contract with Ellet the same day they received John's letter.[28]

Ellet's own proposal came in the same day, a mere sketch with only a handful of details and lots of caveats. He estimated the cost of the bridge at $145,000 ($20,000 more than John's final bid) and thought that he could be finished by November 1848. Ellet did not expect to be in Wheeling for much of the work. Instead, it would be supervised by his hand-picked assistant. Ellet's own "visits will be arranged to suit the state of the world, on which point the board must confide to my judgment, trusting to my intention to protect their interests, and my own reputation," he concluded. One can only imagine what the board thought about their favored engineer after reading that.[29]

John's plan was defined by his experiences in Pittsburgh, especially the debates around his Monongahela and tripartite spans. Both had turned on the question of clearance, which is where John began his proposal. "As great and combined efforts will be made to have this first bridge over the Ohio declared a public nuisance . . . great caution should be exercised in its planning, so as to avoid disastrous litigations for the future." Given the heights of the various steamers plying the Ohio, John felt that "an elevation of not less than 100 feet in the clear" was needed. Anything less would end in the courts; anything more was unnecessary. Should the river reach the heights of, say, the 1832 flood— the highest on record—it would barely matter what the clearance was. "When the river overflows the highest banks and wharves, no freight can be taken in or discharged [and] no loading effected [and] the navigation may be considered as suspended for the time."[30]

In order to guarantee sufficient clearance, John needed help. The riverbank at Wheeling was much higher than on the opposite shore, leading John to plan a two-span bridge with a central pier, much as he had at Cincinnati.[31] Such a plan would be cheaper to build and would lift the trajectory of the roadway upward toward the central pier, not downward to the opposite shore. In addition, it created less disruption than building a huge tower in the middle of the docks, all of which was functional but hardly bold and inspiring. John wanted to be practical, but he needed to be visionary, a lesson he learned over time.[32]

If John favored clearance, Ellet favored a clear 1,010-foot span and a clear vision. John's proposal was too wordy, too faithful to setting out problems and solving them. It was filled with potential worry, not potential wonder. Ellet, by contrast, just set out his specifications and simply asserted that they met all eventualities. His official plan finally arrived on October 26, 1847. It was confident and assertive, and it began by attacking John. "There is . . . no excuse for placing a pier in a navigable channel in any position," Ellet asserted. It was far preferable "to cast an arch of 1,500 feet, than to encounter the cost and the future expense of maintaining a pier," especially one "properly founded, and constructed in a mode capable of resisting the action of the water and the ice by which it is liable to be assailed." A single span "has the advantage of leaving the navigation of the great river unimpeded" while presenting an edifice of "far greater beauty and much more commanding effect."[33] It would also be strangely asymmetrical. John's plan worried about the unequal balance between the opposing shores; Ellet's just ignored it, meaning the bridge would slope slowly downward.

Two of the most significant differences between John's and Ellet's proposals provide keys to their characters and the state of the art at the time. In almost all respects, Ellet stuck to his roots in the French technical literature he had first encountered in the early 1830s and the bridges he had seen at Remoulins and Tournon-sur-Rhône. John, by contrast, appropriated and innovated. A good example was their respective cable systems. Wire ropes and cables were John's business and his preoccupation. He thought about them, he made them, he developed ideas about them, he knew how to situate them, and he held patents for them. Ellet stuck with the "garland" cable system developed by French engineers in the 1820s without alteration or modification. As he had done in Philadelphia with his Schuylkill Bridge, Ellet employed twelve cables festooned in pairs on either side of the bridge. These cables were made onshore, tied intermittently with metal bands every two to three feet—not wrapped and bundled—and hauled into place.[34]

John strenuously objected to this method. Fully wrapped and bound cables were protected against the elements and were significantly stiffer and much easier to set in uniform tension, one of the most important elements of a suspension cable. Should a "heavy gale" hit a bridge with a garland cable system, John wrote, no one would be able to predict how each separate strand would behave. Some wires would "move up [while] others may swing down [rendering] perfect uniform resistance . . . impossible." Or worse, it could spell the destruction of the entire system as individual strands ruptured and broke, placing increasing stress on the remaining ones. But should all those small cables be gathered and bound into a single unit, "no such variableness can exist." Ellet's cables could let in water (which then expanded when frozen) and failed to prevent oxidization. John suspected that cables made in this manner were much lighter and less sturdy than his own. Additionally, the dragging process as they were hauled and manhandled into place "injures them much," wrote John; "they will spread out, spring up and become much disordered." Worse, the process failed to create uniform tension in the wires. That every wire should bear exactly its share of the load was the key to a cable's strength. Anything less was effectively guesswork and "very objectionable."[35]

John disparaged Ellet's bridges as "French," though his were too in several important ways. The French preferred (and pioneered) wire cables, just as John did, whereas such eminent British engineers as Telford, Brunel, Clark, and Stevenson favored "solid chains of bar iron." In addition, the French system was hardly monolithic or unchanging. Navier, the Seguins, and Dufour all brought their cables to their bridges, but that wasn't the end of the story. Beginning in the early 1830s, right after Ellet returned to America, Louis Vicat began to conceive an approach that solved the problem of uniform tension. His solution was to construct suspension cables *in situ*, directly between the towers. The process took a lot longer, but it led to stronger, tighter cables and a more precise curve, he argued. John agreed, albeit somewhat later, adopting the same approach on his bridges. It is difficult to gauge how aware John was of Vicat's ideas, but he was "confident that my mode of constructing wire cables for suspension bridges, when more generally understood, will supersede the old mode altogether," he wrote in his Wheeling proposal. Cable spinning in situ is now the least disputed aspect of suspension bridge construction, especially for long spans. Ellet, it seems, left France a little too early.[36]

———

Modern suspension bridges represent the transformation of a primitive architectural form into a powerful new technology by the application of a new structural material: iron. They struggled through the early decades of the nineteenth century and grew in popularity in the 1830s and 1840s, but not without opposition and significant growing pains. "The insecurity of suspension bridges, as exhibited in the many accidents [and] the vibratory motion to which they are subject during gales," wrote the *Civil Engineer and Architect's Journal* in 1838, "ought to determine the engineer never to adopt them under any circumstances." "In the course of time when the material of the suspension portion of the Menai Bridge, shall have perished, and been consigned to ruin, and worn to dust by the destroying powers of the atmospheric agents," they continued, "the granite bridges of London and Waterloo will then exist in the same freshness and vigour of duration as that in which travellers now find the ancient granite monuments of Egypt, after a lapse of more than thirty centuries."[37] The journal was right, at least as far as the accidents, the gales, and the "vibratory motions" were concerned.

The Menai Suspension Bridge suffered significant damage three times in the 1830s thanks to gales. Engineers responded by increasing the bridge's dead weight. Unfortunately, as it was perched on the edge of the Irish Sea, one of the windiest places in Europe, the winds could always match the weight. In 1839, a third of the bridge's suspension rods broke during a storm, after which the span's roadway was entirely rebuilt. A similar fate awaited Samuel Brown's Brighton Chain Pier, which fell down during a gale in 1833 and then again in 1836. On May 2, 1845, the Yarmouth Bridge "collapsed under weight of large crowd that had gathered to watch a famous clown sail down the River Bure in a washtub pulled by geese," a fate very similar to that visited upon the Broughton Suspension Bridge, which collapsed—with "a sound resembling an irregular discharge of firearms"—on April 12, 1831, while seventy-four soldiers were marching over the span. Soldiers marching in step, like gale-force winds, act on a suspension bridge in a similar way, creating a small but expanding series of oscillating vibrations (resonance) that if left unchecked can tear a span apart.[38]

One of the more instructive bridge failures of the early nineteenth century occurred in a remote town in western Scotland. Built by Samuel Brown, the

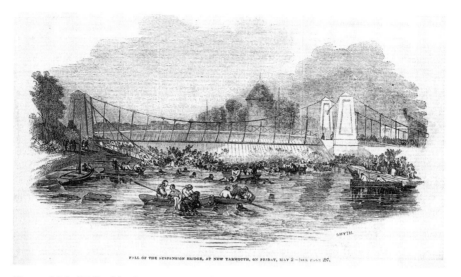

Figure 13.3 "Fall of the Suspension Bridge at New Yarmouth," *Illustrated London News,*
May 10, 1845.

Montrose Suspension Bridge was opened in 1829 and fell down almost immediately when a large group of people took to the bridge to watch a boat race.
Four people were killed and several injured, but "luckily, beyond the tearing of
clothes, and loss of shawls and bonnets, no damage was sustained by the [rest of
the] terrified crowd in their rush to the land."[39] The ruin was inspected by none
other than Thomas Telford, who advised replacing all the hardware and adding
extra strength to the suspension mechanism in the form of heavier and stronger
bars and chains. The bridge was subsequently rebuilt and finally reopened in
the summer of 1838. It lasted another few months before being swept away in
a storm.

Engineer Charles Pasley inspected the bridge in the immediate aftermath.
Witnesses told Pasley that "they felt the bridge vibrate in the most violent
manner . . . just before it gave way . . . and that they had always experienced
the same sort of vibration in a greater or lesser degree during every strong gale
of wind." Pasley likened the effect to accounts of the Menai during gales: "No
transverse vibration ever took place during the most violent storm [instead] the
whole of it undulated longitudinally like the waves of the sea." Pasley inspected a
number of bridges in the wake of the Montrose disaster and did much research
into bridge failures, eventually concluding that most bridge roadways were just
too flimsy to resist the effects of gale-force winds. It was no mere case of weight
but rather one of rigidity. When the Brighton bridge tore itself apart in 1836, for
example, no major structural failure occurred until "the side railings [were] shattered to pieces and blown away, after which the undulations became perceptibly

more violent, and ended in the carrying away of the roadway also." Conversely, the Hammersmith Bridge possessed "four lines of strong trusses along the whole length of the roadway . . . so firmly connected by iron bolts and plates . . . that it [was] quite impossible for the strongest gale of wind to produce any undulations in the roadway." "The roadway of every suspension bridge having only light side railings . . . will sooner or later be carried away by some future hurricane," he concluded.[40]

The Montrose Bridge was rebuilt by James Rendell, who agreed wholeheartedly with Pasley and ultimately with John. Rendell "had long been convinced of the importance of giving to the roadways of suspension bridges the greatest possible amount of stiffness, in such a manner as to distribute the load or the effect of any violent action over a considerable extent. The platforms of larger bridges, in exposed situations, are acted upon in so many different ways by the wind," he wrote, that the only plausible solution had to lie in the span's essential design. Neither weight nor counter-stays nor any other "unnecessary and even dangerous furniture," as Charles Bender described it, would suffice.[41] The "force of momentum brought into action . . . ought rather to be resisted by the form of the structure" itself. To this end, Rendell rebuilt the Montrose roadway in a manner that may have influenced John. The roadway was stiffened "by a compact mass of braced wood-work, the diagonal planking giving the horizontal stiffness, and the two trussed frames insuring the vertical rigidity." With no small sense of pride, Rendell later declared that the rebuilt span "has borne without injury heavy gales . . . and the stiffness has given confidence in the strength to all who have examined it."[42]

Unstiffened roadways were one of Navier's legacies and one of Ellet's chief practices. Both engineers "overlooked the influence of wind acting from below on the floor" and failed to include "those important stiffening elements [that] are inseparable from any good suspension bridge."[43] Neither saw flexibility as a threat. On the contrary, both thought of it as a vital and essential aspect of suspension bridges. Following the lead of his French teachers, Ellet believed that "a bridge floor must remain flexible to relieve itself of the imbalance created by loaded vehicles" and more specifically that a "suspension bridge enables a light and weak structure to yield repeatedly to a heavy body passing over it . . . and return to its former situation as soon as the disturbing force is withdrawn." In other words, a flexible floor helped account for a moving live load. Yes, trusses supplied rigidity, but "an artificial rigidity" not subject to the laws that "control . . . the system of suspension." Ellet believed that "the framed flooring and the flexible cable do not act in concert," leading him to conclude that "stiffness was incompatible with the true structural action of suspension bridges." Instead, "permanent strength . . . can be most cheaply obtained in suspension bridges of very great span, by the addition of weight," not the addition of stiffening trusses.

As Washington noted, with no small measure of derision, "He indulged in vague notions of stone flagging on a bridge to create mass and dead weight and thusly resist undulations. For wind bracing he indulged in the hope that the Lord would let him off easy and not send a big wind."[44]

Ellet had a desultory response to the need for rigidity. Not John. "Storms are unquestionably the greatest enemies of suspension bridges," he declared in his first major article on the subject, "but a stiff and well constructed floor will offer a great resistance." He believed bridges should be built "in such a manner that every portion will add to the stiffness of the structure."[45] John first toyed with the idea of incorporating a Howe truss as a solution to the need for adequate rigidity in 1847, while working on plan for a railroad suspension bridge. John was very aware of the problems that had plagued the Menai and Montrose bridges, and he spent a great amount of time working on a more comprehensive approach to the problem. Rather than solving it, he overcompensated based on observation and experience. There was no way to fully comprehend dynamic response or calculate aerodynamic force at the time, so John tried everything he could think of. His railings weren't true stiffening trusses, but he tried to make them act like a truss, and he combined them with stays and bound cables. Ellet, by contrast, used railings on his Fairmount Bridge mainly for their ability to stop people falling off. John failed to solve the problem—the first true stiffening truss wasn't developed until 1861, fourteen years after John played with the idea—but unlike Ellet, he did worry about it and work on a solution.[46]

Ellet saw the problem of oscillation purely in terms of weight, strength, and load, not dynamic failure. And the implications for the work he was about to undertake at Wheeling were significant. A large number of the suspension bridges that collapsed in the 1830s and 1840s were brought down by "vibratory motions" of one sort or another, whether gales or marching soldiers. Yet Ellet didn't see the storm clouds gathering over his own bridge. John did. A reporter for the Pittsburgh *Commercial Journal*, allegedly "heard Mr. Roebling say that the first violent storm which [the Wheeling] bridge should encounter would destroy it."[47]

———

It took Ellet two years to build the Wheeling Suspension Bridge, during which he grew increasingly disillusioned with the business and politics of large-scale construction. Still, he felt a great sense of pride and accomplishment as his bridge neared completion. "The city was alive with strangers, and people from the surrounding country, thronging the shore," wrote the *Wheeling Daily Gazette*. On the opening day itself, "the morning was ushered in by the sound of cannon, and at an early hour strangers began to gather in from all quarters, the bridge was lined with vehicles, and all around seemed life and animation. At 6 o'clock, the lamps, hung upon the wires, were lighted almost simultaneously and presented an elegant and graceful curve of fire, high above the river." It was rumored that Henry Clay had taken one look at the span and declared, "Take that down! You might as well take down a rainbow."[48]

Ellet's bridge was instantly hailed as a major achievement. It was the longest suspension bridge in the world and regarded by many as the single most important engineering achievement of the nineteenth century thus far. It was praised by sightseers, politicians, businessmen, and builders alike, and by Europeans as well as Americans. Karl Culman's influential report "Der Bau der eisernen Brücken in England und Amerika" (The construction of iron bridges in England and America) described it as one of the highest achievements in modern bridge building and one of the few structures he had come across that exceeded his expectations.[49] Yet despite its reputation, Ellet's bridge failed to spawn any copycat

Wheeling Suspension Bridge.—Front view.

Figure 13.4 One of the few images of the Wheeling Suspension Bridge with its original "French" cable system. From Eli Bowen, *Rambles in the Path of a Steam Horse* (1855). Courtesy of the Milstein Division of United States History, Local History and Genealogy, New York Public Library, Astor, Lenox, and Tilden Foundations.

spans and attracted no disciples, nor did it point the way forward. It was more accurately the final flowering of a set of ideas. Suspension bridges took off in the wake of Wheeling—dozens were built across America in the 1850s—but they did so on native plans, not the French one. The job of moving the structural form on into the future, instead, belonged to John. Ellet's bridge was the French system's last hurrah.[50]

The impact of Ellet's bridge was felt much less in the fields of technology and structural engineering than in issues of interstate commerce. The bridge proved to be a legal nightmare. As John had predicted, clearance was the key, and to the residents of Pittsburgh, Ellet's bridge wasn't high enough. Led by Edwin Stanton and fueled by interstate rivalry and a desire to command the Ohio, the state of Pennsylvania sued the Wheeling and Belmont Bridge Company, declaring the bridge a "public nuisance." The case went all the way to the Supreme Court, which decided against the bridge in 1852. Faced with the prospect of having to dismantle the span, Wheeling set about frantically lobbying Congress. As an extension of the National Road, the bridge ought to be declared a post road, they argued, which came with special privileges and made it exempt from clearance restrictions. Having lost at the Supreme Court, the bridge company won in Congress and saved their bridge. Further troubles lay ahead, some of which led straight back to their choice of engineer. But in the meantime, and for just a few weeks, Wheeling was the winner, as was the Washington establishment itself. The post road issues helped expand the regulatory powers of the Congress. It also helped establish the Supreme Court's jurisdiction over the Constitution's Commerce Clause.[51]

———

The upstate New York landscape John found around him in late August 1847 was far from the calm, bucolic pastoral it is today. It was wild and strange, and much more dangerous. Wolves howled at night, while rattlesnakes and copperheads slinked around the undergrowth. Bears, panthers, and bob cats were all native to the isolated region. John would often "complain of the utter loneliness of his surroundings in the upper Delaware, no society, no habitation or farms—all woods and rocks," Washington recalled. Still, despite the solitude and all the "woods and rocks," work was progressing on his piers and abutments, even with a little labor strife. Some of Jervis's "aqueduct hands," it seems, held firm views on wages and conditions, and they downed tools, demanded raises, and walked out. Charles Dupuy, Lord's eyes and ears at the construction site, fired the ringleaders, hired several local boatmen, and raised wages generally, after which things quieted for a while. Within a few months, however, a boy named William Banks—who had been fired that summer and "intended to make up for it!"—took to sneaking around the worksite, throwing John's tools into the canal.[52]

Word of the disputes failed to reach the *Railroad Journal*, which declared that the D&H had "been singularly fortunate in the selection of able and *faithful* men for the construction and management of its important works." In fact, John and Dupuy clashed frequently with the superintendent. "This work is costing a great deal of money—more I fear than it should," Dupuy wrote Lord in November, "yet I do not see that I can change it." He had pushed Watson hard, but to no avail. "He is not suited to take charge of a work of so extensive a character," Dupuy concluded. Still construction continued, if more slowly than hoped, and with the occasional accident. Three laborers were "seriously hurt by a blast," and in November a crane "hoisting one of the largest Pyramid stones" collapsed, fortunately injuring no one. The Delaware's three piers were all finished by November 20, while the completion of the abutments and anchorages was expected by the end of December. Dupuy hoped to be able to "allow Roebling to put on his wires this winter—but it will take every moment of time." John, for his part, was more than ready, having endured yet another painful encounter with Ellet.[53]

While preparing his wires and anchorage chains, John received word that the Niagara Bridge Company had invited him to present his plans for a suspension bridge up at the falls on November 1. "Although I entertain little hope to overcome Mr. Ellet's influence and get the contract, I have concluded to go there," John wrote Lord to explain his absence from the bridge site. He planned to leave October 20, but John promised there would be no delay in the construction.[54] Despite the chance to secure his revenge on Ellet, Roebling "returned without being successful in his Niagara Bridge," Dupuy wrote Lord. To add insult to injury, the events that dogged John at Wheeling played themselves out again, almost exactly. Despite a plethora of proposals—"two from *Glasgow Scotland*"— and much planning, calculating, and soliciting by John, Ellet was appointed chief engineer, despite not submitting a plan. John did not think the project would ever get started, however, "for the simple reason they cannot raise the money," Dupuy informed Lord.[55]

The work at the Delaware continued well through the winter of 1847–48. On January 21, Lord wrote to Wurts, "The masonry of the Delaware aqueduct is completed and ready for the superstructure. . . . We contemplate getting this work ready for use during the fall of 1848." John finished the wires on the Delaware Aqueduct at the end of March and moved on to the Lackawaxen, whose central pier was finished by April. Heavy and constant rains arrived almost immediately, to the point where most of the crew moved to the nearby village of Deerpark, "there being nothing to do at the Delaware Aqueduct." Spring floods held up the work for weeks, as did the delivery of some planks made from "*old dead trees.*" "There is neither fibre, strength nor life in this wood, and it would not last 2 years in the Aquaduct," John wrote, before adding that the planks "have deceived us all." Tensions between John and the superintending staff also continued to dog the construction. Lord was in overall command of the operation, meaning John exercised little or no authority over many of the hands at the worksite. John found the situation difficult, but he managed to live with it, writing to Lord on numerous occasions to complain about his foremen. "Mr. Johnston does not appear to understand the nature of the [work] and I believe, is *not* willing to," John complained. Thankfully, Lord's trust in John was strong, and most of these messages were relayed without question.[56]

The most significant cause of conflict during the construction involved the rival railroad. As John's spans were being raised, the New York and Erie Railroad was heading up the west bank of the Delaware River, opposite the D&H. They met and crossed at the mouth of the Lackawaxen, very close to where John was spinning his cables. A provision set out by the board of the D&H called for the Erie to "take special care, that their contractors and their men so conduct themselves, and prosecute their work, as not to injure the canal & its appendages" during the construction of their railroad, which turned out to be nothing more than a faint hope.[57] As the railroad worked its way up the Delaware, clashes between railroad workers and canal men were frequent and bloody. Just before the heavy rains of April, Dupuy complained to Lord that the railroad was "blasting on the Delaware Section of the Rail Road [scattering] *stone into the canal. They were not large enough to make the boats stick* but if it continues it will be sufficient to make traveling on the towing path *dangerous.*"[58] Large fragments of blasted rock rained down on the canal, the worksite, and Lord's laborers for several weeks. Traffic was disrupted as boatmen abandoned their barges, fearing injury or worse.

The trouble stemmed from the laborers as much as the work, as well as the Erie's inability to keep them within the bounds of the law. They worked hard, but they also liked a fight and were prone to "frequent riots and conflicts . . . often resulting in the loss of life." Worse, they were armed. Boatmen "have frequently passed along the tow-path and canal while balls were flying amid them," Lord informed Wurts. Under the circumstances, it is little wonder the violence escalated from workplace malice to direct confrontation. On June 3, "a large party of railroad hands, while returning from a turmoil, made an attack upon the boatmen . . . which resulted in a serious conflict, several of the men on both sides receiving serious personal injuries. Subsequent to that collision some of the police officers from the city of New York, together with the sheriffs of Sullivan and Pike counties, were employed by the Delaware and Hudson Canal Company, and remained on the Delaware section as peace officers until about the middle of November." By the end of the year, the railroad had thankfully finished its tracks, spanned the Lackawaxen, and moved on.[59]

Both the Delaware and Lackawaxen aqueducts were finished by January 1849, at a total cost of $51,800. They were opened for use three months later on April 26, 1849, on the first day of the season. A large crowd was on hand to see the aqueducts filled with water and the first boats sent across. There was a measure of concern initially, then wonder as the assembled dignitaries and locals stared out at the peculiar sight of a boat gliding by on a bridge of water, high above the onrushing Delaware. John was once more fêted and celebrated. Even the notoriously cranky and hard-to-please Johnson thought the aqueducts "approached perfection nearly as can be claimed from human hands." Johnson also commended John, "whose competency as a mechanical engineer was not excelled and rarely equaled among men," which was rare praise.[60]

The *Honesdale Democrat* printed a full and complete description of the structures: "The trunks are composed of timber and plank, well joined and caulked, and suspended to two wire cables, one on each side," they wrote; "the cables rest in heavy cast iron saddles, which are placed on top of small stone towers of about four by six feet base, rising four to five feet above the tow path. The trunks are wide enough for two boats of the present capacity to pass, and on each side of each trunk is a towpath. . . . The masonry of the piers and abutments, which support the little towers, has been executed in the most substantial

Figure 13.5 The Delaware Aqueduct and the slack-water dam, ca. 1880. Courtesy of the Minisink Valley Historical Society.

manner. . . . The beds of the face stone are all cut, the backing is large and well bonded, and the whole laid in hydraulic cement. Nothing has been spared to in-sure the safety of the foundations, and by the construction of good ice breakers, top guard the piers against the heavy floods and ice which in this river prove sometimes very violent and destructive. . . . The cables are made in one length across the rivers, from abutment to abutment, and connected at their ends with anchor chains, manufactured of solid wrought iron. . . . The cables are protected against oxidation by a copious varnish and paint, and closely encased by a tight wire wrapping, which gives them the appearance of solid cylinders, they may be considered as indestructible. The woodwork is subject to decay, but will last longer in these works than in common timber structures, and can be renewed at any time."[61]

Despite the great success of his spans, John privately noted several small flaws, none of which were ruinous or disabling, but which certainly seemed to irritate the engineer. The saddles, for one, were entirely too wide, which flattened the wires, causing "unequal tension." In addition, John's wrapping machine was "too long and too wide," meaning "the barrel move[d] with great difficulty [down the cables] without making a very compound wrapping." John struggled with his cables at the Delaware, a problem noted by the New York *Independent*, which observed the "curious fact" that "during the hot days of summer a very slight leakage was discovered at each abutment, which continued only through the heat of the day, and was doubtless owing to relaxing of wire cables by the increased temperature; they returned to their usual tension by night and the leaking stopped." John devoted considerable time and energy to the problem of laying and adjusting his wires so they occupied the correct position and achieved uniform tension, and then to wrapping the cables, a problem compounded by the winter weather. "Great attention is necessary in adjusting the wires, when the temperature changes from the wind or sun, the wires are constantly rising & falling, this is very important in large spaces," he wrote in his diary. "Cloudy dark and sunny clear day[s] are the best. Stormy weather very objectionable, moving the wires & traveling wheels, choose the good season, whenever it can be done." His spans worked well, but John had reservations. The Delaware wires were "made in one span. No good plan. Great difficulty to adjust the wires in such a great span. . . . Better to shorten the span and deflection and let the reminder out upon supports," he scribbled in his notebook.[62]

The D&H disagreed. "The Delaware and Lackawaxen aqueducts were brought into use last spring and have proved invaluable improvements to the navigation, being also substantial and permanent structures, sustaining all that has been claimed for the utility of wire suspension aqueducts," read the company's annual report the following year. From April until December, the last day of the season, the canal operated "with less interruption than usual, furnishing conclusive evidence in favor of the strength and permanence of the new work." As Lord wrote to Wurts on February 6, 1850, John's spans were "substantial and permanent structures, sustaining all that has been claimed for the utility of wire suspension aqueducts," and a marvelous addition to the canal: thanks to "the aqueducts the navigation has not been interrupted [once] during the season."[63] They were so taken with John's work that they decided to hire him to build two more aqueducts, work John was pleased to have in the wake of his disappointments at Wheeling and Niagara.

———

The Delaware was the D&H's top priority, but there were other bottlenecks and problems on the canal. A rickety old two-span wooden bridge, designed and build by Jervis twenty years earlier, carried the canal over the Neversink River at Cuddebackville, and a two-span stone arch structure served the same function over the Rondout Creek at High Falls. Both were rather ramshackle by the late 1840s and almost obsolete. The canal had been enlarged around them both several times, leaving the spans meager and inadequate, especially in the light of Wurts's ambition and Lord's new plans. The D&H's board thought retrofits would be costly and ineffective. Better just to tear both bridges down and build new ones in their place, they decided. Fortunately, they had an expert already planning a couple of aqueducts farther down the line.

Keen to exploit the inside track, John had plans for the next two bridges finished by the end of 1847, before he had really started on the first two aqueducts. He designed a 120-foot span over the Rondout at High Falls (to cost $20,000) and drew up two different plans for the Neversink: a single span of 170 feet (to cost $25,000) and a two-span affair with each span measuring 90 feet (to cost $18,000). In John's opinion, "Two spans are decidedly preferable," but he left that decision to the company, which ultimately disagreed. Ice floes battered Jervis's two bridges relentlessly each winter, leading to frequent repairs and delays. There was no getting across the Delaware without piers in the river, but circumstances were different at Cuddebackville and High Falls. After having spent thousands of dollars dealing with the after effects of spring floods and autumn's deluge, the D&H always preferred a clear span if it was feasible.[64]

John and Lord corresponded intermittently about the new bridges through most of 1848, as did Lord and Wurts. John submitted his official proposal to the board on November 11. He would construct a 170-foot span over the Neversink for $24,900, "my work to include all the iron, wire & wood work." The trunk would be the same dimensions as the Delaware Aqueduct, supported by 9½-inch cables anchored at each end with "solid chains & Oak timber foundations, similar to the Del[aware] plan." For $20,400, John would get the canal over the Rondout with a single span of 140 feet clear, supported on 8½-inch cables, with—again—most of the details and specifics being the same as on the Delaware.[65] The board accepted John's rather slight proposal on December 2, and by December 16 all the contracts had been signed and sealed. John announced the contract early the next year in the *Railroad Journal*, while alluding to a bigger prize: "I have contracted with the company, for two more aqueducts, one over the Roundout river . . . requiring cables of 9½ inches diameter, large enough for the support of a suspension bridge over the Niagara river, at the site in contemplation below the falls." D. K. Minor welcomed the news, as usual: John would lose none of "his well-earned reputation" by his efforts on behalf of the D&H, he editorialized.[66]

Preliminary work was begun at both sites in January and continued through the spring and summer. By August, workers were digging the anchorages, and John seemed pleased with every aspect of the job, as he was with the new locale. The Neversink valley was "attractive, with good farming lands," wrote Washington. "Life here was more endurable [for John], communications better, provisions and labor more plenty, while the village of Port Jervis was always a scene of bustling activity." John boarded with William Rose, the "principal citizen" of Cuddebackville, while shuttling back and forth between the two worksites. With the longest span and the thickest cables, the Neversink was the more strenuous job, but excepting the occasional accident all proceeded well and on time.[67]

One rather predictable problem arose early. "Mr. Jonathan Rhule has given me *no satisfactory* answer to my offer, therefore do not calculate on him—*I do not wish to engage him now*—if he would come," John wrote to Swan in early 1849, before quickly recruiting Rhule's brother David. The younger brother became an essential part of John's bridge building team, acting as master carpenter and "boss cable maker," a trade he had to learn on the job. "He was conscientious, faithful and honest," wrote Washington, and more importantly, "he possessed the faculty of getting along with [John], a rare quality." Of course, working alongside John for so many years, David had no choice but to go along with his boss's mania for the water cure. "The two spent their leisure hours in packing each other in sweat packs, douching, squatting in tubs," Washington disclosed with no small sense of derision. As for David's more independent and less pliant brother, John had some pointed words of warning for Swan: if he should come looking for work, he said, "I wish you to say as little to him as you can in relation to me & the works."[68]

———

While John was away building aqueducts, John A. Roebling's Wire Rope Company was outgrowing the confines of John's backyard. As orders increased,

John began to contemplate a move. His outdoor ropewalk was far from his major customers, and it relied on a shipping system that was slow, expensive, and closed for the entire winter. John had a great product and something of a monopoly for the time being, but should anyone manage to set up a reliable wire rope factory on the Eastern Seaboard—as the LC&N had done, although with little commercial value—John would find himself at a distinct disadvantage. He had moved to western Pennsylvania to be near the American future, but the future of wire rope, at least for now, was in the east. In effect, John decided to do to his business what the D&H was doing to its canal: streamline, enlarge, and head off new competition. As he wrote Archbald toward the end of 1847, "In consequence of the increased demand of Wire Rope, I am now contemplating the establishment of another Rope walk, East of the Allegheny Mountains, in the neighborhood of Philadelphia or New York." Within a year, he had settled on Trenton and had sent Swan to prepare the way and get everything set up.[69]

John picked Trenton partly because of advice, but mainly because of location. Washington certainly thought his father "followed the advice of Peter Cooper"— whose son Edward had just established the Trenton Iron Company in partnership with Abram Hewitt there in 1847—in moving to Trenton, a narrative that has become the standard account. Cooper, it is said, thought Roebling's wire works would be a good neighbor. They would need iron rods to make wire, a product Cooper's shop could easily supply. The proximity would be good for both businesses. The actual series of events is a little more difficult to pin down. On December 23, 1847—the same day he wrote to Archbald—John also wrote to Cooper saying that he wished "to establish a wire-rope manufactory near Trenton, and would like to know if five or ten acres of dry level ground could be obtained near the railway and canal," implying that John had picked Trenton before communicating with Cooper. Cooper's reply, if there was one, has been lost, but by the following summer the two manufacturers were neighbors. In August 1848, John bought a twenty-five-acre parcel of undeveloped farmland about a mile from the center of Trenton for three thousand dollars. The property fronted the Camden and Amboy Railroad and the Delaware and Raritan Canal.[70]

It is much more likely that John chose Trenton for the same good reasons as Cooper. Land there was relatively cheap, the labor market was strong, and transportation was excellent. Positioned midway between New York and Philadelphia, Trenton was close to customers, suppliers, raw materials, and the coalfields of eastern Pennsylvania. And it was well connected to the region's fledgling railroad system and the network of canals that still shifted most of the region's goods. Trenton was ripe for growth, but it had already been a home for the Northeast's iron industry for over a century.

John's arrival was announced in a short article in the Trenton *State Gazette*. "Mr. Roebling of Pittsburgh has purchased a site for a wire rope factory . . . between

White Horse Road and the Canal, a short distance below the new rolling mill," wrote the local paper. The manufacturer "enjoys a high reputation," they informed their readers, "and his business will no doubt be a large one," hopefully "creat[ing] a new source of wealth in this city." The following March, John sent Swan to start building his new factory. John did all the planning, down to the smallest detail, while Swan carried it all out. He was to put up three buildings: a two-story brick house for John and his family, along with a "small wire mill" and a building to house a boiler, steam engine, cleaning house, and "the machinery for driving the rope walk." "I am anxious the house should be completed as soon as possible," John wrote Swan in July, and that "we can commence making ropes" by September 1. He also added: "In case there should be a public auction about Trenton, you might attend and buy for me some furniture, if good yet & cheap for one or two rooms."[71]

Throughout the summer, John sent constant instructions and directives. "The building for pickling & Annealing had better *not* be commenced until you are through with *all the other carpenter work*," he demanded. "You can put up the Oven in its right place and erect a *temporary Board* roof over it and over some of the pickling vats, which will answer very well for a few weeks." Later, upon arriving at High Falls to commence his new aqueduct, he instructed, "I wish you to hurry on with our works *as fast as it can be done*. . . . We must commence making rope *before* the 1st of October." All proceeded well with the factory under Swan's supervision, which was more than could be said for the needs of John's family. As the move grew closer, John's directions got a little more frantic, as if the whole thing had escaped his attention. A week before the move he was urging Swan to go to Philadelphia to look at stoves, "for cooking as well as common use. . . . I must get a cooking stove and one for the lower room before my family arrives."[72]

John also sent a steady stream of mainly German machinists and wire workers who descended on Trenton throughout the summer, to be trained by Swan and put to work. Needless to say, John also sent a set of instructions for each man. Carl Lange, for example, was "very faithful and good dispositioned," but Swan should "not suffer him smoking during work. . . . I believe he was the cause of a fire, which broke out in the shanty yesterday." John seems to have developed a bit of a mania about smoking during his time at the Delaware. "Last winter we had a most dreadful accident in this neighborhood, when a large shanty burned down and 3 men lost their lives, the whole caused by smoking amongst bedding," he informed Swan. "I have now strictly prohibited smoking up stairs amongst bedding . . . and I want you to insist on it and carry out the same rule at Trenton, without exception. Do not let anybody smoke up stairs. I would rather discharge a good man, than lose a building by his carelessness," he declared, before instructing Swan to tell another worker "that he must either quit smoking up stairs or quit work. Do never depart from this rule."[73]

That Swan could put up with John's insistent micromanaging and petty bookkeeping—John once charged Swan thirty-four cents for forwarding him a letter—is testament to what Washington described as his "good disposition and [his] happy faculty of getting along with" his boss. Conversely, Swan became perhaps the only person John ever came to trust implicitly. He was honest, competent, and good-natured. As described by Hamilton Schuyler, Swan "appears to have been one of those loyal, trustworthy, patient souls, entirely devoted to the interests of his employer, and willing and anxious to subordinate himself in all respects to the wishes of his chief." He also became the driving force behind John's wire rope business, the de facto boss of a flourishing industrial enterprise.[74]

In addition to managing John's business, Swan also served as the official greeter when the Roebling family arrived in Trenton. John wrote to say he had instructed his wife to "leave Saxonbg on the 17th Sept so that they will arrive at Trenton on the 21 or 22." John himself "planned to leave High Falls for Never Sink in a few days, stay for a day, head to NYC and be in Trenton on the 23rd," but he never made it farther south than Cuddebackville and only arrived the following month. The Roeblings spent the summer of 1849 preparing for the move. "The children were glad, but my mother wept and the old folks went under compulsion," wrote Washington. The family was forced to arrange many of the details themselves, John being focused on his bridges and his factory. They held a public auction for all belongings they would not need in Trenton and raised money to finance the trip. The moving party consisted of John's wife, his in-laws (who returned to Saxonburg in 1854), his five children—twelve-year-old Washington, along with Laura (nine), Ferdinand (seven), Elvira (five), and Josephine (two)—and a couple of friends of the family, who intended to help with the rope making. Such a journey would have been a handful for even the stoutest wife and mother. That it was expected to take a week and involve multiple forms of transport made the ordeal much greater. And worse: Johanna was also six months pregnant at time. Even by the standards of nineteenth-century gender roles, John's decision to saddle his wife with the responsibility of shifting his large family and her aging parents with so little help was deplorable, let alone not being in Trenton to greet them.[75]

As the only one who spoke English fluently—German was the language of Saxonburg—Washington ended up as default party leader. "We left on a Sunday afternoon in the middle of September for Freeport in 4 wagons," he wrote of the journey. "The whole village turned out to see us off—many cried, all looked sad. . . . We left the friends and companions of 20 years, most of whom were never to see each other again—I think my mother grieved more than anyone, the change in her life was to be so great—Ten years later I visited the place, but I was already a stranger." They spent Sunday night at a hotel in Freeport, "sleeping on sofas and even the floor, it was so full," and found themselves roused at 3:00 a.m.

Monday morning in order to make the Philadelphia packet, after which they got themselves all loaded up and stuffed into the boat and settled in to enjoy the journey as much as they were able. "The weather was fine, we sat on deck, laid down flat every time we passed a bridge, read books, threw stones at things on the shore, admired the scenery and enjoyed the eating which I thought was very fine, because we had rice pudding for dessert every day," Washington later reminisced. They passed by "the noble gorges where the river breaks through the Chestnut ridge and the Laurel ridges" where John had spent time surveying ten years earlier, before unloading again at the Portage Railroad. Washington was ecstatic to see his first locomotive but unimpressed by the Portage Railroad itself, which was "neither steep nor very long."[76]

The idyll of the journey's first leg was dashed as soon as they were back on the canal. Low water at Hollidaysburg grounded them for a day, after which they were forced to find room for the passengers of another boat "producing the most intolerable crowding, especially for the female passengers." "At night we slept on the floor and tables and daytime we walked on the towpath." The Roeblings reached Philadelphia around nine in the evening on Friday, September 21, and stayed at the Allegheny House, "a rusty hostelry." They reached Trenton the following morning: "The weary party trudged down the muddy towpath, and finally entered their new home where Mrs. Swan was cooking dinner. . . . A shade of disappointment passed over the faces of most of us, at first impress of the new home, yet we were all so glad to be under our own roof once more. . . . The house was small for so many—before everything was regulated there were many bickering, and divisions of opinion."[77]

John finally turned up in October "and stayed awhile. We children had seen so little of him for a year or so that we had become a little wild and did not take kindly to the restraint." Washington was "promptly packed off to school with the Hon. Dr. Ewing, a gentleman of the old school, resembling old Benj. Franklin with his silk knee breeches and embroidered vest." On December 12, 1848, almost three months after arriving, Johanna gave birth to her sixth child, Charles, in her threadbare and cramped new home. "The boy as he grew up was more like his father than any of the others," Washington wrote; "he resembles [him] more in features, stature, walk, manner and mental peculiarities, exhibiting much of the same intensity and force of action, but while he had a kinder heart after it was formed, he lacked a certain breadth of mind, polish of manner, and that comprehensive intellect, which stamped Mr. Roebling senior a great man among his fellows."[78]

Swan and his men began drawing wire in early October and laying ropes by November, prompting the local paper to declare that "the new wire rope factory is going ahead as fast as a large body of men can push it."[79] The factory itself was in most respects a larger, mechanized version of the Saxonburg ropewalk.

There were two parallel ropewalks: one for strands and one for ropes (there had been only one in Saxonburg). And they seemed to produce excellent ropes, albeit using a convoluted, cumbersome method. John patented the machinery he designed for his Trenton works in 1854—although no one ever sought to use it—and it was abandoned about ten years later. "I think of all the men on the place only my father & Swan understood the operation of the whole system—certainly no outsider ever got it through his head," wrote Washington. He and Swan called it "Old Siege," implying some form of medieval technology. A reporter for the Trenton *State Gazette* wrote that the "machinery is so perfect that every strand of wire rope will bear its due proportions of the strain to which the whole shall be subjugated," yet he "could not give our readers an intelligent description of the [mechanism if he] should try."[80]

John's factory was little more than a handful of small brick and wood buildings, surrounded by a well-tended garden, but it would grow into a huge sprawling plant and an industrial empire by the early twentieth century. John continued to employ mainly German workers—as he did on his bridge projects—and they in turn remained loyal. During the panic of 1857, John instructed Swan to retain as many employees as possible by stockpiling ropes in advance of actual orders. The

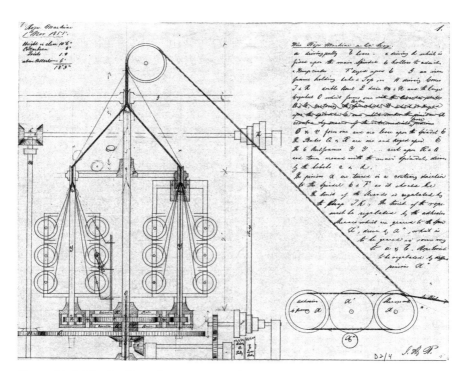

Figure 13.6 John Roebling, "Wire Rope Machine, Nov 1855." Courtesy of the Institute Archives and Special Collections, Rensselaer Polytechnic Institute.

move paid off. Sons followed fathers, and the company payroll remained largely unchanged for decades, except for the addition of new staff as the business expanded. Such measures created a remarkable continuity of expertise and community that allowed John's business to thrive beyond all expectations.[81]

———

Only a few weeks after Ellet opened his Wheeling Bridge, John went to his ropewalk to check on a 3,600-foot-long rope he was laying up for the South Carolina Railroad Company. The day's work had begun, the machinery fired up and in motion. While surveying the smooth running of the room, John absent-mindedly placed his left hand on the drive rope that powered the operation. It snagged somehow and, as John watched in horror, dragged his hand into the maw of the sheave mechanism. His "cry of agony" alerted Swan, who came running. He reversed the machine and helped withdraw "the mangled arm," after which John fell backward, "apparently lifeless." James B. Coleman, Trenton's foremost surgeon, was sent for and "attended to the crushed wound which had lacerated the tendons of his left hand & fingers." John's condition improved, although he remained "permanently injured," unable to play the flute or the piano (except one-handed). He also found it difficult to draw and, at least for several months, difficult to write. Recovery was slow and tedious, and of course John self-medicated with the water cure, much to Coleman's disgust. Slowly, however, his wounds healed. His fingers would remain "stiff for life," and "movement of the hand at the wrist" was greatly impaired, but John was able to keep working, ultimately planning and building his greatest bridges without the full use of both hands. Needless to say, he attributed his recovery entirely to the water cure.[82]

After the injury, John was bedridden for about a month, by which time he had been away from his two bridge sites for over four months. He took Washington with him to serve as his "amanuensis"—despite the boy being only twelve years old "with an underdeveloped handwriting of my own, the cause of much parental complaint"—and to act as "a sort of young nurse, a part I played for 2 or 3 years." It was the first time Washington had spent significant time on the job with his father. In frigid conditions, father and son traveled to New York and took the boat to Piermont and the Erie Railroad to Otisville, after which came a "sleighride of three miles down the hill to the Neversink in the face of a driving Northern sleet storm—Having no overcoat or underclothes I nearly perished from cold—never shall I forget that ride." When they finally made it to Rose's house, they were rewarded with "a substantial supper." They ventured out to the bridge site the following day and "found that a few of the laboring men had remained in the shanties over the winter—these were banked up with earth and resembled underground dwellings to keep out the cold." Stonemasons were out working on the anchorages and abutments, while carpenters were working on the trunk. All seemed well, despite the unforgiving cold and John's prolonged absence, and the Roeblings stayed just a few days, the trip having already overtaxed John.[83]

John was sufficiently healed to manage another trip in May. Several D&H officials came along this time to check on the progress, leaving no room in the stagecoach from Port Jervis for Washington, who had to ride alongside on an ox. "The motion is like that of a dromedary producing sea sickness and spinal concussion," he groused. "I stood it for 3 miles when I rolled off his round back." The ox then promptly fled, leaving Washington lost and alone in the New York forest. The errant son finally got picked up by a friendly team of drivers and taken to Cuddebackville, where he "had to be rubbed with grease to assuage the pain" of his saddle sores. "Here it was beautiful, fine scenery and surroundings, the aqueduct forming a conspicuous feature in the landscape," he marveled between treatments. John and his son pushed on quickly to High Falls, where Washington came across "plenty of black eyes and sore heads, and learned that a few days previous there had been a grand fight between the two Irish factions, the Corkonians and the Far downers." According to the local press, the rivalry between the two groups was a running source of bitterness and violence across Irish work camps at the time. "Without knowing or caring what are the abstract grounds of difference between the [factions], we do know that the grog shops are the parents of the fight," wrote the *Rondout Courier*. Johnson was equally dismissive: "When thus doubly inflamed by passion and whiskey and joined in conflict, the Irish of those times were, in a large degree dangerous to people to houses and to families with whom they came in contact." Drunk "exasperated" Irishmen "wielded their shelalales [*sic*] promiscuously, upon friend and foe alike. . . . It became an interested object on the part of both contractor, their assistants and the citizens to prevent these collisions and their bloody effects by every means at their commend." In April they failed, and a huge riot broke out between the two clans. "The battle waxed so hot that priests had to be sent in to stop it," Washington reported.[84]

Fights and conflicts among the workers caused significant delays during 1850, as did Superintendent Watson, who again proved unable to manage the job effectively. To this was added the unlikely discovery of quicksand during a "deep cut of excavation on the new line at the High Falls." But as the year turned, the finishing touches were applied and the aqueducts completed. Both were put into operation as soon as the season opened, although with much less fanfare than greeted the opening of the Lackawaxen and Delaware spans. There was not much of a celebration, just the expectation that John's bridges would be well-made, watertight, and work perfectly. John in fact was home in Trenton when the aqueducts were opened, having finally received word of the commission he had coveted for the last four years. By the time he received the final payment for his two aqueducts on May 16, John was already hard at work on his Niagara plans.[85]

By any measure, the D&H's enlargement was an incredible success and a fine testament to its canny managers. Coal shipments for the 1851 season were twice those of 1846 and four times those of 1841. By the following season, eight thousand tons of coal was passing though the D&H's Kingston depot every day. The enlargement also allowed for bigger, riverworthy boats that didn't have to unload, but could instead move on to all points south, and north if needed. The extra capacity reduced shipping rates by about half, allowing the canal to compete with the Erie Railroad until well into the 1870s, while simultaneously increasing toll revenue, which increased from an average of $34,827.65 during the 1840s to a high of $652,362.94 in 1855.[86] Although the enlargement had proven costly and taken over three years to complete, it paid for itself within a few years. John's work for the D&H helped to keep the company viable and hugely profitable in the face of new technologies and new competition. It also helped make John's fortune, as he invested in company stock and reaped excellent dividends. Lord, somewhat perplexingly, sold all his shares in the D&H in September 1847, just as the enlargement was getting underway.[87]

After working together on the D&H aqueducts, John's and Lord's careers diverged. John prospered. Lord did not. Being almost constantly at the canal made for a rough, itinerant life. Lord's first wife, Mary Ann Garret, was much younger than Lord. They had three children but were not a happy couple. She died young just as the enlargement was going. On January 29, 1849, Lord married Lizzie M. Scott, soon to be future president Benjamin Harrison's sister-in-law. One wonders how he found the time amid the canal work. Certainly, there was no time for a proper courtship, and perhaps predictably the couple fought bitterly to a general, silent disunion. They had a daughter whom Lord later disowned. By the late 1850s, Lord was drinking heavily, which exacerbated his already nasty temper.[88]

By 1862, Lord and John were back in contact. Massive spring flooding caused significant damage to the Lackawaxen Aqueduct. Lord attempted to fix the problem himself, but his mental state and general lack of sobriety led him to botch the job. He didn't seem to understand he was doing more harm than good until a subordinate discovered the underlying problem. John was then summoned. He brought David Rhule along, and together they worked up a plan for rebuilding. John later wrote kindly to Lord, "You have done *well*, better than I anticipated" after he heard that boats were passing over the aqueduct again on July 15, 1862. He was a little less kind—or at least more direct—the following year when the D&H wrote to ask about enlarging the Neversink Aqueduct. "To widen the trunks and enlarge any of those works is in my opinion impossible," John advised. "If you must have more capacity, there is no other remedy left, but to duplicate and build another aqueduct alongside the old one." Lord wrote back to say the D&H was considering his proposal, but John had moved on to bigger projects and was polite but firm in his response. "I am not in a situation to supply your wants," he wrote, not only because of the Civil War raging to the south, which made it costly to procure sufficient raw materials, but "in consequence of the great importance and magnitude" of his current work. "It will be entirely out of my power to give your enterprise any personal attention."[89]

The year 1863 was Lord's last with the D&H, and to their credit the company "dealt gently with a man who, although only 60, had broken himself in their service."[90] At a board meeting on June 2, 1862, it was decided that "the health of Mr. R. F. Lord . . . was so impaired as to require relaxation from the cares of business." They granted him six months' leave and offered to pay for a trip to Europe to "make such observations as may be of use to the company." Lord refused the offer and battled through one more year of service before tendering his resignation at the close of the 1863 season. The D&H promptly granted Lord a lifetime pension, one of the country's first. He lived for only three more years in a miserable, unhappy state, a human casualty wrecked by delirium tremens, passing away in July 1867. "He was shackled with fatal elements that defaced his grandeur [and] brought him to a grave unwatered by a tear and ungraced by the undivided respect of a human being," wrote Johnson, yet "for fully 30 years he traveled the canal on horse back, through heat and cold, many times in the year as its government required, and carried in a portmanteau lashed to the front of his saddle, the millions of money required for its expenses, without the loss of a single dollar to the company." Under Lord's watch, the D&H enjoyed its greatest years as one of the most profitable, reliable, and influential companies in the United States.[91]

———

John's aqueducts served the D&H almost flawlessly, needing only routine maintenance, until 1898, when the canal was shut down and its parts abandoned. The Delaware span gained a level of fame and notoriety during the late nineteenth century not normally reserved for aqueducts, finding itself featured in songs and paintings, and even making an appearance in William Cullen Bryant's famous and influential *Picturesque America* (1874). The span was subsequently adapted for commercial road traffic—at first for wagons and carts, then automobiles— passing through several phases of ownership before being acquired by the National Parks Service in 1980, which set about restoring it. "The more we got into it, the more we saw of the actual thought and detail," Sandra Speers, chief of planning and support services, told the *New York Times*; "there are so many minutiae of detail, like the wrought-iron metal work that was all hand-crafted for each section." Described as "one of the nation's most significant engineering treasures," the Delaware Aqueduct was declared a National Historic Landmark in 1968 and a National Historical Civil Engineering Landmark in 1972. Today it stands—its cable system intact, its roadway rebuilt by the Parks Service to resemble its original trunk formation—as the oldest suspension bridge in the United States, beating out the still extant, and also substantially rebuilt, Wheeling Suspension Bridge by seven months.[92]

There was little anyone could do to make the other aqueducts useful, nor did anyone seem to want to.[93] They all limped on as casual footbridges for a while. The High Falls bridge survived until 1921; the Lackawaxen lasted perhaps as late as the early 1940s. Both were brought down by fire and their ironwork harvested by local scrap dealers. Most of the abutments survive to this day in various stages of neglect. In 1928, H. C. Boynton, a metallurgist at John A. Roebling's Sons,

Figure 13.7 The Delaware Aqueduct during its second life as a makeshift automobile bridge, photographed ca. 1970–73. David Plowden, "Delaware & Hudson Canal, Delaware Aqueduct, Spanning Delaware River, Lackawaxen, Pike County, PA." HAER PA,52-LACK,1-. Library of Congress, <www.loc.gov/item/pa1234/>.

was able to get some of the wires from the High Falls Aqueduct after it was taken down. "The material was not galvanized or coated with any metal, yet the corrosion of this wire, while marked was not excessive [and] there was relatively little pitting of the surface," he declared. The cable was "still amply strong for its intended use," while the wire had "lost none of its valuable physical properties since the bridge was erected." Quite the contrary, the wires seemed to have grown "a little stronger with age." Most "theoretical metallurgists" believed cold-worked iron to possess "elements of structural instability" in comparison to modern techniques, he concluded, yet the High Falls wire "has the most honorable service record of absolute dependability."[94]

By the spring of 1851, John had built six bridges. All were somewhat modest, especially in comparison with Ellet's massive Wheeling Bridge, and five weren't even true suspension bridges at all. But six was still far more than any other engineer in America, and together they served as excellent case studies in problem-solving issues of form and function. Suspension bridges are designed to support moving loads, but rarely constant heavy loads. Suspension aqueducts, by contrast, are designed to do both. They have to be strong to support a moving load, but also stiff so that they can carry their own weight. They are something of a suspension/truss hybrid, with each element liable for a separate body of weight. Such projects forced John to think in new ways, especially when it came time to build bridges that were more strictly and conventionally suspended. John's early bridges weren't record-setting, but they helped him immensely when it came to designing and building the longer spans that defined the latter part of his career. By the time he finished the D&H commission, he was fully ready for his next challenge. On April 29, 1851, even before a single boat had floated over his High Falls and Neversink spans, John was back up at Niagara Falls to meet with the directors of the Niagara Falls International Bridge Company. Ellet had botched his chance up at the border. John wouldn't.[95]

Crossing Niagara (1846–51)

As John turned forty years old, he found himself standing before the rushing cacophony that was the Niagara Falls, hoping to execute one of the most stupendous engineering feats of the age. He arrived during a boom in tourism and development. Just as the mighty waters of Lake Ontario poured into the Niagara River, crashed over the mighty cataract, and into Lake Erie, so serious sightseers, spellbound gawkers, and daredevils of all stripes traveled across the continent and descended on the falls, to enjoy the overwhelming natural beauty, connect with the sublime, or make their fortunes. Artists, intellectuals, showmen, politicians, and inventors made the falls at mid-century one of the most visited, written about, and exciting places in the country.

In the fall of 1848, Abraham Lincoln stood at the falls and wondered, "By what mysterious power is it that millions and millions, are drawn from all parts of the world, to gaze upon Niagara Falls?" "Its power to excite reflection, and emotion, is its great charm," he thought, but also its links to the planet's shared past and future project. "When Christ suffered on the cross—when Moses led Israel through the Red-Sea—nay, even, when Adam first came from the hand of his Maker—then as now, Niagara was roaring here. The eyes of . . . the Mammoth and the Mastodon . . . gazed on Niagara, as ours do now." Margaret Fuller agreed: there was "no escape from the weight of perpetual creation" at Niagara, nor from a penetrating sense of the eternal. For others it was the "inexpressible, inconceivable beauty," but also of the changes being wrought on the land. "The Americans have disfigured their share of the rapids with mills and manufactories, and horrid red brick houses, and other unacceptable, unseasonable sights and signs of sordid industry," Anna Jameson lamented.[1]

While some celebrated the falls as an awe-inspiring spectacle or lamented the passing of the wilderness and its remote sublimity into industrial blight, still more saw the cataract through increasingly prosaic eyes. In 1845, fifty thousand people descended on Niagara, twice the number of visitors of just five years before, overrunning local transit networks, while trade across the peninsula between British Canada and the United States continued to grow. The minds behind Canada's Great Western and the burgeoning upstate New York railroad system cast their eyes on the region and began to plot. "Railroads transformed Niagara, exploited it, glamorized it, cheapened it, and created on the banks of the gorge what has been called 'the center of a vortex of travel,'" writes historian Pierre Berton, but they also brought remarkable opportunity, especially for experienced engineers like John. Stretching a set of railroad tracks over the Niagara River—the region's great schism—was no easy task in an era when the technology behind both railroads and bridges was still in its infancy and thus far coupling them had proved disastrous.[2]

The first serious proposal to span the Niagara River was put forward by Francis Hall in 1824. Hall claimed to have assisted on the Menai Bridge before arriving in Canada, and his plan was effectively a miniature version of that bridge, with "piers raised on each side of the river . . . and chains to be wrought on the spot." Twelve years later he proposed an even wilder plan: "By [my] design it is proposed to pass from the Canadian shore by a Suspension Bridge of 990 feet span, to an Island in Niagara River, from thence by a Tunnel under the bed of the river 500 yards in length to Goat Island; passing over the same by a common road to a second Suspension Bridge of 594 feet span, to the American shore." The total cost of all this was to be a rather modest £32,000. Another opinion was provided by Captain R. H. Bonnycastle of the Upper Canadian Royal Engineers, who believed a bridge could be thrown over the river just north of the falls themselves—"the least [favorable] in consequence in a commercial point of view, but the greatest in a national one [showing off the region's] magnificence and grandeur"—or somewhere near the Niagara Whirlpool where the shores were closer together and "future Rail Roads could be brought into it." This last option "would perhaps combine the magnificent with the useful" more than any other. A few years later, a local builder proposed to build a single arch stone bridge for $120,000 at a point where the river was only 332 feet wide. The bridge would have room for a railroad track, a carriageway, and a sidewalk for foot passengers. "It is supposed that an Iron Suspension Bridge could be constructed at a less rate, but . . . the public would not have perfect confidence in its safety," commented the *Rochester Advertiser*, which was likely very true.[3]

By the 1840s, there was an ever-increasing need to span the Niagara River. The region was developing; commerce was increasing. Numerous ferries plied the river servicing this need, but the swift-moving current made the journey troublesome and dangerous. Much like the Ohio, the Niagara was chocked with ice for most of the lengthy winter and blocked for navigation. Even during the fine summer months, the ferries that plied the Niagara could hardly keep up with the traffic. Into this situation strode William Hamilton Merritt. As a young man Merritt had helped promote and build the first Welland Canal between Lake Erie and Lake Ontario, before moving on to railroads. He envisioned Upper Canada (roughly southern Ontario) as the site of a major new trade route between Great Britain and the United States.

During a beautiful summer day in 1844, Merritt took his wife for a picnic on the shores of the Niagara just above the falls. They picked up their mail on the way and read a letter from their eldest sons, William Jr. and Jedediah, then traveling in Europe. Of all the sights, both ancient and modern, they had been especially impressed by "a wonderful suspension bridge . . . spanning the River Sarren in the midst of a mountainous country"—Chaley's massive Fribourg Bridge in Switzerland. Gazing out at the steep gorge and the swift-running Niagara, Merritt apparently remarked, "I wonder if a suspension bridge could not be made to span this river."[4] A bridge on its own would serve little purpose but for sightseers and road traffic, neither of which was likely to raise the sort of money needed to erect an eight-hundred-foot-long suspension bridge. To make the span commercially viable Merritt would need a railroad sponsor. To this end he teamed up with Charles B. Stuart, a young civil engineer with plenty of experience with railroads and politics. Stuart worked for the Great Western Railroad and, like Merritt, saw the route from Buffalo through Upper Canada as "the *central link* in the extended chain of railways reaching from New York and Boston to the Mississippi River."[5]

Merritt began to sound out Charles Ellet on the subject of suspension bridges in October 1845, just as John was getting started on his Monongahela span. By the end of the month John's rival was touring around the proposed route of the Rochester and Niagara Falls Railroad with Stuart, helping to explain the science of suspension bridges and the soundness of their design. In November the two were spotted surveying the Niagara River just below the falls. "A suspension Bridge across the Niagara river at the Falls, with a fiery locomotive and its long train of flying cars passing through the air, some 200 feet above the foaming stream, and, perchance, encircled with the rainbow of heaven, would be a magnificent sight," editorialized the Buffalo *Commercial Advertiser*. Word of the venture spread. Ellet was shocked one night in Utica to overhear two men talking about him and his plans to span the mighty Niagara. By the close of 1845, Ellet was already fully enmeshed within the leadership team, making any subsequent sense of a competition illusory.[6]

By his own admission, Ellet had long coveted the project. "Some twelve years ago I went to inspect the location," he wrote Stuart, "and I have never lost sight of the project since."[7] In November 1845, the *Rochester Democrat* published a letter Ellet had written to the chairman of the Great Western Railroad Company and the president of the Niagara Falls and Lockport Railroad Company, when both men had inquired about the feasibility of running a railroad bridge across the gorge. Ellet had examined the area below the falls and decided it was eminently practical. The best site would be "a short distance above the Whirlpool" where the river is only 700 feet wide, where a suspension bridge could run a single railroad track flanked by "two lateral ways for common travel and two foot ways." The cost of such a bridge would be $220,000. "The structure itself will be a beautiful and durable object," Ellet declared, "and the investment a great deal better and more profitable than that of any Railroad line now in use on this continent." With Ellet's "favorable opinion," the *Rochester American* believed "the matter begins to wear less the aspect of a Quixotic enterprise."[8]

By early 1846, parallel US and British companies had been formed and the requisite royal approval granted by Queen Victoria. Prompted by Ellet's open letter, John and D. K. Minor also started to talk. Publicly, the *Railroad Journal* predicted a "spirited competition" between John and Ellet over the contract, although John hadn't as yet been approached about the project. "I am glad to learn that you are moving in the matter of the Niagara Bridge," Minor wrote John on January 2, "& advise you to be as *active* as Mr. E[llet]—[who] is indefatigable in whatever he undertakes." John "must make a noise if you would succeed" and "move in this matter, *promptly vigorously* & *judiciously* if you would inscribe your name on the Rocks of Niagara Falls for all time to come," counseled Minor. He should make himself "*known*" in Rochester and at the falls, "before Mr. Ellet or Mr. *anybody else*, could get to [*sic*] firm a foothold."[9]

John heard from Stuart the same day. The engineer apologized for taking so long to reply to John. He had been "dangerously ill"—a doubtful claim given the frequency of his meetings with Ellet—but was now happy to inform John that all was ready and set for the bridge. "Chas Ellet Jr of Philadelphia will take the contract, and will probably complete the work the early part of next fall," wrote Stuart, before promising to send on copies of Ellet's report and to "visit Pittsburgh this winter & see your bridges and also make your personal acquaintance."[10] Nonetheless, Minor continued to urge John on. "Unless Ellet has got a long start we will give him a pull. . . . You must push for competition, or take more stock than E if need be," he advised. "You must not let your modesty ruin you, nor keep you back, *puff-puff* is the order of the day, & if *you* do not *puff*, others *will*, & you might as well be out of the world as out of *fashion*." "*Action, action* is necessary," he concluded; that and "a little 'soft soap.'"[11] John was terrible at puffery, unfortunately, and could hardly take action, given everything else he was involved with: finishing the Monongahela span; drawing up plans for the Ohio, Wheeling, and tripartite bridges; and growing his wire rope business. If he was to stand any chance with the Niagara contract, he needed to be up in the frozen wilderness of Upper Canada, promoting and glad-handing, as Minor was urging. Additionally, John still understood competition as essentially professional in nature, believing that proposals won or lost on their technical merits alone. The loss of the Niagara contract underscored John's continued failure to understand the terms on which the competition for large-scale construction projects was conducted.

Despite Stuart's confident assertion—and Minor's own belief that "Stuart & E have an understanding, & *mutual* interest"—there had been no official declaration about the bridge. John dutifully submitted a bid of $180,000 on January 7, 1847, after which Ellet immediately lowered his bid from $220,000 to $190,000. John rather unwisely left his plans in the hands of Stuart, hoping—naively— "that no advantage will be taken of this, when competing with others."[12] He also visited the falls in May, making good headway with the commissioners. "We listened to [Roebling's] suggestions and examined his plans but no assurances were given and we expressly reserved our opinions," wrote Washington Hunt, a local lawyer. "Some have been persuaded that Mr. Roebling's mode of construction secures greater strength, but I do not think it is the general opinion," he added. Ultimately, however, John was working against a more formidable foe. Not Ellet this time, but a man named Lot Clark. Clark was a politician, lawyer, and banker, a major player in local affairs, and a master manipulator, as Ellet would himself find out within the year. He was also the largest stockholder in the fledgling company, and he controlled many of the decisions, firmly but quietly. "Mr. Roebling was here," Clark wrote Ellet in June; "they all formed a very good opinion of him, some believe that the company should engage him if practicable, others would be satisfied with either. . . . I have never seen him, but I doubt not he is a very competent man." That said, "like others I have my opinions & preferences [and] I prefer that you should be the architect. My reasons are such as would rapidly suggest themselves to any one—we began intercourse with you on the subject, & on that account as well as some others it would please me better to observe with you to the end." By July, this preference had given way to a definite inclination: "Clark [has] expressed himself quite in favor of giving you the Bridge to construct—*and he controls a majority of the stock*!!!," Stuart wrote Ellet. By the end of August, Clark was certain: "This letter is unofficial [but the two bridge companies] have a desire that you should be appointed their engineer," he wrote Ellet. As for John, the board "has had a letter from an Alleghany friend at Pittsburgh in which he requests in particular that *he* [Roebling] may not be deprived of a fair chance to present his claim for competition." Slyly and singlehandedly, Clark decided that the letter would "not be answered until after the 24th," the preliminary date for the final decision.[13]

Ellet was "selected to survey the river, and the site of the Bridge" at a meeting of the commissioners on September 24. No mention was made of John. In response, James Dickinson, Ellet's principal assistant at Wheeling, wrote that he was "delighted to hear of the appointment as I knew it would gratify you . . . after the unmanly and unfair course pursued by Mr. R. of Pittsburgh." Ellet himself was much less pleased when he was officially appointed chief engineer of the Niagara Falls Suspension Bridge in early November, after all the machinations and double-dealing. "There are innumerable under-currents and obvious intrigues," Ellet wrote his wife while waiting for the final decision to be handed down. "The Engineer of the Welland Canal has a plan, and although before I came, he and Mr. Roebling were at issue, and directly opposed in views, interests and opinions, it is now well understood that they have suddenly compromised, agreeing that one shall be contractor and the other engineer." As for the competition: "I do not know how to get out: for it seems bad to succeed and perhaps worse to fail." But "if I get the appointment, [I will] make what I can of its advantages, and if I fail, to congratulate myself on my escape." At least "Mr. Clark acts all through up-rightly and as straight forwardly as the tortuous courses of those he is concerned with will permit," thought Ellet, rather naively, given how much chicanery had already emanated from that quarter. More prescient was the simple declaration written to his wife a day earlier: "The whole thing is disgusting. I do not like the people, and have little confidence in them or in their intentions."[14]

Not everyone was as concerned as Ellet, especially outside the fraught dealing and decision-making. Typical of many commentators, the Buffalo *Republic* was enraptured by the prospect of the shape of things to come: "The location which the directors have settled upon is one of such awful grandeur, that, when this magnificent production of art shall be added to it . . . it will become a more in-teresting point of attraction than the great Cataract itself. [The rapids] roaring like a thousand earthquakes; the beetling cliffs on either side which nearly chills the blood of the hardiest adventurer who dares to thrust his head over the awful chasm, with the great whirlpool below . . . will present a spectacle which prob-ably will have no equal on earth. We cannot doubt that the completion of this great work of art, will permanently double the number of annual visitors to that stupendous work of Nature."[15]

Within a few weeks of beginning work, Ellet was writing his sister that "the facilities for carrying on work are far greater than I would have expected—and I have never before been able to get underway with so little exertion."[16] Shortly after that, a reporter for the *Morning Courier and New-York Enquirer* paid a visit. "I have been intensely interested to-day in listening to a description . . . of the great bridge over the gorge that separates the dominions of the Queen from those of the President," he wrote in a review that was reprinted all over the country. "This glorious work is already begun, the money for its cost paid in and available, the excavations commenced. . . . Its firmness is to be such that with all the burden of a powerful locomotive and a long attendant train of cars it is not to vibrate one inch in the centre." A road of this kind over the Niagara would soon be "world famed." "It will be an iron link of civilization between the two ruling powers of the world, and will never be severed," they concluded rather optimistically, especially since no one had worked out "how the [first] wires are to be thrown across."[17]

Ellet, it seems, favored using a rocket "to throw his first line across the gulf." John had privately planned to get the first wire across using "a balloon, large enough to carry 6 to 10 lbs of wire." Others thought towing a cord over on a boat would answer the call much better, despite the fact that that the Niagara was choked up with ice. A local man named Frisk thought Ellet could solve his problem much like Ben Franklin, who had summoned electricity from the clouds with a kite. Always happy to encourage a spectacle, Ellet agreed and soon set up a competition to see if any local lads could manage to fly a kite across the Niagara gorge in the wild winter winds of late February. Dozens tried over the course of a week, but eventually a youngster named Homan J. Walsh was able to get his kite over, winning ten dollars from Ellet in the process. "I felt," Walsh later related, "that I had leaped from boyhood to manhood. I had joined two countries."[18]

Once a line had been strung between the two cliffs, a cable could be dragged over and draped over the two twenty-five-foot-tall wooden towers Ellet had erected. The ends of the cable were then securely fastened on either side, "and there it hangs . . . 250 feet above the rapids . . . a band of iron connecting firmly and lastingly those neighboring nations," as one local newspaper described it. A series of grooved pulleys were placed on top of the cable, from which was hung "a basket of commodious and graceful form" that could be pulled back and forth over the abyss. It was reached by a staircase leading to a landing on the wooden towers. "By this simple contrivance, which works smoothly and beautifully," Ellet had "obtained a most convenient ferry over this hitherto impassable gulf" with just "a few weeks unostentatious labor in the most inclement season of the year."[19]

The basket was designed and built by Theodore G. Hulett, Ellet's superintendent at the falls. It was made of iron bands bolted together, and its shape was suggested by putting two rocking chairs together.[20] The basket was first used on March 13, 1848, when Ellet became the first man to cross over the Niagara "on wire, from one empire to another," a day "forever . . . remembered by all who witnessed the awful and sublime spectacle." As described by the *Toronto Colonist*, Ellet took his seat in his strange contraption while "a breathless anxiety filled every heart." When he reached about halfway across, "our fears gave way for his safety, and a shout of joy broke forth [which] overpowered (in our ears) the thunder of the great falls. "Truly we live in a wondrous age," they editorialized, "to see a gentleman floating through the air, 250 feet above the waters, on wires such as are used in electricity; when we reflect upon it our imagination is raised so, that the mind . . . is lost in astonishment." Ellet's daughter Mary gave a more personal description: "There was dead silence as the basket slipped on its way down the incline till it reached about over the middle of the river; then the crowd yelled while the basket swung for a few moments suspended—too long—my mother screamed at them—there were groans and cried of anguish— then Father rose and waved his hat—the obstacle was overcome and the basket rose to the top of the company elevation on the Canada side." Ellet himself thought Hulett's contraption was "a beautiful and curious ferry and will work admirably." "The sight from the centre is grand," he continued; "the cataract to the left—the rapids beneath and to the right, and the cliffs all around, present a most beautiful ensemble." Over the next several months, Ellet's "fairy basket" provided stout and sterling service, eventually hauling more than two thousand sightseers across the gorge (for a modest fee of one dollar), not to mention all the workers, tools, and equipment needed to build Ellet's bridge.[21]

With the help of his basket, Ellet proceeded to build a temporary wooden suspension bridge over the next four months. He finished the work—the first bridge to span the mighty Niagara—on July 29 and marked the occasion with a typical piece of derring-do. With five hundred feet of railing still unfinished on either side, Ellet bundled himself into a horse and buggy and set off across the bridge. "The horse was rather a fractious one and blind of an eye," reported the *Baltimore Patriot*, yet "Mr. E. stepped into the carriage with great composure, started his horse, and rode over in triumph." He then switched to two horses, and "as the horses and vehicle passed over, the bridge would gradually give way under their feet, bending and rising up again, like thin ice when venturesome boys are skating on it. The scene was full of terrific excitement. So confident, however, was Mr. Ellet in the strength and security of his bridge, that he rode upon it without the slightest emotion of fear."[22] Shortly after, in a touching moment of parental trust and pride, Ellet took his daughter out onto the span, providing her with a signal memory of her father and his work: "Upon this bridge this writer—then a little girl of nine years, was led by her father to the middle of the river where . . . she gaped into the mighty abyss below [and] in the brilliant light saw the wonderful sight, the great chasm, the magnificent rush of the great massive Falls . . . beneath our feet." "From this time forth no one was afraid to use the Bridge. The spell was over, the danger was over," Mary observed.[23]

The bridge was constructed from white pine. The roadway was 7½ feet wide, 759 feet long, and supported by eight wire cables, each composed of seventy-two strands of wire. These were bound together by smaller wire, forming a rope about an inch and a half thick. The cables were 1,160 feet long. They were anchored in solid rock at the ends, two hundred feet from the edge of the cliff.

The cables were draped over wooden towers, fourteen feet square at the base and fifty-seven feet high. In total the bridge weighed seventy-five tons. Ellet built the span as a service bridge to aid the larger project of the railroad suspension bridge, which was itself rather a perplexing decision. It took seven months to build and cost somewhere between $24,000 and $30,000, or a quarter of the time budgeted and somewhere between 12 and 16 percent of the total cost. In the meantime, no tangible work was done on the main structure: no granite towers built, no anchorages dug, no approaches surveyed.[24] What it did herald was a tourism and publicity boom.

Reporters from all over the Northeast converged on Ellet's span. "Stepping upon the bridge . . . you find yourself suspended in the air several hundred feet above a mass of jagged and flinty rocks over and among which the waters of Niagara plunge with terrific velocity. To add to the sensations of terror . . . you find the bridge oscillating and bending beneath your weight. It requires considerable nerve to cross this aerial structure, and there are few who have firmness enough to look over the side into the awful surf," wrote the *New York Herald*.[25] Almost everyone else agreed. "You look down the giant chasm to the alternate green and white current moving so majestically beneath and realize that the height of the Falls has not been exaggerated," wrote the *Tribune*. "If a hundred men were on the Bridge and it should part or its fastenings at either end give way, there is not a chance that a single one of them would ever breathe again . . . yet you see men seated across two ropes overhead, weaving and fastening this dainty fabric in apparent unconcern, with two hundred and forty feet of pure air beneath them and no choice of a place to alight at the bottom."[26] The *Rochester Democrat* thought it "impossible to give the reader a clear idea of the work." "If you are below it, it looks like a strip of paper suspended by a cobweb. When the wind is strong the frail gossamer looking structure sways to and fro, as if ready to start from its fastenings, and it shakes from extremity to centre under the firm tread of the pedestrian. . . . You find yourself suspended in the air, with the roaring, rushing, boiling Niagara two hundred and fifty feet below you. . . . And yet the sensation is not altogether unpleasant. The ride itself, as the old lady said about skinning eels, 'is nothing, when you get used to it.' "[27]

"The Bridge is a great triumph of art, and is universally regarded with wonder," wrote the *Salem Register*, and if the experience of treading its boards—"feeling it bend and surge" beneath your feet—didn't "make you dizzy, you can safely turn aeronaut." According to Benson Lossing, "The light structure bent beneath the weight like thin ice under the skater, yet the passage is considered perfectly safe." The fifteen-year-old Alexander Liholiho agreed, while also providing a little religious perspective: "The wind was blowing somewhat stronger than when we crossed, and looking over the bridge, we could see it rolling just like a ship. Here I was strongly reminded of that passage of Scripture—'He shall give his angels

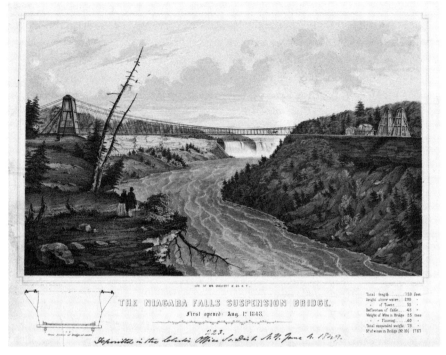

Figure 14.1 Ellet's temporary bridge at Niagara. William Endicott, "The Niagara Falls Suspension Bridge" (1848). Library of Congress.

charge concerning thee, &c.' . . . I'll admit I breathed a little more freely after I got across."[28]

Publicly, all seemed fine as July turned into August. "The *main difficulties* are already overcome; hereafter all will be plain sailing," editorialized the *Buffalo Courier*, spectacularly misreading the situation.[29] The bridge was opened to sightseers on August 1, and they came in droves. Behind the scenes, however, everything was falling apart. Within a matter of days, Ellet was out as chief engineer, and within weeks a series of pitched battles and violent confrontations were waged on the bridge over its ownership. All work ceased within days of Ellet's famous ride, and no further work was ever done on his Niagara Bridge, except to take it down.

———

Beneath the rosy reports emanating from the press was a tense, deteriorating relationship between the two boards and the principals involved. Undergirding the whole venture was a constant struggle for money and control. Both Clark and

Stuart (among others) wanted to move in concert with local railroads, not ahead of them, and in early 1848 they found a cooling national economy and sluggish track development. They supported Ellet's decision to build a footbridge—mainly because of the revenue it seemed to promise—but only if costs could be kept below ten thousand dollars. Unfortunately, Ellet was planning a bridge, while they were planning an entire system.[30] Ellet spent most of March and April pleading for money to pay his construction bills. "I am compelled again to write to you on the subject of funds," he wrote with evident exasperation in March. And he was also worried about his own reputation should the venture fall apart. "It is my *character* which is at stake," he fumed two months into the project.[31] Ellet's mood darkened with a series of discoveries over the first few months of the work. In February, he discovered that Stuart (and some others) had begun selling some of their stock and in March that many of the largest Canadian stockholders had not yet paid their installments, leaving the companies in a precarious situation, administratively and financially.[32]

The situation was compounded by dysfunction in the two boardrooms and a seeming fear of transparency. The venture was financed and overseen by two different companies operating in tandem, although not always in concert: the Niagara Falls International Bridge Company (US) and the Niagara Falls Suspension Bridge Company (Canadian). The joint boards met for the first time in five months in April, a baffling three months into construction. Ellet was "permitted to remain hours in an adjoining room" without any opportunity to address the meeting or confer on important decisions. This was maddening, especially as Ellet owned as much stock as all but two of the fourteen board members. The boards resolved "that the engineer be authorized to build the Bridge so as to possess . . . not less than one half the strength required by the plan," at a cost that "shall not exceed $145,000 instead of $190,000." And the situation was no better outside of official channels. Writing to Washington Hunt on April 2, Ellet claimed that his meeting with Clark "was far from satisfactory. I found him concealed and mysterious, recollecting things which I could not recollect and forgetting others which were impressed vividly on my memory." "I have been a good deal disgusted," he concluded; "my confidence has been shaken and cannot easily be restored."[33]

By the middle of April, John's prediction that the project was being run by "men of straw" was proving prescient, despite Clark's public pronouncements, made less than six months earlier, that "every dollar of stock" had been taken "by men fully able to pay."[34] The board continued to drag its feet supplying funds and honoring Ellet's bills. A resolution was passed that both Canadian and American companies were to share costs equally, despite the Canadian treasury being mysteriously "exhausted," followed by another resolution "that the company on the New York side will not pay for the liabilities incurred . . . in carrying on the work faster than payment is made in the Canada side." By the middle of May, Ellet was writing his former champion "with no disposition to prolong a correspondence which consumes time that ought to be given to public duties and which I can always employ more profitably" seeking legal advice about his position. The crux of his worries was simple: Was he an independent contractor or merely an employee? As such, was he ultimately responsible for the bills and entitled to the revenue, or were the companies? As he complained to the joint boards in June: "On the one hand, I am responsible for all the liabilities which I incur, because I am *contractor*; and you maintain that you are entitled to the revenues of my work, because I am only *agent*."[35]

In a gesture of reconciliation, Ellet agreed to hand over all revenue derived from the tolls—which was by no means inconsiderable—in return for a promise to furnish the money needed to move forward. The board agreed and then promptly sent him a letter informing him he had missed the deadline for the third installment on his stock options and was consequently in "default" and liable to lose his shares, a rather savage affront given that Ellet had furnished much of the cost of construction thus far. The engineer was understandably indignant: "You must have known that I do not intend to trust my money in your hands while the business is conducted in this way," he wrote back, after which he confided to his wife, "I now think it necessary to break the whole concern." Ellet wasn't alone in protesting the board's behavior. In June, a local stockholder wrote to the *Niagara Chronicle* worried about the company's finances. The correspondent had recently visited the bridge site and was shocked to find many of the men discharged, the construction at a standstill, and the project effectively suspended. He demanded the books be opened and the finances examined at a public meeting. After all, if the company had run out of money only a few weeks into construction, then what had happened to everyone's investment? The man worried that the board was being less than honest with ordinary stockholders.[36]

The board subsequently retreated from the scene, cutting off all money and all communication, except a curt pronouncement on Ellet's professionalism delivered by Merritt on July 11:

> The language and spirit of your various letters preclude any further reply. Having refused to furnish the Board with a detailed statement of the cost of the bridge, to enable them to judge of its monthly progress. From the high price paid for material; the increased cost of work, neglect in its execution, with the exorbitant demands made on the Board, they have with great reluctance been compelled to withdraw the confidence they formerly reposed in you; and in order to protect the interests of the shareholders, they feel it their duty to use every means in their power to place the bridge in charge of another Engineer.

They resurfaced on August 5 with a public announcement that "in consequence of the course pursued by Charles Ellet in regard to the construction of the Niagara Falls Suspension Bridge, the Companies find themselves unable to proceed any further with him."[37] Four days after his triumphant ride—just as he was being praised and fêted all over the local and national press—Ellet was fired from the project.

It is difficult to know what Ellet was thinking spending that much money and that much time on a service bridge, a mere platform. He didn't do so at Wheeling, a much longer bridge. The footbridge was a moneymaker to be sure but equally a massive distraction from the job at hand. On Merritt's urging, the board eventually ordered Ellet to stop ferrying tourists back and forth and to use his bridge and basket to actually build them a railroad suspension bridge. Equally, the whole venture was an administrative nightmare, filled with half-truths, hidden motives, and competing personalities. Clark controlled the board but was not universally popular. Some privately hoped Ellet would act as a "wholesome check on Lot Clark." Still others, especially Merritt, seemed to harbor little affection for either party. The whole venture couldn't have been further from John's experience with the D&H, which placed their confidence and their money in Lord and Roebling and then left them alone to do their jobs. Ellet, by contrast, found himself dealing equally with two different companies, headed up by two very different groups of people, operating out of two different countries, all supposedly in a single effort.[38]

The timing of Ellet's firing had less to do with principles than with proximity. The feisty engineer left Niagara for Wheeling on July 29, right after his famous ride, and the joint boards jumped into action. As Ellet explained, they "kept amusing me with proposals for compromise and arbitration until I had got fairly out of reach." Within hours of Ellet's departure, Judge Samuel DeVeaux, a Clark confidant and member of the US board, visited Hulett and the assistant engineer Jonathan Baldwin to inform them that Ellet had been discharged and that a decision had been made to abandon the original plan and instead to strengthen Ellet's footbridge and fit it out for horse and carriage traffic. This, the judge explained, "would be a more profitable investment than a bridge costing $190,000." DeVeaux wished to know if Hulett and Baldwin would "go on with the work, recognizing them (the Directors) instead of the Contractor." The judge also asked that the conference be kept "a secret for the present." Hulett and Baldwin were evasive, hoping to buy some time to mull things over, but they quickly decided to repay the trust Ellet had placed in them, at least initially. They had "received nothing but kindness and gentlemanly treatment from

Mr. Charles Ellet," while the board's actions in Ellet's absence seemed "strongly tinctured with unfairness." Being unwilling "to be made a 'cats-paw' in the hands of the Directors," they wrote to Ellet that evening.[39]

Ellet received the news on August 8 and immediately set about firing off letters and telegrams. "You are now my sole agents," he telegraphed Hulett and Baldwin. "Hold the bridge. Keep possession. Recognize no one. Collect the tolls. Pay the men. Be firm but temperate. Use force if necessary, but not violence. Hold on to the bridge, ground, tools, materials. All are mine. I will protect you. Carry out my plans. Permit no interference. Be firm and fear nothing." And later that day: "I have legal and rightful possession and if they come on the work and interfere they do it at their peril." "Act as you would act in defending your own property from any trespasser." Ellet also wrote to Joshua Spencer for legal advice. He had no desire to abandon his contract, but he also needed a sense of his options. Could he "hold the bridge and compel them, if possible, to go on and fulfill the contract"? And if not, could he hold the bridge and collect the toll revenue? In his considered opinon, Spencer thought the joint boards had no claim on the bridge unless "by the decree of lynch law."[40]

Up at the falls, Hulett was happy to inform Ellet that every single one of the workmen had "volunteered as a *body guard for the bridge*" and that they had established "comfortable quarters inside of the towers on both sides for the guards to occupy at night."[41] Still, a confrontation was looming. On August 12, a notice signed by company secretaries J. C. Colton and W. O. Buchanan claiming sole authority to make contracts or engagements on behalf of the company was posted on the bridge. Two days later, a crowd arrived at the Canadian end of the bridge headed by the local sheriff and a bench of magistrates. The sheriff demanded possession of the span, saying that anyone who refused to comply would be subject to an immediate five-pound fine that would subsequently, and somewhat inexplicably, double—to ten, twenty, forty pounds—every five minutes the fine remained unpaid. While these demands were being made, Hulett and Baldwin noticed some of the board of directors massing on the American side, clearly hoping to take possession of the entire structure. Baldwin rushed to the American side to stop the directors from gaining the bridge, while Hulett "erected a barricade upon the national boundary, and placed an effective guard," which proved ineffective. Baldwin, along with Ellet's brother Alfred, who had arrived four days before, were dragged "with barbarous brutality fourteen miles to Niagara jail, incarcerated and confined without bail or charges for two days, until the American side of the bridge had fallen into the directors' hands, thanks to a temporary injunction preventing any of Ellet's men from "interfering with the Bridge property."[42]

Opinion in the press was divided. For the *Buffalo Commercial Advertiser*, "Mr. E. appear to be in the right." Over the border, the *St. Catherine's Journal* deplored the thugs who had "violently resisted" the directors, even going so far as to "raise an axe to strike the sheriff." On the bridge itself, an uneasy armistice lasted most of August and September, while the issue worked its way through the courts. "All is commotion and fear at the Bridge," Hulett wrote Ellet; "a guard of 6 men upon each side of the Bridge keeps it safe [they] have at least 2 rusty muskets each . . . but rely upon bravery and the 'glittering bayonet.'" Privately, Ellet continued to offer terms to the joint boards. He was willing to submit to independent arbitration but remained worried that any such group would be stacked with "personal friends" of the directors. He was also willing to be bought out of the entire venture. For their part, the directors rather unreasonably demanded to be released from their contract, all while Ellet continued to hold forty thousand dollars' worth of their stock.[43]

Justice Samuel E. Sill of the Supreme Court of New York dissolved the temporary injunction on September 23, after which Ellet wrote to the joint boards to request they relinquish control of the bridge. Hulett and Baldwin meanwhile plotted. They spent the evening of Friday, September 29, visiting their "*captains*" and "matur[ing] our plans for the attack." The next morning at nine o'clock they all approached the bridge with a copy of Judge Sill's decision and demanded entrance. W. O. Buchanan—Clark's man at the bridge—refused. Hulett mounted the bridge gate anyway, looked down, and "saw at least eight clubs raised for my 'special benefit' each swearing 'they would split me through if I descended.'" He did so anyway, dropping himself "in their midst" before setting about smashing the locks with a hammer. "Never give up the Bridge," Buchanan ordered, "until his voice was hushed by my *feeling of his windpipe*, which had the effect to check [his] ambition," as Hulett described it. Buchanan was then grabbed by Ellet's men, who "passed him feet first on his back" out of the bridge "and left [him] in the embrace of the rocks."[44]

He didn't stay there for long, unfortunately for Baldwin, who took off for the "*monarchical half*"—as the *Niagara Chronicle* described it—without much backup. The board's forces on the British end "were perhaps not as prepared as they'd normally prefer, being possessed of only one bayonet, rather rusty, with the point a good deal blunted, one musket, minus a lock, several crowbars, a few spades and any quantity of pickaxes," according to the *Niagara Mail*. They did, however, have plenty of rocks on hand, which they rained on poor Baldwin. He dodged a few shots, but eventually the rocks began to find their mark. "Taking advantage of this brutal injury four men rushed upon him and struck him four blows with clubs on the head—one upon the back of his head which struck him temporarily blind." Baldwin eventually made it to the tower, where Buchanan held a musket to his head and swore to "shoot him if he did not run." "Shoot and be Damned, I'll never run," Baldwin replied, before a group of Ellet's men rushed up, snatched Baldwin, and dragged him back to the American side, his "body horribly mutilated by stones," "his head broken in," and his "clothes completely covered with clotted blood." Hulett ended the day sorry "he had not killed Buchanan" when he had the chance.[45]

As soon as Ellet's men retreated with their injured comrade, the Canadians "immediately threw up a barricade after the Parisian fashion . . . and retired to obtain some refreshments! And hold a council of war!" They had been meeting "but a few moments when a cry was heard in the distance: 'Come on! Come on! Ye sons of Mars!' 'To the barricades! To the barricades!' . . . And behold! Ellet's party was seen approaching, armed with glittering axes, which would certainly have struck terror and dismay into the hearts of any but the brave spirits who were behind the breastwork. They came on with determined resolution to the center of the bridge" before halting, bending down, and starting to dismantle the bridge. Relived, the Canadians "gave three or four hearty cheers for themselves and a like number for the Queen, which showed great loyalty on their part." And there "hostilities ended for the present and the bridge [was] rendered useless."[46]

Hulett placed a "three pound cannon loaded with 400 buck shot" on the bridge and had "an axe secreted near the anchorage of the cables for *actual* use in case of necessity to drop this *bone of contention* out of Lot Clark's reach," after which the two sides began trying to negotiate their way out of the stalemate.[47] Lawsuits were filed for trespass; arrests were made for rioting; court orders were passed and rescinded. Underlying the entire process were two battles: one over physical ownership and the other over damages and compensation. There was little either party could do with one end of a bridge but negotiate, a fact that Ellet understood perfectly. Ellet stuck to his plan but had no problem resorting to hard-nosed tactics. "If they steal my materials fire on them," he told Hulett. "Pick out the most guilty." "Maintain a belligerent attitude and negotiate with loaded guns," he advised on another occasion.[48] Eventually, many in what Hulett had taken to calling "the Niagara Suspension *Guerilla* Co." grew weary of the fight. The Canadian Board grew frustrated with their American counterparts and vice versa, and they began to bicker among themselves. "I think this is the *death struggle of the Vipers*," Hulett noted with his usual vicious derision.[49] At the end of the year, a US grand jury finally threw out both Ellet's suit against the companies and the companies' against Ellet, leaving everyone where they had started. Within days, and with Ellet back up at the falls, a settlement was finally agreed to. The company agreed to indemnify all bills and accounts incurred by Ellet previous to August 6, to pay the combative engineer twelve thousand dollars in damages, and to take all his stock at par. Both sides were released from all further obligations under the terms of the contract. The agreement was signed on December 27, 1848. "All I wish is never to be in that part of the world again— it is a most undesirable atmosphere for an honorable man," Ellet's wife, Ellie, remarked. Ellie also provided perhaps the most fitting tribute to her husband's achievements up at the falls. "They cannot deprive him of the reputation he has won there. He must always be the first, whose skill triumphed over the natural difficulties of that vast chasm—and others can only accomplish what he has shown them how to do," she wrote to her mother-in-law in September 1848.[50]

———

Ellet was already in deep conversations with several people about new bridge projects by the time he arrived back in Virginia. In August he had begun a conversation with Amos Tryon of Lockport about a bridge there, and by the end of the year it was rumored he had received a contract to span the Niagara again, this time a little farther north at Queenston. Ellet also renewed his interest in spanning the Mississippi, writing to Mayor John M. Krum of St. Louis suggesting the city rethink its previous opposition to a suspension bridge. His most sustained effort, though, took place where John had tried so hard and failed two years earlier.[51]

In December 1848, Ellet was invited by a group calling themselves the "Cincinnati Bridge Committee" to visit the Queen City with a view to spanning the Ohio "without piers," a reference perhaps to John's flawed proposal. Ellet visited the city, surveyed the site, and collected as much information as he was able, even writing to a committee member for a copy of John's 1846 proposal. He published the fruits of these labors soon after as *Letter on the Proposed Bridge across the Ohio River at Cincinnati*, his plan for a 1,400-foot-long suspension bridge to vault "La Belle Riviere" in a single span. Sadly, Lot Clark's vindictive anger followed Ellet to southwest Ohio. Unsolicited, Ellet's former boss wrote a letter to Judge J. C. Wright, editor of the *Cincinnati Gazette*, advising him not to employ Ellet. The engineer had "expended & wasted considerable money" up at Niagara, Clark explained, before being summarily fired, leading to "mobs & some lawsuits." "We all of us and every one of our stockholders have a very bad opinion of him," he concluded. Rather put off by Clark's arrogant presumption and meddling interference, Wright gave the letter to William Johnson of the bridge committee, who felt Clark's letter was so unlike anything he had heard about the engineer that he forwarded it directly to Ellet in an effort to make him "aware of this busy-body."[52]

Ellet's Ohio project never got off the ground. His plan was sound, but the finances were not. By April, after several weeks on the market, only a hundred shares of the Ohio Bridge Stock had been subscribed. Ellet would never again seriously compete for a bridge contract.[53] His Wheeling Bridge, the world's longest span, was finished and opened to the public seven months later, but it would be his last. Fed up with share options and boards of trustees, he instead poured his energies into plans to improve the flood plains and navigation of the Ohio and Mississippi Rivers, an effort instigated by the US government.[54] John and Ellet would not reconcile personally, but Ellet wasn't above using John's name when it suited him. And John wasn't above taking his rival's side either. Ellet used John's 1846 Ohio River proposal to bolster his case before the Supreme Court that the Wheeling Bridge did not impede navigation, a case to which John was also called. Despite being used by the defense, John was actually called to testify by the opposition, perhaps figuring he would turn on his old rival. But John defended Ellet's bridge, making them unlikely allies in what was one of their last interactions: the fight to establish and validate the suspension bridge.[55]

Ellet and John also found themselves on the same side nine years later when seven southern states seceded from the United States, throwing the nation into bloody civil war. John was a Union man through and through, although he saw no action, unlike Ellet, who was commissioned by Edwin Stanton, Lincoln's secretary of war, in March 1862 to build and command a small flotilla of iron-clad naval ram ships to help patrol the Mississippi River. The steam rams saw their first action at the Battle of Memphis that June, playing a decisive role in the Union victory, but the glory for Ellet was short-lived. He died from wounds sustained during the battle on June 21, 1862, ending his service in the Civil War and his unique and wide-ranging contributions to the national enterprise, a fact John himself very much understood. Although he fundamentally disagreed with Ellet on numerous technical matters, John recognized his profound courage and skill, touchingly calling his old rival "a true hero" for his actions during the war, and not just for paying the ultimate price but for signing up in the first place when he could have easily afforded a substitute.[56]

For some, Ellet's Niagara fiasco best illustrates the erratic engineer and his idiosyncratic career, showcasing his flair, his technical skill, and his bold decision-making, alongside his pigheaded inability to work with others and his failure to bring the project to a successful conclusion.[57] This seems true as far as it goes, but also harsh. His failures at the falls had more to do with other people's money and other people's sense of control than with Ellet himself, who seems to have done more to keep the peace than anyone else. His crew was unfailingly loyal, and his bridge was in many respects a strong and well-designed triumph (in March 1849, for example, two hundred head of cattle and an unnamed number of oxen were driven over the bridge without incident). It was also a moneymaker, which may have ultimately exacerbated the other problems. Toll receipts averaged $1,544 per month in August and September, an 8 percent return, an irresistible golden egg for a board of trustees struggling to bring in money.[58]

When required to sum up his old Niagara ally in 1871, Stuart recalled that "when wronged, [Ellet's] pride was quickly aroused, even to an appearance of conceit." This he "attributed to [his] strong convictions of being right, and a consciousness of superiority over those by whom he was unjustly treated." More generally, Stuart also believed that "the engineering profession in this country has never had a more industrious worker, or intelligent and original thinker. [Ellet's] vigorous mind challenged, with the greatest satisfaction, enterprises of a bold and difficult character. His views were broad and far-seeing; his judgment on matters pertaining to his profession, aided by his superior mathematical knowledge, was rarely at fault, although his opinions were often in advance of the times."[59] John certainly never had a more significant or worthy rival, and he knew it. The two men had vastly different temperaments and affections, but both were driven, bristling with ideas, and burning with energy. Both were "representative men," to use Emerson's phrase: doers, designers, makers, builders. If anything, Ellet was the more successfully wide-ranging of the two, turning his hand to political economy, travel, farming (successfully), river management, and military strategy, as well as suspension bridges—and the more heroic and self-sacrificing too.

In many ways, Ellet was as talented as John, but he split his attention among too many ideas and projects and ended up doing many things well but few perfectly. John, by contrast, did one thing: build bridges. Even his wire rope business was an adjunct to his bridge-building career, which from 1844 onward took up almost all of his time. He was awful at many other things he tried, farming and medicine especially. Worse, he was disingenuous and illogical, often believing in things no rational scientist could explain or fully hold to. John could plan, design, and build huge structures of startling technical ingenuity, capable of carrying massive live loads over broad rivers, yet, equally, he believed that carrots and cabbages were all but poisonous, that thrice-daily doses of charcoal were the key to healthy digestion, and that a tightly wrapped wet sheet could somehow draw illness out of his body.

———

The joint boards moved on within days of sacking Ellet, before they'd even secured Ellet's bridge or properly disposed of their engineer. "I returned from Niagara Falls a few days ago and can tell you an amusing story about Ellet's famous foot bridge," John wrote Archbald on September 12, 1848, just over a month after Ellet's initial dismissal. "He has been dismissed by the Co. which has engaged my services *preliminary*, they being out of funds for the present."[60] John had peddled this story before to Stuart almost two years earlier. But this time he knew his only serious rival was a spent force. Official word finally came once Ellet was out of the picture early the next year. John Roebling, "celebrated engineer, and one much experienced in the erection of suspension bridges," had been engaged to carry out the new project, reported the *Niagara Mail*, which thought everything would get underway in the spring. John was certainly up at the falls in April, but there was no money there to greet him. John spent the next three years as the chief engineer of a project with no budget. He filled his time completing his work for the D&H, helping Swan get the wire rope factory in Trenton up and running, responding to requests for plans and estimates for other bridges—most of which never got off the ground—and contributing to the world of public affairs and intellectual inquiry.[61]

As his earlier thoughts on slavery, expansion, and national character attest, John was always interested in social questions and public affairs. He had spoken about ethnicity and assimilation at the German convention in Pittsburgh in 1837 but thereafter worked on developing his career, his business, and his reputation. As he did so, John's thoughts and ideas on US society naturally settled on issues of technology and transportation, albeit flavored by a strong social vision. John's first foray into public speaking took place while he was also fighting to secure the D&H aqueduct contract. As he showed Lord around Pittsburgh, he delivered before the Board of Trade a long, substantial lecture titled "The Great Central Railroad from Philadelphia to St. Louis." The talk was a detailed argument for a specific technology and a specific route, but it also set out a specific national vision and embodied a specific philosophy.

"Railways appear to be destined to supersede all other means of intercommunication. Among the great mass of modern inventions and improvements, none perhaps are of greater importance, and will contribute more to the great and *common* interests of mankind than RAILROADS and TELEGRAPHS," John began. While such revolutionary inventions could be harnessed by national interests, they could never be easily confined and simply controlled,. In Russia, for example, ruled by "an Autocrat," a "system of iron bands may first prove another powerful mode of enslaving more thoroughly the masses of people," but equally and ultimately "it will [also] surely aid in their eventual emancipation." "Railroads and Telegraphs," he continued, "may be hailed as the latest offspring of the spirit of the present age; they have imparted a new and most powerful impulse to the social movement, from which will yet flow a vast train of beneficial results." Or, as he stated elsewhere, "Man is a social being, and the interests of society can only be advanced and maintained by rapid and easy means of transit. Indeed the advance of a nation may justly be measured by its facilities of intercommunication; there is no better scale," no more important factor in "American life," than "commercial, social and political contact."[62]

If anyone was wondering how exactly communications affected the "social movement," John was happy to clarify. "One of the best proofs of the advancement of mankind in *true* civilization is, that the industrial efforts of nations are no longer squandered upon the creation of vast amounts of pride and of war. . . . Like a *magic wand*, they [instead] open the slumbering resources and long-hidden treasures of the earth; convert stone and iron into gold; draw into bonds of union and amity isolated individuals, as well as communities and nations; unchain long-cherished prejudices and selfishness, and cause to be made more simultaneous, exertions in all that is useful and good." Such statements showcase John's social ideals and suggest a very unlikely comparison with Walt Whitman, America's great poet of inclusive optimism and national promise. John was about as likely to issue a barbaric yawp as he was to invite the local minister over for a friendly, good-natured chat about the merits of the established church or to sing happily about anything, but both were clearly traveling down the same philosophical path—one, as Raymond Merritt explains, trodden as often by engineers as by poets in the nineteenth century. Engineers saw railroads and telegraphs, along with bridges and other great works of connection, as great works of technology *and* of moral advance, as physical things embodying functional design *and* philosophical principles. Whitman agreed, writing of "the strong light works of engineers / Our modern wonders" and celebrating technology's unifying *ethnical* potential: "The New by its mighty railroad spann'd, / The seas inlaid with eloquent gentle wires . . . / The earth to be spann'd, connected by network, / The races, neighbors, to marry and be given in marriage, / The oceans to be cross'd, the distant brought near, / The Lands to be welded together."[63]

Railroads were the "mighty lever of modern commerce and intercourse," as John later stated, "the nurse of modern civilization," that would band people together, heal divisions, and make neighbors out of rivals and free people out of the enslaved. Or, as he put it, several years ahead of Whitman: "Draw into bonds of union and amity isolated individuals . . . communities and nations; unchain long-cherished prejudices and selfishness." It was often said, John continued, that "the geographical features of the Mississippi valley . . . afford the best guarantee for the stability of this Union." He thought otherwise: "With greater confidence yet, we may entrust the future fate of our country to that great net of railways and telegraphs which soon will spread over the vast extent of its surface." Whitman's confidence often proved a little misguided, as did John's, especially when he went on to claim that "railroads, in fact, will vastly contribute to prevent long protracted wars—civil, as well as national."[64]

John finished his talk on the Great Central Railroad by setting out a set of principles that he thought ought to guide the development of a national transit system: (1) "No two roads shall be made where one can accommodate the business"; (2) "The whole country should be divided into railroad systems, with main trunk lines forming direct communication between the most important commercial towns, and lateral branches extending thro' the adjacent country"; (3) "The main lines should be so located as to interfere as little as possible with each other"; (4) "The main part of the travel should be accommodated by passing through the principal centers of population." Together these ideas were themselves something of a philosophy. Here, competition is a ruinous cause of inefficiency, a hindrance to the national interest. "One company can afford to work to the advantage of the community at large, by making a good road in the first instance, keeping it and its machinery in good repair, running more numerous trains, more regular and faster, and all this at a lower rate of charges," John explained, betraying a level of economic naiveté, but also a genuine sense of the logic. Few things annoyed John more than waste and bad management.[65]

In 1850 John set out a lengthy plan for a transatlantic cable in the pages of the New York *Journal of Commerce*. His advocacy of the idea followed the same logic as his thoughts on the Grand Central Railroad to St. Louis. In a more immediate manner than railroads even, telegraphs would bind the disparate peoples of the world together and "annihilate" space and difference, John believed, much as Whitman had eight years later when Cyrus Field announced his plan to lay a cable from Newfoundland to Ireland. "This Telegraphic Cable is not alone a material bond for the transmission of news of the rise and fall of stocks, and of news gossip generally," Whitman declared, "but it will subserve a higher purpose—that it will link together nations that in heart and feeling are hereafter to be one." One of these purposes was the very work of much nineteenth-century engineering: the attempt to unite mankind by harnessing material physics to social ends. As John explained in his article on the transatlantic cable, "The application of electricity for transmitting intelligence through the medium of metallic wires, on an extensive scale, is a most beautiful illustration of how matter can be rendered subservient to mind."[66]

John was not the first to propose a transatlantic cable, but he was among the first to propose a workable plan. A handful of schemes were suggested during the 1840s—notably Alonzo Jackman's "Grand Submarine and Overland Magnetic Telegraph"—most of which were either chimerical or entirely impractical, including one to establish a "floating telegraph" by means of buoys stretched from New York to London. John's plan was to lay a "Sub-Marine Telegraphic *Wire Rope*" on the ocean floor from the eastern end of Long Island to Land's End in England. Composed of 20 strands of no. 14 wire "perfectly separated from each other" and isolated with a coating of gutta-percha, then wrapped with a "coat of cotton" also soaked in gutta-percha, John's plan anticipated the first successfully submerged international telegraph cable laid down later that same year between Dover and Calais by John and Jacob Brett. The Bretts' cable was a single strand of copper wire but almost identical to John's proposed cable in almost all other particulars.[67]

John was also ahead of the curve advocating for a more systematic approach to technical education, more specifically the creation of a "national university for practical science." "The great want of our time is a Polytechnic Institute, or a University for the teaching of practical and natural sciences," he wrote in

October 1851. While there were plenty of places for young men to study law, theology, or medicine, for example, "there is no institution where young men, whose pursuits in life will be of a practical nature, can obtain a thorough education. There are no schools for the young merchant, mechanic, or manufacturer; still less opportunity is offered to the civil and mechanical engineer, and none at all to the miner," he lamented. West Point trained the Army Corps of Engineers, but its primary business was military, not mechanics. This situation seemed absurd to John, and in desperate need of correction. "The advance of our country is, in a great measure, owing to the activity of our mechanics, engineers, and miners," he reasoned. Do they not "deserve to be supported by intelligence—well-trained intelligence, which is thoroughly familiar with the laws of nature?"[68]

John wasn't wholly accurate in describing the paucity of engineering schools. Rensselaer Polytechnic Institute in Troy, New York, had been granting engineering degrees since 1835, as had the universities of Michigan and Virginia, along with Hanover College in Indiana. Numerous other colleges offered courses in engineering, if not actual degree programs. Still, a vast majority of American engineers were trained in the field, not in a lecture hall. They learned their trade surveying railroad routes and digging canals, a state of affairs that John deplored. "In engineering and mining, the ignoramus is frequently considered the most practical man, simply because he is devoid of science and sneers at it. There is also an unfortunate idea prevailing among moneyed men that science and practice are not compatible and consequently the mere empiric is generally preferred." What American engineering needed was hard science to accompany the tinkering and the tramping around. "While immense appropriations are placed at the disposal of our civil engineers in the construction of public works, we cannot afford to give them an education which would render them competent for the discharge of their duties," he bemoaned.[69]

John's plan called for the United States to adopt the "free and liberal system of the German University." Students should spend three to four years at their studies, with the first eighteen months dedicated to "purely scientific" matters so as best to prepare them for the practical courses to follow. Only with a sound basis in the principles of hard science, John argued, could students move on to the task of applied or "practical science." "An ignorant man is a helpless being," he wrote, "but let his mental capacities be trained and directed to the discovery of the laws of matter, which is surrounding him and constitutes his nature, and he at once becomes a mighty agent; he no longer remains the slave of circumstances and of chance, but controls them as a master!" Miners, engineers, mechanics all needed to learn the universal laws governing matter and needed to do so under the tutelage of trained professionals, before they could begin to think about digging a canal, a mine, or an anchorage. "Our materialism is yet of that coarse and vulgar nature, which treats matter as inanimate dead substance, void of innate force and properties," he warned. "But nature frequently punishes such ignorance by the most frightful manifestations of its hidden powers."[70]

John also had a larger project in mind, one to which he would himself devote several years: the relationship between philosophy and science, or between mind and matter. "The external part of creation is evidently arranged in perfect harmony with the innate powers of man," he wrote, and while "the nature of these faculties has been the profound and exclusive study of the best minds of all ages . . . it is now well understood, that a true philosophy of the mind can only be grafted upon a true philosophy of the laws of matter." Only when this work was done could mankind move forward. In John's formulation, the work of a national university would accompany the work of civilization. "Our national progress has been owing, in large measure, to the natural intelligence and indomitable energies of our people, aided by the most ample resources," he concluded. "We now appeal to the Genius of Science to preside over our future destinies, and we see the most magnificent prospects opened before our vision. Increased knowledge will increase our power and will make us more just to ourselves and to others; our nation will become a *lode-star* destined to guide others, and eventually all mankind, into the haven of freedom and independence!"[71]

John's call would be answered in time by the Cooper Union (1859), MIT (1861), Virginia Polytechnic Institute (1872), the Colorado School of Mines (1874), the Georgia Institute of Technology (1885), and a host of other educational organizations, making the country a global leader in technical education. His appeal found few immediate supporters, however, although one was significant. Writing to the *Railroad Journal*, a man with the initials E. W. S. wrote from New Brunswick, Canada, to praise the "able pen" of John Roebling. "The scientific student has nowhere to go to seek that thorough knowledge which alone can fit him rightly to act his part on the great stage of life," he agreed, a "truth" that was "well-known and to be deplored." And while "nothing less than hard work will accomplish such an undertaking," he continued, "the benefits of [such an] institution" would soon "be acknowledged by all classes of the community." "Let every intelligent person interested in the cause do his utmost to further its object," he exhorted, before concluding, "I have not the pleasure of knowing Mr. R personally, [but I] think, perhaps, if he was solicited, he might be induced to take the initiative in some such plan as he had suggested." Although the author declined to provide his full name, he could have been none other than Edward Wellman Serrell, who was in Saint John to build his second suspension bridge. The previous year, at the age of just twenty-five, he had thrown his first across the Niagara River.[72]

In 1850, Serrell was hired by a group of local merchants and entrepreneurs to build a suspension bridge over the Niagara River between the villages of Lewiston and Queenstown. Serrell had bid for the same contract that entangled

John and Ellet, but his proposal had been all but ignored. Luckily, the towns-people farther north were glad to avoid the public battles that had attached themselves to Ellet's bridge and were happy to take a chance on the youngster. Construction was begun in 1850 at the base of an escarpment just south of the two villages. The cables were suspended from short stone towers located near the top of the cliffs, while the roadway was hung much lower down near the river. This resulted in a rather odd-looking bridge, 1,040 feet long between the towers, but with a roadway of just 841 feet: "a fairy-like structure composed of metallic cords, over 1000 feet in length, drawn from the bowels of the earth, refined, at-tenuated, twisted and suspended in the air, from shore to shore," as one local guide described it.[73] Still, Serrell's bridge—opened on March 20, 1851—was a great success, carrying pedestrians, carriages, and heavy pack wagons reliably from one side of the Niagara to the other. Within a year, John would be asking Swan to send his "slippers" up to the falls, where he had finally found himself with a similar opportunity. Only this time he would have to build something strong enough to carry the world's heaviest—and most daunting—mode of transport: a fully loaded twenty-eight-ton locomotive and full train of twenty ten-ton cars.[74]

Securing Niagara (1852–55)

Railroads were the distilled essence of the nineteenth century. They harnessed the locomotive power of the steam engine and set it upon firm tracks of iron, "the foremost element of civilization," as John described it. They collapsed space and improved communication. They fueled the industrial and market revolutions and drove the expansion of Europe and North America. Trains were one of the most consequential inventions in a century packed full of them. And they would have had little or no impact without bridges. "The rapid extension of railways has given an extraordinary stimulus to the art of bridge-building," reported Samuel Smiles in 1868. "The number of such structures erected in Great Britain alone, since 1830, having been above thirty thousand, or far more than all that previously existed in the country." Unlike traditional road engineers, those in charge of a railroad line had few choices. They had to "take such ground as lay in the line of his railway, be it bog, or mud, or shifting sand [while] navigable rivers and crowded thoroughfares had to be crossed without interruption to the existing traffic." If trains were to fulfill their social function in America—as John hoped—and contribute to the "*common* interests of mankind," they would need to span great gorges and mighty rivers and run across the whole continent. In Smiles's phrase, they would have to be "capable of bearing heavy railway trains at high speed, over extensive gaps free of support," and for this new methods for bridging space would have to be designed and employed. If railroads were to define the United States, as they had Britain, they would need stronger, stiffer, and more dependable bridges.[1]

John was happy to answer this call. "Whenever necessity calls for new works of art, new expedients will be discovered, adapted to the occasion," he wrote in 1852. "It will no longer suit the spirit of the present age to pronounce an undertaking impracticable. Nothing is impracticable, which is within the scope of natural laws."[2] Stone arch bridges had been the standard in the early days of railroads, but they were expensive and politically tricky, always threatening to interfere with navigation. Wooden bridges such as Julius Adams's 250-foot Cascade Bridge (1848) or the Chicago and Rock Island Railroad's Mississippi

River Bridge (1856), a six-span, 1,581-foot-long Howe truss timber bridge, enjoyed a brief vogue but were so prone to fire as to be a liability. John had been mulling the idea of running railroads over a suspension bridge ever since building his very first span. Ultimately, he came to believe that "Suspended Railway Bridges of large spans was a practical question of great importance to the country, intersected as it is by numerous large rivers and deep gorges."[3] In 1844, he drew up rudimentary plans for a double-track three-hundred-foot span over the Lehigh River for the Beaver Meadows Railroad. A year later, D. K. Minor asked if a suspension bridge wouldn't be "first rate for a *railroad bridge*" and invited John to write an article on the subject for the *Railroad Journal*. John declined, but he continued to work on the problem. In 1846, he drew up designs for three different railroad suspension bridges: a thousand-foot span to cross the Connecticut River at Middleton, a two-span 475-foot-long fully trussed affair to get the New York and Erie Railroad over the Lackawaxen, and a massive span over the St. Lawrence at Montreal.[4]

John's most fully developed plan was put together for the Hornellsville and Attica Railroad in 1847. Stretching 600 feet from tower to tower with a single track and two cables 320 feet above the Genesee Gorge, John's bridge would be "perfectly safe for the heaviest trains at any speed," he predicted.[5] Betraying the timidity that plagued almost the entire industry, the company opted for an immense timber viaduct, 234 feet high and 800 feet long that opened in 1852 and lasted until 1875—much longer than most wooden spans—when it was consumed by a massive fire.[6]

Other engineers had also been wondering whether suspension bridges could answer the call of the railroad, with much less impressive results. The first railroad suspension bridge ever constructed was put to work in December 1830, and it was an absolute disaster. Designed by Samuel Brown, one of Britain's foremost suspension bridge engineers, the Stockton and Darlington Railroad Suspension Bridge over the River Tees in the UK was 281 feet long, its unstiffened deck was sixteen feet wide, and the whole thing weighed a mere 113 tons. According to one eyewitness, "it was fearful" when a loaded train "went over the first time." The deck flexed so badly that "there was a wave before the engine of something like 2 feet, just like a carpet," while the whole thing shook, creaked, and barely held together. The tower on the Yorkshire side "swayed and cracked." The train's coupling broke in the middle, and half the train's cargo ended up on one side of the river, with the rest on the other. In the words of engineering historian James Sutherland, "suspension bridges for railways have been damned in Britain ever since."[7]

Brown's bridge's inadequacies were glaring and obvious.[8] Robert Stephenson—son of "father of the railways" George Stephenson and author of the seminal article "Bridges of Suspension" (1822) that John read in Berlin—was

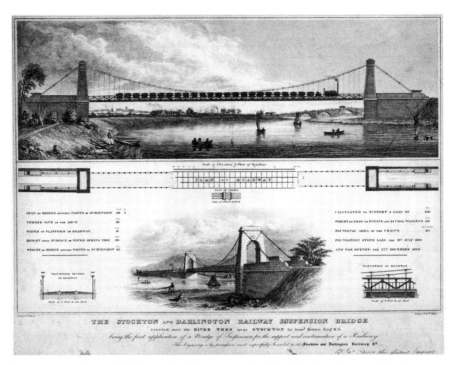

Figure 15.1 The world's first railroad suspension bridge. "The Stockton and Darlington Railway Suspension Bridge" (1830). Getty Images.

brought in to design and build a replacement, this time a cast iron and masonry arch bridge. What Stephenson learned about the debacle over the Tees informed one of the most momentous engineering feats of the mid-nineteenth century and put him on a collision course with John.

The legacy of Brown's failure over the Tees was uppermost in Stevenson's mind when he was approached by the Chester and Holyhead Railway in 1844 to design a railway bridge to span the Menai Strait between mainland Wales and the island of Anglesey. Stephenson's initial thought was whether he could adapt Telford's Menai Suspension Bridge to the task, but "as the strength of the suspension-bridge was deemed inadequate for carrying safely railway trains and ponderous locomotive engines," he toyed with the idea of establishing terminals on each side of the bridge, detaching the cargo, and using old-fashioned horse-power to lug it across. This seemed wildly inconsistent with establishing a new speedy route to Dublin, so his thoughts turned to an arch bridge, which was then vetoed by the Admiralty, who were more concerned with clearance than with train lines. "In this position of affairs," Stephenson wondered whether it was not possible to "stiffen the platform of a suspension-bridge so effectually as to make it available for the passage of railway trains at high velocities." His answer was no. "The injurious consequences attending the ordinary mode of employing chains in suspension-bridges, were brought under my observation in a very striking manner on the Stockton and Darlington Railway . . . which had proved an entire failure," he wrote in defense of his ultimate plans for his massively expensive tubular beam bridge. He was more forthright before the House of Commons: "I do not approve of [suspension bridges] for the passage of locomotive engines, on account of the undulation into which the platforms are usually thrown."[9]

Stephenson thought a more feasible solution might involve a "combination of the suspension chain with deep trellis trussing" so as to form "a roadway surrounded on all sides by strongly trussed framework. A structure of this kind would no doubt be exceedingly stiff." In fact, he continued, such an approach had already "been applied successfully in America on a large canal aqueduct," the one John had built in 1844-5 over the Allegheny River. "The application, however, of this system to an aqueduct is perhaps one of the most favourable possible," he thought, "for there the weight is constant and uniformly distributed." In a railway bridge, however, the load is much heavier and more mobile and transient. If the Stockton and Darlington Bridge had taught Stephenson anything, it was the inability of a suspended structure to adequately address a constantly moving "superincumbent weight." There would never be sufficient stiffness to balance the stress placed on the cables or the roadway.[10]

Stephenson's solution was to look elsewhere. First and foremost, he needed rigid sides that sat securely on a rigid base. And if he wanted a fully stiffened structure, capable of resisting the force and motion of a heavy, loaded moving railway train, he needed to close the top loop and think in terms of "a huge wrought-iron rectangular tube, so large that railway trains might pass through it, with suspension chains on each side." At this point he realized he was no longer dealing with a suspended bridge at all but with a beam bridge; the chains (or cables) were at best "auxiliary," at worst "incompatible." He didn't need the strength: a wrought iron tube of 460 feet would be self-supporting. And he didn't need the structural competition. With chains and tubes the span would be composed of "two parts," the stability of one conflicting with the stability of the other. A passing train, for example, with its "unequal distribution of weight," would "pull" on the line of a suspended cable as it moved across the span, bending it out of a natural curve, in the process lifting the bridge behind it, creating "undulation." Chains or cables—incorporated initially to help support the weight of the tubes—would instead compromise the span's essential rigidity, the most vital aspect of any railroad bridge.[11]

Stephenson's Britannia Bridge—four hollow wrought iron tubes resting on two abutments and three mid-river piers, for a total length of 1,512 feet—was opened with great fanfare on March 5, 1850. The great engineer's achievement over the Menai was the backdrop to John's efforts at Niagara, especially once it was announced that Stephenson would design a similar bridge to cross the St. Lawrence at nearby Montreal. The *St. Catherine's Journal* thought anyone looking to build a railroad bridge over the Niagara ought to pay close attention to Stephenson's "Tubular Sheet Iron Bridge." William Merritt even seems to have had a conversation with Stephenson who "gave his opinion that a wire suspension bridge over the Niagara could not be made practical for railway communication." The *American Railroad Journal* chimed in, just as the construction was about to get underway, saying that "it is well known that Stephenson, the Magnus Apollo in engineering . . . has decided against the suspension principle as applied to railway bridges," meaning that if John could wrestle his bridge successfully across the gorge, he would "be doing that [which] has not merely never been done before, but what has been pronounced by the highest authority, impracticable." John took the whole thing in stride. "Although the question of applying the principle of suspension to railroad bridges has been disposed of in the negative by Mr. Robert Stephenson," John wrote to Charles Stuart in 1847, "I am bold enough to say that this celebrated Engineer . . . does no justice to the question [and] has not at all succeeded in the solution of this problem." "The only question which presents itself," John felt, was quite simple: "Can a suspension bridge be made stiff enough, as not to yield and bend under the weight of a railroad train when unequally distributed over it; and can the great vibrations which result from the rapid motion of such trains and which prove so destructive to common bridges, be avoided and counteracted?" He responded in the affirmative, maintaining that "wire cable bridges, properly constructed, will be found hereafter the most durable and cheapest railroad bridges for spans over one hundred feet."[12]

A persistent myth—begun by either John himself or Ashbel Welch and repeated by historians—has it that Stephenson told John, "If your bridge succeeds, mine is a magnificent blunder."[13] There is no evidence that Stephenson ever said such a thing, nor that the two engineers even met until after John's bridge was finished, but clearly Stephenson believed that suspension bridges were inadequate for railroad traffic. He would revise this belief in the years to come, paying professional homage to John's achievements at Niagara. Still, there is much to connect John's and Stephenson's vastly different bridges. They both began with the same problem—attaining sufficient stiffness—but they ended in different places and with different choices, although they passed through very similar stages. Both began with the need to span very long distances without employing falsework, therefore precluding an arch bridge. Both engineers then began to think in terms of what Stephenson called a "stiff lattice cage" supported by suspension cables, which almost perfectly describes the solution John ended up with. Where they diverged was in local conditions and structural commitment.

Figure 15.2 Stephenson's Britannia Bridge, opened in 1850. Francis Bedford, *Bangor, The Britannia Bridge, from Anglesey* (1860).

Stephenson was a railroad engineer who built bridges, whatever best suited local conditions. John was a suspension bridge engineer, committed above all to a single structural type. John was also more constrained than Stephenson, who had the luxury of a rock in the middle of his river. John had to vault over eight hundred feet in a single span. Stephenson only had to get his bridge 460 feet from pier to pier, at the longest. John's dilemma at Niagara was different from Stephenson's in this regard. His bridge had to span the sort of distance only a suspension bridge could manage.

The battle at Niagara was in some respects a battle over the future of railroad bridges, between John's suspension plan and Stephenson's tubular plan. Neither of them won, as it happens. As Henry Petroski notes, Stephenson's Britannia Bridge was already a "dinosaur" by the time it was opened, doomed by the sheer scale of its cost. The *Journal of the Franklin Institute* suggested that a $200,000 suspension bridge "would cost but little, if any, more than the interest for one year, at six per cent, of the cost of the tubular bridge across the Menai Strait." Over at the *Railroad Journal*, Minor was incredulous at the "eminent English engineers opposed [to] suspension bridges for railroads" who nevertheless approved of a bridge that was "projected to cost in the region of $2,500,000!!," he spluttered. By the time Stephenson's Victoria Bridge was opened in 1859, tubular bridges were widely regarded as a structural "anachronism."[14]

Despite Minor's support, suspension bridges fared little better than tubular bridges. They had their adherents but few, if any, practitioners.[15] As Stuart noted in 1871, looking back to the Niagara competition, the idea of a railway suspension bridge "was a novel and bold undertaking, and generally believed to be impracticable. . . . A circular letter was addressed to a number of the leading Engineers of America and Europe, asking their opinion of the undertaking. Various replies were received, some in open condemnation of the project, others expressive of grave doubts of its practicability and safety at any cost."[16] This was confirmed in practice. The Louisville and Frankfort Railroad built the first railroad suspension bridge in the United States over the Kentucky River in 1850, and it lasted barely five years. By 1854, "the masonry of the towers . . . had become shaken, and badly fractured by the vibratory action of the cables, and notwithstanding every effort to preserve it in repair, it had long been considered unsafe for heavy engines to cross."[17] Stephenson heard about this bridge from "a big engineering authority in that country," remarking, "From the information in my possession, the work alluded to can scarcely be looked upon as a permanent, substantial, and safe structure. Its flexibility, I was informed, was truly alarming."[18] In Europe, Frederick Schnirch, builder of the Prague Suspension Bridge, completed the Vienna Railroad Bridge in 1860, but it was subject to such severe strains and to such ever-increasing deflection that "great alarm was felt," and it was taken down in 1884. In 1862, George Turnbull, chief engineer of the East Indian Railway, drew up plans for a combined railway and carriage traffic bridge across the Hooghly River, sixteen miles above Calcutta, based almost entirely on John's Niagara span, but the project never got off the ground.[19] As locomotives got heavier, suspension bridges got less attractive, while rigid steel truss spans, whether arch, girder, or cantilevered, grew in popularity and dependability. By the close of the nineteenth century, there were no more supporters and no real railroad suspension bridge successes.

Long-span steel and iron truss bridges took off in the second half of the nineteenth century, dooming both suspension and tubular bridges as railroad options. William Bollman began building iron truss bridges for the Baltimore and Ohio in 1850, and they caught on. From 1859 to 1870, the New York Central, the Pennsylvania, and the Lehigh Valley railroads all built medium-span truss bridges. In 1871, the 1,300-foot-long Viaduc de la Bouble was completed in France, while three years later the three-span Eads Bridge was opened in St. Louis. In 1882 the thousand2,000-foot-long Kinzua Viaduct was built by the Erie Railroad in Pennsylvania; Gustave Eiffel's magnificent 1,854-foot-long Garabit Viaduct followed two years later. There were many failures, but these were due more to material—fatigue and fracture—than structural type. New steelmaking processes devised by Bessemer (1856), Siemans (1867), and others revolutionized the iron bridge industry, which culminated in the victory of the steel truss bridge over all other options. As if to illustrate the point, the Michigan Central and Canada South built a massive cantilever truss railroad bridge across the Niagara in 1883 parallel to John's aged pioneer.[20]

The example of the Pittsburgh and Steubenville Railroad illustrates the problems railroad suspension bridges faced. In 1852, John had high hopes for a contract with the company to build a railroad bridge across the Ohio at Steubenville. He drew up a number of handsome plans and even had the ear of the company's chief engineer, David Mitchell, yet even these advantages were not enough. Writing to John in 1852, Mitchell confessed, "The consulting engineer and I disagree as to the plan and we could not come together—he contended for the How[e] truss with arches and piers and I for the suspension with one pier—I would not yield the impracticability of the suspension although I must confess that the experiment of the Bridge over the Tees at Stockton given by Mr. Stevenson looks rather unfavorable, and I believe I stand alone in the west in my advocacy of the plan." A decision was postponed, but in 1857, two years after John's Niagara railroad suspension bridge was opened amid global fanfare, the Pittsburgh and Steubenville began work on a Howe truss bridge.[21]

———

John's first fully realized plan to span the Niagara River was drawn up in May 1847, and it began with a simple founding observation: "For the uninterrupted passage of numerous and heavy trains, it would be inadmissible and altogether unsafe, to place the railway track and the roadway upon the *same* platform. . . . Horses meeting rail road trains with their puffing and panting locomotives, will always scare and become frightened." If one wanted to secure passage for wagons, carriages, and trains and "to avoid serious accidents . . . it becomes therefore absolutely necessary, to place the roadway *below* the Railroad track," John wrote, "and secure it so that frantic animals cannot jump off." This initial design decision separated John from any other bidder and seemed to promise a more complex and expensive design. John was slowly becoming an adroit promoter, and he used this skill to address Stephenson's primary complaint about using suspension bridges for railroads. "The necessity of constructing one road above the other," he wrote, "can be advantageously turned to very good account, as thereby a great depth of framing will be formed . . . which will greatly add to the stiffness of the structure." "Suspension bridges may be destroyed by their *own weight*," he continued, plowing a furrow that defined his career, "if such is allowed to rise and fall repeatedly in consequence of the vibrations of the superstructure." The great objective in the designing of such bridges was "to apply all the means which are calculated to improve their stiffness, and rather sacrifice that character of lightness, which has proved fatal to more than one suspension bridge."[22]

In constructing the body of his bridge, John hit upon the idea of a lattice structure "possessing a high degree of stiffness," similar in some regard to Stephenson's solution. Both were effectively boxes, with John's span formed by a rudimentary wooden truss system rather than a solid iron tube. Such a design, John reasoned, "would weigh less than any other structure of similar stiffness," thus allowing the requisite length to get from shore to shore, and would also mitigate against the effects of high winds and gales. Open sides would reduce buffeting and undulations and improve stability. Under the floors stays "anchored in the rocks" would maintain "vertical and horizontal stability." Tightly wrapped wire cables nine inches in diameter would could carry John's bridge over the Niagara. Its maximum load, "including cars, superstructure, 20 four horse teams, the impact of a moving train and even 1 foot of snow," would be 1,265 tons. John normally quadrupled the "strength which will barely support the maximum tension," but in this case he was more cautious, aiming for five times. He even gave some thought to the aesthetics of the job: "To add to the appearance of the work and to produce a striking effect at a distance I propose to paint the lattice white, and the cords black. The railings of the Susp. Bridge over the Monongahela river at Pittsburgh, are painted in the same style and present a very beautiful appearance." John also proposed to whitewash everything inside "for the purpose of preserving it and improving the gloomy aspect of a covered passage."[23]

John's final proposal, submitted in November 1847, was an effort to cover all bases. He had corresponded with Merritt and done plenty of due diligence as regards the Great Western Railroad and its likely development. As he wrote in his notebook, "The prospects of the N. Br. will depend upon the success of the R.R." Still, "if the prospects of the R.R. become distant, Mr. Merritt will take the Bridge . . . into his own hands." Merritt, it seems, thought the bridge would pay for itself—"unconnected with the R.R."—purely through "common travel." With this information in hand, John proposed three different bridges: "a box bridge for R.R. 170,000," a bridge "omitting upper floor & cables putting up side railings 120,000," and a "Bridge for common travel only, 30 feet between the railings R.R. track in the Center 135,000." If the Great Western were truly interested in running rails over the Niagara, then all was well and good. But if not, John—with a sideways glance at Merritt—was still primed to pick up the contract. He had accounted, he thought, for all eventualities. As he concluded: "I was invited to furnish a design for a R.R. Bridge and such I have done and will stake my reputation upon this issue." He was not called upon to stake his reputation, but he was the first one they contacted when things began to sour with Ellet.[24]

Lot Clark struck up a correspondence with John about Ellet's bridge and the future of the entire venture in early September, about a month after the bridge company had fired Ellet. Clark was worried about the "large expenditure [occasioned] by the erection of the present temporary foot Br[idge]" and wondered if it was "of any essential use in the erection of a permanent Br[idge]" such as the company had in mind. John thought not, but was polite about it, resisting the urge to openly criticize Ellet. Certainly they were occasionally used on chain bridges, but never to John's knowledge on a wire bridge. There were plenty of ways of spinning a cable "across deep rivers & chasms" without resorting to an independent platform. John's own method—patented just the year before—would cost no more than $1,500 for "machinery and temporary fixings," a bad piece of news for a company that had just spent almost $30,000 on a temporary bridge. As for the present state of the footbridge, John thought the span was capable of supporting itself along with about twenty tons "provided such a load is uniformly distributed over the floor and is at rest. A greater load than 20 tons would tax the power of the cables over 1/3 of their ultimate strength, and would therefore be unsafe." As for whether the bridge could survive "a strong gale," that would depend on whether the cables had been laid in uniform tension and if there were adequate stays. Without stays, John wouldn't "consider the bridge safe [for longer than] 24 hours."[25]

With Clark's encouragement, John was back working on his Niagara plans in October 1848—even while Ellet was fighting for control of his footbridge—eventually filling up over forty pages of a notebook with specifications and accounting.[26] John had never had the Niagara job out of his mind, he informed Clark, and was able to produce such a plan "as will reduce the cost of the Br. to the lowest practicable sum, without destroying any of the primary objects of the work," a dubious claim, as it turned out. His 1848 plan was a compromise. In a desperate effort to secure the contract, John proposed a much cheaper, significantly reworked span. Gone was the double-deck structure that defined his first system. In its place John proposed a single floor, twenty-nine feet wide, with two four-foot-wide walkways and two seven-foot-wide carriageways flanking a "R.R. track in the Center" supported by two cables 9½ inch in diameter resting on isolated sixty-foot-high columns. The total cost would be $128,000 (excluding the rails), a strategic reduction no doubt designed to account for the fact that the bridge company had already sunk $30,000 into the span with little to show for their efforts. "*Unnecessary* strength and magnificence, which would be considered, if a more liberal expenditure could be made, is of course avoided by the plan now proposed," John added, "but at the same time, I maintain without hesitation, that no design has been produced as yet by any party, which will make as beautiful and graceful a structure" as his. John also advised Clark against strengthening Ellet's bridge and against any "further temporary expenditures." Anything added to Ellet's bridge would just have to be removed at a later date and would only interfere with the construction of a permanent bridge, which the company desperately needed to "restore the confidence of the Public in the undertaking and in the stock."[27]

By the end of the year John was writing to Clark to "express to you *individually* my sincere thanks for the interest you assume to take in my appointment. This disposition on your part is so much more grateful to me, as I did not and had no cause to expect it. I can only assure you, in case I am charged with the construction of the N. Br. . . . that you will not find yourself deceived in me, as far as competency and integrity is concerned."[28] Although there was no official contract, John continued to visit the falls during the next couple of years surveying the location and refining his plans, returning them to their origins, as it turned out. He was there April 16–18, 1849, making detailed notes about the location and checking to see how much of a hindrance Ellet's bridge would be to his plans. "It appears that the cables of the foot bridge will just pass the masonry of the new towers," he concluded.[29] A year later, on June 19–20, 1850, he returned to conduct an official inspection of Ellet's bridge, which did not seem to be holding up too well.[30] The old cables were "considerably strained," their tension "no longer equal"; the floor had sunk eighteen inches, and the anchorages—although fine and in good working order—were full of "sulphur water." The towers, however, were the main problem. The eastern tower was "1'9" out of plumb" and "continues to lean over," thanks to a set of rusted and broken cable rollers on top of the tower. "Since the rollers on the tower appear to be perfectly stationary and do not move, a further yielding of the American tower appears to me unavoidable," John concluded. He didn't think there would be any "immediate danger, as long as there is sufficient strength in the timber itself to support the weight." Unfortunately, he then discovered that "the quality of this timber . . . is very bad." John's brief report concluded that the bridge would be good for approximately "2 years" of use, beyond which nothing could be guaranteed "with any degree of safety," which turned out to be rather accurate. He was asked to submit a further set of estimates the following year, including one for a 1,300-foot-long footbridge at Victoria Point, but it was not until June 25, 1852—two years and five days after his inspection report—that John accepted the appointment as chief engineer of the Niagara Falls International Railroad Suspension Bridge. "Professionally there is no man that stands higher than Mr. Roebling," commented the *Niagara Falls Iris*.[31]

His only motive for taking the contract, John avowed, was "to gratify my professional pride of having accomplished a difficult task in Engineering." Compensation was "no inducement because I am independent in circumstances." He could happily accept any of the other offers that arrived daily—all of which would pay him "at least $20,000," he boasted—but he had decided to place his talents in the service of his profession and the bridge company (covering up that he had chased this contract quite relentlessly for almost six years). After all, railroad suspension bridges had been John's "study for a number of years," which, when coupled with his "experience as a contractor of Wire C. & Rope," meant that his "practical knowledge in that sphere is probably greater than that of any other living man." In executing this mammoth task, he was happy to "take all the responsibility upon myself but at the same time shall claim all the Credit which shall be attached to the work." As for the specifics of his proposal, he wrote, "I cannot submit my plans for approval because I consider myself the more competent. Alternatives might be suggested, but not every alternative is an improvement. Moreover it is difficult to harmonize the original designs and ideas of different engineers." He would set them out, but he would not debate them or subject them to outside scrutiny or second-guessing.[32]

Despite being "considered by most engineers, if not impractical at least very doubtful," the task of wrestling a successful railroad suspension bridge over the Niagara River, he continued, was neither difficult nor especially complicated. All the "principles" involved were "exceedingly simple, and do not involve any intricate question." The only "real difficulty" was in its "novelty," he thought. In fact, the feat involved merely two "considerations": adequate strength and stiffness. The question of strength was simple: "To support a heavy weight, nothing safer can be employed, than a well-made wire cable or rope. It is not only the strongest, but also the most economical." Stiffness, John believed, could only be guaranteed by three methods, all of which he had planned for: using longitudinal girders and heavy timbers in the construction of the floor to distribute pressure over a larger area; building a truss system into the main body of the bridge; and using stays, both internally, running from the towers to the roadway, and externally, from the bridge to the surrounding riverbank. The most significant of these was the makeshift truss system John adopted for the bridge's roadway. The bridge's double floor, he wrote, would form a "hollow, straight beam, of 20 feet wide and 18 feet deep, composed of top, bottom, and sides." The upper and lower floors were connected by vertical wooden side posts positioned every fiveevery feet and by twin cables hung with a 10-foot difference in deflection. Stiffness was generated by wrought iron rods, one inch in diameter and 27 feet 4 inches long, which were screwed and bolted into the posts and ran diagonally and at right angles to each other, from the top and bottom of the first and fifth posts. The system wasn't a true truss, but it was very truss-like. The posts and rods helped transfer pressure and energy around the bridge and lent it "a high degree of rigidity and stiffness."[33]

John's 1852 plan reverted to many of the ideas he had initially proposed in 1847. His truss system was modeled on his original lattice plan, allowing for "great lightness" and providing "little surface to the action of the wind." The stays—upper and lower—were also retained and would help "produce a degree of stiffness, sufficient . . . to admit of the passage of the heaviest trains at full speed, without producing any injurious vibration." That said, John decided to limit the "ordinary speed of trains . . . to five miles per hour." By his calculations, a fully loaded train (complete with twenty-seven fully loaded double freight cars) running the entire length of the bridge would weigh 491 tons. If the weight of the superstructure (782 tons) were added to the weight of the lower floor crowded to capacity with 4,443 men (one for every three square feet of room), each weighing 140 pounds (for a total of 310 tons), it meant the bridge would have to support a potential weight of 1,583 tons. An act of Parliament had called for a total strength of 6,600 tons. John himself opted for 10,000 tons.[34]

Four cables, each 9½ inches in diameter, would support the roadway. Two upper cables would primarily support the upper deck, while two lower cables would run down the sides of the carriageway and support the lower one. When a train ran over the span, the upper cables would "be taxed," John understood, but he also knew that his box system would transfer pressure down through the posts and rods to the lower cables, in effect ensuring the four cables acted in concert when needed. The cables would rest on four separate towers, each sixty feet high (fifteen feet square at the base rising to eight feet square at the top) and made of "compact, hard limestone," which would "bear a pressure of 500 feet upon every square foot." If anyone was worried about the lateral stability of independent towers, John reassured, "Their own weight and the great pressure they have to support" would keep them honest and upright. The total cost of the entire venture John pegged at $196,866, a significant increase on the cut-rate prices he had been offering over the previous couple of years.[35]

———

The most noticeable aspect of John's plan was its style. If money were no object, he envisioned "imposing gateways, erected in the massive Egyptian style, and joined by massive wings, the cables watched by sphinxes, with parapets, and all the rest of the approaches, put up of appropriate dimensions and in suitable style." He settled for a more modest vision, the grand display replaced by four huge square towers in the style of fluted Egyptian columns with palm capitals. His "bridge, when viewed from the upper floor, where all the foot passengers will resort, will, however, present a very graceful, simple, but at the same time substantial appearance. The four massive cables, supported on isolated columns of very substantial make, will form the characteristic of the work, and this will be unique and striking in its effect, and quite in keeping with the surrounding scenery," John believed.[36]

John's choice of an Egyptian Revival theme was new for him, but the style had been popular across Europe and America for over fifty years, ever since Napoleon's troops had returned from Egypt in 1801, although it was on the wane and much less fashionable by the time John began to build his Niagara Bridge.[37] John never explained his decision to adopt an Egyptian theme, and in fact he seems to have decided upon it rather late. Just as his structural plans altered and evolved over the previous five years, so did his aesthetic choices. His initial plans in 1847 were eclectic and convoluted—a Gothic arch beneath a pointed classical pediment, flanked by simple rounded sectional columns—as if John were simply unable to follow architectural conventions. By 1848, he had turned his attention to the Egyptian Revival style, but, restless and rarely satisfied, he continued to test different approaches. In 1850, he was playing around with a rounded Roman arch with matching pediment and flanking columns, in addition to a rather monstrous set of crenellated towers complete with decorative embrasures (arrow slits), enclosing a Gothic arch, perhaps inspired by Thomas Telford's Conway Suspension Bridge (1822–26), which at least had the excuse of being built adjacent to Conway Castle. By 1852, John was toying with various different Gothic approaches: a Gothic arch with Egyptian details and a classical pediment, or a Gothic arch with a castellated cornice. He even drew up a design for unadorned double Gothic arches, a design he later employed on the Brooklyn Bridge. Even as late as June 1852, a month before issuing his final official report, he was still considering simple rounded Roman arch towers with raised sides.[38]

Such tinkering and wavering suggests John had more in mind than pure economy. Or it at least raises the question of what he intend to convey, if indeed he intended anything. Was he looking to exploit or appropriate the symbolism of Egyptian architecture? Or was he trying to conjoin design and purpose? Critics have made much of John's later bridge designs, especially how his bridges were "expressive of the purpose for which [they were] built," to use A. J. Downing's phrase.[39] Was this also the case at Niagara?

By the time John came to consider an Egyptian motif, almost every important architect in the United States had worked in the genre, and it was current across John's landscape. Gone was the eighteenth century's romantic obsession with nature's inevitable conquest over the works of man, with ruins and decay. Engineers of the nineteenth century wanted to convey a sense of triumphant endurance, of strength and durability, especially in the realm of such new—and to some still unproven—technologies as railroads and suspension bridges. For engineers, Egyptian Revival architecture provided this shorthand. Many railroad stations were built in the Egyptian Revival style, as were suspension bridges, beginning with Brunel's initial plans for the Clifton Suspension Bridge in 1831. "Egyptian architecture is particularly applicable to engineering work, particularly for their piers, &c., of suspension bridges," wrote one architect in 1834, while another thought it was "most suitable for engineering purposes: being massive; having few and bold details; and consequently, not requiring very nice or expensive workmanship or materials." Explaining his decision, Brunel

Figure 15.3 John Roebling's design sketch for a Niagara railroad bridge, incorporating Gothic, classical, medieval, and Egyptian elements (1848). Courtesy of the Special Collections and University Archives, Rutgers University Libraries.

thought the grandeur of the Egyptian form was appropriate to the grandeur of the site, and John might have felt a similar pull. The description of his plan from 1852 sounds very much like Brunel's, especially with its "imposing gateways, erected in the massive Egyptian style, and joined by massive wings, the cables watched by sphinxes."[40]

When reaching for comparisons, especially in terms of size and longevity, some newspapers naturally settled on Egyptian works. "When finished [John's bridge] will surpass any work of the kind that has been attempted either in

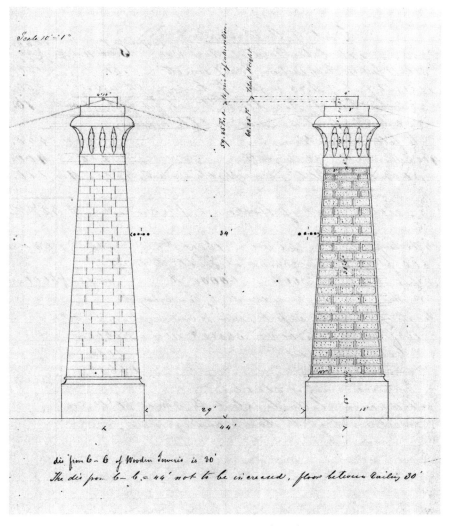

Figure 15.4 A draft sketch of John's Egyptian towers (1852). Courtesy of the Special Collections and University Archives, Rutgers University Libraries.

ancient or modern times," the *St. Catherine's Journal* believed. "The Egyptian pyramids and the Grecian temples have been the wonders of ages, but we confess that neither of them excites us with such admiration for the skill and power of the human mind, as these suspension bridges. The tombs of the Pharaohs are evidences of stupendous combinations of muscular or mechanical power . . . but the suspension bridge suggests an idea of difficulties overcome, and of the wise adaptation of the means to an end, which seem to us among the highest achievements of man."[41]

Egyptian architecture, built to last for eternity, stood for strength, solidity, and immortality; Egyptian civilization suggested hidden knowledge, ancient wisdom, and deep mystery. Such an understanding helps answer the rather curious question of how exactly—as John maintained—four huge sixty-foot-tall man-made Egyptian columns would be "in keeping with the surrounding scenery" of Niagara Falls. The overwhelming scale of the towers and the bridge's roadway bespoke awe-inspiring scale, much like falls themselves—the upward sweep of the towers from a thick, massive base bespoke uplift and soaring solidity—while their ability to evoke both fear and attraction was equally vital. But the power of Egyptian Revival architecture to evoke the same sense of ancient mystery that defined the falls might best explain both John's choice, along with his sense that the two icons could be "in keeping" with each other: both powerfully sublime yet still shrouded in secrecy, romance, and the enigma of time. As historian William Irvin notes, John's bridge helped link the world's oldest civilization with "America's timeless geologic antiquity." It might also explain John's long dalliance with the Gothic form too, a style that, like the falls, conveyed religious significance and devotional awe.[42]

———

John spent the summer of 1852 up at the bridge site, organizing, hiring, overseeing, and planning. He had to let the masonry contract out three different times before he found a dependable team. "Mrs. Roebling wishes me to come home," he wrote Swan in late July. "This I cannot. If I leave, everybody will." By August, the press was reporting a significant uptick in activity around the worksite, and John had begun to relax a little. "Rhule is here," he wrote home in the middle of the month with evident relief. The region around Ellet's bridge was still a far cry from that envisioned by Clark, Stuart, and Merritt five years before. It was lush and wooded but still a rather spartan place, with neither settlement nor railroad. But that changed over the course of the next three years as a new village sprung up around John's bridge and the railroad depot it served. Appropriately, everyone called it Suspension Bridge, an "ugly, bustling little village growing up around the American extremity of the bridge" as *Harper's* described it.[43]

The work proper began in September with the digging of the anchorages and the construction of the masonry. Eight shafts were sunk into solid limestone, four on either side of the river. Into each shaft was placed a huge cast iron plate, 6 feet 6 inches square and 2½ inches thick, to which was attached an immense chain made of eight seven-foot-long links and one ten-foot-long link. Each link was made of seven and eight bars (alternating) of wrought iron sandwiched together—not welded—to form one solid piece. Each link was riveted firmly to its neighbor with a 3½-inch-diameter iron bolt. The chains were sixty-six feet long and built to withstand four times the weight of the superstructure and "any load that will ever be placed on it." The chains reached the surface just to the rear of the base of the towers. Once up at the surface and in position, the shafts were filled with masonry, then cement mortar, and finally grouted "copiously." "My experience has given me ample proof, that cement grout will take a firm hold of iron, and will effectually guard it against oxidation," John declared, understanding instinctively the need to prevent rust, but not a similar need to guarantee the free movement of his suspension cables from anchor plate to anchor plate. The decision would eventually imperil his bridge.[44]

While the shafts were being dug, John's huge Egyptian towers were being constructed next to Ellet's rickety span. At every motion Ellet's "frame work vibrates and trembles," reported the *Boston Morning Journal*, perhaps due to all the digging and blasting going on around John's bridge.[45] Separate companies were responsible for the two sets of towers, John Brown in Canada and Latham and Gage in New York. The work took almost the entire year and was finally completed in November 1853. With everything in reliable hands and the Niagara project progressing according to his precise instructions, John spent much of the year on the move, drumming up new business, chasing new bridge contracts, and beginning new projects. His business—overseen on the ground by Swan—in Trenton was booming, and he was increasingly bombarded with requests for bridge designs and estimates. He worked up partial plans for over ten different bridge projects in the early 1850s. His letters to Swan give a sense of his schedule and the toll it must have taken on him and his relations with his family. On January 24, 1853, he was in Danville, Kentucky, but, he wrote, "will leave here tomorrow [and] shall remain several days at Lexington & Cincinnati, there I go to the Falls where I expect to stay about one week only, then I will go to New York by way of Worcester to examine Washburn's Mill. In New York I will examine C. M. Erickson's Engine. I will be in Trenton before or about the middle of Febry." Almost all of John's letters ended with some appeal to Swan to "please read this letter to Mrs. Roebling and give my love to the whole family," but he was rarely there with them.[46]

John's dedication to his work—and the blind eye he seems to have turned to his family—reached a rather absurd point by the turn of the year. The spinning of the lower suspension cable was begun early in December, shortly after which John wrote to Swan to say that he wasn't sure if he would make it back to Trenton for Christmas but that he would certainly be there for New Year's. Eleven days later, he wrote to say that the middle of January was the earliest he could possibly leave the bridge. On December 29 he wished Swan a "happy New Year to yourself and to both families" and said that he "should like to be at home just now, but must wait, until a whole operation of Strand making is gone through." "My machinery here works very well and hands are getting practiced, the whole operation is very interesting and creates much interest," he continued. And the next day: "We are in spite of the cold & stormy weather getting along so rapidly, that I believe the 2 first Strands will be completed in 3 days and that by the end of the next week the 2 next Strands will be commenced." It soon turned out that John was forgetting something at home, or that someone was forgetting him. "You say in your last, that *Mrs. Roebling* & *the child* are pretty well," John wrote Swan on January 6; "this takes me by *surprise* not having been informed at all of the delivery of Mrs. R. Or what do you mean? Please answer by return of mail." John's surprise is perplexing and revealing. Either he had no idea his wife was pregnant or no one thought to inform him of the birth of Edmund, his seventh child. Less in doubt is the fact that he was clearly more interested and invested in his cable spinning than in his wife or his family. For a professional engineer on the cusp of a global accomplishment, this preoccupation is perhaps understandable, if a little damning, as was his next communication on the subject of his wife, almost a month later: "Tell Mrs. Roebling I bought one Gal. of syrup and paid for it, will be shipped tomorrow." Worst of all, perhaps, John referred to Edmund as Edward in his will, drawn up fourteen years later, as if he didn't know the names of his own children.[47]

John saw precious little of his children, but he was capable of affection and consideration, even if, as Washington claims, his children "lived in terror of him." His diaries contain gift lists—"Laura: silk dress; mother: pocket books; Wash: walking stick and gold pen; Ferd: cap; Joseph: indian work; Charlie: toy"—a task he did not delegate to Johanna. And his children returned the favor, fretting over what to buy their father for Christmas most years. One of his diaries for 1853 contains a lengthy and rather sentimental passage John copied out verbatim from Donald Grant Mitchell's bestselling *Reveries of a Bachelor: A Book of the Heart* (1850), apparently one of Emily Dickinson's favorite books. There is no explication or comment, but the effect is disarming. Under the heading "Reconsider Ferdy going to Germany!" John wrote out:

> Let the father, or the mother think long, before they send away their
> boy—before they break the home-ties that make a web of infinite fine-
> ness and soft silken meshes around his heart, and toss him aloof into
> the boy-world, where he must struggle up amid bickerings and quarrels,

into his age of youth! There are boys indeed with little fineness in the texture of their hearts, and with little delicacy of soul to whom the school in a distant village, is but a vacation from home.... But there are others, to whom the severance ... gives a shock that lasts forever ... and the sobs with which the adieux are said, are sobs that may come back in the after years, strong, and steady, and terrible.[48]

Ferdinand—"little Ferdy"—was John's favorite, but also a source of worry and concern. "I am very desirous that my son Ferdinand, who is progressing but very slowly, should receive private instructions," John wrote in 1854. Four years later, Johanna wrote to Washington, "So far as Ferdinand is concerned, it is difficult to have a very definite opinion. He is still so confused and playful.... It is absolutely necessary that he should get into a different environment for a while, and that he should be separated from his playmates." Ferdy ended up in what he called "a one horse College town" otherwise known as Washington, DC, where he attended Columbian College (now George Washington University). "The students are most all of them southern loafers," he informed his brother; "the best fellow among them is the one that can make the largest pool of tobacco juice on the floor." A year later, he was even more candid. "Things are going rather roughly out at the College now," he informed his father; "most of the students have been drunk the greater part of the vacation, five or six have been in the guard house and were fined for being drunk in the streets." Shortly after this, Ferdy rather unsurprisingly transferred to the Polytechnic College of Philadelphia, where he thrived. Ferdinand eventually took the financial reins of John A. Roebling's Sons Company and ran the company with great acumen and success for over fifty years, turning it into an industrial titan.[49]

John was often quite judgmental with his children, as he was with almost everyone who came within his orbit, a fact made plain in a rather ludicrous letter John took time out to write Swan in June 1854 while he was trying to erect the world's first successful railroad suspension bridge: "Say to Mr. Harris that he must be more particular in directing letters, I mean as to style, penmanship & position of address. The last letter was addressed in the old fashioned mode.... This will not do. He must take pains to improve his handwriting and examine attentively well written letters, which you receive, and which may serve him as patterns. Addressing letters, the direction should never be put up high in the upper part of the Envelope, but rather below the Center, else it looks uncommercial like, for instance"—here John included a drawing of an envelope properly addressed— "Mr. Harris must pay attention to these matters and improve."[50] For John, it was never too much trouble to point out a person's shortcomings.

The construction was pushed forward with great dedication and energy through 1854, a pace matched by John, who managed to publish three new articles in May and June on typically eclectic subjects.[51] All the hewing and hefting had sunk the anchorages and raised the towers and spun out the lower cables by mid-April, after which Rhule and his crew of carpenters descended on the bridge to piece together the lower carriageway. By the end of May, the bridge was "progressing with as much speed as so ponderous a work can, regard being had to its strength, durability, and safety." The "massive cables" were nearly completed, "and the timber work is all in readiness to be suspended." Marcus Adams, an early settler and diarist, watched as John's men began to assemble the bridge's roadway. On June 5, he reported, "Floor timbers rapidly going in for carriage bridge," and two days later, "Carriages will pass over the bridge next Monday, if rain does not prevent laying the timbers." He "went over to Canada [a couple of days later] to see the new bridge as far as it was put up" and "was much amused" to watch numerous different individuals pass "up a pair of stairs from the old to the new bridge. Some men seemed almost paralyzed with fear. The women were quite as little alarmed as the men." Grading for the new railroad station depot was begun on June 27, 1854, while on July 14 the bridge's cables were being fastened to the carriageway. Once all was fixed and secured, the lower roadway was quietly opened for any person or vehicle wishing to cross.[52]

The construction was not without its misfortunes, however. "About 3 o'clock on Friday [March 10] one of the carriages containing 4 men employed in winding the wire round a cable of the new Suspension Bridge, gave way, and two of the men . . . were precipitated down the bank of the river some 70 feet and instantly killed. . . . The other two saved themselves by clinging to the cable." Later in the year, John's "principal carpenter Mr. Kenzie" was—"without sufficient caution," according to John—taking down the heavy framework of timber, constituting the old towers of Ellet's bridge, when he lost control and was "struck across the face" by a falling beam and seriously injured, while two of his companions "were precipitated into the river." "His recovery will take time & is doubtful under the bad medical treatment, which he has. I am now in a bad fix, and compelled to complete the work without him," wrote John. There were other mishaps, but very few were serious, surprisingly for such a massive project. The most significant architectural disaster in the entire venture—what John later called "the greatest disaster of the kind on record"—happened far away, about three hundred miles to the south.[53]

On the morning of May 18, the *Wheeling Intelligencer* reported news of a massive calamity. "With feelings of unutterable sorrow, we announce that the noble and world renowned structure, the Wheeling Suspension Bridge, has been swept from its strong holds by a terrific storm, and now lies a mass of ruins," ran the story. "Yesterday morning thousands beheld this stupendous structure

in undisturbed repose and in undiminished strength, a mighty pathway spanning the beautiful waters of the Ohio, a link in the unbroken chain of trade and
travel between the East and the West, and looked upon it as one of the proudest
monuments of the enterprise of our citizens. Now, nothing remains of it but the
dismantled towers looming above the sorrowful wreck that lies buried beneath
them! A giant lies prostrate in the Ohio, and against his huge and broken ribs,
and iron sinews, snapped asunder, the waves are dashing scornfully, sending up
a sound the most doleful that ever fell upon the ears of our citizens."[54]

The destruction was over quickly but had built up for several hours. A "high
storm of wind" swept through the Ohio Valley in the late morning, "breaking
vessels at their moorings and causing great devastation." The gale was stronger
by noon and was raging with still greater force by three o'clock when a local
reporter for some reason thought they might take a walk across the Wheeling
Bridge "for pleasure, as [they] have frequently done, enjoying the cool breeze
and the undulating motion of the bridge." Once there he "discovered that one
of the guys or small iron cables extending from the flooring to the wall, near
the base of the east abutment, was broken from its fastenings, and several of the
stones wrenched apart." About a hundred yards farther on, he found a broken
suspender. "These were but small damages," he remarked, "but as we had never
before seen the bridge effected [*sic*] even to this extent by gales, and as it began
to sway violently, we thought it prudent to retrace our steps." He had been off the
bridge only a couple of minutes before the "whole structure of cables and flooring
[began] heaving and dashing with tremendous force." "For a few moments we
watched it with breathless anxiety, longing like a ship in a storm; at one time it
rose to nearly the height of the tower, then fell, and twisted and writhed, and was
dashed almost bottom upward. At last there seemed to be a determined twist
along the entire span, about one-half of the flooring being nearly reversed, and
down went the immense structure from its dizzy height to the stream below,
with an appalling crash and roar. Nearly the entire structure struck the water at
the same instant, dashing up an unbroken column of foam across the river, to the
height of at least forty feet," while a broken cable on the opposite shore "gyrated
around in almost every direction, and the huge thing is now coiled and twisted,
and looks much like a serpent grown stiff in the act of striking a mortal blow."[55]

The destruction was more or less total. All the cables except two on the north
side "were torn from the towers"; all the cables on the south side were "torn from
their anchorage"; "the entire wood work" ended up "in the river"; the tollhouse
was completely swept away; and the large iron gate at the end of the bridge "was
shivered to atoms." With little stiffness and no resistance to dynamic force, the
bridge had succumbed to huge torsional pressure and ripped itself apart. As John
later wrote, the Wheeling Bridge "was destroyed by the momentum acquired by
its own dead weight, when swayed up and down by the force of the wind," and

while weight is an essential element of resistance to gales, "it should not be left to itself to work its own destruction."[56] John's bridges were purposely designed to resist such forces, yet the incident sent him into a panic. As soon as he heard the news, John wrote to Swan for another two thousand feet of wire rope "*as soon as you possibly can.*" "I want this rope for Stays below the floor, and will need it in 2 weeks, when the floor will be up." A day later he was more certain and equally hurried. "The destruction of the Wheeling Bridge is a fact," he wrote Swan before again urging that he send rope as soon as possible. "You can use any bridge wire for this rope," he wrote, less concerned by size or gauge than by his ability to secure his bridge. Coincidentally, news of the hurricane in western Virginia arrived at the falls just as a "very severe squall" blew through the region, increasing John's concern. "I feared [it] would break down the old bridge," he wrote Swan, "but it stood the whirl well. I am anxious however to secure the new floor well by Stays."[57]

John was more confident a couple of weeks later but still cautious and in need of more rope. "I want a good deal more rope for Stays than I first ordered," he wrote Swan on June 8. Still, "my bridge is the admiration of every body, the directors are delighted."[58] He had also, it seems, heard from a couple of "competent eye witnesses" who described the destruction and helped corroborate John's impression of events. "Mr. Baldwin states that the floor surged in the center from 25 to 30 ft above its ordinary level, it tore into 3 sections, the eastern one of 500′, middle one 200, West 300." "Cause of destruction is *total want of stays or guys*," both above and below the floor, he determined. John also learned from Baldwin that "the gale was not strong enough to tear up the trees or houses," and that no other damage was done by the wind. The destruction, he concluded, "was therefore effected by a comparatively small force," a fact confirmed by the *Intelligencer*: "The storm did other damage in the city, but nothing of a serious character," they wrote a week after the storm.[59]

On July 13, John learned—with evident disappointment—that "the Wheeling Bridge is going up again, the same as before," which wasn't entirely accurate. Ellet arrived in Wheeling on May 21 at the board's request and began the process of rebuilding. The span was reopened for traffic on July 26 with a much narrower, one-way roadway, at a cost of seventeen thousand dollars. This lasted for another five years until the board of directors hired Captain William McComas to rebuild the roadway, restoring it to a two-lane highway. As part of this effort, the board paid for McComas to visit John's Niagara Bridge, while Washington visited Wheeling in 1860 to offer some informal advice. McCombs's rebuilt bridge was opened on July 28, 1860. The six garland cables on either side of the bridge had been consolidated into a single wrapped cable—as was John's practice—while the deck was stiffened with a wooden Howe truss and vertical iron rods, much like the Niagara Bridge. A set of inclined stays were added to the bridge in 1871, along a plan devised by Washington, furthering the process by which Ellet's bridge was slowly "Roeblingized." Further stays added in 1886 completed the process. These later additions have led many historians to claim, incorrectly, that John rather than Ellet rebuilt the Wheeling Bridge. In fact, John played no part whatsoever in the rebuilding. The fact that the Wheeling Bridge now looks like a Roebling bridge is not evidence that John rebuilt the bridge, especially when the minutes of the board of trustees tell a very different story. This is a part of the obfuscation of Ellet's contributions to the world of nineteenth-century engineering. Ellet's cables have been replaced and reconfigured, much as they have on almost every bridge of a similar age, including on John's, but the towers remain, beautiful monuments to the engineer's creativity and enduring influence.[60]

———

The events in Wheeling reverberated around the country, unleashing a new wave of doubt and suspicion. An anonymous article published in the Buffalo *Democracy* a week after Wheeling took aim at John's unfinished bridge and at suspended spans more generally. "Undulations produced and propagated in the chains and platforms of suspension bridges, are of the most serious consequences to these structures," the article began, and not so much in terms of the span's inherent structural integrity but in the structural material itself. "There is . . . an inherent and latent defect in Iron, that will forever make it an unreliable material for Bridge Structures, of the Suspension form," the author asserted. "When constantly subjected to concussion, tension, and vibration, the metal granulates. It loses in a greater or lesser degree, that peculiar relation and arrangement of its constituent particles, which gives to it the quality of tenacity." The article cited the Angers Bridge disaster, the collapse of the Broughton and Brighton Chain bridges, the broken rods on the Menai, and the recent wreckage at Wheeling— "completely blown down and flung a wreck into the water, bottom side upwards"—as evidence of trusting too fully in iron. If anything should happen to a bridge perched so far "above the greedy waters of the Niagara," they concluded, "not a man, woman, or child, would escape the horrible ruin."[61]

The *Niagara Falls Gazette* was incensed. The editors could not understand why the *Democracy* had "thrown the weight of its influence" against "one of the noblest and most interesting fields of modern engineering." Yes, many bridges fall down, the paper continued, suspended ones and otherwise, but many also stay up. To give up on suspension bridges is to give up on the idea of progress, they declared. Bridges that stay up—the Frybourg, the Hammersmith, the Menai, and the Chain Bridge at Budapest, which successfully carried "two retreating armies, consisting of infantry, cavalry and heavy military trains . . . during the late Hungarian struggle" of 1848—are proof that bridges are safe when "properly constructed." The fall of the Wheeling Bridge was "undoubtedly worthy of serious attention and study" but should not doom the fate of all suspension bridges. "From the particulars that have reached us"—via John presumably—the *Gazette* had no hesitation in blaming "the want of sufficient stays" for the disaster. Ellet clearly "relied too much on the weight of the suspended structure to resist the vertical as well as the lateral force of the wind." Had he added a fleet of stays "to check any considerable vibrating or undulating motion," most likely his bridge would have remained upright.[62]

Over the next several weeks, the *Democracy* and the *Gazette* fired claims and counterclaims across their editorial sections. The *Democracy* continued to assert that iron granulates under the stress of vibration, losing its "fibrous character" and becoming "crystallized," and that the consequences were potentially catastrophic. The *Gazette* remained incredulous. Iron does not suffer under use, it declared, but "only by *misuse* and violence."[63] If tension and vibration destroy iron, then how could all the iron bridges that are still standing be explained, the *Gazette* concluded. The naysayers all seem to forget that iron was used by every bridge builder in one form or another.[64]

The debate between the *Democracy* and the *Gazette* was part of a larger discussion about the sort of bridge John was trying to raise and about the innate nature of the materials he was using and how they would perform when called into constant use. After the Wheeling disaster, could one continue to rely on suspension bridges to solve the growing need to vault rivers and span long distances? More significantly, could iron—what John Locke called "the father of arts and author of plenty," the very foundation on which the global Industrial Revolution was built—be trusted to perform under pressure?[65] Could it reliably undergird and support a new era of expansion and development? Slowly, but with gaining momentum, iron was being called into action to support a new national and global economy, but also—in the form of trains, bridges, new buildings, railroad lines—the lives of millions of people. Was it up to the job? The fate of John's bridge would in some measure help answer that question.

———

John felt himself to be the master of at least two different branches of applied science: engineering and medicine. The destruction of the Wheeling Bridge tested his expertise in the first, ultimately validating and confirming his stature as an engineer of the first rank. A similar test soon arrived in the realm of public health, and the results showed John's abject failure as an effective physician, even while it affirmed his energy and humanity.

"Probably no locality in this country has ever suffered so severely [from] a most fatal visitation of Cholera [than] Suspension Bridge, near Niagara Falls," reported Stanford Hunt, a young doctor drafted up to John's shantytown in 1854 in an effort to contain the outbreak. "The disease was principally confined to the large foreign population engaged in the excavations and public works. It was characterized by a peculiar malignity. . . . Some sixty deaths occurred during the first week. The panic was indescribable." "Treatment, in the majority of cases, availed but little. . . . We frequently found men left alone, with a bucket of water by their side, to die uncared for. Aside from the neglect of patients induced by the panic, other effects were evident in the desperation, frantic fear, or cold apathy and fatalism, manifested by many." The Buffalo *Evening Post* was more pointed: "The seat of the epidemic was stated to be among the laborers at the Suspension Bridge, and the fatality was said to have been fearful."[66]

Dr. R. J. Rogers was the only physician working in the village of Suspension Bridge at the time, and he remained on duty from the outbreak to the close of the epidemic, "giving himself little or no rest day or night, until compelled to do so in consequence of his own illness." Tragically, Rogers's wife was the very last person to succumb to the disease there. According to Rogers, a group of German emigrants appeared in the village in early July, several of whom were diagnosed with cholera. One died quickly, while the others "were sent West." The same day, three laborers boarding at the Bellevue House came down with the disease, as did the innkeeper's mother, after which the contagion spread out from the hotel. In one of John's shanties on the Canadian side, an "Irish laborer was taken sick and died that afternoon. They had a wake that afternoon over the corpse (which means whisky), and, of those engaged in the wake, five died of cholera within twenty-four hours." By the twenty-fourth, the cases had become so numerous that it was impossible for Rogers to see them all, much less to give them any assistance. Word also spread to the village. Marcus Adams was certainly aware of the outbreak, noting on July 15, "Sickness here and at the Falls is creating somesome alarm,"," and, two days later: "Cholera is no doubt among us. Eight deaths as the Falls yesterday." By July 20 he was reporting that "the tenements where the cholera had broken out [had been examined] and the amount of filth found was astounding." The following day, "the Bridge tender was at his post in the morning, but at 10 p.m. was dead," an event that confirmed everyone's worst fears. By the twenty-fourth the people of the village and the surrounding area had "become panic-stricken," and many fled, "thus leaving fewer victims for the disease to feed upon." With so many workers ill, all work on John's bridge was suspended, even after John raised the daily wage to three to four dollars a day, twice the normal rate. But no able-bodied men were willing to take the risk.[67]

Cholera in the nineteenth century was an especially fearsome disease. No one knew how it worked, how it spread, or how it was cured, but they did know it could fell a full-grown healthy adult in a matter of hours and was excruciating to watch. Contemporary observers reported an unreal "pinched blue or purple pallor; eyes sunk, lips dark blue; the nails were livid"; skin was drawn, leaden, and puckered, "losing its contractility, the pulse deserting the wrist, the tongue becoming cold, and the voice husky"; and the "hands shriveled, called washer-women's hands." Accompanying the physical deterioration was the expulsion of vast quantities of colorless and scentless water though the bowels, containing only tiny white particles, what doctors at the time called "rice-water stool," along with profuse sweating, cramps, vomiting, and a crushing thirst.[68] The disease occasioned neither fever nor delirium, and thus no respite from the awful, acute consciousness. "While the mechanism of life is thus suddenly arrested, the body [is] reduced to a damp, dead, clay-cold mass," reported the *London Medical Gazette* in 1849, "the mind within remains untouched and clear—shining strangely through the glazed eyes, with light unquenched and vivid—a spirit looking out in terror from a corpse."[69]

"It was almost impossible to get at the number attacked," Rogers reported, "but it has been ascertained that there were at least eighty deaths on the two sides of the river; and, when we consider the proportion which this number bears to the actual population at that time, this result is appalling. . . . The actual population was decimated by the disease in about ten days." "Fully one half [of the victims] were employed in the construction of the bridge—wiremen, blacksmiths, and carpenters." "Three bridge tenders are dead and many men working on the new bridge dead," reported Adams. "Watson, principal foreman on the bridge, a Scotchman of much experience in this business, died this pm." With no known cure, the local authorities decided on a scorched-earth policy following some initial attempts at contact. In late July, two bodies in an advanced state of decomposition were discovered in one of the shanties near the bridge, where they had lain for some days. "So strong was the effluvia arising from the corpses, that it was deemed hazardous to go near the building." Fifty dollars was offered to two local men if they would go into the house and place the bodies in coffins for interment. They tried but were "deterred by the foulness of the air" and gave up. Some other men were contracted at a hefty wage to remove bodies from the shanties or to clean away the filth around the shacks—filth, along with sinfulness and poverty, was long held to contribute to diseases of all stripes—but they were never paid, because none survived. After this failure, officials took to burning any shack or shanty containing a dead body. Within days the disease was arrested, and by August 2 work was resumed on John's bridge, at signifi-cantly increased labor costs. "The [cholera] visitation was remarkable for the suddenness of its appearance, its short duration, the number of cases, and its terrible fatality," concluded Rogers.[70]

Trading ships moved cholera around the world, and it likely came to Suspension Bridge with the nameless "Germans" via the St. Lawrence River. Cholera first appeared in North America in 1832, and it came through the port city of Montreal before quickly spreading south. Such conditions, along with its subsequent identification with the crowded tenements of New York City, helped forge a link between cholera and immigration—between disease and a culture of poverty, crime, sin, and filth. As John Pintard, a prominent merchant, banker, and the founder of the New-York Historical Society, clearly believed, cholera was "almost exclusively confined to the lower classes of intemperate dissolute & filthy people huddled together like swine in their polluted habitations. . . . Chiefly of the very scum of the city." Pintard was right that the disease was chiefly limited to the lower classes, not because of their supposed habits but because of the conditions in which they were forced to live.[71]

Cholera—or more precisely *Vibrio cholerae*—is a bacteria, and to flourish it needs to be swallowed. It can't be transmitted through the air or through any bodily fluids except diarrhea. "Drop it into a setting where excrement eating is a common practice," writes Steven Johnson, "and cholera will thrive—hijacking intestine after intestine to manufacture more bacteria." It is the perfect disease for cramped quarters and unsanitary conditions, exactly like those found in the worst urban tenements or the most congested work camps, especially those like John's where "water stood in pools around the shanties that were huddled pretty close together on the low ground," helping to intermingle waste and drinking water. Once ingested, the bacteria make their way to the small intestine, where they thrive. *Vibrio cholerae* pathogens attack in two ways: they reproduce at an astonishing rate, forming a thick, multilayered "mat" that coats the intestine, and at the same time they produce a toxin that disrupts the intestine's ability to regulate water balance, one of its primary functions. Normal, healthy intestines absorb more water than they secrete. The cholera toxin reverses this process, however, forcing the intestines to expel water at a prodigious and alarming rate—eventually leading to massive dehydration and eventually organ failure—which is the reason a victim's diarrhea is clear and odorless. It is not actually waste but just water, mixed with damaged and ejected lower intestinal cells (the rice in the rice-water), along with millions of *Vibrio cholera* bacteria. The disease effectively converts the body into a machine for making and then expelling itself, to be reingested by a new host, where the process starts all over again. If the *Vibrio cholerae* bacteria have nowhere to go, they die, as does the wider outbreak, which is where a scorched-earth policy becomes effective, especially in the absence of any known cure or preventative.[72]

The solution to the conundrum of cholera was just a few months away when it struck John's camps at Suspension Bridge. In September 1854, physician John Snow would establish a connection between cholera, waste, and drinking water during the Broad Street cholera outbreak in London. Up at Suspension Bridge, however, there was just guessing even among the experts brought in to help. Hunt thought the most significant factors were the "epidemic constitution of the air," "high heat and humidity," and "soil poison." "The intelligent correlation of these three factors will control any of the great and sweeping epidemics and largely control the strictly contagious disorders," he declared, an opinion his colleague Frank Hamilton shared.[73] Rogers was less certain—"We know better than our predecessors what the cholera is not, but we do not know what it is"— but thought, like most, that the disease was airborne. By 1854, the debate over cholera, both in Europe and in America, was split between contagionists and miasmatists, with the latter very much in the ascendancy, especially in urban areas defined by their stench. As the British social reformer and public health advocate Edwin Chadwin famously declared, "All smell is disease."[74]

Some of the local newspapers simply denied that cholera existed at the falls. Others reflected the dominant belief that the disease only affected the "destitute and reckless class," and that sober and honest citizens had little to fear. "Rational people will remember that temperance, equanimity, employment, without over-fatigue and exposure, preservation of the functions of the skin by copious use of water and pure air, are necessary to avert the first approach of the disease," wrote one paper. Others were keen to prescribe treatments and cures. On July 26, the *Niagara Mail* printed a "recipe for cholera" sent in by a helpful reader: one ounce of cloves, one ounce of cinnamon, one ounce of ginger root, one ounce of nutmeg, and half an ounce of cayenne pepper "mixed into a pint of the best Brandy, left to sit for three days and shaken often," which sounds more like a holiday cocktail than a medical cure. The *Gazette* prescribed 18 grains of "sugar of lead," 24 grains of pulverized camphor, 6 grains of pulverized opium, and 10 grains of cayenne pepper. John, of course, prescribed water.[75]

As reported by Rogers, "Swathing the patients in wet sheets was thought at first to be beneficial, for it removed the dark leaden color of the skin al-most immediately and restored the natural color, the absorption of the water compensating, in a measure, for the loss of the serum of the blood; but in the end it all seemed 'vanity of vanities'" and very likely contributed to the spread of the disease. "Homeopathy and hydrotherapy were alike tried by one or an-other of the sufferers, and they alike failed," he continued; "the latter form of treatment was tried most thoroughly by Mr. John A. Roebling, the distinguished engineer. He was a great admirer and personal friend of Priessnitz, and, fully believing in his theory, on the morning of that very fatal day, he improvised a hospital and had eight patients subjected to that form of treatment, but they *all* died before night."[76] John was a little prouder of his achievements, even if the results were more or less the same. "I have saved 2 by *water treatment*, all the rest are in the grave," he wrote Swan soon after the outbreak. "The Doctors had bad luck. Watson is dead, died from sheer exhaustion, the medicine had so far undermined his digestive functions, that he could no longer support life. Under the water treatment, as I recommended it to Mrs. Roebling, the patient soon gets hungry and eats, Keep off *fear*—this is the great secret. Whoever is afraid of Cholera, will be attacked, and no treatment can save him," he concluded, in the process shifting the blame from treatment to the patient. Washington's judgment was a little less kind: "My father had a touch of it also, but cured himself by what would be called 'Christian Science' at the present day—pacing the floor all night & muttering to himself—I have it not! I have it not!" As John advised Swan: "Should the Cholera appear at Trenton, keep up your courage, and do not fear, but be determined, that the disease should not attack you. Best not to think of it at all. I recommend you to wear a compress upon the Abdomen, and to take a short sitsbath every day. If your bowels get loose at all, go at once to work and apply cold cloth upon the abdomen & upon the spine."[77]

Ironically, the cure for cholera is water, albeit huge amounts of it. John douched and wrapped his patients and warned against psychological intimidation when he ought to have just hydrated them and kept them that way.[78] John did not run from the deadly outbreak, as many did, but set up a makeshift ward and tried to cure his workers. He seems to have thought nothing of his own safety. He may well have thought he had all the answers, but he also felt responsible for his workers. John's local Trenton paper reported much later that, during the outbreak, "Mr. Roebling had an idea he could cure cholera by a modification of the hydropathic treatment," wrote the anonymous author. "There was plenty of patients and he began in the morning with a little child, and before night had five cases in one shanty. At midnight they were all dead, and Mr. Roebling disconsolately abandoned the practice of medicine, though he was about as successful as any of the doctors. Everybody who was smitten on that sultry Saturday died. There was nothing strange in the affair, except the heroism of the man in his desire to alleviate human misery. The further history of that shanty is really remarkable. Mr. Roebling cheerfully assumed the expense of the interment, but there was a particular horror of that place, and in the panic that prevailed, he could induce no person to approach it. He then offered $50 to anyone who would throw the bodies off the bridge into the Niagara. No one would do it. His next move was to inform the authorities that if on Monday morning the bodies were still there he would set fire to the shanty and dispose of his unwelcome charge by cremation. The threat was of no avail, and he kept his word. But a hemlock shanty furnishes little fuel and the bodies were only scorched and this funeral was still upon his hands. He finally paid two bravadoes from Lockport to bury them where they lay. They were howling drunk and full of blasphemica. Both went back to Lockport and died the next night. That closed the tragedy. With all his talents, Mr. Roebling as a doctor or undertaker was not a success."[79]

———

John began the work of suspending the upper floor at the end of August, before moving on to what Washington called the "*experimentum crucis*," uniting the two floors and setting the two cables in position. In an effort to "make due allowance for the lower cables which had already been stretched and force the upper cables down to their ultimate place," John loaded "the upper floors with 400 tons of stones, thus stretching the upper cables artificially," a plan that "succeeded admirably." The two sets of cables—each composed of 3,640 wires—were hung on an incline, the upper cables much more so to equalize the length across all four cables. "The appearance of the cables is not only pleasing, but their massive proportions are also well calculated to inspire confidence in their strength," John stated, an impression echoed by a correspondent for the *Salem Observer*: "I walked down to the Suspension Bridge, and every time I look at it the more it magnifies my ideas of mechanical genius. New ropes of wire are drawn across the abutments to sustain a railroad bridge which is now nearly completed. . . . A train of cars passing midway between earth and sky, with everything above and below visible, I fancy will be rather an electrifying sight, both for the looker on, and for actor in this terrestrial balloon." John even wound some of Ellet's wires into the cables, having found them "about the same quality as that in the new cables . . . its strength and toughness scarcely impaired."[80]

John's cables were finished by the end of the year, and they were quickly tested by a "tremendous gale" in late January. "The wind blew so strong that wagons were blown from one side of the [bridge's] carriage way to the other," wrote the *Niagara Falls Gazette*, and they were only "kept on the bridge by the [span's] side timbers." Eventually, John closed the bridge for fear of its customers tumbling off the span. Despite the tempest, the bridge held firm. "The motion, if any, was so slight as to be unnoticed," reported the *Gazette*. John himself thought his bridge was "remarkably sturdy." There was "very little motion in the center" and "scarcely any motion perceptible" elsewhere, owing to the service of the stays and the iron floor girders, he believed.[81]

Washington Roebling thought that "Niagara [was] a melancholy place. The constant roar of the rapids produces a numbing of the finer sensibilities—a sort of daze which draws one thither and yet you feel you want to get away from it." Others disagreed. Marcus Adams was entranced and amazed by the place, especially by its growth and burgeoning potential. He had set up home in a lonely field and found himself, just a couple of years later, in a small thriving village. "I never before realized what a place we are, until having a full view of all the bustle and noise which prevail here. It was with amazement that I witnessed the cars, carriages, men rushing in all directions." As would prove the case nationwide over the next fifty years, development followed in the wake of railroad tracks. The failure of the Great Western to raise sufficient funds to commence its extension plans had clearly played a silent but nonetheless vital role in the Ellet debacle, leaving the poor engineer in charge of building a railroad bridge with no sign of a railroad or any railroad money. But with the securing of significant American investment in 1851 the project was again up and running, as was the need for a railroad bridge across the Niagara. Work on the Great Western Railway extension, from Hamilton to Suspension Bridge, was finally begun in 1852, eventually employing over 7,600 men. The first train passed through the Niagara Peninsula in November 1853, eventually arriving at the Canadian bridgehead on November 11 to great crowds and wild cheering. The *St. Catherine's Journal* noted "with astonishment as well as pleasure, that the Iron Horse was seen passing along in all the dignity of steam." Once at the bridge, the passengers had no option but to take a carriage across, but the upper floor was pieced together and the tracks laid out as the day of the bridge's first crossing drew closer. With no industry-standard gauge, the bridge eventually housed three different tracks. The upper floor was leased in perpetuity to the Great Western Railroad at a yearly rate of $45,000—it was also used by the New York Central and the Elmira, Canandaigua, and Niagara Falls Railroad—which added to over $20,000 in toll receipts and accounting for labor costs of only about $5,000 per year, left a healthy and handsome yearly profit of $60,000. It was not bad income from a $400,000 investment, especially for John, who took stock in the venture and was also given twenty additional shares "as a complimentary act" of gratitude once his bridge was completed.[82]

———

On March 7, the *Gazette* predicted the bridge would be finished by April and open by May.[83] The following day, however, a twenty-three-ton locomotive called *London* lumbered across the bridge "at a moderate speed" producing little or no vibration—"less trembling than under the effects of some heavy teams on the lower floor," wrote John in a notebook—and causing "a slight depression of the superstructure, which, in the centre, measured 3½ inches," or "no more than a fly on a clothes' line," according to Adams. The first crossing was a structural stress test organized by John, and "extraordinary efforts" were made to keep the event secret. This was impossible in such a small world and with so many people involved, and by three o'clock, as reported by Adams, "the whole engine and tender was covered with men" as it chugged into position.[84] "Amid the cheering of the multitude," and with John, along with nine invited friends, the train made its way slowly to

> the center of the bridge, where it was stopped, and three times three cheers were given for John A. Roebling, who stood canopied by the stars and stripes, and the royal cross of St. George. Then with a deafening whistle . . . that reverberated through the rifted chasms and along the boiling waters of the Niagara below, and booming up into the azure heaven, the *London* moved over to the American side. . . . On returning to the Canada side and making another trip, every fear seemed to have left even the most timid, and both engine and tender seemed to be a struggling mass of human beings each clinging in the excitement, wherever they could get a foot-hold.[85]

"This day will long be remembered by the people of this village," wrote Adams. The *Niagara Mail* crowed that John had "reared a monument of the greatness of his mind, which will be lasting," while the Buffalo *Republic* cheered the "annexation of the British Provinces to the United States, by rail."[86] For the

Figure 15.5 "The passage of trains is a great sight." William England, "A locomotive crossing the Railway Suspension Bridge over the Niagara River" (1859). Getty Images. William England/Stringer.

Western New-Yorker, "nowhere upon the western continent is there a work of anything like the importance and magnitude which this possesses." "Omnipresent and omnipotent steam has at last laid its hand on the fierce waters of the Niagara River and conquered them," they continued. Once the *London's* whistle "rolled and echoed and clattered back and forth among the astonished cliffs [and] the splendid engine moved towards the American side . . . tumultuously greeted with rapturous huzzas such as only Yankees can give . . . the success of this once doubtful enterprise [was] rendered certain," they affirmed. The first day and the first tests had gone well, but John knew that heavier, more robust freights would need to be carried for the bridge to be regarded as a complete success.[87]

John repeated his experiment the following day, this time with a much more laden train. The *Pluto*—one of the largest in Canada—weighed thirty-four tons, traveled at eight miles per hour, and pulled a "well-filled" passenger car. Again there were "no vibrations whatsoever." In fact, several men on the carriageway remarked that had they not been looking, "they could not have told when the train passed." "Strange as it may appear," John added, "a number of loaded [wagon] teams produce more motion than results from the transit of a train. But for the rumbling noise over head, such transit would not be noticed by persons on the lower floor." As for deflection, the depression in the center of the span was a mere 5½ inches, which John took as full confirmation. "The success of the work may be considered as established," he concluded, and everyone agreed. Train conductors threw their hats in the river; a band played "God Save the Queen," "Hail Columbia," and "Yankee Doodle"; spectators cheered; and newspapers celebrated.[88] "The opening of this mighty and magnificent structure—well worthy of being classed with the world's wonders—really forms an epoch in the history of the world," wrote the editor of the *Rochester Daily Democrat,* who had taken the inaugural voyage. "This is indeed a great triumph of genius. Anyone who ever looked down into the fearful gorge which it spans must consider it one of the mechanical wonders of the world, and as reflecting the highest credit upon American enterprise and skill," wrote the *Salem Observer,* whereas the *Niagara Falls Gazette* took aim at those who had tried to cast doubt on John's plans. "Cavilers, editorial or others, stand confronted with the triumph of this great work," they editorialized. "A wire suspension bridge for railway purposes is no longer a theoretical matter, it is an established fact." John's victory over the Niagara Gorge was so complete, reported the *Gazette,* that "Mr. Roebling is himself disappointed that his success is so perfect."[89]

Much was also made of the man at work on his second tubular bridge at Montreal. "The predication, by that justly celebrated engineer Stephenson, that no wire suspension bridge could ever be used for railway purposes has . . . been proved erroneous," wrote the Buffalo *Express.* "He must have looked with a jealous eye from his own favorite Tubular Bridge upon this great design, and

Figure 15.6 William England, "The top-tier of the Railway Suspension Bridge over the Niagara River, built in 1855 by John A Roebling to carry the Grand Trunk Railway between Canada and New York State, USA" (1859). Getty Images. William England/ Stringer.

allowed his professional prejudices to warp his excellent judgment," they speculated. Others joined in. "Thus has been accomplished what was supposed by the great Engineer of the day, Mr. Stevenson [*sic*], to have been impossible," wrote the *Hamilton Gazette*, while the *St. Catherine's Journal* thought John deserved "the plaudits of the world for having brought to successful completion an undertaking supposed to have been impossible by those whom the world pronounced competent judges." According to the *Atlantic Monthly*, "If America does not show a Thames Tunnel, a Conway or Menai Tubular Bridge, or a monster steamer, [still] she has a railroad bridge of 800 feet clear span, hung two hundred and fifty feet above one of the wildest Rivers in the World."[90]

Stephenson's failure of judgment was as much a theme of the opening reports as John's triumph. "The idea of a perfectly rigid structure, such as a tubular bridge," was a misguided and expensive chimera as far as John was concerned. While his bridge had cost "less than $400,000 . . . the same object accomplished in Europe would have cost 4 millions without serving a better purpose, or insuring greater safety," by which he meant if it were built as a tubular bridge. "We can only obtain a *comparative* degree of rigidity in *any* kind of structure," he continued, "no matter whether it is a stone or cast-iron arch, iron or wooden truss, or a hollow wrought-iron beam." "The Conway tube of 400 feet span"—Stephenson's other Menai bridge—for example "deflects 3 inches under a weight of 300 tons, placed in the center," leaving John to wonder, "How much would a tube of 800 feet span deflect under the same load, provided such a tube had the requisite depth and strength?" No less than nine inches, he decided, which compared very well with his bridge, "calculated to deflect ten inches under a weight of 326 tons." "To construct a Suspension Bridge which shall not sink under heavy loads, or by an increase of temperature, cannot be done," John declared, and neither could it with a tubular beam bridge either. The ultimate equation, as John understood it, was simple: different forces produced almost the exact same results, yet for wildly differing costs. This led him naturally to conclude that "in a country where the Engineer's task is to make the most out of the least, the Suspension principle will henceforth take the lead of the tubular, in all ordinary localities. For extraordinarily long spans the tube cannot compete on any terms."[91]

Stephenson was a little more generous when forced to confront the controversy. He remained skeptical of John's plan during its construction, remarking that while "great skill has been shown" in tempering the "tendency to flexibility," such a span would prove "more expensive to maintain, and far inferior in efficiency and safety."[92] He was more appreciative and enthusiastic after visiting John's newly opened bridge. "You are aware, that during my last visit to Canada, I examined this remarkable work, and made myself acquainted with its general details," he wrote the directors of Canada's Grand Trunk Railway. "Since then Mr. Roebling has kindly forwarded to me a copy of his last Report . . . in which all the important facts connected with the structure, as well as the results which have been produced, since its opening for the passage of railway trains, are carefully and clearly set forth." "No one can study the statements contained in that Report without admiring the great skill which has been displayed throughout the design: neither can anyone who has seen the locality fail to appreciate the fitness of the structure for the singular combination of difficulties which are presented," Stephenson continued politely, especially given the criticism his ideas had received in John's report.[93]

Stephenson also sent Alexander Ross—the Grand Trunk's top engineer—to visit John's bridge, after which the two conferred, coming to very similar conclusions: first, that John's span was a fitting and appropriate structure for the place and use for which it was intended, and second, that a bridge constructed along such principles would prove wholly inadequate to serve the Grand Trunk's purposes at Montreal. "Mr. Roebling has succeeded in accomplishing all he had undertaken," wrote Ross, by which he meant "safely to pass over railway trains at a speed not exceeding five miles an hour." If such speeds were maintained over the St. Lawrence, it would take a train three-quarters of an hour to cross, and "allowing reasonable time for trains clearing and getting well out of each other's way" would mean the bridge could serve no more than twenty trains in any twenty-four-hour period. This seemed wildly inefficient to both Ross and Stephenson. The existing demand alone "require[d] four or five times this accommodation."[94]

Stephenson was never going to admit to having made a costly error over the Menai, but he was happy to reserve some praise for John. "I beg that this observation may not be considered as being made in the tone of disparagement," wrote Stephenson; "no one appreciates more than I do the skill and science displayed by Mr. Roebling in overcoming the striking engineering difficulties by which he was surrounded." His only objection lay in that "unavoidable defect in the suspension principle," its failure to achieve sufficient rigidity, which would severely retard speed. Thankfully, the Victoria Bridge's comparatively small spans solved the problem for them. Not needing to span the large distances John was confronted with at Niagara, Stephenson was able to design a massive 6,512-foot-long, twenty-four-span tubular bridge across the St. Lawrence. Stephenson was fully invested in his tubular design, but he also made a somewhat reasonable engineering decision. He prioritized speed over cost, building a significantly more expensive bridge so as to allow for faster passage. The problem of pace versus price would have led to a very different set of decisions several years later with the advent of steel truss bridges, but those options were as yet unavailable, leaving the Grand Trunk few palatable options, despite securing the services of such an accomplished railroad engineer. Stephenson's bridge cost £1,500,000 (the equivalent to about $6,600,000 at the time), the interest on which proved crippling for the Grand Trunk for many years.[95]

———

John continued to conduct almost constant tests through March and April, recording every single shift, strain, and movement. By March 18, he was ready to remove the restrictions and declare his bridge open for the regular passage of trains. The first train across "was the heaviest freight train that will ever pass, and was made up on purpose to test the bridge," John reported to Swan back in Trenton. "With an engine of 28 tons we pushed over from Canada to New York 20 double cars each loaded with 10 tons, cars weighing 7 tons, making a gross weight of 386 tons." The train "very nearly covered the whole length of the floor between the towers" and was "literally covered with passengers among them a great number of ladies," not only on the inside, but on the platform and on the top. Midway across the train stopped "to let an artist take a daguerreotype impression," which was soon endorsed by John and on sale in the pages of the *Rochester Daily Democrat*.[96]

John spent part of the day "sitting upon a saddle on top of one of the towers" of his bridge studying his work and no doubt gazing out at the sublime surroundings. "During the passage of a train, moving at the rate of 5 miles an hour," John felt less vibration up on his massive Egyptian obelisk than he did in his "brick dwelling at Trenton, NJ, during the rapid transit of an Express Train over the New Jersey RR, which passes my door within a distance of 200 feet." He noticed that the saddle rollers moved about half an inch forward with the passing of each heavy train but that "everything returned to its place, after the Br. was relieved." Equally, owing to a slight incline at the New York terminus, some trains needed an assistant engine or two to get over the bridge. Still, twenty trains passed over in the first twenty-four hours, increasing to thirty trains by March 23, making a mockery of Ross and Stephenson's predictions. "No one is afraid to cross," John wrote Swan; "the passage of trains is a great sight, worth seeing it. Please communicate the above to Mrs. R. this will save me writing to her."[97]

On May 1, he submitted his final report to the board of trustees, a document filled with pride, elation, and no small amount of self-congratulation. Thanks to John's efforts and innovations "the great rivers of this continent will no longer offer an insurmountable obstruction to the formation of uninterrupted lines of Railways," he began, while "at the completion of the first road to the Pacific we shall possess continuous lines of Rail of over 3000 miles extent, over which, if desirable, cars loaded with treasure at San Francisco, may be passed to New York without breaking bulk." Two-thousand-foot-long suspended railway bridges "that would admit the passage of trains at the highest speed" would soon be with us, he predicted. John finished with gracious thanks to the board of trustees, who had accorded him a level of freedom and trust they had not offered Ellet. "In reporting to you the final and successful completion of the Bridge, I would be doing injustice to my own feelings as a man, if I did not avail myself of this opportunity, to thank you publicly for the unwavering confidence, which you have always placed in my professional ability. When Engineers of acknowledged talent and reputation freely expressed their doubts as to the success of this work, a wavering of confidence on your part would have been but natural. But I am happy to state here, that in all my operations I have always met with a cordial support [and] mutual confidence."⁹⁸

John stayed at the falls for another few weeks, doing odd jobs, monitoring how his bridge stood up to a tornado that did "great damage" to homes and trees in Niagara but "did not produce the slightest motion in either floor," and finding himself embroiled in a failed attempt to sound the Niagara River from his bridge. Having thrown a forty-pound weight attached to a "strong wire" off his bridge, John watched it fall 225 feet to the river below, but it resurfaced "a second later" a hundred feet downstream and proceeded to "skip along like a chip until it was checked by the wire." At this point John started to slowly haul the weight back, "which made the iron bounce like a ball" before "a cake of ice struck it and ended the sport." "I am satisfied that *no metal* has sufficient specific gravity to pierce that current—even with the momentum acquired by a fall of 225 feet," he concluded. But as May ended, John was itching to move on to a new venture, one that would take him west to the Great Plains, not home. "My personal intention is to leave for Iowa next Saturday morning or evening," John wrote Swan in mid-June; "address me at Iowa City, Iowa, Care of A. G. Gower & Bro."⁹⁹

———

John's bridge was a triumph. Travel writer John Disturnell called it "the grandest and the most distinguishing achievement of Art in this world." Novelist and post office surveyor Anthony Trollope thought the bridge "of marvelous construction." Others believed John's bridge—"stretching over the fearful chasm, and apparently suspended by gossamer threads, whose graceful curves describe lines of true sublimity"—was "the last great triumph of human genius and engineering skill . . . its grace and beauty lost in its great utility." The *New York Daily Tribune* thought John's span—"giddy and exciting [but] with feelings of perfect security"—was "worth a journey across the wide continent." Even Prince Albert, eldest son of Queen Victoria, took a jaunt up to the falls to see "the beautiful suspension-bridge, like a web of iron, thin and delicate as a net."¹⁰⁰

All who came were impressed, except Mark Twain. When "you drive over to Suspension Bridge, [you] divide your misery between the chances of smashing down two hundred feet into the river below, and the chances of having the railway-train overhead smashing down onto you," he grumbled. "Either possibility is discomforting taken by itself, but, mixed together, they amount in the aggregate to positive unhappiness," he concluded. Twain was in the minority, and the bridge quickly established itself as an icon to rival even the falls themselves. "Niagara is a handsome thing," a guest at the Monteagle House told Charles Mackay, "but what is it to the bridge? The bridge! Why, I hold *that* to be the finest thing in God's universe!" Charles Woodman spoke for many when he wrote that the bridge was a symbol of progress, reflecting America's profound love of technology: "Every locomotive that thunders over the Suspension bridge, rushing through space, over the seething torrent, bids us to beware of imitating the examples of those who, by utter disbelief, expressed by contemptuous sneers, have attempted to stop the world's progress and arrest the onward march of civilization."[101]

For others, the bridge added to the transcendent appeal of the falls, placing the natural and the technological in symmetry and balance, just as John had hoped and predicted. The bridge was "one of the few structures that not only harmonizes with the grand scenery of the vicinity, but even augments its impressiveness," wrote local historian George Holley, affirming John's vision. For Walt Whitman, the beauty and grandeur of the falls was echoed by the view from the bridge. Several years later Henry James was struck by how "this obstructive bridge tends in a way to enhance the first glimpse of the cataract. Its long black

Figure 15.7 The lower deck of the Niagara Bridge, designed as a "hollow, straight beam" to improve rigidity and stiffness. William England, "Foot passengers inside the Niagara suspension bridge, connecting Canada and the USA over the Niagara River" (1859). Getty Images. William England/Stringer.

span, falling dead along the shining brow of the Falls, seems shivered and smitten by their fierce effulgence, and trembles across the field of vision like some enormous mote in a light too brilliant."[102]

Images of the bridge that proliferated after the span's opening were often less interested in showing a harmonious relationship with the landscape than with presenting "a great monument dominating the scene, its own grandeur outstripping that of Niagara," as Elizabeth McKinsey describes it. Such images as the anonymous *The Railroad Suspension Bridge near Niagara Falls* (1856), Currier and Ives's *The Railroad Suspension Bridge* (1857), or any of Joachim Richardt's sketches (1856) or William England's photographs of the bridge (1859) all depict the spectacle from a similar angle, slightly below the bridge, looking up at the massive structure, and with the falls themselves behind the span.[103] Thanks to the foregrounding and perspective, the bridge appears the more lasting and permanent of the two icons; the falls are in the distance, faint and seemingly inconsequential when juxtaposed with the bridge. In these images, the more important feature is hardly in doubt.

Perhaps the most elaborate, evocative, and loving tribute came from the pen of William Dean Howells, the "Dean of American Letters":

> Of all the bridges made with hands it seems the lightest, most ethereal; it is ideally graceful, and droops from its slight towers like a garland. It is worthy to command, as it does, the whole grandeur of Niagara, and to show the traveller the vast spectacle from the beginning of the American Fall to the farthest limit of the Horse-Shoe, with all the awful pomp of the rapids, the solemn darkness of the wooded islands, the mystery of the vaporous gulf, the indomitable wildness of the shores, as far as the eye can reach up or down the fatal stream. . . . The exquisite structure, which sways so tremulously from its towers, and seems to lay so slight a hold on earth where its cables sink into the ground, is to other bridges what the blood horse is to the common breed of roadsters. . . . The thrill was a glorious one, to be known only there.[104]

The bridge proved important to a whole host of people. It was the perfect platform on which to watch the myriad high-wire walkers who were drawn to the falls over the next thirty years, from Blondin—who walked over on stilts, in a sack, blindfolded, and once carrying his manager on his back—in 1859 to Signorina Maria Spelterini, in 1876, the first woman to walk over from the United States to Canada. "Twenty-three years of age, with dark Italian features, superbly built," Spelterini made the crossing "attired in flesh-coloured tights, a tunic of scarlet, a seagreen bodice, and neat green buskins." Additionally, she made the trip blindfolded, then shackled at the ankles and wrists, and finally with big clumsy peach baskets on each of her feet.[105] But above all, John's bridge was important to America's massive enlaved population.[106]

As one of the primary eastern links with the Canadian border, the Niagara Peninsula looms large in the history of American abolitionism. An active stop on the Underground Railroad had long existed at the falls. In the words of the anonymous poem "A Fugitive Slave's Apostrophe to Niagara" (1841), "Over thy rugged brow / Changeless and bright, the bow of promise bends" from "where BASTARD FREEDOM broods her mongrel horde." With the opening of John's bridge, the strenuous work of crossing the raging Niagara River was reduced to a simple walk or a brief train ride. No wonder that slave catchers often stood guard at the bridge's American entrance or that Frederick Douglass funneled countless "colored chattels" onto the Rochester mail train bound for the Suspension Bridge.[107] Black activist William Still documented dozens of examples of enslaved men and women escaping to "freadums shore" in Canada, much as Albert Metter described his own journey over the "railway Suspension Bridge" in May 1855.[108] In his autobiography, noted ex-slave and abolitionist Samuel Ringgold Ward tells a dramatic story of a fugitive slave who arrived at Niagara pursued by his master.

> In an instant, he ran—almost flew—from the margin of the river, to gain the suspension bridge close at hand, and cross it. His master pursued. On he flew: he gained the bridge; so did his master. He ran for life, and liberty—the master ran for property: the former had freedom to win, the latter feared the loss of chattel. . . . The keeper of the toll-gate encouraged the Negro, who, though breathless, redoubled his energies . . . until he reached the Canadian end of the bridge—when he suddenly stopped, his haste being over, the goal having been reached, the prize won. He looked his former master, who had just "arrived in time to be too late," calmly in the eye, with a smile of satisfaction and triumph overspreading his features. The two were equals: both were free. The former slave knew it right well.

Such stories, it seems, were legion.[109]

John's bridge is most closely identified with Harriet Tubman, the region's most famous abolitionist. Tubman escaped from slavery in 1849 and by 1851 was active in the St. Catherine's branch of the Underground Railroad, about ten miles from the Niagara Whirlpool. St. Catherine's remained her base of operations until about 1857 or '59, during which time she helped usher dozens of escaped slaves over the bridge and into Canada and helped inspire a popular song: "I'm now embarked for yonder shore, / There a man's a man by law; / The iron horse will bear me o'er, / To shake de lion's [England's] paw." In 1897,

Tubman told Harvard researcher Wilber Siebert that she herself had crossed into Canada at "the Suspension Bridge" thanks to the effort of "the fugitive slave, Frederick Douglass," and letters reveal that her associates were accustomed to "forward all [fugitive slaves] directly to the Bridge" to await her aid. There also exists some evidence that Tubman brought her own parents into Canada over John's bridge.[110]

Sarah Bradford recounts a number of stories she heard from Tubman about John's bridge during their dozens of interviews. One, involving a young man named Joe, shows Tubman at her caring and inspiring best:

> They passed along in safety, and at length found themselves in the cars, approaching Suspension Bridge. The rest were very joyous and happy, but Joe sat silent and sad. . . . The cars began to cross the bridge. Harriet was very anxious to have her companions see the Falls. William, Peter, and Eliza came eagerly to look at the wonderful sight; but Joe sat still, with his head upon his hand. "Joe, one look at de Falls! Joe, you fool you, come see de Falls! It's your last chance." But Joe sat still and never raised his head. At length Harriet knew by the rise in the center of the bridge, and the descent on the other side that they had crossed "the line." She sprang across to Joe's seat, shook him with all her might, and shouted, "Joe, you've shook de lion's paw!" Joe did not know what she meant. "Joe, you're free!" shouted Harriet. Then Joe's head went up, he raised his hands on high, and his face, streaming with tears. . . . "Joe, come and look at de Falls!" called Harriet. "Glory to God and Jesus too, One more soul got safe." was all the answer.[111]

Tubman left the region just prior to the outbreak of the American Civil War, after which Niagara became a center for Confederate intrigue and activity and the topic of countless fraught rumors relating to Britain's relationship to the United States. At a board of directors meeting on December 21, 1861, the question was asked what would become of the bridge if the two countries went to war. It was the board's unanimous and rather startling opinion "that it would be considered a military necessity to destroy the Bridge in order to prevent the passage over it of troops, and munitions of war etc." Alternatively, it was discussed whether—"to save the bridge from total destruction"—"it might be best for us to render it impassable by taking up a portion of the Bridge between the towers, and laying it away until peace should be restored." John was asked whether he would superintend the work, although any answer has so far been lost to history. But a gun—loaded with three ounces of powder and two and a half pounds of buckshot—was placed at the bridge's entrance "to help repel the expected rebel raiders." Who "would be injured the more, in case the gun was fired, those in front of the gun or those behind it?" wondered a local wit. This wasn't the first time the subject of dismantling John's bridge was aired in public. Despite having successfully carried trains across the Niagara Gorge for several years, John's bridge was scrutinized, inspected, and queried almost from the very beginning.[112]

Modest repairs were carried out over the years, along with periodic bolt tightening and the adjustment of loose stays. Eventually the carriageway was reinforced, the beams replaced (white oak replacing pine, which was too soft), and rubber washers replaced with iron.[113] But there was always an undercurrent of doubt that lingered around John's bridge, little of it emanating from the engineering world. Inference and a long-standing feud fueled the first warnings. On March 12, 1857, a swing bridge on the Hamilton-to-Toronto railroad came "out of joint," precipitating "a scene of unequalled horror" as a train jumped the tracks and plunged into the Des Jardins Canal, killing almost 60 percent of those on board.[114] It was later discovered the fault lay with the engine—a broken axle—rather than the bridge, but that didn't stop a writer from denouncing John's bridge in the *Buffalo Express*. "Somebody of no account will be slightly censured—the affair plastered over—[yet] the cars, before the poignant grief for the dead gets cold, will go whirling and thundering over [John's] bridge as before [crowding] the road to death as to a festival." "Modern engineering planned this bridge," he continued, "the greed of monied capital built it, and the travelling public caring little, and knowing less [will] trundle recklessly over it . . . until a thousand shrieks, and an awful sudden plunge announce that there has been a—short and terrible funeral!" "*Fall, that bridge will*," was the writer's conclusion. "We do not date the time—but mark, that *Bridge will fall!*"[115]

Most of the regional papers pounced on the writer's sloppy reasoning and shoddy understanding of the disaster. The *Gazette* thought the refrain "The bridge will fall" seemed to forget that "iron is the universal fastener" and ignored the legion of suspension bridges that had been operating for decades, including one in Pittsburgh ("Roebling's") that "has been 'vibrating' and 'granulating' under loads covering its double track from shore to shore during sunlight for 16 years." The *Buffalo Republic* pointed out that the disaster had everything to do with a faulty train and nothing at all to do with the bridge. Nonetheless, the writer denigrated the watchmen and switch tenders who worked on John's bridge as "common hirelings . . . guzzling beer half the time in the first drunkery at hand, as the multitude of accidents occurring weekly all over the county, under just such regulations, witness." As for John's claims and assertions: "I care just as little about Mr. Roebling's 'full written reports'—such reports are always good enough until some frightful accident occurs, and then some 'defect' is found to have existed." He was prepared to admit that John's bridge had held up so far, but "so did the Hamilton bridge till it fell and slaughtered near a hundred people."[116]

Aspersions from other quarters were cast in the direction of John's bridge. The following year the *London Quarterly Review* ran a review of the span that praised it as "an ingenious work" that "does [Mr. Roebling] much credit," yet went on to claim that "when the wind is strong, the gossamer-looking structure swings to and fro as if ready to start from its fastenings, and it even shakes under the firm tread of the passing pedestrian." The *Gazette* called the article "an unmitigated falsehood," clearly written by someone "firmly wedded to some rival plan for building bridges, and ready to use unfair means to cast discredit upon all others," which was likely quite true, but that did not stop the rumors. In August 1859, an alarming story began to make the rounds of the New York press. Written by an anonymous source up at Niagara, the report claimed that while John's bridge used to sag two or three inches under the weight of a train when it was first opened, it now sagged up to twenty inches. "The general impression in the neighborhood is that this great work of art will one of these days give way and fall into the river," it reported. The story was reprinted and discussed. The *American Railway Times*, whose reporter had recently visited the bridge and witnessed its robust health, thought the report was complete rubbish. "The public seem determined to talk that bridge out of existence," it declared, yet "the structure, however, seems disposed to stand a stubborn fact." The local *Buffalo Daily Courier* conducted a "careful examination," finding that reports of excessive sagging had "not the slightest foundation in fact." The *Herald* shot back that they were sending "two commissioners" to inspect the bridge and report back, although their threats were never realized. But the press coverage forced John to respond and then conduct his own official inspection.[117]

John knew the only people he really had to convince were the bridge's board of trustees, few of whom could be relied upon to grasp the technology and the physics at play. And without some definitive statement, distrust continued to dog the span. To this end, John journeyed up to Niagara in July 1860 and spent three days conducting a thorough examination of the work. His final report, issued on August 1, concluded that the "cables of the Niagara Bridge are made of a superior quality of material; that they possess an abundance of strength; that they are free from vibration; that they are well preserved and taken care of; and consequently that they may safely be trusted for a long series of years. . . . The durability of the cables have undergone no change since 1855," he affirmed, when the bridge was opened. In fact, "they have only been strengthened by additional experience." As to their life expectancy, John was "unwilling to estimate at less than several hundred years."[118]

As was his way, John got a little philosophical in his explanation. "The material universe is not by any means constituted under the principle of *immutability*," he mused. Instead, "material existence is but a theatre of change, of breaking down, of reduction and of reconstruction of the elements of matter. . . . And as all human fabrics being but material constructions, will have to succumb to the same inexorable law, we can not expect that the Niagara Bridge will form an exception." Only two ways were known, though, to affect "the strength of iron," he explained. One was granulation, a process John believed of no importance unless "great heat" was acting on the iron. The other was oxidation, or rust. John had gone to great lengths on all his bridges to guard against this creeping evil. He oiled and painted and protected "all iron and wire within reach" and did the same with the wires in the anchorages, before filling the whole thing with masonry and expanding cement to form "a solid envelope, excluding air and moisture." This seemed an excellent solution to the problem of oxidation, but in solving one problem, John completely overlooked another, buried deep in his anchorages.[119]

John's first important breakthrough in the science of suspension bridge engineering took place in Bamberg in 1830, when he witnessed firsthand the ruinous effects of fastening and fixing suspension cables to towers. It was a practice that failed to account for the fact that iron is elastic; it expands and contracts with changes in temperature, but also acts within a structure as a buffer or a shock absorber. Suspension bridge cables need to move to account for changes in temperature, but also to account for the vibratory force caused by transitory loads. Bridge cables need to move slightly, to account for a moving weight, the traffic that travels from one end of the span to the other. If they don't, they will pull at what impedes their movement. In the case of the Ludwigsbrücke in Bamberg, as John noticed, the force of a moving load acting on the suspension cables got as far as the towers, where it was suddenly and violently halted. With such a design, something had to give. Either the metal would weaken, strained by the artificial limits on its elasticity, or the masonry would, which is exactly what happened. After only a year's service, the towers of the Bamberg Bridge were marked by cracks and fissures, the result of its cables constantly pulling against the supporting masonry.

It was a lesson John never forgot, at least regarding towers. What he failed to consider in his zeal to prevent oxidation was that he was replicating almost the exact same thing in his anchorages, fixing the anchor chains in a masonry seal. Sooner or later, the vibratory (and thermal) force acting on those chains would play out in the anchorages, tugging on John's "solid envelope," slowly loosening the cables from their cement casing. Once those tiny cracks had formed, gravity would do the rest, allowing moisture to trickle down into the anchorages and collect near the cable ends. This was potentially disastrous when coupled with the overall scheme. In an open anchorage, the cables can be inspected and repainted and repaired. In a closed anchorage, there was no way to tell what was happening to the anchors, the very things that are holding the whole bridge up.[120]

Ellet was somewhat unique in believing in open anchorages, especially given his otherwise strong adherence to the French system of suspension bridge construction. The French generally favored closed and sealed anchorages, up until 1850, that is, when the country witnessed the worst suspension bridge disaster in history. In Angers, capital of the Maine-et-Loire department, on April 16, 1850, several hundred soldiers were marching over the Pont de Basse-Chaîne when a heavy gale hit the city. The storm caused the bridge's deck to bend and twist. As usual, the troops had been ordered to break step when crossing the bridge, but this proved almost impossible once the torsion began, which only amplified the twisting. Corporal Charles Duban reported that when almost all of the soldiers were on the bridge, "a terrible crash was heard: the end of the deck from the city's side of the river began to break up! The enormous weight of men and horses jostled . . . and plunged into the river. . . . They were thrown pell-mell spilling into each other." The soldiers fell thirty-six feet into the water below, where they were bombarded by huge lumps of stone and iron as the disintegrating bridge rained down on them. To make matters worse, the soldiers had been asked to march with their bayonets affixed to their rifles in an effort to look more impressive, so many were inadvertently stabbed by their colleagues during the fall. "I've seen in my career, many war events, terrible catastrophes," wrote Duban, "but never, no, never have I seen a picture as horrible, so sad!" By the end of the day 223 soldiers were dead.[121]

A commission of inquiry set up after the disaster concluded that the bridge's deck had sufficient strength to support the troops but that the action of the soldiers marching over, coupled with the effects of the gale-force winds, had caused one of the bridge's cables to fail and snap, a process hastened by oxidation in the anchorages, unbalancing the whole structure—in short, that the bridge would have held were it not for the presence of rust hidden deep and undetected below ground. The bridge's cement seal had cracked and let in the two substances most damaging to iron: water and air. After that the cable had succumbed to rust. After Angers, the French virtually abandoned the suspension bridge, a form they had embraced like no other nation over the previous twenty years. John's reaction to the Angers bridge disaster was complete silence, an extraordinary response for a man who diligently kept himself abreast of every new bridge, every new report, and certainly every failure or problem. That he failed to either comment or alter his methods suggests that he was unaware of both the disaster and its official report or willfully ignored them. The first seems preposterous; the second seems bizarre. Perhaps he felt he had learned all there was to know about the science of suspension bridges, although four years later he took keen interest in the Wheeling disaster and made changes to the Niagara Bridge in consequence. Equally, the fact that the Angers report was published in France and written in French seems of no account, since John could read French as well

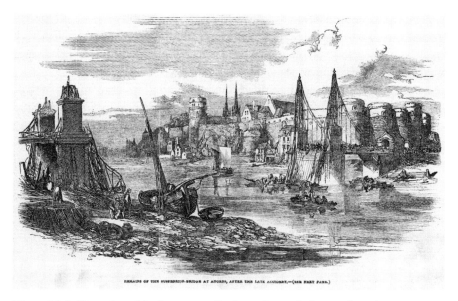

Figure 15.8 "Remains of the Suspension Bridge at Angers," *Illustrated London News*, April 27, 1850.

as he could read English. In fact, according to Washington, John "especially delighted in French professional reports which are noted for their clear diction."[122]

A more plausible set of answers might emerge from John's supreme self-confidence and his efforts to establish himself as a preeminent bridge builder and innovative designer. Much of John's thinking on almost any subject grew out of his sense that only he was an expert, be it religion, medicine, or engineering. Once he had decided where the correct answer lay, nothing could dissuade him. He had decided that cement-sealed anchorages were the answer to oxidation, and little could shift his opinion. In addition, John's 1846 patent "Improvements in the Wire Cable or Chain Suspension Bridge" went to great lengths to stress the novel and superior thinking behind his anchorages. Even in the face of contrary evidence, he was hardly going to admit he was wrong. Privately, the idea was repugnant to John, but professionally, the damage to his reputation would be worse.[123]

Despite John's 1860 report, problems and concerns continued to dog the bridge and its board of trustees. But with tourist dollars just as important as freight, the decision to conduct a major inspection—perhaps leading to a major renovation—was constantly postponed, until February 1877, when John's error was quietly unearthed by Thomas Clarke of the Phoenix Bridge Company, who had been asked to excavate a small section of the anchorage and conduct an examination. On reaching the section where the cables connected to the anchor chains, Clarke found "several of the wires corroded quite through and others partially so." The "mischief was not very extensive," though, and new wires were spliced in to replace the damaged ones. The Great Western—currently running thirty to forty trains per day over the bridge—immediately demanded a more thorough study, and the bridge company drafted a distinguished team of engineers, including Milnor Roberts, W. H. Paine, T. E. Sickles, T. C. Clark, and a brilliant young engineer named Leffert Lefferts Buck. Buck and Paine—who was also working as an assistant engineer on the Brooklyn Bridge at the time— quickly discovered that the damage inside the anchorage was serious. Corrosion was minimal near the surface, where most of the wires were "sound and bright" and "in as good condition as when first put in," but widespread and extensive further down. The problem, they soon discovered, was exactly the same as that which had brought down the Angers bridge. "The evident cause of this corrosion was the elongation and contraction of the strands under passing loads which had loosened the cement from the outside strands, allowing moisture to work in and finally reach the lowest point," wrote Buck in his official report.[124]

It was soon evident that new anchorages needed to be dug and set, and Buck was chosen for the job. He began in September 1877 and had the whole job finished in less than eight months, including replacing the entire wooden superstructure. It was a remarkable feat of skill. While supervising the work, Buck noticed that John's limestone towers were beginning to disintegrate under the pressure of the load they had been carrying for over twenty years, combined with the effects of frost and moisture. Structural steel was still in its infancy and not yet at the stage where "all of the required shapes could be promptly and economically obtained," but Buck thought the bridge's trustees would need to consider the option in the near future. And they did. On November 18, 1885, after Buck had again inspected the towers and found them "badly cracked" and with some stones "ready to fall out," the decision was made to replace John's stone towers with steel, and once again Buck was chosen to complete the task.[125]

Buck not only built new steel towers around John's old Egyptian obelisks and then managed to wrestle the cables from the one set of towers to the other, but he did so without interrupting traffic for a single day. The *Engineering Record* thought it was "probably one of the most remarkable engineering achievements of our age, performed so modestly that until it was completed and the dangers of the work were explained by other men, few people knew that such an enterprise was even contemplated."[126] Such an engineering triumph—as impressive as it was—couldn't halt the march of time and scale. By 1893 the Great Western was paying forty-five thousand dollars per year to use John's bridge despite being unable to run many of their trains over it. The size of an average locomotive grew sevenfold between 1855 and the end of the century, and the bridge was too weak to carry the heftier railroad traffic from one side of the Niagara to

Figure 15.9 View of the end of the Niagara Railway Suspension Bridge showing the excavation of the anchorage cable, ca. 1877–78. Courtesy of the Institute Archives and Special Collections, Rensselaer Polytechnic Institute.

the other. The decision to abandon John's bridge was made in early 1896, and Buck was again hired to solve the problem. He designed a two-level steel arch bridge that still stands today, the oldest span across the Niagara. "The tearing down and dismantling of the old structure seems almost a sacrilege," lamented the *Gazette*. "Nearly half a century of pleasing memories cling around it. . . . The tens of thousands—yes millions—who have admired its symmetrical beauty and the view from its dizzy heights, the madly rushing rapids of Niagara, for more than forty years, will gaze upon the fall of this structure with a feeling of inexpressible sadness." The work of razing John's first great success—the work that brought him worldwide renown and elevated him to the first rank of world engineers—was begun shortly afterward, while Buck's new arch bridge was built on top of the old span. The last traces of John's bridge were removed on August 27, 1897. "Even the date stone with the Roebling name on it has disappeared," lamented Washington several years later, "a victim to the envy which lies deep in all men's hearts."[127]

—

John's Niagara International Railroad Suspension Bridge lasted for just over forty-two years, but its influence on the region, the country, world of engineering, and John's reputation was huge and enduring. It singlehandedly created a new settlement—the village of Suspension Bridge, ultimately incorporated into the city of Niagara Falls in 1892—and fed it with a constant stream of trade and tourists. It helped fuel the sense that America was a nation of can-do problem solvers, able to overcome obstacles with native ingenuity and abundant elbow grease. Achievements in engineering were the perfect symbol to encapsulate America's distinct greatness, its ability and efficiency. While John's bridge may have been the only successful railroad suspension bridge ever built, its impact on the development of suspension bridges themselves—and on the public's perception of them—was enormous. It showcased to the world the length, strength, adaptability, and efficiency of the suspension form. By combining wire stays, parabolic suspension cables, and a stiffening truss, it brought structural stability to a system sorely in need of it. From its opening until the present day, John's bridge has been lauded as a magnificent achievement and a vital inspiration by historians and professional engineers alike.[128]

John of course never suffered from a lack of confidence. He knew he could build the Niagara Bridge safely, securely, and efficiently. The doubt and questions all lived in the minds of other people: investors, engineers, and the general public. But with the successful completion of the Niagara span, much of the apprehension—about John and about long-span suspension bridges, especially post-Wheeling—vanished. The Niagara Bridge wrought great changes in the trust and regard in which John was held professionally. As recently as three years earlier he had been building small wooden aqueducts up and down the Delaware & Hudson Canal. Now his achievements were on the front page of the *London Illustrated News.* He was suddenly an engineer of substance, the world's preeminent suspension bridge builder, in the eyes of the world. In fact, even as John was finishing up at Niagara, he was hard at work on a much longer railroad suspension bridge and in the final stretch of securing the long-held prize of spanning the mighty Ohio at Cincinnati. Both, if realized, would be longer than any other suspension bridge ever built.

The Kentucky, Ohio, and Allegheny (1851–60)

John went chasing railroad suspension bridge contracts all over the nation in the early 1850s. He designed a 600-foot double-decked railroad and highway bridge to cross the Genesee River, a short span for the New York and Erie Railroad at Lackawaxen, a mammoth 1,200-foot bridge for the Steubenville Railroad, a 1,000-foot railroad bridge over the Connecticut River at Middletown, and a massive two-span 1,600-foot-long bridge to stride the Hudson River for Erastus Corning's recently consolidated New York Central. Yet despite devoting countless hours and much effort to designing, corresponding, and traveling, John's only success outside of Niagara proved to be an absolute albatross.[1]

Railroad development in the early nineteenth century was intensely regional. Most railroads operated over relatively short distances, forcing customers to switch from one operator to another if they intended to get very far. In addition, while there were numerous roads in the Northeast, the Midwest, and even in the South, there were no connections between the northern and southern states.[2] Of course, much trade and many travelers relied on the Mississippi River, but even with such a trusted route, large swaths of the inland country found themselves outpaced and inconvenienced. For such burgeoning Midwest cities as Cincinnati, a southern railroad link was a "chronic want." The Lexington and Danville Railroad—chartered in May 1850—promised to gather and centralize the lines approaching from Knoxville, Nashville, and Memphis and "throw them upon" the recently chartered Covington and Lexington road, terminating at Cincinnati, creating the first link between Ohio and the South. "Although but a short link," reported the *Railroad Journal*, "it is a most important member of the railway system of Kentucky and adjoining states."[3]

The problem of connecting Lexington with all points south was a deep and impassable gorge known as the Kentucky River. Flowing "between two walls of limestone rock [each] 300 to 450 feet high [and] almost perfectly vertical, and varying from 1,000 to 1,300 feet apart," the river was "extremely tortuous." It was fast-moving and prone to flooding, precluding mid-river piers. In addition, the bedrock on the north shore "was covered with a treacherous soil, full of springs [and] easily scoured [making] the question of foundations on that side a very serious one, both as to cost and safety."[4] As at Niagara, if anyone was going to run a railroad over the Kentucky River, they would need to trust a suspension bridge. They would need to trust John A. Roebling.[5]

John began to correspond with George Schaefer, the Lexington and Danville's chief engineer, in the spring of 1851, initially offering to build a six-hundred-foot-long railroad bridge for $30,000 (excluding the cost of masonry) before upping his bid to a thousand-foot span slated to cost $127,000. "I will build [the] bridge and offer to superintend the work for $6,000," John wrote Schaefer, "provided the erection of the superstructure can be postponed until I am through with the Schuylkill bridges," he added, in what would prove to be a growing tendency to exaggerate his fortunes and play off seemingly competing employers, a strategy that seems to have worked with the people up in Niagara. He would not agree to the Kentucky Bridge "until I should hear from your company," John wrote Samuel DeVeaux on February 7, 1852. "At our last meeting I mentioned that I should hold myself in readiness to take charge of your work, so long as no other more certain engagement would be offered. As this is now the case, you will see the necessity of acting on the part of your Co. towards myself. If you do not intend to commence the work vigorously next spring, I shall feel inclined to go to Kentucky." He did this anyway, but not before the Niagara concern had clearly panicked and offered John a contract.[6]

John continued to correspond with the Lexington and Danville through the rest of the year, eventually submitting a formal proposal on November 29, 1852, just as he was beginning work on his Niagara towers. John had examined the site selected by Schaeffer earlier that year and found it "judiciously and well selected," but with a single unavoidable drawback: "To cross such a fearful chasm with a Rail Road by the ordinary means of bridging appears indeed impracticable, except at a most extravagant cost." Taking a page from his successful Niagara bid, he devoted the early part part of his proposal to a defense of railroad suspension bridges. "The question of the practicability of R.R. Susp. Br. is [now] being settled permanently by the contractors of the Niagara Bridge, under my charge," he declared. The only doubts still entertained by the engineering profession arose from "their supposed want of stiffness," he continued with a breezy confidence. Should one hang "a roadway of common construction" and expect it to service a railroad, the results would be swift and ruinous. Instead,

John combined a "substantially built truss" with iron girders to "a united depth of 18 ft" to create "inherent stiffness, which will render all vertical oscillation utterly impossible within a distance of several hundred feet." As at Niagara, John also planned a complex system of stays "to guard against the rising of one, extensive portion of the Bridge, while the other is being depressed by the action of the train, and vice versa." "These stays will hold the structure down in such a uniform and permanent manner that its equilibrium cannot be disturbed to any extent that will interfere with the passage of Rail Road trains," he concluded.[7]

John played around with the arrangement of the stays, especially the upper stays, over the next few years. Primarily, this was an effort to improve stiffness, to use the cable stays as their own structure—something resembling a triangular corner brace—that would build rigidity into the span. He also increased the total cost of the bridge periodically, from $160,000 to $180,000 to $244,939.[8] But much of the plan stayed the same. Two cables—eleven inches in diameter composed of 3,845 wires—would support a 1,200-foot roadway carrying a single railroad track. The cables would rest on 86-foot high towers, tapered from 16½½'-by-24½' at the base to 7'-by-8' at the top, constructed of local masonry and connected "by an arch some distance below the top." "No other projections, cornices, or moldings are to interfere with their simple outlines," John announced, while the appearance of the towers "will be greatly improved by the cast iron ornament which crown their tops." As usual, his anchorages would follow his customary flawed plan: sunk, filled, and sealed.[9]

The company brought in Julius Walker Adams, first to consult on John's plans, then to direct them. Adams—a second cousin of John Quincy Adams—was one of America's foremost engineers, part of "a group of brilliant, solid and enterprising men who established civil engineering as a coherent and organized profession on this continent." He was also, according to John, "an old friend of mine, who has full confidence in my abilities." Adams was educated at West Point, served as chief engineer for a series of different railroads, and eventually became one of America's foremost experts on sewers and sanitation, designing the country's first modern sewerage system in Brooklyn and writing several books on the subject. Adams's obituary singled him out as "an artist, a soldier, a writer, an editor, an architect and an engineer, and like Leonardo of handsome and dashing presence."[10]

Recounting the story thirty years later, Adams noted that Mr. Barkley, the president of the Lexington and Danville, recruited him in December 1852, a week or so after John had submitted his first plan, for the purpose of finding "an engineer who would be willing to endorse" a 1,250-foot-long railroad suspension bridge. "After a proper study of the subject," and allowing that a truss bridge on piers was out of the question, Adams "did not hesitate to pronounce the plan as entirely practicable and safe," after which Barkley offered him the position of chief engineer of the entire railroad. "In justice to Mr. Roebling," Adams later explained, he was not responsible for "designing any part of the suspended structure, but simply for supervising its construction, under plans and specifications prepared and submitted by the contractor of the bridge, Mr. Roebling."[11]

Washington tells an altogether different, more intriguing story. While Schaeffer ("an old friend") was in charge, John caused no trouble, but when Adams—"who had ideas of his own about suspension bridges"—took over, "trouble began and became so violent as to lead to blows and the expulsion of the Col. from the works." Legal proceedings were apparently entertained "claiming that as engineer of the road he had a legal right to examine and follow up all the processes of the cable work, etc." John claimed that Adams's only right and obligation was "to inspect the completed work and if it did not come up to the requirements, to condemn it." According to Washington, the two engineers "had clashed once before in the matter of a design for the New York crystal palace in 1851," and they "remained bitter enemies." It is uncertain how true this version of events is. John could be a hothead, and he hated being bossed around or judged, especially in regard to his engineering acumen. Still, he barely mentions Adams in any correspondence. And only a single letter between the two—dated June 2, 1853—remains, in which John asks Adams to look at the question of load. "If you and the directors should decide on heavier trains . . . then the bridge's strength will need to be increased," he points out fairly and without a trace of malice, adding that "I would charge only for the additional materials." Further, he seems to have included Adams in a list of "invitees"—written out in a notebook in February 1856—to some unnamed function, which also included news editors and prominent businessmen in all the towns where he was hoping to work.[12]

By the beginning of 1853, John was beginning to get impatient with the Lexington and Danville. On January 1, he wrote to urge "an immediate and prompt decision" from Barkley. John had been "offered by parties in Pittsburgh the construction of two large Rail Road Bridges, the one over the Monongahela river for the Pittsburgh and Steubenville RR, the other over the Allegheny river for a connection between the Central Penn[sylvania] road and the Penn[sylvania] & Ohio road." "Indeed," John continued, "the Pres[ident] of the latter road Gen[eral] Robinson *insists* on an *immediate* commencement of the latter work," which again seems like John trying to play off rival projects. Although John drew up several fine drawings for these bridges and certainly spent time in the region "examin[ing] the proposed site," there is no existing evidence that a contract was offered. The bridges themselves remained unbuilt for another ten years, suggesting the company was in no rush, while John continued to lobby for the contract and work on his designs for another two years. But John was in a hawkish mood with Barkley and had clearly learned the political skill of creating and using leverage. He had offered to construct the Kentucky Bridge for $180,000 not five weeks earlier, he wrote, but the price of iron was rising so quickly that "to adhere under these circumstances to my former propositions and estimates, would prove a ruinous business to me." Instead, he had written to make "a new and distinct proposition," displaying a newly ruthless ability to force the issue. "I offer to *contract* for your bridge for the sum of $215,000, *provided* you accept it within 15 days and acquaint me of your decision by *telegraph* before the 16th of this month. If I do not hear from you in relation to this *new* proposition *before* the 16th I shall consider myself free from all engagements." "Although I can do much better by under-taking those works in Pittsburgh," he concluded, "I am willing to undertake yours first, providing I can do so without running any risks and with a reason-able prospect of making a fair profit." Forced into a corner, the Lexington and Danville offered John a contract.[13]

John shuttled between Danville, Trenton, and Niagara almost constantly in 1853, never staying longer than a week in Trenton and rarely more than three weeks at either bridge site. He was in Kentucky—seven hundred miles from Trenton and six hundred miles from Niagara, in an age when such journeys took several days and numerous different modes of transit—on nine different occasions in 1853. My father was "always complaining of the long journey (be-fore Pullmans)," wrote Washington. John started setting up shops and shanties in May right near the Shaker village of Pleasant Hill. One can only imagine the interactions that must have taken place between the Shakers—so detached, so diligent, and so devout—and the ironworkers and bridge jockeys who made up John's industrial crew. Maybe they saw John's bridge itself as a spare and simple structure after their own hearts, a carefully made thing worthy of praise. More likely they would have frowned on such worldly and complex things. Still, "they were a hospitable lot," Washington informs us, "never ceasing to wonder at the miracle passing near them."[14]

The work progressed fitfully over the following year. John professed himself "very well satisfied with the looks of things" in July and by the end of November could report that the stone towers were finished and the anchorages dug, the necessary plates and saddles hoisted on the towers, and some of the wire and lumber delivered. Built of local limestone, the tapered towers were 85½ feet high and 33⅓ feet apart. The connecting arch was positioned 13⅓ feet below the top of the towers. They looked like "two trim Bunker Hill monuments," according to one source. Cable-making shops were set up early in 1855, and John's Niagara team was ready to relocate south. According to Washington, "another 18 months [at this point] would have completed the work."[15]

But the work was never completed. Things ground to a halt in early 1855 and were never renewed. "The two massive towers for the suspension bridge over the Kentucky river have been erected at a cost of $97,667," reported the *Railroad Journal*, yet "further work on the bridge has had to be temporarily suspended for the want of means to pay Mr. Roebling his monthly estimate." Money problems had been chronic from the very beginning. John's letters to Swan throughout 1853 and 1854 are littered with references to the company's dwindling cash flow. "The progress of the KY Bridge is a little *doubtful* on account of money matters," he wrote on October 23, 1853. The following August he thought "the prospects in KY are as bad as can be" and that he couldn't "calculate upon the KY Br. going on." By the end of 1854, right after finishing his towers, John admitted that "the prospects of the KY bridge are not very bright." The Lexington and Danville's financial status further worsened in early 1855. According to the published accounts, the railroad had raised all the money it was ever likely to—their bonds were proving increasingly more difficult to dispose of—yet were already twenty-six thousand dollars in debt, and nothing had been finished. There was no railroad and no bridge. There were parts of both—two sets of towers, a couple of deep anchorage pits, and about thirteen miles of railroad track—but nothing they could use or lease to generate any major revenue.[16]

Figure 16.1 The towers of John's unfinished Kentucky High Bridge. "High Bridge Station, High Bridge, Kentucky" (1907), Detroit Publishing Company. Library of Congress.

Still, the bridge continued to be mentioned in the press as an ongoing concern, as if the work was current and completion imminent. Two and a half years after construction ground to a halt, General Leslie Combs, president of the Lexington and Danville, felt himself able to declare, "Our suspension bridge will at once become the object of curiosity and attraction to citizens and strangers *having the longest single span in the world, and twenty-five feet higher over the water than that at Niagara!*" A further three years after that, *Scientific American* wrote that "a suspension bridge is now being constructed by Mr. J. Roebling over the Kentucky river, on the Lexington and Danville Railroad, which will have a span of 1,224 feet from center to center." John himself never seemed to believe the project was ever truly out of reach. He revised and he tinkered, always keen to settle the question of the suspension bridge as a fitting solution to the conundrum of railroad bridge construction. In September 1855, he drew up plans for the "enlargement and strengthening of KY Bridge" for a new final cost of $342,131, raising the price on a company that had run out of money. In his report on the condition of the Niagara Bridge (1860), John suggested that he would resume construction of the Kentucky Bridge soon, in the process proving he could adequately stiffen a suspension bridge to the point where freight trains could pass at much higher speeds. In between, in October 1858, John again wrote to the company offering to complete the bridge for $225,000, completely oblivious to the company's precarious financial position. "I should like to be able to expend a little more upon the work," he noted, "but if the resources of the Co. will not permit, I feel satisfied that the above sum will be sufficient to put up a structure that will not only possess ample strength & stiffness, but . . . will be durable for an indefinite period." John closed with a simple declaration: "I am willing to interest myself in your enterprise to the extent of my ability," which was both a heartfelt plea and a response to the world. The panic of 1857 had helped shut down most large-scale building projects, including John's oft-dreamed project of a bridge over the Ohio at Cincinnati. The panic had squeezed America, and as a result John was keen to secure work. Still, the Kentucky Bridge remained a tease and a taunt in John's mind. It was a job he had secured and started but one that he had been forced to walk away from, leaving (potentially) the world's longest suspension bridge unfinished. John had had the Kentucky Bridge, and he had lost it, although through no fault of his own. And it haunted John. He was halfway there, halfway to a finished bridge. Unfortunately, he would be halfway there for the rest of his life.[17]

The irony of John's letter was made plain about three weeks later when the Fayette County District Court ruled that, in lieu of its debts, the Lexington and Danville—including "a large quantity of Wire, Wire Rope and Bridge Timber, at the Kentucky River, intended for the bridge"—had to be sold at auction. Even that didn't stop John from continuing to pursue the bridge. A group calling themselves the Lexington and Danville Railroad Association bought the company and its assets for $132,150 on November 18, 1858, and John was among their number. His share of the total was $15,000, paid out in six installments over two years. "We have got a very good bargain," he wrote Swan; "all the men, composing our association are good [while] the whole association is got up so that every member is safe." With his usual unbridled commercial optimism, John thought that a further expenditure of fifty thousand dollars fixing and finishing up the railroad and leasing it would net the new concern at least twenty thousand dollars in much-needed revenue. But little work was done on the line in the next couple of years, after which the country was plunged into sectional conflict. "Of course, additional work on our road is now dead," wrote one of John's agents on December 2, 1860.[18]

With his father sidelined during the Civil War, it was Washington's turn to end up on the banks of the Kentucky River. As the Union Army swept down the Confederacy's western flank in 1863, General Ambrose E. Burnside put Washington in charge of surveying the site of his father's old endeavor, with a view to completing the bridge, in an effort to support the Union's advance. Washington's report to Burnside recommended a temporary suspension bridge—using his father's towers and anchorages—with a single track twelve feet wide to "admit of the passage of a single line of wagons with ample room on one side to pass horsemen and men on foot between the wagons and railings" and span between the towers of 1,350 feet. Washington priced his bridge—"very approximately"—at $145,561. In a personal note, Washington admitted that with such a price tag it was "very doubtful" that the bridge would be built. Still, as he wrote Swan, "I should like very well to go and build it." After submitting his report to Burnside, Washington must have sent a copy to his father, who unsurprisingly worked up plans to turn the temporary bridge into a permanent railroad bridge—all to no avail.[19]

On April 4, 1874, the still incomplete Lexington and Danville Railroad was sold to the Cincinnati Southern Railroad for $300,000, and shortly thereafter the new company reopened bidding for their Kentucky River railroad bridge. John was dead by this time. Still, John A. Roebling's Sons—John's wire rope company, now in the hands of his sons—submitted a proposal—likely put together by one of Washington's assistant engineers—on the suspension plan as originally intended for $410,000. The plan proposed using John's towers, which had been examined by the Cincinnati Southern's chief engineer in 1873 and declared still "in good condition and fully adapted to its purpose." But the company decided instead on a plan for a three-span, 1,125-foot-long iron Whipple truss railroad bridge drawn up by Charles Shaler Smith, which was completed and opened in 1877. John's bridge towers remained, acting as a gateway to Smith's bridge, "standing in the wilderness for many years, monuments of mystery and objects of pilgrimage," Washington wrote rather fancifully. They survived until 1929, when the railroad broadened the roadway to accommodate another set of tracks. There simply was not enough space between John's towers, so the railroad tore them down. They used some of the masonry to help build a retaining wall on the adjacent roadway, the only existent physical reminder—except a plaque put up in 1970—that John had ever been there.[20]

————

With his Kentucky project on indefinite hiatus and his Niagara triumph complete, John found himself in need of a new adventure. And he found one, albeit briefly. At the height of his fame as a bridge builder, and just when his wire rope business was blossoming, John started buying land in Iowa, not as a land speculator but as someone who was planning a return to farming, despite his failures of twenty years earlier. Perhaps it was John's ceaseless desire to keep moving; after all, he had no contracts or projects lined up. Perhaps it was a need to prove himself a success at the one thing he had so spectacularly failed at. Either way, John started buying land in Iowa in 1855, and he continued until 1861, eventually owning about 1,100 acres in Grundy and Black Hawk Counties, in and around what was slowly becoming the town of Waterloo. He made his first investment—$9,297.34—and took his first trip there in 1855, right after finishing up at Niagara. "I shall leave tomorrow for the West," he wrote Swan on June 15. No one heard from him for the next six months.[21]

In many respects, Iowa was a natural choice for John, even if the idea of him resuming farming was decidedly not. Iowa's population by 1855 was an even mix of Midwestern transplants and northern European immigrants, almost a third of whom were German. Arriving in 1851, William Fischer thought half the people in Iowa must be German. "One hardly realizes that he is in America because everywhere you hear German spoken," wrote an astonished Fischer before predicting that "in ten years Davenport will equal the first cities of Germany."[22] Iowa was also morphing into familiar ground politically, in an era whose politics was often as violent as its expansion. John had refused to settle in a slave state on principle in 1831, and there was little chance he would do so in 1855, just as the issue of slavery's expansion and protection were dominating the national agenda. Unlike nearby Kansas, Iowa was not violent, unpredictable, or a pawn in a national game of territorial chess. It was already fiercely antislavery—Coker Fifield Clarkson established a stop on the Underground Railroad in Grundy County in 1854, close to where John began buying land—and decidedly free soil. By 1856, in fact, the state was part of what state historian Leland Sage describes as the "miracle of political biology" that saw the Republican Party "conceived and born in a thousand places" across the country between 1854 and 1856. In the elections of 1856, Republicans won the governorship, carried the General Assembly, and cast their Electoral College votes for John Frémont, the first Republican candidate for president. In addition, it served as the only northern "lifeline" to Kansas after proslavery vigilantes closed the Missouri River, helping funnel some of the state arsenal to "the service of Kansas freedom."[23]

John kept few mementoes during his life, but buried in his papers is an intact edition of the *Waterloo Courier* from May 22, 1860, acquired presumably during one of his subsequent visits to the state. Emblazoned along each of its column inches is the news that the Republican National Convention had nominated Abraham Lincoln for president of the United States. The engineer and the rail splitter shared a mighty vision of a unified United States and several core principles. Neither were active abolitionists at that point in time, but both men detested slavery and believed in the inalienable right of all people to freedom. Likewise, both believed devoutly in the ideal of the "self-made" man and the fundamental right to the fruits of one's labor. That this was the only newspaper that John ever kept speaks to his affinity with the Great Emancipator and his hopes for his adoptive country.[24]

Iowa was fertile ground for a free soil, antislavery German in the 1850s, but it was for the fertile ground itself that most people came. "As black as your hat and as mellow as a[n] ash heap," Oliver Ellsworth wrote his brother in 1837. If they moved there, they could "live like pigs in the clover," he decided. Thousands followed. "Beautiful rolling prairie [with] mostly rich black productive ground suitable for crops of every kind," Fischer wrote fourteen years later. In 1854, Frances Gage, the noted writer, feminist, and abolitionist, sent back a glowing report to *New York Tribune*. "In many places Nature seems to have laid out the farm expressly for man's use," she wrote about her first trip to the state. It "is the most beautiful country that I have ever seen, and when the land of active industry and energy has overcome the difficulties necessarily attendant upon a new country, and art and wealth have embellished what nature has made so grand, it will be, as the old man said, 'almost the Garden of America.'"[25]

The prairie—"like a great green sea," as Herbert Quick described it in *Vandemark's Folly* (1922)—was some of the richest agricultural land in the United States, and it beckoned to many who were struggling to make ends meet in the East. "The immigration into Iowa the present season is astonishing and unprecedented," wrote one East Coast editor in June 1854. "For miles and miles, day after day, the prairies of Illinois are lined with cattle and wagons, pushing on toward this prosperous State." One Iowa City editor predicted that the state's population would increase by fifty thousand before Christmas—an opinion he expressed in September. He may have exaggerated, but from 1854 to 1856 the state's population increased by almost two hundred thousand, which had been the state's total population in 1850. Reports circulated that the Rock Island ferry was running a hundred trips a day, yet was still backed up. "Seek whatever thoroughfare you may and you will find it lined with emigrant wagons," wrote one witness.[26]

The conduit for John's Iowa adventure was one Alexander Greenwood Gower and the fact that—"like most Americans of the day"—John seems to have contracted "land fever," at least according to his son. As described by Washington, "It came about in this way—needing a resident assistant at the Ky. Bridge, he found him in the person of a professor of mathematics at a Ky. College of the name of Gower, who had drifted down from his native state of Maine in search of a fortune—Big & fat, suave, oily, unctuous and persuasive he was the prince of promoters and schemers—He unfolded to my father the possibility of big money in land—Land bought with soldiers warrants could be bought for a dollar and a quarter an acre, to be sold later on for 7 to 10 or more—My father could not resist." Gower was in fact taken as a very young boy to Iowa by his father, who migrated in 1841 and later served as a member of Iowa's State Constitutional Convention. He later worked for John on the Covington and Cincinnati Bridge and as a traveling agent for John's lingering Kentucky Bridge dreams, but eventually resigned. "No great loss," according to Washington. "He was a big fat heavy hunk, no acrobat whatever, couldn't climb a ladder, walk cables or do any of the lofty stunts required on a suspension bridge—but he could soft soap people and sooth the hardest kicker. It was dangerous to lend him money," he concluded rather mean-spiritedly. Gower was a faithful friend to John, as their correspondence attests, and John in turn valued Gower for his acumen and honesty.[27]

It is plausible that John's move was motivated by speculation, but the countless notes and plans in his notebooks are about seeds, horticulture, and botany. He copied down almost verbatim, for example, an article entitled "An Experienced Hedge Grower's Advise to Plant Osage Orange Seed" from the *Iowa State Register* and made extensive notes on "Mr. Bruce's system for feeding cattle & hogs during winter." He bought oxen and "farming utensils" and even built a house, "contract[ing] at Waterloo for all the boards you can get . . . for roofing, flooring and doors" and so on and for "tarred paper roofing." By all accounts, John had concrete plans and intentions, even if they did not materialize. Still, speculation was rampant, and people made good money buying up unused government land warrants—public land given out to US citizens in lieu of military service—and selling them on for a profit.[28]

That John would return to farming is puzzling—as is Washington's contention that his father "took a notion to live . . . and farm in open free country of God"—but not beyond the bounds of reason. That he would indulge in some capricious speculative venture also fits, for John was drawn into crazes and quirks on a regular basis. Strange ventures accompanied by poor choices and an odd cast of swindlers and hustlers littered John's life. The rational and logical existed alongside the confounding and perplexing. From raising canaries and silkworms to fad diets and bizarre cures, John was surprisingly easily taken in by a host of people. He would always take ownership of the idea, but there was always someone like an Etzler, a Bourne, or a Gower to sow the seed. John was certainly a genius, a man of great learning and knowledge, but he could also be a complete sucker. Regarding Iowa, John was likely at loose ends, taken in by Gower's vision, and perhaps nostalgic for the hopes and dreams he had shared with his much more agrarian brother. One thing is certain, however: Washington's descriptions of his time in Iowa with his father are some of the most fascinating and entertaining portions of the biography he wrote about John.

In May 1856, while proslavery forces were sacking the town of Lawrence, Kansas, and Charles Sumner was almost beaten to death by Preston Brooks on the floor of the US Senate, John Roebling set out for Iowa to "find" some of the land he had bought. With Washington freshly finished with his second year studying for a degree in civil engineering at Rensselaer Polytechnic Institute (RPI), John took him along. They made their way first to Cincinnati so John could meet with "his bridge people" before heading off through Indiana and Illinois and crossing into Iowa at Rock Island and taking the railroad to Iowa City. A stagecoach took them from there to Grundy County.[29]

John and Washington spent four months in Iowa during the late spring and early summer of 1856, and it seems to have been a fraught but energizing period—at least for Washington—full of hard times, strange happenings, and terrifying encounters with both the land and sky. And there was even a touch of tender sentiment. A day after Washington was apparently "nearly killed by a meteorite," he "met a prairie rose who had apparently fallen down from heaven also. Phosy Alderman was her name—while looking at her I fell down a gopher hole and nearly severed my thumb with a hatchet." "I bear the scar yet," he later griped. Later that summer, the two Roeblings took to the land and got lost, spending a whole day frantically roaming the prairie looking for help. The "memory still clings to one," Washington wrote with a shudder. Fortunately, they "struck a Norwegian woman baking pies" after dark and were saved.[30]

While out with John, Washington "learned to plough and break the prairie sod," an activity one pioneer described as sounding "like someone ripping cloth," given the long, entrenched roots of the plants on the prairie, while another thought it sounded more like "a volley of pistol shots."[31] His plow team "comprised 4 big oxen," two of whom he named Buck and Breck (after James Buchanan and John Breckinridge, his running mate), while the others he christened Sampson and Goliath. "I learned how to plow a straight furrow a mile long and swear in Ox talk," Washington boasted, not that John's plans "to live [happily] and farm in open free country of God" weren't going any better that they had in Saxonburg. They had to slaughter poor Sampson soon after and eat him. "Provisions had given out," and the Roeblings were soon "reduced to one bag of dried apples and what prairie chickens [Washington] could shoot." "Swans were not good to eat," they discovered. Eventually even "Powder & shot also gave out," meaning they "were forbidden to shoot rattle snakes." "There was one every 10 feet," Washington complained, a fact corroborated by Fischer, who "killed approximately thirty" rattlesnakes during his first three weeks in Iowa. Instead, on John's orders "they were to be trampled to death." Washington's father "had a pair of cowhide boots and never hesitated to trample on the biggest rattlers— We thought sure he was a maniac—none of the rest dared do it—One of the men died mysteriously from putting on a pair of boots—which had belonged to a previous victim of a rattler—it seems the fangs had been pulled loose & stuck in the leather—putting them on he scratched his calf and promptly died." "There is no moral," Washington concluded with evident exasperation.[32]

Clashes with his father seem to have been frequent and taxing. John, for example, "had learned Dutch surveying," while Washington had been trained in American surveying techniques, and "the two would not mix." The ensuing commotion—"a perpetual volley of curses all day and all next day till everyone got tired"—brought into sharp relief John's volatility and anger. "If I dared to hold an opinion then came a storm of vituperation followed by a hurricane of personal abuse and attacks on my life," Washington wrote about his father. "In his frenzied rage, the spit would fly, his arms clove the air, he jumped & swore and cursed with horribly distorted features—any man with more spunk than I had would have killed him." Sadly, "after the paroxysm was over it was usually found that one or two dispassionate words could have settled the whole discussion," but such was rarely the case. "There are times when every man must fight for himself," Washington lamented, "I did not fight enough." Just nineteen years old at the time, Washington might not have fought enough, but he was certainly learning to question his father and even disagree with him if necessary. It is fascinating to contemplate the two men traipsing around Iowa, falling out and screaming into the wilderness, both growing up a little, confronting one another and perhaps even beginning to realize some things about themselves and each other.[33]

Washington eventually returned to RPI in August, and his father was not far behind him. A day or so after his son had left, John received a letter from Cincinnati announcing that sufficient money had finally been raised to secure the building of an Ohio bridge. John would return to Iowa periodically, but the promise of a new bridge had broken his land fever. John left William Meissner, his sister's newly emigrated son, in charge; he sank eighteen thousand dollars into the venture over the next two years, all to no account. In a comically colossal blunder, Meissner traveled down to Kentucky the following year, bought twenty-five prize boars (seventy-five dollars each), and took them back to Iowa, where every single one of them froze to death the following winter. He was "certainly the most unfortunate farmer I ever heard of," John lamented. Still, two-thirds of John's Iowa lands were ultimately sold "at good profits," while the rest were sold by Washington at "good prices" after John's death.[34]

———

The Ohio River bridge project never really went away. Ellet briefly revived John's plan in 1849 with his *Letter on the Proposed Bridge across the Ohio River at Cincinnati*. Five years later, the local press reported that "energetic businessmen have the matter in hand . . . perfecting the preliminary arrangements with all the dispatch the nature and importance of the work admits of." The public should expect to hear something in "about a month," they concluded. Around the same time, an engineer by the name of D. Griffith Smith proposed a 1,400-foot-long span to spring forth at Columbia Street and leap Front Street with a "malleable iron bridge of a Tubular girder pattern." "Three lines of wire cables," each consisting of four cables, would carry a thirty-two-foot-wide roadway "between two stupendous towers of suspension." Unfortunately, the early months of 1854 were not a great time to be advocating for a suspension bridge, either nationally—especially after the destruction of the Wheeling Bridge on May 17—or locally. Erected in 1853, John Gray's 550-foot Licking Bridge between Covington and Newport introduced the region to long-span suspension bridges. For many local boosters, the span was a dress rehearsal for the larger and more ambitious Ohio bridge, and the initial impressions were encouraging. The bridge was opened December 28, 1853, to some acclaim. While touring Covington, British writer William Ferguson walked over and declared it "a light handsome structure," although he also noted how it did "vibrate considerably." A writer for *Ballou's Pictorial Drawing-Room Companion* called it "a fine and substantial piece of building," so it might have come as a surprise to many when, a little over two weeks later, it "tumbled into the river a shapeless wreck," thanks in large part to a couple of horses and some cows.[35]

On the evening of January 16, 1854, two horseback riders were trotting over the Licking River on Gray's new bridge, making their way from Covington to Newport, while eighteen head of cattle ambled over in the other direction. Driver Joseph Millridge, "doubting the security of the bridge, stood at a little distance" watching his cattle. Just as the two parties were about forty feet apart, the bridge suddenly gave way and took a "dizzying plunge amid crashing timber and iron into the icy river." In its descent, the bridge "turned bottom up, twisting the cables as if they had been so many light cords [landing] with a tremendous crash." Both men survived the seventy-foot drop, as did most of the cows and one horse. One of the equestrians described his experience: "Like a true American, he slapped his hand on his pocket-book, which was in his breeches pocket, and held on for dear life, and once or twice during the frightful descent, wondered 'what the old woman would do for market money.' "[36]

A civil engineer by the name of James Hogane conducted an inspection and found four major design flaws in Gray's bridge. First, the "approaches were *independent* of the span"; second, the cables were "not wrapped the full length with fine wire"; third, the "joists were improperly attached to the suspension rods"; and finally, the "forces of the anchorage were *miscalculated*; and herein was the immediate cause of the accident." Overall, Hogane proved himself a man after John's engineering heart. The "characteristics of a superior suspended bridge," he noted, are "rigidity of structure, strength to carry the load and be built of materials which possess the greatest lasting qualities." Yet even "the most superficial observer" looking at Gray's bridge "would at once perceive that a small force would start the oscillation of the whole structure . . . ultimately, indeed making it commit suicide." Worse, after only a few weeks, the cables were marked by significant rust from the inadequate wrapping. To this was added the poor quality of the iron used in the anchorage. "There is no part of a suspension bridge in which an excess of strength is more needed than in the anchorage," Hogane wrote. "Here lie the muscle and sinews of the structure." A bridge should contain six or seven times the "strength sufficient for ordinary purposes," he maintained. Gray built his bridge with a working strength of 140 tons when it should have been built to around 714 tons. Twenty head of cattle combined with "the natural oscillation and undulation [easily] made a wreck of its fair proportions."[37]

Gray rebuilt the bridge and reopened it later that year, but the damage done to the larger Ohio project was significant. As the *Covington Journal* observed, with no small level of regret, "The accident which befell the Licking Bridge has unsettled the confidence of some persons in the principle of suspension for works of this character."[38] Needing not just legislation but significant funds, the project was in crisis. If a respected engineer couldn't get a suspension bridge over a river the size of the Licking nor one over the Ohio at Wheeling, then what chance was there that someone could span the mighty Ohio at Cincinnati? Or more appropriately, who would commit several thousand dollars of their own money to find out?

———

The Ohio project was almost completely abandoned in the wake of the Licking and Wheeling disasters, and it might never have been revived without the effort of a local businessman named Amos Shinkle. Shinkle had worked a variety of jobs up and down the Ohio and Mississippi Rivers before eventually settling in

Covington in 1846, where he made his name and his fortune as a coal merchant. After ten years, he was a vocal advocate of public education, a player in the real estate market, and a leading light in civic affairs. In early 1856, he also bought stock in the Covington and Cincinnati Bridge Company and got elected to the board of directors.[39]

Washington could be singularly unpleasant about Shinkle, calling him a "skinner [and] a wharf rat [and] as close and mean as he could be," not to mention doing all he could to "wear off the plebian stains which stuck all over the Shinkle hide."[40] But there is no doubt that Shinkle's energy and vision saved the Ohio bridge project. Within two days of being elected to the board, he had rewritten the bylaws, suggested crucial charter amendments, initiated several new resolutions, and formed a committee to lobby both the Ohio and Kentucky legislatures in favor of the changes. The most significant alterations included raising the company's capital stock to seven hundred thousand dollars and lowering the bridge's mandatory central span from 1,400 to 1,050 feet. The latter opened up the possibilities immeasurably, although it did not go far enough for John, who later complained that he would have much preferred an eight-hundred-foot central span, flanked by two four-hundred-foot spans but that "that plan had been forestalled by previous legislation."[41]

John was often critical of the legislative process surrounding the Ohio bridge, sometimes rightly so. One act to amend the bridge company's charter—passed for seemingly no discernible reason on March 20, 1850—declared, "No lands shall be entered on and appropriated . . . except such as lie between Walnut street and Western Row in the said city, and exclusive of the lands now used for public travel upon Vine, Race, Elm and Plum streets," meaning in effect that the bridge could not align with any existing thoroughfare.[42] "A work of such magnitude and appearance . . . if located in the line of either of those streets, would have converted them into the finest and most magnificent avenues on this continent," John later complained. "No avenue in any of the large capitals of Europe could now compare in beauty of grandeur with that long vista which would be presented by the line of Vine street on the one side, continued in a straight course by Scott street on the opposite shore, and connected across the river through the imposing arches of the great towers of the suspension bridge," he continued. "As it is, both approaches are abruptly terminated by cross streets; all the immense traffic has to turn sharp corners, and nobody can discover the hidden entrance until it is reached. Or perhaps passed." "The location of this bridge will remain a standing reproach to those short-sighted property holders who have fought us during the last twenty years," he concluded with palpable anger.[43]

Shinkle's charter amendments passed the Kentucky legislature on February 25, 1856, and the Ohio legislature a month later, beginning the process that got the project back up and running. The measures passed surprisingly easily in

Kentucky, given the previous concerns there over runaway slaves, but ran into problems in Ohio. A group of abolitionists demanded all reference to slaves be expurgated from the charter, especially its notorious Section 10. Instead, the legislature approved the less drastic language they had added in 1849, which left the question of permission in place ("It shall be unlawful for said company, their agents or officers, to suffer or permit any slave or slaves to pass over said bridge without a written request of the owner") while eliminating questions of value and repayment ("No action shall be brought for the value of any slave or slaves, suffered to pass over the said bridge"). This was a poor compromise for a dedicated abolitionist but acceptable to most Ohio politicians. It was also a fair reflection of the state of race relations in Cincinnati at the time, given how deeply the issue of slavery had divided the city.[44]

In 1856, Cincinnati was at once the most northern of the southern cities and the most southern of the northern ones. Its large German population was distinctly antislavery, while its Irish residents—often forced to compete for jobs with blacks—were decidedly of a different opinion. Additionally, its transplant population was roughly split between New Englanders and southerners, all of whom managed to somehow do business with each other. Then came Margaret Garner to roil this uneasy mix, just two months before the Ohio legislature debated Shinkle's amendments. Garner fled over the frozen Ohio with her husband, her children, and several other enslaved people on January 28, after which they made their way to a house by Mill Creek, but they were soon cornered. At this point, Garner committed an act that would ensure her notoriety—providing the inspiration for Toni Morrison's *Beloved* (1987)—and place Cincinnati at the heart of the national debate about slavery. She took a large slaughtering knife and cut the throat of her two-year-old daughter, avowing later that she would rather kill her girl than see her returned to bondage.[45]

The Garner case emboldened Ohio abolitionists and very likely played a role in their decision to push for a full repeal of Section 10. They knew how many fugitives fled over the Ohio and into Cincinnati—175 in January 1856 alone, according to one count—and how crucial a physical bridge would be for runaways, especially if they weren't required to show "a written request." The bridge did and would loom large in the collective cultural imagination as a means to pass from bondage to freedom. An advertising card issued in Cincinnati shows an aged black man toting a carpetbag and a walking stick standing before the completed bridge saying, "Yes sah! I'll jes' exodust Kaintuck, and don't you forget it!"[46]

The Fugitive Slave Act (1850) best explains Kentucky's seeming nonchalance about the issue that had doomed the project in 1846. With the national policy in place and enforced, Kentucky did not need to fret too much about compensation for runaways. Kentucky slave catchers now carried the rule of slave law into Ohio whenever they crossed the river. It also allowed the *Covington*

Figure 16.2 "Yes sah! I'll jes' exodust! Kaintuck, and don't you forget it!" Postcard, ca. 1860s.

Journal—northern Kentucky's most influential newspaper—to be virulently pro-bridge and proslavery, an impossible position in 1846. In an editorial on the subject addressed "To the People of Cincinnati," published just as the bridge project was being revived in the legislature, the paper complained that the United States had "fallen upon evil times." "Justice is withheld," they charged, while "the rights of property are disregarded . . . the supreme law trampled upon and degraded . . . its plainest provisions unheeded and its solemn sanctions derided. . . . The Chases, the Sewards, the Sumners, the Wilsons, and the Greelys [all committed abolitionists], are striking out boldly on the dark wave now rolling over the North. . . . Must this last hope of Freedom—this more perfect Union be dissolved to gratify the unhallowed passions, the inordinate ambition of wicked and selfish men?" It was also the case that by 1856 the bridge project was "almost exclusively a Covington enterprise. Cincinnati looked on, if not with a jealous eye, at least with great indifference and distrust." Making the bridge company pay for escaped slaves would have meant Kentuckians footing the bill for Kentucky runaways. It would be much easier to effectively police the bridge and let the slave catchers take care of the rest.[47]

If Shinkle brought renewed energy to the bridge project, John brought renewed belief and conviction. "Faith in the principle of suspension somewhat shaken by the falling of the Wheeling and Licking bridges has been completely reestablished by the triumph of the principle in the Niagara suspension bridges," wrote the *Covington Journal* soon after Shinkle had been elected to the board of directors. Covington hosted an enthusiastic and successful public meeting in early February to discuss and adopt measures to secure the bridge's construction, the upshot of which was a plan for the town to subscribe to $100,000 of bridge stock. Such a plan would require a tax increase and two votes, one to levy the tax and another to subscribe. Although controversial, both measures passed easily at a public meeting later that month, leading the *Journal* to proclaim that Covington "needs only the magnificent suspension bridge across the Ohio river to make the place one of the most desirable, whether for residence or business purposes, in the Western country."[48]

In May, the company opened their books to receive stock subscriptions and posted a notice in all the local papers. "In making this announcement the undersigned appeal to the friends of the enterprise, in the confident hope that they will . . . ensure the erection of a structure, imperatively demanded by the requirements of commerce, indispensable to the prosperity of our cities." A letter from John avowing the practicality of the bridge and promising that it would not impede navigation accompanied the notice. Stock subscriptions reached $127,000 by the end of May, not including the $100,000 promised by Covington. The *Journal* complained that numerous wealthy Covington citizens had so far "refused to subscribe a dollar." The paper hoped they would come forward "like men" before it was too late. "Covington expects it, and has a *right* to expect it." Few did. But by the time the board of directors next met on June 27, total subscriptions had risen to $175,000, which, if combined with the promised Covington money, got the company within $25,000 of the amount they needed on hand to begin the project. A committee was formed and charged with raising the amount of the shortfall, and the decision to begin construction was made. The directors contacted John, who returned to Cincinnati and on August 18 signed a contract.[49]

———

The city that greeted John on his return from Iowa was a heaving, messy hive: clean and elegant, neat and aspirational in some places, in others it was run-down and filthy, noxious and dangerous. British traveler Isabel Bishop thought Cincinnati was "a second Glasgow . . . one of the most remarkable monuments of the progress of the West." "Heavily-laden drays rumbling along the streets—quays at which steamboats of fairy architecture are ever lying—massive warehouses and rich stores—the side-walks a perfect throng of foot-passengers—the roadways crowded with light carriages, horsemen . . . galloping about on the magnificent horses of Kentucky—an air of life, wealth, bustle, and progress." She was equally horrified, however, by the town's main business: pigs—"lean, gaunt, and vicious-looking"—that "riot through her streets." "All Cincinnati is redolent of swine," wrote Charles Mackay. "Swine prowl about the streets and act the part of scavengers until they are ready to become merchandise. . . . Barrels of them line all the quays; cartloads of their carcasses traverse the city at all seasons; and palaces and villas are built, and vineyards and orchards cultivated, out of the proceeds of their flesh, their bones, their lard, their bristles, and their feet."[50]

If pigs ran riot down Cincinnati's streets, up above it was just as dismal. Cincinnati "is crowned with a coronal of perpetual and very dense black smoke, so black and dense as almost to hide it from . . . view," wrote Mackay. "Next to Manchester and the great manufacturing towns of Yorkshire . . . it may be called the smokiest city in the world." Russian visitor Alexander Lakier arrived expecting a "Promised Land . . . a realm of pure equality" but was surprised to find "a cloud of smoke as sooty and black, if not so dense, as the one over Pittsburgh" over the whole city. Descending from his steamer to the levee, he marveled at the scene, "crowded for full three miles [with] steamboats. . . . Their smokestacks, without exaggeration, seemed like a black, charred forest and I wished for the sake of diversity that there were just one white sail."[51]

The levee itself—adjacent to John's worksite—was a riot of sounds and smells. The noise of loading and unloading competed with steam whistles, horses' hooves, and dozens of different accents: Irish brogue, barked German, clipped Yankee, genteel Quaker, African American vernacular, Southern drawl. All around was the pungent smell of the town's numerous glassworks, iron mills, and distilleries, mixed with the scent of sweet molasses, bitter coffee and all the strange and exotic aromas coming from "vast quantities of merchandize spread out all over the vast levee." Overhanging the whole scene was the fetid odor of the town's main business: the stockyards, abattoirs, and packinghouses that processed upward of six hundred thousand pigs a year, from live animals to packed, barreled, and salted commodity. Its primary byproduct, a vast quantity of dung, stunk up the town and created a wonderful nest for flies. Swatting these pests all day was a small army of roustabouts—"a society of wanderers who have haunts but not homes"—many of whom repaired at the end of the day to a nearby "congregation of dingy and dilapidated frames, hideous huts, and shapeless dwellings," as Lafcadio Hearn described it. The whole settlement—marked by "tortuous ways [and] long shadows of the weirdest goblin form"; its "silent frames with nailed-up entrances and roof[s] jagged with ruin"—"striving, through conscious shame, to bury itself under the earth," while the great Ohio rolled by. Into this scene, on September 1, 1856, descended John and "about one hundred hands," all ready to build the world's longest suspension bridge.[52]

Even though it took over ten years to get started, the project's beginnings were rushed and fraught. Certainly, the Ohio was as low as it had been in years—excellent conditions for excavating the towers—and the board felt it had the right man in charge and sufficient money on hand. John had no experienced and no dependable people on the ground or in the region, however; no physical presence, no workshops, no tools, no machinery; and no real time to prepare and plan. He signed a contract with only experience and a general framework, and then two weeks later he began. In between, he had to gather a team, set up shop, and think through the most significant problems and obstacles, especially regarding the towers. John had used existent piers when constructing his Allegheny and Monongahela bridges in Pittsburgh, and his Niagara towers, the first he had ever built, were both small and skinny (fifteen feet square at the base, rising to eight feet square at the summit) and constructed on dry land. By comparison, his Ohio towers were to be eighty-two feet wide by fifty-two feet long and built in the middle of a fast-moving, heavily trafficked, and commercially vital river. These problems were new to everyone, and assembling a competent team would require more luck than management. This was especially the case with the masonry contract. As John explained, "No contractors made acceptable offers, because none had experience in such work."[53]

Building up his towers would be taxing and difficult, but first John needed to dig down through the riverbed to bedrock in order to lay his foundations. Even with the low river, this would prove much harder than anyone had imagined, although it also displayed John's problem-solving skills. John's team built a cofferdam—a large watertight structure built within a body of water that enables people to work beneath the waterline—quickly enough, but keeping it dry proved impossible, especially after John discovered that "the great depth and extent of the foundation" had managed to drain most of the wells "along the rising ground, back of Cincinnati." This left John's laborers with "masses of soft mud and sand" and a constantly refilling pool of water, armed with nothing more than shovels. What John needed was a pump, but the only pumps available in Cincinnati were those outfitted on riverboats, which were tiny in comparison and could not handle gravelly water. "Raising clean water is an easy process, but to raise large masses of soft mud and sand is not so easy," John later wrote. He then tested out "some patent rotary pumps," which took up several weeks and still failed to work. With conditions so advantageous and time running out, John decided to just make one himself. He needed to sink his foundations and build up his towers so they would stand above high water when the river finally rose with the coming of winter. Every day was vital, and it would take weeks to have a proper steam pump built at any of the shops in Cincinnati. Accordingly, John designed a couple of crude box pumps out of three-inch pine plank, twenty-four square feet with an Indian rubber flap valve, then jury-rigged them to the engine of one of Shinkle's towboats. And they worked. They threw "mud and sand as effectively as pure water," John bragged, and in quantities that were "enormous," wrote the *Enquirer*.[54]

Once commenced, the excavation employed seventy men working "night and day, without interruption." Two "large floating warehouses" were constructed and floated out into the Ohio to hasten the work. The foundations—110 feet long, 75 feet wide—caused far fewer problems on the Covington side than on the Cincinnati side, and little pumping was required to keep the pit dry. By early October, "a deep layer of coarse sand and gravel" about five feet beneath the riverbed was laid bare inside the cofferdam on the Covington side, and a decision was required "whether to go to the [bed] rock, to pile, or to lay down a solid timber platform" right there on the compact bed of shale. John decided on the latter, the next best thing to a solid rock foundation ("provided that unequal settling is guarded against"), for reasons of time and geology. The Cincinnati foundation continued to give John "a great deal of trouble," but eventually the workers got to bedrock in late October, which was a mere twelve feet beneath the Ohio's riverbed.[55]

While John's tower crew dredged, the levee crew worked on the approaches and the abutments, digging and demolishing from Front Street to the river. His crew's inexperience showed almost immediately when a heavy winching beam, straining to lift a block of stone, broke and landed "a violent blow" on a laborer's head, leaving him "in a dangerous condition." Then just as his mud-filled cofferdams had fully engaged John's attention, his workers—"supposing they could take advantage of the urgency of the work," as the *Journal* understood it— went on strike, just ten days into the construction. Two gangs had been working around the clock and earning one dollar per day, but on the evening of September 10, just as the night shift was about to start, one of the workers stepped forward and demanded a wage increase of fifty cents. George W. Fulton—John's assistant engineer—promptly refused the demand. "Immediately the spokesman of the party gave a loud whoop, which was echoed by the rest of the gang, and re-echoed from this shore," after which the laborers on both sides of the river put down their tools and left the worksite. They continued to "cluster in large squads around the works, and threaten annihilation to any other laborers who should engage with the contractor," a strategy that eventually required a police presence. Shinkle tried to negotiate and managed to convince several strikers to return to work. John's approach was typically blunt. He fired all the workers, mainly Irish, and replaced them with Germans.[56]

With the massive pits sunk, John could start to build his foundations. Laborers laid heavy square logs, from ten to fifteen inches thick, snuggly side by side in the pit and then grouted the whole with cement. Another layer of timber (and grout) was placed at right angles to the one beneath it and attached with twenty-inch bolts. The Covington side required six courses of timber, while the Cincinnati tower required eleven. John then built a strong cofferdam around these huge structures—"to prevent inundation" from the rising Ohio—which he covered in cement to render it airtight. The result was a solid platform, 110 feet wide, 75 feet deep, and 8 feet tall on the landside and 12 on the river, "a foundation nearly as good as rock, provided it is guarded against undermining," John believed, upon which he would build the towers. The Covington platform was finished in early November and the Cincinnati one by the end of the month. Thankfully, the river was still very low, so John got to work immediately on his towers in an effort to build up sufficient weight to secure the foundations in such manner that they would resist the action of floods or ice floes. Four hoisting barrels, worked by friction clutches, lifted the stones into position. Derricks and guy wires positioned the stones and helped set them. John used Dayton limestone for the first twenty-five feet above the foundation, after which he opted for Buena Vista sandstone from Scioto County, Ohio, primarily because it contained petroleum, which he believed would help protect his towers against water damage. Unfortunately, what it promised in protection it delivered in blight. "The appearance of the lower masonry . . . has been somewhat injured by the oozing out of petroleum, and consequent blackening of its face," John later admitted.[57]

The weather in December continued to be mild, allowing John to push on late into the year. He eventually suspended work on the Covington side on December 20 "for want of the right kind of stone" and on the Cincinnati side on Christmas Eve with the approach of winter. The bridge project had thus far been one big race against time: to get the towers set on a firm foundation, to get them strong enough to resist a potentially brutal winter, and to position them high enough to stay above the river. Fall and winter rains could raise the river as much as twenty feet in a little over a week and easily drown a project. Likewise, a frozen river would test a masonry tower, subjecting it to huge amounts of force through both crushing and collision. Confirming a builder's worst fears, the winter of 1857 was long and hard. The Ohio froze over within days of John suspending the construction, and it stayed frozen for over a month. The mighty squeeze of an ice-bound river was nothing compared with its release, which arrived in early February. On the morning of February 5, 1857, Cincinnati woke to "the ringing of steamboat bells and the shrieking of steam whistles." The Ohio was cracking up and beginning to move. Within an hour, thousands had gathered on the landing to watch the spectacle and to watch over their interests, either as owners or as employees. Cincinnati was a principally a river town, and a frozen river all but shuttered the place, leaving little work and less commerce. Over the next few days the ice groaned, creaked, and splintered, slowly unbuckling itself from its moorings. It moved in a destructive wave of lumbering motion, slowly and incrementally at first, then with great urgency and force. The sight was terrible, as was the destruction. Huge blocks of shifting ice staved boats. Devastation ruled the levee and all things between Covington and Cincinnati, except for John's towers, which stood undaunted and intact through the whole episode.[58]

After the frigid winter came the spring rains, raising the Ohio steadily and making work all but impossible. By May the Ohio was still swollen, and money was growing tight. The board had set about suing several delinquent stock subscribers and sent President Ranson to New York in March for fund raising. He returned a month later empty-handed. The courts were only a little kinder, bringing in a mere $2,800. Some feared the company's indebtedness was already greater than the charter allowed, a fact the company refuted but which did not inspire general confidence or, more importantly, any new investment. And money would need to flow freely should the work commence.[59]

With the Ohio still much too high, John decided to take a trip. Along with numerous other well-known Americans—Henry Ward Beecher, Stephen Douglas, Lewis Cass, and George Bancroft, among others—John had been invited by the Ohio and Mississippi Railroad (O&M) to celebrate the coming of the railroad to St. Louis, an event he had advocated for ten years before. Begun in 1852 and completed in April 1857, the O&M ran parallel to the Cincinnati and Whitewater Canal from Cincinnati to East St. Louis, Illinois, linking the two towns. Trains loaded with dignitaries and officials left Baltimore's Camden Station in late May, arriving in Cincinnati on June 3 for the beginning of what became known as the Great Railroad Celebration of 1857. Festivities began at Cincinnati's Burnett House, an opulent hotel described by one visitor as "more like a royal palace than anything else" and by the *London Illustrated News* as "the best hotel in the world." Located at the northwest corner of Third and Vine—about 350 yards from the bridge site—the 340-room Burnett was also John's preferred haunt in town. He was there when the O&M trains rolled into town and the hotel hosted a "grand fashionable ball" to mark the occasion. John sadly failed to record what he made of the "exceedingly brilliant" occasion.[60]

Two mornings later a packed set of trains full of "a fair representation of the wealth and power of the country," as the *Cincinnati Times* described it, and including John, left Cincinnati at six in the morning for the eighteen-hour journey to St. Louis. John planned to stay with his old friend Ernest Angelrodt, who had balked at settling in Saxonburg in 1832 with the Mühlhausen Emigration Society. John arrived at Angelrodt's palatial home well after midnight after a long train journey, a ferry ride across the Mississippi, and a coach through St. Louis. It was John's first time in the city and his first encounter with this stretch of the Mississippi.[61]

John told Swan to send all correspondence "by telegraph, direct care of *E. C. Angelrodt*," although nothing has survived, nor have any of John's communications from St. Louis, if he wrote any. John likely spent his time catching up with his millionaire friend, making his way through the dense crowds that packed the city, and enjoying the various events that took place all week in St. Louis: speeches, musical performances, dinners, gatherings. He missed the fireworks display and the huge opening ceremonies—a massive parade from the levee up to the Fair Grounds, followed by speeches—as did most of the Cincinnati contingent. Word from the O&M was that the fête would not begin until Monday, but St. Louis had already decided to begin on Friday while many of the invited guests were still en route. John likely also spent some of his time on the waterfront, planning, thinking, and surveying, with an eye to a possible future project. The question of bridging the Mississippi at St. Louis had long been in the air. John would have known this, just as he would have realized instantly that while the O&M terminated in East St. Louis, what was really needed was a railroad bridge to vault the Mississippi and take the trains into St. Louis. He would devise his first Mississippi plan four years after his first visit and would continue to mull over the problem until his death.[62]

John returned east via Niagara Falls and New York, but he was back in Cincinnati in late June, just as the Ohio finally descended to a workable level. Work on the towers and approaches recommenced in early July, and all seemed to be back on track and progressing well. "The most precarious portion of the work is accomplished," wrote one newspaper in late July, as huge blocks of stone littered the levee and the towers continued to rise. The bridge was living proof of the "tangible union between the North and the South," wrote another, a startling claim for a country on the verge of civil war. But enthusiasm was infectious in southwest Ohio in the summer of 1857, although also cruelly short-lived, cut down by what historian Kenneth Stampp called "an unfortunate sequence of dismal events, great and small." The opening of the O&M had led the *Enquirer* to brag about Cincinnati's "marvelous greatness." Its current state presented "a picture of progress heretofore unknown in the history of cities," they declared. By late August, the *Daily Commercial* was boasting that "the prosperity of Cincinnati is growing into a proverb." "Her area of improvements is expanding with magic celerity," they wrote. "All things in truth, point luminously to the brilliant destiny of our fortunate city," they concluded with optimistic gusto. Meanwhile, in New York, the Ohio Life and Trust Company—the "most important banking institution in Cincinnati"—had suspended payments, and they failed soon after. Less than a week after the *Commercial*'s proud bombast, the Panic of 1857 was in full swing, leading the *Pittsburgh Gazette* to claim, "The specialty of Cincinnati appears to be suicide."[63]

The financial collapse of 1857 snuck up on the country despite clear evidence that trouble was looming. The country's increasingly sectional politics was growing more bitter and divisive. There was rioting in New York and Washington, DC, serious discussions in the South about annexing Cuba and reopening the Atlantic slave trade, William Walker's bizarre and ill-fated invasion of Nicaragua, the aftershocks and ramifications of the *Dred Scott* decision, the potential for a military occupation of Kansas in an effort to impose slavery on a free-state majority, and the reality of the national army marching on the Territory of Utah. The country's financial condition was no better. National prosperity peaked in the early to mid-1850s and declined thereafter, despite soaring sentiment. The hard financials of government land sales, commodity prices, railroad profitability, the Californian gold supply, and domestic and international trade all fell after the highs of 1855, while land speculation was rampant, creating paper millionaires and complex lines of credit, along with a misbegotten sense of invulnerability. With the end of the Crimean War in March 1856, Russia reentered the global wheat market, puncturing America's brief agricultural predominance. US wheat production was up in 1857, but there were far fewer places to sell it, leading to lowered prices and confidence. The effects of all this on a declining US stock market were unsettling, leaving the country's financial institutions weakened, at which point European banks started to call in their loans. Soon the panic was on.[64]

Initially, most people felt insulated from the banking crisis in New York. Certainly, a large financial institution had failed, but it had speculated and gotten what it deserved. The country would come to realize slowly over the coming weeks how intertwined the economy was, not just nationally but globally. The rest of the country scoffed at the idea that a speculative bubble could bring them down. Their regional economies rested on tangible goods: grain, cotton, beef, pork, tobacco, and indigo. Yet banks nevertheless slowly started to collapse around the country. Then on September 25, 1857, Philadelphia's seemingly impregnable Bank of Pennsylvania failed, telegraphing the panic across the entire country. Bank runs and failures accelerated, production and construction stopped, and everything seemed to grind to a sudden and decisive halt. By the first week of October, the collapse was national.[65]

John reacted to the panic like a man trying to plug a sieve. His factory had orders coming in, each of which would require significant amounts of time, labor, and material. Yet he could no longer rely on all his customers to pay. Each rope was less a commodity than an investment, and he needed to choose wisely which orders to fill. His was a national business, reliant on national moods and conditions, and he needed to understand these forces. He also needed to chase down debtors, to salvage and strategize, and to figure out who was vulnerable and who to trust. "No more orders filled, except Cash *before* shipment," he wrote Swan in October; "this must be the Rule hence forward. You can trust no Co[mpany]." "I will rather close my mill than do any more work on credit," he added. By early October, he had decided to lay off some workers and reduce his factory hands to a "*winter force*." "We must prepare for the *worst*," he added; "there will be *no* demand for Wire rope next year, at least such is my present opinion." As for his current orders, he reasoned, perhaps Swan could "spread the making of them over the whole winter, so that we could keep a half force of our men at work or at least enough employed to keep them together." Two days later he had made the decision to pay half his laborers' wages in coal and provisions, which he asked to be kept "under lock and key" in his cellar. "This will not only be a Saving all around, but also a great Service to our hands," he explained. "We may be able by this means, to employ our old good hands all winter & make rope ahead." The burden of course fell on Swan and Johanna. "Say to Mrs. Roebling, that she must not buy any more provisions & groceries in Trenton—all must come from Ph[iladelphi]a at wholesale prices, bought for bills of the Ph[iladelphi]a Bank."[66]

John's knowledge of banks and their standings often seemed encyclopedic, as was his knowledge of his holdings. By 1857, John was a wealthy man, with stocks in dozens of companies and cash deposits in almost as many banks. None of this helped when the panic hit. Like most other Americans, he was cautious but not overly worried through early September, but when the financial titans of Philadelphia began to fall, the desperate scrambling began. On September 28, he instructed Swan to move some of his money to New York. "We must make safe all we can, while there is time," he warned, and convert all incoming checks into gold immediately. He worried that thethe Trenton Bank was "*not safe* in times like these," although thankfully "the Old Pittsburg [*sic*] Bank . . . keeps up well, paying specie, [despite] a *hard* run." "The NY banks are good," he decided, although "there will be more failures, particularly in Ph[iladelphia] & Penn[sylvani]a." He feared it was only beginning "in the West," and he "expected all the Ohio B[an]ks will have to suspend."[67]

As it happened, Ohio banks survived the panic surprisingly well, thanks primarily to a regional panic two years before that wiped out all the weaker banks. But that alone couldn't keep the West from bankruptcy and ruin. "No B[an]k in the Country is safe now," John declared; "things in the West look very gloomy. Half the merchants will fail—all the mills will stop," a prediction that proved accurate. John's diagnosis of the country's afflictions was surprisingly solid. "As the winter approaches, [conditions] will be getting worse instead of better. The embarrassment is universal. The last reduction of the Tariff"—"Democratic work," he sniffed, as a staunch Republican—"has closed our manufactures and increased our importations, thereby expanded and facilitated sales on Credit." "To this," he continued, "comes the bankruptcy of most of our Rail Roads and total depreciation of all our Securities." "No wonder . . . the country should be universally prostrated in spite of our good crops," he concluded shrewdly.[68]

For Washington, John endured the entire panic "in a horrible state of excitement," which may have been a true assessment of his father or payback for enlisting his whole family in a mad dash to move the family's cash deposits. In one bizarre episode, John seems to have sent Washington and Swan to the National Shoe and Leather Bank in New York to remove between twenty and thirty thousand dollars in gold he had deposited there. "For a day the bank demurred," Washington recalled, "but finally gave in." The money "was so heavy that we could scarcely carry it," he complained, after which, "we dug a hole in the cellar, put it in & sat on it for a long time until Mr. R. came home. After a while, things having quieted down, we were told to take it back to the same bank who received us with great derision. This roiled Mr. R. and subsequently he moved his account to [New York's] Chemical Bank." John's take on the matter was slightly less dramatic, however: "I think it would be advisable to withdraw the [money] and put it away in my Safe at Trenton & let Washington sleep in that room. The N.Y. B[an]ks are not out of the Woods. Think about this. You might take Ferdy along & a good bag to bring the gold home." But the result was still the same. The Chemical Bank shuttered its doors shortly afterward. How much John had in the bank is unknown.[69]

The collapse of 1857 "was a *fast* panic," wrote North Carolina newspaper editor William Holden, "and therefore in entire keeping with this fast age." Most of the surviving banks had stabilized by the end of the year and were again issuing specie. Nevertheless, broken people, stalled projects, and ruined livelihoods littered the country. Over a year later, John wrote that "the country cannot remain prostrate for years." Work on his Ohio bridge continued as the panic gripped the country, but not for long. The project was already light on cash, and it never fully recovered from the economic crash. Work ceased in November after torrential rains made working in a fast-moving, rising river treacherous. And the following year began with serious disaffection in Covington, which still hadn't raised the hundred thousand dollars it had promised the project. A new property tax was proposed, debated, and soundly defeated, which left Covington with little option but to dispose of its shares "at a liberal discount and on easy terms of payment," further crippling the already cash-strapped venture.[70]

The project limped on through the rest of the year with almost no cash on hand, working only with contractors who traded their time and raw material for stock. By the end of the year, the Covington tower stood seventy-five feet above the low-water mark, and the Cincinnati tower was forty-seven feet, less than half their intended size. To prosecute the work with all due haste would require "the co-operation of the stockholders," wrote the *Covington Journal*, but no further money was forthcoming. On March 11, 1859, John was given notice by Henry Bruce, president of the bridge company, that all work on the bridge would be suspended for twelve months, as would the company's need of his services. "There is no prospect of doing any thing . . . this season," John wrote Swan. By the close of 1859, the company had spent all money it had on hand and exhausted all its bartering options. "We have heard nothing of the Cincinnati and Covington Bridge Company. What has become of it? Are the two half finished piers to remain as they are, eternal monuments of financial distress," asked the *Cincinnati Times* the following year, to which the *Journal* replied that "if Cincinnati would but do her part . . . the half-finished piers will spring up to their magnificent proportions, and become eternal monuments to the enterprise of Covington and Cincinnati." As John himself noted, there was a general distrust of "all incorporated public undertakings," leaving the project stuck. The directors announced a final, rather desperate and delusional bid to get the project restarted in April 1861 through the issue of a preferred stock option, but prices had risen so drastically since 1856 that the cost of the project now topped a million dollars. More importantly, two days later, Confederate troops opened fire on Fort Sumter, after which attempts to link the North with the South took a less friendly turn.[71]

———

The Panic of 1857 put an end to most of the country's building projects, but not all of them. In Pittsburgh, where John still enjoyed good contacts and an enviable reputation, there was a growing need to replace the St. Clair Street Bridge, just upriver from the aqueduct John built in 1845. Constructed by Sylvanus Lothrop in 1819, the St. Clair was a four-span covered wooden arch truss bridge running between Federal Street in Allegheny City and St. Clair Street in Pittsburgh. It cost $92,500 and was the first span to cross the Allegheny. The city celebrated the opening with a banquet spread across almost the entire length of the span. The bridge proved to be quite a romantic spot during the day— "a delightful promenade . . . many people in summer pay the toll, 4 cents, just for the pleasure of walking over on one side & back on the other," wrote Elizur Wright—but a site of robbery and rough justice at night. It was also an excellent investment, "constantly alive with human beings, horses, cattle, carriages, wagons, and drays," paying a 15 percent dividend most years. By 1857, however, it was in a deplorable condition. Even back in 1845, the *Chronicle* thought it was "beginning to show evident signs of decay, as it shakes terribly under the weight of a heavy wagon." "It cannot last much longer," they concluded, but it soldiered on for another twelve years.[72]

The St. Clair Bridge did such good business that by the time it needed replacing, the bridge company had plenty of cash on hand to finance the venture and every reason to believe it would continue as a profitable concern.[73] The president of the bridge company advocated for a suspension bridge over the objections of some of the stockholders, who thought such a span would cost too much. But they all knew John and what he could do. He had already successfully built two bridges in Pittsburgh, had just finished the world-renowned Niagara Bridge, and recently started to build what promised to be the longest suspension bridge in the world. Once persuaded, the Allegheny Bridge Company was content to give John "*carte blanche* to do as he saw fit." What John designed was an ornate but also rather pedestrian feat of engineering, at least by his own standards. The new St. Clair Street Bridge would be a four-span affair, with three piers in the river. The total length would be 1,036 feet, two central spans of 344 feet flanked by side spans of 177 and 171 feet. The two main suspension cables—7½ inches in diameter—held up the 20-foot-wide central roadway; two smaller outside cables—4½ inches in diameter—held up the 8-foot-wide sidewalks on either side that ran between the cables. The towers—45 feet tall when finished—were the most striking and lavish of John's career: four cast iron columns braced by cast iron latticework and crowned with an ornamental iron cap. John estimated the total cost at $239,411.[74]

An announcement appeared in the local press in late July that "the celebrated bridge architect" John Roebling would replace the St. Clair Street Bridge starting in just a few weeks. The new bridge would be "the handsomest structure of the kind in the country," declared the *Gazette*. Lest anyone worry about interruptions, the bridge company stressed that John "intended to proceed with the new bridge without removing the old one" so that traffic would not be "incommoded." By August 23—the day before the Ohio Life and Trust Company shuttered its doors—John had let out the masonry contract and work began the following week. By October, a large body of workers were "laying broad and deep the foundations of the abutment" on the Pittsburgh side, while a series of workshops dotted the shore "to accommodate the mechanics who are or may be engaged in this great work." The masonry team had begun excavating the riverbed using a variation of the pump technique John had developed the year before in Cincinnati. Derricks were being built, and everything needed to prosecute the "important work" was in place.[75]

John spent most of the fall in Pittsburgh. In late August, his aqueduct had sprung a leak, and the new owners summoned him to supervise the repairs. A month later, the city began to renovate his Monongahela span, "putting the superstructure of this fine bridge in complete repair." The city again brought John in to consult and supervise. One wonders if John's mind turned to the huge effort that had raised his first two bridges in little over a year and a half, to the decisions he had made, and to the city that had since grown so much in size, population, and industry. As in 1844, John again found himself standing at the Allegheny

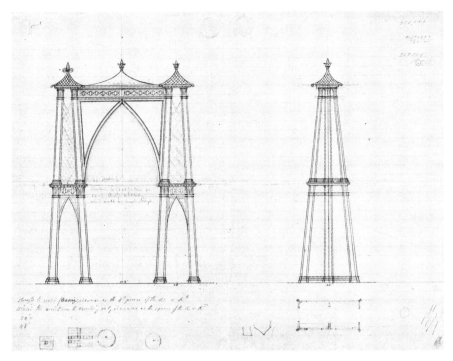

Figure 16.3 One of John's original design sketches for the Allegheny Suspension Bridge (1857). Courtesy of the Institute Archives and Special Collections, Rensselaer Polytechnic Institute.

shore, enveloped by what Lakier called Pittsburgh's "dismal atmosphere"—the "dense smoke," the "black and unhealthy faces," and "the houses covered with soot"—staring out across the river, planning, calculating, imagining. He was unknown thirteen years earlier, whereas now the press reported on his projects all over the nation and throughout Europe. John was not inclined to too much introspection, but he must have sensed how far he had come and understood his changing role. He was again in Pittsburgh to build a bridge but also to begin to train his eldest son. As the year turned, Washington completed his studies at Rensselaer—designing a suspension aqueduct for his senior thesis—and journeyed to Pittsburgh to join his father.[76]

Washington earned ten dollars a week initially as his father's assistant, which then rose to fifty dollars a month beginning July 1. He later complained that it "barely sufficed for [his] existence," betraying an increasing propensity to feel sorry for himself. John seems to have enjoyed having his son around, writing cheerily that Washington was "getting along well here [and] is about the work and doing very well." Washington always had mixed feelings about working for his father, however. He understood his genius, and perhaps his own good fortune to be able to learn from it, but he also understood his father's volatility. "I have long been of the opinion that a graduate should not work with his father, at least such a father as I had," Washington wrote in his memoir. "When I ventured to have a different opinion on some professional problem I was called a fool—my teacher was a damned fool—but what my father had learned was right and always would be right." Still, John seems to have trusted his son regardless. He left him in charge of the bridge project from time to time when his business took him elsewhere, including during the early months of 1860 when the bridge was nearing completion. Despite Washington's characterization of his father, he was able to make changes on his own authority, writing to his father that the girder rivets were too short (and too thick) and to say that he had had other parts recast.[77]

Work continued on the piers and abutments all summer as John flitted between Pittsburgh and Cincinnati, overseeing one project and trying to breathe life—or more accurately money—into another. Fortunately, the Allegheny Bridge Company was a going concern with a predictable market and an established income, while the Covington and Cincinnati—a much larger, more daring, and expensive venture—was more of a shot in the dark. The St. Clair Street Bridge had paid a 15 percent dividend for as long as anyone could

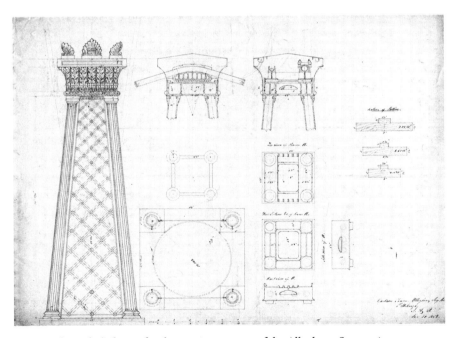

Figure 16.4 John's design for the cast iron towers of the Allegheny Suspension Bridge (1858). Courtesy of the Institute Archives and Special Collections, Rensselaer Polytechnic Institute.

remember, meaning new investors were easy to find in Pittsburgh, whereas they were impossible to identify in Cincinnati. "Our new [Allegheny] Bridge Stock *all* sold the other day at auction *at par*, surprising everybody," John wrote Swan in August, while lamenting that he had "not got as much [stock] as [he] wanted." "People have great confidence in this Bridge," he announced, while privately concealing that faith in his Ohio span was waning.[78]

The public's confidence in the nation, its institutions, traditions, and future, was also waning in 1858, especially as regards steamboats, the primary means of moving people and produce around America's massive inland waterways. At 6:00 a.m. on June 13, 1858, the riverboat *Pennsylvania* was calmly gliding up the Mississippi River about sixty miles south of Memphis when it suddenly erupted into flames. Four of its eight boilers had exploded, and huge clouds of escaping steam scalded and scorched the passengers and crew. People—in parts and wholes, bloody and twisted—flew into the river, while agonized screams and dreadful wails rent the air. Some were born aloft on blasts of boiling water, only to fall back onto the torn and tangled remains of the ship, or onto the hot ruins of the shattered boilers. A priest from Milwaukee was boiled alive; others were burned and blasted, decapitated and impaled. The explosion completely annihilated the boat's front third, while leaving the rest of the ship a useless hunk of blasted wood and ruptured metal splattered in blood and littered with bodies. The smell of burned flesh filled the air. The river turned an ugly red.[79]

The *Pennsylvania* was one of the worst disasters in steamboat history. Well over half of the 450 people onboard perished, while dozens of bodies were never recovered. Among the casualties was Mark Twain's younger brother Henry, and almost Twain himself, who had worked as a cub pilot on the *Pennsylvania* as recently as a week before the explosion. Twain quit before the fatal voyage after falling out with head pilot William Brown, who he described as "a middle-aged, long, slim, bony, smooth-shaven, horse-faced, ignorant, stingy, malicious, snarling, fault-finding, mote-magnifying tyrant." Brown perished in the explosion, and his body was never found.[80]

John had been thinking about steam boilers and steam engines for twenty years, dating back to his first published essay in the United States.[81] In the aftermath of the *Pennsylvania* disaster, he took up his pen again to write about steam power and to urge action. His stance was no longer solely scientific and technological but public and political. The "human lives . . . sacrificed" on the Mississippi had urged upon him, John began, the fundamental question: Would the United States allow this "sad catastrophe to pass away again without an inquiry," without understanding what caused the devastation and whether anything can be done to avoid further loss of life? No country on earth used steam power as extensively, and no one had more at stake in understanding its limitations and dangers. "Kind nature did not place one of her choicest gifts at our disposal without the means of applying it properly and rationally," he explained. Yet "all natural forces are within the form and control of the intellect of man! Man stands at the head of creation, and nature is his school wherein to practice his faculties and gain experience. What is yet buried in mystery will become plain in the course of time," John believed, "to subdue natural forces and apply them for the practical purposes of life, is one of the objects of existence."[82]

Luckily, John continued, humanity already knew enough about steam to "arrest its dangers in most cases." All we need is to apply the "proper remedy, legislative and mechanical." In France, for example, there were laws about such things. The government made and sold special "fusible [lead] plugs" that melted at a lower temperature than the iron boilerplate into which they were inserted, thus allowing steam to escape whenever the pressure or temperature rose above a certain level. Boiler explosions were nonexistent in France, John wrote, and Sir William Fairbairn, president of London's Institution of Mechanical Engineers and an expert on the subject, agreed, citing the French system as one of the safest and most reliable. "What a sorry contrast between our rough and tumble democracy and that French scientific despotism [that] insure[s] their citizens against explosions!" John declared. "Is it really impossible to raise our standard of national virtue and intelligence high enough to prevent such wholesale human slaughters?" he wondered. "These so called accidents cannot very well be charged to the account of a special providence—they are in most cases but the legitimate and direct result of a culpable carelessness and gross stupidity!" In America, the safety of American passengers depended entirely on the "watchfulness and intelligence of the engineer on duty," he complained.[83]

Fairbairn understood the need for effective safety valves and well-made boilers, a serious problem in America. A French technologist by the name of Dureau poured scorn on American boilermakers in 1851, after visiting a US workshop. "Iron plates with but half the thickness required by law in France and badly joined together," he scoffed, "loose rivets, cast-iron boiler heads carelessly fastened, internal flue without bracing, inadequate safety devices, and the failure to prove the finished boiler." John himself noted in his article how used boilers were often patched up and sold on, two or even three times. They had likely not been strong enough when initially built, he complained, given the propensity to cut corners, use shoddy materials, and ship off products that had been neither tested nor evaluated. As for safety valves, the "daily sober experience" of steamboating proved they were often "loaded down, so that it cannot open," in an effort to increase pressure and speed. "The sober truth is that steamboat running is a bold game between life and death, all the time!" John concluded, while "the real wonder . . . is not the *great* number of annual explosions we hear of, but the *small* number!"[84]

John was calling for government regulation but also for a check on break-neck commercial activity at all costs. Regulations would force people to make safer boats and operate them in a safer manner, but they would also bring with them necessary delays and inconveniences. After a "blow out," a ship could only replace its lead plugs once the boilers had cooled down sufficiently. This might take half a day, slowing down the journey time and angering passengers perhaps, but it would also ensure safety. John thought it was too easy to blame the nation's rivermen, since they existed in a cutthroat commercial world that valued pace and profit. "Our rivermen are no fancy men; they go in for high pressure and speed. Nor are *they* to blame; *they* risk their lives along with the rest; it is the public body that is to blame!" John believed. When a population demands speed and efficiency and owners demand unbridled income, then it is up to politicians to do the hard work of maintaining standards and security. John finished by appealing to the boards of trade in Pittsburgh, Cincinnati, Louisville, St. Louis, and New Orleans to hold special meetings and demand from their representatives in Congress that a special commission be created to examine more fully the causes of steamboat explosions and to rewrite existing statutes to guarantee "more safety than the ones now in force."[85]

John meant to "keep [the matter] stirred up, until the proper legislation had been obtained," but he soon returned to his bridges, and steamboat explosions continued to menace western waterways. Seven years later, on April 27, 1865, the steamboat *Sultana* exploded, killing 1,700 people. But the age of the steamboat was gradually giving way to the age of the railroad. Steamboats were better made and better inspected in the second half of the nineteenth century, but they were never again as popular as in the 1850s. Rail tracks were cheaper and quicker than waterways, which, as John understood, was always the bottom line.[86]

———

All John's piers and abutments were set by the beginning of 1859, leaving just the flooring and the cables to take care of. His carpenters started "unroofing the old bridge" in March before setting to work building the new floor. A first test of the span came in early 1860 when "the river [was] full of heavy floating ice." "It is a fine sight to see a large cake strike one of our piers and split up the whole length," Washington wrote John, who was away on business. By spring 1860, forty-two carpenters were drilling, hammering, tightening, forging, connecting, and "driving as hard as [they] could" toward completion on the bridge. Above and around them, the cable gangs manhandled huge skeins of wire rope. As Washington explained, there was "more difficulty in the adjustment and in the perseverance of equilibrium under moving loads" in a multi-span (as opposed to a single-span) suspension bridge, which led John to forgo saddles and instead to attach his cables to bell cranks within each tower's ornamental cap. The object was to "secure a more sensitive adjustment in the strains of the cables under passing loads," but the effect was disappointing. Without saddles, "the vibration of the bridge [was] increased perceptibly by the lightest passing load," complained *Scientific American*. In reviewing the span, *Engineering* agreed: "The cranked saddles allow[ed] only a restricted motion, which increase[d] the vibration of the bridge." They further worried that "the constant 'chattering,' moreover, of this arrangement under the lightest possible load speaks ill for its durability."[87]

John was ready to open his new bridge by the beginning of May. The span was not entirely finished, but it could support traffic, and the city was desperate to start moving goods and people across the Allegheny again. No fancy opening ceremonies greeted the first horse and cart on May 2, nor were there any special dinners or toasts as there had been in 1845 when his aqueduct had opened to such fanfare. But there was pride and a genuine sense of accomplishment. "Our bridge stands well & is firm, less shaking than on a wooden Br[idge]," he wrote Swan, which proved extremely useful when "a fool of a fellow . . . sitting in a tub on a river & propelled by 4 geese" sailed by in late May. An "immense crowd" collected on one side of the bridge before suddenly "surging" over to the other as the fool—a clown from Rogers and Spalding's Circus—and his geese passed under, severely taxing the span. "The load was so unequal on the different spans" that some of John's bell cranks shifted three inches in either direction, he noted. But they soon returned to center, and the bridge passed its first test.[88]

After the goose-boat adventure, John and Washington left for Kentucky and Cincinnati to check on John's other bridge projects, but they were soon back in Pittsburgh. "We are now finishing & putting up ornamental work & tollhouses. . . . When entirely completed this Br. will make a splendid appearance, Gilded domes on the towers & well shaped spires on the tollhouses, with cornices . . . so as to cover the sidewalks." "The bridge will be beautiful, when entirely completed," he wrote with evident pride. Residents agreed. Independence Day found people in huge numbers "having a great time" on the span under the seemingly happy influence of "Patriotism, whisky and Lager Beer." The *Evening Chronicle* thought the span a "fine structure"—"one of the noblest and most substantial bridges of the character in the United States"—and noted that it was "doing an immense business." The Duke of Newcastle, "a very practical man" and a member of the Prince of Wales's entourage as he passed through Pittsburgh later that year, conducted a thorough inspection of the bridge and described it as "the best bridge he had ever seen." As late as 1868, traffic over John's bridge was "unceasing," wrote one eyewitness.[89]

John's bell cranks did not doom his bridge. Progress ultimately did, although not before fire and decay had both tried to bring the span down. At noon on

Figure 16.5 John's Allegheny Suspension Bridge in operation. "Sixth Street Bridge" (1890). Courtesy of the Heinz History Center, Pittsburgh.

Sunday, June 19, 1881, the bridge was crowded with foot traffic when smoke began to rise from around the span. No one could quite work out where it was coming from, so the city put a fire engine on a flat boat and sent it out into the Allegheny to investigate. Flames started to lick around the bridge as the firemen probed and searched, and when the flames leaped over the sides, it seemed like "only a question of a few hours" before it would "fall into the river entire." Eventually, the firemen cut open a section of the roadway above the north pier and uncovered "a huge mass of fire" and finally set about extinguishing the conflagration. The Pittsburgh *Dispatch* estimated that about fifty thousand people watched the spectacle, crammed around the shore, on rooftops, and on the river itself. Several thousand were already there before anyone had even turned on a hose. A Sunday school teacher was so intent on watching the confusion that she got in the way when the water started to flow and was "cast upward several feet" by the blast, landing "face downwards on the bank with her skirts wrapped in promiscuous confusion around her head." No one ever discovered how the blaze got started. Some blamed a leak in the gas line that ran across the bridge; others blamed arson, or the tar that covered the roadway timbers, or even spontaneous combustion. Bridge company president John Harper blamed the sparrows that nested beneath the bridge for stuffing the span with hay and straw, which then went up when a stray spark from a smokestack found its way there. Harper should have shouldered some of the blame himself, at least for the damages, which ran to about thirty thousand dollars. It seems he thought the bridge all but indestructible, so he carried no insurance on it.[90]

The bridge company installed perforated water pipes along the whole length of the span so it could be instantly drenched should a similar event occur, but fire proved much less of a worry than corrosion. As with John's Niagara Bridge, it was his anchorages, not his cables per se, that were the bridge's weak link. In August 1883, about three months after the triumphant opening of the Brooklyn Bridge, Washington Roebling sent Francis Collingwood to inspect his father's Allegheny span. Washington and Collingwood had known each other at RPI, were both excellent engineers, and trusted each other. Washington, however, did not trust his father's anchorages. He grew anxious about the Allegheny Bridge, not only as an engineer but also as a major stockholder, so he sent his most trusted lieutenant.[91]

Collingwood examined the cables at the point where they emerged from the masonry and started to excavate. A reporter from the *Pittsburgh Telegraph* stood by and was shown over the "combination of iron and wood by Mr. Collingwood, who took pains to explain minutely" what he was doing. Before the cables had been surrounded by canvas and encased in masonry, they had been "embedded in asphaltum [boiled tar], applied in a hot state, so that neither air nor water can reach it." But the paintwork had cracked, and "grave defects" had appeared in the masonry, allowing air to "percolate to and fro" and water to slowly collect. When Collingwood burrowed farther down, he found that "the tar had partially disappeared, and that the cavity was nearly full of a dirty, greyish liquid," which, according to the *Telegraph*, "contained chloride, carbonate, and other salts of ammonia, which ate the iron. Some pieces of wire were dotted with little holes, like small-pox pits, where the rust had gnawed away the material, and when the wires were uncovered and a strain put upon them they snapped like straws." Collingwood opened a second cable, with similar results. There was "extensive rusting of the wires, so that the seizing-wires . . . were in many places rusted through, and the cable-wires deeply pitted."[92]

Collingwood commenced repairs immediately. He carefully scraped and overhauled each wire. Wherever he found rust and pitting, he cut it out and spliced in a new section, which was delicate and difficult work, as the tension in each wire had to be uniform. It was tedious work in cramped quarters, but "it is well that the scrutiny took place," the *Telegraph* concluded, "for the bridge was in danger of being ruined by the sagging and even by the breaking of the cables." By the end of the repairs, Collingwood's men had made 484 separate splices. They also repointed much of the masonry, replaced defective stones in the piers, and completely refashioned the anchorages. "Although all of the damaged wires were less than 10 percent of the total 5,600 wires in the four main cables," writes Donald Sayenga, "the scary part of the story was the realization that the damage was constantly underway at the weakest sector of the wires, in a sealed location which could not be inspected." Collingwood rectified this by building a water-tight "brick tunnel . . . provided with iron water shedders and covered by iron plates, which can be lifted when it is necessary to repaint or repair the cables in future."[93]

Another of Washington's men was back at the bridge in 1888, when Wilhelm Hildenbrand explored converting the span to "the cable system of rapid transit." Hildenbrand cleaned, re-oiled, and inspected the anchorages, concluding that they were "so thoroughly protected that they are good for at least 100 years, and that the wires, where they passed around the shoes, will need no examination for the next 20 or 25 years." Still, with cable cars and light rail replacing horse and cart, traffic was much heavier in the 1890s than in the 1850s, and John's Allegheny Bridge was less and less capable of shouldering the additional weight, much as John's Niagara Bridge was struggling under the weight of heavier locomotives. "It was a fine structure for its day, but of late years has not been equal to the traffic demands," wrote the *Railroad Gazette* in 1892, the year the city finally took John's bridge down. The city needed "a structure capable of carrying the heavy loads customary in an iron city," and they turned to Theodore Cooper, an RPI graduate. Cooper designed a bow-string truss bridge that served the city until 1927, when it was replaced by a self-anchoring chain bridge, the last of the iconic "Three Sisters" spans built over the Allegheny in the late 1920s.[94]

John's Allegheny Suspension Bridge was a product of its time. It served the public taste, and it worked handsomely for what John built it to do. *Scientific American* believed it was "express[ing] the general opinion among engineers and architects when [it said that it] is one of the most elegant structures of its class on the continent." "Nothing can exceed the grace of its outline when seen from a favorable point of view," they thought. And it was a fortunate structure in lots of ways too. The board contracted for it at the right time and with ample money and confidence. John got it finished in time—during the last peaceful summer the United States would know for several years—unlike his Ohio span, whose half-built towers stood as lonely witnesses to the passing of time. While Pittsburgh was celebrating its new bridge, the Covington and Cincinnati Bridge Company announced a new stock issue, which was a rather preposterous effort in the face of almost total uninterest. No one had performed any work on the bridge in almost two years, nor had anyone raised new money. Very soon, civil war would halt any hope of further work on the span. During the wartime years, John was unable to build anything. Instead, he retreated inside his own head and worked on problems—philosophical, practical, technical, and national. Over the next three years, he dashed off reams and reams of written thoughts on all subjects and of all descriptions. Taken from the riverbanks that had been his home for so long and forced to stay at his desk, he kept himself busy and productive the only way he knew how. He wrote. And wrote and wrote and wrote.[95]

And the War Came (1861–65)

As the state capital of New Jersey, Trenton was a busy place during the Civil War. Military and political leaders gathered; troops were housed. Camp Olden in Chambersburg—the town's first garrison—was joined by Camp Perrine on South Broad Street in 1862 and by the Trenton Barracks on Olden Avenue in 1864. All over town, troops were mustered, organized, recruited, and fed. The main markets on Broad Street were kept busy day and night feeding the new residents, while munitions, provisions, equipment, and clothing were shipped in via carriage, railroad, and canal. Trenton was abustle, and so was John's rope works. Business was "brisk," according to John. More than ever, coal needed to be mined and hauled to fuel the Union Army, and the business was also producing "a good deal of rigging" for the navy. The company's main problem was a lack of sufficiently skilled workers to keep up with its orders. John had long ago ceded day-to-day control of his factories to Swan, who by this point knew the business far better than John. The war left him with little to keep him occupied, although he did his best.[1]

John bought war bonds and donated to various local charities during what he called "the gigantic Southern rebellion," primarily favoring destitute women's homes and children's charities. Early in 1860, he donated a thousand dollars to William Phelps's Union Association of Children's Home—designed to educate "the poor and friendless children" of Trenton—enclosing with his contribution a letter that Phelps begged John to have reprinted in the local press. "I have seen tears of gratitude shed this day over the contents of your letter by more than one . . . noble women," he wrote. John declined, but there was no hiding his name and good deeds from the local press, who lauded John's "magnanimous and un-solicited" generosity, while Mary James, one of the home's managers, wrote that John's "cheering communication [had] darted a glorious beam of light upon our pathway."[2]

He also journeyed out to Iowa in the summer of 1861 with Gower, who was trying to sell some of John's land to a religious colony, and to New York with Johanna in the autumn to attend the wedding of his nephew Charles Meissner and to visit his daughter Laura, who was living on Staten Island.[3] "This will be a little wholesome diversion for mother, who feels the loss of Willie acutely," John wrote Washington in reference to the recent and sudden loss of his youngest child—the four-year-old William—from diphtheria, an event that shook the family and the normally unflappable John. "Little Willie's death has produced a great vacancy in our family, which will be long felt by mother & myself," wrote a grieving John. "Such a sweet little boy, with such a loving disposition and so intelligent & mature is not easily forgotten. I had no idea that any death could affect me as much as this has done." Rarely were John's emotions so unguarded.[4]

John also kept himself busy to ward off the grief. He worked on a host of requests to provide plans and estimates for several small suspension bridges, although few larger than a couple of hundred feet. He even heard from someone looking to build a bridge across a "river in the Andes of South America for mule transportation."[5] The most daring and outrageous plan he pondered had been brewing for a decade over in Europe, namely, the creation of physical link between England and France. In 1851, Hector Horeau believed he could lay a tubular tunnel—to house two railroad tracks—on the sea bed of the English Channel for a total cost of £87 million. Four years later James Wylson proposed suspending a tunnel in the Channel at a uniform depth by means of ties and buoys. In 1856, Thomé de Gamond—who had been thinking about a Channel tunnel since 1834 and did more than anyone to popularize the idea in the public mind—proposed constructing a series of thirteen islands in the Channel to facilitate and link a tunnel. Napoleon III was impressed, as was a commission of eminent French engineers, but the plan was abandoned as a threat to navigation.[6]

John thought de Gamond's plan deserved "no support"—"The cost of such a work can scarcely be estimated, and when done, who will go through a tunnel 19 miles long, if he can avoid it?" he reasoned—and on January 25, 1861, he sat down at his desk to see if he could work out an alternative plan, by which he meant, of course, a suspension bridge. Such a project "is perfectly practicable and can be put up at such a cost as will prove a good investment," he claimed, despite it needing to be nineteen miles long to stretch from Dover to Calais. John's plan was understandably short on details, perhaps hinting at the impossible scale of the job, but he sketched out the basics. There would be thirty-eight spans, each 2,640 feet long—or over twice as long as the current longest single-span suspension bridge—strung between "massive & strong" wrought iron towers. The structure would employ John's trademark network of cables, suspenders, and stays, all to be made from steel wire. His roadway could carry two railroad tracks and be encased in a series of long steel trusses connected to each other with slip joints so "the stays will go and come with the cable." The "best plan," he decided, would be to manufacture separate cables for each span and connect them on the towers" by passing them around "2 wrought [iron] shafts or cylinders" attached to a "bedplate or saddle," much as he had done on his Monongahela Bridge in 1845.[7]

The plan was something of a throwaway idea, but John returned to it seven years later. This time John's bridge would comprise a series of composite structures, each of which would be 3,300 feet long. Each of the bridge's sections would contain three separate spans—two 1,000-foot spans surrounding a central 1,300-foot span—and be anchored at either end by double piers "each at liberty to expand and contract by itself." Still, such a framework would presumably need about thirty of these composite sections, making the whole venture a massive chain of approximately ninety suspended spans. John's rough drawings seem to indicate a suspension / steel arch hybrid similar to William Hill's initial design for the Clifton Suspension Bridge, and he was clearly the only engineer daring enough to think about throwing a bridge across the Channel at the time. The first bridge proposal didn't arrive until 1889, a twenty-mile-long steel truss cantilever bridge proposed by Hildevert Hersent and Henri Schneider in conjunction with the English engineers John Fowler and Benjamin Baker, the minds behind the Forth Bridge outside Edinburgh.[8]

———

If the war didn't occupy John physically, as an engineer, it certainly occupied him mentally and emotionally, as a thinker, a citizen, and a father. "The troublesome political condition which preceded the rebellion excited him very much, as he had little sympathy with the south," wrote Washington, and "as the excitement in public affairs increased my father's excitement . . . increased, so that it was almost impossible to live at home. He constantly lamented that his health and age would prevent him from taking an active part in the conflict." Unfortunately, few of John's letters from the period survive but he saved enough of his correspondence to convey a flavor of the reactions he expressed to others. During the presidential election of 1860, he kept up a lively correspondence with Gower, who was in Lexington, Kentucky, and clearly in agreement with John on many of the issues facing the country. As the election grew near, Gower grew worried and fearful. "I find in the south all there . . . rank advocates of *disunion* & I am very fearful if they should carry the south generally it will be construed as a majority," he wrote three days before election day. "Destruction & disunion will follow," such an outcome, he predicted, "then revolution. You perhaps can not realize to what extent that matter is seriously entertained. The extent that this has taken hold of the . . . people." Other correspondents didn't seem to grasp how popular disunion was either or how readily the south would seize upon the idea. George Schaffer from the Patent Office in Washington had just been in Georgia and couldn't "for a moment believe . . . that millions of sensible men [would] at the dictation of a few demagogues act in *opposition* to their own sense of right and wrong." But Gower—a northerner and a Republican—clearly did. He had received offers of work in the South, he wrote shortly after Lincoln's election, "but I do not feel like going to a country where I have got to take a coffin with me."[9]

As more and more voices were raised in secessionist anger, Gower wrote to John, "I share your views on the political troubles of the day, although the secession wave may be pushed further than people generally in the northern & middle states are willing to credit." John had sent him an article on the subject from London's *Saturday Review*, "which is decidedly the best thing I have seen & the most philosophical." Gower agreed. The article poured scorn on southern rhetoric, southern intentions, and the South's reaction to the election. "Americans," they charged, "have accustomed themselves, on all political occasions, to talk in superlatives, without foreseeing the influence which language may exercise when it becomes necessary to act." As a result, "irritation at once assumes the form of irreconcilable hostility, and the expression of discontent commences with treasonable declarations and with threats of civil war." Thus had the South talked themselves into a corner, out of petulance and short-sighted arrogance. "To foreigners the provocation which has been offered seems ludicrously disproportioned to the resentment which is called forth," they continued. Lincoln had no interest in interfering with slavery "where it exists," nor much power—on his own—to prevent its extension. And further, no one could reasonably claim he bore any responsibility for any of the "personal liberty" laws enacted by various northern states in the 1850s in response to the Fugitive Slave Act (1850), "which constitutes the most substantial grievance of the south." If the election of a Republican president broke any laws or any articles of common faith, they claimed, the objection should have been made "when the candidate was proposed, not because he has been elected." After all, the Constitution allows for the election of differing political visions. Despite the temper tantrums and foot-stomping, "the seceders can only treat the result as a decisive proof that the enemies of the extension of slavery have at last acquired the control of the federal government."[10]

Ultimately, the *Review* thought secession made no sense—not physically, not politically, not economically—but that some of the slave states would secede anyway, then after a time "seek readmission to the union." "Americans," they believed, were "an eminently practical people, with an innate capacity for escaping from insoluble dilemmas," and they will most likely "prevent the history of which they are so proud from breaking off at one of its earliest chapters." Gower was less sure. He had recently been in Tennessee, he informed John, and was surprised by the "terrible hatred being cultivated in the south towards northerners." To his mind, any compromise "must & can only be more or less temporary." Gower believed the conflict over slavery was "irrepressible," and while he was convinced the institution would eventually die away, he also thought that "the animal will die hard & doubtless bound many in its dying throws." This "universal hatred will sooner or later seperate [*sic*] the union," he concluded.[11]

———

John's most heartfelt engagement with the war came through his son Washington, who served from April 16, 1861—four days after the eruption at Fort Sumter—until January 21, 1865, when he retired at the impressive rank of lieutenant colonel. By his own account, and in a story he told repeatedly throughout his life, Washington was sitting at the family table when his father suddenly looked at his son and barked: "Washington! you have kicked your legs under my table long enough, now you clear out this minute!" A potato that Washington "was guiding to [his] mouth fell to the plate" after which he stood up, put on his hat, walked out and headed straight to New York to enlist. The story seems far too dramatic to be accurate. John didn't order any of his other sons to "clear out," even though Ferdinand, for example, was a strapping twenty-year-old at the time. And while Washington eventually enlisted as a private in the Ninth Regiment of the New York state militia, he did so in June 1861, after two months in the Trenton National Guard.[12]

It is possible Washington may have been ready to enlist as a means to escape the pressures and expectations of being John's eldest son and joining the family business, a tradition he did not endorse. "Because an engineer has a son, it does not follow that the son would also be an engineer—my own son should have been a doctor—my father's father was a tobacconist and rolled cigars. To imagine my father rolling cigars would make a horse laugh."[13] If it was independence and adventure Washington was after, then the war provided the perfect setting. He put all his skills to good use: physical, intellectual, technical, administrative. He fought, he served, he built; he was a gunner, a scout, a historian, a balloonist, an engineer, and an aide-de-camp. He even assembled a ballroom and then staged an actual regimental ball. As described by Theodore Lyman, Washington was "a character . . . with a countenance as if all the world were an empty show. . . . He goes poking about in the most dangerous places, looking for the position of the enemy, and always with an air of entire indifference. His conversation is curt and not garnished with polite turnings. 'What's that redoubt doing there?' cries General Meade. 'Don't know; didn't put it there,' replies the laconic one." On reconnaissance one morning, Washington got lost behind enemy lines and managed to stumble upon Confederate major general "Jeb" Stuart and his staff having breakfast. While journeying to Fort Monroe, he watched the showdown between the *Merrimack* and *Monitor*. During a rather comic reviewing of the troops later in the war, he witnessed the "unmerited and humiliating torture"

Figure 17.1 Portrait of Washington A. Roebling as a student at Rensselaer Polytechnic Institute in 1856. Courtesy of the Institute Archives and Special Collections, Rensselaer Polytechnic Institute.

of his president. Lincoln—"evidently not a skilled horseman"—was atop "a fractious horse" when "his tall hat fell off; next, his pantaloons which was [*sic*] not fastened on the bottom, slipped up to the knees, showing his white home-made drawers, secured below with some strings of white tape, which presently unraveled and slipped up also, revealing a long hairy leg."[14]

Washington's first posting was as a private in the New York State artillery, and he saw action almost immediately. At the First Battle of Bull Run, "the guns were so hot from the rapid firing that even after retreating 5 miles . . . they were hot enough to light a match," he wrote Swan. Two months later, at the Battle of Ball's Bluff, Washington found himself "dancing around . . . without shelter or protection, trying to dodge the hail of bullets from the bluff above." He only escaped with his life after "a little piece of brass" in the pommel of his saddle managed to stop a bullet heading straight for his midriff. Washington's next close call came in April 1862, when he was ordered to Washington to consult with the army brass about the effectiveness of building and using suspension bridges in the field. Five days later, while Washington was still in the capital, his regiment was ordered into action at the Battle of Williamsburg. "Perhaps it saved my life," he wrote later, "as many in the whole battery were killed."[15]

The order fundamentally altered his experience of the war. Detailed to special duty, he became something of a free agent. For the next fifteen months, he fought occasionally and served on staff duty, but mainly he lived away from the front lines trying to build bridges. When the military finally realized that suspension bridges weren't the answer to any of their problems, Washington found himself assigned to General Gouverneur K. Warren. As Warren's aide-de-camp, and later a member of his general staff, he was often in Washington and away from the principal fighting. Just as importantly, he was increasingly a man of consequence: an engineer in charge of building bridges and a member of a general's staff. His days of meager rations, long marches, sleeping outside under a threadbare blanket—in short, the life of a private—were mainly over.

Washington's career as a military bridge engineer did not prove particularly rewarding. The military understood the need to maintain paths and routes of travel and communication, especially over strategically important bodies of water, but not the material needs and time frames under which engineers work. They expected suspension bridges to function like pontoon bridges: simple to make, quick to construct, and applicable to just about every situation. Washington's first job was to write a manual on the subject for wide dissemination across the entire army. The result—"The Construction of Military Suspension Bridges" (1862)—was detailed and impressive, but it was never printed up and distributed. Quartermaster General Montgomery Meigs even "caused to be prepared three complete sets of equipment for the construction of suspension bridges of wire rope," although there is no evidence they were put to any use. In early June, Washington was complaining to John that he still hadn't been asked to build any bridges. He came "very near" to building one "over Goose Creek" in northern Virginia, but the army decided it was "not worthwhile to build bridges for the secessionists" to use. They did send him to Front Royal when they discovered that a flood had swept away a bridge over the Shenandoah. Washington spent five days trying to cobble something together—"the nearest place to get plank is Alexandria [over 70 miles away]," he wrote Ferdinand with clear exasperation, before a retreat was called and the plan abandoned, not, however, before Washington had to swim across the fast-moving river with a tape in his mouth "to get the length of the spans."[16]

Washington's next assignment was to raise a bridge across the Rappahannock at Fredericksburg using the piers of the old Chatham Bridge. The experience gave him a taste of the military's interminable red tape and a real sense of the destruction and scarcity that were following in the war's wake. "The country beyond Fredericksburg is becoming a desert," he wrote his brother; "everything worth eating or stealing is taken." But he managed to wrestle a thirteen-span suspension bridge across the river in only three weeks, using "contrabands" (freed slaves) and southern captives, along with cables from his father's factory and wood pillaged from local barns and abandoned houses. He marched a cavalry brigade over his thousand-foot-long bridge to test its strength in late July. It "will be a great convenience for citizens, if they are allowed the privilege of using it," wrote the local newspaper. Washington himself questioned whether the whole endeavor was worth the trouble. "Certainly not as far as I was concerned," he concluded. It had been a deeply frustrating experience working with meager, untrained hands, after which the bridge only lasted about five weeks before being blown by General Ambrose Burnside in early September.[17]

After almost a year and a half of fighting, Washington's disillusion was starting to bleed out into his letters home. After the First Battle of Bull Run he had shown his disdain for the Union Army's leadership. "McClellan, the ass, lost nothing," Washington lamented, while "we lost thousands." After the Second Battle of Bull Run a year later, he was openly scornful. The army's "generals seemed perfectly content to sit still and allow the enemy to do what he pleased," even calling for a retreat when they were clearly on the verge of victory. Washington was "utterly sick, disgusted, and tired of the war," he told his father. The soldiers "fight without an aim and without enthusiasm [and] they have no faith in their leaders." Back in Trenton, John kept the faith. He worried greatly about his son and thought McClellan's strategy "difficult to understand," a sentiment he shared with almost all of the north, including President Lincoln. But he was generally upbeat, a sentiment that grew as the war progressed.[18]

On general assignment, Washington traveled to Sulphur Springs to consult on a bridge, performed some reconnaissance work for General Irwin McDowell in Northern Virginia, and served as a staff officer during the Second Battle of Bull Run and again at the Battle of Antietam under Major General "Fighting Joe" Hooker, before heading downriver to Harper's Ferry for more bridgework. By October, the order had been approved by McClellan himself, and Washington set to work throwing a suspension bridge over the Shenandoah under the command of General John Kenly, a man Washington regarded as cowardly and "uncertain." The general "has very clear ideas about bridges," he wrote his father, "considering that they are merely avenues by which the rebels might get after him and are therefore very dangerous structures." In consequence he refused to allow Washington to lay any plank on the bridge, "not even a gangway for the men to walk on." "As none of my men could fly," Washington laid down a double track of planks anyway, only to receive "a great lecture upon the enormity of the crime committed" and an order to have every plank removed by the next morning. Luckily, the only thing that happened the following morning was Kenly's replacement. General Benjamin Kelley, an acquaintance of John's from his days negotiating over the Wheeling Bridge, took over command of the region and "ordered the bridge to be completed at once."[19]

Kelley gave Washington all the men he needed and even allowed him to bring in David Rhule as a civilian expert. With sufficient support and the right materials, Washington made good time and erected a bridge "more solid and substantial" than he had first imagined. Two outside cables, complete with stays, and a central cable hung in three spans of between 132 and 136 feet long held up a 550-foot-long double-track roadway. It was "very stiff, even without a truss railing," Washington remarked, even with the "cavalry charging over." Rhule agreed, and he would know. He was not a speller or a stylist, but he was a fine craftsman, without whom none of the Roeblings' bridges would have been as longstanding or as impressive as they were. "It is a good gob & my friand W. A. Roebling de serves grait credit for a good gob he maid of it," he wrote.[20]

By the spring of 1863, the army "was tired of military suspension bridges," and Washington found himself passed from general to general. He eventually landed with Warren, who thought his new aide "a splendid young man rich and talented and accomplished."[21] For his part, Washington "contracted a lasting friendship" with Warren and served with him "during the remainder of the war," most notably at the Battle of Gettysburg. In the late afternoon on the second day of the battle, with the Union Army in a defensive position and the Confederates launching an all-out assault on their left flank, General Meade bellowed at Warren—or so Washington later recalled—"I hear a little peppering going on in the direction of the little hill off yonder. I wish that you would ride over and see if anything serious is going on." Warren later suggested it was he who suggested to Meade he should be sent to reconnoiter and "examine the condition of affairs," which seems more likely. Arriving at Little Round Top, with Washington in tow, Warren discovered that Major General Daniel Sickles's troops were badly out of position, that the confederates had already taken nearby Devil's Den, and that the only people on Little Round Top were signalmen with nothing more than semaphore flags to beat back the rebel army. If the confederates could break the Union line at Little Round Top, they could flank Meade's forces, routing them from the rear, and the battle would be lost, and maybe even the war. Warren was appalled, and he burst into action, directing his aides to ride hither and yon in search of backup and firepower. Washington helped lug cannon and shot up the hill and stayed to defend the spartan redoubt. The fighting lasted until nightfall, by which time the hill was still in Union hands after Colonel Joshua Chamberlain and his men finally and decisively beat back the rebels with a bayonet charge after they ran out of ammunition. Washington was there for the entire fight, an active witness to the great turning point of the Civil War. "There was no credit to running up that little hill," Washington later recalled, "but there was some in staying there without getting killed."[22]

After Gettysburg, John believed, "The backbone of the rebellion has been effectually broken." By the following year, he had high hopes that "Grant, bulldog fashion, will hold onto Lee, until he's torn him to pieces," although he still worried about Lincoln's ability to summon the necessary grit and gumption to press for final victory. He thought the "only man fit for steering the union out of its present perils" was Benjamin "Beast" Butler, a pugnacious radical Republican loathed throughout the South after a stint as an authoritarian military governor of New Orleans. John's leanings in that direction reveal much about his desire for some ruthless backbone coupled with a little moral indignation over both slavery and the South's conduct. Still, he did admit that "Mr. Lincoln's reelection is 'certain,' [which] together with a few more great military successes will reduce the rebel forces to such straits, that a general collapse of the confederacy becomes a certain and fixed fact before next spring," a prospect he looked forward to with no small sense of glee.[23]

While John grew hopeful, Washington grew weary. "It is the same old story every day," he wrote in the summer of 1864: "kill-kill-kill." Four days later he wrote that the Union "must put fresh steam on the man factories up north; what they demand down here for killing purposes is far ahead of the supply; thank God however for this consolation that when the last man is killed the war will be over." "This war you know differs from our previous wars in having no object to fight for," he remarked in rather a telling manner; "it can't be finished until all the men on either the one side or the other are killed; both sides are trying to do that as fast as they can because it will be a pity to spin this affair out for two or three years longer." Washington fought for the Union, and not for any other reason. He always referred to Southerners and members of the Confederate Army as "sesechers," or occasionally rebels, as if their crime was always their secession, not their system. Washington was often complimentary about his Southern foes, commending their bravery and resourcefulness, even enjoying the company of a captured Southern sniper—a "good fellow though"—who worked on one of his bridges. He described the Southern defense of Petersburg as "very noble," a sentiment his father would never have entertained. "No Democrat can be trusted," John wrote Swan in the middle of the war; "they are all disloyal and treacherous more or less."[24]

Washington seems not to have cared about the fate of enslaved people or black Americans generally. In fact, he hated working with them when they were seconded to his bridge projects. To a man, he thought they were lazy and stupid.

He treated them with contempt in person and ridiculed them in his letters. "Our colored retainers are especially disgusted," he wrote Warren's sister Emily, by this point Washington's fiancé; "it seems that the Brooklyn 14th (red legs) observe a time-honored custom of licking every nigger that shows himself; the first recipient of the bounty was his serene majesty Wolford whom they knocked down in the mud, stole his hat and pulled his wool." "I trust the operation will be repeated from time to time," he wrote with ready approval, "the effect having been decidedly beneficial." When his own aide—a man named Banks—took a furlough, the army sent Washington "an aboriginal genius" with the rather unfortunate name of Jeff Davis. "A tail is all that is wanting to constitute him a perfect ape," wrote Washington. "We amuse ourselves by pointing a pistol at him occasionally," he added; "he runs until he finds a sandheap into which he sticks his head; then he is safe," he added.[25]

Such was of course a common sentiment in the North, but it was not one shared by Washington's father. John cared about the fate of black Americans, a theme he wrote on with great clarity and passion after emigrating and returned to repeatedly in his writing throughout the war. In general terms, John certainly shared many of the assumptions of the nineteenth century about race, especially those espoused by Hegel in his *Lectures on the Philosophy of History*. He thought the "general development of the human race" looked something like the ages of man, with some races older and more advanced than others. Perhaps unsurprisingly, John thought the "African race" was "the child race." "Truly the child[ren] of nature," they were "joyful, full of animal life, perfectly careless, not caring for tomorrow, highly imitative; obedient to authority and submissive." Crucially however, John didn't believe that blacks were trapped by their nature or their place in history. Their "self consciousness is only awakening, dim and shadowy," he wrote. John believed that the "Caucasian race [currently] takes the lead in the great historical development," but the "other races will be following slowly, one by one in the path, pointed out before them." The "white race" was ahead, but it would not stay there. "In that eventual spiritual elevation, to which all races aspire," John concluded, "the Negro will not remain much behind the Caucasian."[26]

The trouble for "Africans" was embedded in the national framework. In "The Condition of the US Reviewed by Higher Law," one of the dozens of unpublished articles he wrote during the Civil War, John wrote of the conflict at the heart of the American enterprise. "The principle of free development does not harmonize with the principle of tyranny and oppression; the one is light, the other darkness, they are opposites." Yet despite the noble sentiments contained in Jefferson's Declaration of Independence—a document "not in harmony with slavery," John was at pains to point out—these opposites had been enshrined as the law of the land. The "corrupt seed" was planted in the Constitution by the founding fathers, and "the tree has been seditiously nourished in its growth" ever since. Now, "we are reaping the fruit." John did not fault the founders entirely. They too believed in change and advancement, just as John did. "Human nature is not yet perfection, but is heading towards it and is progressing at a slow rate," he wrote. "Jefferson & his compatriots knew this and trusted to the future." Unfortunately, "the future has come & passed, but the improvement had not. Advancement has been retrogression; the claims of humanity have been lost sight of during the splendid reign of King Cotton."[27]

John's reference to King Cotton implicated the country's economic system, one underpinned by a concept John was keen to rephrase. He began with a question: Can a social community be governed by the same principles as a commercial partnership? In the latter, people are "governed exclusively by their interest, real or imaginary," he explained, as perhaps they should be in a community. After all, "self interest is the great lever of actions, and if correctly understood, it ought to be the sole motive power that sways men's minds and directs their actions." But before anyone could get the wrong idea, John clarified exactly what he meant by self-interest: "My own true interest does not only involve a few short years spent on the surface of this globe, but it embraces the eternity of a future," a future that would always be "a reflex of my present acts." John believed his "own true interests [were] indissolubely [sic] connected with those of [his] fellow men" and that the respect of mutual claims was a "condition *sine qua non* of a sound partnership in commerce," as in fact it should be in "a partnership of states." Such ideas had an element of contract and trust but also of social and environmental harmony. For John, the earth "is not assigned to the present generation of men as a property over which they can wield unlimited control." Instead it was "only held in trust, not for the few individuals, who just now happen to occupy a state or Territory, but for all future generations." "Men live there only in the capacity of stewards, who have to account to future generations," he concluded. Self-interest for John was national and global, and it stretched out into the coming millennia.[28]

John loved the old proverb—which he discovered in the preface to Goldsmith's *The Vicar of Wakefield*—"Handsome is that handsome does." It perfectly captured the idea that appearances are "deceptive and may mean anything, but [that] actions speak for themselves," which is maybe why he ended up writing "A Few Truths for the Consideration of the President of the US" in October 1861, a clear call to action on the issue of slavery. Its medium is short declarative statements, often phrased in terms of opposites. "All progress is positive & affirmative," he began, while "All failure is negative & conservative." By progress he meant the slow overcoming of evil by good. "To overcome Evil by Good is not done by conserving the Evil, but by instituting the Good, and allowing the Evil to perish for want of support." By contrast, "The Conservation of Evil is Evil itself," which moved John to his subject: "Slavery is Evil," and "the effort to conserve it, is still more Evil." What was required was a sudden national shift. "Earthquakes & tornadoes are as necessary to the world's process as are sunshine & rain," he reminded his audience. "God's providence acts by revolutions as well as by peaceable means." John doesn't seem to have mailed his "Few Truths," but it was clear whom he was addressing. "You Mr. President are now the most responsible [for the fate of slavery] because the most prominent Agent of Divine Providence, and as such Providence will make you individually accountable for all your deeds." Would the president prosecute the war to abolish slavery or wage the war to save the union? Or neither? For John, the "truths" were clear. "When a whole Nation has been steeped for a whole century in the sins of inequity, it may require a political tornado to purify its social atmosphere. You can direct this tornado either for lasting good or more Evil. Future generations will either honor your memory or curse it," a perspective Lincoln himself certainly understood.[29]

John held a dim view of the series of events that had led the human species to the battlefields of Antietam, Chancellorsville, and Gettysburg. "We cannot close our eyes to the appalling fact that the events of human history are made up of long series of individual and national crimes of all sorts, of enmity, cruelty, oppression, massacres, persecution, wars without end," he wrote. Such compulsions had warped and shaped humanity, leading to what John understood as "the ruling destiny of this age": "Gross all-absorbing materialism, selfishness allied to intense activity, enslaving one portion of the race for the sole purpose of enriching the other—these are the rules by which we act." "They are to be sure, not admitted theoretically, *as ruling*," he added, "neither in church nor State, but they nevertheless *do* rule our actions. These callow professions of Christianity on the one side mask selfish activity on the other." As he cast around the nation in April 1862, John saw little to celebrate and much to mourn. "When error, superstition & bigotry have assumed the garb of truth; when men have lost much of that intuitive perception of wright [*sic*] and wrong; when the mercantile balance sheet and a false political aspiration [have] become the sole arbiter of a nation's fate; when even human slavery and human misery are sanctioned in the forum and in the pulpit," he declared, "then indeed is that nation's future history shrouded in darkness!"[30]

Thankfully, John was able to separate the past and the present from the future. He never lost sight of hope, nor did he ever truly abandoned his optimism. From the day he set foot on the *August Eduard* in Bremen to the darkest days of the Civil War, with his eldest son on the front lines and his adoptive nation on the brink of collapse, John believed wholeheartedly in human progress as an inexorable force. His ideas were as often spiritual and metaphysical as they were material and social, but they fed an unshakable belief that the world was full of potential and that humanity was headed toward a much better place. "Why is this splendid domain entrusted to our care?" John wondered. "Is it that we should enslave our brothers of a darker color, or that we should employ nature's forces, making them our slaves?" Clearly not. This would only lead to more "strife & jealousy," which failed to jibe with what John saw as mankind's rapidly improving material condition, not to mention its spiritual need for brotherhood. John thought such destructive behavior would soon "cease & give way to national pursuits which will make plenty for all," after which humanity would "go to work . . . on a large scale . . . with those stupendous forces at our command, and change the face of the desert of Sahara in Africa [and] sink audacious wells of 1000 ft deep to water the young forests which we are bound to plant in the great basin." As he wrote elsewhere: "As comforts increase and become more plentiful, more within the reach of every human being, in the same ratio social distinctions will be leveled down and common fellow feeling will be cultivated. It is the great mission of science, to abolish slavery, human and natural, and to establish perfect freedom in its stead. Perfect freedom consists in perfect emancipation from natural as well as spiritual bonds. The church refuses to assist, therefore science is left alone for a while."[31]

In its emphasis on natural resources as a democratizing influence, John's vision echoes that of Etzler and other nineteenth-century advocates of technological utopianism. "With the vast power of physical nature under our control, a deep insight into her invisible workings . . . the day will come . . . when in consequence of a general diffusion of all essential comforts and even luxuries the now almighty dollar will have lost its charm and will have lost its controlling power! Then and not until then will man be prepared to inaugurate another era in the history of his race." John styled this "the *era of redemption,* the beginning of the true millennium." But he was smart enough to realize that technology alone couldn't effect change, that mankind also needed a profound moral adjustment, the sort envisioned by the legions of radicals and reformers who tried to establish self-sustaining utopian communities around the country in the early nineteenth century. "As the spiritual shall gain ascendancy over the cold calculating intellect, so will a new epoque in the history of man be inaugurated," he wrote. "Human selfishness and exclusiveness will abate, and the true freedom of the mind shall be achieved. Man's sympathies will be enlarged; the human family will become one fast brotherhood, and the weak as well as the strong will be embraced." And should anyone "doubt of such a calming advent," John was happy to lend his confidence. "I am firmly convinced of its approach. Even now I can discern slight pulsations in the great heart of humanity which indicate such an approach," he wrote, without offering any more helpful specifics. "How will you account for the determined position of one half of a nation to the enslaving attempts of the other half?" he continued. "Do you listen in vain to the voice of humanity, which now and then makes itself heard?"[32]

John didn't see how "this happy era" could be inaugurated "until positive science has solved the greatest problem of all: the reconstruction of society on the principles of humanity, or what is the same, on the simple principles of Christianity," by which John meant the philosophy of Jesus, not the dogmas of the established church. (As he stated elsewhere, Jesus's "immortal injunction"— Do ye unto others, as you would them do unto you —"is the great law which applies with equal justice and with equal force to man individually as to man collectively"; it is "the alpha and omega of true religion, and at the same time of true morality.") The problem for John was that while many efforts had been made to reconstruct society, none of them had worked, "having met with strenuous opposition by government and society at large." Still, John believed that "the day is fast approaching when even this question . . . will claim a great party, and will force its way with the impetus of a moral avalanche through the combined resistance of an old foggiest conservatism in church and state. . . . If man cannot be forced in harmony with nature, then we are led to conclude that there is something essentially wrong in the government of the world." Needless to say, John had a few thoughts about this.[33]

———

In a remarkable unpublished document called "An Appeal to the Philanthropist," John set out some ideas on how to start planning for a new society and a new future. He addressed his manifesto to the *New-York Tribune*, although it seems unlikely that it was ever sent, and it was certainly never published. Horace Greeley, the *Tribune*'s editor, was, however, a natural choice. He was virulently antislavery and almost as enthusiastically a friend of "association," the polite term the communitarian movement used to describe itself. Greeley was converted to utopian socialism by Albert Brisbane, whose *Social Destiny of Man* (1840) was one of the defining texts of the movement. Greeley gave Brisbane a regular column in his paper after reading his book and promoted his ideas for years. And the *Tribune* was friendly to John too, calling him "an enterprising German" in a glowing review of his early work as a bridge builder in 1846, and giving him valuable column inches in 1857 when he was attempting to get his East River bridge project off the ground. Greeley later referred to him as a model immigrant, capable of "a higher order of industrial activity."[34]

John began his letter with the words of the spiritualist mystic Andrew Jackson Davis, from his book *The Principles of Nature, Her Divine Revelations and a Voice to Mankind* (1847): "Make men love truth by causing their interests to correspond to truth, and then truth will be received by a natural influx from their superior situation. But leave men inferiorly conditioned as to their social and external affairs, and all their opinions will correspond precisely to the inferior state in which they are existing." These fine words came with a warning and some counsel. "Deception . . . exists in the world, and all descriptions of dissimulation. But these things do not flow from the interior of man's nature, but arise merely as a consequence of his unholy, imperfect, and vitiated situation, in reference to his fellow-beings. Unholy situations produce unholy effects . . . and hence, in order to banish evil from the earth, a change must occur in the social condition of the whole world." Humanity needed to forge a new reality, a new "social condition," one based in "truth," as John understood it.[35]

The world had made efforts before to solve these problems. So why had they failed? To John, the answer was plain: "You cannot rear a holy structure with materials unholy & vitiated. But such has been the case." At great personal sacrifice and "at a risk of incurring the censure & ridicule of unreflecting multitudes" men had tried, but they had also made fundamental mistakes in their methods and membership. But social harmony and brotherhood could "only be developed properly in a congenial situation," John believed. Men could be virtuous and pure, it's true, but "when exposed to vicious influence, when misdirected under the guidance of wholly imperfect & vitiated examples," mankind's "beautiful passions" turned to "violence and corruption." Humanity's moral landscape was built up slowly and inexorably from a young age through habits and "modes of thinking." Therefore "no one can be a fit member of an Association, who has long been under the influence of a vitiated society and who has been trained in the scool of disimulation [*sic*]." John believed that "any attempt to build up an Association with persons, whose habits and feelings have not been trained in the school of virtue, must prove a failure." Clearly he had contemporary America in mind.[36]

Despite his own professional successes, John seems to have understood American society as rotten to the core, so rotten that nothing less than a complete break was required. When he asked himself, "Where can men be found good enough to associate?" his answer was a bleak "no where!" All were tainted by the sins of the nation. All previous attempts at social engineering had failed, John claimed, because they tried to "remodel the very *trunk* of the existing generation." But this trunk had already grown in an enfeebled atmosphere of cruelty and hypocrisy and would prove useless as a basis for a new start. Instead, John proposed to focus on the next generation. "All experience teaches that lessons, good manners & habits must be learned when young," he wrote, and that "the principle and practice of association may be enduringly engrafted upon the feelings and affections of such children, as have been selected with especial regard to their physical and mental endowments." Therefore, "for the first experiment only children of the most perfect organization should be admitted," John counseled. "O friends of suffering humanity," he continued, "let us unite and collect means to carry out a plan of Association with one thousand appropriate children of both sexes, selected with due regard to their natural capacity. One thousand of the most perfect specimens of the rising generation are to be congregated into one association, there to receive a most perfect education, physically, morally & intellectually, to be brought up in righteousness and truth, so as to prepare them for the full engagement of a . . . happy & holy life . . . and to live true to the high principle of their noble nature."[37]

John's ideas were deeply rooted in nineteenth-century utopian thinking. The Shakers, for example, believed they could only institute and maintain their particular brand of social organization away from the corrupting influence of the larger world. All the other great utopian experiments of the nineteenth century followed suit, closing their doors to preserve the integrity and purity of their systems. For some this was just the beginning, a prototype to stabilize and perfect before taking their plan on the road. Robert Owen believed his system would spread around the globe once established, as John did. "The first experiment, thus successfully carried out, will be a practical demonstration of the teachings of Christ and other great reformers," John wrote, hinting at how he understood Jesus's relationship to church and society. "It will form the nucleus of an expansive system, which to embrace the world is amply prepared." Granted, "the social regeneration of nations will be the work of ages, even as time will reduce the temper of opposing forces & prejudices," John wrote, and there "are many well meaning persons, who look upon associations with great distrust . . . or are habitually opposed to all reforms." But once the example was there for all to see, the world would acknowledge, accept, and adopt. "The great intellectual moral & practical movements, which now agitate mankind" were all leading to that "one great point," John asserted, to the "emancipation of human nature."[38]

As was often the case with John, his plan was long on rhetoric and short on details. The "idea of an Association of Children" would cost a million dollars, he thought, money that would be raised by subscription. The venture itself would be "entrusted to such noble men & women as are distinguished by their superior intellects & moral worth; who have proved themselves perfectly independent in their mental researches & free from all sectarianism and who are also deeply imbued with the divine spirit of Association." These noble men and women "must be constitutionally well adapted for the teaching and training of children; their minds must be pure, their affections tender, their sympathies strong." Beyond this, there is little of substance. But the document is only a draft of a letter, not a fully worked-up proposal, like his 110-page emigration plan. Still, John wove many of his grievances and remedies—along with his joyous enthusiasm—into his conclusion: the "glorious era" is approaching, he declared, "when distributive justice will pervade the social world, when virtue and morality will bloom with an immortal beauty." Then and only then, he added, again taking his cue from Davis, will "the sun of righteousness . . . arise in the horizon of universal industry and shed its genial rags over all the fields of peace, plenty & human happiness!"[39]

In line with almost every other communitarian plan in nineteenth-century America, John occupied himself with the problems he saw as vital to the health of the nation. "Is the human race not sufficiently afflicted with moral & physical diseases?" John asked rhetorically. After all, "gross all-absorbing materialism, selfishness [and] enslaving one portion of the race for the sole purpose of enriching the other" were "the rules by which we act." They were also the things that needed fixing. As John Humphrey Noyes—founder of the Oneida colony—long ago realized, the through line of America's utopian movement was a blend of religious revivalism and socialist enthusiasm. John's ideas walked this line perfectly, between a focus on Christian morality (as espoused in Jesus's philosophy) and a more equitable social system. John wanted to achieve "virtue and morality," but he also wanted "distributive justice." He believed that slavery and capitalism were morally corrosive and failed to create the basis of a just society. When the "mercantile balance sheet" and the "almighty dollar" become "the sole arbiter of a nation's fate," serving at the same time to enslave an entire group of people, then that nation could only survive with a complete overhaul. Whether John believed the Civil War would achieve that seems ambiguous, which may be why he failed to pursue his plans much beyond a sketch. He cheered on the Union in his letters and his public deeds, but clearly despaired at the rotten trunk of the United States in private.[40]

———

John couldn't fix a broken world, except perhaps in his head, which is exactly where he spent much of the Civil War, developing, fixing, and trying to explain what his son derisively called his father's "philosophy of the whole universe." Beginning in the winter of 1861, John steadfastly sat at his desk and produced hundreds of pages of amateur philosophy, technical exposition, and spiritual enquiry. He wrote and rewrote, less perhaps to revise as to restate and rededicate himself. With his son at war and his country in chaos, John seems to have found the experience therapeutic and assertive; certainly much of what he wrote in 1864 differs little from what he wrote in 1862, for example. Despite his son's dismissive attitude, these jumbled, scrawled, and scattered pages are a vital window into John's strange and mystical soul. Together they reflect few things more than his need for understanding and harmony in the world. "It is a want of my intellectual nature, to bring in harmony all that surrounds me," John wrote in 1856. "Every new harmony I discover, is to me another message of peace, another pledge of my redemption."[41]

Few individuals were less constituted to live with doubt and uncertainty than John. Ever since Napoleon's troops turned the European world upside down, he had craved order, certainty, and balance, eventually adopting them as the central pillars of his life and philosophy. In this he saw the world through the gaze of his profession: as a fixer, a builder, and an inventor. "Like the building or rearing of an enduring superstructure," he wrote on January 8, 1863, "the human mind intuitively requires a solid foundation." During the bleak days of the Civil War, John had admitted to himself that the United States had been constructed on the twin, corrupting foundations of slavery and the "almighty dollar." His writings during the war were an attempt to reconstitute and rebuild the world, in his own mind if nowhere else; to take life down to the studs, so to speak, and start afresh. Like an engineer, John set out to layer knowledge and understanding upon each other in an effort to mold an "enduring superstructure." Humanity's "instinctive endeavor to understand ourselves," he wrote, "is but the craving of our unsatisfied nature towards the higher; it is the sacred fire that keeps up a healthy enthusiasm of the soul." John's understanding would veer dangerously into the realms of nineteenth-century mysticism—into spirit worlds, pseudoscience, and "Odic forces"—but it also brought peace, clarity, and harmony, at least for him.[42]

Broadly, John's writings from this period can be separated out into two areas, both of which were planned as books but never published. One of them dealt mainly with the physical sciences: the laws and forces that shape the world and human life in it. At the heart of this effort is a 250-page unfinished manuscript entitled "Enquiry into the Nature and Origin of Matter," primarily a technical survey of the state of contemporary scientific knowledge.[43] Covering such subjects as heat and molecular change, electricity (and electromagnetism), conductivity, optics, and metallurgy, it is comprehensive and deeply learned. John appears to have read just about everything written on the subject of electricity, for example, along the way quoting from a dizzying array of experts—including Ambrogio Fusinieri, Sir David Brewster, William Wollaston, Martin van Marum, Joseph Priestley, Edward Nairne, William Brooke O'Shaughnessy, André-Marie Ampère, Edmond Becquerel, Claude Pouillet, Sir Humphry Davy, Sir William Harris, Michael Faraday—a mighty undertaking for someone for whom the topic had little practical application in his work. This is the public John Roebling: sober, technical, sophisticated, dedicated to professional standards and professional knowledge. John called his other great project from this period "The Truth of Nature," his effort to explain—philosophically and theologically—the history and meaning of life: who we were, where we came from, and where we were going. This is the other John: philosophical, speculative, abstract, unorthodox, and often deeply strange, at least to the twenty-first-century mind. It is John's *On the Origin of the Species*, his *Phenomenology of the Spirit*, and his *Nature*. If his "Enquiry" concerns the tangible forces that

Figure 17.2 John Roebling, etching from a photograph, ca. 1866–67. Courtesy of the Institute Archives and Special Collections, Rensselaer Polytechnic Institute.

control our lives, his "Truth" is primarily about the unseen "immaterial" forces that govern our journey.

John began with a declaration of principle and intent, of his right to enter the fray and to speak. "It may appear strange that a person unknown to the scientific world should undertake to write a work on the truth of nature," he wrote, and while it might be "customary for an author to excuse himself . . . and to crave the kind indulgence of [the] critics," John "asked no pardon." "It is true I have no claims as a philosopher," he wrote. "Most of my active life has been spent in the honest pursuits of civil engineering, and only the leisure of declining years in decided philosophical researches. But is this field of knowledge forbidden ground?" he asked. "Do the champions of truth form a circumscribed cadre, whose precepts can not be overstepped without sacrifice by uninvited outsiders?" Absolutely not. "The light of truth invites all, it is not the doctor's privilege alone," he declared.[44]

John believed there was always room for "more light, for more understanding," and that they could emanate from uncommon or divergent sources. Philosophy shouldn't be left to philosophers, and neither should religion, a branch of knowledge that accords "no liberty of free inquiry to the laymen." All the "momentous inquiries, upon which the solution of the question of human life depends, have been left too long in the exclusive safekeeping of theology," he complained. Thought, knowledge, and understanding all needed to be democratized. "I claim for myself the same freedom of inquiry, which is professionally claimed by theologians, even on the question of religion," he declared. "There can be no objection to religious or any other association, provided that object is the promotion of human welfare," he affirmed. "All associations, civil as well as ecclesiastical should respect the inalienable right of man's freedom of mind." "Without this freedom all is lost," and humanity is left "chained in mind [by] dogmatical belief." John of course hated to be chained, and his pronouncements remind us of Walt Whitman's "Song of Myself," his great poem of personal autonomy and democratic inclusion. Both the poet and the engineer began by affirming their place in the world and their right to think (with "Creeds and schools in abeyance"), to speak ("at every hazard"), and to believe ("in you my soul"), as Whitman put it. Or as John declared: "I have no apology to offer. I therefore claim for myself entire an absolute freedom of mind."[45]

In the beginning, in John's understanding, the universe was "chaos" and "chaotic space." Then a "great active creation" commenced. The great solar systems and the planetary groups "sprung up from the womb of unformed chaos." Life commenced in "universal motion throughout the vast realm of space." "System within system, sphere within sphere, this vast machinery began its regular course." Light appeared, and "nature was called forth." "Lifeless space was condensed into natural matter and imbued with the principles of motion, development and progression. After countless ages of nebula aggregation, the different planetary systems were formed, . . . matter consolidated, and various chemical elements, which constitute the present phases of nature, made their appearance." On one level this sounds like the modern big-bang theory, but John was headed in a different direction. "It is now generally admitted by scientific man," he wrote, "that the space of the material universe is filled with an imperceptible extremely subtle fluid, which serves as the medium of communication between the numerous stellar and planetary bodies, which form the great cosmos of creation," which was quite right, at least in the context of the times. Isaac Newton believed that space was a substance, as did many late-nineteenth-century physicists. But John wasn't thinking of a primordial soup or of luminiferous aether, the substance several contemporary physicists believed allowed light and sound waves to move through space, however. John believed in a different kind of "ether," a substance and a concept he borrowed almost wholesale from the German naturalist and philosopher Lorenz Oken.[46]

Ether, for John, was a material, a medium, and a spirit: the "virgin" stuff of all creation. It filled "all space; it is the atmosphere of the universe, the element in which the world lives and moves . . . the note from which the material world was created." It was also a "manifestation" of the "universal ideal spirit." All physical things were formed out of ether and imbued with an unseen, immaterial force, which shaped and controlled the world. "The Spiritual" was the mainspring of all life and creation: "the great first cause . . . the origin of all life, of all energy, of all motion, of all activity." The spiritual "impregnated" ether, creating a "universal cementing essence, which connects and pervades all creations, visible and invisible." It "is the cause of all actual life, of all motion, of all action; it forms that chain of universal sympathy and intelligence which encircles the great whole." "Every something" was but an outflow from this "universal fountain," and together, they were the living stuff of God.[47]

John believed in God, even if he did not believe very much in churches or religion as practiced by his contemporaries. But he believed in a very specific idea of God, perhaps closer, as he admitted, to "the *Great Spirit* of the untutored Indian." "There can be no variety of spirits," however, but only one, "one all-powerful, all present, all wise and intelligent," which pervad[es] the whole universe." From "the roar of a cataract [and] the howling of a tempest [to] the sweet sounds of a singing bird or the harmonious strains of a good vocalist," God spoke through his creations. And not as "an *outside* being," above the world somewhere, looking down and playing with his creation "as with a football." "God lives in all things," John declared, "his spirit animates every object in creation. And every creature is an organism through which his wisdom and love are experienced." He was "universal spiritualized . . . substance as well as a spirit," John wrote. He is "the great philosopher, the great mathematician, the great architect," who works not by "induction" or deduction" but "by reflection alone. He simply reflects himself and all is right." His light "proceeds from the center towards the periphery" breathing life into all of creation.[48]

John was incapable of living, thinking, or existing without a reason. There had to be order and balance. Nothing could be messy or random. There had to be a logical means to understanding the world. There were things—flowers, sunlight, mustaches, mosquitoes—so there had to be a reason that was fixed and solid, explainable by reference to a guiding authority or agent that moved everything into place and set it working. Something had to have happened for all the stuff of the world to come into existence. John simply couldn't move his brain into the realm occupied by "materialists," that newfangled bunch of naturalists who questioned whether there was a divine hand nudging the world onward. A world made of nothing more than self-organizing atoms, unrelated to each other except by a common drive to survive, struck John as ridiculous and terrifying. Self-sufficiency of matter was "tantamount to atheism," as most nineteenth-century Americans (and Europeans) knew instinctively. In a world emptied of God, what of morality, meaning, or order? With only isolated, unconnected life running around, competing and self-developing—what Sir J. F. W. Herschel famously characterized as "the law of higgledy-piggledy"—then the world was suddenly traveling down the path of a pointless and senseless existence. John couldn't follow. "Is harmony a result of accident or design?" he wondered. "Surely where there is harmony and order, there is also design and law?" When the mind is lost in the "perplexity and bewildering multiplicity of the minor creations," he continued, "lift your thoughts and behold the stupendous grandeur of the order and harmony, which reigns in the heavens! No unsophisticated mind will doubt, that the great absolute is equally competent to govern the parts as well as the whole!" There had to be an intelligent motive force behind it all, a "cause"; and if there was a cause, there had to be an effect.[49]

Cause and effect were the watchwords of John's philosophy. When he looked around, he saw effects everywhere, effects that needed explaining. So explain them he did, by developing his own hermetic, linear system, albeit one that owed much to metaphysical and transcendental thinking. All of existence was dependent on "the unity of cause and effect," which were interdependent. "Neither the one nor the other has existence by itself; there is no matter without spirit, neither is there spirit without matter," he wrote. "They are to each other as cause and effect, and cannot be separated." Consequently, there was no such thing as "passive inactive matter, or matter without life" in John's mind. Whatever exists does so by "virtue of its inner life, and not by control of an exterior power. The spirit of God pervades all and controls all." John believed there were two worlds: the unseen, immaterial, spiritual world and the outer, visible, material world of nature. These two worlds existed in "stability and harmony," the one shaping and regulating the other. "A material object is but an outer manifestation of an inner life or principle," John wrote.[50]

"The universe is a formalization of divine thoughts," John argued. "The natural or outer universe is an outside manifestation of the spiritual or inner universe." God had no existence outside of the material world, which in turn had no existence outside of God. Together they form "a great dance . . . one grand harmonious symphony, its celestial tones vibrat[ing] through" all of space and time. In response to those "who believe that nature is nothing but a wonderful material self regulating mechanism, without any further meaning," John was blunt. "In the great workshop of the creator there is no chance, all is law and premeditated design, all is system and order," John declared, in what might well be accounted a case of finding exactly what one is looking for. But John believed. All of nature took the form dictated by its "inner principle." At the apex of this principle was man, "an individual revelation of God's own personality," the pinnacle of self-reflection.[51]

For John, "man is a two-fold being: inner and outer, spiritual and material, cause and effect . . . the fulfillment of God's design in his creation." While we each take individual form, we are not possessed of individual souls. "There is but . . . one *spirit—One great spirit*—The spirit of the universe." John did, however, seem to believe in an inner individual of some description. "Whoever has reflected upon himself and examined himself carefully, can doubt the existence of an inner organism?" he asked. "If you never have watched your own inner being, try and do it now," he counseled. "Think and speak within yourself, silently, do not open your mouth, do not move one of the articulating muscles: can you not speak rapidly, articulate every syllable, annunciate, and even exclaim violently, and all in perfect silence, only using your inner organs of speech? . . . So with your organ of vision, close your outer eyes, collect your thoughts and concentrate them on anything, you wish to see, and you will see, with your outer eyes closed. The most gorgeous spectacles and the brightest shows and colors," he declared, seeming to mix up his imagination with a more mystical sense of his interior being.[52]

The entire world—seen and unseen, spiritual and material—acted in concert, and humanity needed to understand this fact to realize that "our mind is one with the Great Universal Mind." This matter alone, John believed, forms "the grand basis of the harmony of creation." Without understanding, without acceptance, humanity would never achieve its object, its purpose. "Bring your own interior nature in unison with the outer world, and harmony will be established," John wrote. Discord—a failure to realize and believe—will destroy the balance, however, tipping the world into chaos. "Every sentiment of our mind forms a note in the music of creation, and will either as a *discordant or consonant* [note] depress or swell the harmony of the whole."[53]

John's God was completely of the New Testament. He rallied against the "changeable God" of Moses: a "grand man, endowed with grand attributes and also with grand human passions," because he contradicted himself. At one moment, he was a God of "justice and of love," and then at another he was full of "wrath and vengeance." How could such a being maintain harmony and balance? Violence and retribution could play no part in God's love or human nature. "Will the principal of 'a tooth for a tooth, and an eye for an eye' calm down those fearfully turbulent passions; will man's law of vengeance act like oil upon the troubled waters?" John asked. There could be no such God in John's world. There could only be a God of love and forgiveness. "Love and wisdom make up the Spirit of God, therefore they should also be the foundation of man's law," John wrote. "Man has no right to take revenge on his brother."[54]

John's critique of religion was the key to much of his philosophy. There needed to be consistency within and across the terrain of human understanding and human knowledge. Contemporary religious practice wasn't free, it wasn't consistent, and it wasn't harmonious. It lacked deep commitment—"Outward praying and ostentatious church service does not constitute true worship," he protested—and was "destitute of spiritual life." John believed in God, in Jesus, and in some vague idea of Native American spirituality, because they were all pointed in the same direction. They all spoke of a similar relationship, at least in John's mind. "The mind of man & the mind of nature is one," he wrote. "The simple Indian beautifully expresses himself, when he calls the Earth his mother, and the Great Spirit his father. We are truly the children of nature, impregnated by nature's god. How does it come that we can appreciate the beauty & diversity of colors, the sound of noises?" Religion—true religion—in John's conception was that which "produces harmony." "When my own being is in full harmony with nature and nature's God, consequently at peace with myself and all that exists, then I am truly religious." But when looking to "injure my fellow man"— for whatever reason—"then I commit an irreligious act, a wrong."[55]

John placed much of his hope and belief in the figure of Jesus Christ, whom he saw less as the son of God—in truth, he saw every man as the son of God— and more as a philosopher and "reformer." "The value of the Christian religion consists in the simple fact of Christ's life," John wrote, "and because [the] good deeds of his life come nearer to perfection than any other man's, so also his teachings partake of the same sublimity." All who believed that Jesus had died for our sins were wrong. The central fact of Jesus's life was his life, not his end. "He alone is a follower of Christ who endeavors to act as he did, not by professions and ceremonies but by actual deeds," John affirmed. John believed, and repeatedly stated, that "Do ye unto others, as you would them do unto you" was "the great law which applies with equal justice and with equal force to man individually as to man collectively." Oddly, this placed John in complete agreement with that archmaterialist Charles Darwin, who declared, "The golden rule, 'As ye would that men should do to you, do ye to them likewise,' . . . lies as the foundation of morality."[56]

John scorned materialists. "Almost without exception, the great bulk of scientific men have become materialists," he charged. "Many of them will not admit this change, but their arguments prove it. Some indeed make strong religious professions but their professions are not in harmony with their scientific convictions," which is an accurate description of the tightrope many of John's contemporaries were trying to walk. John was troubled by the limitations of science as a branch of knowledge. He believed man was "bewildered" by "the many disconnected branches of the ever spreading tree of knowledge." Modern science was excellent at gathering knowledge and finding out new things but it could not and did not put them all together into a coherent narrative that explained existence. "Beyond the practical aggregation of scientific discoveries, science is without interest, because it has no aim, beyond itself." Science promised no future but come what may. And John couldn't live with that. There had to be a point, and neither religion nor science seemed capable of comprehending it. "A barren theology pursues its old worn out track regardless of the enlargement of truth," while science has "no compass, no rudder, to steer the exploring intellect on this ocean of mind." Mankind needed answers. Science could "acquaint us with the facts of existence," but not with the "comprehension" of those facts, not with their "relations." Only philosophy could "reason in the abstract" and grasp the "truth of science." "Scientific knowledge leads not to wisdom," John explained, "but philosophy does." Philosophy saw beyond superficial facts and "simple effects" to see "the inner truth of things."[57]

Philosophy was a higher order of thinking whose "true office" was "to trace the connection between cause and effect" and "establish the connection between the creator and his creation." But it couldn't function without the base supplied by other ways of knowing and understanding. The fault in the way we sought to process the world around us stemmed from our propensity to retreat behind little bodies of knowledge. If we wanted insight into the deepest aims and ideas about life, we needed to adopt a broader methodology. Science, religion, and even philosophy were all wrong when they claimed the entire field for themselves. Their conclusions were impoverished by their narrow focus. Science and religion were both "handmaids to philosophy," in John's conception, but together they were the glue that held our understanding of the world together. Those who thought philosophy was "degrading" to either science or theology "possess no clear idea about either," John declared.[58]

In 1856, John wrote a rather fanciful introduction to a piece he called "The Harmonies of Creation." He began by imagining "an observing friend perched up . . . high up in the heavens, far enough away to [see] the outlines of the globe at one glance." From such a platform, one could "comprehend the situation and movement" of all things, "all that breathes and moves, all that is organized." John's surrogate scanned the globe, eventually training his sights on the North Pole, where he came across "a fearful desolate sight, a trackless waste, an accumulation of indeterminable masses of snow and ice." Such a bleak scene, he thought. No "green oasis to relieve this dreadful desert," no "life giving sun—no sound to break upon the stillness of the scene!" And then, all of a sudden: the "winds begin to howl and the storms rage with terrific fury! All hell appears to be let loose—nature is destroying itself! It is the grand semblance of a raving

maniac, blank in mind pursuing but one destructive and desolate idea!" Our
friend despairs and can't comprehend. Then slowly, he turns his glance south
to the "vast oceans," and "for an instant his eyes are dazzled by the sight; he
believes himself suddenly transported to those wonderful scenes, described by
the Arabian Bards, when Emerald Isles were swimming through the Oceans,
wafted by gentle breezes from one happy shore to another!" Yet on closer examination "these imaginary swimming abodes of happiness & bliss" are merely
icebergs, torn from "their ancient seats high up in the north" by the "fearful onslaught" and "the resistless tide." "Why does nature cause the unyielding masses
to move south, and impede the mariner's way?" The mystery is soon solved. "As
he turns his glance further south, he is met by great currents and streams, which
move with a majestic sweep from the tropics to the poles, disseminating genial
warmth, as they proceed, and thus tempering the region of the higher latitudes,"
while the icebergs move south and melt away, helping to "temper the extreme
heat of the south. By the action of simple hydraulic laws a grand system of circulation" is thereby established and maintained "in those vast extent of waters,"
while "an important part of nature's sublime economy is carried on." Without
each of the elements, the various bodies and movements and changes in temperature, "the waters of the ocean and the air of the atmosphere would become
stagnant. The great current of the ocean would not be maintained."[59]

"Chaos and destruction" give way to "order and system," and "our philosopher" begins to wonder if this is all chance "*or do these fixed and determined relations* . . . all point to a common origin and to Unity?! The answer is plain and
suggests a vast train of reflections," but also a set of principles. The harmonies
of creation require a broad, totalizing perspective. They require the patience to
observe, the faith to infer, and the imagination to reason.[60] For too long, "theology, philosophy and science have been at war," and "not because of any internal
disagreement between the three, but because its champions simply imagine so."
They had all crowded in on themselves when they should have formed an alli-
ance and learned from each other. "The unity of the human organism embraces
all modes of investigation," John wrote, whether inductive or deductive, ob-
servant or reflective. For mankind to live harmoniously, to live in truth, "all his
faculties must come into play, not only his observing but also his reasoning
faculties, as well as his affections and religious endowments." Our approach to
knowledge—to our world and our lives—must become more inclusive, more
accepting and embracing. "When my own being is in full harmony with nature
and nature's God, consequently at peace with myself and all that exists, then I am
truly religious," John wrote. "Is not this same great end also the endeavor of true
philosophy [and] in the same large sense [of] all true science?"[61]

John could often sound like Ralph Waldo Emerson in his evocation of nature's purity and virtue, which was hardly surprising. An assiduous reader who cast about widely for inspiration and ideas, he poached and borrowed. Emerson was perhaps his favorite native thinker, but many of John's ideas fit the transcendentalist mold. Taking his lead from the Unitarian minister William Ellery Channing, a huge influence on both the engineer and the transcendentalist movement, John believed that "all evidences of Christianity may be traced to this great principle—that every effect must have an adequate cause." John would also have heartily agreed with Channing's claim that "the principle in human nature from which religion springs" was not the need to serve, venerate, or sanctify but "the desire to *establish relations* with a being more perfect than itself."[62] When asked to define transcendentalism, George Ripley wrote that its adherents "believe in an order of truth that transcends the sphere of the external senses. Their leading idea is the supremacy of mind over matter. Hence they maintain that the truth of religion does not depend on tradition or historical facts, but has an unswerving witness in the soul. There is a light, they believe, which enlighteneth every man who cometh into the world. There is a faculty in all—the most degraded, the most ignorant, the most obscure—to perceive spiritual truth when distinctly presented," a definition that almost perfectly describes John's philosophical-theological project.[63]

John called Emerson a "profound thinker" full of "sublime ideas," but also found much justification in his writings for things he already felt and knew. More precisely, Emerson confirmed John's thinking as much as it informed it, which reflects their shared interest in Hegel, Swedenborg, J. B. Stallo, and other intellectuals. Both sought to understand what made the world move and where to find the source of the world's great animating force, and both found it in a spiritual communion with the natural world. The philosopher and the engineer sought to free themselves from the dry theory and established dogma of individual churches, and to forge a set of beliefs centered in moral and ethical behavior and in the natural world, not in a liturgy and a building. Mind, reason, and spirit were vital to this process. They were the "cement" (in John's phrase) that bound the world together, linking man and God, the outer and the inner worlds, the material and the immaterial. Emerson "believed completely, implicitly, and viscerally in the reality and primacy of the spirit," as did John, and both believed in the "existence of the material world as an expression of the spiritual."[64]

The idea that "particular natural facts are symbols of particular spiritual facts" is key to Emerson's great essay "Nature" (1836), as is the idea that our "moral law . . . lies at the center of nature and radiates to its circumference." Together they remind us of the relationship between matter and mind, between nature and thought, and our relationship—our debt and dependence—to "the Universal Being." The whole of creation is suffused with the divine spirit, and in turn each small thing accordingly holds the spiritual source code for all the rest, a point on which John and Emerson agreed completely. "I believe in the omnipresence; that is; that the all is in each particle; that entire Nature reappears in every leaf and moss," wrote Emerson. John made almost the exact same point when he argued that "an acorn contains within itself the whole principle of a full grown oak, so does the human organization contain within itself the principle of the whole man, the fully developed man, the universal man, the divine man, the great God himself." Both John and Emerson came to believe very strongly in Johann Fichte's idea, interpreted by Thomas Carlyle, that "there is a 'Divine Idea' pervading the visible universe; which visible universe is indeed but its symbol and sensible manifestation. . . . To the mass of men this Divine Idea of the world lies hidden: yet to discern it, to seize it, and live wholly in it, is the condition of all genuine virtue, knowledge, freedom; and the end, therefore, of all spiritual effort."[65]

Emerson borrowed one of *the* organizing metaphors of "Nature" from Emanuel Swedenborg—the "great Swedish master of the imagination"[66]—a writer whose ideas also exerted a large influence on John. Everything that existed in the physical world had a counterpart in the spiritual world. Swedenborg called this the doctrine of "correspondence." "The grand truth, that mind is nothing but a material realization of the spiritual, was first clearly announced by Swedenborg," wrote John, "but his sources of knowledge were beyond the reach of human faculties, and philosophers were inclined to discredit the genuineness of his inspirations," he continued, referring to Swedenborg's claims to have found all this out by regularly visiting the spirit world and communing with angels, phantoms, and other apparitions. Still, John didn't think it could "be denied, that [Swedenborg's] doctrines of analogies and correspondences, which control the relations between mind and matter, and which were taught by the learned Swede, have had a most important influence on the leading philosophies of the present day." Between the "gross materialism" of Locke on the one hand and the "pure idealism" of Kant on the other, the world of nature had been dropped from the philosophical project. Swedenborg's "profound" achievement for John was demonstrating that "nature is only a reflection of the mind that actuates it . . . that there exists perfect correspondence and harmony between the deity and his works."[67]

Swedenborg's reputation has declined since the nineteenth century. But thousands of Americans were attracted to his ideas and experiences in the 1850s. Whitman thought Swedenborg would have "the deepest and broadest mark upon the religions of future ages here, of any man that ever walked the earth." Emerson prized the mystic's energy, commitment, and imagination. "To the withered traditional church yielding dry catechisms, he let in nature again," he wrote approvingly. He understood the old "spook hunter" (as Kant called him), giving him his due and applauding his achievements, much as John did. Swedenborg and John disagreed on many things, the existence of hell being one.[68] But Swedenborg's sight was vital to John's knowing. "When I concentrate my mind upon a subject and I reflect intensely, then new ideas appear to flow into me," John wrote following Swedenborg's lead. "These ideas are not created within myself, but they come from without, from above. My brain appears to be surrounded by an ocean of ideas, they rush in as the mental floodgates are open. Once within my brain, they are appropriated, individualized through my mental organism. Thus is my mind enriched from the universal fountain of knowledge." It would take John a few more years to start believing in spirits, but even by 1862 he believed he could listen to and communicate with other realms.[69]

"The vast array of scientific discoveries in the different departments of nature, accumulated during the last 100 years, has crowded up on the human mind an avalanche of detailed facts, so overwhelming," John wrote, "that no one single individual, no matter how gifted, possesses enough of capacity for that perfect appropriation and systematic digestion." Our understanding of the world was spinning out of control even if our knowledge of it was increasing. Amid the centrifugal forces of an increasingly modern world, humanity needed an anchor, an organizing principle. Civil war, evolution, industrialization, paleontology, the market economy, and the technological revolution all heralded a new world, one lacking a path and a plan. For John, the more we discovered, the less we knew, and for a man dedicated to order and certainty, such an inference was frightening. It sent him ultimately to the certainty of books, not into the messy world of events. After all, what do philosophers do? They make order. Or they find it.[70]

John read widely, and he often found exactly what he was looking for: people who agreed with him. He plowed through Harriet Martineau's two-volume *The Positive Philosophy of August Comte* (1853), finding the Frenchman's ideas ambitious and compelling but ultimately unpersuasive. Comte's positivism was too deeply rooted in the pure veracity of science to let in a metaphysician like John. He read and approved of the intensely anticlerical Henry James, Sr.—one of America's foremost Swedenborgians—especially his essays "Man" and "The Principle of Universality in Art" from *Lectures and Miscellanies* (1852). John also made extensive notes on James's *Shadow and Substance* (1863), selecting for special praise the observation that "life and mind are convertible terms." "*Life and Mind are identical*," John wrote, happy no doubt to have yet more confirmation of one of his core beliefs. The Universalist William Fishbough's *The Macrocosm and Microcosm; or, The Universe without and the Universe within: Being an Unfolding of the Plan of Creation and the Correspondence of Truths, Both in the World of Sense and the World of Soul* (1852) was also very much to John's taste, with its focus on the unity of human experience, encompassing both the scientific and the religious. Johann Spurzheim's *A View of the Philosophical Principles of Phrenology*

(1825) was also a favorite. "Phrenology . . . has a great mission to perform, and deserves to be placed at the head of the great science of human physiology," John remarked. He was also attracted to Baron Carl Von Reichenbach's concept of "Odic force," an idea that posited the existence of some type of vital, invisible force that binds together and links all things, or, as John put it, "the existence of imponderable essences and powers, which appear as emanations from all natural bodies." "Reichenbach's discovery of Odic phenomena, promise[s] to give us true insight into the nature of matter," John wrote.[71]

Odic force appealed to John in the same way that Oken's ideas on ether did: they reinforced John's sense of a controlling authority behind all of nature. "Ether is the first instance of God becoming real and simultaneously his eternal position," wrote Oken in his *Lehrbuch der Naturphilosophie* (Textbook of natural philosophy; 1811), "God and ether are identical. Ether is the foundational matter of creation. . . . It is the ultimate divine element, the divine body, or substance." It is perhaps easy to criticize this approach, as many did at the time, complaining that Oken's definition of God was so broad that it must also include "mint liqueur and such." But if we substitute "nature" for "ether," we likely have not strolled very far from the core beliefs that drove Emerson and his fellow transcendentalists. Oken believed that *"the philosophy of nature is the science of God's own eternal transformation within the world,"* a sentiment that would not have been out of place in an Emerson essay or a Unitarian sermon.[72]

A name conspicuously absent from any of John's manuscripts is Peter Kaufmann, who Heinrich Rattermann remembered John meeting "frequently, anywhere where philosophy was the topic of conversation" and especially at "Nikolaus Schmitt's wine tavern" in Cincinnati in the 1850s. Kaufmann was a prolific author and philosopher who had published his first book—*Betrachtung über den Menschen* (Meditations on man)—in 1824 when he was just twenty-four years old. Kaufmann had worked as a language instructor for Rapp at Economy and by 1857 had struck up a correspondence with Emerson, whom Kaufmann revered to a degree "such as God alone could barely surpass." In 1858 he published *The Temple of Truth; Or, the Science of Ever-Progressing Knowledge; containing the Foundation and Elements of a System for Arriving at Absolute Certainty in All Things; Being a Message of Never-Ending Joy, and the Abiding Herald of Better Times to All Men of a Good-Will, or Desirous of Acquiring It,* "the condensed result of [Kaufmann's] most earnest and active research after *absolute truth,* prosecuted during a period of thinking existence and amidst an interior and exterior experience, infinitely copious and multiform in variegation, in extent and amount, of nearly half a century in duration." At their meetings John's eyes, "from which his genius twinkled, would light up," Rattermann recalled.[73]

G. W. F. Hegel was the first philosopher John ever encountered—back in Erfurt in 1822—and he remained the most important thinker in John's world for the rest of his life. John's comprehension of the great theorist was formed through a detailed reading of Hegel's works, but also through contact with several of his disciples in the New World. Principal among this group were the Ohio Hegelians, especially the philosopher and jurist John Bernard Stallo. Like John, Stallo was a German expatriate who had emigrated to the United States in the 1830s. Stallo's *General Principles of the Philosophy of Nature, with an Outline of Some of Its Recent Developments among the Germans, Embracing the Philosophical Systems of Schelling and Hegel, and Oken's System of Nature* (1848) caught the attention of America's thinking class almost immediately. Theodore Parker reviewed the tome for the *Massachusetts Quarterly*, calling it "a grand, solid book . . . the best thing upon the profound subjects to which it relates that has ever appeared on this side of the water." Emerson made notes on the book in his journals, copying out several striking passages, even using and endorsing some of Stallo's ideas in such essays as "Poetry and Imagination."[74]

Stallo's *General Principles* was devoutly Hegelian, devoted to breaking down the barriers between objective and subjective knowledge, between mind and spirit, and John loved it. He quoted from it time and time again in his writings, often including only large chunks of Stallo's text under certain headings, as if he himself had nothing to add or amend. Stallo's reliance on Hegel allowed him "to provide a sweeping perspective on man's total environment and place in it. He was able to show how the same principles which operate in a grain of sand or one man's reflections are also manifest in the solar system, and the sweep of history. All these phenomena are essentially self-revelations of Mind or Spirit."[75] No wonder John was captivated.

John admitted that it had taken him years to come to terms with Hegel's ideas, and Stallo's book may have been a key. But John clearly pored over Hegel's *Encyclopedia of the Philosophical Sciences* (1817)—a grand overview of Hegel's entire system, split into three sections: the science of logic, of nature, and of mind—as the presence of three different, well-thumbed German editions in John's personal library attests. He found answers there that fundamentally informed and undergirded his understanding of the world. Hegel was perhaps the only individual whom John celebrated unconditionally, the only person he praised, not because they agreed with him but because John agreed with them. John called Hegel a "profound genius" and "truly the spiritual philosopher of modern times." He regarded Hegel's "science of logic" as "a monument of mental depth and breadth for all future time" and a "beacon light of truth." John doesn't seem to have developed any special insights into Hegel's thought, though, and seems to have understood him as his contemporaries did. In *The Secret of Hegel* (1865), James Stirling characterized the universe as "a materialisation [and] an externalisation . . . of the thoughts of God." For Moncure Conway, the essence of Hegel's system was "the conception of an absolute idea which has represented itself in Nature, in order that by a progressive development . . . may gain consciousness in man, and return as mind to a deeper union with itself." John would have readily agreed with both definitions.[76]

John's debt to Hegel was threefold: the great philosopher reconciled mind and matter, provided a sure sense of trajectory, and allowed for a recasting of belief. All along, he brought light to questions of knowledge and understanding. "Before mind can comprehend its outer effects, it must comprehend its own working," John wrote, which was one of "the tasks of Hegel's logic; not to log down mechanic and arbitrary rules of thinking but to demonstrate the nature of thought itself." Hegel's bedrock—and John's—was "the perfect identity of matter in mind." Man had come to conceive of the spiritual and the material as enjoying "two separate existences," but Hegel had established "that neither has existence by itself; the spiritual alone exists through the material, and the material has no existence without the spiritual." Such an insight, John believed, allowed man to comprehend the "unity of nature," its "perfect accord and correspondence." This fusion underpins Hegel's concept of Geist, an idea often translated as "spirit" but that also suggests a broader sense of the mind's interaction with a larger group culture, or, as Hegel wrote, the "I that is We and the We that is I." Geist was immanent in nature—thus in the "Divine Spirit"—but also in the sweep of history and the movements of social life. Geist was the truth of history, and it was always unfolding and developing, revealing itself, asserting its freedom, and expressing itself in time and space. The concept allowed John to read the unfolding of a divine plan in Hegel's system, one untethered from the sort of established religious narratives he loathed. Back in Berlin, Hegel had angered his most pious critics not by his atheism so much as by his propensity to see God inside the world, not outside. God and man weren't separate, and neither were God and the infamous mouse droppings. Hegel couldn't accept the sort of dualism that defined the Christian church in the early nineteenth century, which didn't necessarily mean he didn't believe in God. Like John, he just went looking for him in very different places. John found God in everything, especially in Hegel.[77]

John summed up his sense of and debt to Hegel in "The Truth of Nature." "For a rigorous proof and logical demonstration of the truth, that the spiritual and natural form one inseparable unit; that all existences are but parts of one great intelligent organism; and that the different phases of life are but so many stages, so many moments of one grand universal process for the establishment of these grand and sublime doctrines," he wrote, "the world is in debt to the mastermind of Hegel. Hegel's god is a spirit and at the same time a substance; the absolute substance is both material and spiritual. Existence is a process in which the material is nothing but an outward display of the immanent spirit."[78]

John's philosophy encapsulates and epitomizes him, throwing into relief all his bizarre contradictions and inconsistencies. It is a direct experience of what it was like to live inside his head. To read page after page of John's thoughts is to be awed by the effort, intrigued by the ideas, surprised by the shortsightedness, and puzzled by the conclusions. The hundreds and hundreds of pages he produced during the Civil War reveal a technical genius able to assimilate and adapt new information, the philosophical naïf who longed for certainty, and the quack who bought snake oil on a regular basis. As was a pattern in his life generally, his ideas were a combination of rigid beliefs and honest seeking. It blended true insight and knowledge with foolishness and humbug; the professional with the amateur; the keen intellectual with the gullible patsy. John was both, and he was always both and consistently, often blending all the ideas in his life into a rough compound of unlikely—inconsistent and untenable—belief. He wanted to make a science of philosophy and a philosophy of science and turn both to the question of faith. He trusted Michael Faraday and Baron von Reichenbach; he believed in conductivity and Odic force, and he always used Hegel to mediate, to provide the fulcrum on which to balance the competing ideas. It was all rather wild and improbable, but it was also most often in the service of a higher ideal.[79]

Much of John's philosophy reads as so much mumbo jumbo, at least to the modern mind, but it also showcases a society struggling to reconcile the rising influence of science with the declining authority of faith and religion. Many nineteenth-century Americans wanted to establish empirical grounds for religious belief amid the growing cultural authority of science. Others retreated into more "internal and intuitive sources of religious experience," hoping to set their belief on the grounds of personal experience, not on an inherited hierarchy. John wanted both. He was a believer and a scientist; a romantic and a realist; a transcendentalist and technologist. He straddled the blurred line that ran straight through the nineteenth century, shaping its unsteady but inexorable onward march. John is a reminder that in a world of flux and uncertainty, people can be many things, and that contradictions aren't always so clear as they are with hindsight. Arthur Conan Doyle, the mind behind literature's most rational brain, was a doctor, ophthalmologist, and botanist who studied at one of the United Kingdom's most prestigious medical schools. He was a full-throated advocate of vaccinations, a man who understood the crimes of colonialism and stood up to them. He also believed in fairies. One recalls Dr. Hesselius in Sheridan LeFanu's famous short story "Green Tea" (1872), a brilliant German physician yet who nevertheless believes "the entire natural world is but the ultimate expression of that spiritual world from which . . . it has its life [and] that the essential man is a spirit, that the spirit is an organized substance." If you substitute physician for engineer, you have John in a nutshell.[80]

In many respects, the closest contemporary comparison for John might be the hated materialists. Both sought certainty in a world that was unmoored and changing rapidly, and they looked for it deep in the heart of every living thing, not up or outward to some celestial being overlooking all of creation. Both believed in a sense of common ancestry, that all things had flowered from a common source and had not been crafted individually in an everlasting, unchanging form. Both believed in a teleological view of the world: the planet was an ongoing project, always in motion, always changing, always developing; that the world was fundamentally mutable, a blasphemy to all but the most radical in the mid-nineteenth century. John even quoted approvingly from Robert Chambers's sensational bestseller *The Vestiges of the Natural History of Creation* (1844), a pre-Darwinian take on "transmutation" and evolution that also found room for the idea of a creator. Yet ultimately John—admittedly not a botanist, a biologist, or geologist—couldn't go where Darwin went. It is difficult to overstate how religious the nineteenth century was, how hard it was to think beyond or around it. Giving up on God was the strenuous, all-consuming work of an entire lifetime for Darwin. "It is like confessing a murder," he wrote Joseph Hooker, his most trusted friend. John could imagine a different narrative, a different way of thinking and believing, but he simply could not give up God. He couldn't lose the "great steel anchor" of his life.[81]

Transmutationists and materialists didn't have any clear idea of where life was going, only that it was going. But John did. If there was a first cause, an absolute cause, then there had to be an aim, a final destination. Order requires symmetry and harmony, not open-ended notions extending out into the furthest reaches of time. The same certainty that led John to believe in a beginning—a start—also led him to belive in a trajectory and an end. The world was not perfect. There would be no point to a world made perfect. But it was certainly the job of the world to get there, to attain perfection, through a slow process of growth and insight. Reason and self-reflection were the keys to this growth, for bridging the inner and outer worlds, for connecting humanity to its spiritual dimension, bringing them ever closer to the divine spirit, to their own destiny as children of God. Reason was the "union of heaven and earth," the "grand ultimate purpose" by which humanity could fulfill "the deity's designs." As the spiritual asserts itself more and more, so humanity's "cold reason and calculating intellect" will abate and a new age commence. Cruelty and selfishness will cease, and "true freedom of the mind shall be achieved." "Man's sympathies will be enlarged; the human family will become one fast brotherhood, and the weak as well as the strong will be embraced by the same common Bond of Christian love and forbearance. Man's inferior perceptions and his inner sight will be opened. What now remains a sealed mystery to man's intellectual curiosity will then become plain to his spiritual gaze."[82]

One might ask what one would see with this new "inner sight," with this "spiritual gaze." John's answer was simple and rather beguiling. We would know wisdom and we would see love. "True wisdom . . . is the purest, most disinterested, and most universal love," he affirmed. "In doing good to others, and loving my neighbor like myself; in utterly divesting myself of that coarse material of selfishness, and devoting all my powers and energies to the good of my race; in the performance of these acts my spiritual self becomes conscious of its own elevation and finds its reward in its own heaven." John believed that "love and wisdom united in acts, constitute supreme happiness, supreme heaven," which led directly to "the deep truths of those beautiful injunctions of Christ: 'Love you one another'; 'Do ye unto others, as you would them do unto you.' Are there any more laws required, then these self evident truths, in order to really regulate the conduct between man and man?" he asked. "And does not the same law of nature also enjoin upon man the same measure of sympathy and justice towards all creatures? What more laws are needed for man, to guide him safely through his earthly career?" he wondered. In April 1863, John was trying to write an epigraph for his mighty philosophical treatise. He tried out several, all on a single theme: "One God, one creation, one law, and this law is love!"[83] Amid the tumult of civil war, the atrocities of slavery, the challenges of evolutionary science, and the fading authority of the established churches, and with the "wolffish [*sic*] part of human nature" seemingly everywhere ascendant, John cast his thoughts around his battered world and settled on love as the only foundation on which the world could move forward. "Love and wisdom make up the Spirit of God, therefore they should also be the foundation of man's law," he wrote. "All nature is blended in love. . . . All harmony consists in love."[84]

————

The John Roebling that emerges from these Civil War–era writings is a completely new man: unknown to almost everyone; rarely glimpsed by previous historians, or, seemingly, his eldest son. This isn't the "man of iron" spoken of by Henry Estabrook at the dedication of John's statue in Trenton in 1908 ("Iron was in his blood, and sometimes entered his very soul"), nor is it the successful immigrant and industrial titan found in the pages of Hamilton Schuyler's *The Roeblings* (1931). It isn't the stern genius, forged in the long, hard years of America's struggle, presented by David Steinman's *The Builders of the Bridge* (1945), nor even the brilliant and austere polymath from David McCullough's *The Great Bridge* (1972). Most assuredly this is not the terrifying and overbearing John Roebling of Washington's memoir—full to the brim with fault-finding, complaints, and accusations—the primary account of him. Washington's John Roebling is mean and violent, brutal and intolerant. "His domestic life can be summed up in a few words—dominating tyranny only varied by outbursts of uncontrollable ferocity," wrote Washington. "His wife and children stood in constant fear of him and trembled in his presence." "It was a fortunate thing that his engineering engagements kept him away for prolonged periods, otherwise his children would all have died young," Washington added ominously. Yet the John of "The Truth of Nature," along with almost everything else he wrote in the late 1850s and early 1860s, is generous and hopeful, full of warm feeling and universal brotherhood. This John believed that "the principle of optimism prevails throughout the creation" and that "sympathy and love" were the only bonds that could hold humanity together. That John—Washington's John—had "something of the tiger in him."[85]

John and Washington were vastly different people. Their letters are a study in contrast: John's formal and measured, Washington's lighthearted and exuberant. Both "styles," however, hide important truths. Despite his stuffy way with words, John's letters to his children are loving and full of warmth, as are those he received in return. Writing to her father in March 1860, sixteen-year-old Elvira Roebling, John's fourth child, demanded that when John had "done" with his latest bridge—over the Allegheny at Pittsburgh—"you must come home and have a good long rest. You have never been home in the spring have you?" she wrote, lamenting John's constant traveling; "you don't know how beautiful it is." "I wanted to hear from you so much," she concluded, hardly the sentiments of someone overcome by "constant fear" and trembling.[86]

By comparison, Washington's jovial manner sometimes helped disguise a rather mean streak and a tendency to feel sorry for himself. His comments about A. G. Gower, written in 1894, are cruel and unpleasant—as are those about Amos Shinkle, many of which are also patently untrue[87]—and they hardly stack up against Gower's own letters to John or his (seemingly) tireless work on behalf of John's interest in the Lexington and Danville Railroad. Nor do they stack up very well with Washington's own letters to his father thirty years earlier when he asked John to pass on his " respects" to a man he later called "oily, unctuous . . . the prince of promoters and schemers."[88] Such conundrums dog Washington's memoir. Apt to see things in a profoundly negative light, Washington is a frequent complainer, often criticizing people's actions and motives. John, by contrast, rarely has a bad word to say about anyone. He was by no means above correcting people's behavior, but he was never mean or caustic. Washington often makes the claim that John kept his wife and family in poverty, even after becoming a wealthy man. Yet there is nothing in Johanna's letters to Washington to support this except a rather jovial admission that she was "always and forever the poor one" while preparing for the upcoming holidays. "If I had a bag full of money, it would probably be gone," she added. The family was able to afford most modern conventions and conveniences, including dancing and

Figure 17.3 The house John built in Trenton, later used as a home by his daughter Elvira after her marriage to John Stewart, then later as the main office building of John A. Roebling's Sons. Courtesy of the Institute Archives and Special Collections, Rensselaer Polytechnic Institute.

music lessons and one of the first commercially available sewing machines. In addition, John was extremely generous with local charities and with gifts. His notebooks often include lists of presents he bought his family, while his eldest daughter, Laura, thought her "father had better buy a lot of watches at whole-sale," as everyone in the family "wants one." "I have quite a number of wants this winter which cost something, and if father does not choose to be a little generous," she continued, "I shall be quite poor compared with other girls." Needless to say, she wasn't.[89]

Regarding John's Iowa adventure, Washington casts blame in every direction. After John was called away to Cincinnati, the concern passed into the hands of John's nephew William Meissner, who mismanaged the project, sinking eighteen thousand dollars into the venture, all to no account. "This made Mr. R. mad & he stopped the whole farce," Washington writes. John's letters from the time—to Washington no less—tell a different story. John was inordinately tolerant of his nephew, even though he believed William "himself is to blame & not the bad luck." But he let William make his own decisions and refused to tell him how to run the business he had put him in charge of. "Preaching to young men . . . is of no use, you know, they must find out by their own experiments how nature wants to be treated," John wrote evenhandedly, without even a trace of the abundant fury we come to expect of him from reading Washington's memoir.[90]

A similar set of problems dog Washington's time in Pittsburgh when he was helping his father build the Allegheny Suspension Bridge. To read Washington retell the experience is to hear a tale of constant browbeating, deprivation, and misery. "My principal duty," he wrote, "was to serve as a talking post. All his outlandish notions on Religion, chemistry, politics, and everything else were first thrashed out on me and if I could not or would not understand I was dubbed an ass and a scoundrel & was glad to escape with my life." All day, it seems, John "hurled [his ideas] at me with fierce declaim," and should Washington be anything but accepting, his father "would damn my atoms until a large crowd assembled, then I ran away to a saloon & replenished my mind, spirit & atoms with some bread & cheese & beer." As regards his living arrangements, Washington hated the long Sundays. "I always went supperless to bed—My boarding house shut up at 6 on Sundays, while he had a fine supper at the Monongahela house without inviting me." "Little things like this are never forgotten," he wrote tellingly. Yet the letters Washington wrote at the time tell a very different story. He wrote to Swan about the "very pleasant boarding house" where he was staying: "The table . . . is very well filled [and] each one digs in and helps himself." And about a Trenton friend named Clark Fisher who had just passed through Pittsburgh: "He cant [sic] imagine how anybody can live here and enjoy life," he wrote Swan. "For my part, I feel quite sorry that I will have to leave it. . . . I am perfectly at home in this place."[91] Oddly, Washington seems to have had a fantastic memory. In 1924, for example, he was apparently able to remember the names of every family that was living in Saxonburg in the 1840s. So one wonders what accounts for those periods in his memoir that are puzzlingly inaccurate or just mean-spirited.

No relationship was more important to John than the one he had with his eldest child, but equally none of John's children bore the brunt of John's life and ambition as much as Washington. His eldest son was raised and trained to take his father's place in the world. It was to Washington that the burden of finishing his father's greatest project fell, an enterprise that left Washington broken and confined to a wheelchair after two excruciating attacks of the bends. By the time the Brooklyn Bridge was completed and opened, Washington was a virtual shut-in, confined to a darkened room in a brownstone in Brooklyn Heights, while his long-dead father was praised as an engineering genius and exemplary American. Washington lived the majority of the rest of his life in his father's shadow—undeservedly. It was he who built the Brooklyn Bridge, not John. It was he who along with his brothers helped raise John Roebling's Sons into an industrial powerhouse, known the world over. That he still had to explain to people that he wasn't John clearly rankled. And when he came to write his account of his father—composed over forty years after many of the events described—his memory was perhaps less at fault than his temperament. He had given large chunks of his life and health to his father. In their place had grown a bitterness that is both understandable and somewhat uncomfortable, but that also doesn't engender total confidence in his account. As he wrote late in life: "No matter what you do, the people at large will rise in their bitter ignorant, jealous hate and destroy everything, merely to gratify unreasoning passion. . . . Man carries his own destruction within him."[92]

It is an almost impossible job to piece together the relationship between a father and a son. John and Washington spent so much time together, often alone, out of earshot. They spoke and argued and debated—maybe even laughed— and yet there were precious few other witnesses to their relationship, and much of what they shared was private and is lost to history. Ultimately, Washington tells one story, while John tells another; most likely, the truth of their lives blends both sides. Yet Washington was plainly afraid of his father on some basic level, as was made clear when he wrote to announce his engagement to Emily Warren.[93]

Washington was terrified of telling his father of his engagement, clearly fearing his father's wrath on some pretext or another, afterward even admitting he'd have gladly paid a hundred dollars to have the whole thing "cleared up" without his involvement. But John was overjoyed both at the news and that Washington had chosen to marry for love. He trusted that Washington knew what he was doing and that Emily—whom he had never met—was fully deserving of his son's love and commitment. He let Washington know the young couple would always be welcome at the parental home, that he would gladly build them a home in Trenton, and that if they needed any money, they need only ask. Never florid or effusive, John signed off "with the request, that you assure your young bride of my most affectionate regards . . . before I shall have the pleasure of making a personal acquaintance. Your affectionate father." The overall effect is charming, but also a little sad. Washington had worried for nothing, and he had clearly misread his father. Washington's fears were no doubt based on something, but John was delighted and generous, all of which took Washington by surprise. When forced to comment on his father's amateur philosophy, Washington was dismissive. "I cannot read it," he sniffed. Maybe he should have. He may have found there a much different father from the one he subsequently remembered.[94]

Unfinished Business (1863–69)

Unfortunately, John wasn't heading toward perfection. He was heading toward Cincinnati to reconnect with the half-built bridge he had left standing in the Ohio. As 1863 dawned, and with the war still raging throughout the United States, Amos Shinkle announced that "all the late issue of stock" issued in 1861—amounting to a newly raised $500,000—had finally been subscribed and that construction would recommence in the spring. Equally important, a bill appeared before the state legislature to amend the charter of the Cincinnati and Covington Bridge Company so as to reduce the height of the bridge from 120 to 100 feet above the low-water mark. John had long championed the lower clearance, on financial, technical, and practical grounds, but the move was controversial. Some feared a lower bridge would scare off trade, interfere with navigation, or lead to a rival landing established below the bridge. Someone even wrote an in-depth pamphlet on the subject. For others, the case was clear. The cost of moving a hogshead of tobacco from Lexington to the railroad depot in Covington (about ninety miles) was about the same as getting the same item across the river to a warehouse on Front Street in Cincinnati (one mile). With such conditions, the question of elevation hardly mattered. "Will a bridge benefit the city?" asked several of the city's newspapers. Undoubtedly yes, especially if "it can be done without material injury to any *great* interest of the city or its people. All legislation should be in favor of the interests of the people of a community rather than in favor of a class," wrote the *Gazette*. "Private interests . . . must always yield" when in "conflict with the interests of a community."[1]

———

Covington and Cincinnati were far from the wartime fighting, but the people were still divided in their loyalties, as were the bridge company's board of trustees. "The day is fast approaching when every citizen of this commonwealth [Kentucky] will necessarily be compelled to take his stand on one side or another," wrote Shinkle in 1861, and he chose the Union. By contrast, Henry

Bruce—the president of the bridge company and a slaveholder—picked the South. Such a state of affairs could be maintained while the fighting took place elsewhere, but on the rare occassion when danger did approach—as it did in the fall of 1862—choices had to be made, about loyalties, about defense, and about infrastructure.[2]

In the late summer of 1862, Confederate generals Braxton Bragg and Edmund Kirby Smith led a joint-pronged charge into Kentucky, hoping to shift public (and political) sentiment in their favor, in the process drawing neutral Kentucky into the Confederacy. A second prize seemed available in capturing Cincinnati itself, a major industrial center with much-needed manufacturing and materiel. Smith routed Union forces at the Battle of Richmond at the end of August and set his sights on southern Ohio. By the end of the month, he had taken Lexington and stood poised to control all of northern Kentucky. Over the river, a public meeting was held on September 1 to discuss "surrender versus pillage and destruction." The press, luckily, was more resolute. "The time for playing war has passed," wrote the *Gazette*; "the enemy is now rapidly approaching our doors. Kentucky has been successfully invaded and Cincinnati is now, for the first time since the commencement of the rebellion, seriously threatened." "The great duty of the people now is to unite and rise like one man and prepare to resist the approaching foe." Later that day, Major General Lew Wallace—future author of *Ben Hur*—arrived, declared martial law, and took charge.[3]

Unfortunately, there were barely any actual troops in Cincinnati. "The war had been a horror to them," Wallace later recalled, "read of as so distant it could not be brought to their doors." In fact, when word went out that the enemy was coming, the most frequent reply seems to have been "What enemy?"[4] But under Wallace's command, the people of Cincinnati rallied and responded. A call for mass mobilization yielded an astonishing sixty thousand recruits. Unfortunately, assembling a large army on one side of a wide river might save a city from invasion, but it wouldn't keep anyone from coming right up to their doorstep, menacing the river, and laying siege. If Wallace was to steal a march on Smith, he would need to set his defenses in Kentucky and beat back the enemy from there. But how was he to transport his militia across the Ohio in such a short period of time? Wesley Cameron, who had worked on John's span, suggested a pontoon bridge, if the city could rustle up sufficient barges. Thirty hours later, Wallace's militia was marching down Walnut Street, over the Ohio on Cameron's bridge, and up Greenup Street in Covington to take up their positions. Wallace set up defenses along the hilltops from Ludlow in the east to Highlands Heights. Smith's advance scouts arrived in Covington on September 6 and soon realized what they were up against. After a brief skirmish at Fort Mitchell, they abandoned the area, and the Confederacy all but abandoned Kentucky. Cincinnati praised Wallace's "moving spirit" and steadfast resolve to save the Queen City "in the

Figure 18.1 Cincinnati under siege during the Civil War, with John's half-built bridge towers as a backdrop. "Cincinnati Bridge half built, Union troops crossing from Cincinnati to Covington," from *Frank Leslie's Illustrated Weekly*, September 27, 1862. Library of Congress.

very face of death and his victorious hordes from Richmond." They also began to realize all over again how necessary bridges were. "The pontoon bridge . . . was of incalculable utility to the City, and a lesson never to be forgotten," wrote the *Gazette*, shortly after which Shinkle finished selling the company's new stock and John got his height reduction.[5]

The bridge company was soon in touch with John, who made his way out to Columbus in March 1863 to urge passage of the charter amendment. The legislation was duly secured, and by April John was back in Cincinnati. His towers were exactly as he had left them four years earlier, although the city itself seemed vastly changed. Cincinnati "is full of strangers," he complained. "Everybody is anxious to see the bridge work go on as rapidly as possible," he wrote Swan; "the bridge is very much needed." John was also lucky to have his two old assistant engineers back: Gower and George Fulton (described by Washington as "a fine type of the American engineer, ready for anything"), along with the ever dependable David Rhule.[6] Unfortunately for John little else was the same. The prices of almost all raw materials had doubled since the war began, as had the price of labor. Worse, the economy was being run on a wartime footing. As John well knew, his bridge was "the only public work in the country [being] carried on by private enterprise; to crush the rebellion, all the energies of the nation [were] being centered on the one military task." There were no companies to bid on the contract to finish John's towers. If the towers were to be built, John would need to do it himself. He would need to design every section of his machinery and then build it, no small feat during a civil war. But he managed it. He designed a dolly and ramp system to get the blocks of granite to the base of the towers, where they were hauled up to the top on a wire rope controlled by a steam-powered winch. Once up at the summit, the blocks were put on a little trolley and moved around, eventually being lowered into place by a setting derrick.[7]

By May there was a considerable force of workmen engaged on the Cincinnati shore, and by June everything was progressing nicely. On July 13, John wrote to Swan to report that he had finally gotten his derricks made and working and that he'd right then be "laying masonry, if martial law had not been declared." "Our city is wild with excitement over the near approach of John Morgan and his force of 5,000 guerrillas," reported the Democratic *Enquirer*. General Morgan and his band of Confederate raiders had been making their way through Kentucky and Indiana burning bridges, government stores, water stations, and railroad depots, all while stealing horses, cutting telegraph wires, and tearing up rail tracks. As of July 13, 1863, they were in Miamitown, only fourteen miles away. Fresh from blowing up Washington's Rappahannock Bridge, Ambrose Burnside—the new commander of the Ohio—decided to suspend all business and order all white male citizens to assemble at the prescribed points and organize themselves into companies "under the Militia Law." Morgan and his band of wildcats had no taste for large, well-guarded cities, and they headed north instead.[8]

Morgan reminded "a city unused to the din of war and its impediments" that there was a conflict raging all around them. John, however, knew this implicitly. He knew the pressure it exerted on wages and the strife political differences could wreak on a workforce. He also had decided opinions on the matter himself. "No Democrat can be trusted, they are all disloyal and treacherous more or less," he wrote Swan, before laying out the labor troubles dogging the project. "I have some trouble here with my laborers who struck this morning for a rise. I have paid them so far 1.25 and do not feel inclined to raise the wages. If I do every other builder in the city will be compelled to follow suit," he feared. Worker dissatisfaction had plagued the construction since the very first week, and John was certain about who was responsible. "I want to get rid of the Cinc[innati] wharf rats at any rate," after the latest rounds of demands, "and engage Germans in their place. . . . The Germans about here are mostly loyal, the Irish alone are disloyal." For John, the bridge and the Union were as one. Loyalty was key. John would never pay an honest wage to a disloyal worker—disloyal to him or to the country.[9]

John's towers continued to rise without incident until the middle of December, when the weather turned frigid and work was suspended for the season. John returned home to his family for the holidays. As usual, he busied himself with financial matters in January, going over the company books, auditing his investments, and planning for the coming year. His concern for Washington was evident in most of the letters he wrote in the first half of the year, though Washington was ironically nearby in Washington most of the time, attending functions and falling in love with his commanding officer's sister. By the end of March, John was back in Cincinnati, where the weather was "so raw and cold" that he was unable to get anything done, except place orders and wait for the weather to lift. The masonry work was recommenced on May 9, about the same time that "a heavy force" was busy "in the anchor pits." The towers rose about five feet per week, while the buttresses were being formed and the arches set. It was hoped that both towers would be completed by winter, but the slow pace of hauling and setting left them unfinished by December 10 when work ceased for the season. John was back in Trenton by this time, however, and barely paying attention. Two weeks earlier, he had been summoned from Covington by Swan with a rare and urgent telegram: "Mrs Roebling died this PM—Can you come home—Answer at once." Death, it seems, had come to the Roebling family, not to take his eldest child, as John had long feared, but to take his wife.[10]

———

Johanna Roebling is a conundrum. Like so many women in history, she left behind children and little else to tell us about the life she led. Her name appears only once in the index to the massive Roebling archives at Rutgers University and Rensselaer Polytechnic Institute: "Johanna Herting's baptismal certificate, May 22, 1831," filed—perhaps unsurprisingly—under "John A. Roebling / Personal Miscellany." The only image of her—a portrait done in 1860 as part of a set depicting her and her husband—shows a plain and sober woman with sad eyes and a weary look. Her clothes are black, and her hair is pulled back and tied. She epitomizes the burdened nineteenth-century housewife and appears much older than her forty-two years. A few of her letters to her children also survive—showcasing her elegant handwriting, which seems to belie the sense of her as uneducated—and they tell a different story, characterizing a woman of warmth, given to gentle ribbing, and possessed of a mildly irreverent streak and an appreciation of beauty. Writing to Washington in 1858, she tells of the coming of spring to Trenton. "It is lovely everywhere . . . now that nature is putting on her loveliest dress," she writes. "Yesterday was such a beautiful Sunday.

I am sure you and Papa [who were both in Pittsburgh] went out to enjoy the lovely spring air?" As usual, Johanna spent part of her Sundays at church. Uncle Riedel had preached at the local Lutheran services. "Uncle's preaching is entirely different from that of" their usual pastor, Johanna remarked. "One certainly doesn't fall asleep over it," which seemed like something of a mixed blessing. Johanna missed being "lull[ed] so nicely to sleep" as she normally was. Later that year, after the beautiful spring had given way to a brutal summer— "Everything looks as though it has been cooked," Johanna wrote with lyrical resignation—she again wrote to Washington to pass on a rumor that Annie Train, a local girl, had married a young man from the normal school. Ms. Train had "is said to have declared that she could have had Washington Roebling any time she wanted to," Johanna teased. She wasn't above making fun of her husband either. A couple of years later, Elvira wrote to her father, "Mother wants to know if you awoke when you fell through your bed the other night. She thinks it advisable to send for some . . . wire rope." Nor was she slow to compliment him either. After John and Swan went horseback riding in early August 1862, Johanna wrote to Laura to tell her what a good rider her father was. About a month before she passed away, Johanna told her daughter Elvira that John used to promise her a quarter every time she helped him wrap himself up in a wet sheet as part of his water cure. He never paid, but the moment and the memory seem playful, not demanding.[11]

Johanna's command of English was never strong; indeed, her letters to her children were in German, which often left her somewhat isolated in her husband's company. Washington felt this to be a curse that kept his mother "aloof from society" and contributed to what he took to be her "hard life." Yet she went frequently to local lectures and concerts (especially with her daughters), received many guests and friends at her home, was an active gardener, and served as an organist at her church. She also made trips to see old friends and family in Saxonburg. Her letters of the early 1860s certainly suggest that she felt very keenly the increasing absence of her children, with Washington fighting in the war, Laura on Staten Island, and both Ferdinand and Josephine at school. One imagines that her home must have felt newly and painfully diminished. As for John, Johanna was rarely actually in her husband's company over the years, although she clearly discussed his work with him, knowing, for example, that he was traveling to Columbus, Ohio, in 1862 to convince the legislature to alter the charter of the Covington and Cincinnati Bridge. She also followed his exploits in the papers and seems to have developed an appreciation for the issues involved. "I read in the newspaper that the Lexington and Danville railroad has been sold," she wrote Washington, a day after John had written to his son to break the news. "That probably means that construction will soon start again," Johanna predicted, and that sadly "we'll probably see very little of you two at home" over

Figure 18.2 Johanna Herting Roebling, ca. 1860. Courtesy of the Ferdinand W. Roebling III Archival Center of the Roebling Museum.

the next few years. "Those who built the railroad have not rescued much of their capital," she noted; "the second company will make out better."[12]

Much of what is known about Johanna comes from the pen of Washington, a complicated witness. If Washington could be damning of his father, he was vituperative in describing John's relationship with his mother. "The poor woman was glad to die, even at 48," he wrote—somewhat dismissively—of Johanna and her experiences. "She had had a hard life—worn out with hard incessant work [and] many children—her nerves wracked by the never ending, everlasting, continuous, senseless useless scolding on the part of her husband." "The few rays of sunshine fell on her path only when her husband was away on a long engineering trip," he continued, which actually seems to suggest that her life was filled with sunshine, since John came "home [only] once or twice a year." Ultimately, in Washington's mind, his mother "gave up [her life] in despair," which seems like a bold statement, given how rarely he had seen his mother in the last ten years of her life, and that she still had four children under twenty years old in her care.[13] Running a large nineteenth-century home was no picnic, of course, but it's hard to imagine Johanna "worn out with hard incessant work," especially with a cook and a fleet of chambermaids. Additionally, none of Johanna's letters to daughter Laura betray any anger or frustration with John, except perhaps that the house would be so quiet after he leaves for Cincinnati. "It is good that people can get used to anything," she wrote as John prepared to leave for the Queen City, "even loneliness," seeming to undermine Washington's claim that she cherished John's absence.[14]

Washington thought his father "would allow [his mother] no doctor," which is untrue. In April 1864, John wrote Swan to ask who her physician was— "Nobody had informed me"—and to "request you *as a friend*, to talk *on my behalf* with her physician and ask him, to give you a correct *diagnosis* of her disease, in *writing*, also the history of her illness, and if he chooses, his treatment and candid opinion. I have among my friends here three distinguished physicians, with whom I shall consult, as soon as I am supplied with the correct description of her disease." Certainly, John tried to recommend treatment and doctors to his faraway and ailing wife, all while admitting that Johanna "never has paid the least attention to anything I've said or done on the subject of health." In a rather grisly passage, John recounted to Swan his recent struggles with illness as "ample proof of the efficiency of judicious water treatment." John had "been very sick & reduced," while away in Cincinnati during the early months of 1864, always "on my legs and about the river, taking new & fresh colds, as it were, every day." At home he could have rested up and taken care of himself, "but not so here, exposed to the cold damp chilly river air from morning to night" as he was. In consequence, he had been stuck with "a violent cough for four weeks." "Homeopathic medicines were without effect," he wrote Swan, leaving him with no choice but "*to return* to my own treatment," which "at last succeeded." "The whole mischief has at last left my throat & chest & *gone down* to my legs, which *look like raw meat*," he continued. "I could scarcely walk, but a few applications of my Pricker & the oil bring out the mischief & I am now getting entirely well. My mucous membranes have cleaned themselves & the coughing ceased then of itself. Give my love to all," John signed off, "and read this to Mrs. Roebling," who one imagines promptly shuddered with horror and sent for her physician.[15]

Rather than forbidding any doctors, John seems to have tried quite a few. "Dr. Borden has run her down; the N.Y. physician has done no better & totally misjudged the case; Dr. Rauhe has given her up," he wrote with evident exasperation just a month before Johanna's death. John eventually asked Dr. Brinkman— a "physician of much experience and intelligence"—to monitor his wife, which may have been foolish but was also neither cruel nor unthinking. Brinkman was a water adherent like John, and Washington certainly believed his mother "literally died from being stuck in cold water all the time," which might have been true. With his wife worsening and no one seemingly able to help, John took greater and greater charge of his wife's treatment. "We are deep in the water cure now and it is a great deal of work but I think it is doing mother good," Elvira wrote Laura in October 1864. Her mother still felt weak, but her racing pulse had slowed, and "she has a good appetite and does not throw up what she has eaten. She eats four meals a day but little at a time [and] feels a great deal freer in her head than she has for a long time. Her face begins to color again too, it has lost that ghastly yellow look."[16]

Laura was less convinced by her father's methods, a fact that soon found its way to John's ear. "I read your letter to Elvira," he wrote his eldest daughter while home in Trenton on an emergency visit to check on Johanna at the beginning of November. "You express a fear that the *wet sheet* might affect mother too much etc etc etc. Now I wish to caution you against using in your future letters any such expressions which are calculated to take away mother's confidence in *my treatments*. So long as my prescriptions will be pursued *faithfully*, so will her life be safe, and she will eventually recover her former health," John continued with his trademark confidence. Should she "on the other hand, return to medicine, then her doom is sealed." If Laura wished to help, "cheering her up will have a good effect & that is what she needs," John advised.[17]

We have no idea what sort of medicine Johanna had taken or who prescribed it. We do know that nineteenth-century medicine was often no better than a coin toss in its effectiveness and that Dr. Coleman—another of Johanna's doctors—thought "she has had enough [medicine] stuffed into her" over the previous months. John didn't think Coleman "knew enough about water" or "had a just idea of her disease." But he consulted with him anyway, "because he is honest and intelligent," which makes a mockery of Washington's statement that Dr. Coleman had to be "smuggled in [past John, after his mother's death] so as to be able to give a death certificate."[18]

John's iron certainty may well have contributed to Johanna's death—although equally, so did the work of at least four other qualified doctors. Yet John clearly worried about his wife, a fact even acknowledged by Washington at the time. Writing to his fiancée in June 1864, Washington told Emily, "Father is very much worried about mother's state of health" and believes "that one of the principal causes of it is the anxiety and worry she is in about my safety." John asked Washington "to write home just as often as possible in order to quiet their fears there" and had earlier in the year worried that Johanna was "left quite alone at Trenton [with] nobody at home but Ferdy." When she began to fall ill in April 1864, John wrote to Swan about how anxious he was "to see her health restored and her life spared." None of which is to say that John enjoyed a particularly loving marriage, or that he held his wife in high esteem, neither of which was unusual for the time. He could certainly treat Johanna with little or no concern, was away for vast stretches of his married life, and seems to have communicated most often with her via Swan. Whether this indicates disdain for his wife or a rigid commitment to his career is hard to say. But John did understand that love was the central pillar of married life, which makes him somewhat enlightened for his time. After hearing of Washington's engagement in 1864, John wrote happily that he took "it for granted, that love is the motive, which actuates you, because a matrimonial union without love is no better than suicide." Whether John believed that he had committed suicide in Saxonburg in 1836 by marrying Johanna we will never know. But John mourned his wife. He wrote of her in the family Bible—"In a higher sphere of life I hope I shall see you again Dear Johanna! And I also hope that my own love and devotion will then be more deserving of yours"—and eventually tried to contact her in the afterlife. He even wrote to Washington in mid-November to say, "Mother is improving slowly, but I think surely [and] that her entire recovery will take a year." Unfortunately, Johanna was dead soon thereafter in yet another show of John's unwavering certainty running headlong into reality.[19]

———

John returned to Trenton after receiving Swan's telegram but was soon corresponding with business associates and his men in Cincinnati, where a "severe" winter had descended. Gower wrote to say he was leaving "on a *petroleum hunt*" and later that the ice in the Ohio had ruined all the company's workboats. "Nothing can be done with them," he wrote his boss. John wrote nothing about his wife's death, and neither, it seems, did any other member of the family at the time. Johanna was buried in a plot in Riverview Cemetery in Trenton, next to her beloved son Willie. In time, she would be joined by John, Elvira, and her wayward and troubled son Edmund. John lies fittingly between his favorite daughter, Elvira, and Willie, whom he first adored and then mourned. Johanna lies between her last two children, one of whom lived a tragically short life and the other a tragically long one. All are marked with short, plain gravestones, behind which is a much larger and much grander monument to John. In death, as in life, John cast a large shadow over his family.[20]

The family's gloom dissipated somewhat with the coming of the New Year and the approaching wedding of Washington and Emily Warren. They were married in Emily's hometown of Cold Spring, New York, on January 18, 1865. Shortly afterward, it was announced that Washington would join his father in Cincinnati as his assistant engineer, where he was forced to board with the pro-Confederate Ball family. Emily had long feared falling into the life Johanna had led, bound to the home while with her husband was off for months at a time. And she fought with Washington over it. Emily was smart, ambitious, and opinionated. She was among the first group of women to attend New York University's Women's Law Class and even had an essay excerpted in the *Albany Law Journal*, an article on the subject of the legal status of married women. "The sacred rite of marriage conferred upon" woman little more than "the honor of ranking in legal responsibilities with idiots and slaves," she argued. Emily fully intended to be a partner in her marriage, not a subject of it, and after several months in Trenton—helping Elvira manage a household that was bereft of both mother and father, but which still included Josephine (seventeen), Charles (fifteen), and Edmund (ten)—she joined Washington in Cincinnati. What the sister of a Union general made of having to board with a family with decidedly Southern Confederate sympathies was not recorded, but no doubt strained moments followed in the wake of President Lincoln's assassination in April 1865. "The sad bereavement of the nation by the foul assassination of President Lincoln has produced a strong and deep feeling of bitterness against the rebels about here," John wrote Swan.[21]

Washington was amazed at what he found when he arrived out west. "Our bridge here is an immense thing," he wrote Emily; "it far surpasses my expectations, and any idea I had formed of it previously." His presence must have delighted John, who had fretted over his son's fortunes for almost four years, but it wasn't without its dilemmas. John already had two assistant engineers, and he could hardly bring his son—a trained engineer, married, and recently brevetted from the Union Army as a lieutenant colonel—all the way to Ohio without appropriate work. So John made way for Washington. He fired George Fulton, while Gower resigned. He gave his reasons as having just leased some "very promising oil territory in the mountains of Kentucky," but he may have anticipated what would happen to his position once Washington joined the project. Washington claims Gower's resignation "disgusted" his father "because it threw more work on him," but this seems to be another instance of Washington's cranky temperament and mean-spirited memory. John never had a bad word to say about Gower—in fact, Gower promised to continue to help John "as far as I can" in any of his ventures, despite resigning—and seems to have understood his friend's move. As he explained to Washington the previous year: the central problem in Gower's life was "that neither farming nor engineering is a money making business," so he was always having to cast about for something more permanent and substantial.[22]

John and Washington directed the completion of the towers through the spring and summer of 1865, and by August, with both towers standing 230 feet above the river, they were ready to begin the cable spinning. First they had to construct a temporary footbridge that would allow workers to lay, group, and bind the cables. The first wire was taken across by a steamboat at the end of August, and the entire crossing was in operation by the beginning of October. The footbridge was only about two and a half feet wide and a nightmare in a gale. John didn't allow any workers up in such conditions, as the whole thing was liable to buck its riders or tear itself apart. According to Washington, John made his son repair the footbridge—"always at the risk of my life," he added—which seems an odd thing to ask of one's second-in-command and a son whose safety John had worried over repeatedly for the last several years. (The truth was less dramatic, as Washington relayed to his brother at the time. "Climbing the towers is perfectly awful," he wrote Ferdy. "I used to go up on the rope until father positively forbid [*sic*] it.") Still, people lined up in their hundreds to apply to cross the temporary span, which John didn't allow, leading some to sneak across. One man stole past the guards just before dawn and marched across the river, only to find himself "perched a hundred feet above the water, on an exceedingly frail structure, which was creaking and swaying to and fro in a most unpleasant manner." Seized with complete fear he sat down, listened to "the awful grating of the wires," and edged himself slowly over the river. No such suffering or dread plagued two "Miss B's" from Covington who were sighted later that year "as if they had just come from the opera," laughing and singing on the footbridge, after which they "actually ascended to the top" of the Cincinnati tower and took "a promenade and moon-light survey of the surroundings."[23]

The wire for John's cables began to arrive at the Cincinnati landing on September 10. As on the Niagara Bridge, the wire was ordered from Richard Johnson in Manchester, England, to John's mind the most consistent and superior manufacturer. The wire arrived in eight-hundred-foot lengths coiled around huge drums. It was soaked in raw linseed oil, after which three more coats of boiled linseed were applied, before the wire was spliced together and then run out over the Ohio. To make a splice, the two ends of the wire were beaten out and flattened, notched, bound together with fine wire, and then painted with red lead. Tests proved these splices to be as strong as the wire itself. Because the cables covered such long distances, John set up portable splicing tables, complete with vice, notching tool, and anvil. To spin out the cables, an endless looped rope, powered by a steam engine, carried two grooved pulleys, which moved back and forth between the two anchorages. A wire rope was attached to the anchor chains and spun out over the Ohio on one of the pulleys in a huge loop, while the pulley on the opposite side moved in the other direction. It took eight minutes to make the passage across the river, and the whole operation looked like "a mammoth spider crawling along its web up to its den." The cables were attached to the anchor chains at the end of each pass, adjusted to maintain uniform sag and tension, and sent back. The work was exacting, its principles "simple," as John explained, but its practice painstaking and burdensome. Each wire had to do "its allotted duty," bearing the exact same weight under the exact same tension as each and every one of its 5,180 neighbors. The cables sat on top of a cast iron saddle set on rollers and a massive bedplate atop each tower. It took 740 wires to make a strand and seven strands to make a cable. Starting in November 1865, about seven tons of wire were carried across the Ohio each day. The last wire was run out on June 23, 1866, by which point 10,360 wires had been woven into the cables, for a total weight of five hundred tons. The cables were 12½ inches in diameter. Once spun out over the Ohio, the strands were collected and wrapped to form one solid mass, then painted with white lead "until they resemble polished cylinders, bright as a silver dollar fresh from the mint." John used the special wrapping collar he had outlined during his patent application back in 1846 and used on the Allegheny Aqueduct, his first bridge. The tightly bound cables were then painted in a mix of brown pigment, lampblack, and linseed oil. Wire stays running from the tower to the roadway provided a stabilizing force that could account for a moving live load and help keep the whole thing rigid.[24]

The riverfront and abutments on both sides of the Ohio were covered with workshops from the winter of 1865 to the spring of 1867. The entire area hummed with the incessant sounds of steam engines, whipsaws, forge hammers, and other industrial instruments. Orders were barked, instructions issued, warnings made. Over two hundred men were employed spinning the cables, hewing wood, and finishing the ironwork. Covington played host to the woodworking—a drying house and a planning mill to season and cut the half million feet of lumber that would be used to build the roadway—while all the rope and ironwork was conducted on the Cincinnati side. Hundreds of spools of

Figure 18.3 Cable making and construction for the Covington and Cincinnati Bridge across the Ohio River (1866). Courtesy of the Institute Archives and Special Collections, Rensselaer Polytechnic Institute.

wire rope sat alongside almost seven hundred massive iron floor beams recently shipped from Buffalo. The scale of the work was huge, and at the center of it all was John, "the master mind of this great work," as one newspaper described him. "Mr. Roebling is a singularly modest man in appearance and demeanor," they continued. "He is now sixty years of age, but does not look to be more than fifty, of medium height, dark complexion and iron-gray hair, with features full of the characteristic expressions of great energy combined with deliberateness." "Every stone laid, every wire stretched, has received the attention of Mr. Roebling," they wrote.[25]

———

In the spring of 1866, with John's cables almost complete, a reporter for the *Daily Commercial* visited the construction site and was lucky enough to be guided around for a few hours by Washington. After a brief tour of the workshops, they headed up a series of ladders "into the dizzy altitude" on top of the abutment, where they could look down into the "terrible depth[s]" at the hundreds of men working on the wharf. "A man of weak nerves must not approach near to the edge of this mountain of stone," wrote the alarmed reporter, "for the inclination to look straight down, and then perhaps, to cast himself headlong, will seize him." But let him walk away from this danger, to the middle of the structure, "and he may enjoy, with a pleasurable sense of security, a truly charming view of nature and art": the surrounding cities with their "tens of thousands of houses" and "hundreds of miles of streets," "the encircling and closing hills with their wealth of forest and meadow verdure," and "far away to north and to south, rolling peacefully through all this, and looking not unlike a band of silver, gracefully curls the Ohio River, mighty with its swollen torrents." "In the construction of this bridge, far more than in any work," the reporter continued, "does one obtain an idea of the fertility of man's ingenuity, of his indomitable energy in creating dumb agents and inspiring them with a power, which, when he brings it to bear, makes of him a Titan." To watch the construction was to marvel at man and at what he can do. "Creeping along these iron strands, balancing themselves where a false step or a slip means death," John's workers "labor as rapidly as though they were standing upon solid earth, far away from any danger."[26]

From the abutment, Washington led the reporter up the footbridge toward the first tower. As he did so "a feeling of ill-defined uneasiness" started to creep over the journalist. "The frail structure rocks in the wind and the wires creak and rattle and sigh like a hundred Æolian harps," wrote the "ill-at ease pedestrian" as he recalled glancing down at "the gulf of nothingness over the water." "Doing the bridge is nothing," remarked Washington to his increasingly terrified companion, but "climb this ladder to the cradle"—forty to fifty feet above the temporary bridge—"and you will be the first to do it," except for those working up there. "Come!" he commanded as he sprang upon the ladder and began to ascend, scaring the living daylights out of the writer, who was forced to follow. "The first three steps suggested a grave without a coffin," he wrote, "grasping the ropes " [which] swayed too [*sic*] and fro fearfully, and creaked and groaned with a noise which seemed equal to thunder." Unable to resist, the reporter looked down. "The sensation was horribly sickening." His "knees began to tremble, and the perspiration began to pour. To look again through that terrible distance would be to fall." So he screwed up his courage, moved up, got onto the cradle, "stood erect, looked as though the affair was nothing, and remarked that it was rather hard climbing." A workman immediately gave him the side-eye and with a stony voice responded, "Rather."[27]

With the cables finished and the local press awed and ecstatic, all John had left to do was hang the roadway. Two huge nineteen-foot-long I-beams were riveted together end on end and hung from vertical suspenders on either side of the bridge. The suspenders were attached to the suspension cables every five feet by means of an iron strap that was worked by hand and hammer in a portable forge (designed by John) and then bent around the main cables before the suspenders were attached. The spacing helped maintain the cable's shape and ensured a level roadway. The deck frame was made of iron, while the roadway was made of three courses of oak, each coated in coal tar and rosin to prevent rot. Rigid side railings were designed to help with stiffness, as were two long wrought-iron trusses that separated the central roadway from the sidewalks on either side. All were connected using slip joints to allow some movement. By September, the press was reporting that the work was being "push[ed] forward . . . with an energy and rapidity seldom seen in any great public work." By the end of November, it was ready for limited use.[28]

———

Much was still left to finish by December 1, 1866, but John and the bridge company threw the bridge open to pedestrians anyway. The day—a Saturday—was bitterly cold with a "keenly-cutting wintry wind whistling along the river," but a huge crowd turned out all the same, as many as forty-six thousand by some estimates. Even more appeared the following day, when the weather was much better and "people were [more] generally at leisure." The streets approaching the bridge were crowded from ten in the morning until after dark, with every inch of the bridge covered from one end to the other. The *Gazette* thought it might have been the largest gathering in the city's history, while John thought it was "probably the greatest test of strength the bridge will ever have," with the final tally topping one hundred thousand. "There was really something wonderful in the immensity of the masses of people—men, women and children, young and old, rich and poor, all classes in fact—that passed over the great suspension bridge yesterday," wrote the *Commercial*. "The bridge was something wonderful to look upon. . . . All day, from sunrise to sunset, there was an unbroken throng crossing from the Ohio side, and another equally continuous, from the Kentucky side." The *Daily Times* noticed several "heavy gentlemen" jumping up and down trying to "budge" the span, grabbing "hold of the cables to demonstrate whether or not they could be shaken." Another of their reporters hoofed over the span at night the following week and was rewarded with "a picture grand and beautiful," the bridge "dimly lit by lanterns . . . creating just sufficient light to guide one's feet," while all the heavens were reflected in "the clear stream below." The vision was so magical that the journalist very nearly strayed "into the sublime void beyond the graceful outlines of the wiry monster" and into the icy Ohio.[29]

Perhaps the oddest event surrounding the bridge's opening took place the following Sunday, when the Reverend A. D. Mayo delivered a sermon at the Church of the Redeemer entitled "The Suspension Bridge: Politically, Socially, Morally and Religiously Considered." The reverend began with the observation that there were more people on the bridge the previous Sunday than in all the churches of Cincinnati combined. "The new Suspension Bridge was emphatically the preacher to the people of this city" that day, Mayo concluded, and his

Figure 18.4 The view from the river. The Covington and Cincinnati Bridge, ca. 1870. Courtesy of the Institute Archives and Special Collections, Rensselaer Polytechnic Institute.

task was simply to "interpret" what the bridge's "sermon" had been. He came up with many things, of course. The bridge spoke of "grace," "sublimity," and "wondrous beauty," but most of all it seemed to promise "the coming of a new era of Christian Light and Love," a development that would take many forms. On the one hand, John's handiwork was "an eloquent preacher of Union and Liberty," "one more link in that social chain which, more than laws and political policies, must finally bind this Republic into one," a sentiment John very much agreed with. "Thus united by strong cords of wire," John hoped, the bridge—a "truly national highway" permanently attaching the north to the south—would unite the "two great commonwealths" on either side of the river "commercially, as well as socially and politically," he later wrote. For Mayo, Ohio and Kentucky represented the "conflicting elements of our national life." With the war over and "every great principle of free society" established, it seemed fitting to the good reverend that John's bridge should stand "as the highway over which our New America shall march in her triumphal progress to the Gulf," bringing "light" to the "ruins of slavery" and "free schools" and "free industry" to people that "have long sat in darkness." Mayo envisioned free newspapers winging their way south bringing "freedom of thought and liberty of speech" to the "desolated southwest," helping to establish a "true American society, in which all men shall be equal in civil rights and wisdom and worth." All would pour over the bridge, which would be "filled by the presence of the Lord."[30]

On the other hand, the span would also inspire the land to the north of the bridge to take a fresh look at itself, to "no longer be content with many things we now meekly endure." The city of Cincinnati "must no longer reek with filth," while its people "shall no longer drink a museum of geological, vegetable and animal remains in every glass of water." (A friend of John's once remarked that consuming a glass of Cincinnati drinking water was very much "like eating and drinking at the same time.") The city's upper class, he continued, rather a little too optimistically, would no longer "feel happy" to live "amidst their sumptuous gardens on the hills," while everyone else huddled below "in our smoky Tartarus, without breathing space or park." Instead, "they will give us public halls, academies of music, great libraries and galleries of art." They will build homes with "speedy ways of reaching" them and "crush those infamous monopolies in the necessities of life which stand like highwaymen by every citizen's door." Taking John's span as its inspiration, Cincinnati "must build a new bridge . . . between Labor and Wealth," for "already a deep and turbid flood of distrust roars between the few who own and the multitude who toil." This must be addressed, and a "new reverence for human nature and a new respect for labor" must be cultivated. Only "then will all our bridges, and all our highways, and all our footpaths, converge to one broad avenue . . . beautiful as the rainbow . . . over which God shall perpetually descend to earth, and man shall ever more aspire to God."[31]

John might have laughed at such a notion, and he certainly had his tussles with the local clergy. According to Washington, John got into a shouting match the previous year with Pastor Michael J. Cramer, a brother-in-law of General Ulysses S. Grant, whom John "routed with great slaughter" and then "spat out of the house." But John would also have applauded Mayo's thoughts on human nature, especially his human nature. "A quiet, modest man"—the reverend had clearly never met John—"stands upon our river bank, marshals his army of intelligent mechanics, summons his materials from two continents, and thinks an iron pathway across our valley," he preached. "Who can look on this sublime achievement of the spiritual nature within us and not feel that man is something greater than he has been held to be? The obstinate materials of nature melt like wax in his skillful hands," while the builder himself "must feel the presence of a spiritual nature higher than his own," Mayo continued, unwittingly echoing a sentiment John had written privately many times over the previous decade. "Only through knowledge of themselves can men rise to a knowledge of a God whose laws are eternal order and justice, and whose being itself in infinite love," he concluded.[32]

John finally opened his bridge for vehicular traffic on New Year's Day 1867. Heavy ice in the Ohio meant the decision couldn't be delayed much longer. The bridge was serviceable even though it wasn't finished, which was more than could be said for all the ferry boats docked fast on either side of the river. An impromptu cavalcade was gotten up, featuring a band and a hodgepodge of carriages and wagons. John and Washington rode over from Covington with Amos Shinkle at about noon, while his assistants rode behind with other members of the board. The procession set off from the company's offices on Greenup Street, went over to Cincinnati, collected some wagons that had just paraded down Vine Street, and headed back to Covington to march through the streets and "serenade well-known citizens." As had happened the previous month, the people came out in droves, jamming the streets around the bridge. All morning, the cheers of the crowd and the "stirring music of the band" blended together into a cacophony of approval. Wait times at the tollbooths were about half an hour all day, even though the span had been opened to pedestrians a month earlier.[33]

Word of John's newest success spread quickly and easily. Images of the span were emblazoned across *Harper's Weekly* and *Scientific American*. Descriptions and reviews appeared all over the country and throughout Europe, and everyone agreed: John's span was a triumph. It was strong and beautiful, a milestone in the history of engineering. Back in Ohio, everyone seemed bridge crazy. Within months, talk of a railroad bridge between Cincinnati and Newport was being hotly debated and endorsed in all the papers, the beer halls, and the corner stores. "Nothing but bridges over the Ohio now attracts public attention," wrote the *Daily Times*. John wrote to endorse the project, but his time on the Ohio was finally over. His labor on the Covington and Cincinnati Bridge had begun in the early months of 1846 and had finished almost twenty-one years later, which coincidentally may have been the most opportune moment. Just as the crowds were flooding over John's newly opened bridge, temperatures in New York City were dropping precipitously, and its waterways were solidifying. The deep freeze that had crippled the Ohio ferry system also brought many of the docks and harbors in the North to a standstill. On January 23, New York's East River froze solid—nearly bringing the entire town to a grinding halt—and in a matter of

Figure 18.5 The view from the roadway. "Cincinnati and Covington Bridge over the Ohio River" (1870). Stereocard, J. H. Hoover photographer. Library of Congress.

days the whole city was clamoring for relief, for movement, and for a world-class bridge builder. John left Washington to act as chief engineer and finish up the remaining work—and repair the nearby Licking Bridge after it fell victim to a big gale—and set off east. Within four months he had signed a contract to throw a massive bridge over the mighty East River, one of the most sought-after projects in global engineering.[34]

———

Before arriving in New York, John stopped in Trenton, where on February 6, 1867, he suddenly married Miss Lucia W. Cooper. Little is known of John's second wife. According to a notice of her death, published in the *New York Times*, she was the daughter of James Cooper, "a wealthy civil engineer of Dublin," and his wife, Catherine, "daughter of Toler, the Lord Chief-Justice of Ireland." Her family immigrated to the Hudson Valley, where Lucia—the youngest of ten— was born in 1820, making her three years younger than Johanna. Lucia had remained unmarried, and she spent the bulk of her maiden life living with her sister in Niagara, which is where John met her. This account contains a couple of inaccuracies, but also—perhaps—some truths. John Toler was actually chief justice of the common pleas for Ireland, not lord chief-justice, but he also had no children named Catherine. Washington confirms John and Lucia's meeting, remarking, almost matter-of-factly, that his father "suddenly returned from" Niagara Falls with Lucia in May 1854, which raises numerous questions about their relationship, some of which might be answered by an obscure diary kept by the English writer and illustrator Thomas Butler Gunn, author of *The Physiology of New York Boarding-Houses* (1857), who seems to have known Lucia in the late 1850s.

In 1857, Gunn was boarding at 132 Bleecker Street when he met a young lady called Lucia Cooper who had just arrived from Niagara. Lucia was the sister of Gunn's landlady, Catherine Potter, and the daughter of Mrs. Lucia Cooper—a mightily unpleasant old woman, it seems—who also lived in the house. Lucia split her time between her sister's boarding house on Bleecker Street and Niagara, where another sister—Eliza Griffin—ran a series of hotels on both sides of the river. Lucia seems to have lived a relatively quiet existence and with few options. "'Tis pity Miss C. isn't married," Gunn wrote on December 2, 1858; "her position can hardly be a satisfactory one. They say she had plenty of opportunities once. She honestly regrets having let them pass, now." Lucia nursed her disagreeable mother "assiduously" and was "tormented" by "a pretty and grossly ignorant" woman by the name of Elizabeth Gourverneur, a rather colorful friend of the family possessed of "all sorts of indefinite hankerings after men, by the score." Elizabeth eventually married Lucia's brother Theodore, after which she seems to have spent her time "flirting with the entire village, even with her coachman and waiters, and vampiring Miss Cooper after her old fashion." Lucia called her "a wicked woman."[35]

Gunn's diary doesn't mention John, but it seems to suggest that if he did bring Lucia back from Niagara in 1854, he didn't bring her to stay, either with him or the family. Perhaps she was brought to Trenton to serve as a governess or in some other formal capacity. None of the other members of the family mention her in their letters of the time or later, however. While it is certain John met Lucia during his time at Niagara in the early 1850s, it is unclear what their relationship was for the next thirteen years. Gunn's diary doesn't establish that, but it provides the only substantial description of Lucia, the woman John elected to spend his final years with, and the central problem that afflicted her life and those of so many women of her era. "Miss C. honestly confesses she would like to be married—doubtless, naturally, hopes yet to be so, though the chances are dead against her, for she is poor, not young—especially for America—not brilliant, nor accomplished," Gunn wrote. "I think she has concluded that if a husband is to be had, it is only by dint of steady, perpetual, martyrising persistence in amiability." "She carries this out so, that though it may be unjust, you can't help suspecting its entire genuineness. You would be relieved if she would only dissent from you." Gunn remembered Lucia lamenting how pretty her friend Weighty Griffin was and how it allowed her so much leeway in her character and conduct. "I don't wonder that poor Lucia, without any prospect of being married, should revel in her woman's heart at the loose praises bestowed on perhaps a shallower person," Gunn confided to his diary. "I didn't feel inclined to laugh at the revelation," he continued, "rather to be sad. Oh what a crushing down and drying up of a woman's hopes must have occurred before she could take up this role of amiability. How she must long to be bitter, to give vent to her injuries—for what injury can be greater than to condemn a woman to be unloved all through life?" he concluded with evident sympathy.[36]

John seems to have had sympathy for Lucia and some genuine affection. The only existent letter he wrote her begins with "my dearest" and ends with "your loving husband," phrases he never used with Johanna while she was alive. Likewise, his will refers to her as "my beloved second wife." His children reacted less well to a stepmother, however. According to Washington, there was "a hell of a time" when John installed Lucia in Trenton. "Mr. Roebling having been away so much, his children . . . began to think the place their own," Washington reports, and they "made trouble." Washington met his father's new wife in March 1867 when he returned briefly to Cincinnati. He thought Lucia was "a harmless creature who ought to have been married to a different type of man, twenty years sooner." He thought John "regretted [his second marriage] before his demise," although the evidence from his letters suggests otherwise. John certainly knew

Figure 18.6 John's second wife, Lucia W. Cooper (n.d.). Courtesy of Antonia Malone.

that "the harmony [of his] family relations [had] been disturbed by his marriage with Miss Cooper," but he also seems to have believed that it was due to "the opposition of his children to that marriage" and not to any fault of his or Lucia's.[37]

John spent the last two years of his life married to Lucia, but it might be more accurate to say that he spent those years in the company of both his wives, at least in his own mind. Lucia was John's earthly companion, while Johanna appeared to him during séances. John had long embraced the ideas and theories of Andrew Jackson Davis, a man described by Arthur Conan Doyle as "one of the most remarkable men of whom we have any exact record" and by the *New York Times* as "an unnecessarily tedious . . . uneducated and densely ignorant person." Known as the "Poughkeepsie Seer," Davis was the leading figure in a rationalist reconfiguring of theological belief that sought to incorporate the presence and agency of spirits—and the ability of people to communicate with them—into everyday religious life. He was a Swedenborg for American democracy, ripping apart ecclesiastical hierarchies, and John idolized him. Despite a devout belief in spiritualism and the spirit world, John's first encounter with a medium only took place in Cincinnati in 1866, and he was hooked. "Last evening, Tuesday Feb 27 . . . Father and Emily & I went to Mr. Colchester the celebrated medium," Washington wrote Ferdy. "We are all confirmed Spiritualists now; father & I are good mediums. From Willie we have several communications, also from mother, and numerous other dead relatives and friends. Little Willie seems highly delighted that he had a chance to talk to us and promised to communicate often with father. Among other questions I asked what you are doing that particular moment; the answer was that you were quite indisposed that evening, and had already retired. This was about 9 o'clock in the evening. I wish you would write to me in regard to yourself whether that was in fact."[38]

John's interest in spiritualism was consistent with his own personal beliefs and with his times. A surprisingly large number of prominent Americans took to spiritualism in the second half of the nineteenth century: judges, journalists, abolitionists, historians, military officers, politicians, businessmen, and poets. "Scarcely another cultural phenomena affected more people or excited more interest," writes historian R. Laurence Moore. Everything seemed to be in flux, but also possible and within reach: new ways to build, communicate, and think; new places, materials, and laws to discover; even perhaps communing with the dead. It was a time of openness and optimism, but also of huge loss. War, disease, and large-scale migration separated family members, often forever. The confluence of loss and discovery fed the fake science of spirit photography, much as a restless search for answers created and fed an "antebellum spiritual hothouse" that in turn helped promote spiritualism. If the religious impulse represents the search for answers in the face of the panic of complete annihilation, then spiritualism offered a comforting, plausible solution to a bewildering era that took away as much as it promised.[39]

John's spiritualism was no embarrassing aberration, as it might now seem to us about so many major nineteenth-century figures when we imagine otherwise sensible people closeted in darkened rooms waiting for the dead to knock or raise a table. It was entirely consistent with what he thought and believed and the certainty he strove for. Spiritualists were often rational people looking to satisfy religious, personal, or social needs. In fact, few practices leaned so heavily on rationalism or "worked as hard to borrow [science's] prestige." Spiritualism sought to make the afterlife a verified, observable fact. It was the point where mysticism met empiricism, where poppycock found its proof. Many Americans weren't fooled, of course, but if John's life tells us one thing, it is that he was often easily fooled. John's immersion in the practice followed an established pattern. Most people attended their first séance after the death of a close relative, most often a spouse. Most went looking for contact, a chance to talk once again to a mourned and beloved partner, which is exactly what happened to John.[40]

John took part in séances at his home in Trenton for almost a year, beginning on November 10, 1867, and the list of people he believed he was talking to is large and revealing: Johanna; Johanna's mother, father, and sister; his own mother, father, and two brothers; his grandmother; Willie; Hannah, his second daughter who had passed away after only a few weeks in 1840; Lucia's mother; Overman; and several other friends and acquaintances. According to Ferdy, their cousin Edmund Riedel, who was employed in the rope works, was the medium. The séances seem to have come about in a rather random manner. After the Colchester meeting with Washington and Emily, John took part in no further séances until November 9, when Ferdy and Edmund were together at the family home. Out of the blue, they heard three knocks right under Ed's chair, and he "did not know what to make of it so they examined the room and porch and all around [yet] the knocks still followed." They told John about it the next morning, and in the evening they formed a circle in John's office and tried again. They "got no communication, but as soon as Ed went to his room & *pulled his boots off* he heard the knocks, then they called father & all went into the kitchen, where there is no carpet and the knocks were louder," all of which might seem to suggest a prankster. John, however, assembled an alphabet and tried to discover whose spirit they were in contact with. As Ferdy wrote excitedly to Washington, "The latest sensation we have had here are spiritual communications from Mother." John quickly discovered that Johanna wouldn't speak through anyone other than Ed, but also that she could summon numerous other spirits to the table. "Various questions were asked, father suggesting them," Ferdy wrote Washington, "but none of any account and finally she said she would come back again in two weeks."[41]

Once the initial "contact" had been established, regular meetings were held in Trenton over the next year.[42] Although he "talked" to many different spirits, John's primary contact was Johanna, with whom he spoke with great tenderness. "While in this body, you never thought of yourself, you always thought of others," he recalled, before asking if "your devotion to the welfare of others . . . your great love and attachment to your family brings you back to your earthly home." It had. "Your labors then are those of love and good will towards others," John replied. "How delightful and blissful such a life? You are very happy in your spirit home, are you not?" John was always careful, it seems, to both find out about the afterlife and confirm his own theories on the matter. "The greatest spirit is he who has the least selfishness?" Yes. "Selfishness kills spiritual life, here as well as hereafter?" Yes. "True happiness can only consist in living for others & doing good to others, is this so?" Yes. John also seemed keen to understand his wife's death, likely to absolve himself from any blame on account of her medical treatment, or maybe just in search of more certainty about what had happened. "Could your earthly life have been prolonged by better medical treatment?" he asked.

No, came the reply. "It is plain therefore that none of the physicians understood your care?" he continued, to which he failed to receive any reply. Still, he clearly hoped that she had been spared any pain and even hoped for much more. "Your transition from physical to spiritual life was to you a pleasant sensation, a beautiful exhilarating process?" The answer was yes.[43]

John seemed overjoyed to be in touch with Johanna, calling her "my dearest" and declaring, "To me it is a great delight to communicate with yourself & thus to realize that you are living." He also wanted to know if little Willie had any "desire to communicate with his father." He did, and he appeared a few weeks later, rapping out, "Good evening all of you," on the table. John's reply was a rather touching, almost wistful "Willie are you grown any?" Still, he seemed happy to talk to almost anyone who came to the table. "How delightful to hold friendly conversations with all of you," he announced after a brief "chat" with his sister's husband, Karl Meissner. Less delightful was the state of his household in light of his recent marriage. Lucia seems to have attended the séances and, according to Gunn, had long been exposed to the world of spiritualism, having attended lectures by Cora L. V. Hatch (née Scott) in New York in 1858. John raised the issue with Johanna in a bizarre manner, seeking to confirm—from his dead wife, not his living children—that his marriage had disturbed the harmony in the house. "You now come back on an errand of Love," he asked Johanna, "you wish to restore the former harmony in [the] family?" She had. "You are counseling Love and mutual forbearing, is this so?" he asked, finding himself in the socially awkward position of talking to his (dead) first wife about the impact of his second marriage on their children while seated next to the woman who had replaced her. Never one to notice such things, John even had the temerity to ask Johanna if she had "any message for Miss Cooper." No, came the rather obvious reply.[44]

John's questions increasingly focused on the form and structure of the afterlife, rather than on Johanna herself or any of John's old acquaintances. "Besides your labors of love in the care of others, are you engaged in studies and in the pursuit of higher knowledge?" he enquired. (Apparently, Johanna's favorite lecturer in the spirit world was the Unitarian minister and intellectual William Ellery Channing, who had passed away twenty-five years earlier.) John asked about the effort it took to make the knocks, how they made them, and how easy it was to summon other spirits. He was also keen to find out how religion was viewed in the afterlife. "Are you taught religion?" he asked. No. "Have you got a bible there?" No. "Is the Christian Bible considered by the advanced Spirits a mixture of truth and error?" Yes. "The Christian bible, the Jewish scriptures, the Turkish Koran, and all other books, which lay claim to a divine origin & divine inspiration, are all human compositions, therefore liable to error?" Yes. Religion in the afterlife "embraces all churches and creeds, is this true?" he wished to know, to which he was told there were neither idols, priests, nor churches in the afterlife. Should one believe in "the saving machinery of church & priesthood?" he asked. No. Then Jesus was but a man—"a great moral reformer & spiritual teacher"—"but he was gifted with a highly refined spiritual organization, which enabled him to a divine life, to teach divine truths, and at last to die at the cross for the good of his fellow men, is this view correct?" Needless to say, it was.[45]

With each new meeting John's questions got longer, more specific, and more absurd. "Whatever your mental vision desires to see will appear in your surroundings," he stated. "If you desire to be clothed in a silken dress of a certain color and pattern," for example, "the spiritual Ether, which surrounds you, will assume the form of this garb, and it is there, ready woven, dyed and fitted. All your desires will thus be realized?" he asked. "We mortals can fashion and form matter into certain shapes, as for instance the sculptor does his marble, but this attended by actual labor. By the sweat of the brow and the application of sinew and muscle do we perform our tasks. But you enjoy a superior power. The spiritual matter, which surrounds you, is perfectly obedient to your desires & wishes; while our matter only yields to material force, is only measurably plastic, your matter is perfectly plastic, ready at your bidding, to assume any shape or form which you desire?" In addition, the higher you progress in "spiritual life," the great your power of creating. Eventually, John surmised, "when sufficiently advanced in love & wisdom you will become fit instruments through which the Creator governs his creations?" Yes.[46]

For John, the afterlife clearly offered a utopia of beauty, harmony, and sympathy. "Are you surrounded by beautiful spiritual scenery corresponding to the natural scenery in earth, but far more beautiful and transcendent . . . than the human language can describe?" he asked. They were. They were also taught by Channing that the essence of "the unfathomable Divine Principle" is

> the union of Perfect Love & Perfect Wisdom; that the greatest Law of all laws is the Law of Love. The Creation itself is the result of Love & Wisdom. God, the great first Cause, is the everlasting fountain of pure, holy, unsullied love! What an encouraging and consoling thought, that God is Love, Love which embraces all his creatures, all his children, good & bad, advanced, or retrograde! In this bosom of unfathomable love all can rest, all can confide. Like the maternal Love of an exalted unselfish mother, but immeasurably richer, this divine Love has manifested itself throughout the Creation, it is the eternal source, which satisfies and energizes the living aspirations of all spiritual being!

After which, in the margins, John wrote the simple, almost preposterously austere: "yes."[47]

Such was the way John's séances went, after the initial burst of excitement. Brief enquiries were replaced by increasingly esoteric questioning, as his friends, family, and loved ones drop out of the picture. John was especially keen to confirm Davis's ideas about there being seven spheres of existence one worked through after one's death. Each sphere surrounded the earth and belonged to it. Individuals who were "sufficiently purified and advanced in spiritual perfection" were admitted to more "universal spheres," the highest of which Davis called the "super celestial" realm, or "Summerland." He was equally keen to confirm his suspicions about "materialists": "Through a discovery of the laws of nature they hope at last to comprehend the hidden causes of nature? Will they succeed?" he asked. No, came the reply in the séance room, which had always been something

Figure 18.7 John A. Roebling (1868). Courtesy of Donald Sayenga.

of an echo chamber. For an entire year, John had spoken his beliefs and received affirmation. As the months went by the transcripts of the meetings start to read like his Civil War philosophy, just with question marks at the end of each sentence: huge statements of belief, with multiple clauses and conditions, almost all of which end with a laughably brief "yes," shorn of all clarifying nuance. This might not have been John's fault. He was a believer, and like all believers, he was the subject of fraud on some level. He was looking for confirmation, but he very likely also believed he was getting it.

———

Few years are more representative of John's life than 1867–68, when he spent his days thinking through and designing one of the nineteenth century's foremost feats of engineering and his evenings contemplating spirits and the spirit world. Both efforts required intense thought and imagination, and John certainly conceived of them as part of the same essential history: the world of scientific discovery. That he could equate spirits and suspension bridges (on some level) is a testament to John's worldview, but also to a century when so much was in flux and had yet to be established. Spiritualism was certainly a fad, but wire suspension bridges were hardly entrenched either. They were distrusted by many, and when they failed, they failed spectacularly. Even John's Niagara Bridge was dogged by fears over its safety for almost its entire serviceable life. It is entirely possible that more people may have believed in spirits in 1867 than in suspension bridges.

Luckily, a group of influential New Yorkers and Brooklynites believed in them, or at least in John, and they were willing to subscribe to stock and shepherd legislation to bring a venerable dream to life. The need for sure and steady passage across the East River—actually a tidal strait, not a river—was as old as the Lenape tribes that populated the region in the years before European settlement. A chaotic system of ferries served the needs of New Netherlands and New York for over two hundred years, but in the face of strong winds and erratic currents, the journey across the East River was arduous and wildly unpredictable. Rowboats were forced to endure strong shifting tides; often, sailboats would catch a stiff breeze and end up on either Governor's Island or Blackwell's Island. Robert Fulton's invention of the steamboat—which could make the journey between Beekman Slip and Ferry Street in just six minutes—solved most of the problems of time and navigation, but once the notion of bridging, tunneling, or otherwise overcoming the East River had been raised, it could not be silenced for long.[48]

The first serious public debate over the merits of bridging the East River took place in Brooklyn in 1800 and was recorded by Jeremiah Johnson in his private diary—the "idea has been treated as chimerical, from the magnitude of the design; but a plan has already been laid down on paper, and a gentleman of acknowledged abilities and good sense has observed that he would engage to erect it in two years' time"—while the first official proposal appeared two years later in Alexander Hamilton's *New-York Evening Post*. Thereafter plans and schemes came thick and fast. John Stevens—an engineer, inventor, and railroad pioneer—proposed a floating bridge with drawbridges for river traffic. Benjamin Latrobe, the architect who designed the US Capitol, studied the subject, concluding that such a bridge was entirely feasible, but that no municipal government or private organization would be able to afford it. Some suggested tunneling under the river; others even suggested filling the entire thing in and creating one massive landmass, composed of New York and Long Island. John started to think about the idea in 1847, when he jotted down ideas about a bridge at Blackwell's Island. These plans and ideas were rudimentary, though, set down in a crowded notebook and dashed off during a spare moment. But bridging the East River was a goal, one John returned to several times in his career before he secured the contract in 1867.[49]

John passed through New York frequently during the early 1850s, occasionally making the trip across the East River. In April 1853 he visited Julius Adams at 122 Livingston Street in Brooklyn Heights to discuss his Kentucky River bridge, and perhaps they discussed an East River span. Within a decade, both engineers would draw up plans for such a bridge. John was formally drawn into the wider discussion in 1856 when a group of businessmen solicited his thoughts on the subject. Fresh from his success at Niagara, John met a member of the group "on the ground" in New York and put together an official proposal. He was still thinking about Blackwell's Island as his base, offering the simple explanation that "no other part of the East River offers a locality so favorable." His bridge would be a three-span affair, with side spans of eight hundred feet linked by a center span over the island of six hundred feet. It would cost $1,200,000 and sit 150 feet above high water. John promised "a first class structure, in point of convenience, strength, permanency & beauty," which did not persuade anyone. John's interest in Blackwell's Island faded after 1856, even as his interest in the East River sharpened.[50]

John next cast his eyes farther south to the region around Fulton Ferry in a letter he wrote to Abram Hewitt—his neighbor in Trenton and an occasional guest at his family's New Year's Day celebrations—the following January. Hewitt was so impressed by John's letter that he had it printed in the *Journal of Commerce*, hoping, no doubt, that it would move the business community to answer John's call. It didn't, despite Hewitt and the *Journal*'s hearty endorsement, but it did help move the East River bridge into the realms of possibility. "The following communication, on the subject of a bridge from New York to Brooklyn," wrote the *Journal*, "is from a gentleman well known as the greatest living authority on the subject of Suspension Bridges, and as he never expresses an opinion or makes statements without due deliberation, reliance can be placed on the estimate of cost as well as upon the feasibility of the project." Finally, the call for a bridge had been answered by someone who could actually design and build one.[51]

John's letter began with some practical realities. Yes, a bridge between New York and Brooklyn was "an absolute necessity" and "perfectly practicable," but it would also "involve an amount of cost and damages" that would cause both citizens and those likely to invest "for the sake of dividends" to balk at the project. With this in mind, costs and approaches needed to be rethought. Normally such a large span would require lengthy approaches on either side of the river. These would be damaging to the surrounding urban fabric, hugely expensive, and deeply unpopular. John, however, believed he could erect a bridge so that "no ground will be permanently occupied by the work or even temporarily interfered with." He would built two massive stone towers three hundred feet high on either side of the river from which he would suspend an arched roadway "over which more passengers can be transported, at any time of the year, and in less time, and more comfortably, than can now be done on all the existing ferry boats taken together." Trains would run in either direction at all times of the day; John estimated it could carry 288,000 passengers a day. The whole project would cost $2 million, providing "a handsome dividend" to investors.[52]

John's letter to Hewitt wasn't meant as a full-scale proposal or a public declaration, but he soon realized he would need one if he wanted to maintain momentum. To this end he wrote to Horace Greeley's *New-York Tribune* a couple of months later with a more polished, far more rhetorical, but essentially similar set of ideas. He also worked up several different tower designs: a hulking, overworked Egyptian arch with intricate palmed lintels and cornices, adorned with what seems to be a face blooming from some sort of plant, the other a tall and elegant Romanesque arch with a ribbed cornice. John began his letter to Greeley with a vision of the East River "fifty years ahead" when millions of people would crowd both shores and the river would be a tangled mess of boats. Collisions and gridlock would rule. Commercial activity would rise along with the population, while transit would slow down, ending up at a standstill. "It is plain . . . that necessity will demand some other means of crossing." John restated most of the points in his Hewitt letter while adding new details. The bridge would only require enough room for the towers' foundations on either side of the river. Its main span would be 1,500 feet, which would descend "at a gentle rate . . . forming a series of [four] large spans"—successively 600, 500, 400, and 240 feet—"which will extend over several squares without touching the roofs of the houses until the high ground is reached on which the approaches will be located." The total length of the bridge from end to end would be gargantuan, almost 5,000 feet. As at Niagara, John would build a double-deck roadway, with railroad tracks up top and ordinary traffic below. The railroad cars would be "connected and propelled" by an endless wire rope attached to a "stationary engine" on one end of the span. A thousand passengers "will be conveyed every trip with all the ease and comfort that well-constructed, ventilated and warmed cars will afford." As a work of engineering, it would be unrivalled, John declared; as a work of art, it would stand as one of the "grandest and most attractive features" in the whole region, so much so that tourists would "make a trip for the sole purpose of enjoying the grand sight such a passage will present," he claimed. A bill was soon introduced before the legislature to authorize the construction of a suspension bridge, but again it went nowhere. The city—especially the harbor interests—was not ready.[53]

John never failed to mention the need for an East River bridge in any official report or communication, and he always kept his ear to the ground for rumors, interested parties, or public discussion. In March 1860, the *Architects' and Mechanics' Journal* ran a lengthy, rather florid article on the subject. New York was justifiably famous for its Croton Aqueduct, wrote the *Journal*, "but there is still another enterprise which she is destined to accomplish, and which will be the crowning effort of her growing strength." An East River bridge "is imperatively demanded by the greatness of the two cities now separated . . . like lovers eager to rush into each other's arms," they continued. The *Journal* expressed some doubt, however, as to the "stability and steadiness" of a 1,824-foot-long suspension bridge—the distance from Fulton to Dover Streets—so they counseled a tubular bridge to span the East River at Blackwell's Island. John was quick to pick up his pen and reply. He had continued to study the problem in the three years since he had last written on the subject, and he was convinced its success would be governed by three fundamental considerations. First, no plan could interfere with navigation, and only a suspension bridge or a tunnel could achieve this; second, the bridge would need to house a railroad if it was to do its principal job, which was to move upward of a half a million people per day between New York and Brooklyn; and third, the merits of the project as a financial investment were "*undoubted.*" John then addressed himself to the technical problems of construction—especially when compared with a tubular bridge—but he had already done his most important work. He had spoken to the river and harbor interests, to answer their fears about navigation; he had spoken to the people of both cities to assure them that the bridge would solve an urgent and growing civic problem; and he had spoken to Wall Street to assure them that the investment was sound. As he concluded, the bridge will "convey passengers from the centre of one city to the centre of the other in 5 minutes time at a rate of 3 cents per head. What more could be desired by all parties?" The *Journal* admitted they found the idea of such a long bridge—over twice the length of the Niagara

Bridge—"rather startling" at first but were happy to allow that "Mr. Roebling's large experience entitles his opinion upon this point to great weight."[54]

The bridge debate raged in the parlors of Brooklyn Heights and in the pages of the local press throughout the 1860s. Busy with his Ohio bridge, John could do little but trust to his reputation and keep one eye trained on events. Julius Adams seemed to have the inside track as John was finishing up in Cincinnati. Adams had been working on a plan since 1864 and, being a Brooklyn resident at the time, had direct access to all the important players. In fact, it seems likely that Adams was at the meeting that launched the entire enterprise. On the evening of December 21, 1866, William Kingsley and Judge Alexander McCue boarded a carriage in Brooklyn Heights and drove down to the home of Henry Cruse Murphy in Bay Ridge. Murphy was the foremost politician in Brooklyn, a lifelong resident, and for many the patrician voice of the entire city. Kingsley was two decades younger than Murphy but already a prosperous contractor and a hard-nosed deal maker, well versed in Gilded Age politics. No records were kept of the meeting, but once it was over everyone was committed to the project. Murphy would sponsor the legislation and lend it his considerable prestige; Kingsley would manage the process and superintend the construction in all practical ways. Another local politician, James T. Stranahan, was subsequently recruited, as was Thomas Kinsella, editor of the *Brooklyn Daily Eagle*, the city's most influential newspaper.[55]

A bill chartering and empowering the New York Bridge Company was submitted to the legislature on January 25, 1867—using Adams's plans and estimates—and passed on April 16. The act fixed the capital stock at five million dollars and required the company to build a bridge from the intersection of Main Street and Fulton Street in Brooklyn to some point at or below Chatham Square in New York. It was to be finished by June 1870, which even then must have seemed like wishful thinking. A meeting was held shortly after the passage of the bill at the Brooklyn County Courthouse. Officers of the bridge company were elected, and the issue of who to appoint as chief engineer was raised. Adams seemed like the front runner, but he had never built a bridge of much size before. He had his supporters, but amid the debate someone raised John's name. Hadn't he just completed the world's longest suspension bridge over the Ohio? And wasn't he at that moment in Trenton, not sixty miles away, with nothing very much to occupy his time? Kingsley wrote to John on February 23 "anxious to see you in relation to the Bridge." The two met several times over the next few weeks, and on May 23 John signed a contract to design and supervise the construction of a bridge between New York and Brooklyn. He would be paid eight thousand dollars per year, and he would be free to design almost any type of structure he decided upon. For his part, Kingsley knew the project needed a big, reliable name, someone the public could trust implicitly. After all, they were hoping to construct the world's longest suspension bridge between two of the four largest cities in the United States. Given the landscape of bridge engineering at the time, no one would trust such a project to anyone but John A. Roebling.[56]

John spent the summer at home with his new wife and his new project, with an occasional trip to the East River to conduct surveys and to Cincinnati to show his bridge to Murphy. He sent Washington off to Europe on July 1 to study the installation and use of pneumatic caissons, an engineering technique that would be vital in setting the tower foundations and to meet with Richard Johnson in Manchester to discuss how the wire manufacturer could best meet John's up-coming needs. John resurfaced in September with his official report, which he had printed up and then read in front of the board of trustees on September 7, 1867. "The contemplated work, when constructed in accordance with my designs, will not only be the greatest Bridge in existence," he began, "but it will be the great engineering work of this continent, and of the age. Its most conspic-uous features, the great towers, will serve as landmarks to the adjoining cities, and they will be entitled to be ranked as national monuments. As a great work of art, and as a successful specimen of advanced Bridge engineering, this struc-ture will forever testify to the energy, enterprise and wealth of that community, which shall secure its erection." John set out his vision in seven categories: loca-tion, general description, practicability and strength, towers and foundations, anchorages, approaches, and estimated cost. Under the category of location John set out three distinct lines, each emanating from the junction of Main and Fulton in Brooklyn. John favored the park line, running to the foot of City Hall Park, even though it was the longest. It would involve less destruction of valuable property; in fact, it might even "greatly beautify and improve this part of the city, which appears to need it more than any other." It would also "collect and accom-modate more travel." "For the next fifty years to come, City Hall Park will remain the great focus of travel, from which speedy communications will ramify in all directions," John wrote.[57]

The whole length of the bridge would be 5,862 feet, of which 3,480 feet would be suspended: 1,600 from tower to tower, with side spans of 940 feet on either side, and approaches of 1,337 feet on the New York side and 837 feet on the Brooklyn side. These approaches—constructed from "small piers of ma-sonry"—would contain "stores, dwellings or offices" and vault over existing streets on iron girders. Railroad cars would run over the bridge twenty-four hours a day, which would be convenient should there be "an invasion by a for-eign enemy, landing on the Long Island Shore" and the military suddenly found itself needing to move half a million troops into Brooklyn. Current figures for the Union Ferry Company showed that almost 110,000 people used the ferries each day. John's railroads would have a carrying capacity of over twice that number. In thinking about his railroad, John decided to flip the scheme he had stayed with since designing the Niagara Bridge. Railroad tracks would run on the lower—not upper—level, flanked by a roadway for regular traffic, a notion he had explicitly rejected twenty years earlier when planning the Wheeling Bridge. Above the roadway, John positioned an *"elevated promenade . . .* the principal use [of which] will be to allow people of leisure, and old and young invalids, to promenade over the Bridge on fine days, in order to enjoy the beautiful views and the pure air. I need not state that in a crowded commercial city, such a promenade will be of incalculable value. Every stranger who visits the city will at least take one or two walks on this promenade." John's central walkway would prove to be the span's most unique and enduring feature, the place where a fourteen-year-old Alfred Kazin experienced his first epiphany; where Lewis Mumford found his inspiration; where Thomas Wolfe, Jack Kerouac, and Marianne Moore were beguiled by the intricate web of the bridge's cables; where Hart Crane believed he had found the answer to America; where countless artists from Childe Hassam to Walker Evans to Georgia O'Keeffe stood transfixed and enraptured; and where millions of tourists and natives have flocked to stand and stare, to be encased and engrossed.[58]

John was more than happy to vouch for the bridge's excessive strength. He planned to use steel wire in the bridge's cables—not iron—and to employ four main suspension cables, 280 stays, and a set of lateral trusses. "Ordinary transitory loads will make no perceptible impression upon the work, and least of all will the motion of the passenger trains be felt," he wrote. It "will not be affected by the heaviest gales [nor by] the severest hurricanes." The cables would run over two massive towers, "the great features of the work," 134 feet by 56 feet at its base tapering through a series of buttresses (or "sloped offsets") up to 120 feet by 40 feet at the summit. The towers would be defined by what John called two "pointed arches" through which the roadway would pass. "The impression of the whole will be that of massiveness and strength," he declared.[59]

John closed his report with an appeal to the historical moment. New York was on the brink of claiming its place as "the great commercial emporium, not of the continent only, but of the world." The flow of civilization has always been from east to west, and so it seemed inevitable that "the old and the new are to meet on this continent," here in New York. "Lines of steamers, such as the world never saw before, are now plowing the Atlantic [while] the same means of communication will unite the . . . coast of Asia." New York, John reasoned, will mark and remain "the centre where these lines meet." With this in mind, New York and Brooklyn would only grow, as they had exponentially during the nineteenth century. "Am I wrong in estimating the travel across the East River at eighty millions of people annually ten years hence?" John asked, as well as that "this general increase of population is sure to take place in the whole country as well as about the city of New York, *Bridge or no Bridge*?" Given this certain reality, "it remains for the people of Brooklyn to decide whether they will attract their legitimate portion of this additional increase or not," John remarked, throwing out something of a challenge. No sane individual could predict anything but a sparkling future for the cities and the bridge. The operating expenses would be small, while the revenue would be "so immense, that the bridge company, in a few years after the completion of the work, will feel justified to put up great magnificent depots and portals at both termini, which shall be a credit to the two cities," he announced, clearly hoping to attract a few capitalists. John signed off predicting—remarkably—the bridge's dividends would cover the initial investment—$6,675,357, which John knew was a hefty underestimate—in "less than three years."[60]

Accompanying John's report was a large rendering of the bridge in all its projected glory. Its huge masonry towers and Gothic arches loom over everything around it: the warehouses at its feet, the ships and ferries that cluster on the river, and the city behind it. Its network of stays, cables, and suspenders sweep majestically over the East River from shore to shore. It is a study in monumentality but also in simplicity and restraint. It was devised to awe and promote, of course, but it also says much about John as an architect and an engineer in pursuit of the same goal. Washington thought his father would have made a good architect, although he also thought there were instances when he should have hired one. John was certainly an excellent draftsman who trained in both engineering and aesthetics while in Berlin, unlike most contemporary engineers, including his son, whose program at RPI was rigorously and exclusively scientific. In fact, such a combination was rare in nineteenth-century civil engineering, where things were either designed to work well and efficiently— not necessarily to express or represent anything—or they were overdesigned with several different goals in mind. Suspension bridges often featured overelaborate ornamentation that was meant to mask or distract from the structure's essential functionalism, or they were designed with absolutely no thought to the aesthetics. Unlike nineteenth-century railroad stations, which often did an inspiring job of marrying architecture and engineering, bridges that managed this were rare. John did about as much as any American engineer to think about structures from both perspectives, and even he had found it rough going.[61]

John's design for the Brooklyn Bridge was the culmination of an admittedly uneven aesthetic development. None of the designs for his previous bridges were able to marry function and expression anywhere near so successfully. His Monongahela Bridge was pure utility, drawn up hurriedly as a retrofit. In consequence, it looks like what it is, and no more. Even the bridge's lattice columns seem to suggest a compromise between strength and economy rather than anything else. John's aqueducts were likewise exercises in serviceability, where much of his work was hidden beneath a huge wooden flume. They contain neither adornment nor artifice. His Niagara span evoked the ancient mystery of the falls and the timelessness of Egyptian monuments, but all the stays radiating randomly from the underside of the bridge suggest uncertainty, maybe even frailty, as if a carpenter had finished his work and then—a little unsure of himself—banged in a whole bunch of extra nails just to make sure, which in large measure is exactly what happened. Most of the stays were added for stability after large sections of the Wheeling Bridge had been swept away a year before John's bridge was finished.[62]

The process that led to John's Niagara Bridge gives us some sense of him as a fledgling designer. It was in many respects rather scattershot. He played with different design elements, alternating, subtracting, and adding, as if he had a set of stock motifs and parts that just needed interchanging until the final form was decided upon. Many of his designs were eclectic to the point of complete incoherence. His initial plans drawn up in 1847 included a Gothic arch surrounded by a classical pediment and columns. In 1850, he toyed with a design that included Gothic, Roman, and castellated features. Two years later, he added Egyptian motifs to a Gothic arch with a classical pediment, as if he were simply unable to follow established architectural conventions. Many of John's unbuilt projects show a similar propensity. Although he built only nine bridges in his lifetime, John designed dozens, for many of which he worked up preliminary sketches. These designs tended to follow a similar path as his Niagara plans. Between 1852 and 1855, for example, John campaigned to build a railroad suspension bridge for the Steubenville Railroad, in the process drawing up a succession of different designs. One was a sleek and clean dentil structure with a high Italian arch; another had an Egyptian motif with a square arch and towers; yet another was pure eclecticism with a Gothic arch, castellated top, and six-sided towers with fake arrow slits and a low spire with flagpoles. Other bridge designs feature Tudor arches with minarets and battlements or Roman arches with Byzantine turrets. The effect is bewildering and perplexing, yet each design was surprisingly similar: differing architectural elements and styles flung together willy-nilly.[63]

John's designs that called for iron towers were somewhat similar, although often better proportioned and much less confusing. His design for the Girard Avenue Bridge (1851) to span the Schuylkill at Philadelphia called for cast iron towers with diagonal bracing, a rather delicate set of Corinthian columns with a sunburst motif in the middle. Worked up the same year, his design for a bridge to span the Allegheny at Bayardstown near Pittsburgh was much more pared down, with simple iron columns braced with lattice slats and topped by a simple metal dome. Unfortunately, when John came to design the Allegheny Bridge, he seems to have lost much of the moderation that had marked his previous work in cast iron. It is overworked and overly ornamental, as if John were striving to make something beautiful and attractive simply by adding features.

Figure 18.8 The drawing that accompanied John's initial East River bridge proposal. Wilhelm Hildenbrand, "East River Bridge" (1868). Courtesy of the Institute Archives and Special Collections, Rensselaer Polytechnic Institute.

Aesthetically, it is the very definition of busy. The four suspension cables, the stays, sidewalk railings, lattice columns, and ornate cupolas all compete for attention, their lines intermingling and confusing the viewer. It is like looking at five different drawings all overlaid upon each other. The span's greatest distraction, however, is the tollhouses positioned on either side. They are too large, too heavy, and out of proportion to the bridge; their roofs are out of proportion to what they cover. Atop each is a large, somewhat Moorish spire that is almost as tall as the tollhouse itself, which seems larger than the suspension towers, which in comparison almost seem like perfectly pleasant pieces of architecture.[64]

The Covington and Cincinnati Bridge represents the beginnings of John's maturation as a designer. It was the first time he grappled with the issue of how to integrate masonry with iron, an architectural problem—as cultural historian Alan Trachtenberg notes—"virtually without precedent" in the United States. It

Figure 18.8 (Continued)

was both unimaginable and impossible to construct metal towers of sufficient size and strength in 1856, as has been the norm since the late nineteenth century, allowing engineers to think of a bridge as a single coherent whole. This left John with two very different materials—which each performed very different functions (the cables in tension, the towers in compression)—that were both at odds with each other yet also worked together to keep the bridge up and running. Trying to think of them as a single piece made up of complementary parts forced John to think of his Ohio bridge in ways that went well beyond traditional engineering. He needed to build something that worked and that meshed visually. He needed integration. He needed economy, balance, and symmetry. "It is a difficult task to produce a proper architectural effect when designing towers for a suspension bridge of large dimensions," he wrote in his final report to the bridge trustees. "Highly ornamented masonry may be built, but it looks out of place, when the general impression should be that of simplicity, massiveness and strength. On the other hand, a public work, which forms a conspicuous landmark across a great river which separates two large cities, both abounding in highly ornamental facades, should also serve as a model of appropriate architectural proportions. Public works should educate public taste," he wrote; "in the erection of public edifices, therefore, some expense may and ought to be incurred in order to satisfy the artistical aspirations of a young and growing community."[65]

Such ideas led to the Ohio bridge's most prominent flaw—the superfluous small spires that sat atop the two towers—while highlighting John's great aims and the bridge's great strengths. While the Moorish embellishments are at odds with the Romanesque arch that otherwise defines the towers (overall they seem to exist as if John simply had to put something up there in an effort to reflect the "highly ornamental facades" of Cincinnati)), the span's evident strength is achieved through simplicity of design and proportion, and without an overwhelming sense of bulk. "Where strength is to be combined with lightness and elegance," he wrote, "nature"—always John's benchmark—"never wastes heavy cumbrous masses." Neither did John. He achieved his aims with a high, "fined tuned arch"—airy yet "artistical" without detracting from its function—and through his use of buttressed walls. "Mediaeval architecture is distinguished for its remarkable lightness and great strength at the same time, owing principally to the judicious use of the buttress," he explained in his report. Such themes found a parallel with his cables, themselves remarkably light yet possessing great strength. The cables of course helped relate the towers to the roadway, providing a thematic link. Neither could be allowed to overwhelm the other in appearance, and neither could the roadway, which itself was considered in the design process. "Without stays and trusses, the elevation of the bridge floor would be too light in appearance as compared to the massiveness of the towers," John noted. "As it is, the whole has a pleasing effect, and at the same time, presents strong and reassuring proportions, which inspire confidence in the stability of the work." Balance was the key, between all elements, and when successfully achieved it could advance and educate public taste. After its opening, John's Ohio bridge drew much praise as an aesthetic object. Washington believed the towers "were noble pieces of architecture." More recently, it has been remarked that "its design is a superb study in contrast. The massive towers . . . support a delicately arched roadway. The tension is established between the towers and the filigree of tightly strung cables emanating from them."[66]

John's East River bridge design continued this work, refining and clarifying his aesthetic. Gone are the embellishments—the efforts at ornament—in favor of a more holistic, pared-down, and expressive approach. He retained the prominent use of buttresses and swapped out a Romanesque arch for double Gothic arches, which add size, symmetry, and thematic coherence. While Gothic and Romanesque are both medieval architectural styles, the former is far more in keeping with a buttressed wall than the latter. Gothic arches and buttressed walls are also both aesthetic forms and engineering techniques. They both grow out of the medieval desire to stretch upward toward the divine, best exemplified in the great Gothic cathedrals of Europe. Visually they move the viewer's gaze upward, just as they allow a building to rise upward. They combine this with a wonderfully iconic sense of a gateway: the great arches as a passageway and an entrance to an inspiring, even spiritual place, a feature that brings the bridge's roadway and elevated promenade into play, linking the vertical with the horizontal, the masonry with the steel. It is from the walkway that one best experiences the bridge as a portal, but also the web of cables that speak to the geometry of the city rising around the bridge—the destination—and draw one's attention back up to its Gothic arches. Walkway, cables, towers: John's plan calls for architecture and engineering to exist in harmony. He designed his last bridge as "a principle of order," subsuming form, function, history, and culture, refracting and reflecting our experience of passage and revelation.[67]

Unlike much of the work of the Gothic revival that flourished in the United States from 1840 on, John's use of the motif sought to put an old style to a new use. It is forward-looking, not nostalgic, a fact noticed immediately by Vladimir Mayakovsky—"the plenipotentiary of Soviet poetry"—in 1925. Mayakovsky's architectonic masterpiece "Brooklyn Bridge" (1925)—his "shout of joy," as Colum McCann wonderfully describes it—portrays the bridge as an arbiter, as the meeting ground of past and future. Standing on "this steel-wrought mile" where "my visions come real / in the striving / for structure / instead of style," Mayakovsky saw the future unfold, the dynamism of steel "unfurling" out through both time and space into a new future, flowing from and taking the place of past achievements. Many followed the poet's lead, celebrating John's design with infectious enthusiasm and giddy abandon. Others didn't. Henry James called it a "monster," a "colossal set of clockworks, [a] steel-souled machine-room of brandished arms and hammering fists and opening and closing jaws," but James almost never liked anything new, and this was perhaps the point. The Brooklyn Bridge was—and was intended to be—something new, a fact that stymied Montgomery Schuyler, who wrote the first serious architectural consideration of the bridge to mark the span's opening on May 24, 1883. Schuyler liked the bridge as a piece of engineering and hated it as a piece of architecture. Most of his complaints focused on the towers, which he felt referenced old forms while disguising their contemporary uses. The trouble for Schuyler was that he had to invent a rather unfair conceit in order to get there. Imagine the scene in hundreds of years, he wrote, when a future archaeologist might happen upon a ruined and deserted New York. Should he discover the bridge, its cables would most likely have rusted and fallen into the river, leaving just the towers. With this scene before Schuyler's imagined voyager, could he decipher the functions of these lonely sentinels? No, he decided. On their own the towers expressed

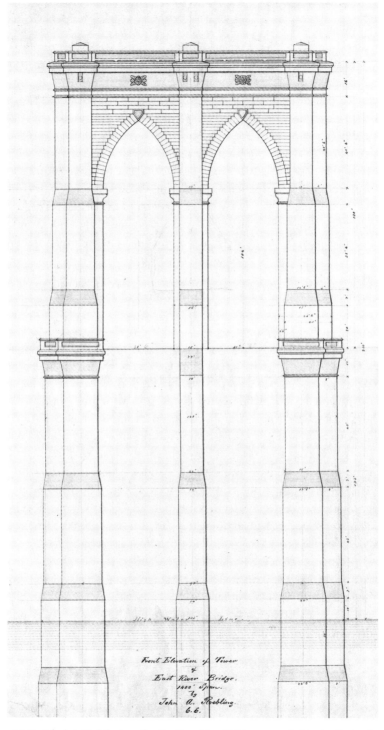

Figure 18.9 John's initial designs for the Brooklyn Bridge, remarkably similar to the finished structure. John Roebling, "Front Elevation of Tower of East River Bridge" (1867). Courtesy of the Institute Archives and Special Collections, Rensselaer Polytechnic Institute.

nothing of their function: that they were there to shoulder four large suspension cables that held up a mile-long roadway. As the first critic to recognize the
bridge's significance, Schuyler deserves credit, but his criticism seems unfair and
beside the point. John designed the various parts of his bridge to balance each
other, to work in harmony. To take away either part—be it the towers or the
cable structure—is to shift the terms on which it was designed. One wouldn't
dream of assessing *King Lear* after first removing one or more of the daughters,
or Frank Lloyd Wright's Fallingwater without its natural setting. In addition, one
might also reasonably ask what else might two large gateways stuck in the middle
of a river between two cities be but a bridge.[68]

"It so happens that the work which is likely to be our most durable monument, and to convey some knowledge of us to the most remote posterity," wrote
Schuyler, rather disparagingly, "is a work of bare utility; not a shrine, not a fortress, not a palace, but a bridge." John, ironically, would have been overjoyed
with such an assessment. "The present age is emphatically an age of usefulness,"
he wrote in his Ohio bridge report. "The useful goes before the ornamental. At
the time when Grecian culture was shaping the human mind," he continued, "the
reverse was the accepted rule; first the ornamental, then the useful." But "it is evident that the general interests of mankind are [now] more promoted by the present than it was by the ancient maxim. No matter what may be charged against
the material tendencies of the present age, it is through material advancements
alone that a higher spiritual culture of the masses can be attained." "In this sense
the advancement of the sciences and various arts of life may well be hailed as the
harbingers of good; its laborers are our friends, not our enemies. The works of
industry will be soon broadcast over the surface of the earth, and want will dis-
appear." John cared not a fig for shrines or palaces. Neither were useful; neither
were "the harbingers of good"; neither would solve the problem of "want"; neither advanced the "higher spiritual culture of the masses." As David Billington
notes, John believed the spirit was "uplifted by understanding technology and
by creating out of it superior works that people can afford, that they can openly
use, and that they can aesthetically use." These were the meanings he tried to
weave into the design of his final bridge. It was the same message he wove—
albeit obliquely and esoterically—into much of the writing he set down during
the Civil War. These were his ideals and his principles.[69]

———

The great East River bridge project was ready to go by the fall of 1867 in all areas
but financing, which as John well knew was always a fraught business, heavily
dependent on politics and public opinion, neither of which seemed to be on
his side. The respected *Scientific American* allowed that John's bridge "might be a

curiosity as a work of art, and monument of engineering skill [but] it might also be a monument of the folly of its builders." By the beginning of 1868, four months after John's report, the *New York Times* was wondering, "What has become of the Brooklyn Bridge? Has the project fallen through?" Last they had heard three months earlier, the work was slated to begin at once. "Have the directors found it difficult to raise funds?" they asked. Kingsley and Murphy quietly and smoothly arranged for Brooklyn to subscribe to three million dollars of stock, but they also needed a commitment from New York—in other words, from William "Boss" Tweed, the grand sachem of the Tammany political machine. Little moved in New York politics, public works, or even public opinion without Tammany's assent, usually secured through cash delivered to Tammany headquarters. Murphy and Kingsley knew this, and so did John once they told him. There is "a strong combination made against the measure by a ring," Kingsley wrote John, and they "want to be bought." Without the necessary grease, Tammany aldermen would see to it that the project ground to a halt, even going out of their way to malign anyone involved. In April 1868, Alderman James Ingersoll made public a letter from John from 1866 stating that an East River bridge could be built for $4 million. Why was the cost of such a structure so much higher only two years later? asked the alderman. And more importantly, why should the people bear the brunt of this new "taxation"? Alderman Ingersoll even had Brooklynites rethinking their own contribution, which they subsequently withheld until the end of the year. "There is a great danger that the East River Bridge project, of which we have lately heard so much, will, for the present, at least, end in smoke," wrote the *Times*.[70]

Ten years later Ingersoll was named extensively in the special committee report by the board of aldermen into the frauds perpetrated by the Tweed Ring, but in 1868 his influence was vast and needed to be countered. To this end, Murphy visited Tweed. The only record of the meeting was supplied by Tweed during his trial for corruption and embezzlement, but if he is to be believed—and he was remarkably candid about the affair—Murphy was told what he already knew: that "an appropriation could be passed by paying for it." The cost would be $55,000 or $65,000—Tweed couldn't recall exactly—and Murphy agreed. Several weeks later, Kingsley boarded a ferry and crossed over the East River to New York to deliver the money to a Tammany hack named Thomas Coman, who kept some for Tweed and distributed the rest among the board of aldermen, including Ingersoll. The appropriation was made, and all the requisite ordinances were approved. Heavily discounted shares would follow, and half the seats on the six-man board of trustees. Washington later wrote that once his father understood that Tweed meant to use his bridge to rob the public coffers, "he made up his mind to get out," but he was certainly hard at work on the bridge up until the very end.[71]

John bided his time waiting for the politicians to do their work and the press (especially the *Eagle*, which promoted the bridge assiduously in the fall of 1868) to whip up public approval by fretting over politics—especially recent Democratic gains in Congress—and reading about his third grandchild. His namesake, Johann August Roebling II, was born to Washington and Emily in

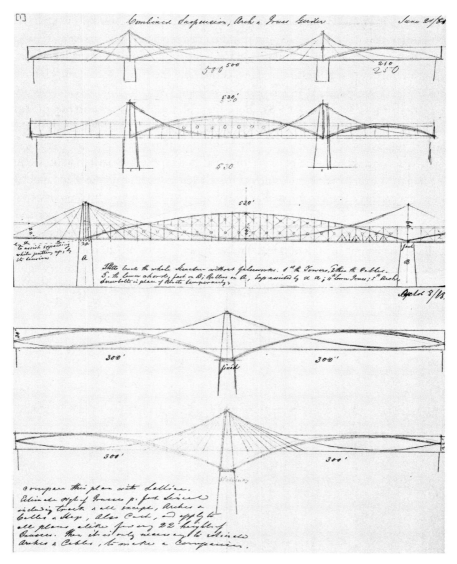

Figure 18.10 John Roebling, "Combined Suspension, Arch & Truss Girder" (1868). Courtesy of the Special Collections and University Archives, Rutgers University Libraries.

Mühlhausen on November 21, 1867—while they were in Europe so Washington could research pneumatic cassions—and baptized in the same font as John had been sixty-one years earlier.[72] John also turned his attention to a couple of projects he had been ruminating on for the past eight years. The first was a technical treatise on long- and short-span railroad bridges, which he had started making notes about in 1860 while working on his Allegheny bridge. It was the culminating effort in John's mainly unsuccessful twenty-year campaign to establish suspension bridges as acceptable means of conveying railroads over rivers and other ravines. This was no pure restating of a previous idea, however. He had clearly done some further thinking on the issue. In his final Ohio bridge report, John predicted that all future bridges would take the form of either upright or inverted (i.e., suspended) arches. His new scheme was both. In the search for adequate stiffness, John placed a parabolic truss alongside suspension cables. The result is visually elegant, but it found neither adherents nor even much in the way of discussion after it was published the following year.[73]

The second was a series of plans for a bridge over the Mississippi at St. Louis he had also been working on since at least 1860.[74] Captain James Eads had recently won this contract and had already begun to erect a beautiful and innovative steel arch bridge, but John wasn't perturbed. The Mississippi, he reasoned, would likely need bridging several more times as St. Louis grew. His main plan called for a center span of 600 feet flanked by side spans of 420 feet, after which a continuation of small spans 150 feet long would take the bridge to a suitable grade on either shore. (John drew up four other designs, all essentially the

Figure 18.11 Detail from John's "Plan of a Bridge over the Mississippi River at St. Louis," from John A. Roebling, *Long and Short Span Railway Bridges* (1869). Courtesy of Digital Bridges, Lehigh University.

same—all with two towers firmly planted in the river—but with different span lengths.) Again, a double deck would be employed with common travel above and a railroad below. The most interesting feature of the bridge is its hybrid nature. It is clearly a suspension bridge, employing four main suspension cables and John's signature set of stays, but it is also a truss bridge. And an arch bridge. The span contained three double trusses—two outside and one in the center—all of which are undergirded by an arch made of steel piping, another subject he had written about favorably in his Ohio report. Despite the looming work in New York—or maybe because of the looming political work still to be done there—John decided to write to the St. Louis press about his ideas and seems to have been given a fair hearing. "After the able letter of Mr. Roebling" on the subject of suspension bridges, wrote Eads, the man John was on some level seeking to discredit, "I feel I can say nothing to add to its force."[75]

———

Things began to move in New York as the winter of 1869 started to dissipate into spring. The money had been secured, and public opinion was turning in favor of the project. Sensing the shift, John suggested to the trustees that they recruit a board of consulting engineers. John understood how damaging the previous year had been and that his reputation alone couldn't silence the questions. It might be good politics to have a cadre of experienced and trusted professionals to back him up. Seven names were quickly decided upon, all "well-known engineers," according to *Scientific American*: Julius Adams; Horatio Allen, a noted engineer, inventor, and industrialist; James Pugh Kirkwood, a "stubborn, hardheaded Scotchman" who had designed the Starrucca Viaduct and surveyed the Pacific Railroad from the Mississippi to the Rocky Mountains; Benjamin Henry Latrobe, son of the architect behind the US Capitol; William Jarvis McAlpine, president of the American Society of Civil Engineers; John J. Serrell, the only one among them who had actually built a suspension bridge; and J. Dutton Steele, chief engineer of the Reading Railroad. John held regular meetings with these men at the Brooklyn Gas Light Company on Fulton Street, laying out his plans and explaining his thinking, his theories, and his methods. Each meeting was then "followed by an eminently satisfactory collation of chicken salad, lobster—champagne etc [which] helped to soothe down the acerbities of the fierce discussions." Needless to say, John wasn't looking for input or advice, but strict assent, much as he had when soliciting endorsements for his wire ropes in 1841. As almost everyone was at pains to point out, John was the foremost suspension bridge engineer in the country, if not the world. There weren't many people who could surprise him when it came to throwing a suspension bridge over a wide body of water, and neither did he expect anyone to. But he understood the politics of the situation and the need for public assurance, which is what he achieved.[76]

According to Washington, who sat in and took notes, the meetings weren't always as smooth as John might have wished and even presumed. "It required courage and resolution on the part of Mr. Roebling to defend his thesis as it was against all comers," he added. John's plan called not only for the largest span ever built but just as importantly for the deepest and largest foundations ever undertaken. John could be trusted implicitly with the first, but perhaps not with the second. His foundations at the Ohio had been paltry in comparison. Borings taken in 1868 suggested John would need to dig down up to one hundred feet—"a most appalling depth, never before reached or attempted"—to set his New York tower. Such an undertaking would require dozens of men working inside an upturned wooden box—upon which a huge masonry tower was being built—deep below the riverbed in air compressed to the force of fifty pounds per square inch. The whole plan seemed sure to invite death. And it ought to be accounted a feat for John to have persuaded his consultants, who rendered their verdict on March 13, after having sat for weeks "carefully examining the details of the plans and theories of Mr. Roebling." A subsequent full report was issued to the board in June and reprinted in the *Eagle*, stating, "It is beyond doubt entirely practicable to erect a steel wire suspension bridge of 1,600 feet span, 135 feet elevation, across the East River, in accordance with the plans proposed by Mr. Roebling, and that such a structure will have all the strength, stability, safety and durability that should attend the permanent connection by a bridge of the cities of New York and Brooklyn."[77]

No doubt with the lawsuits that had plagued the Wheeling Bridge in mind, the board also hoped to have their bridge declared a US post road. They enlisted the help of the US congressman for Brooklyn, General Henry Slocum, an active participant at Gettysburg and during Sherman's March to the Sea, who reached out to Secretary of War John Rawlins. Rawlins then sent three army engineers— Generals Newton and Wright and Major King—to visit John and review his plans in late March. With much of the official explanatory work behind him but some decisions still pending, John then suggested a short trip to tour his other bridges, as both a celebration and a guide to what might be to come. The bridge party was large, comprising John and Washington, Kingsley (who was paying for the trip), Kinsella of the *Eagle*, all seven consulting engineers, the three officers appointed by the secretary of war to study John's plans, numerous members of the political and business team that were shepherding the project, several assistant engineers John had already recruited to work on the span, and a black servant named Joe who apparently "contributed largely to the well being of the party."[78]

The party left Brooklyn on Wednesday, April 14—"all sober," quipped the *Eagle*—and journeyed to Jersey City, where they boarded a "palace car" provided by the Pennsylvania Railroad, then traveled on to Trenton to pick up John. The train sped through New Jersey and into Pennsylvania as everyone relaxed. "Have you ever noticed how agreeable and genial men can really be if they try, and when they intend to spend five or six days together?" wrote Kinsella, who penned an account of the trip for the *Eagle*. A set of "uninviting sandwiches" couldn't spoil a mood lightened by a series of champagne cocktails, unlike John's request that everyone be up at five o'clock the next morning "to hail the sun rise and light up the Alleghenies." The party pulled into Pittsburgh—"the muddiest, smokiest, most thriving city of the country"—mid-morning, to inspect John's Allegheny span. John lectured everyone on the principles behind suspension bridges, pointing out that even though the spans of the bridge they were standing on seemed modest—350 feet—the same principles also secured John's 820-foot span at Niagara and his 1,057-foot bridge at Cincinnati, much as they would a 1,600-foot span over the East River. In fact, spans of up to feet were perfectly feasible, John told the assembled crowd, if price were no object. John also addressed himself to the equally important question of revenue. The Allegheny paid a dividend of 15 percent, even though it was not the only bridge to connect the city to the surrounding area. John knew this very well, being a large shareholder, just as he was for all the commercial bridges he had built. John's guests then took a stroll on his span "while the street cars were crossing and the ordinary traffic flowed past, and noticed no more tremor than is observable on an ordinary trussel bridge," wrote Kinsella.[79]

The bridge party left Pittsburgh "like a great sooty blotch" early the next morning and set off for Cincinnati. A damaged tunnel forced the party onto a different train and into a half-mile walk, but they were soon off again at the "awful" rate of fifty-four miles per hour, which had some of the party thinking they'd soon be "compelled to wind up the game of life." But they made it to Cincinnati safely and on time and checked into the Burnet House, where everyone was packed off to bed with John's injunction to be up and ready by nine the next morning, a command Slocum thought "barbarous." Everyone agreed, and "the untiring Old Man Roebling yielded an hour's grace."[80]

Everyone was in good spirits the next morning as they set off to see John's longest bridge, "the stateliest and most splendid evidence of genius, enterprise and skill, it had ever been my lot to see," as Kinsella described it. The party "walked to and fro upon it for an hour, and it seemed as solid and as stable beneath our feet as the earth on either side of the river. Yet as we stood under it, and saw it swing in the air so high, so graceful, and yet so secure, it was indeed a work to excite amazement and wonder." They met up with Shinkle and asked him about John. "He is an extraordinary man," he remarked, "and if you people in Brooklyn are wise you will interfere with his views just as little as possible. Give the 'old man' his own way, and trust him." Eminently satisfied, the party then took a stroll down Fourth Street "with its great crowd of elegantly dressed people called out by the beautiful weather," catching the attention of the local press, who recognized John and interviewed a couple of his party, who seemed somewhat shocked by all the bustle. "I had no idea there were so many people in Cincinnati," remarked one of John's companions.[81]

The party departed for Cleveland later that day, arriving the following morning amid "the blue sky and the blue waters of Lake Erie." They made a tour of the "Forest City" (as Cleveland was known in the nineteenth century), which impressed Kinsella as almost as attractive as Brooklyn. The last stop on the tour was Niagara, where John again walked his party over his bridge, explaining each of its features in great detail. The region had something of a glut of suspension bridges, which John was happy to show his group. The day was capped off with a group photo taken by Charles Bierstadt—brother of renowned landscape

Figure 18.12 Bridge Review Panel at the Clifton Suspension Bridge (1869). John, *front right*, in the tan overcoat. Courtesy of the Institute Archives and Special Collections, Rensselaer Polytechnic Institute.

painter Albert—on Samuel Keefer's recently finished Niagara Fall and Clifton (or Upper) Suspension Bridge. It is one of only three photographs of John and the only one where John and Washington are pictured together. John is immediately recognizable in a tan duster, looking at ease, confident, and comfortable as he stares up at the camera. No signs of age or infirmity cloud his face or mark his posture. His beard is gray, but he seems healthy and friendly, a distinct contrast to his two other photographs—both posed—that show a stiff, rather severe-looking man. Washington appears curious but happy to stand in the crowd, somewhat anonymously, and gaze up at the photographer. The image nicely captures the two men at a relaxed but distinct moment in their lives. The group enjoyed a final meal together, at the end of which General Slocum rose to say that that day he had looked upon the only thing for which he would be willing to forfeit his war record: John's Niagara Bridge. The next morning everyone boarded "a special car well furnished with refreshments" and headed back to New York for the job of building the world's longest suspension bridge.[82]

After the bridge tour, Washington made his way to Brooklyn to help with the final preparations. He rented a house at 137 Hicks Street for Emily and his young son. John spent most of his time in Trenton, traveling to Brooklyn once a week to interview a revolving stream of workmen, artisans, contractors, and engineers and to meet with investors and officials. While in Brooklyn he stayed at a Turkish bath on Hicks Street. The first and most pressing job facing the project was to survey the bridge's center line, a task that fell mainly to Washington. Each morning he would set out for the waterfront with Colonel William Paine—a self-taught surveyor from New Hampshire who had performed sterling work for the Union Army behind enemy lines—to take sightings and lay marker pins, establishing a baseline and slowly working backward inland. They laid markers in the middle of roads, on docksides, and in the sides of buildings. They clambered over whatever lay in their way, or the way the bridge would take, climbing up on top of stores and warehouses, over churches, through worksites, and through people's homes. Washington kept minute notes in his notebook, and slowly he and Paine became a familiar sight on the waterfront, scurrying, planning, chatting, and conferring. John would come down from the bridge offices on Fulton Street to check on the progress, see his son, and perhaps enjoy the breeze.[83]

Throughout June, Washington kept his father abreast of developments with the War Office, where approval seemed less than certain. General Slocum was again dispatched to Washington, DC, to exert whatever influence he could on Secretary of State Hamilton Fish, "who put in his personal influence against the bridge," a fact he later denied to Murphy. Washington even persuaded his brother-in-law Gouverneur Warren to take a trip south to "see how the matter stands down there." All were on tenterhooks in Brooklyn awaiting word from the capital, which finally arrived on June 21 when Brigadier General A. A. Humphreys wrote to Henry Murphy to say that Secretary of War Rawlins "approves the plan and location of the East River Bridge." Everything was now fixed and in place. All the money had been raised, the certifications approved, the personnel rounded up, and the plans made. John immediately made his way to Brooklyn to check on Washington's progress and to start work.[84]

On the afternoon of June 28, 1869, John walked down to the waterfront to inspect the site where the Brooklyn tower was to be built. He was standing on a beam attached to the inside of the fender (or outer) pilings that ran around the ferry slip when he noticed a boat coming in. The fender pilings were designed to cushion the impact of an incoming ship, so John stepped back onto a beam that ran around a set of rigid inner pilings, but he did not get far enough away. The impact of the ferry coming to dock pushed the outer beam onto the inner catching John's foot in the process severing all but the fifth toe "like a big pair of shears would do." By chance, Paine was in the bow of the incoming ferry— having spent the morning "making observations from several high buildings on the N.Y. side"—and saw the whole thing. "What folly, what folly," John cried before quickly giving orders for the "application of water." The pain must have been excruciating, but John kept on giving directions to Paine for some minutes without moving from the spot of the accident. Most likely he was in shock, but he soon succumbed and slid to the ground. Washington immediately took his father to the Turkish bath, where John's foot was placed into a bath of "cold water for hours removing it only to have the parts necessary [four crushed toes] severed"—"the large toes merely hung by a strip of skin," reported the *Eagle*— and the foot bound up. After this John "limped to the door without assistance" and was taken to Washington's house and bundled up the stairs and into bed.[85]

"Father had the toes of his left foot cut off today accidentally," Washington wired Ferdy once he had a spare moment. "He is quite comfortable and there is no danger of losing the foot." Later he sent his brother a fuller account of the day, assuring him his father "endures the pain bravely" and asked Ferdy to "please tell Mrs. Roebling not to be alarmed as the rest of the foot [is] safe," which seems to have been the consensus opinion. Paine wrote in his diary that "Mr. Roebling's foot has been getting along very well" and the *Eagle* reported that John's doctors thought "his health is so good that there is not reason to doubt he will be able to be about as normal in two to three weeks," which may well have been true if something else hadn't happened: John had somehow been infected by the *Clostridium tetani* (tetanus) bacteria. He had contracted lockjaw. According to Washington, John dismissed his doctors the next day, declaring that he would "take command of his own case." He ordered a tinsmith to construct a large round dish, into which he placed his foot. A hose positioned above the dish supplied a constant stream of water, and the distinguished engineer sat back to await his recovery. One of the doctors returned to warn John that he was "inviting sure death," but the engineer was bullheaded. He banished the doctor and returned to his bucket and hose.[86]

Unfortunately John's malady was "of a more painful and permanent character than we [at first] apprehended," wrote Kinsella shortly after John's accident, as news of its serious nature started to spread slowly around Brooklyn. But a week later John, who reported to have felt "no physical pain since the amputation" and expected to be out surveying again in a week or two, seemed busily engaged on the plans for the bridge "while his injured foot [was] so placed that a constant stream of cold water is poured on it." "The distinguished engineer has his own notions about surgical treatment," the *Eagle* reported, a fact that Washington had long deplored. John's eldest son chastised himself for not taking his father immediately to a hospital or insisting on better or more appropriate treatment, but in 1869 there was little to be done for infection. There was no vaccine for tetanus in 1869. John's tin bucket didn't help, but it didn't kill him either.[87]

Tetanus works on the central nervous system and results in violent muscle spasms, often leading to bone fractures and muscle tears. The muscles in the face slowly tighten as the lips curl back, the jaw locks, and the throat ceases to work. Eating becomes impossible, but death often results from asphyxiation as the patient can no longer control their own breathing, if they haven't already died from a heart attack or the pain brought on by the violent spasms that twist and rack the body, all of which are accompanied by an accelerated and irregular heart rate, elevated blood pressure, fever, sweating, and a complete inability to communicate. Tetanus is truly the body in extremis, and it was visited upon John in all its savage misery during his last days, ensuring that his end was wildly horrific.

Paine visited John almost everyday during his illness and left a full record of his treatment and deterioration. On July 15, the engineer "was attacked with stiffness of the throat which has been . . . alarming," leading to "his throat becom[ing] so constricted as not to admit food to pass. His jaws have become set," Paine continued, "and his whole spinal column has become stiffened and he remains sleepless." Two days later, the *Eagle* reported that John was "dangerously ill." John soon lost the ability to speak, which left him with the awful prospect of facing his death with almost no way to communicate. Although unable to speak and barely able to hold a pen, he tried to write orders about the bridge and when that failed he took to giving orders "by signs." Still, John gave no indication of giving up, even though he believed devoutly in an afterlife that would see him evolve to the next stage of life, closer to God and to man's perfection. "Mr Roebling . . . has considerable strength and still controls the details of all that is done for him," wrote Paine in the morning of July 21. "He even finished the drawing of a plan to have himself raised with more ease but the spasms seem to be more frequent and he lays much of the time in a disturbed semi-consciousness. He is wholly sustained by [morphine] injections."[88]

Whether he knew his body was failing is hard to say. John often misread evidence and circumstances, and he was supremely fallible despite his many achievements. But everyone else seemed to know. In the afternoon of July 21, a man "of the Union"—neither the name nor the nature of the "Union" are specified—"who claims to be able to loosen contracted muscles by laying on his hands" was summoned. "I was not able to see any amendment," Paine reported. That evening John was "put in a warm bath—102°—His face lost all color and it was thought he was dying when first put in but he soon revived and liked it. Cold water was poured on his spine and he remained in the bath for an hour." After that, he "was taken out and wrapped in a blanket. His muscles seemed somewhat relaxed and he appears easier." The spasms that racked his body almost constantly by this point seemed "lighter" but when he "took a little water and attempted to swallow [he] choked so badly that one had hard work to keep life in him." By 9pm that night Washington insisted that Paine—who had been at John's side for over 24 hours—go home and get some rest.

Washington and Edmund—who had arrived in early July—tended to their dying father throughout the night, along with Lucia who never left her husband's side during the whole ordeal. "I was the miserable witness of the most horrible tetanic convulsions, when the body is drawn into a half circle, the back of the head meeting the heels, with a face drawn into hideous distortions," wrote Washington; "hardened as I was by scenes of carnage on many a bloody battle-field, these horrors often overcame me." John's body jerked uncontrollably all night, his facial muscles petrified, welding his mouth shut in a demonic grin. Yet he "continued to control all the arrangements about him to the last," Paine gleaned the following day. "His mind showed great rigor and seemed to be employed in a careful attention to his own symptoms and the treating of them. Hopefulness seemed to predominate and God only knows the effect of all this upon his own mind and heart." The fight was slowly fading from the great engineer however. He began to "surrender in his mind" in the middle of the night before suffering two massive "spasms" in the early morning. All that was left was to sweat through another hour of excruciating torment before death came for him. At his own request, he was "lowered partially on his side" during which "he breathed his last" at six in the morning on July 22, 1869.

Epilogue

"I am my own Judge"

At 11:00 a.m. on Sunday, July 25, 1869, the doors to the Roebling mansion's south parlor were slowly opened, and the assembled throng was allowed to enter. A constant stream of men, women, and children passed through. All were silent, all removed their hats, all waited patiently. Some were tearful as they took their turn to gaze on "the inanimate form, of the man who had so often proved himself their friend." Dressed in a fresh black suit, John was laid out in a solid rosewood coffin lined with white satin. Some were shocked at how thin he was, having not been able to eat for the four weeks leading up to his death. The viewing lasted until 1:00 p.m., when a train whistle pierced the silence, announcing the arrival of a special railroad car from Jersey City packed with officials and other luminaries from New York and Brooklyn. Several other railroads had made special arrangements for those attending from Philadelphia and elsewhere. With the crowds still thick around John's coffin, the visiting dignitaries were ushered into John's study, where they were met by Washington and a selection of city officials, including the mayor, president of the common council, and the county court. The press estimated that approximately two thousand people were gathered around John's mansion by the early afternoon, the majority of whom "belonged to the working classes." "It was a very sad and affecting sight to see tears in the eyes of many of the powerfully-built mechanics as they passed out of the room in which the body of their deceased master was lying," wrote the *Eagle*. Services were held inside the Roebling home and were presided over by members of the First Presbyterian Church, the Lutheran Church, St. Paul's Episcopal, and Trinity Episcopal churches.[1]

The Reverend Hall of First Presbyterian spoke of John's kindness and charity, much of which he concealed even from his family. Hall had just that morning, for example, found out that John had "for many a year" given one thousand dollars annually to the Pittsburgh Orphans' Asylum, in a city he had not called home for over twenty years. If all of John's charitable works "could be discovered they would tell as stirring a story of his heart as these other monuments [his wire

rope company and his bridges] tell of his brain," he added. Others recalled the
last gathering of the Roebling family at the mansion for Elvira's wedding to John
H. Stewart, just five weeks earlier. John "was then full of life and happiness, and
everyone could see how genial he was in his family circle." For Reverend Brown
there was no greater evidence of the high regard in which Trenton held John than
that the reverend's office "was crowded by people of all denominations" hoping
for news of John once the accident had become known. Charles Hewitt, vice president of the Trenton Board of Trade, was prompted "to think less about the greatness and more about the goodness of our friend." "Perhaps there is no trait in
his character that will remain brighter in [Trenton's] recollection than that of his
personal kindness—a kindness that was steady and knew no shadow of turning."
"A common grief pervades all classes of our community," he concluded.[2]

After the services, a huge procession gathered and set off. Their destination
was a short ride from the family home: Myrtle Cemetery (now Riverview) on
Clinton Street, where Johanna and Willie were already buried. The clergy and
members of the Roebling family rode at the head, followed by local officials and
invited dignitaries, after which marched one hundred members of the Trenton
Board of Trade, two hundred employees of the New Jersey Iron Works, and 150
men from John's rope works, followed by two hundred orphans from the Trenton
Children's Home, to which John was a frequent and liberal donor. Workers
from the city's other ironworks and sundry other people and professions were
next in line, brought up in the rear by members of all the local fire companies.
The procession was said to be about a mile and a half long, with almost 1,500
participants. Those not marching were watching. By all accounts the sidewalks
were thronged, with every window of the buildings occupied. Some said that
nearly half of the city had turned out to honor John's memory. Only a fraction of those who turned out were able to fit into the cemetery for the burial,
which almost seemed like the day's least important event, after the viewing and
the speeches and the parade. The pallbearers—Henry Murphy, Julius Adams,
Horatio Adams, Andrew Green, Charles Hewitt, Timothy Abbott, Samuel
Wilson, and Alfred Livingston—shouldered John's coffin, walked slowly to his
grave, and watched as John was laid to rest after a life of almost constant activity.
Only a few quick words were said before everyone drifted off slowly, to get on
with their lives. One imagines that John would have approved.

———

On some level, a funeral should showcase a man's life and achievements, whether
professional or personal. John's was a testament to the life he had built in the
United States since disembarking onto the Philadelphia docks thirty-eight years
earlier: the family he had sired, the manufactory he had created, the many social

orbits in which he moved, the people he knew and had influenced, the lives he had made, the charities he had sustained, the loyalties he had inspired, the things he had built and achieved, the things he believed in and cherished. "In all his business relations he was a man of perfect justice," declared the Reverend Hall, who, while "not able to speak positively as to [John's] religious convictions," also knew that "next to occupying his mind with mechanical pursuits was his love for investigations of this character," providing a sense that John's private musings on the nature of being were perhaps not so private. Others talked of how "Old Man Roebling" was "always affable" with his workmen and how he "endeared himself to people of every class" in Trenton. He was, in the words of almost everyone, "a good man." His impact on the town had been huge, his death "a public calamity." John had been president of the Board of Trade as well as the Literary and Philosophical Society, not to mention a member of both the Eagle and the Delaware fire companies. While the country mourned a man "who had elevated her among the nations of the earth" and the scientific world would "feel the void caused by the extinguishing of one of its most brilliant stars," Trenton mourned a friend, a man of "charity and virtue." Shortly after his death, William Phelps sent the *State Gazette* a copy of the letter John had declined to have published in 1860 when offering to underwrite the establishment of an orphan's home. "I trust that in a community where there is so much treasure spent cheerfully for the rearing of elegant temples of worship, there will be found enough practical sympathy left to heal the most putrid sores of an outraged and crying humanity. Let us go to work at once and accomplish it," John had written. The Trenton orphan's home also received a large bequest in John's will, which allocated one-sixth of his "personal estate"—"to an amount not exceeding ninety thousand dollars"—to various charities in Trenton and western Pennsylvania, including thirty thousand dollars for Trenton's Widows and Single Women's Home. Everywhere he had lived, John had been a friend to the poor and the needy.[3]

In the wake of John's death, tributes poured in from all quarters. The mayor and town council of Mühlhausen sent a letter expressing their "profound sympathy" and their pride in their former resident. *Scientific American* believed that "few men have lived whose history can record a series of more brilliant successes than that of Mr. Roebling. He leaves behind him monuments of his greatness, and his name will pass into history among the brightest of those who have achieved immortality by benefitting the human race." The *Eagle* called John "first among the mightiest class of men—men who subdue the elements and bend the forces of nature into the service of the people. The engineers are the representative men of the nineteenth century," they continued, because they were "the most practically useful men of the day." John's death was major news, not only in New York, Trenton, Boston, Baltimore, Cincinnati, St. Louis, and Washington, DC, but in such places as Iowa, Michigan, Salt Lake City, Dallas, St. Paul, and New Orleans.

It was the only story on the front page of *Harper's Weekly* the week of August 7, 1869. The national magazine called John "the most talented [bridge] engineer of the age," who "won the love and respect of all who knew him, and in his works has left behind him a nobler monument than could be shaped in marble." The sense of pride felt by German Americans was palpable and ably expressed by Carl Reemelin in Cincinnati's *Der Deutsche Pionier*: "No order of the eagle covered his chest, and yet so much of an eagle was inside him. He let his eyes wander through the field of technology, but he also looked at [life's] details with the greatest precision." *Beecher's Magazine* couldn't think of "any death among scientific men that has occasioned a more profound sense of national loss, or been the subject of such universal regret by the press at home and abroad." Befitting some of John's more idiosyncratic tendencies, the *American Phrenological Journal* also gave their opinion: "Mr. Roebling had a full-sized brain on a well-proportioned body; a very active mind, in keeping with his clearly marked motive-mental temperament. His Constructiveness, Concentrativeness, Firmness, and Self-Esteem were large," they reported helpfully.[4]

—

John's death left a void in Trenton's social fabric and in the world of American engineering. More pressingly, it left the project to construct the world's largest suspension bridge without its master builder and guiding light. All work ceased on the East River bridge while John was buried. But with so much at stake and so many hands waiting to get to work, no one could afford to be sentimental. The subject of who would take over as chief engineer was discussed as soon as Kingsley, Murphy, and the others boarded the train back to New York after John's funeral. On August 3, 1869—barely two weeks after John's death—the board of trustees met and appointed Colonel Washington A. Roebling chief engineer of the New York and Brooklyn Bridge. The decision was easy but risky. No one had undertaken a bridge of this magnitude except John and Ellet, both of whom were now dead. Washington knew his father's plans and had worked closely with him on his previous two bridges. John himself said on at least a couple of occasions that his son was more than capable of building the bridge he had designed. Still, the trust shown in thirty-two-year-old Washington was staggering, and he repaid it several times over, with his energy, his expertise, his commitment, and ultimately his health. Washington ably and heroically carried the bridge project to its conclusion, perhaps even more ably than John might have, eventually throwing the massive span open on May 24, 1883.

Washington did not merely realize John's plans. He made crucial choices and decisions at every stage of the operation, altering John's plans to suit his own ideas, not his father's. The Brooklyn Bridge was the first Roebling bridge built with an open anchorage, covered only against the elements—John had planned his usual sealed and cemented arrangement—thus saving the Brooklyn Bridge the same fate as almost all of John's bridges. In 1867, John had claimed that the only part of his Ohio span "that will ever need repairs is the wooden floor," but by 1895 a major overhaul was needed. Wilhelm Hildenbrand was placed in charge. The engineer had worked on the Brooklyn Bridge under Washington and had met John in New York in 1867, helping him to draft the drawings that accompanied his initial East River bridge report. Hildenbrand's renovations changed much of the look and feel of the bridge—replacing almost all of the hardware and adding another set of suspension cables—but they also ensured the bridge remained in service.[5]

After John's death, his second wife, Lucia, inherited an eighth of his estate, "retired from society," and moved to New York, where she "devoted her whole time to charity, which she dispensed in the most unassuming and modest way." "She was a lady of the highest refinement," according to the *New York Times*, "of a cheerful and tender-hearted disposition, with a deep religious training. She was very fond of poetry, and was able to quote from memory long passages of the best English poets." She spent her remaining days visiting the poor, relieving them with "material support and friendly advice." She died at the Bristol Hotel in Midtown Manhattan on December 28, 1884. If Gunn is to be believed—that Lucia wanted few things but to be married and not poor—she presumably died happy.[6]

Back in Trenton, Swan continued to help run John's wire rope business, but the concern passed into the hands of his sons, who took a far more active role than their father. John had hoped his sons would make Swan a partner, but his sons were reluctant to cede either control or revenue. Rather disingenuously, Washington wrote to Swan to make the case that he would earn more as an employee than as an owner and "avoid all risk" into the bargain. Before John's estate had even been appraised, a deal was struck to make Swan a well-paid "Manager and Superintendent of the Wire Rope Works" but not a partner. Under the wise and skillful leadership of Ferdinand (who took control of the company's finances), Charles (who was in charge of the plant and production), and Washington (who looked after engineering), John A. Roebling's Sons expanded exponentially, becoming an industrial behemoth by the early twentieth century, employing thousands of hands and generating a staggering amount of wealth for all members of the family. When Charles died in 1915, John A. Roebling's Sons Company was worth almost 240 times as much as when the brothers had inherited it in 1869. This outcome, alongside Washington's successful completion of the Brooklyn Bridge, leads to the rather irony that the two things John is best known for were brought to fruition by his sons, not by him. John remains the most famous, however, a source of great personal pain to Washington, who spent much of his life having to persuade people that he was not his father and that he had built the Brooklyn Bridge.[7]

Trenton has yet to raise a statue to any of John's sons or any of their descendants, or name a park after any of them, but the town is littered with John's name. In 1908, a statute of him was erected in the city's Cadwalader Park—although, perhaps fittingly, Washington had to pose for it—and two separate parks bear the Roebling name, as do a shopping mall and a condo development. A similar situation has helped sustain and nurture John's fame in Covington. A statue of a bizarrely flamboyant John was erected in 1988. Four years previously, the Covington and Cincinnati Bridge was renamed the John A. Roebling Bridge, another historically inaccurate alteration, given the retrofit performed by Hildenbrand in 1895 and the lopsided effort put into the construction by Covington. Somewhat worse, the span was repainted a garish blue in 1976 during the country's bicentennial celebrations, leading local historian Phillip Spiess to remark, "If John Roebling were alive today, he'd die." Perhaps the most enduring monument to John, however, lies on the Delaware River at Lackawaxen between Pennsylvania and upstate New York. John's Delaware Aqueduct has been in almost constant service since 1849. Its massive flume was dismantled and then rebuilt decades later, but the cables and the piers have continued to do their work for almost 170 years, carrying canal boats during their heyday and automobiles during theirs. It was the place John repaired to after the disappointments of the late 1840s, when his dreams were so large and his contracts so small. He had dreamed of spanning the Ohio at Wheeling, or at Cincinnati, or the Niagara up by the falls. And he had ended up at Lackawaxen, where he built a much less impressive, much more workaday structure, but one that he built to the very best of his ability and one that endures to this day.[8]

—

John wasn't the smiling, theatrical showman imagined at the Covington waterfront, but he also wasn't the strict and unbending curmudgeon historians have often portrayed him as either. Heinrich Ratterman, one of the nineteenth century's most prominent German American intellectuals, knew John in Cincinnati and wrote a short biography of him in German after his death. "Röbling was an exceptional man. His powerful, high forehead arched above his energetic brow and somewhat deep-set eyes. Upon meeting him for the first time you would think he was an angry, inaccessible character; however, if you were around him often, you were easily convinced that he was just the opposite. He was not only talkative but gladly allowed his sociable temperament to be understood." (In this, perhaps, historians have acted much like those who met John in the flesh.) "He had an impressive physique, built tall and broad-shouldered,"

Ratterman continued. "His mouth and nose depicted determination, power and audacity. At first glance one sensed the goodness of his heart and the great modesty (that was his nature), as well as the geniality in his dealings; however, if you were around him often, you would not only perceive these characteristics, you would witness them." John was perhaps a hard man to know, but he was knowable, and he was always hardest on himself. "A man may be content with the success of an enterprise; he may have succeeded in overcoming all obstacles . . . in achieving a great task; solving a great mental problem or accomplishing a work which was previously pronounced impossible & impracticable," he once wrote. Yet after he is "admired & is proclaimed a public benefactor [and] feels himself elated, and in his own estimation, a great man, if not a true man," he is forced to face himself. "Retiring in one calm moment within the recesses of his own inner self, he reviews his past deeds, his thoughts and motives of action. And before the judgment of his own consciousness he stands condemned, an untruth, a lie to himself. But no body knows! Does he himself not know? Who can hide one from myself? Vain conceits!" "I am my own judge, and from my own inner judgment either happiness or misery results!" he declared.[9]

Despite living a life full of achievement, John didn't really believe in happiness. "Perfect happiness & contentment has not fallen to the lot of men," he wrote. "Perfect happiness can only result from perfect harmony; but perfect harmony presupposes absolute perfection. God alone is absolute perfection, is absolute Harmony. . . . To feel happy & contented, a man is compelled to work, to improve himself, to progress spiritually." John believed in working toward perfection. He believed it was his duty to get things moving, that his physical actions would move himself and the world closer to spiritual perfection. John's beliefs and his actions rarely diverged, so the fact that his sons realized what he began fits John's vision of the world perfectly. This vision was developed in response to dozens of different ideas and theories, but it was profoundly American at heart. It is the idea of the unfinished pyramid waiting to be completed, the republic to be perfected—that it is the job of the present generation to start things that others will finish. John understood his role in all this as an engine, helping to propel the present into the future.[10]

John was well suited for this task. He was fundamentally a seeker and a believer. It's why he emigrated and why he was at the Brooklyn waterfront in June 1869. It's why he left so much unfinished work on his drafting table and why he left a bridge for his son to finish. He would always have left something for Washington to finish. So much of John's life had been spent reaching toward a goal that was just out of reach, be it another shore or a new way to build or to organize society or the afterlife. He always had his eyes on something new. Washington could be cruel about his father and even dismissive, but he could be admiring too, especially on this point. "Few people that I ever met possessed

such an amount of vital energy, coupled at the same time with an amazing perseverance which never rested, week day or Sunday—from early morn to dewy
eve and later. His mind was incessantly at work—We all know that mere thought
without expression or action is useless—His every thought was at once put
down in the shape of a drawing, a plan or in writing—Of these I have hundreds and thousands packed away in boxes—all antiquated by this time, mere
memorials of past activities surpassed by the *combined* progress of innumerable
other minds, each one of which is however an essential unity, without which the
whole cannot exist." Historians have tended to portray John as rigid and closed
off to new ideas, but he was remarkably open in all sorts of ways. He was certainly very sure in his beliefs, but he was accepting of dozens of ideas that were
new in his lifetime. Looking through the "memorials of [John's] past activities,"
one is struck by the candor with which he wrote about his own ideas and his
willingness to learn.[11]

In this, and in other areas of his life, John was a thinker, an ideas man. And he
had thousands. Many were foolish; others were ridiculous. Most missed the mark
in one form or another, but some didn't, and those ideas helped change the face
of a nation. Washington understood this, but in a limited way. He saw his father's
genius but not its context. He enjoyed the gifts he was handed—much as he
suffered unfairly under the obligations—but he also missed the lessons of John's
character. "What he really believed," Washington wrote in his memoir, "I never
found out, fortunately it does not matter a particle." No sadder sentence exists
in the whole storied chronicle of the Roebling family, through all their years of
effort and innovation. What John believed was central to who he was, to what
he built, wrote, thought, and planned so voraciously, and to why he boarded the
August Eduard, so full of energy and enthusiasm. It was the reason he devoted
his life to bridging great distances, to what he understood as the job of uniting
the nation. That he remained so incomprehensible to his beloved eldest son was
the great hole at the center of his life, the great failing that throws everything else
into relief. John could communicate through the things he built and wrote, but
not through the life he lived with his son. If a life, like a bridge, is a delicate balance of countervailing forces, John's achievements were too grand and his focus
too firmly fixed on the opposite shore. With fewer ideas and fewer beliefs, he
may have been a better father, although hardly a better engineer. Perhaps in this,
as much as in anything else, John's life encapsulated the great sweep and shift of
the nineteenth century.

NOTES

Abbreviations

MVEC-M	Memoires of Mary Virginia Ellet Cabell, Papers of William Daniel Cabell and the Cabell and Ellet families, Special Collections, University of Virginia Library, Charlottesville
NFC	Niagara Falls Collection, Niagara Falls Public Library, Niagara Falls, NY
PHMC	Pennsylvania State Archives, Pennsylvania Historical and Museum Commission, Harrisburg
RFP-RPI	Roebling Family Papers, Rensselaer Polytechnic Institute, Troy, NY
RFP-RU	Roebling Family Papers, Rutgers University, New Brunswick, NJ
RL-UM	Rochester Ladies Anti-Slavery Society Records, University of Michigan, Ann Arbor
RLP-MVHS	Russel F. Lord Papers, Minisink Valley Historical Society, Port Jervis, NY
SPL	Local History Collection, Saxonburg Public Library, Saxonburg, PA
SRL	Some Roebling Letters (1821–1927) and incidental matters/selected and arranged by Clarence E. Case, Transcript Books no. 3a–3c, Roebling Family Papers, Rutgers University
TBG	Thomas Butler Gunn Diaries, 1849–1863, Missouri History Museum, St. Louis
TFP-JHHC	Thaw Family Papers, 1787–1981, Thomas and Katherine Detre Library and Archives at the Senator John Heinz History Center, Pittsburgh
WAR	Washington August Roebling
WFP	Wurts Family Paper, Manuscripts and Archives Department, Hagley Museum and Library, Wilmington, DE
WPP	William H. Paine Papers (MS 475), New-York Historical Society, New York
WRF	Donald Sayenga, ed., *Washington Roebling's Father: A Memoir of John A. Roebling* (Reston, VA: American Society of Civil Engineers Press, 2009)
WP	Gouverneur Kemble Warren Papers, New York State Library, Albany

Introduction

1. *Diary*, 81–83.
2. *WRF*, 40.
3. Surprisingly, the last biography of Roebling—David Steinman's *The Builders of the Bridge: The Story of John Roebling and His Son* (New York: Harcourt, Brace, 1945)—was published over seventy years ago. Despite being woefully under-researched and riddled with inaccuracies and presumptions, it is still regarded as the definitive book on Roebling, primarily in the absence of anything else. Fourteen years previously, Hamilton Schuyler published *The Roeblings: A Century of Engineers, Bridgebuilders and Industrialists* (Princeton, NJ: Princeton University Press, 1931), a mostly accurate but very scant family history, focused much more on the family and its business than on John himself. Clifford Zink's wonderfully illustrated *The Roebling Legacy* (Princeton, NJ: Princeton Landmark Publications, 2011) is in the same vein. David McCullough's *The Great Bridge: The Epic Story of the Building of the Brooklyn Bridge* (New York: Simon & Schuster, 1972) contains a very short biographical summary of Roebling's life, perhaps best described as the life sketched in very broad outlines. Thankfully, much excellent research into John's life has been published in Germany recently, especially by Nele Güntheroth, Andreas Kahlow, Eberhard Grunsky, and Christiane and Horst Vielhaber. See the essays in Güntheroth and Kahlow, eds., *Von Mühlhausen in die neue Welt: Der Brückenbauer J. A. Röbling (1806–1869)*, Mühlhauser Beiträge 15 (Mühlhausen, Germany: Muehlhäuser Museen, 2006); Eberhard Grunsky's "Von den Anfängen des Hängebrückenbaus in Westfalen," *Westfalen* 76 (1998), 100-159 and "Von Eslohe, Freienohl und Finnentrop bis Niagara, Cincinnati und New York," *Sauerland* 1 (2004), 20–24; Christiane and Horst Vielhaber's "Von der Lenne-Brücke zur Brooklyn Bridge. Über Johann August Röbling's Esloher Jahre," *Esloher Museumsnachrichten* (2008), 3–7. Additionally, the essays published in Theodore Green, ed., *John A. Roebling: A Bicentennial Celebration of His Birth, 1806–2006* (Reston, VA: American Society of Civil Engineers, 2007), are wide-ranging and useful. Finally, the work of Don Sayenga over the past forty years deserves special praise. His comprehensive and diligent investigations into almost

every aspect of Roebling's life, as a bridge builder and wire rope manufacturer, are where everyone interested in Roebling's life must start. See especially, but not exclusively: "Roebling's Pittsburgh Aqueduct," *Canal Currents: Bulletin of the Pennsylvania Canal Society* 61 (1981), 3–6; "Roebling's First Rope," *Wire Rope News* 3, no. 3 (1982), 10-12; "Roebling's Second Rope," *Wire Rope News* 3, no. 4 (1982), 9–12; *Ellet and Roebling*, 2nd ed. (Easton, PA: Canal History & Technology, 2001); "The Saxonburgh Ropes," *Wire Journal* 32 (May 1988), 88–99; "The Early Years of America's Wire Rope Industry, 1818–1848," *Canal History and Technology Proceedings* 10 (1991), 149–180; "'Pittsburgh Aquaduct': Reconstruction of the Pittsburgh Aqueduct by John A. Roebling," *Canal History and Technology Proceedings* 14 (1995), 73–90; "The Archbald/Roebling Correspondence," *OIPEEC Bulletin* 83 (2002); *Washington Roebling's Father: A Memoir of John A. Roebling* (Reston, VA: American Society of Civil Engineers Press, 2009); "Cement Shoes," *Wire Rope News and Sling Technology* 35, nos. 5–7 (2015), 20–24, 28, 30–31; 8–10, 12, 14–15; 18, 20–22, 24, 26, 28, 30.

Chapter 1

1. For the history of Mühlhausen see Christian Gottlieb Altenburg, *Die Chronik der Stadt Mühlhausen in Thüringen* (Bad Langensalza, Germany: Rockstuhl, 1999 (1824)).
2. See Abraham Friesen, *Thomas Muentzer, a Destroyer of the Godless: The Making of a Sixteenth-Century Religious Revolutionary* (Berkeley: University of California Press, 1990), 217–68.
3. Christoph Wolff, *Johann Sebastian Bach: The Learned Musician* (New York: W. W. Norton, 2000), 104.
4. Wilhelm Auener, *Johann August Röbling* (Mühlhausen, Germany: Verlag des Altertumsvereins, 1931), 3–4.
5. Ibid., 4–5; *WRF*, 3–4.
6. J. R. Seeley, *Life and Times of Stein: Or, Germany and Prussia in the Napoleonic Age*, 3 vols. (Boston: Roberts Bros, 1879), 1:80; Charles Esdaile, *Napoleon's Wars: An International History, 1803–1815* (New York: Viking, 2008), 138.
7. See James J. Sheehan, *German History, 1770–1866* (New York: Oxford University Press, 1989), 233–34; Christopher Clark, *Iron Kingdom: The Rise and Downfall of Prussia, 1600–1947* (London: Penguin, 2006), 292–93, 300, 346; Esdaile, *Napoleon's Wars*, 240.
8. Alistair Horne, *Napoleon: Master of Europe, 1805–1807* (New York: William Morrow, 1979), 196–97; [Reinhard] Jordan, *Chronik der Stadt Mühlhausen in Thüringen*, vol. 4, 1770–1890 (Mühlhausen, Germany: Danner'sche Buchdruckerei, 1908), 67. As Paul Schroeder succinctly notes, Prussia chose to be a "lion only after trying so hard to remain a jackal." See Paul W. Schroeder, *The Transformation of European Politics, 1763–1848* (New York: Oxford University Press, 1994), 303.
9. Schroeder, *The Transformation of European Politics*, 74–76; Alexander Grab, *Napoleon and the Transformation of Europe* (New York: Palgrave Macmillan, 2003), 99–103; Owen Connelly, *Napoleon's Satellite Kingdoms* (New York: The Free Press, 1965), 185; Sheehan, *German History*, 259–61; Herbert Fisher, *Studies in Napoleonic Statesmanship: Germany* (Oxford: Clarendon Press, 1903), 295.
10. Connelly, *Napoleon's Satellite Kingdoms*, 196, 207–9; Schuyler, *The Roeblings*, 4–5; *WRF*, 5; Johan Georg Schollmeyer, "Einige Worte zur Beherzigung für Väter und Mütter," *Neues Mühlhäusisches Wochenblatt* 45 (1806) quoted in Nele Güntheroth, "The Young Roebling, Biographical Notes," in Green, *John A. Roebling*, 4.
11. See for example Henry D. Estabrook, "Address Is Mr. Henry D. Estabrook," in *John A. Roebling: An Account of the Ceremonies at the Unveiling of a Monument to His Memory* (Trenton, NJ: Roebling, 1908), 25–26; Steinman, *The Builders of the Bridge*, 4–6; Schuyler, *The Roeblings*, 9–10.
12. *WRF*, 4; Güntheroth, "The Young Roebling, Biographical Notes,", 4–5.
13. Johann's loathing was hardly unique. By the end of the Napoleonic Wars a popular phrase entered the Prussian repertoire: "Exterminate the French; God at the Last Judgment will not ask you why." According to his son, however, Johann's attitude did change toward the very end of his life after he read Louis Adolphe Thiers's *The History of the Consulate and the Empire of*

France under Napoleon (1845–62), so that "his German views were sufficiently modified for him to admit that Napoleon was one of the greatest men that ever lived." See *WRF*, 5.

14. See Eric Hobsbawm, *The Age of Revolution, 1789–1848* (London: Abacus, 1999 (1962)), 110; Frederick Hertz, *The Development of the German Public Mind*, 2 vols. (London: Allen & Irwin, 1957–62), 2:420; Terry Pinkard, *Hegel: A Biography* (New York: Cambridge University Press, 2000), 228.

15. Esdaile, *Napoleon's Wars*, 516; Sheehan, *German History*, 318–19; Friedrich Meinecke, *The Age of German Liberation, 1789–1815*, ed. Peter Paret, trans. Peter Paret and Helmuth Fischer (Berkeley: University of California Press, 1977), 119; Jordan, *Chronik der Stadt Mühlhausen in Thüringen*, 92–93.

16. W. O. Henderson, *The State and the Industrial Revolution in Prussia, 1740–1870* (Liverpool: Liverpool University Press, 1958), 81–83.

17. Hans G. Schenk, *The Aftermath of the Napoleonic Wars* (London: Kegan & Paul, 1947), 120; Hagen Schulze, *The Course of German Nationalism: From Frederick the Great to Bismarck, 1763–1867*, trans. Sarah Hanbury-Tenison (Cambridge: Cambridge University Press, 1991), 38–39; Sheehan, *German History*, 392, 408–9; Clark, *Iron Kingdom*, 402–5.

18. Karl A. Schleunes, "Enlightenment, Reform, Reaction: The Schooling Revolution in Prussia," *Central European History* 12, no. 4 (1979), 315–42; Brendan Simms, *The Struggle for Mastery in Germany, 1779–1850* (London: Macmillan, 1998), 75; Eric Dorn Brose, *The Politics of Technological Change in Prussia: Out of the Shadows of Antiquity, 1809–1848* (Princeton, NJ: Princeton University Press, 1993), 109–12.

19. Schleunes, "Enlightenment, Reform, Reaction," 317, 325; Brose, *The Politics of Technological Change in Prussia*, 110–11; Mathew Levinger, *Enlightened Nationalism: The Transformation of Prussian Political Culture, 1804–1848* (New York: Oxford University Press, 2000), 199; Nele Güntheroth, "Realien und Karriere: Röbling's Ausbildung zum Baumeister und Ingenieur," *Mühlhauser Beiträge* 15 (2006), 9–11.

20. Güntheroth, "Realien und Karriere," 8–9; Sheehan, *German History*, 436–37; Hobsbawm, *The Age of Revolution*, 232–34.

21. Johan Georg Schollmeyer, "Ueber die Äußern und Innern Beschaffenheiten des Gymnasiums Berichtet der Rector Schollmeyer" (1817), reprinted in Güntheroth, "Realien und Karriere," 9–11.

22. Ibid.

23. Amalia Röbling to Friedrich Karl Röbling, April 29, 1822, in SRL.

24. Güntheroth, "Realien und Karriere," 11.

25. See Johann Charles Hochhuth, *Erinnerungen an die Vorzeit und Gegenwart der Stadt Eschwege in Thüringen* (Leipzig: Weygand in Komm, 1826).

26. See Nele Güntheroth, "Ephraim Salomon Unger: Röbling's Erfurter Mentor," *Mitteilungen des Vereins für die Geschichte und Altertumskunde von Erfurt* 68 (2007), 7–11; Güntheroth, "The Young Roebling, Biographical Notes," 6–7.

27. JAR to Friedrich Karl Röbling, March 24, 1823, in SRL.

28. Ibid.

Chapter 2

1. Anthony Read and David Fisher, *Berlin: The Biography of a City* (London: Pimlico, 1994), 78–83; Ronald Taylor, *Berlin and Its Culture: A Historical Portrait* (New Haven, CT: Yale University Press, 1997), 121–25; W. O. Henderson, "Peter Beuth and the Rise of Prussian Industry, 1810–1845," *Economic History Review* 8, no. 2 (1955), 222–31; Henderson, *The State and the Industrial Revolution in Prussia*, 113.

2. Gottfried Riemann, "Schinkel's Buildings and Plans for Berlin," in *Karl Friedrich Schinkel: A Universal Man*, ed. Michael Snodin (London: Victoria and Albert Museum, 1991), 16–26; Brose, *The Politics of Technological Change in Prussia*, 108–10.

3. See Henry E. Dwight, *Travels in the North of Germany, in the Years 1825 and 1826* (New York: G. C. H. Carvill, 1829), 114–16.

4. JAR, "Student book #1a," RFP-RU, 6; Güntheroth, "Realien und Karriere," 15.

5. GuentherothGüntheroth, "Realien und Karriere," 16; *Diary*, 108; E. T. A. Hoffmann, "My Cousin's Corner Window," in *The Golden Pot, and Other Tales*, trans. Ritchie Robertson (New York: Oxford University Press, 1992), 378–80.

6. Güntheroth, "The Young Roebling, Biographical Notes," 8.

7. See Horst Althaus, *Hegel: An Intellectual Biography*, trans. Michael Tarsh (Malden, MA: Polity, 2000), 159–60; Pinkard, *Hegel*, 516.

8. On the legend see Steinman, *The Builders of the Bridge*, 13; *WRF*, 6–7. John only seems to have referred to his experiences with Hegel twice. In December 1862, he noted that "in the year 1824 I enjoyed the good fortune to tend to his [Hegel's] lectures in the University of Berlin. Youth and a prevalence of material conceptions of course were great stumbling blocks in my way." And the following April he again referred to the time he "attended Hegel's lectures in Berlin" when he was "too young and too material in my conception." See JAR, "The Truth of Nature," box 4, folders 12 and 14, RFP-RU.

9. See Georg W. F. Hegel, *Lectures on Logic*, trans. Clark Butler (Bloomington: Indiana University Press, 2008), especially 227–33; Georg W. F. Hegel, *The Philosophy of History*, trans. J. Sibree (Buffalo, NY: Prometheus, 1991), 19; Althaus, *Hegel*, 175.

10. See Georg W. F. Hegel, *The Science of Logic*, trans. A. V. Miller (Amherst, NY: Humanity Books, 1969), 825–44; Pinkard, *Hegel*, 474–75.

11. JAR to Polycarpus Röbling, March 30, 1844, in SRL; *WRF*, 42. Also see Georg Wilhelm Friedrich Hegel, *Lectures on the Philosophy of Religion*, 3 vols., ed. Peter C. Hodgson, trans. R. F. Brown, P. C. Hodgson, and J. M. Stewart (New York: Oxford University Press, 2007); Franz Wiedmann, *Hegel: An Illustrated Biography*, trans. Joachim Neugroschel (New York: Pegasus, 1968), 74; Pinkard, *Hegel*, 529.

12. Althaus, *Hegel*, 157.

13. *WRF*, 41–42, 209.

14. Hegel, *The Philosophy of History*, 12; JAR to Polycarpus Röbling, March 30, 1844, in SRL; Thomas Paine, *The Age of Reason*, in *The Complete Writings of Thomas Paine*, ed. Philip S. Foner, 2 vols. (New York: Citadel, 1969), 1:464.

15. Dwight, *Travels in the North of Germany*, 132, 165–66; Thomas Hodgskin, *Travels in the North of Germany*, 2 vols. (Edinburgh: Archibald Constable, 1820), 1:33–34; *Diary*, 113. The retreat from associational culture was Europe-wide. Visiting the United States in 1831, Alexis de Tocqueville was struck by the vibrancy and openness of public debate, leading him to realize how largely "apathy" had come to define his home continent, to the point "that society seems to vegetate rather than thrive." See Alexis de Tocqueville, *Democracy in America* ed. Olivier Kunz, trans. Arthur Goldhammer, 2 vols. (New York: Library of America, 2012), 1:104.

16. Alexandra Richie, *Faust's Metropolis: A History of Berlin* (New York: Carroll & Graf, 1998), 116–17; JAR, "Student book #5," RFP-RU; Read and Fisher, *Berlin*, 67; Schulze, *The Course of German Nationalism*, 59.

17. Güntheroth, "Realien und Karriere," 13–14; Andreas Kahlow, "Johann August Röbling (1806–1869): Early Projects in Context," in Green, *John A. Roebling*, 37.

18. Tom F. Peters, *Transitions in Engineering: Guillaume Henri Dufour and the Early-19th-Century Suspension Bridges* (Basel: Birkhäuser Verlag, 1987), 9–11; Eda Kranakis, *Constructing a Bridge: An Exploration of Engineering, Culture, Design, and Research in Nineteenth-Century France and America* (Cambridge, MA: MIT Press, 1997), 11.

19. See J. F. W. Dietlein, *Perronet's Werke: Die Beschreibung der Entwürfe und der Bauarten der Brücken bei Neuilli, Mantes, Orleans, Louis XVI* (Halle: Hemmerde & Schwetschke, 1820); J. F. W. Dietlein, *Auszug aus Navier's Abhandlung über die Hängebrücken* (Berlin: G. Reimer, 1825); J. F. W. Dietlein, *Grundzüge der Vorlesungen über Strassen, Brücken, Schleusen, Canal, Strom, Deich und Hafen Bau; Gehalten in der Königl Bauakademie zu Berlin in den Jahren 1824 bis 1831* (Berlin: G. Reimer, 1832).

20. Güntheroth, "The Young Roebling, Biographical Notes," 9; JAR, "Student book #1," RFP-RU.

21. *WRF*, 7. See JAR, "On Steamships—Engines, Propellers, Boilers, etc." (1841), box 5, folder 52, RFP-RU; JAR, "Hints on the New Steam Frigates for the United States," *Scientific American*, June 10, 1854, 310; JAR, "On Marine Boilers," *Scientific American*, June 17, 1854, 318.

22. Antoine Picon, "Navier and the Introduction of Suspension Bridges in France," *Construction History* 4 (1988), 21–34; Kranakis, *Constructing a Bridge*, 97–118; Honoré de Balzac, *The Village Rector*, trans. Katherine Prescott Wormeley (Boston: Roberts Brothers, 1893), 242.

23. JAR, "Student book #1a"; C. L. M. H. Navier, *Rapport à Monsieur Becquey et Mémoire sur les Ponts Suspendus*, 2nd ed. (Paris: Carilian-Goeury, 1830), 64.

24. Picon, "Navier and the Introduction of Suspension Bridges in France," 23–24; Robert Stephenson, "Description of Bridges of Suspension," *Edinburgh Philosophical Journal* 5, no. 10 (1821), 237.

25. Kranakis, *Constructing a Bridge*, 163.

26. See Navier, *Mémoire sur les Ponts Suspendus*, 226–34; Kranakis, *Constructing a Bridge*, 165–69.

27. Navier, *Mémoire sur les Ponts Suspendus*, 61, quoted in Picon, "Navier and the Introduction of Suspension Bridges in France," 25.

28. See H. J. Hopkins, *A Span of Bridges: An Illustrated History* (New York: Praeger, 1970), 174–77; Daniel W. Gade, "Bridge Types in the Central Andres," *Annals of the Association of American Geographers* 62, no. 1 (1972), 95–100; Stephenson, "Description of Bridges of Suspension," 238–39.

29. James Finley, *A Description of the Chain Bridge* (Uniontown, PA: William Campbell, 1811), 11; "Iron Bridge," *Farmer's Register* (Greensburg, PA), May 22, 1802, 2. On Finley see Donald Sayenga, "A Gazetteer of Finley Patent Bridges," *Canal History and Technology Proceedings* 27 (2008), 105–26; Emory L. Kemp, "James Finley and the Origins of the Modern Suspension Bridge," *Canal History and Technology Proceedings* 27 (2008), 133–54; Kranakis, *Constructing a Bridge*, 17–39. Also see James Finley, "A Description of the Patent Chain Bridge," *Port Folio* 3, no. 6 (1810), 441–42.

30. Kranakis, *Constructing a Bridge*, 62–65.

31. Albert Gallatin, *Report by the Secretary of the Treasury on the Subject of Public Roads and Canals* (Washington, DC: R.C. Weightman, 1808), 738–39; Lee William Formwalt, *Benjamin Henry Latrobe and the Development of Internal Improvements in the New Republic, 1796–1820* (New York: Arno, 1982 (1977)), 276.

32. Magazine articles also helped spread word of Finley's bridges. See the descriptions of Finley's Potomac and Merrimack bridges in *The Monthly Magazine; or British Register* 26, no. 4 (1808), 344, and 31, no. 2 (1811), 361; *The Gentleman's Magazine and Historical Chronicle* 81, no. 2 (1811), 275.

33. Thomas Pope, *A Treatise on Bridge Architecture* (New York: Alexander Niven, 1811), 189. On Pope see Alan Trachtenberg, *Brooklyn Bridge: Fact and Symbol*, 2nd ed. (Chicago: University of Chicago Press, 1979), 24–29, and Richard Haw, "Bridging the East River: The History of an Idea, 1800–1867," *Long Island Historical Journal* 20, nos. 1–2 (2007–8), 88–93. Oddly enough, Benjamin Latrobe also endorsed Pope, or at least wrote reference letters for him, and tried to secure him work, much as he did for Finley. See Talbot Hamlin, *Benjamin Henry Latrobe* (New York: Oxford University Press, 1955), 419–20.

34. Richard Shelton Kirby, *Engineering in History* (New York: Dover, 1990 (1956)), 234.

35. Stephenson, "Description of Bridges of Suspension," 239–40; Emory L. Kemp, "Samuel Brown: Britain's Pioneer Suspension Bridge Builder," *History of Technology* 8 (1977), 8–11.

36. Emory L. Kemp, "National Styles in Engineering: The Case of the 19th-Century Suspension Bridge," *Journal of the Society for Industrial Archeology* 19, no. 1 (1993), 24–27; Thomas Day, "Samuel Brown: His Influence on the Design of Suspension Bridges," *History of Technology* 8 (1983), 68–73. Also see Gordon Miller, *Samuel Brown and the Union Chain Bridge* (Berwick-upon-Tweed: Friends of the Union Chain Bridge, 2017).

37. See Michael Mende, "'Not Only a Matter of Taste but . . . of the Laws of Mechanics': The Adaptation of British Models in Nineteenth-Century Continental Suspension Bridge Design," *Journal of Design History* 6, no. 2 (1993), 79; Henderson, *The State and the Industrial Revolution in Prussia*, 99; Georg C. Mehrtens, *DA Hundred Years of German Bridge Building*, trans Ludwig Mertens (Berlin: J. Springer, 1900).

38. See Joseph Louis Etienne Cordier, *L'Histoire de la Navigation Intérieure et Particulièrement de celle des Etats-Unis D'Amerique* (Paris: Firmin Didot, 1820), 172–83; Charles E. Peterson, "The Spider Bridge: A Curious Work at the Falls of Schuylkill, 1816," *Canal History and Technology*

Proceedings 5 (1986), 244–5; Kathleen A. Foster, ed., *Captain Watson's Travels in America: The Sketchbooks and Diary of Joshua Rowley Watson, 1772–1818* (Philadelphia: University of Pennsylvania Press, 1997), 57–59, 125, which contains a sketch of the bridge.

39. Samuel Brown, "Improvement in the Construction of a Bridge by the Formation and Uniting of Its Component Parts in a Manner," British Patent no. 4137, July 10, 1817, 3–4.

40. See Louis Joseph Vicat, "Ponts Suspendus en Fil de Fer sur le Rhône," *Annales des Ponts et Chaussées* 1, no. 1 (1831), 93–145; Emory L. Kemp, "Links in a Chain: The Development of Suspension Bridges, 1801–1870," *The Structural Engineer* 57 (1979), 259; Charles Stewart Drewry, *A Memoir on Suspension Bridges* (London: Longman, Rees, et al., 1832), 75–81, 150; I, *Transitions in Engineering*, 68–74; Dominique Amouroux and Bertrand Lemoine, "L'âge d'or des Ponts Suspendus en France, 1823–1850," *Annales des Ponts et Chaussées* 19, no. 3 (1981), 53–63.

41. Davies Gilbert quoted in R. A. Paxton, "Menai Bridge (1818–1826) and its Influence on Suspension Bridge Development," *Transactions of the Newcomen Society* 49 (1977–78), 97.

42. Güntheroth, "The Young Roebling, Biographical Notes," 9–10; *WRF*, 5–6.

43. JAR, "Student book #3," 10.

Chapter 3

1. Henderson, *The State and the Industrial Revolution in Prussia*, 47.

2. Brose, *The Politics of Technological Change in Prussia*, 68.

3. JAR, "Student book #3"; Heinrich Heine, "The Harz Journey" (1826), in Heinrich Heine, *The Harz Journey and Selected Prose*, trans. and ed. Ritchie Robertson (New York: Penguin, 1993), 65.

4. See Henderson, *The State and the Industrial Revolution in Prussia*, 46–49; Voltaire, *Candide, or Optimism*, trans. and ed. Theo Cuffe (New York: Penguin, 2005), xiv; Michael Mende, "Early 19th-Century Suspension Bridges on the Upper Ruhr: John August Roebling's 1828 Freienohl Project and the 1839 Bridge by A. Burns at Laer Manor," The International Committee for the Conservation of Industrial Heritage, http://www.ticcihcongress2006.net/paper/Paper%207/Mende%207.pdf, accessed November 8, 2010.

5. See Christiane Vielhaber and Horst Vielhaber, "Von der Lenne-Brücke zur Brooklyn Bridge: Über Johann August Röblings Esloher Jahre," *Esloher Museumsnachrichten*, 2008, 3–5; Güntheroth, "The Young Roebling: Biographical Notes," 10; JAR, "Eslohe Highway," box 6, folders 25–29, RFP-RUP.

6. JAR, "Eslohe Highway," box 6, folders 25–29, RFP-RUP, 4–5; Andreas Kahlow, "The Role of Archetypes in the Development of Structural Thinking in Bridge Building in the 1820s," University of Évora, http://www.cidehus.uevora.pt/centro/arquivo/arq03/eng03/TKahlow.pdf, accessed November 3, 2010; JAR, "Ödingen Road—Designs for the Warden's House & Stables," box 6, folder 34, RFP-RUP.

7. JAR, "Student book #3"; Vielhaber and Vielhaber, "Von der Lenne-Brücke zur Brooklyn Bridge," 3, 6.

8. Vielhaber and Vielhaber, "Von der Lenne-Brücke zur Brooklyn Bridge," 3.

9. JAR, "Student book #3"; *Magazin der Neuesten Entdeckungen und Erfindungen* 3 (1828).

10. JAR, "Student book #3"; Adam Burg, "Zusammenstellung mehrerer sehr interessanter Versuche, welche über die absolute, respektive und rückwirkende Festigkeit verschiedener Materialien, als des Eisens, des Bauholzes u.s.w. neuerlich angestellt worden sind," *Jahrbücher des Kaiserlichen Königlichen Polytechnischen Institutes in Wien* 5 (1824), 215–87; Kahlow, "The Role of Archetypes," 1, 5; Nele Güntheroth, "Realien und Karriere," 21; Kahlow, "Bridge-Building and Industrial Revolution," in *Proceedings of the First International Congress on Construction History*, ed. Santiago Huerta (Madrid: Reverté, 2003), 1181.

11. Thomas Nipperdey, *Germany from Napoleon to Bismarck, 1800–1866*, trans. Daniel Nolan (Princeton, NJ: Princeton University Press, 1996 (1983)), 163; Friedrich Harkort, "Eisenbahnen)," *Hermann*, March 30, 1825.

12. JAR to WAR, January 7, 1868, in SRL; Güntheroth, "Realien und Karriere," 20; Andreas Kahlow, "Röbling als Konstrukteur," *Mühlhauser Beiträge* 15 (2006), 134.

13. The proposal was only recently discovered buried in the archives of the Count of Westphalia and is reprinted in Eberhard Grunsky, "Johann August Röbling's erster Entwurf für eine Hängebrücke," *Mühlhauser Beiträge* 15 (2006), 28–75.

14. Kahlow, "Johann August Röbling (1806–1869)," 39–40; Kahlow, "Röbling als Konstrukteur," 138; Grunsky, "Von den Anfängen des Hängebrückenbaus in Westfalen," 134.

15. See Eberhard Grunsky, "Von Eslohe, Freienohl und Finnentrop bis Niagara, Cincinnati und New York," *Sauerland* 1 (2004), 23; Kahlow, "Early Projects in Context," 42; "Aufsätz, zusammengestellt aus den von dem verstorbenen Geh. Regierungsrath Henz während seiner Reise in Nord-Amerika im Jahre 1859 gesammelten Notizen: Die Hängebrücken des Mr. Röbling," *Zeitschrift für Bauwesen* 12 (1862), 373–74; Henry Petroski, *Engineers of Dreams: Great Bridge Builders and the Spanning of America* (New York: Vintage, 1995), 387–88.

16. Kahlow, "Bridge-Building and Industrial Revolution," 1185; Grunsky, "Von den Anfängen des Hängebrückenbaus in Westfalen," 135; Mende, "Early 19th-Century Suspension Bridges on the Upper Ruhr," 3.

17. Mende, "Early 19th-Century Suspension Bridges on the Upper Ruhr," 1, 6.

18. Güntheroth, "The Young Roebling," 12; Mende, "Early 19th-Century Suspension Bridges on the Upper Ruhr," 2; Vielhaber and Vielhaber, "Von der Lenne-Brücke zur Brooklyn Bridge," 6.

19. Güntheroth, "Realien und Karriere," 21.

20. See Kahlow, "The Role of Archetypes," 5; Grunsky, "Johann August Röbling's erster Entwurf für eine Hängebrücke," 30.

21. Güntheroth, "The Young Roebling," 12.

22. JAR, "Student book #3"; Grunsky, "Johann August Röbling's erster Entwurf für eine Hängebrücke," 30.

23. Grunsky, "Johann August Röbling's erster Entwurf für eine Hängebrücke," 29.

24. Kahlow, "Johann August Röbling (1806–1869)."

25. Grunsky, "Johann August Röbling's erster Entwurf für eine Hängebrücke," 29–30; Grunsky, "Von Eslohe, Freienohl und Finnentrop," 23.

26. Kahlow, "Röbling als Konstrukteur," 139.

27. *Journal für die Baukunst* 3 (1830), 462–64.

28. Part of this concern centered quite rightly on the nature of chains themselves, which were very much the dominant means of suspending a bridge's floor, especially in the United Kingdom. Unlike cables, chains are only as strong as their weakest link, meaning a single frail connection could doom an entire span.

29. For the history of suspension bridges in Germany, see Georg Christoph Mehrtens, *Vorlesungen über Ingenieur-wissenschaften: Eisenbrückenbau im Allgemeinen* (Leipzig: Wilhelm Engelmann, 1908), 369–81.

30. See Gottfried Bandhauer, *Verhandlungen über die Artistische Untersuchung des Baues der Hängebrücke über die Saale bei Mönchen-Nienburg* (Leipzig: Hartmann, 1827); Charles Birnstiel, "On the Collapse of a Cable-Stayed Bridge at Nienburg: A Nineteenth-Century Disaster Revisited," in *Bridge Management*, ed. J. E. Harding, G. A. R. Parke, and M. J. Ryall (London: E. & F. N. Spon, 1996), 516–22.

31. See especially C. P. Beuth, "Über die Nienburger Kettenbrücke," *Verhandlungen des Vereins zur Beförderung des Gewerbfleißes in Preußen* 5 (1826), 65–76, 120–29.

32. Quoted in Grunsky, "Von Eslohe, Freienohl und Finnentrop," 23; JAR, "Student book #3"; Kahlow, "Johann August Röbling (1806–1869)," 43; WRF, 8; Güntheroth, "Realien und Karriere," 23.

33. Vielhaber and Vielhaber, "Von der Lenne-Brücke zur Brooklyn Bridge," 7, and JAR, "Student book #3."

Chapter 4

1. Auener, *Johann August Röbling*, 14; Güntheroth, "Realien und Karriere," 76. For Etzler see Patrick Ronald Brostowin, "John Adolphus Etzler: Scientific-Utopian during the 1830s and 1840s" (PhD diss.: New York University, 1969); Joel Nydahl, introduction to *The Collected Works of John Adolphus Etzler* (Delmar, NY: Scholars' Facsimiles & Reprints, 1977).

2. JAR, "Student book #3"; *Morning Star*, March 1, 1845, 2; Güntheroth, "The Young Roebling: Biographical Notes," 13. See Paul C. Weber, *America in Imaginative German Literature in the First Half of the Nineteenth Century* (New York: Columbia University Press, 1926); Hans-Jürgen Grabbe, "Weary of Germany—Weary of America: Perception of the United States in Nineteenth-Century Germany," and A. Gregg Roeber, " 'Through a Glass, Darkly': Changing German Ideas of American Freedom, 1776–1806," both in David E. Barclay and Elisabeth Glaser-Schmidt, eds., *Transatlantic Images and Perceptions: Germany and America since 1776* (New York: Cambridge University Press, 1997), 19–40 and 65–86.

3. John Adolphus Etzler, *The Paradise within the Reach of All Men, without Labor by Powers of Nature and Machinery: An Address to All Intelligent Men* (Pittsburgh: Etzler & Reinhold, 1833). On Etzler's influence see Henry David Thoreau, "Paradise (to Be) Regained," *United States and Democratic Review* 13, no. 65 (November 1843): 451–63; Bernard De Voto, "What the Next Hour Holds," *Harper's Magazine*, June 1936, 109–12; Thomas P. Hughes, *Human-Built World: How to Think about Technology and Culture* (Chicago: University of Chicago Press, 2004), 33–37; Steven Stoll, *The Great Delusion: A Mad Inventor, Death in the Tropics, and the Utopian Origins of Economic Growth* (New York: Hill & Wang, 2008).

4. JAR, "The Personal Diary of J. A. Röbling [handwritten in the "Old" German; His Travels and Observations, 1830]," trans. Renate Fine, CZC, 5, 6, 25–29.

5. Ibid., 28–29.

6. Tilmann Breuer and Reinhard Gutbier, *Die Kunstdenkmäler von Bayern: Stadt Bamberg, Innere Inselstadt* (Munich: R. Oldenbourg Verlag, 1990), 1256–75; *Die Neue Ludwigsbrücke in Bamberg: Erste Kettenbrücke in Bayern* (Bamberg: n.p., 1830).

7. "The Personal Diary of J. A. Röbling," 14.

8. Ibid., 11, 14, 15–16, 20.

9. Ibid., 7.

10. Ibid.

11. Ibid., 33.

12. H. George, "Röbling und seine Werke," *Deutsche Bauzeitung*, May 27, 1869, 263.

13. JAR, "Student book #3"; Kahlow, "Röbling als Konstrukteur," 143–44; Mehrtens, *A Hundred Years of German Bridge Building*, 12.

14. Clive H. Church, *Europe in 1830: Revolution and Political Change* (London: George Allen & Unwin, 1883), 40–56.

15. Nipperdey, *Germany from Napoleon to Bismarck*, 324–25; Sheehan, *German History*, 604–7; Charles Breunig and Matthew Levinger, *The Revolutionary Era, 1789–1850*, 3rd ed. (New York: W. W. Norton, 2002 (1970)), 243; Church, *Europe in 1830*, 31–32, 36.

16. Martyn Lyons, *Post-Revolutionary Europe, 1815–1856* (New York: Palgrave, 2006), 98; Frederick B. Artz, *Reaction and Revolution, 1814–1832* (New York: Harper & Bros., 1934), 263; Sheehan, *German History*, 604.

17. Sheehan, *German History*, 605.

18. Ferdinand Bähr to Friedrich Carl and JAR, June 11, 1831, box 1, folder 14, RFP-RU; Schuyler, *The Roeblings*, 26–27; Leo Damrosch, *Tocqueville's Discovery of America* (New York: Farrar, Straus & Giroux, 2010), 95.

19. Mack Walker, *Germany and the Emigration, 1816–1885* (Cambridge, MA: Harvard University Press, 1964), 65; Kilian Spiethoff, "America, Land of Refuge: Emigration, Emigration Societies and the Idea to Establish a German State in the New World (1816–1834)," in *Aufbruch in die Utopia: Auf den Spuren einer deutschen Republik in den USA / Utopia: Revisiting a German State in America* (Bremen: Falkenberg, 2013), 31; "Ein Besuch bei Friedrich Muench," *Der Deutsche Pionier* 7, no. 2 (1875), 55.

20. Contract between JAR and E. W. Röbling, Mühlhausen, September 18, 1830, box 8, folder 22, RFP-RU; *Allgemeine Ansicht der Vereinigten Staaten von Nord-Amerika für Auswanderer, nebst Plan zu einer gemeinschaftlichen Ansiedlung daselbst* (Eschwege: E. W. Roebling, 1830); Walker, *Germany and the Emigration*, 126–29.

21. Eugene E. Doll, "American History as Interpreted by German Historians from 1770 to 1815," *Transactions of the American Philosophical Society* 38 (1948), 472–501; Grabbe, "Weary of Germany—Weary of America," 65–66, 74; T. S. Baker, "America as the Political Utopia of Young Germany," *Americana Germanica* 1, no. 2 (1897), 62–65; Richard O'Connor, "Dreams

of Germania-in-America," in *The German-Americans: An Informal History* (Boston: Little, Brown, 1968), 67–97; Spiethoff, "America, Land of Refuge," 44–52.

22. Güntheroth, "Realien und Karriere," 77; "The Personal Diary of J. A. Röbling," 39–60.

23. Frederic Trautmann, "New York through German Eyes: The Travels of Ludwig Gall, 1819," *New York History* 52, no. 4 (1981), 444. Also see Ludwig Gall, *Meine Auswanderung Nach Den Vereinigten-Staaten in Nord-Amerika im Frühjahr 1819* (Trier: n.p., 1822).

24. Gall, *Meine Auswanderung Nach Den Vereinigten-Staaten*, 444–45; Trautmann, "Pennsylvania through a German's Eyes: The Travels of Ludwig Gall, 1819–1820," *Pennsylvania Magazine of History and Biography* 105, no. 1 (1981), 60–62. All-consuming greed was a common compliant among German visitors. "A Niagara-voice would be needed to teach these rascals that there are higher gods than those struck off the mint," complained poet Nikolaus Lenau: "functional man unfolds [here] in fearful banality." See Grabbe, "Weary of Germany—Weary of America," 71–72.

25. Trautmann, "New York through German Eyes," 456; Trautmann, "Pennsylvania through a German's Eyes," 45–47.

26. Trautmann, "Pennsylvania through a German's Eyes," 65.

27. Marcus L. Hansen, *The Atlantic Migration, 1607–1860* (Cambridge, MA: Harvard University Press, 1940), 149; Weber, *America in Imaginative German Literature*, 117.

28. See "Appendix I: Textual Emendations Made in the Edition of 1834," and "Editor's Introduction," in Gottfried Duden, *Report on a Journey to the Western States of America, and a Stay of Several Years along the Missouri (during the Years 1824, '25, '26, 1827)*, ed. and trans. George H. Kellner, Elsa Nagel, Adolf E. Schroeder, and W. M. Senner (Columbia: University of Missouri Press, 1980 (1829)), xx–xxi and 262–8.

29. Ibid., 67, 70, 207–44.

30. Duden's picture of pastoral ease ought to be compared with those of Frederick Muench, who also settled in Missouri: "Many evenings my limbs were so tired that I could hardly bring the fork to my mouth, or my head sank to the table as I fell into slumber. During the harvest, I often had to change my sweat-drenched clothes 2 or 3 times a day while my head burned with the constant swishing in my ear." Quoted in Rolf Schmidt, "Departure and Journey of the Giessen Emigration Society," in *Aufbruch in die Utopia*, 154.

31. Weber, *America in Imaginative German Literature*, 120–59; Duden, *Report on a Journey to the Western States*, 245–61; Karl J. R. Arndt, *George Rapp's Harmony Society, 1785–1847*, rev. ed. (Rutherford, NJ: Fairleigh Dickinson University Press, 1972 (1965)), 333. Rapp's Harmony movement was famous throughout Europe by the mid-1820s. Byron mocked the movement in his unfinished *Don Juan* (canto 15, stanza 35), while Goethe modeled the emigrant state depicted in his *Wilhelm Meisters Wanderjahre* (1829) on Rapp's colony.

32. Karl Bernhard, Duke of Saxe-Weimar-Eisenach, *Travels through North America during the years 1825 and 1826*, 2 vols. (Philadelphia: Lea & Carey, 1828), 2:107, 110–11, 160–61, 163–64. As a communitarian settlement, New Harmony lasted a scant two years, from 1825 to 1827.

33. Bernhard, *Travels through North America*, 107, 108, 112, 115, 161; J. E. Alexander, *Transatlantic Sketches, Comprising Visits to the Most Interesting Scenes in North and South America, and the West Indies*, 2 vols. (London: Richard Bentley, 1833), 2:130; Arthur Bestor, *Backwoods Utopias: The Sectarian Origins and the Owenite Phase of Communitarian Socialism in America, 1663–1829*, 2nd ed. (Philadelphia: University of Pennsylvania Press, 1970 (1950)), 160–201; Robert Dale Owen, "My Experience of Community Life: A Chapter of Autobiography," *Atlantic Monthly* 32 (September 1873), 343.

34. Friedrich Gerstäcker, *Nach Amerika! Ein Volkbuch* (Leipzig: Costenoble, 1855), quoted in Günter Moltmann, "Three Hundred Years of German Immigration to North America," in *Three Hundred Years of German Immigrants in North America, 1683-1983* ed. Klaus Wust and Heinz Moos (Baltimore: Heinz Moos Publishing, 1983), 14.

35. JAR, "Vereinigte Staaten," box 4, folder 49, RFP-RU.

36. See "Was Für ein Land Sind die Vereinigten Staaten von Nord Amerika für Deutsche Auswanderer?," *Columbus: Amerikanische Miscellen* 2 (1830), 264–68.

37. *Allgemeine Ansicht der Vereinigten Staaten von Nord-Amerika für Auswanderer* (1830), 3; "Plan zur Gemeinschaftlichen Auswanderung Nach Nord-Amerika," *Columbus: Amerikanische Miscellen* 2 (1830), 446–51.

38. JAR, Johann Etzler, Friedrich Dachröden, and Heinrich Harsheim, *Allgemeine Ansicht der Vereinigten Staaten von Nord-Amerika für Auswanderer, nebst Plan zu einer gemeinschaftlichen Ansiedlung daselbst*, trans. Josiah Simon (Eschwege: E. W. Roebling, 1831), 59–63.
39. Ibid., iii–xi.
40. Ibid., 34, 37, 47.
41. Ibid., 35–43.
42. Ibid., 43–47.
43. Ibid., 45–46, and Alexander, *Transatlantic Sketches*, 1:130. The settlement of Zoar was established by German Separatists in 1817 in Ohio and flourished for over eighty years.
44. JAR, Etzler, et al., *Allgemeine Ansicht*, 55.
45. Ibid., 64.
46. Ibid., 65–66.
47. Roderick T. Long, "Towards a Libertarian Theory of Class," *Social Philosophy and Policy* 15, no. 2 (1998), 304–5.
48. Johann would return to the concept of self-interest many years later, reading the idea as explicitly connected with the fate and condition of "his fellow men." See JAR, "The Condition of the US Reviewed by Higher Law" (n.d.), box 5, folder 40, RFP-RU.
49. Günter Moltmann, "The Pattern of German Emigration to the United States in the Nineteenth Century," in *America and the Germans: An Assessment of a Three-Hundred-Year History*, vol. 1, *Immigration, Language, Ethnicity*, ed. Frank Trommler and Joseph McVeigh (Philadelphia: University of Pennsylvania Press, 1985), 22; Johnston Birchall, *The International Co-operative Movement* (Manchester, UK: Manchester University Press, 1997), 4; JAR, Etzler, et al., *Allgemeine Ansicht*, 67.
50. Auener, *Johann August Röbling*, 15–16; Güntheroth, "Realien und Karriere," 79; Agnes Bretting, "Organizing German Immigration: The Role of State Authorities in Germany and the United States," in Trommler and McVeigh, *America and the Germans*, 26–27, 30.
51. Güntheroth, "Realien und Karriere," 79.
52. Ibid., 79–80.
53. JAR to Bürgermeister Gier, February 24, 1831, box 1, folder 12, RFP-RU.
54. Güntheroth, "Realien und Karriere," 80.
55. WRF, 10; WAR, *Early History of Saxonburg* (Butler, PA: Butler Country Historical Society, 1924), 7; Schuyler, *The Roeblings*, 27; JAR to Karl Meissner, June 15, 1834, and January 2, 1836, box 3, folder 41, RFP-RU.
56. WRF, 11; "Contract," in "Sundry Letters and Reports by John A. Roebling," Transcript Book #1, 1–4, RFP-RU.
57. *Diary*, 2.
58. Auener, *Johann August Röbling*, 6, 15–16.

Chapter 5

1. *Diary*, 2–3, 12.
2. See Bretting, "Organizing German Immigration," 32; Kathleen Neils Conzen, "Germans," in *Harvard Encyclopedia of American Ethnic Groups*, ed. Stephan Thernstrom (Cambridge, MA: Harvard University Press, 1980), 410; Ernest Bruncken, "German Political Refugees in the United States during the Period from 1815–1860," *Deutsch-Amerikanische Geschichtsblätter*, special pamphlet (1904), 15.
3. *Diary*, 3–7.
4. Ibid., 9–13. As was the custom, the *August Eduard* was not docked in Bremen itself but at Brake, thirty miles down the River Weser toward the North Sea.
5. Ibid., 82.
6. Ibid., 3, 15, 18–19, 37, 75.
7. Ibid., 27, 40, 50, 70, 94.
8. Albert Bernhardt Faust, *The German Element in the United States*, 2 vols. (Boston: Houghton Mifflin, 1909), 1:36–38, 73–74, 149, 161, 177, 226, 357; Walker, *Germany and the Emigration*, 5–6. Also see Spiethoff, "America, Land of Refuge," 19–23.
9. *Allgemeine Zeitung*, December 9, 1816, quoted in Walker, *Germany and the Emigration*, 1.

10. Quoted in Spiethoff, "America, Land of Refuge," 22.

11. Walker, *Germany and the Emigration*, 24–28; Friedrich List, "Protokolle der Auswanderungsbefragungen des Rechnungrats List in Heilbronn, Weinsberg und Neckarsulum vom 30. April bis zum 6. Mai 1817," reprinted in *Aufbruch nach Amerika: Die Auswanderungswelle von 1816/17*, ed. Günter Moltmann (Stuttgart: J. B. Metzler, 1989), 128–66.

12. John Arkas Hawgood, *The Tragedy of German-America: The Germans in the United States of America during the Nineteenth Century—and After* (New York: G. P. Putnam's Sons, 1940), xiv–xv, 93–103; Richard O'Connor, *The German-Americans* (Boston: Little, Brown, 1968), 67–79; Garrett Davis, "Speech of Hon. Garrett Davis upon His Proposal to Impose Further Restrictions upon Foreign Immigration" (1949), in *Historical Aspects of the Immigration Problem*, ed. Edith Abbott (Chicago: University of Chicago Press, 1926), 770.

13. The pamphlet's title was *Aufforderung und Erklärung in Betreff einer Auswanderung im Grosen aus Deutschland in die nordamerikanischen Freistaaten* (Call and declaration concerning an emigration en masse from Germany to the North American states) (J. Rickers: Giessen, 1833).

14. Ibid.; "Sagengeschichte einer deutschen Auswanderung-Gesellschaft," *Der Deutsche Pionier* 1, no. 1 (1869), 22. Also see Spiethoff, "America, Land of Refuge," 15–83.

15. Ibid., 20–22, 44, 54.

16. Ibid., 53.

17. See Johann August Röbling, *Tagebuch Meiner Reise von Mühlhausen in Thüringen über Bremen Nach den Vereinigten Staaten von Nordamerika im Jahre 1831, Geschrieben für Meine Freunde* (Eschwege: E. W. Röbling, 1832).

18. *Diary*, 7–9, 28–33, 58–60.

19. Ibid., 45–46, 48.

20. Ibid., 50, 56–57, 67, 80, 86.

21. Ibid., 46, 68–69, 73, 76.

22. Ibid., 76–79, 84. Joseph Conrad, *Lord Jim: A Tale* (New York: Oxford University Press, 1983 (1900)), 115.

23. *Diary*, 93–95.

24. Ibid., 98–99.

25. Ibid., 99–101.

26. Ibid., 101–3. Johann later admitted that this idea "disappears as soon as one observes the interior and perceives the plan of the city."

27. Nicholas B. Wainwright, "The Age of Nicholas Biddle, 1825–1841," in *Philadelphia: A 300-Year History*, ed. Russell F. Weigley (New York: W. W. Norton, 1982), 261, 263, 269, 275; Marion V. Brewington, "Maritime Philadelphia, 1609–1837," *Pennsylvania Magazine of History and Biography* 63 (January 1939), 117, and *United States Gazette*, November 6, 1829, 3.

28. Bruncken, "German Political Refugees in the United States," 17–18; E. Manso, G. Genss, JAR, and F. C. Röbling to Dachröden, Harsheim, and Hupfeld, August 13, 1831, box 7, folder 32, RFP-RU; JR-FB, 5–6; "Passages Relating to 'Mr. Etzler' in Omitted Portions of the Two John A. Roebling Letters Published in the *Western Pennsylvania Historical Magazine*," MS, JHHC, 1.

29. Quoted in Rolf Schmidt, "Departure and Journey of the Giessen Emigration Society," in *Aufbruch in die Utopia*, 139.

30. Manso, Genss, JAR, and F. C. Röbling to Dachröden, Harsheim, and Hupfeld, August 13, 1831; JR-FB, 5–6.

31. Manso, Genss, JAR, and F. C. Röbling to Dachröden, Harsheim, and Hupfeld, August 13, 1831; "Passages Relating to 'Mr. Etzler' in Omitted Portions of the Two John A. Roebling Letters," 2.

32. *Diary*, 106–7; Charles Dickens, *The Life and Adventures of Martin Chuzzlewit* (Harmondsworth, UK: Penguin, 1999 (1844)), 263–64.

33. *Diary*, 106–9; Wainwright, "The Age of Nicholas Biddle," 263, 281; *United States Gazette*, August 30, 1828, 2; Charles Dickens, *American Notes for General Circulation* (Harmondsworth, UK: Penguin, 1972 (1842)), 110; Frances Trollope, *Domestic Manners of the Americans*, ed. Pamela Neville-Sington (New York: Penguin, 1997 (1832), 201–4).

34. *Diary*, 110–11; Samuel Hazard, *The Register of Pennsylvania* 7 (1831), 172–73; Wainwright, "The Age of Nicholas Biddle," 293; William Lloyd Garrison, *An Address Delivered before the Free People of Color in Philadelphia, New York and Other Cities* (Boston: Stephen Foster, 1831), 3; Julie Winch, *A Gentleman of Color: The Life of James Forten* (New York: Oxford University Press, 2002), 236–58.

35. *Diary*, 111–13.

36. Ibid., 114–15; Manso, Genss, JAR, and F. C. Röbling to Dachröden, Harsheim, and Hupfeld, August 13, 1831 JAR; JR-FB, 6 and 196. Little is known of the Mühlhausen Emigration Society's southern venture after this, but two years later, in 1833, Dachröden turned up in Missouri, living with Ernest Charles Angelrodt. A Thuringian native and a friend and correspondent of Johann's, Angelrodt immigrated to the United States in 1832 as a member of the Mühlhausen Emigration Society's second wave but was unhappy with the lands picked out by Johann, and he continued on west, eventually settling in St. Louis, where he prospered. See Thomas McCormack, ed., *Memoirs of Gustave Koerner, 1809–1896*, 2 vols. (Cedar Rapids, IA: Torch, 1909), 1:312–13. Christian Hupfeld's letters home to his brother Herman—a professor of theology at Marburg—were published in Germany in 1834. See Herman Hupfeld, *Briefe eines deutschen Ausgewanderten aus Nordamerica, besonders eine Ansiedlung in Alabama betreffend* (Letters from a German emigrant from North America, especially concerning a settlement in Alabama) (Marburg, Germany: R.G. Elwert, 1834).

37. *Diary*, 13, 114–15; JR-FB, 7; Manso, Genss, RJAR, and F. C. Röbling to Dachröden, Harsheim, and Hupfeld, August 13, 1831.

38. *Diary*, 116–18; JR-FB, 8–9.

39. *Diary*, 116–18; JR-FB, 8; JR-OFI, 76; Louis P. Masur, *1831: Year of Eclipse* (New York: Hill & Wang, 2001), 38–39. For a firsthand account of the "slave insurrection in New Orleans," see J. E. Alexander, *Transatlantic Sketches, Comprising Visits to the Most Interesting Scenes in North and South America, and the West Indies*, 2 vols. (London: Richard Bentley, 1833), 2:227.

40. *Diary*, 116–18.

41. When Johann penned his assertion of principles, Frederick Douglass was still a young slave, seven years from freedom, while William Lloyd Garrison's *Liberator* had thus far published only a few issues. Such important tracts as Lydia Maria Child's *An Appeal in Favor of That Class of Americans Called Africans* (1833), William Ellery Channing's *Slavery* (1835), or the works of the Grimké sisters were all in the future, as were the establishment of the African-American Female Intelligence Society of Boston (1832), New England Anti-Slavery Society (1832), and American Anti-Slavery Society (1833).

42. William H. Freehling, *The Reintegration of American History: Slavery and the Civil War* (New York: Oxford University Press, 1994), 12–34, 199–200; Seymour Drescher, *Abolition: A History of Slavery and Antislavery* (New York: Cambridge University Press, 2009), 97; Dorinda Outram, *The Enlightenment*, 2nd ed. (New York: Cambridge University Press, 2005), 60–76; JR-OFI, 75.

43. Owen S. Ireland, "Germans against Abolition: A Minority's View of Slavery in Revolutionary Pennsylvania," *Journal of Interdisciplinary History* 3, no. 4 (1973), 685–703; Duden, *Report on a Journey to the Western States of America*, 182–85; *Aufforderung und Erklärung in Betreff einer Auswanderung*, 17–25; Hawgood, *The Tragedy of German-America*, 50–51.

44. T. Vigne, *Six Months in America*, 2 vols. (London: Whittaker, Treacher, 1832), 2:33–38; Henry Tudor, *Narrative of a Tour in North America*, 2 vols. (London: James Duncan, 1834), 2:68–72; Thomas Hamilton, *Men and Manners in America*, 2 vols. (New York: August M. Kelley, 1833), 2:73; David Brion Davis, *The Problem of Slavery in the Age of Emancipation* (New York: Knopf, 2014), 261–70; Sándor Bölöni Farkas, *Journey in North America, 1831*, trans. Arpad Kadarkey (Santa Barbara, CA: American Bibliographical Center, 1978), 178–79.

45. See Tocqueville, *Democracy in America*, 1:365–476. Gustave de Beaumont, Tocqueville's best friend and US traveling partner, certainly agreed, publishing his angry, impassioned, and incendiary antislavery novel *Marie; ou L'esclavage aux Etats-Unis, Tableau de Moeurs Americaines* three years after returning home to France. Beaumont's novel is one of the first American novels to feature a black hero, and a fully sympathetic one at that. It predates Richard Hildreth's *The Slave; or, Memoirs of Archy Moore* by two years. See Gustave de Beaumont,

Marie; or, Slavery in the United States, trans. Barbara Chapman (Baltimore: Johns Hopkins University Press, 1999 (1958)).

46. The threat of violence from Native American tribes was of course all too real, in the wake of the Indian Removal Act (1830) and with the Black Hawk (1832) and Second Seminole (1835) wars still to come.

47. *Diary*, 115–16, 118, 121, 123, and JR-OFI, 76–77.

48. *Diary*, 119, and Manso, Genss, JARJAR, and F. C. Röbling to Dachröden, Harsheim, and Hupfeld, August 13, 1831.

49. E. Manso, G. Genss, JAR, and F. C. Röbling to Dachröden, Harsheim, and Hupfeld, August 13, 1831; JR-FB, 5–6; *Diary*, 123–24.

Chapter 6

1. W. Bernard Carlson, "The Pennsylvania Society for the Promotion of Internal Improvements," *Canal History and Technology Proceedings* 7 (1988), 178. By 1823, the value of the traffic moving through the port of Philadelphia was half what it had been in 1796, while the value of traffic in New York increased by 140 percent over the same period.

2. *American Daily Advertiser*, January 28, 1825, 2.

3. J. Lee Hartman, "Pennsylvania's Grand Plan of Post-Revolutionary Internal Improvement," *Pennsylvania Magazine of History and Biography* 64 (1941), 439–57; Willard R. Rhoads, "The Pennsylvania Canal," *Western Pennsylvania Historical Magazine* 43, no. 3 (September 1960), 203–38.

4. JR-FB, 9–10.

5. Peregrine Prolix [Philip Nicklin], *A Pleasant Peregrination through the Prettiest Parts of Pennsylvania* (Philadelphia: Grigg & Elliot, 1836), 48–58; JR-FB, 9–10; George Wilson Pierson, *Tocqueville in America* (Baltimore: Johns Hopkins University Press, 1996 (1938)), 543.

6. JR-FB, 3, 10–11, 20; JR-OFI, 77–78.

7. Michel Chevalier, *Society, Manner and Politics in the United States: Being a Series of Lectures on North America* (Boston: Weeks, Jordan, 1839), 169. In addition, while Johann was initially very enthusiastic about the prospects of settling in Ohio, he changed his tune once he had heard that that state's climate was "unhealthy."

8. Edward Park Anderson, "The Intellectual Life of Pittsburgh, 1786–1836," *Western Pennsylvania Historical Magazine* 14, nos. 1–2 (1931), 9.

9. Leland D. Baldwin, *Pittsburgh: The Story of a City, 1750–1865* (Pittsburgh: University of Pittsburgh Press, 1937), 191–221; Vigne, *Six Months in America*, 2:15–16; Tudor, *Narrative of a Tour in North America*, 1:92; Sarah H. Killikelly, *The History of Pittsburgh: Its Rise and Progress* (Pittsburgh: B. C. & Gordon Montgomery, 1906), xi.

10. Russell Errett, "Pittsburgh in 1829," *Magazine of Western History* 7 (November 1887), 33–34; James Stuart, *Three Years in North America*, 2 vols. (New York: J. & J. Harper, 1833), 2:295.

11. JR-FB, 13; William Tell Harris, *Remarks Made during a Tour of the United States of America in the Years 1817, 1818 and 1819* (London: Sherwood, Neely & Jones, 1821), 89.

12. JR-FB, 144; JR-OFI, 80.

13. JR-FB, 178; Chevalier, *Society, Manner and Politics in the United States*, 169; Edward Hahn, "Science in Pittsburgh, 1813–1848," *Western Pennsylvania Historical Magazine* 55, no. 1 (1972), 66, 70, 72; Anderson, "The Intellectual Life of Pittsburgh," 16, 25, 102.

14. Collins was a "lady of considerable wealth ... doubtless one of the first females in Pennsylvania, on every account," according to Anne Royall, who met the widow a couple of years before Johann. See Anne Royall, *Pennsylvania; Or, Travels Continued in the United States*, 2 vols. (Washington, DC: Anne Royall, 1829), 2:88.

15. Samuel Jones, *Pittsburgh in the Year Eighteen Hundred and Twenty-Six, Containing Sketches Topographical, Historical and Statistical; Together with a Directory of the City* (Pittsburgh: n.p., 1826), 149; Russell Errett, "Pittsburgh in 1829," 36; JR-FB, 17, 23, 182, 186, 190; Ralph Goldinger, *Historic Saxonburg and Its Neighbors* (Saxonburg, PA: Saxonburg Historical and Restoration Commission, 1990), 9.),

16. James McKee, *History of Butler and Butler County, Pennsylvania and Representative Citizens* (Chicago: Richmond-Arnold, 1895), 462. The official records of Saxonburg's United

Presbyterian Church list August Grabe as one of twenty-five founding members of the congregation. See Ernst Weiss, "The History of the Evangelical Protestant Community of Saxonburg, PA: The Years, 1837–1887," trans. Walter E. and Audrey L. Gerlach (1973 (1887)), MS, SPL, 6. The Grabes' indenture contract required confirmation "by a lawful authority" upon landing in America. It's quite possible that this wasn't done and that the contract was therefore rendered invalid. It may also be that Johann didn't possess the resources to clothe, feed, and otherwise care for the entire Grabe brood, thus reneging on his side of the bargain. See Goldinger, *Historic Saxonburg and Its Neighbors*, 149.

17. Ibid., 18, 25–26.
18. JR-OFI, 82; JR-FB, 22, 24; Butler County Office of the Register and Recorder, Deed Book G, 480–82.
19. JR-FB, 21, 23, 171–72.
20. Karl J. R. Arndt, *George Rapp's Harmony Society, 1785–1847*, rev. ed. (Rutherford, NJ: Fairleigh Dickinson University Press, 1972 (1965)), 43–50, 61–71, 133–34. Rapp initially hoped to settle in Louisiana and even managed to secure Napoleon Bonaparte's approval and an official land grant, before the First Consul reneged and sold the territory to the United States. See Farkas, *Journey in North America, 1831*, 170.
21. Arndt, *George Rapp's Harmony Society*, 6, 394, 414; Farkas, *Journey in North America, 1831*, 168, 174.
22. See Farkas, *Journey in North America, 1831*, 170; Arndt, *George Rapp's Harmony Society, 1785–1847*, 322; *Niles' Weekly Register*, October 27, 1827, 133.
23. JR-FB, 173; Arndt, *George Rapp's Harmony Society, 1785–1847*, 293–94, 381.
24. JR-FB, 173.
25. See Arndt, *George Rapp's Harmony Society, 1785–1847*, 449–98; "An Affray at Economy, Pennsylvania," *Pittsburgh Manufacturer*, reprinted in *Niles' Weekly Register*, May 4, 1833, 151; JR-FB, 3–4.
26. Muench quoted in Schmidt, "Departure and Journey of the Giessen Emigration Society," 146.
27. On Rapp's successes with silk production see *Niles' Weekly Register*, October 8, 1831, and L. R. Cortambert, "Colonie d'Economy et Secte des Harmonistes," *Nouvelles Annales des Voyages*, April 1842, 65–74. Also see *WRF*, 17; JAR to Harmony Society, February 17, 1836, MG-185, Microfilm Roll 60, AOEV.
28. JR-FB, 4, 26, 175–76.
29. Ibid., 176, 192–94; JR-OFI, 78; *WRF*, 25; Muench quoted in Rolf Schmidt, "Departure and Journey of the Giessen Emigration Society," 154.
30. JR-FB, 176, 185, 195.
31. Simms, *The Struggle for Mastery in Germany*, 142, 154; JR-FB, 176–77; JR-OFI, 89, 107.
32. Masur, *1831*, 202–3; JAR quoted in Auener, *Johann August Röbling*, 12.
33. JR-FB, 78–79, 180–81.
34. Ibid., 180–81.
35. Ibid., 177.
36. Leonard Krieger, *The German Idea of Freedom: History of a Political Tradition, from the Reformation to 1871* (Chicago: University of Chicago Press, 1957), 6; Breunig and Levinger, *The Revolutionary Era, 1789–1850*, 164; Robert C. Williams, *Horace Greeley: Champion of American Freedom* (New York: New York University Press, 2006), 130.
37. Eric Foner, *The Story of American Freedom* (New York: W. W. Norton, 1998), 69–94; Francis Lieber, *On Civil Liberty and Self Government* (Philadelphia: Lippincott, 1853), 1–27; Williams, *Horace Greeley*, 50, 147, 161; Reeve Huston, *Land and Freedom: Rural Society, Popular Protest, and Party Politics in Antebellum New York* (New York: Oxford University Press, 2000), 107–31.
38. JR-FB, 1831, 23, 177–78.
39. Ibid., 184, 188, 197.
40. See Masur, *1831*, 9–19, 39, 135–67, 170–71; J. Cutler Andrews, "The Antimasonic Movement in Western Pennsylvania," *Western Pennsylvania Historical Magazine* 18, no. 4 (1935), 255–56; Charles McCool Snyder, *The Jacksonian Heritage: Pennsylvania Politics, 1833–1848* (Harrisburg: Pennsylvania Historical and Museum Commission, 1958), 27–28; Joel Myerson, ed., *The Selected Letters of Ralph Waldo Emerson* (New York: Columbia University Press, 1997), 112.

Chapter 7

1. *WRF*, 23; Pierson, *Tocqueville in America*, 543; JR-OFI, 86–87. Johann's son Washington was "constantly amused" by his father's "enthusiasm" for the land he had bought and the prospect of farming. It can only be counted a minor miracle that Johann's patience and belief weren't strained to the limit by the bleak winter scene he encountered.

2. *WRF*, 31; JR-OFI, 84, 86, 105.

3. WAR to John A. Roebling II, n.d., 1893–4 in SRL; JR-FB, 3; *WRF*, 32, 58; WAR, *Early History of Saxonburg*, 11; Helen Stuebgen, "Old Sachsenburg," *Historia* (April 1972), 8; Weiss, "The History of the Evangelical Protestant Community of Saxonburg, PA," 1–2.

4. JR-OFI, 93; R. C. Brown, *History of Butler County, Pennsylvania* (Chicago: R. C. Brown, 1895), 72; Goldinger, *Historic Saxonburg and Its Neighbors*, 10; WAR, *Early History of Saxonburg*, 9.

5. JR-OFI, 75.

6. Ibid., 78.

7. There are many reasons to question both the role of Carl in the emigration venture and Johann's representation of him, but ultimately no evidence. As the eldest brother, one might naturally assume Carl to have been the dominant partner. One might also question why Johann would go farming when he was clearly more suited to engineering. There were certainly plenty of reasons for Johann to emigrate in 1831, although becoming a farmer doesn't seem to fit any of them, unless it was Carl's idea and Johann went along with it. In these respects, the history and the dynamics seem illogical. Yet Johann's version of events is the only one we have. In addition, it was to Johann that the mayor of Mühlhausen wrote on the eve of departure, not Carl, and it was also Johann who took the lead in communicating with friends back in Mühlhausen.

8. JR-OFI, 87, 100–101. Johann and Carl's money worries were alleviated in May 1832 when Johann heard from a Philadelphia bank that six thousand dollars had arrived from Bremen on behalf of the next wave of settlers.

9. JR-OFI, 102. See "Ist die Auswanderung nach Fernen Zonen Nothwendig?" *Gemeinnützigen Unterhaltungsblatt* 50 (December 1832); Güntheroth, "Realien und Karriere," 85, 88.

10. JAR to Ferdinand Bähr, January 1831, JAR Correspondence #2, 3:26, RFP-RU.

11. Ibid., 103, 107, 181–82.

12. JR-OFI, 75, 88; JAR to Ferdinand Bähr, January 1831, 3:104; Charles Sellers, *The Market Revolution: Jacksonian America, 1815–1846* (New York: Oxford University Press, 1994), 3–33. Predictions of violent slave revolts were common in the United States both before and after Turner's Rebellion.

13. Tocqueville, *Democracy in America*, 2:104–12; Damrosch, *Tocqueville's Discovery of America*, 202; *Diary*, 110; JR-OFI, 75.

14. Tocqueville, *Democracy in America*, 2:98, 110; *Diary*, 111; Damrosch, *Tocqueville's Discovery of America*, 106.

15. *Diary*, 112; Tocqueville, *Democracy in America*, 2:11, 136.

16. Tocqueville, *Democracy in America*, 1:288–300.

17. Brostowin, *John Adolphus Etzler*, 18; "Passages Relating to 'Mr. Etzler' in Omitted Portions of the Two John A. Roebling Letters Published in the *Western Pennsylvania Historical Magazine*," MS, JHHC, 2.

18. Loyd D. Easton, *Hegel's First American Followers* (Athens: Ohio University Press, 1966), 11–27; Johann Etzler to George Rapp, September 3, 1832, Letter File, AOEV.

19. Johann Etzler to Harmony Society, August 26, 1834, Letter File, AOEV; *Pittsburgh Gazette*, June 11, 1833, 2.

20. John G. Whittier, "The City of a Day," in *Literary Recreations and Miscellanies* (Boston: Ticknor & Fields, 1854), 318–20.

21. Etzler, *The Paradise within the Reach of All Men*, 1.

22. Thoreau, "Paradise (to Be) Regained," 451–63. Also see Brooke Hindle, "Spatial Thinking in the Bridge Era: John Augustus Roebling versus John Adolphus Etzler," in *Bridge to the Future: A Centennial Celebration of the Brooklyn Bridge*, ed. Margaret Latimer, Brooke Hindle, and Melvin Kranzberg (New York: New York Academy of Sciences, 1984), 131–47.

23. Etzler, *The Paradise within the Reach of All Men*, 3–4; Alexis Madrigal, *Powering the Dream: The History and Promise of Green Technology* (New York: Da Capo, 2011), 13–16.

24. Thoreau, "Paradise (to Be) Regained," 460–63.

25. See *Der Deutsche Pionier* 1, no. 7 (September 1869), 198–99.

26. "Great Movements in Limestone, Warren County, Penn," *The Present* 1, no. 9 (March 1844), 353; "Etzler's Satellite and Other Inventions," *The Artizan* 10 (October 1845), 208–10; Andrew B. Smolnikar, *Secret Enemies of True Republicanism* (Spring Hill, PA: Robert D. Eldridge, 1859), 175–77.

27. JAR to Polycarpus and Christel Röbling, March 30, 1844, box 3, folder 43, RFP-RU; *Morning Star*, July 4 and 18, 1846; Gregory Claeys, "John Adolphus Etzler, Technological Utopianism, and British Socialism: The Tropical Emigration Society's Venezuelan Mission and Its Social Context, 1833–1848," *English Historical Review* 101, no. 399 (April 1986), 351–75; Stoll, *The Great Delusion*, 138.

28. Eugene DeGeller, "The History of the Evangelical Protestant Congregation of Saxonburg, PA: The Years 1831–1914," trans. Walter E. and Audrey L. Gerlach, MS, SPL, 15.

29. Ferdinand Bähr to JAR and F. C. Röbling, January 1832, box 1, folder 17, RFP-RU; *WRF*, 20, 55–56; WAR, *Early History of Saxonburg*, 18.

30. *WRF*, 55, 57, 59; WAR, *Early History of Saxonburg*, 26, 33, 38; Goldinger, *Historic Saxonburg*, 25.

31. Brown, 468; Weiss, "The History of the Evangelical Protestant Community of Saxonburg, PA," 1–2; WAR, 28; Thomas McCormack, ed., *Memoirs of Gustave Koerner, 1809–1896*, 2 vols. (Cedar Rapids, IA: Torch, 1909), 1:312–13; Carl E. Schneider, "The Establishment of the First Prussian Consulate in the West," *Mississippi Valley Historical Review* 30, no. 4 (1944), 507–20.

32. Amelia Meissner to JAR, September 20, 1832, reprinted in Schuyler, *The Roeblings*, 41.

33. *WRF*, 33; WAR, *Early History of Saxonburg*, 17, 9, 26, 32; Goldinger, *Historic Saxonburg*, 25, 105, 110. A Dr. Koch arrived in 1843 and served as the village's first resident physician. Koch pulled Washington's "best *sound* back tooth" the next year. "I miss it yet," he wrote eighty years later in 1923.

34. WAR, *Early History of Saxonburg*, 10, 25–35; Goldinger, *Historic Saxonburg*, 17, 114; Stuebgen, "Old Sachsenburg," 7–8.

35. David L. Taylor, *Saxonburg Historic District*, nomination document (Washington, DC: National Park Service, National Register of Historic Places, 2002), http://www.dot7.state.pa.us/CRGIS_Attachments/SiteResource/H115567NOM.pdf, accessed April 17, 2012; JR-FB, 175–76; E. Wiston, "Roebling, Brooklyn Bridge Builder Made First Cable in Tiny Shop in Saxonburg," *Pittsburgh Press*, July 28, 1929, 1.

36. WAR, *Early History of Saxonburg*, 31; Washington Roebling to John A. Roebling II, January 5, 1926, SRL.

37. Taylor, *Saxonburg Historic District*; WAR, *Early History of Saxonburg*, 10; JR-OFI, 82; *WRF*, 35–36.

38. See Solon J. Buck and Elizabeth Buck, *The Planting of Civilization in Western Pennsylvania* (Pittsburgh: University of Pittsburgh Press, 1939), 288–305; *WRF*, 31; WAR, *Early History of Saxonburg*, 10; Schuyler, *The Roeblings*, 42. Ironically, of course, Johann's land was exceptionally valuable, although not as farmland. A few years after Johann sold his land, a gas well was struck on his former meadow. Later, oil was discovered on much of his original property. See Stuebgen, "Old Sachsenburg," 10, and *WRF*, 21.

39. *WRF*, 21, 31.

40. Ibid., 22, 36–67.

41. Ibid., 35–36, 60.

42. Ibid., 21, 23–24; Güntheroth, "The Young Roebling, Biographical Notes," 15; JAR, "Copy Book," box 5, folders 44–45, RFP-RU.

43. "Circular," box 8, folder 23, RFP-RU; DeGeller, "The History of the Evangelical Protestant Congregation of Saxonburg, PA," 5.

44. Goldinger, *Historic Saxonburg*, 14; Weiss, "The History of the Evangelical Protestant Community of Saxonburg, PA," 7.

45. Weiss, "The History of the Evangelical Protestant Community of Saxonburg, PA," 5, 7, 8–10.

46. Quoted in Auener, *Johann August Röbling*, 25. Johanna was born in Mühlhausen on August 18, 1817.

47. *WRF*, 39, 43.

48. Ibid., 44; Estabrook, "Address," 33; Brown, *History of Butler County*, 470.

49. Amelia Meissner to JAR, September 20, 1832, in Schuyler, *The Roeblings*, 41.

50. See, for example, Steinman, *The Builders of the Bridge*, 36; "What Might Have Been," *Oregon Statesmen*, January 25, 1924, 4.

51. See "What Might Have Been," *Oregon Statesmen*, January 25, 1924, 4; "Reverting to Roebling," *Oregon Statesmen*, January 27, 1924, 4; Robert J. Hendricks, *Bethel and Aurora: An Experiment in Communism as Practical Christianity* (New York: Press of the Pioneers, 1933), 1–11, 244–49.

52. JAR to Christel Röbling, March 30, 1844, in SRL; William G. Bek, "The Community at Bethel, Missouri and Its Off-Spring at Aurora, Oregon," *German American Annals* 7 (September 1909), 261.

53. Edward Thierry to JAR, August 2, 1836, box 1, folder 29, RFP-RU.

54. Voucher 6899, September 26, 1836, and Voucher 7662, October 21, 1836, both in File C-6, 78, box 159, Beaver Division, Pennsylvania Canal, PHMC; Robert McCullough; Walter Leuba, *The Pennsylvania Main Line Canal* (York, PA: American Canal and Transportation Center, 1973), 79.

55. Ronald E. Shaw, *Canals for a Nation: The Canal Era in the United States, 1790–1860* (Lexington: University Press of Kentucky, 1990), 123; W. H. Van Fossan, "Sandy and Beaver Canal," *Ohio State Archaeological and Historical Quarterly* 55, no. 2 (1946), 165–67; Ronald Max Gard, *The Sandy and Beaver Canal* (East Liverpool, OH: East Liverpool Historical Society, 1952), 123–32. See Gill's beautiful renditions of Philadelphia's Market Street Bridge in John Weale's *The Theory, Practice, and Architecture of Bridges of Stone, Iron, Timber, and Wire: With Examples on the Principle of Suspension*, 2 vols. (London: Architectural Library, 1843), plates 34, 35.

56. Harry L. Watson, *Liberty and Power: The Politics of Jacksonian America* (New York: Hill & Wang, 1990), 205–6; Errett, "Pittsburgh in 1829," 41; Snyder, *The Jacksonian Heritage*, 115; Daniel Hovery Calhoun, *The American Civil Engineer: Origins and Conflicts* (Cambridge, MA: Technology Press, MIT, 1960), 141–42; Joel Porte, ed., *Emerson in His Journals* (Cambridge, MA: Harvard University Press, 1982), 164.

57. WAR, *Early History of Saxonburg*, 12; WAR, "The Life of John A. Roebling, C.E. by His Eldest Son Washington A. Roebling, Together with Some Personal Recollections of the Latter, Written Partly in 1897 and in 1907," box 10, folders 23–36, RFP-RU. Johann and Johanna had ten children together over the next twenty years, eight of whom lived into adulthood. They were: Washington August Roebling (May 26, 1837–July 21, 1926); Hannah Roebling (July 7, 1838–died after only a few days); Laura Adelheid Roebling (January 24, 1840–January 3, 1873); Ferdinand William Roebling (February 27, 1842–March 16, 1917); Elvira Amalia Roebling (May 22, 1844–January 17, 1871); Josephine Eleanora Roebling (March 22, 1847–1934); Charles Gustavus Roebling (December 9, 1849–October 5, 1918); Edmund Roebling (January 1, 1854–December 21, 1930); and William Elderhorst Roebling (September 22, 1856–September 21, 1861).

58. See JAR, "An Essay on the Obstruction of Streams by Dams, with Formulæ for Ascertaining the Rise of Water Caused by Their Construction," *American Railroad Journal and Mechanics' Magazine*, December 1, 1838, 330–38,38 and "A Treatise on Reservoire [*sic*] Locks," *American Railroad Journal and Mechanics' Magazine*, December 15, 1838, 361–68. Johann also published another article in the *Railroad Journal* that year. See JAR, "Relative Value of the Different Kinds of Steam, from Different Liquids, as a Moving Power," *American Railroad Journal and Mechanics' Magazine*, July 1, 1838, 7–9.

59. JAR to E. H. Gill, June 28, 1837, box 3, folder 42, RFP-RU.

60. Ibid.

61. *WRF*, 31, 39; WAR, *Early History of Saxonburg*, 11–12, 21–22; Brown, *History of Butler County, Pennsylvania*, 467.

62. JAR, "Certificate of Naturalization," box 8, folder 24, RFP-RU.

63. Snyder, *The Jacksonian Heritage*, 112–19; *WRF*, 49.

64. Bruncken, "German Political Refugees in the United States during the Period from 1815–1860," 25–26; Daniel Walker Howe, *What Hath God Wrought: The Transformation of America, 1815–1848* (New York: Oxford University Press, 2007), 5; Watson, *Liberty and Power*, 43–45.

65. See O'Connor, *The German-Americans*, 74–75, and Gustav Philipp Körner, *Memoirs of Gustave Koerner, 1809–1896*, 2 vols., ed. Thomas J. McCormack (Cedar Rapids, IA: Torch, 1909), 1:423–25.

66. Heinrich A. Rattermann, "Johann August Röbling: Berühmter Amerikanischer Ingenieur und Brückenbauer," in H. A. Rattermann, *Gesammelte ausgewählte Werke* (Cincinnati: Selbstverlag des Verfassers, 1911), 421; JAR, "[Speech by J. A. Roebling]," box 4, folder 48, RFP-RU, 4–5.

67. JAR, "[Speech by J. A. Roebling]," box 4, folder 48, RFP-RU, 4–5, 6–7.

68. Ibid., 9.

69. Ibid., 9–10.

70. Albert Bernhardt Faust, *The German Element in the United States*, 2 vols. (Boston: Houghton, Mifflin, 1909), 2:366.

Chapter 8

1. Snyder, *The Jacksonian Heritage*, 124–25; Hubertus M. Cummings, "John August Roebling and the Public Works of Pennsylvania," *Proceedings of the Canal History and Technology Symposium* 3 (1984), 97.

2. JAR, "Student book #3," 137.

3. John Lauritz Larson, *Internal Improvement: National Public Works and the Promise of Popular Government in the Early United States* (Chapel Hill: University of North Carolina Press, 2001), 12–40; David E. Nye, *America as Second Creation: Technology and Narratives of New Beginnings* (Cambridge, MA: MIT Press, 2003), 147–54.

4. Larson, *Internal Improvement*, 25.

5. Ibid., 50; Calhoun, *The American Civil Engineer*, 3–27.

6. File C-6, 139, box 172, West Branch Division, Pennsylvania Canal, PHMC; *Appendix to Volume II of the Journal of the Senate of the Commonwealth of Pennsylvania, Session of 1838–1839* (Harrisburg, PA: Holbrook, Henlock & Bratton, 1840), 168.

7. See "Allegheny Feeder: Report of W. E. Morris, Engineer," *Appendix to Volume II of the Journal of the House of Representatives, Session of 1840* (Harrisburg, PA: Holbrook, Henlock & Bratton, 1840), 168–69; File C-6, 70, box 158, Western Division, Pennsylvania Canal, PHMC; JAR to Charles Ellet, July 16, 1838, box 1, folder 51, EP-UM.

8. File C-6, 70, box 158, Western Division, Pennsylvania Canal, PHMC.

9. *WRF*, 81. See JAR, "Relative Value of the Different Kinds of Steam, from Different Liquids, as a Moving Power," 7–9; "An Essay on the Obstruction of Streams by Dams, with Formulæ for Ascertaining the Rise of Water Caused by Their Construction"; "A Treatise on Reservoire Locks," *American Railroad Journal and Mechanics' Magazine*, December 15, 1838, 361–68; JAR to the Commissioners of Patents, December 7, 1838, box 3, folder 42, RFP-RU; W. L. Ellsworth to JAR, July 2, 1839, in LTJAR; I. A. Hand to JAR, May 5, 1841, box 1, folder 34, RFP-RU; JAR, "Self-Acting Gauge," box 5, folders 46–50, RFP-RU; JAR to Charles Ellet, July 16, 1838, box 1, folder 51, EP-UM.

10. "Report of A. Morris, Superintendent, to the Board of Canal Commissioners of Pennsylvania," *Appendix to Volume II of the Journal of the House of Representatives, Session of 1840* (Harrisburg, PA: Holbrook, Henlock & Bratton, 1840), 169, 170; *Appendix to Volume II of the Journal of the House of Representatives, Session of 1840*, 496, 508.

11. James Parker, Jr., ed., *Memoires of Colonel James Worrall, Civil Engineer* (Harrisburg, PA: E. K. Meyers, 1887), 48.

12. *WRF*, 45.

13. Albert J. Churella, *The Pennsylvania Railroad*, vol. 1, *Building an Empire, 1846–1917* (Philadelphia: University of Pennsylvania Press, 2012), 68–69; Calhoun, *The American Civil Engineer*, 26–29, 53.

14. George Rogers Taylor, *The Transportation Revolution, 1815–1860* (White Plains, NY: M. E. Sharpe, 1951), 85; "Report of C. L. Schlatter, Engineer, on the Surveys for a Continuous Rail-Road from Harrisburg to Pittsburgh," in *Annual Report of the Canal Commissioners, to the Governor of Pennsylvania, with Accompanying Documents, for the Year Ending October 31, 1839* (Harrisburg, PA: Holbrook, Henlock & Bratton, 1840), 222–33, 235, 238; William B. Sipes, *The Pennsylvania Railroad: Its Origin, Construction, Condition, and Connections*

(Philadelphia: The Passenger Department, 1875), 9–10; Cummings, "John August Roebling and the Public Works of Pennsylvania," 98; *Appendix to Volume II of the Journal of the House of Representatives, Session of 1840*, 43–44.

15. W. J. B. Andrews to JAR, August 16, 1839, and Charles Schlatter to JAR, August 23, 1839, both in LTJAR; Schuyler, *The Roeblings*, 46; "Report of C. L. Schlatter, Engineer, on the Surveys for a Continuous Rail-Road from Harrisburg to Pittsburgh," 235–36; "Report of John A. Roebling, Pr. Ass., on the Harrisburg and Pittsburgh Rail Road Survey," in LTJAR.

16. "Report of C. L. Schlatter, Engineer, on the Surveys for a Continuous Rail-Road from Harrisburg to Pittsburgh," 235–36; JAR, "Report of John A. Roebling, Pr. Ass., on the Harrisburg and Pittsburgh Rail Road Survey."

17. "Report of C. L. Schlatter, Engineer, on the Surveys for a Continuous Rail-Road from Harrisburg to Pittsburgh," 235–37; JAR, "Report of John A. Roebling, Pr. Ass., on the Harrisburg and Pittsburgh Rail Road Survey." Also see "Notes on Wire," box 4, notebook 140, and "Wire Rope Order," box 24, notebook 39, RFP-RPI, both of which contain extensive notes made by John on his surveying trips.

18. "Report of C. L. Schlatter, Engineer, on the Surveys for a Continuous Rail-Road from Harrisburg to Pittsburgh," 235, 237; JAR, "Report of John A. Roebling, Pr. Ass., on the Harrisburg and Pittsburgh Rail Road Survey."

19. JAR, "Report of John A. Roebling, Pr. Ass., on the Harrisburg and Pittsburgh Rail Road Survey."

20. Ibid.; Solomon W. Roberts, "Reminiscences of the First Railroad over the Allegheny Mountain," *Pennsylvania Magazine of History and Biography* 2, no. 4 (1878), 373–74; W. L. Perry, *Scenes in a Surveyor's Life* (Jacksonville, FL: C. Drew's Book & Job Printing, 1859), 3, 6.

21. JAR, "Report of John A. Roebling, Pr. Ass., on the Harrisburg and Pittsburgh Rail Road Survey."

22. See *American Railroad Journal and Mechanics' Magazine*, March 15, 1840, 161–68; May 1, 1840, 264–65; August 1, 1840, 66–68; June 1, 1840, 324–28; and December 1, 1840, 325–26.

23. Charles L. Schlatter, "Preliminary Report on the Survey for a McAdamized Road from Laughlinstown to Chambersberg," in *Appendix to Volume II of the Journal of the House of Representatives of the Commonwealth of Pennsylvania, Session of 1841, Containing the Canal Commissioner's Report and Accompanying Documents* (Harrisburg, PA: James & Wallace, 1841), 294; Cummings, "John August Roebling and the Public Works of Pennsylvania," 99–100.

24. JAR, "Engineer's Notebook [c. 1840]," in "Allegheny Portage Railroad Papers 1837–1860," MS, MFF 0072, HSWP; "Second Report of Charles L. Schlatter, Principal Engineer in the Service of the State of Pennsylvania, to the Canal Commissioners, Relative to the Continuous Railroad from Harrisburg to Pittsburgh," in *Appendix to Volume II of the Journal of the House of Representatives of the Commonwealth of Pennsylvania, Session of 1841*, 241, 251–52, 256; Charles Dickens, *American Notes for General Circulation* (Harmondsworth, UK: Penguin, 1972 (1842)), 192–93; Bayrd Tuclerman, ed., *The Diary of Philip Hone, 1828–1851*, 2 vols. (New York: Dodd, Mead, 1910), 1:312.

25. "Second Report of Charles L. Schlatter," 256–61; Solomon Roberts, "Reminiscences of the First Railroad over the Allegheny Mountain," 373–74; JAR, "Engineer's Notebook [c. 1840]," JAR Eng #1 and box 7, folders 26–31, RFP-RU; Cummings, "John August Roebling and the Public Works of Pennsylvania," 99.

26. "Second Report of Charles L. Schlatter," 239, 44; *WRF*, 45; Schuyler, *The Roeblings*, 325.

27. "Second Report of Charles L. Schlatter," 283–88; John N. Boucher, *History of Westmoreland County, Pennsylvania*, 2 vols. (New York: Lewis, 1906), 1:216–17, 220.

28. "Report of C. L. Schlatter, Engineer, on the Surveys for a Continuous Rail-Road from Harrisburg to Pittsburgh," 235; Boucher, *History of Westmoreland County*, 239–40; Charles L. Schlatter, "Preliminary Report on the Survey for a McAdamized Road from Laughlinstown to Chambersburg," 292; William H. Shank, *Three Hundred Years with the Pennsylvania Traveler* (York, PA: American Canal & Transportation Center, 1976), 37; Prolix, *A Pleasant Peregrination through the Prettiest Parts of Pennsylvania*, 95; John R. Stilgoe, *Common Landscape of America, 1580–1845* (New Haven, CT: Yale University Press, 1983), 115.

29. Schlatter, "Preliminary Report on the Survey for a McAdamized Road from Laughlinstown to Chambersburg," 292–94.

30. See Marguerite Holloway, *The Measure of Manhattan: The Tumultuous Career and Surprising Legacy of John Randell, Jr., Cartographer, Surveyor, Inventor* (New York: W. W. Norton, 2013), 234–36; Calhoun, *The American Civil Engineer*, 98–99; "Second Report of Charles L. Schlatter," 241.

31. Shank, *Three Hundred Years with the Pennsylvania Traveler*, 101.

32. See JAR, "The Great Central Railroad from Philadelphia to St. Louis," *American Railroad Journal*, February 27, 1847, 134–35, 138–41, and *American Railroad Journal*, March 6, 1847, 155–57. Also see JAR, "Location of the Central Railroad through Pennsylvania," in "The Great Central Railroad from Philadelphia to St. Louis," *American Railroad Journal Extra*, pamphlet (1847); JAR, "Diary, 1847," box 2, notebook 19, RFP-RPI; *Westmoreland Republican and Farmer's Chronicle*, April 24, 1836, 2.

33. JAR, "Bound Notebook, Railroad Surveys" (ca. 1839–1842), JAR. Eng. #1, RFP-RU.

34. Sipes, *The Pennsylvania Railroad*, 10–11. All of this furious activity hid a painful personal detail. Sometime in March or April 1841, John's second daughter, Hannah, died in infancy. Hannah's death was mitigated somewhat the following year with the birth of a second son, Ferdinand Roebling, on February 27, 1842.

35. See *Poulson's American Daily Advertiser*, September 3, 1838, and September 5, 1838, both 2. Also see Lee H. Nelson, *The Colossus of 1812: An American Engineering Superlative* (New York: American Society of Civil Engineers, 1990), 19–26, 50.

36. George C. Gorham, *The Life and Public Service of Edwin M. Stanton*, 2 vols. (Boston: Houghton, Mifflin, 1899), 1:290; James Dilts, *The Great Road: The Building of the Baltimore and Ohio, the Nation's First Railroad, 1828–1853* (Stanford, CA: Stanford University Press, 1993), 350.

37. W. B. Chittenden to Charles Ellet, March 1, 1836, box 2, folder 36; Joseph C. Cabell to Charles Ellet, July 30, 1835, box 2, folder 30; Charles Ellet to the directors of the James River & Kanawha Co., September 16, 1838, box 2, folder 51, all EP-UM; For Ellet see Gene D. Lewis, *Charles Ellet, Jr.: The Engineer as Individualist, 1810–1862* (Urbana: University of Illinois Press, 1968); Sayenga, *Ellet and Roebling*; Charles B. Stuart, *Lives and Works of Civil and Military Engineering in America* (New York: D. Van Nostrand, 1871), 257–85.

38. Charles Ellet to Mary Ellet, June 15 and November 4, 1827, box 2, folder 8, EP-UM.

39. Calhoun, *The American Civil Engineer*, 29; Herbert P. Gambrell, "Three Letters on the Revolution of 1830," *Journal of Modern History* 1, no. 4 (1929), 594–606.

40. Emory L. Kemp, "Ellet's Contribution to the Development of Suspension Bridges," *Engineering Issues* 99, no. 3 (July 1973), 333; Lewis, *Charles Ellet, Jr.*, 19–26; Peters, *Transitions in Engineering*, 147–50; Charles Ellet to May Ellet, March 1, 1831, box 2, folder 11, EP-UM.

41. "Bridge across the Potomac at Washington," *Journal of the United States' House of Representatives*, no. 374, 23rd Congress, 1st Session (1834), 1–22. Ellet's application was overseen by Roger Taney, later the author of the infamous *Dred Scott* decision.

42. Donald Sayenga, "Fairmount Suspension Bridge," in *Baltimore Civil Engineering History*, ed. Bernard G. Dennis and Matthew C. Fenton (New York: American Society of Civil Engineers, 2005), 282; *Journal of the Senate of the Commonwealth of Pennsylvania, Session 1838–9* (Harrisburg, PA: E. Guyer, 1839), 663; *Public Ledger*, February 8, 1839, 2, and March 20, 1839, 2.

43. Sayenga, "Fairmount Suspension Bridge," 269–70, 273; Shaw, *Canals for a Nation*, 63–64; James Finley, "A Description of the Patent Chain Bridge," 441–42; Joseph Jackson, *William Strickland: The First Native American Architect and Engineer* (Philadelphia: n.p., 1922), 11–12; Charles Ellet to Ellie Ellet, May 6, 1839, box 2, folder 59, EP-UM.

44. See Charles Ellet, Jr., "A Popular Notice of Wire Suspension Bridges," *American Railroad Journal and Mechanics' Magazine*, June 1, 1839, 343–48.

45. Charles Ellet, Jr., *A Popular Notice of Wire Suspension Bridges* (Richmond, VA: P. D. Bernard, 1839), 4–6; *Circulaire aux Préfets en Faveur de la Construction de Ponts Suspendus*, Circulaire 6, École des Ponts et Chaussées (November 1823), 1–7.

46. Ellet, *A Popular Notice of Wire Suspension Bridges*, 6–8; Marc Seguin, *Des Ponts en Fil de Fer* (Paris: Chez Bachelier, 1824).

47. Ellet, *A Popular Notice of Wire Suspension Bridges*, 12.

48. Ibid.
49. Sayenga, "Fairmount Suspension Bridge," 281; Charles Ellet to Ellie Ellet, May 4, 1839, box 2, folder 59; Charles Ellet to Ellie Ellet, May 6, 1839, box 2, folder 59; Frederick A. Graff to Charles Ellet, May 8, 1839, box 2, folder 59; Michael Israel to Charles Ellet, May 7, 1839, box 2, folder 59; Charles Ellet to Ellie Ellet, July 29, 1839, box 2, folder 60, all EP-UM.
50. C. M. Woodward, *A History of the St. Louis Bridge* (St. Louis: G. I. Jones, 1881), 6; Charles Ellet, Jr., *Report and Plan for a Wire Suspension Bridge Proposed to Be Constructed across the Mississippi River at St. Louis* (Philadelphia: Will Stavely, 1840), 5; Lewis, *Charles Ellet, Jr.*, 67–69; The Committee of the Board of Aldermen and Delegates of St. Louis to Charles Ellet, September 23, 1839, box 2, folder 61, EP-UM.
51. Woodward, *A History of the St. Louis Bridge*, 8–9; Ellet, *Report and Plan for a Wire Suspension Bridge Proposed to Be Constructed across the Mississippi River at St. Louis*, 7; St. Louis Comptroller's Office to Charles Ellet, May 30, 1840, box 2, folder 65, EP-UM.
52. Lewis, *Charles Ellet, Jr.*, 69–70; Charles Ellet to Ellie Ellet, July 29, 1839, box 2, folder 60, EP-UM.
53. Sayenga, "Fairmount Suspension Bridge," 284. Ellet and John held a brief correspondence two years before. Writing on July 16, 1838, John hoped Ellet—then chief engineer of the James River and Kanawha Canal—"would excuse the liberty I take in applying to you" before detailing his work as a civil engineer in Germany, on the Beaver Division of the Pennsylvania Canal, the Sandy and Beaver line in Ohio, and the Allegheny Feeder at Freeport. This last work was due "to be completed in a few weeks," after which "should [you] want an assistant for some length of time, I should be very happy to enter your service." The references he supplied were E. H. Gill and a Mr. Charles Cramer. See JAR to Charles Ellet, July 16, 1838, box 1, folder 51, 1838, EP-UM.
54. JAR to Charles Ellet, January 28, 1840, box 2, folder 64, EP-UM.
55. Ibid.
56. Charles Ellet to JAR, February 8, 1840, in LTJAR; JAR to Charles Ellet, February 24, 1840, box 2, folder 64, EP-UM. It is entirely unclear who John meant by "an acquaintance of mine." Most likely it was invented, or an exaggeration, meant to impress Ellet.
57. Charles Ellet, Jr., "Suspension Bridges—Plan of the Wire Suspension Bridge About to Be Constructed across the Schuylkill, at Philadelphia," *American Railroad Journal and Mechanics' Magazine*, March 1, 1840, 129–33; Charles Ellet to Ellie Ellet, May 27, 1840, box 2, folder 65; Mary Israel Ellet to Charles Ellet, June 23, 1840, box 2, folder 66, both EP-UM; Sayenga, "Fairmount Suspension Bridge," 284.
58. *Public Ledger*, June 29, 1840, 2, and July 2, 1840, 2; Charles Ellet to the Commissioners of the County of Philadelphia, July 19, 1840, box 2, folder 67, EP-UM; Sayenga, "Fairmount Suspension Bridge," 285.
59. JAR to Charles Ellet, December 16, 1840, box 2, folder 69; JAR to Charles Ellet, February 1, 1841, box 2, folder 70, both EP-UM.
60. See JAR, "Some Remarks on Suspension Bridges, and On the Comparative Merits of Cable and Chain Bridges, No. 1," *American Railroad Journal and Mechanics' Magazine*, March 15, 1841, 161–66, and "Some Remarks on Suspension Bridges, and On the Comparative Merits of Cable and Chain Bridges, No. 2," *American Railroad Journal and Mechanics' Magazine*, April 1, 1841, 193–96. John also wrote a brief technical description of the Fribourg Suspension Bridge (at the time the world's longest) for the *Railroad Journal* later that year— rather odd, given that, unlike Ellet, he had never seen it in person—but it added little to the ideas expressed in "Some Remarks on Suspension Bridges." See JAR, "Wire Suspension Bridge at Frybourg," *American Railroad Journal and Mechanics' Magazine*, October 1, 1841, 196–97.
61. Iron chains are an inefficient way of supporting a suspension bridge. They are prone to sudden failure, being only as strong as their weakest link.
62. JAR, "Some Remarks on Suspension Bridges, and On the Comparative Merits of Cable and Chain Bridges, No. 1," 165–66.
63. JAR, "Some Remarks on Suspension Bridges, and On the Comparative Merits of Cable and Chain Bridges, No. 2," 193–95.
64. Ibid., 195.

65. Ibid., 194–95.

66. Ellie Ellet to Charles Ellet, March 17, 1841, box 2, folder 71, EP-UM; JAR, "Some Remarks on Suspension Bridges, and On the Comparative Merits of Cable and Chain Bridges, No. 1," 161; Charles Ellet to JAR, March 27, 1841, in LTJAR.

67. JAR to Charles Ellet, April 2, 1841, box 2, folder 71, EP-UM.

68. Andrew Young to JAR, May 3, 1841, and Charles L. Schlatter to Henry Spackman, May 7, 1841, both in LTJAR; Mary Israel Ellet to Charles Ellet, July 19, 1840, box 2, folder 67, EP-UM.

69. Andrew Young to JAR, June 12, 1841, in LTJAR; *North American and Daily Advertiser,* June 14, 1841, 2.

70. Andrew Young to JAR, June 12, 1841, in LTJAR.

71. *American Railroad Journal,* December 18, 1845, 812; Ellet, *A Popular Notice of Suspension Bridges,* 10; Emory L. Kemp, "Roebling, Ellet, and the Wire Suspension Bridge," in Latimer, Hindle, and Kranzberg, *Bridge to the Future,* 50–51; JAR, "The Cincinnati Bridge," *Engineering,* July 26, 1867, 75; Emory L. Kemp, "Ellet's Contribution to the Development of Suspension Bridges," *Engineering Issues* 99, no. 3 (1973), 340.

72. Ellet, *A Popular Notice of Suspension Bridges,* 10–12; *United States Gazette,* November 7, 1841, 2; "The New Bridge," *American Railroad Journal and Mechanics' Magazine,* April 1, 1842, 224; "Monongahela Suspension Aquaduct," *American Railroad Journal,* February 14, 1846, 121; S. M. Wickersham, "The Monongahela Suspension Bridge at Pittsburgh, PA," *Scientific American,* June 16, 1883, supplement no. 389, 6201.

Chapter 9

1. Albert zu Clausthal, "Die Anfertigung von Treibseilen aus geflochtenem Eisendraht," *Archiv für Mineralogie, Geognosie, Bergbau, und Hüttenkunden* 8 (1835), 418–28; Donald Sayenga, "The Birth and Evolution of the American Wire Rope Industry," in *Proceedings of the First Annual Wire Rope Symposium* (Pullman, WA: Engineering Extension Service, Washington State University, 1980), 286–88.

2. E. R. Forestier-Walker, *A History of the Wire Rope Industry of Great Britain* (London: Federation of Wire Rope Manufacturers of Great Britain, 1952), 3–43.

3. Traditionally, pilot wheels were linked to rudders with cordage rope, but with the sharp increase in boat fires thanks to steam boiler explosions, boats could find themselves ablaze and with no means of steering.

4. W. A. J. Albert, "On the Manufacture of Whim Ropes from Iron Wire," *Journal of the Franklin Institute* 19 (1837), 369–73; Sayenga, "Roebling's First Rope," 11; Sayenga, "The Early Years of America's Wire Rope Industry, 1818–1848," 162; Isaac McCord, "Improvement in the Mode of Manufacturing Round Flexible Wire Rope for Steering Vessels and Other Purposes," US Patent no. 1219, July 6, 1839; for Aaron Bull see *Journal of the Franklin Institute* 9 (June 1832), 401.

5. JAR to Charles Ellet, December 16, 1840, box 2, folder 69, EP-UM.

6. Ibid.; Charles Ellet to JAR, March 27, 1841, in LTJAR. Annealing is a process whereby wire is heated and slowly cooled so as to increase its strength and pliability.

7. Wm. E. Morris to JAR, January 12, 1841, in LTJAR.

8. Ibid.

9. Charles Ellet to JAR, March 27, 1841, in LTJAR; JAR to Charles Ellet, February 1, 1841, box 2, folder 70, EP-UM; JAR, "Specification of Wire Rope," March 27, 1841, box 6, folder 1, RFP-RU.

10. Sayenga, "The Early Years of America's Wire Rope Industry, 1818–1848," 165.

11. Thomas P. Jones to JAR, March 24, 1841, in LTJAR; Sayenga, "The Saxonburgh Ropes," 91–92; JAR, "Specification of Wire Rope," March 27, 1841, box 6, folder 1, RFP-RU.

12. Charles L. Schlatter to JAR, June 25, 1841, August 24, 1841, and October 20, 1841; William E. Morris to JAR, April 21, 1841, all in LTJAR; JAR to Charles L. Schlatter, September 23, 1841, box 3, folder 42, RFP-RU.

13. Jesse L. Hartman, "John Dougherty and the Rise of the Sectional Boat System," *Pennsylvania Magazine of History and Biography* 69 (1945), 294–97.

14. JAR to the Board of Canal Commissioners, n.d. [1841], Records of the Land Office, Records of the Board of Canal Commissioners, *Allegheny Portage Railroad Reports and Miscellaneous Documents, 1829–1857*, vol. 2 (1829–1843), 154, PHMC.

15. WAR, "First Wire Rope in the United States," *Bulletin of the American Iron and Steel Association* 27, no. 45 (1893), 355.

16. Andrew T. Rose, "John Roebling's Development and Use of Wire Rope in Western Pennsylvania," in Green, *John A. Roebling*, 66.

17. JAR, "American Manufacture of Wire Rope for Inclined Planes, Standing Rigging, Mines, Tillers, etc.," *American Railroad Journal* 16, no. 430 (November 1843), 321–22; Sayenga, "The Saxonburgh Ropes," 93.

18. See JAR, "Method of and Machine for Manufacturing Wire Rope," Patent no. 2720, July 1842; Roebling, "American Manufacture of Wire Rope," 321.

19. *WRF*, 69–72; Sayenga, "Roebling's Second Rope," 9–10.

20. James Clarke to John A. Roebling, February 2, 1842, in TTJAR; Clarence D. Stephenson, "James Clarke: Father of the Pennsylvania Canal," *Indiana County Heritage* 10, no. 1 (1985), 15–19.

21. JAR to the Honorable President and Board of Canal Commissioners, February 1842, Records of the Land Office, Records of the Board of Canal Commissioners, *Allegheny Portage Railroad Reports and Miscellaneous Documents, 1829–1857*, vol. 2 (1829–1843), 150, PHMC.

22. *Canal Commissioner's Journal*, March 14, 1842, 3790–91; Cummings, "John August Roebling and the Public Works of Pennsylvania," 103.

23. On June 16, 1836, after the Portage Railroad had been in service only two years, the canal commissioners were authorized to survey a rail route through the Alleghenies "with a view to avoid, if possible, the inclined planes on the portage railroad." By 1840, Schlatter's railroad surveys had uncovered a route that required no inclined planes and which increased the overall distance by a mere four miles. John D. Weinhold, "The Inclined Planes of the Allegheny Portage Railroad," *Canal History and Technology Proceedings* 17 (1998), 220.

24. Charles Trcziyulny, "Report of the President of the Board of Canal Commissioners to the Governor of Pennsylvania," *Journal of the Senate of the Commonwealth of Pennsylvania* 35 (1824), 492.

25. David Stevenson, *Sketch of the Civil Engineering of North America* (London: John Weale, 1838), 262.

26. See "The Railroads and Canals of Pennsylvania," *Boston Atlas* reprinted in *Hazard's Register of Pennsylvania* 14 (July 1834–January 1835), 283.

27. The two most useful sources for information about the Portage Railroad are William Bender Wilson, "The Evolution, Decadence, and Abandonment of the Allegheny Portage Railroad," *Pennsylvania Railroad Men's News* 9 (September and October 1897), 289–305 and 317–23, and John D. Weinhold, "The Inclined Planes of the Allegheny Portage Railroad," *Canal History and Technology Proceedings* 17 (1998), 203–49; Dickens, *American Notes for General Circulation*, 199.

28. Stephenson, *Sketch of the Civil Engineering of North America*, 273.

29. Prolix, *A Pleasant Peregrination through the Prettiest Parts of Pennsylvania*, 123–24; Charles Dickens to John Forster, March 28, 1842, in Madeline House, Graham Storey, and Kathleen Tillotson, eds., *The Letters of Charles Dickens*, vol. 3, *1842–1843* (Oxford: Oxford University Press, 1974), 171; Dickens, *American Notes for General Circulation*, 199–200.

30. Chris J. Lewie, *Two Generations on the Allegheny Portage Railroad, the First Railroad to Cross the Allegheny Mountains* (Shippensburg, PA: Burd Street, 2001), 53–55; Sayenga, "The Saxonburgh Ropes," 92; Roberts, "Reminiscences of the First Railroad over the Allegheny Mountain," 379.

31. Weinhold, "The Inclined Planes of the Allegheny Portage Railroad," 214–15; Sayenga, "Roebling's Second Rope," 9.

32. See JAR, "Bound Notebook, Railroad Surveys" (ca. 1839–1842), JAR Eng. #1, RFP-RU; Steinman, *The Builders of the Bridge*, 64; Lewie, *Two Generations on the Allegheny Portage Railroad*, 87; *Hollidaysburgh Register and Huntington County Inquirer*, October 6, 1841, 3; "Dreadful Accident," *Beacon Light*, April 24, 1844, 3; "Great Explosion" and "Adventure and Accident," both *Hollidaysburgh Register and Huntington County Inquirer*, June 28, 1843, 4.

33. Cummings, "John August Roebling and the Public Works of Pennsylvania," 100; *Annual Report of the Canal Commissioners to the Governor of Pennsylvania* (Harrisburg, PA: Holbrook, Henlock & Bratton, 1840), 21–22.
34. Charles L. Schlatter to JAR, April 14, 1842, in LTJAR.
35. Sayenga, "Roebling's Second Rope," 10; John Snodgrass, "Annual Report" (1842), 74.
36. JAR, "Method of and Machine for Manufacturing Wire Rope," US Patent no. 2720, July 1842.
37. Charles L. Schlatter to JAR, April 14, 1842, in LTJAR; Sayenga, "Roebling's Second Rope," 10; Charles L. Schlatter to JAR, December 7, 1842, in LTJAR.
38. See Charles L. Schlatter to JAR, April 14, 1842, December 6, 1842, December 22, 1842, and April 29, 1843, all in LTJAR.
39. Charles L. Schlatter to JAR, January 9, 1843, in LTJAR.
40. Charles L. Schlatter to JAR, n.d. [winter 1842/3] and January 9, 1843, both in LTJAR.
41. See Charles L. Schlatter to JAR, April 29, 1843, in LTJAR; Sayenga, "The Saxonburgh Ropes," 92.
42. *Annual Report of the Canal Commissioners* (1843), in *Reports of the Heads of Department, Transmitted to the Governor of the Commonwealth* (Harrisburg, PA: Isaac G. McKinley, 1844), 22, 56.
43. "Report of the Superintendent of the Portage Railway" (1843), in *Reports of the Heads of Department, Transmitted to the Governor of the Commonwealth* (Harrisburg, PA: Isaac G. McKinley, 1844), 37–38.
44. JAR to the President and Board of Canal Commissioners of Pennsylvania, October 14, 1843, Records of the Board of Canal Commissioners, *Allegheny Portage Railroad Reports and Miscellaneous Documents, 1829–1857*, vol. 2 (1829–1843), 204, PHMC; "Report of the Superintendent of the Portage Railway" (1843), in *Reports of the Heads of Department, Transmitted to the Governor of the Commonwealth* (Harrisburg, PA: Isaac G. McKinley, 1844), 37–38; *Journal of the Board of Canal Commissioners* (1843), in *Reports of the Heads of Department, Transmitted to the Governor of the Commonwealth* (Isaac G. McKinley, 1844), 170. Also see *Beacon Light*, November 10, 1843, 3.
45. See, for example, A. Mountaineer, "John Snodgrass and His Lettings," *Hollidaysburgh Register and Huntington County Inquirer*, March 4, 1845, 3.
46. John Snodgrass to John B. Butler, August 12, 1842, Records of the Board of Canal Commissioners, *Allegheny Portage Railroad Reports and Miscellaneous Documents, 1829–1857*, vol. 2 (1832–1857), 124, PHMC; John Geary to JAR, June 17, 1843, and Charles L. Schlatter to JAR, May 8, 1843, both in LTJAR.
47. *Journal of the Board of Canal Commissioners of Pennsylvania* (1843), 188–90.
48. *Beacon Light*, February 21, 1844, 3; *Journal of the Board of Canal Commissioners of Pennsylvania* (1844), in *Reports of the Heads of Department, Transmitted to the Governor of the Commonwealth* (Harrisburg, PA: J. M. G. Lescure, 1845), 4–9; Charles L. Schlatter to JAR, February 20, 1844, in LTJAR.
49. Charles Cheney to JAR, June 29, 1844, and John O'Neill to JAR, March 27, 1844, and May 18, 1844, all in LTJAR; James Bowstead to JAR, March 16, 1844, in LTJAR; "The Wire Rope at Plane 10," *Beacon Light*, March 20, 1844, 3; *History of the County of Westmoreland, Pennsylvania*, ed. George Dallas Albert (Philadelphia: L. H. Everts, 1882), 632.
50. See JAR, "American Manufacture of Wire Rope," 321–24. The article was reprinted in the *Journal of the Franklin Institute* 7 (January 1844).
51. JAR, "American Manufacture of Wire Rope," 321–24.
52. D. K. Minor to JAR, December 29, 1843, in LTJAR.
53. Louis Hartz, *Economic Policy and Democratic Thought: Pennsylvania, 1776–1860* (Cambridge, MA: Harvard University Press, 1948), 161–63; Snyder, *The Jacksonian Heritage*, 151–71; Lewie, *Two Generations on the Allegheny Portage Railroad*, 58–60; Roberts, "Reminiscences of the First Railroad over the Allegheny Mountain," 384.
54. JAR to the President and Board of Canal Commissioners of Pennsylvania, January 22 and February 16, 1844; Canal Commissioners Office to J. A. Reobling [sic], April 27, 1844, all in Records of the Land Office, Records of the Board of Canal Commissioners, *Allegheny Portage Railroad Reports and Miscellaneous Documents, 1829–1857*, vol. 1 (1844–1857), 46–49, PHMC.

55. "The Wire Rope at Plane 10," 3; Charles Ellet to James Clark, September 17, 1844, in *Records of the Board of Canal Commissioners, General Correspondence, Reports, Surveys, and Related Records, 1816–1860*, 128, PHMC; John Snodgrass, "Report of John Snodgrass, Superintendent of Motive Power and Repairs on the Allegheny Portage Railroad" (1844), in *Reports of the Heads of Department, Transmitted to the Governor of the Commonwealth* (Harrisburg, PA: J. M. G. Lescure, 1845), 6; William Inman to JAR, December 11, 1843; Charles Schlatter to JAR, May 8, 1843, in LTJAR.

56. Sayenga, "Roebling's First Rope," 10; *WRF*, 75–76.

57. WAR, *Early History of Saxonburg*, 13–14; *WRF*, 36, 70–72.

58. WAR, *Early History of Saxonburg*, 15; *WRF*, 74–75.

59. Francis Laube, "Historical Sketches" (1888), SPL, 29; WAR, *Early History of Saxonburg*, 14, 17–24; Goldinger, *Historic Saxonburg*, 108.

60. See Charles L. Schlatter to JAR, June 10, 1843, and July 11, 1843, both in LTJAR; Cummings, "John August Roebling and the Public Works of Pennsylvania," 106; Records of the Board of Canal Commissioners, Columbia and Philadelphia Railroad Reports and Miscellaneous Documents, 1843–7, vol. 3, 151–55, 157–60 and Columbia and Philadelphia Railroad Reports and Miscellaneous Documents, 1848–58, vol. 1, 62, both PHMC.

61. L. Chamberlain to JAR, August 5, 1842, in LTJAR; John's reply quoted in Donald Sayenga, "The Mauch Chunk Wire Rope Factory," *Canal History and Technology Proceedings* 17 (1998), 142.

62. L. Chamberlain to JAR, August 24, 1842, and March 30, 1844, in LTJAR; *Carbon County Gazette and Mauch Chunk Courier*, September 2, 1847, 2.

63. JAR, "Free Trade and Protection" (n.d.), box 5, folder 43, RFP-RU.

64. Horace Hollister, "History of the Delaware & Hudson Canal Company" (1880), 60, bound MS, WFP.

65. Michael Knies, "The D&H Coal Company: New Insights from the James Archbald Papers," *Canal History and Technology Proceedings* 10 (2001), 53–80; F. Daniel Larkin, *John B. Jervis: An American Engineering Pioneer* (Ames: Iowa State University Press, 1990), 16–34; Larry Lowenthal, *From the Coalfields to the Hudson: A History of the Delaware and Hudson Canal* (Fleischmanns, NY: Purple Mountain, 1997), 5–11.

66. Washington Irving to Mrs. Van Wart, August 1, 1841, in *The Life and Letters of Washington Irving*, 4 vols., ed. Pierre M. Irving (London: Richard Bentley, 1863), 3:132–33.

67. JAR to James Archbald, March 16, 1844, and May 11, 1844, both JAP-LHS; JAR to James Archbald, July 23, 1844, and October 6, 1845, both JAP-JHHC; James Archbald to Russel Lord, April 23, 1847, RLP-MVHS.

68. Donald Sayenga, "America's First Wire Rope Factory," *Canal Currents* 55 (1981), 1; Donald Sayenga, "The Archbald/Roebling Correspondence," 26; Harlan D. Unrau, *Historic Structure Report, Historical Data Section: the Delaware Aqueduct, Upper Delaware National Scenic and Recreational River, New York–Pennsylvania* (Denver: National Park Service, 1983), 21–25.

69. Sayenga, "The Archbald/Roebling Correspondence," 26; JAR to James Archbald, July 23, 1844, and December 23, 1847, both JAP-JHHC.

70. E. A. Douglas, "The Letter Book of E. A. Douglas," MS, Eleutherian Mills Historical Library, Greenville, Delaware; Sayenga, "America's First Wire Rope Factory," 3–4.

71. Sayenga, "America's First Wire Rope Factory," 3–4; Sayenga, "The Mauch Chunk Wire Rope Factory," 146; *Carbon County Gazette and Mauch Chunk Courier*, July 13, 1848.

72. Sayenga, "The Saxonburgh Ropes," 97; JAR, "Notebook 1848," box 5, notebook 25, RFP-RPI.

73. Sayenga, "Roebling's Second Rope," 12; Cummings, "John August Roebling and the Public Works of Pennsylvania," 105; R. Townsend to JAR, May 26, 1844, in LTJAR.

Chapter 10

1. *First Report of the Pennsylvania Canal Commissioners* (Harrisburg, PA: Cameron & Krause, 1827), 11–13.

2. Allegheny City remained independent until 1907, when it was absorbed into the city of Pittsburgh.

3. *First Report of the Pennsylvania Canal Commissioners*, 11–19. Also see Robert D. Ilisevich and Carl K. Burkett, Jr., "The Canal through Pittsburgh: Its Development and Physical Character," *Western Pennsylvania Historical Magazine* 68, no. 4 (October 1985), 351–59; McCullough and Leuba, *The Pennsylvania Main Line Canal*, 48–53.

4. John C. Trautwine, "Description of the Wooden Aqueduct Carrying the Pennsylvania Canal across the River Alleghany, at Pittsburgh," *Journal of the Franklin Institute* 4 (1842), 10; Sayenga, "Pittsburgh Aquaduct," 76; Elizur Wright, Jr., to Susan Clark, December 12, 1828, box 1, Elizur Wright Papers, Manuscript Division, LOC; "Great Flood," in *Register of Pennsylvania, Devoted to the Preservation of Facts and Documents and Every Other Kind of Useful Information* 9, no. 2 (February 1829), 125.

5. "Pittsburgh" in *Register of Pennsylvania, Devoted to the Preservation of Facts and Documents and Every Other Kind of Useful Information*, 4, no. 20 (November, 1829), 336; *Pittsburgh Daily Gazette and Advertiser*, May 24, 1845, 3; Dickens, *American Notes for General Circulation*, 200. Lothrop and LeBaron's bridge was based on a British design patented in 1797 by James Jordan. See "Specification of the Patent Granted to Mr. James Jordan, for His New Invention in the Art of Constructing Bridges, Aqueducts," *Repertory of Arts and Manufactures* 6 (1797), 220–34.

6. Trautwine, "Description of the Wooden Aqueduct Carrying the Pennsylvania Canal across the River Alleghany, at Pittsburgh," 1–4, 7–9; Sayenga, "The Original Pittsburgh Aqueduct," 1–2.

7. *Pittsburgh Daily Gazette and Advertiser*, May 24, 1845, 3.

8. See Trautwine, "Description of the Wooden Aqueduct Carrying the Pennsylvania Canal," 1–10.

9. Ilisevich and Burkett, "The Canal through Pittsburgh," 360; *Pittsburgh Daily Chronicle*, September 11, 1843, 2; *Annual Report of the Canal Commissioners* (1843), in *Reports of the Heads of Department, Transmitted to the Governor of the Commonwealth* (Harrisburg, PA: Isaac G. McKinley, 1844), 8.

10. *Journal of the Senate of the Commonwealth of Pennsylvania* (Harrisburg, PA: C. G. McKinley, 1844), 69, 85, 101, 113; *Jeffersonian Republican* (Stroudsburg, PA), January 18, 1844, 2.

11. See *Laws of the General Assembly of the Commonwealth of Pennsylvania Passed at the Session of 1844* (Harrisburg, PA: Isaac G. McKinley, 1844), 12; Cummings, "John August Roebling and the Public Works of Pennsylvania," 107; "An Ordinance, 29 January 1844, of the Common Council and of the Select Council, Presidents Morgan Robertson and Thomas Bakewell, Relative to the Restoration of the Aqueduct Crossing the Allegheny River at Pittsburgh," Records of the Land Office, Records of the Board of Canal Commissioners, Map Books, 1810–1881, Map Book 50, Series no. 17.452, PHMC.

12. See "An Ordinance, 29 January 1844, of the Common Council and of the Select Council"; *Beacon Light*, January 31, 1844, 2; James H. McCelland, Sr., "Diary—1842–1853," in Papers of the McClelland Family, 1821–1977, MS no. 66, JHHC; "Affairs in Pittsburgh," *Philadelphia Inquirer*, reprinted in *New-York Daily Tribune*, July 4, 1844, 2.

13. "An Ordinance, 29 January 1844, of the Common Council and of the Select Council"; JAR, "Allegheny Aqueduct, 1845–46," box 5, folder 2, RFP-RPI; *Pittsburgh Gazette*, May 5, 1844, 2.

14. Marie Bader to WAR, February 11, 1925, in SRL.

15. JAR to Polycarp Roebling, March 30, 1844, in "Correspondence, Letters Sent (1834–1869)," box 3, folder 43, RFP-RU.

16. Ibid.

17. Ibid.

18. Ibid.

19. JAR, "August–October 1853," box 7, notebook 126, RFP-RPI; *WRF*, 6; Ralph Waldo Emerson, "Nature," in *Emerson: Essays and Poems*, ed. Joel Porte, Harold Bloom, and Paul Kane (New York: Library of America, 1996), 5–49. See Easton, *Hegel's First American Followers*, 45–49, 120–21, and Robert D. Richardson, Jr., *Emerson: The Mind on Fire* (Berkeley: University of California Press, 1995), 470–76.

20. Ralph Waldo Emerson, "The Over-Soul," in Porte, Bloom, and Kane, *Emerson: Essays and Poems*, 383–400; Hegel, *The Philosophy of History*, 212–13.

21. JAR to Polycarp Roebling, March 30, 1844.

22. JAR to Christel Roebling, March 30, 1844, in "Correspondence, Letters Sent (1834–1869)," box 3, folder 43, RFP-RU.

23. JAR to Christel Roebling, March 30, 1844.

24. *WRF*, 39–40. It should be noted that John's wife Johanna left no written record of John's temper or brutality, and neither did any of his other children.

25. Ibid.

26. Ibid., 39–40, 41, 43. Also see JAR, "Diary 1847," box 2, notebook 19, and JAR, "Pocket Notebook 1852," box 2, notebook 20, both RFP-RPI.

27. *WRF*, 81; JAR to Mitchell, July 4, 1844, Records of the Land Office, Records of the Board of Canal Commissioners, Western Division, Reports and Miscellaneous Documents, 1825–1859, vol. 2, 1844–1859, Series #17.519, PHMC; John Linton to JAR, July 9, 1844, in LTJAR.

28. D. K. Minor to JAR, July 19, 1844, in LTJAR; *New York Times*, April 20, 1872, 3; Edwin F. Johnson and W. R. Casey to JAR, August 5, 1844, in LTJAR; JAR to James Archbald, July 23, 1844, in James Archbald Papers, 1825–1847, JHHC.

29. JAR, "Specification of the Wire Suspension Aquaduct over the Allegheny River at Pittsburgh," Records of the Land Office, Records of the Board of Canal Commissioners, Western Division, Reports and Miscellaneous Documents, 1825–1859, vol. 1, 1844–1859, Series #17.519, PHMC.

30. Ibid.

31. Ibid.

32. See *Pittsburgh Daily Gazette and Advertiser*, July 22, 1844; July 26, 1844; August 5, 1844; and August 8, 1844, all 2.

33. See *Pittsburgh Daily Gazette and Advertiser*, July 27, 1844, 2.

34. *Pittsburgh Daily Gazette and Advertiser*, July 29, 1844, 2.

35. JAR to R. Galway, July 22, 1844, Records of the Land Office, Records of the Board of Canal Commissioners, Western Division, Reports and Miscellaneous Documents, 1825–1859, vol. 2, 1844–1859, Series #17.519, PHMC.

36. David Steinman reckons there were forty-three competing bids for the aqueduct contract, which is absurd. Both he and Washington seem happy to overstate the level of opposition, as if John were arrayed against the city, the state, the whole of the engineering profession, and every single inhabitant of Pittsburgh. There were certainly competing bids, but they were few in number and much less impressive. John, of course, was by 1844 a very well-respected and admired engineer and manufacturer, and his proposal was by far the most professional. See Steinman, *The Builders of the Bridge*, 83.

37. *Pittsburgh Daily Gazette and Advertiser*, July 30, 1844, 2. "Pittsburgher" piped up again on August 1, a little miffed by John's rather dismissive reaction. "I shall not stay to take notice of the summary and rather supercilious manner in which [Roebling] disposes of . . . my argument," he remarked, "my object being not a personal controversy but a discussion of some of the questions pertaining to the construction of the Aqueduct," which he again detailed at great length. See *Pittsburgh Daily Gazette and Advertiser*, August 1, 1844, 2, and *Pittsburgh Daily Gazette and Advertiser*, August 2, 1844; August 3, 1844, both 2. Guiser wrote to the *Gazette* on the subject of the aqueduct four more times over the next ten days. See *Pittsburgh Daily Gazette and Advertiser*, August 3, 1844; August 5, 1844; August 6, 1844; and August 14, 1844, all 2.

38. *Pittsburgh Daily Gazette and Advertiser*, August 8, 1844, 2. Brown's Chain Pier was repaired and managed to remain in service for another sixty years in fact, until its floor and piers were rotten and decrepit and the whole thing was swept away in a gale.

39. *Der Freiheits-Freund*, August 2, 1844, 2; also see *Canal Commissioner's Journal*, August 12, 1844, in *Reports of the Heads of Department* (Harrisburg, PA: J. M. G. Lescure, 1845), 98–99.

40. Cummings, "John August Roebling and the Public Works of Pennsylvania," 108–9.

41. Sayenga, "Pittsburgh Aqueduct," 78; JAR, "Specification of the Wire Suspension Aquaduct over the Allegheny River at Pittsburgh."

42. Sayenga, "Roebling's Pittsburgh Aqueduct," 3; "Suspension Aqueduct," *American Railroad Journal* 17 (September 1844), 276. While Ellet was competing for the Niagara Bridge contract several years later, rumors circulated that his Schuylkill Bridge was a little too shaky for its own good, prompting the engineer to write to the editor of a local paper asserting that his bridge has never yielded a particle since the day it was finished." "*Rochester American*, January 3, 1847, 2.

43. Robert M. Vogel, *Roebling's Delaware and Hudson Canal Aqueducts* (Washington, DC: Smithsonian Institution Press, 1971), 4–5.

44. See "Suspension Aqueduct," *American Railroad Journal*, September 17, 1844, 276; "The Wire Suspension Aqueduct over the Allegheny River," *American Railroad Journal*, October 9, 1845, 648–49.

45. "The Wire Suspension Aqueduct over the Allegheny River," *American Railroad Journal*, October 9, 1845, 648; Larkin, *John B. Jervis*, 75.

46. Anthony Trollope, *North America*, 2 vols. (Philadelphia: J. Lippincott, 1863), 1:75; James Parton, "Pittsburgh," *Atlantic Monthly* 21 (January 1868), 17; Alex Mackay, *The Western World; Or, Travels in the United States in 1846–7*, 2 vols. (Philadelphia: Lee & Blanchard, 1849), 2:149; B. F. Tefft, "The Smoky City," *Ladies' Repository* 8 (1848), 281. Both Trollope ("The Monongahela is crossed by a fine bridge") and Mackay (who crossed the Allegheny on a "stupendous bridge") also complimented John's handiwork.

47. Baldwin, *Pittsburgh*, 203; Henry Oliver Evans, "Life in Pittsburgh in 1845," *Western Pennsylvania Historical Magazine* 28, no. 1 (1945), 20–25. Also see David Nasaw, *Andrew Carnegie* (New York: Penguin, 2005), 30.

48. Baldwin, *Pittsburgh*, 275.

49. James D. Van Trump, "The Pennsylvania Canal in Pittsburgh and Allegheny" (1969), JVTP-PHLF, 4; Baldwin, *Pittsburgh*, 194.

50. Baldwin, *Pittsburgh*, 189–90.

51. S. M. Wickersham, "The Monongahela Suspension Bridge at Pittsburgh, PA," 6201.

52. "The Wire Suspension Aqueduct over the Allegheny River," *American Railroad Journal*, October 9, 1845, 649. John's anchorage system, birthed on the Allegheny in 1845, was so well thought-out and successful that it required "no essential modification when thirty years later it was applied to a structure on the scale of the Brooklyn Bridge." See Vogel, *Roebling's Delaware and Hudson Canal Aqueducts*, 21.

53. JAR, "Allegheny Aqueduct, 1845–46," box 5, folder 2, RFP-RPI.

54. JAR, "Allegheny Aqueduct, 1845–46," box 5, folder 2, RFP-RPI.

55. WRF, 84; JAR to James Archbald, November 9, 1844, JAP-LHS.

56. S. Campbell to JAR, January 9, 1845, and James Boon to JAR, February 22, 1845, both in LTJAR.

57. WRF, 81; Kahlow, "Johann August Röbling (1806–1869)," 51–52.

58. WRF, 84, 88–89; JAR to Jonathan Rhule, February 18, 1847, "Delaware & Hudson Canal, Wheeling Bridge Notebook," box 5, folder 28, RFP-RPI; JAR to Charles Swan, April 21, 1849, in LTJAR.

59. JAR, "Allegheny Aqueduct, 1845–46," box 5, folder 2, RFP-RPI.

60. Kahlow, "Johann August Röbling (1806–1869)," 51. This description is taken from John's patent application "Apparatus for Passing Suspension-Wires for Bridges across Rivers." As he notes at the end of his application, "The above mode of traversing wires, has in its main features been successfully applied in the formation of the cables of the suspension aqueduct at Pittsburgh, constructed by me." See JAR, "Apparatus for Passing Suspension-Wires for Bridges across Rivers," US Patent no. 4945, January 26, 1847. Also see WRF, 85–87.

61. See JAR, "Specification of Wire Rope," March 27, 1841, box 6, folder 1, RFP-RU; "The Aqueduct," *Pittsburgh Morning Chronicle*, February 25, 1845, 2. Also see Sayenga, "Roebling's Pittsburgh Aquaduct," 4.

62. JAR, "Method of and Machine for Manufacturing Wire Rope," Patent no. 2720, July 1842.

63. *Pittsburgh Morning Post*, January 23, 1845, 2; "The Aqueduct," *Pittsburgh Morning Chronicle*, February 25, 1845, 2.

64. "The Wire Suspension Aqueduct over the Allegheny River," *American Railroad Journal*, October 9, 1845, 649; Roebling, "Allegheny Aqueduct, 1845–46"; JAR, "Report of JAR, C.E., to the President and Board of Directors of the Covington and Cincinnati Bridge Company," in *Annual Report of the President and Directors of the Covington and Cincinnati Bridge Company* (Trenton, NJ: Murphy & Betchel, 1867), 47–48.

65. "The Wire Suspension Aqueduct over the Allegheny River," *American Railroad Journal*, October 9, 1845, 649.

66. JAR, "Allegheny Aqueduct, 1845–46," box 5, folder 2, RFP-RPI; *Pittsburgh Morning Post*, March 3, 1845, 2; *WRF*, 88.

67. William G. Johnson, *Life and Reminiscences from Birth to Manhood* (Pittsburgh: William G. Johnson, 1901), 179; Thomas Mellon, *Thomas Mellon and His Times* (Pittsburgh: University of Pittsburgh Press, 1994), 147; Roebling, "Allegheny Aqueduct, 1845–46." Also see Donald E. Cook, Jr., "The Great Fire of Pittsburgh in 1845," *Western Pennsylvania Historical Magazine* 51, no. 2 (1968), 127–33; Charles F. C. Arensberg, "The Pittsburgh Fire of April 10, 1845," *Western Pennsylvania Historical Magazine* 28, no. 1 (1944), 11–17.

Chapter 11

1. Johnson, *Life and Reminiscences from Birth to Manhood*, 181; Cook, "The Great Fire of Pittsburgh in 1845," 127–33; Robert McKnight, "Diary, 1839–1847," box 2, MS no. 176, JHHC.

2. *Pittsburgh Daily Gazette and Advertiser*, April 11, 1845, 3; McKnight, "Diary, 1839–1847."

3. "Fire at Pittsburgh," *Niles' National Register*, April 19, 1845, 102.

4. Ibid.; Mellon, *Thomas Mellon and His Times*, 147; *Pittsburgh Morning Post*, April 12, 1845, 3.

5. *Pittsburgh Morning Post*, April 11, 1845, 2; *Pittsburgh Daily Gazette and Advertiser*, April 11, 1845, 3; McKnight, "Diary, 1839–1847."

6. *Pittsburgh Morning Post*, April 11, 1845, 2; *Bicknell's Reporter*, April 12, 1845, 3; *Cincinnati Gazette*, June 16, 1845, 2; McKnight, "Diary, 1839–1847"; Heron Foster, *A Full Account of the Great Fire at Pittsburgh, on the Tenth Day of April, 1845: With the Individual Losses and Contributions for Relief* (Pittsburgh: J. W. Cook, 1845), 3.

7. See E. P. Swift, *The Calamity of Pittsburgh* (Allegheny, PA: Kennedy & Brothers, 1845), 18.

8. Foster, *A Full Account of the Great Fire at Pittsburgh*, 3; Wickersham, "The Monongahela Suspension Bridge at Pittsburgh, PA," 6201; Erasmus Wilson, ed., *Standard History of Pittsburgh, Pennsylvania* (Chicago: H. R. Cornell, 1898), 717.

9. *Pittsburgh Morning Post*, April 12, 1845, 3; Andrew B. Stevenson, "Diary for 1845," April 20, 1845, Andrew B. Stevenson Papers, 1836–1910, # MFF 0073, JHHC; *Pittsburgh Morning Post*, April 22, 1845, 4.

10. *WRF*, 89.

11. *Pittsburgh Morning Post*, May 1, 1845, 3.

12. Ibid.

13. A prominent Pittsburgh banker, Thaw was also the grandfather of Harry Kendell Thaw, who murdered Stanford White, the famous architect, in 1906, sparking "the trial of the century."

14. JAR to John Thaw, May 1, 1845, box 2, folder 10 (Monongahela Bridge Company, 1841–1861), TFP-JHHC.

15. *Pittsburgh Daily Gazette and Advertiser*, May 8, 1845, 3; *Pittsburgh Morning Post*, May 8, 1845, 3; *Pittsburgh Morning Chronicle*, May 8, 1845, 3; *Weekly Mercury and Manufacturer* (Pittsburgh), May 10, 1845, 2; "John A. Roebling and the Committee, Contract for Building the Bridge, May 23, 1845," box 2, folder 10 (Monongahela Bridge Company, 1841–1861), TFP-JHHC.

16. Not that there was any reason to expect "any danger to be apprehended from fire," he was quick to point out. There was to be no roof to communicate fire from one span to another, and the spans were disconnected at the piers and separated by masonry, further preventing the possible spread of fire. To which one might counter: if the Great Fire could leap the Pennsylvania Canal and burn down Pipetown, one imagined it could easily jump a short pier.

17. JAR, "Specification of the Proposed Wire Suspension Bridge over the Monongahela River, May 1, 1845," box 2, folder 10 (Monongahela Bridge Company, 1841–1861), TFP-JHHC.

18. See Charles Stewart Drewry, *A Memoir on Suspension Bridges* (London: Longman, Rees, 1832), 80, and Richard Beamish, *Memoir of the Life of Sir Marc Isambard Brunel* (London: Longman, Green, Longman & Roberts, 1862), 178–81.

19. JAR, "Specification of the Proposed Wire Suspension Bridge over the Monongahela River, May 1, 1845."

20. Ibid.

21. Ibid.

22. Ibid.

23. Ibid.

24. "John A. Roebling and the Committee, Contract for Building the Bridge, May 23, 1845."

25. *WRF*, 81.

26. *Pittsburgh Morning Post*, April 12, 1845, 3.

27. *Pittsburgh Daily Gazette and Advertiser*, April 23, 1845, 3.

28. Laube, "Historical Sketches," 27-28; *Pittsburgh Morning Post*, May 1, 1845, 3.

29. *Pittsburgh Daily Gazette and Advertiser*, May 5, 1845, 3.

30. *Pittsburgh Morning Post*, May 22, 1845, 2; *Pittsburgh Daily Gazette and Advertiser*, May 22, 1845, 3; *American Republican and Baltimore Daily Clipper*, May 21, 1845, 1; *Pittsburgh Morning Chronicle*, May 19, 1845, 2; *Indiana State Sentinel*, June 5, 1845, 2. Also see "Destructive Fire in Allegheny City! Loss Estimated at $2,000,000!!!," *Pittsburgh Morning Post*, May 19, 1845, 2.

31. *Pittsburgh Daily Gazette and Advertiser*, May 24, 1845, 3; McKnight, "Diary, 1839-1847"; *WRF*, 88; *Pittsburgh Morning Chronicle*, May 26, 1845, 2.

32. *Pittsburgh Morning Chronicle*, June 2, 1845, 2; *Pittsburgh Daily Gazette and Advertiser*, June 3, 1845, 3; *Pittsburgh Morning Post*, June 4, 1845, 3.

33. *Pittsburgh Morning Post*, January 21, 1846, 3; *WRF*, 88; D. H. Mahan to JAR, September 3, 1845, in LTJAR; D. H. Mahan, *An Elementary Course of Civil Engineering*, rev. ed. (New York: Wiley & Putnam, 1846), 272-76.

34. George Upfold, *The Last Hundred Years: A Lecture* (Pittsburgh: George Parkin, 1845), 14, 57-58; *Pittsburgh Morning Chronicle*, July 28, 1845, 2; McKnight, "Diary, 1839-1847."

35. James Moore Swank, *Progressive Pennsylvania* (Philadelphia: J. B. Lippincott, 1906), 252; Sayenga, "Roebling's Pittsburgh Aqueduct," 5; *WRF*, 43; *Pittsburgh Daily Gazette and Advertiser*, May 24, 1845, 3. Also see *Pittsburgh Daily Gazette and Advertiser*, August 12, 1845, 3, and August 14, 1845, 3; Washington Gill to JAR, July 22, 1845, in LTJA.

36. Sayenga, "Pittsburgh Aquaduct," 86; *Wheeling Daily Intelligencer*, January 16, 1854, 3; Sayenga, "Roebling's Pittsburgh Aqueduct," 5; *Pittsburgh Gazette*, April 16, 1861, 2; Thomas Wierman to JAR, July 4, 1861, "JAR, Letters Received 1827-1869," box 2, folder 33, RFP-RU; JAR, "Notes on Suspension Bridges, 1869," box 7, notebook 131, RFP-RPI; *WRF*, 87-88. John was asked to advise on the construction of a new bridge, and even to help recycle the wire cables for the Mount Union Bridge and Aqueduct near Mount Union, in Huntingdon County, Pennsylvania. He turned down both tasks but did at one point think the job of constructing the Mount Union Bridge from John's old cables would be a perfect job for Washington. See Thomas Wierman to JAR, July 12 and August 23, 1861, "JAR, Letters Received 1827-1869," box 2, folder 33, RFP-RU; JAR to WAR, October 14, 1861, box 10, folder 7, RFP-RPI.

37. *Brownsville Herald*, May 24, 1845, 3.

38. Ibid.; *Genius of Liberty* (Uniontown, PA), May 29, 1845, 2; *Waynesburg Messenger*, June 3, 1845, 3.

39. *Pittsburgh Daily Gazette and Advertiser*, June 14 and 20, 1845, both 2. Somewhat ironically, Pittsburgh made an almost identical argument in 1835 against the building of a Wheeling bridge as Monongahela Valley towns were making now, urging Congress to continue "*removing* the obstructions, and improving the channel, of that river from Pittsburgh to Louisville," not adding to them. "A Remonstrance against Obstructing the Navigation of the Ohio River, by the Erection of a Bridge at Wheeling," doc. no. 188, in *Executive Documents of the House of Representatives at the First Session of the Twenty-Second Congress* (Washington, DC: Duff Green, 1832), 2.

40. *Pittsburgh Morning Post*, June 21 and 23 and June 24, 1845, both 2; *Brownsville Herald*, June 10, 1845, 3.

41. *Pittsburgh Morning Post*, June 24, 1845, 2; L. Diane Barnes, "Urban Rivalry in the Upper Ohio Valley," *Pennsylvania Magazine of History and Biography* 123, no. 3 (1999), 201; F. Frank Crall, "A Half Century of Rivalry between Pittsburgh and Wheeling," *Western Pennsylvania Historical Magazine* 13, no. 4 (1930), 237.

42. JAR, "Specification of the Proposed Wire Suspension Bridge over the Monongahela River, May 1, 1845."

43. JAR to Messrs. Henderson, Bissel, and Jackson, Committee of Monongahela Bridge, May 5, 1845, and "Monongahela Bridge Company in Act. with JAR," both box 2, folder 10 (Monongahela Bridge Company, 1841-1861), TFP-JHHC; JAR, "Wire Suspension Bridge

over the Monongahela Bridge, at Pittsburgh," *American Railroad Journal*, April 4, 1846, 376; Herbert Du Puy, "A Brief History of the Monongahela Bridge, Pittsburgh, PA," *Pennsylvania Magazine of History and Biography* 30, no. 2 (1906), 199.

44. Richard C. Wade, *The Urban Frontier: The Rise of Western Cities, 1790–1830* (Urbana: University of Illinois Press, 1996 (1959)), 323.

45. *Waynesburg Messenger*, June 3, 1845, 3; *Brownsville Herald*, June 10, 1845, 3.

46. Elizabeth Brand Monroe, *The Wheeling Bridge Case: Its Significance in American Law and Technology* (Boston: Northeastern University Press, 1992), 30–31; *Pittsburgh Statesmen*, June 2, 1821, 2; *Northwestern Gazette* (Wheeling, VA), June 16, 1821, 3.

47. Barnes, "Urban Rivalry in the Upper Ohio Valley," 220; Wade, *The Urban Frontier*, 326; Crall, "A Half Century of Rivalry between Pittsburgh and Wheeling," 239. Luckily for Pittsburgh, Wheeling was afflicted by many of the issues that dogged internal improvements generally. Any bridge spanning the Ohio at Wheeling would have one foot in Virginia and the other in Ohio, thus necessitating legislation from both state governments. This was eventually achieved, but legislation was often easier to get than financing. Positioned far away from the center of political life and economic action in Richmond, Wheeling was of little concern to Virginia, which refused to spend a penny on the project. See Monroe, *The Wheeling Bridge Case*, 13; James Morton Callahan, "The Pittsburgh-Wheeling Rivalry for Commercial Headship on the Ohio," *Ohio Archaeological and Historical Publications* 22 (1913), 42–44.

48. *WRF*, 88, 82.

49. Ibid., 6, 41.

50. Henry Burnell Shafer, *The American Medical Profession, 1783 to 1850* (New York: Columbia University Press, 1936), 45–76; John S. Haller, *American Medicine in Transition, 1840–1910* (Urbana: University of Illinois Press, 1981), 100. As Charles Rosenberg notes, there were few more popular trends in Jacksonian America than "do it yourself medicine." See Charles E. Rosenberg, *The Cholera Years: The United States in 1832, 1849, and 1866* (Chicago: University of Chicago Press, 1987 (1962)), 71.

51. *WRF*, 92; Harry B. Weiss and Howard R. Kemble, *The Great American Water-Cure Craze: A History of Hydrotherapy in the United States* (Trenton, NJ: Past Times, 1967), 4.

52. John B. Blake, "Health Reform," in *The Rise of Adventism: Religion and Society in Mid-Nineteenth-Century America*, ed. Edwin S. Gaustad (New York: Harper & Row, 1974), 44; Weiss and Kemble, *The Great American Water-Cure Craze*, 4; [R. T. Claridge], *The Cold Water Cure, Its Principles, Theory, and Practice; by Vincent Priessnitz* (London: William Strange, 1842); Robert Hay Graham, *Graefenberg: Or, A True Report of the Water Cure* (London: Longman, Brown, Green & Longmans, 1844), 34.

53. R. T. Trall, *Hydropathic Encyclopedia: A System of Hydropathy and Hygiene* (New York: Fowlers & Wells, 1854), 4; Weiss and Kemble, *The Great American Water-Cure Craze*, 7, 9.

54. "Confessions of a Water-Patient," *New Monthly Magazine* 75, no. 297 (1845), 1–16; Susan E. Cayleff, *Wash and Be Healed: The Water-Cure Movement and Women's Health* (Philadelphia: Temple University Press, 1987), 26; David S. Reynolds, *Waking Giant: America in the Age of Jackson* (New York: Harper Collins, 2008), 231.

55. *WRF*, 93.

56. "Abolition in politics and pure water in medicine were frequently found together, for their advocates saw them as moral, not political or scientific issues." See Rosenberg, *The Cholera Years*, 162.

57. Sylvester Graham, *Lectures on the Science of Human Life* (Boston: Marsh, Capen, Lyon & Webb, 1839); Cayleff, *Wash and Be Healed*, 17–18; *WRF*, 93.

58. WAR, 92–93; JAR, "Pocket Notebook 1852," box 2, notebook 20, RFP-RPI; Weiss and Kemble, *The Great American Water-Cure Craze*, 51.

59. *WRF*, 41, 92.

60. JAR, "Water Cure 1852," box 2, notebook 21, RFP-RPI; Mary Gove Nichols, *Experience in Water-Cure: A Familiar Exposition of the Principles and Results of Water Treatment* (New York: Fowler & Wells, 1849), 16.

61. JAR, "Water Cure 1852," box 2, notebook 21, RFP-RPI .

62. *WRF*, 82, 88; JAR, "Water Cure 1852," box 2, notebook 21, RFP-RPI; JAR, "Notes 1856," box 7, notebook 129, RFP-RPI; JAR, "Pocket Notebook 1852," box 2, notebook 20, RFP-RPI.

63. Reynolds, *Waking Giant*, 227.
64. One notable example seems to be anesthesia, which John doesn't seem to have experienced, but he did read Walter Channing's *Treatise on Etherization in Child-birth*, calling it "of great importance" at a time when the practice was new and still controversial. See "Directory, 1854–55," box 2, notebook 18, RFP-RPI.
65. *WRF*, 93.
66. *Pittsburgh Daily Gazette and Advertiser*, June 14, 1845, 2; *New York Herald*, June 25, 1845, 3.
67. *Pittsburgh Daily Gazette and Advertiser*, July 2, 1845, 2.
68. Gustav Lindenthal, "Rebuilding of the Monongahela Bridge at Pittsburgh, PA," *Transactions of the American Society of Civil Engineers* 12 (1883), 354.
69. *WRF*, 94; JAR, "Wire Suspension Bridge over the Monongahela, at Pittsburgh," *American Railroad Journal*, June 13, 1846, 376.
70. *Pittsburgh Morning Chronicle*, November 13, 1845, 2; *Pittsburgh Morning Post*, November 13, 1845, 2.
71. *WRF*, 94.
72. Lindenthal, "Rebuilding of the Monongahela Bridge at Pittsburgh, PA," 354; Kahlow, "Johann August Röbling (1806–1869)," 52.
73. WAR to JAR II, January 5, 1926, in SRL; *WRF*, 91, 96.
74. *Pittsburgh Morning Chronicle*, November 19, 1845, 2; *WRF*, 96.
75. *Pittsburgh Morning Chronicle*, December 17, 1845, 3.
76. Du Puy, "A Brief History of the Monongahela Bridge, Pittsburgh, PA," 201–2; *American Railroad Journal*, February 21, 1846, 126.
77. *American Railroad Journal*, February 21, 1846, 126; *Pittsburgh Daily Gazette and Advertiser*, February 2, 1846, 2; *Pittsburgh Morning Chronicle*, February 3, 1846, 2.
78. *American Railroad Journal*, January 24, 1846, 57. Also see bridge clippings from various newspapers in box 2, folder 10 (Monongahela Bridge Company, 1841–1861), TFP-JHHC; *Pittsburgh Morning Post*, November 13, 1845, 2.
79. JAR, letter to the *Ohio Union* reprinted in *Pittsburgh Daily Gazette and Advertiser*, February 14, 1846, 2.
80. *Pittsburgh Daily Gazette and Advertiser*, February 14, 1846, 2.
81. *American Railroad Journal*, February 14, 1846, 121.
82. *Pittsburgh Morning Post*, January 21, 1846, 3.
83. Lindenthal, "Rebuilding of the Monongahela Bridge at Pittsburgh, PA," 355, 374; Puy, "A Brief History of the Monongahela Bridge," 217.
84. James D. Van Trump, "A Trinity of Bridges: The Smithfield Street Bridge over the Monongahela River at Pittsburgh," *Western Pennsylvania Historical Magazine* 58, no. 4 (1975), 449; Lindenthal, "Rebuilding of the Monongahela Bridge at Pittsburgh, PA," 353–54, 355, 377–85, 391.
85. See Lindenthal, "Rebuilding of the Monongahela Bridge at Pittsburgh, PA," 366–69; David Plowden, *Bridges*, 167.
86. *Saturday Courier* (Philadelphia), January 17, 1846, 3. The old aqueduct had cost Pittsburgh $104,000 in 1829. The old Monongahela had cost $110,000 in 1818. See Du Puy, "A Brief History of the Monongahela Bridge, Pittsburgh, PA," 187–88.
87. *Saturday Courier* (Philadelphia), January 17, 1846, 3.
88. Ibid.

Chapter 12

1. *Ohio Union*, February 10, 1846, 2. John's letter was reprinted in Charles Cist, ed., *The Cincinnati Miscellany*, 2 vols. (Cincinnati: Robinson & Jones, 1846), 1:317–18; *Pittsburgh Morning Chronicle*, February 21, 1846, 2.
2. Franz von Löher "passed fleets of steamboats and smaller craft steering merrily through masses of errant wood and uprooted trees tossing on the yellow flood" while journeying up the Ohio, for example, the same year John made his bridge proposal. See Franz von Löher, "The Landscape and People of Cincinnati, 1846–7," trans. and ed. Frederic Trautmann, in *Ethnic Diversity and Civic Identity: Patterns of Conflict and Cohesion in Cincinnati since 1820s*, ed. Henry D. Shapiro and Jonathan D. Sarna (Urbana: University of Illinois Press, 1992), 39.

3. See Daniel Drake, *Natural and Statistical View, or Picture of Cincinnati and the Miami County* (Cincinnati: Looker & Wallace, 1815), 219; "Bridge across the Ohio," *The Cincinnati Directory* (Cincinnati: Oliver Farnsworth, 1819), 155; Wade, *The Urban Frontier*, 326; "Bridge over the Ohio," in *Cincinnati in 1826*, ed. Daniel Drake and E. D. Mansfield (Cincinnati: Morgan, Lodge & Fisher, 1827), 95–97.

4. *Covington Free Press*, March 23, 1839, 2; *Licking Valley Register*, January 15, 1842, 2; *Daily Morning Atlas*, February 20, 1844, 2; *Cincinnati Daily Herald and Philanthropist*, August 30 and September 6, 1843, 2.

5. *Pittsburgh Morning Chronicle*, February 18, 1845, 2; *Kentucky Intelligencer*, February 14, 1845, 2; *Daily Cincinnati Chronicle*, January 13, 1846, 2; *Licking Valley Register,* January 17, 1846, 2; *Licking Valley Register,* November 29, 1845, 2; *Licking Valley Register,* January 24, 1846, 2.

6. "An Act to Confirm the Charter of the Covington and Cincinnati Bridge Company" (1846), reprinted in *Licking Valley Register*, March 21, 1846, 1. The act passed both houses of the legislature on February 13 and was signed into law by the governor on February 17.

7. *Daily Morning Atlas*, February 12, 1846, 2.

8. *Cincinnati Daily Gazette*, February 19, 1846, 2. The council's "Report of the Committee on Federal Relations" was submitted to the Ohio Senate on February 19 and reprinted in the *Cincinnati Daily Gazette*, February 24, 1846, 2.

9. *Cincinnati Daily Enquirer*, February 24, 1846, 2.

10. *Licking Valley Register*, February 21, 1846, 2; *Daily Cincinnati Chronicle*, February 17, 1846, 2.

11. *Daily Morning Atlas*, February 12, 1846, 2; *Daily Cincinnati Chronicle*, February 21, 1846, 2; *Licking Valley Register*, February 14, 1846, 2.

12. *Daily Cincinnati Chronicle*, February 19, 1846, 2. Also see *Daily Morning Atlas*, February 16, 1846, 2; *Daily Morning Atlas*, February 12, 1846, 2; *Daily Cincinnati Gazette*, February 17, 1846, 2.

13. Tocqueville, *Democracy in America*, 1:398–99; Alexander Mackay, *The Western World*, 3:77; Alexander Borisovich Lakier, *A Russian Looks at America: The Journey of Aleksandr Borisovich Lakier in 1857*, trans. and ed. Arnold Schrier and Joyce Story (Chicago: University of Chicago Press, 1979), 144. While visiting Cincinnati in 1855, Lincoln

   > pointed across the river to Kentucky, and said: "Here is this fine city of Cincinnati, and over there is the little town of Covington. Covington has just as good a location as Cincinnati, and a fine country back of it. It was settled before Cincinnati. Why is it not a bigger city? Just because of slavery, and nothing else. My people used to live over there, and I know. Why the other day I went to ship my family on a little railroad they have got down there from Covington back into the country. I went to the ticket office and found a lank fellow sprawling over the counter, who had to count up quite a while on his fingers how much two and one half fares would come to. While over here in Cincinnati, when I shove my money through the window, the three tickets and the change would come flying back at me quick. And it is just the same way in all things through Kentucky. That is what slavery does for the white man."

   See Ralph Emerson and Adaline Elizabeth Talcott Emerson, *Mr. & Mrs. Ralph Emerson's Personal Recollections of Abraham Lincoln* (Rockford, IL: n.p., 1909), 9.

14. Darrel E. Bigham, *On Jordan's Banks: Emancipation and Its Aftermath in the Ohio River Valley* (Lexington: University Press of Kentucky, 2006), 21; "An Act to Confirm the Charter of the Covington and Cincinnati Bridge Company" (1846), in *Charter and By-Laws of the Covington and Cincinnati Bridge Co.* (Covington, KY: Covington Journal Office, 1856), 6. Also reprinted in its original form in *Licking Valley Register*, March 21, 1846, 1. Underground activity along the Ohio was so significant that in 1838 Kentucky sent emissaries to the Ohio legislature to petition the state to pass legislation cracking down on citizens who "interfere with the relations of master and slave in the State of Kentucky." See Ann Hagedorn, *Beyond the River: The Untold Story of the Heroes of the Underground Railroad* (New York: Simon & Schuster, 2002), 180.

15. *Licking Valley Register*, February 14, 1846, 2; *Cincinnati Daily Enquirer*, February 17, 1846, 3.

16. *Daily Morning Atlas*, February 17, 1846, 2; *Cincinnati Daily Herald and Philanthropist*, February 18 and February 25, 1846, 2.

17. *Daily Cincinnati Chronicle*, February 21 and 25, 1846, both 2.

18. Harriet Beecher Stowe, *Uncle Tom's Cabin; Or, Life among the Lowly* (Harmondsworth, UK: Penguin, 1981 (1852)), 108–21; Keith P. Griffler, *Front Line of Freedom: African Americans and the Forging of the Underground Railroad in the Ohio Valley* (Lexington: University Press of Kentucky, 2004), 2.

19. John O. Wattles, *Annual Report of the Educational Condition of the Colored People of Cincinnati* (Cincinnati: John White, 1847), 7; Griffler, *Front Line of Freedom*, 32; Nikki M. Taylor, *Frontiers of Freedom: Cincinnati's Black Community, 1802–1868* (Athens: Ohio University Press, 2005), 139; Andrew Cayton, *Ohio: The History of a People* (Columbus: Ohio State University Press, 2002), 109.

20. Stephen Middleton, *The Black Laws: Race and the Legal Process in Early Ohio* (Athens, OH: Ohio University Press, 2005), 115–56, 177–79; Taylor, *Frontiers of Freedom*, 117–37; Griffler, *Front Line of Freedom*, 51–52; Paul Finkelman, *An Imperfect Union: Slavery, Federalism, and Comity* (Chapel Hill: University of North Carolina Press, 1981), 174–77.

21. Bigham, *On Jordan's Banks*, 6, 13–15, 21; Harold D. Tallant, *Evil Necessity: Slavery and Political Culture in Antebellum Kentucky* (Lexington: University Press of Kentucky, 2003); Coffin, *Reminiscences of Levi Coffin*, 318.

22. *Licking Valley Register*, February 28, 1846, 2.

23. Samuel Wickersham to JAR, October 6, 1845, in LTJR.

24. See "Tripartite Bridge, Pittsburgh," box 38, folder 16, RFP-RPI; *Pittsburgh Daily Gazette and Advertiser*, February 18, 1846, 2; *Pittsburgh Morning Post*, March 20, 1846, 2; *Pittsburgh Morning Chronicle*, March 20, 1846, 2.

25. *Pittsburgh Morning Post*, February 13, 1846, 2; *Pittsburgh Morning Chronicle*, February 16, 1846, 2; *Daily Commercial Journal* (Pittsburgh), February 18, 1846, 2; *Pittsburgh Daily Gazette and Advertiser*, February 18, 1846, 2.

26. *Pittsburgh Daily Gazette and Advertiser*, February 25, 1846, 2; *Daily Commercial Journal* (Pittsburgh), February 16, 18, 19, 20, and 25, 1846, 2–3.

27. *Daily Commercial Journal* (Pittsburgh), February 19, 1846, 2.

28. *Pittsburgh Daily Gazette and Advertiser*, February 19, 1846, 2; *Pittsburgh Morning Chronicle*, February 26, 1846, 2.

29. *Pittsburgh Morning Chronicle*, March 3, 1846, 2.

30. *Pittsburgh Daily Gazette and Advertiser*, February 19, 1846, 2.

31. Ibid., 3; *Daily Commercial Journal* (Pittsburgh), February 19 and 26, 1846, both 2; *Pittsburgh Morning Chronicle*, February 26, 1846, 2.

32. See *Daily Commercial Journal* (Pittsburgh), March 4, 6, and 12, 1846, 2; *Pittsburgh Daily Gazette and Advertiser*, March 14, 1846, 2.

33. *Pittsburgh Morning Chronicle*, April 4, 1846, 2; *Pittsburgh Morning Post*, April 8, 1846, 2. See "An Act Authorizing the Governor to Incorporate a Company for Erecting a Wire Suspension Tripartite Bridge over the Allegheny and Monongahela Rivers," in *Laws of the General Assembly of the State of Pennsylvania, Passed at the Session of 1846* (Harrisburg, PA: J. M. G. Lescure, 1846), 309–12.

34. *Pittsburgh Daily Gazette and Advertiser*, February 18, 1846, 2; *New-York Daily Tribune*, April 9, 1846, 3; "Directory, 1854–55," box 2, notebook 18, RFP-RPI.

35. *Daily Commercial Journal*, April 15, 1846, 2; Joel A. Tarr and Steven J. Fenves, "The Greatest Bridge Never Built?" *Invention and Technology Magazine* 5, no. 2 (1989), 29. The project was revived in 1871, after John's death, but again went nowhere. See *Laws of the General Assembly of the State of Pennsylvania, Passed at the Session of 1871* (Harrisburg, PA: B. Singley, 1871), 500; "Tripartite Bridge," GPC box 11, folder 37, JHHC. John planned a much less ambitious Point bridge in 1855, a project that also failed to find sufficient funding. See "Point Bridge, Pittsburgh, December 1855," box 7, folder 20, RFP-RU.

36. JAR, "Remarks Made on a Tour East in 1846," box 4, notebook 149, RFP-RPI.

37. Ibid.; Donald Sayenga, "The Mauch Chunk Wire Rope Factory," *Canal History and Technology Proceedings* 146; JAR to Superintendent John Ferguson, December 19, 1846, in *Allegheny Portage Railroad: Reports and Miscellaneous Documents, 1829–1857*, vol. 2 (1829–1843), 154, PHMC; "Wire Rope Order," box 24, notebook 39, RFP-RPI.

38. JAR, "Remarks Made on a Tour East in 1846"; *WRF*, 110. John's remarks are contained in the preface to Frederick Overman, *A Treatise on Metallurgy* (New York: D. Appleton, 1852), ii–iv.

39. JAR, "Remarks Made on a Tour East in 1846." Also see John's two water cure journals, box 2, notebooks 20 and 21, RFP-RPI.

40. JAR, "Remarks Made on a Tour East in 1846." John was always impressed by his new friend's healing powers. "Overman cured a *Red Nose* by Charcoal alone in 4 weeks," wrote John at one point with evident amazement.

41. *WRF*, 111; "Directory," box 2, notebook 18, RFP-RPI.

42. "Directory," box 2, notebook 18, RFP-RPI; Overman, *A Treatise on Metallurgy*, iii; *WRF*, 111.

43. JAR, "Remarks Made on a Tour East in 1846"; JAR, "Suspension Bridge, December 1847," box 7, folder 7, RFP-RU.

44. "Suspension Bridge, December 1847," box 7, folder 7, RFP-RU.

45. See "Blackwell's Island, 1856–7," box 16, folder 4, and "Blackwell's Island Bridge," box 54, folder 2, both RFP-RPI.

46. "Taylor Bridge at Falmouth, KY," box 3, folder 6, RFP-RPI; "Barryville Footbridge, 1847," box 38, folder 2, RFP-RPI. The Barryville and Shohola Suspension Bridge was eventually constructed in 1856, and it has been suggested that it was built according to John's designs and with his instructions. This seems unlikely. John's plans would have been nine years old at that point, and further the span that was eventually built doesn't resemble John's design. See Frank T. Dale, *Bridges over the Delaware River: A History of Crossings* (New Brunswick, NJ: Rutgers University Press, 2003), 141–42. For a comprehensive list of John's major unbuilt bridges see *Guide to the Roebling Collection* (Troy, NY: Rensselaer Polytechnic Institute, 1983), 127–28 and boxes 6, 38, and 51, RFP-RPI.

47. See "St. Lawrence River Bridge, 1846," box 38, folder 12, RFP-RPI; "R.R. Bridge over the St. Lawrence," box 7, folder 5, RFP-RU; JAR, "Suspension Bridges, 1847," box 7, folder 9, RFP-RU; *Guide to the Roebling Collection*, 127.

48. "Directory, 1854–55," box 2, notebook 18, RFP-RPI.

49. "Delaware & Hudson Canal, Wheeling Bridge Notebook, 1846," box 5, folder 28; "Wheeling Bridge, 1847," box 6, folder 32; "Wheeling Bridge, Ohio River—Specifications, 1847," box 38, folder 17; "Diary, 1847," box 2, notebook 19, all RFP-RPI. Also see Kemp, "Charles Ellet, Jr. and the Wheeling Suspension Bridge," 20–21; Monroe, *The Wheeling Bridge Case*, 44–46; *WRF*, 97.

50. JAR to Hamilton Merritt, July 27, 1847, in "Niagara Bridge, 1847," box 7, folder 9, RFP-RU.

51. See JAR, "Wheeling Bridge, Ohio River—Specifications, 1847," box 38, folder 17, RFP-RP; D. K. Minor to JAR, January 2, 1846, in LTJR; "Niagara Bridge, 1846," box 7, folder 5, and "Niagara Bridge, 1847," box 7, folder 9, both RFP-RU; Robert M. Stamp, *Bridging the Border: The Structures of Canadian-American Relations* (Toronto: Dundurn, 1992), 14; "Niagara Falls Suspension Bridge Contract," box 3, folder 116, EP-MU.

52. JAR, *Report and Plan for a Wire Suspension Bridge, Proposed to Be Erected over the Ohio River at Cincinnati* (Cincinnati: J. A. & U. P. James, 1846), 10. "Greeted by odours I will not describe," her feet "entangled in pigs' tails and jaw-bones," Trollope was forced to cross streets "red with the stream from a pig slaughter-house." Fanny Trollope, *Domestic Manners of the Americans*, 70.

53. Louis Leonard Tucker, "Cincinnati: Athens of the West, 1830–1861," *Ohio History* 75, no. 1 (1966), 16; Taylor, *Frontiers of Freedom*, 20; Robert C. Vitz, *The Queen and the Arts: Cultural Life in Nineteenth-Century Cincinnati* (Kent, OH: Kent State University Press, 1989), 40; Mildred Crew, "J. J. Ampere's Journey through Ohio: A Translation from His *Promenade en Amerique*," *Ohio State Archaeological and Historical Quarterly* 60 (1951), 74.

54. Tucker, "Cincinnati: Athens of the West, 1830–1861," 17, 23; Harriet Martineau, *Retrospect of Western Travel*, 3 vols. (London: Saunders & Otley, 1838), 2:56; Frank Blackwell Mayer, *With Pen and Pencil on the Frontier in 1851: The Diary and Sketches of Frank Blackwell*, ed. Bertha L. Heilbron (St. Paul: Minnesota Historical Society, 1932), 46; von Löher, "The Landscape and People of Cincinnati, 1846–7," 40–44; Mackay, *The Western World*, 3:77–79.

55. *Daily Cincinnati Chronicle*, September 30, 1846, 2.

56. "Suspension Bridge at Cincinnati," *American Railroad Journal*, December 19, 1846, 810.

57. Roebling, *Report and Plan for a Wire Suspension Bridge*, 11; *Daily Commercial*, December 1, 1846, 2; Vitz, *The Queen and the Arts: Cultural Life in Nineteenth-Century Cincinnati*, 42–43.

58. *Daily Cincinnati Chronicle*, October 13, 1846, 2. John finished his plan and report on September 1, 1846, before sending it to Cincinnati to be printed up, bound, and published.

59. Henry Petroski, *Engineers of Dreams: Great Bridge Builders and the Spanning of America* (New York: Vintage, 1995), 50–52, 67–68; *WRF*, 100. Also see David P. Billington, *The Tower and the Bridge: The New Art of Structural Engineering* (Princeton, NJ: Princeton University Press, 1983), 72–83; Raymond Paul Giroux, "The Relevance of Roebling," *Journal of the Performance of Constructed Facilities* 23, no. 2 (2009), 2–4.

60. JAR, *Report and Plan for a Wire Suspension Bridge*, 4–5.

61. Ibid., 6–7.

62. Ibid., 7, 9.

63. Ibid., 9–19.

64. Ibid., 13–20.

65. Ibid., 29.

66. Ibid., 10, 13–14, 19–22, 30.

67. Ibid., 29–30.

68. "Directory, 1854–55," box 2, notebook 18, RFP-RPI; *Washington Times*, reprinted in *New York Farmer and Mechanic* 4, no. 4 (1846), 134; *Cincinnati Daily Enquirer*, December 21 and 25, 1846, both 2.

69. *Daily Cincinnati Chronicle*, December 1, 1846, 2; *Daily Cincinnati Commercial*, December 1, 1846, 2; "Suspension Bridge at Cincinnati," *American Railroad Journal*, December 19, 1846, 810.

70. *Daily Cincinnati Gazette*, December 3, 7, and 10, 1846, all 2.

71. *Remarks upon Mr. Roebling's "Plan & Report, of the Proposed at Cincinnati"* (Cincinnati: n.p., n.d. [1847]), 1–2, 4–6.

72. Ibid., 10–12.

73. Ibid., 12–18.

74. *Sunday News* (Cincinnati), December 20, 1846, 2; *Cincinnati Daily Gazette*, January 28, 1847, 2; *Cincinnati Daily Enquirer*, January 27, 1847, 2.

75. See "John A. Röbling," *Der Deutsche Pionier* 1, no. 7 (September 1869), 201.

76. Ibid.

77. "Diary, 1847," box 2, notebook 19, RFP-RPI; "Directory, 1854–55," box 2, notebook 18, RFP-RPI; JAR, "The Great Central Railroad from Philadelphia to St. Louis," *American Railroad Journal*, February 27, 1847, 134–35, 138–41, and *American Railroad Journal*, March 6, 1847, 155–57. By the time of his death in 1869, John had accumulated twelve US patents, ranging from the obvious (improvements in the manufacture of wire ropes) to the more surprising (improvements in spark arresters, steam boilers, and "metallic railroad cars"). See box 34, folder 4, RFP-RPI. Also see "New Method of Traversing Wires across Rivers or Hollows for the Purpose of Forming Suspension Cables," box 3, folder 16, RFP-RPI.

78. *WRF*, 81; Sayenga, "Roebling's First Rope," 10; Kahlow, "Johann August Röbling (1806–1869)," 57–59.

Chapter 13

1. *WRF*, 115.

2. The most reliable history of the Delaware and Hudson Canal remains Larry Lowenthal, *From Coalfields to the Hudson: A History of the Delaware and Hudson Canal*, 2nd ed. (Fleischmanns, NY: Purple Mountain, 1997). Also see *A Century of Progress: History of the Delaware and Hudson Company, 1823–1923* (Albany, NY: J. B. Lyon, 1925); Edwin D. LeRoy, *The Delaware Hudson Canal: A History* (Honesdale, PA: Wayne County Historical Society, 1950); Malcolm A. Booth, "The Delaware and Hudson Canal, with Special Emphasis on Deerpark, NY" (MA thesis, SUNY Oneonta, 1965).

3. See *Niles' Nation Register*, February 21, 1829, 433; Henry S. Tanner, *A Description of the Canals and Railroads of the United States, Comprehending Notices of All the Works of Internal Improvements throughout the Several States* (New York: Tanner & Disturnell, 1840), 58; *Albany Argus*, December 20, 1828, 2; John Willard Johnson, *Reminiscences and Descriptive Account of the Delaware Valley* (Walton, NY: Highland Cultural Resources Commission, 1987), 4.

4. For a description of the Delaware crossing see Johnson, *Reminiscences*, 20–21.

5. Ibid., 21; Russel F. Lord to John Wurts, January 6, 1847, *Annual Report of the Board of Managers of the Delaware and Hudson Canal Company*, March 30, 1847, in *The President, Managers, and Company of the Delaware and Hudson Canal Company vs. the Pennsylvania Coal Company: Pleadings and Testimony Taken before J. H. Dubois, Referee*, 8 vols. (New York: W. C. Bryant, 1858), 8:i–ii, x. One should also acknowledge, as Larry Lowenthal does, that the Delaware crossing was still a remarkable operation in many respects. That it was possible, during a single eight-month season, to pull four hundred thousand tons of coal, or approximately eight thousand fully loaded coal boats, across a pooled section of the Delaware, along with all the necessary horsepower to keep them moving down the canal, was a minor miracle of effort and coordination. See Lowenthal, *From Coalfields to the Hudson*, 155.

6. Johnson, *Reminiscences*, 5, 22–23. Also see Lowenthal, *From Coalfields to the Hudson*, 147.

7. *National Intelligencer*, April 18, 1829, 2; Johnson, *Reminiscences*, 11; *Wayne County Herald*, November 22, 1877, 3; Unrau, *Historic District Report, Historical Data Section*, 11.

8. *A Century of Progress: History of the Delaware and Hudson Company, 1823–1923*, 108, 139; John Wurts to Russel F. Lord, September 4, 1846, RLP-MVHS; John Wurts to Russel F. Lord, February 26, 1845, RLP-MVHS.

9. Archbald and Lord were the D&H's principalHC's principle engineers, although they reigned over different areas of the operation. Lord oversaw the canal, Archbald the mines and the railroad. In other words, Lord was charged with moving swiftly along the canal all that Archbald could mine and then deliver to the canal at Honesdale. Both had multiple dealings with John. Lord talked to him about aqueducts; Archbald talked to him about wire ropes. No lesser a personage than John Jervis thought that much of the D&HC's "prosperity was due to the able and faithful engineers (Archbald and Lord)," although when doling out individual compliments it was evident whom Jervis favored most. Archbald "had an excellent engineering mind and great practical sagacity and was eminently upright in purpose," while Lord "was a man of good executive ability and indefatigable industry." See Neal FitzSimons, ed., *The Reminiscences of John B. Jervis, Engineer of the Old Croton* (Syracuse, NY: Syracuse University Press, 1971), 84.

10. JAR to Russel F. Lord, November 14, 1846, RLP-MVHS.

11. WRF, 115; Lowenthal, *From Coalfields to the Hudson*, 152, 154; John Wurts to Russel F. Lord, December 17, 1846, RLP-MVHS; Solan Chapin, "Proposal," RLP-MVHS. As John wrote Archbald in 1851:

> Respecting your treatment by water, I think that you will experience great improvement from the use of douche baths on the diseased limb. . . . You may take a douche two or three times a day when *over excited*. . . . If you have no apparatus for a douche, then get another person to pour the water on your limbs, from a great height, as he can reach, out of a bucket, and use several buckets full at a time.

See JAR to James Archbald, January 21, 1851, JAP-LHS.

12. *Minutes of the Board of Managers of the Delaware and Hudson Canal Company*, January 6, 1847, D&HC.

13. "Diary 1847," box 2, notebook 19, RFP-RPI; JAR, "Specification of the Superstructure of the Wire Cable Suspension Aquaduct [sic] over the Delaware River and Lackawaxen Creeks, February 1, 1847," copy included in "Wheeling Bridge, 1846, Delaware & Hudson Canal," box 5, folder 28, RFP-RPI. Also see "The Great Central Railroad from Philadelphia to St. Louis," 134–35, 138–41, and March 6, 1847, 155–57.

14. JAR, "Specification of the Superstructure of the Wire Cable Suspension Aquaduct [sic] over the Delaware River and Lackawaxen Creeks, February 1, 1847"; JAR, "Notes on Suspension Bridges," box 4, notebook 108, RFP-RPI. Also see Vogel, *Roebling's Delaware and Hudson Canal Aqueducts*, 10–16.

15. John Wurts to JAR, February 12, 1847, RLP-MVHS; JAR, "Wheeling Bridge, 1846, Delaware & Hudson Canal," box 5, folder 28, RFP-RPI; JAR to Russel F. Lord, February 13 and February 18, 1847, RLP-MVHS; "D & H Aqueduct," box 50, folder 4, RFP-RPI; Thomas Tracy to Russel F. Lord, February 2, 1847, RLP-MVHS; Russel F. Lord to John Wurts, January 6, 1847, *Annual Report of the Board of Managers of the Delaware and Hudson Canal Company*, vii.

16. JAR to Jonathan Rhule, February 18, 1847, in "Wheeling Bridge, 1846, Delaware & Hudson Canal," box 5, folder 28, RFP-RPI.
17. JAR to Russel F. Lord, March 13, 1847, RLP-MVHS; Russel Lord to JAR, March 22, 1847, "Delaware & Hudson Canal Correspondence," box 5, folder 24, RFP-RPI.
18. *Annual Report of the Board of Managers of the Delaware and Hudson Canal Company*, lxxii–lxxiii; Vogel, *Roebling's Delaware and Hudson Canal Aqueducts*, 11; Russel Lord to JAR, March 22, 1847, "Delaware & Hudson Canal Correspondence," box 5, folder 24, RFP-RPI; Russell Lord to JAR, March 19, 1847, "Delaware and Hudson Canal Correspondence," box 5, folder 24, RFP-RPI.
19. JAR to James Archbald, May 10, 1847, JAP-LHS; JAR to James Archbald, June 5, 1847, JAP-LHS; JAR to James Archbald, August 25, 1847, JAP-LHS; "D & H Canal Aqueduct—Receipts of Funds, 1847–1848," box 5, folder 27, RFP-RPI.
20. JAR to James Archbald, May 10, 1847, and June 5, 1847, JAP-LHS; "The Bridge at Wheeling," *Baltimore Gazette and Daily Advertiser*, June 14, 1836, 2. Also see Monroe, *The Wheeling Bridge Case*, 42–43; WRF, 89; Wharton to JAR, January 27, March 27, and April 9, 1847, all in "Wheeling Bridge 1847," box 6, folder 32, RFP-RPI. For a potted history of Wheeling's attempts to throw a bridge over the Ohio see *Wheeling Daily Times*, March 30, 1847, 2.
21. Wharton to JAR, March 27, 1847, "Wheeling Bridge 1847," box 6, folder 32, RFP-RPI; Henry Moore to Charles Ellet, April 14, 1847, box 3, folder 111, EP-UM; Henry Moore to JAR, April 14, 1847, and May 18, 1847, both in "Wheeling Bridge 1847," box 6, folder 32, RFP-RPI.
22. Charles Ellet to Henry Moore, April 25, 1847, box 3, folder 111, EP-UM.
23. Henry Moore to Charles Ellet, May 19, 1847, and June 3, 1847, both box 3, folder 112, EP-UM.
24. "Wheeling Bridge 1847," box 6, folder 32, RFP-RPI; James Baker to Charles Ellet, July 14, 1847, box 3, folder 113, EP-UM; Clifford M. Lewis, "The Wheeling Suspension Bridge," *West Virginia History* 33, no. 3 (1972), 209–10.
25. Thomas Sweeney, on behalf of the Wheeling and Belmont Bridge Company, to Charles Ellet, July 14, 1847, box 3, folder 113, EP-UM.
26. Charles Ellet to James Baker, July 17, 1947, box 3, folder 113, EP-UM.
27. Charles B. Stuart to Charles Ellet, August 3, 1847, box 3, folder 113, CP-MU.
28. See Lewis, "The Wheeling Suspension Bridge," 210–13, and Emory L. Kemp, "Charles Ellet, Jr. and the Wheeling Suspension Bridge," in *Proceedings of an International Conference on Historic Bridges to Celebrate the 150th Anniversary of the Wheeling Suspension Bridge*, ed. Emory Kemp (Morgantown: West Virginia University Press, 1999), 21; JAR to Henry Moore, July 20, 1847, "Wheeling Bridge 1847," box 6, folder 32, RFP-RPI.
29. Charles Ellet to the President and Managers of the Wheeling and Belmont Bridge Co., July 22, 1847, box 3, folder 113, EP-UM.
30. JAR, "Wheeling Bridge, Ohio River—Specifications, 1847," box 38, folder 17, RFP-RPI.
31. John drew up two different two-span solutions. One included spans of 531 (from the Wheeling abutment to the pier) and 284 feet (from the pier to the island abutment) for an "aggregate waterway of 815 feet." The other had spans of 556 and 305 feet. Both plans included 100 feet of clearance on the Wheeling side, decreasing to 74 feet at the center pier and 59 feet at the island. Both were also 26 feet wide, with an 18-foot-wide roadway flanked by an 8-foot sidewalk. The suspension cables—9½ inches in diameter—and cable stays were positioned between the roadway and the sidewalks. See JAR, "Wheeling Bridge, Ohio River—Specifications, 1847," box 38, folder 17.
32. John seemed fixated on central piers during the mid- to late 1840s. In addition to his two Ohio proposals—at Wheeling and Cincinnati—he also designed a two-span bridge at Niagara Falls, with a central pier located on Goat Island flanked by two thousand-foot spans. See "Suspension Bridge, December, 1847."
33. Charles Ellet, Jr., *Report on the Wheeling and Belmont Suspension Bridge, to the City Council of Wheeling* (Philadelphia: John C. Clark, 1847), 7–8. Ellet made sure to fit his proposal to the city's ambition, which meant devoting large sections of his report to the subject of railroads. In 1847, the Baltimore and Ohio—the nation's first railroad—was deciding whether to terminate its line at Wheeling or at Pittsburgh. Ellet hadn't designed his bridge to carry railroad traffic, but a quick retrofit would be both easy and cheap, he noted, and would most likely help

Wheeling's cause. In short, his bridge was good for the river and good for the rails. See Ellet, *Report on the Wheeling and Belmont Suspension Bridge*, 35–38; Dilts, *The Great Road*, 314–36.

34. Emory L. Kemp, "Roebling, Ellet, and the Wire Suspension Bridge," in Latimer, Hindle, and Kranzberg, *Bridge to the Future*, 53; JAR, *Report of JAR, Civil Engineer, to the President and Board of Directors of the Covington and Cincinnati Bridge Company*, 49–50; Ellet, *Report on the Wheeling and Belmont Suspension Bridge*, 11. As Emory Kemp notes, "The Wheeling Bridge . . . completed in 1849, represents the final flowering of French design principles. It was a French bridge on American soil erected within 60 miles of three Findley chain bridges." See Emory L. Kemp, "National Styles in Engineering: The Case of the 19th-Century Suspension Bridge," *Journal of the Society for Industrial Archeology* 19, no. 1 (1993), 31.

35. JAR, "Wheeling Bridge, Ohio River—Specifications, 1847."

36. L. Vicat, "Observations Diverses sur la Force et la Durée des Cables en Fils de Fer," *Annales des Ponts et Chaussées* 11 (1836), 206; JAR, "Wheeling Bridge, Ohio River—Specifications, 1847." Charles Bender wasn't afraid to point out the Vicat's method of spinning cables in place "was copied by erecting the Niagara and Cincinnati bridges." US bridges were "to be appreciated as great works of American enterprise and boldness, but exhibit nothing commendable in the way of *invention*." See Charles Bender, "Historical Sketch of the Successive Improvements in Suspension Bridges to the Present Time," *Transactions of the American Society of Civil Engineers* 1, no. 1 (1872), 31, 39.

37. "Suspension Bridge over Kenmare Sound," *Civil Engineer and Architect's Journal* 1, no. 12 (1838), 317.

38. Peters, *Transitions in Engineering*, 169; Bender, "Historical Sketch of the Successive Improvements in Suspension Bridges," 32–33; "Fall of the Broughton Suspension Bridge," *Guardian* (Manchester), April 16, 1831, 3. For the history and theory of stiffened suspension bridges see Dario Gasparini, Justin Spivey, Stephen Buonopane, and Thomas Boothby, "Stiffening Suspension Bridges," in Kemp, *Proceedings of an International Conference on Historic Bridges to Celebrate the 150th Anniversary of the Wheeling Suspension Bridge*, 105–16, and Stephen Buonopane and David Billington, "Theory and History in Suspension Bridge Design from 1823 to 1940," *Journal of Structural Engineering* 119, no. 3 (1993), 954–77.

39. *Spectator*, March 27, 1830, 6.

40. C. W. Pasley, "Description of the State of the Suspension Bridge at Montrose, after It Had Been Rendered Impassable by the Hurricane of the 11th of October 1838," *Transactions of the Institution of Civil Engineers* 3 (1840), 220–22, 227; W. A. Provis, "Observations on the Effect of Wind on the Suspension Bridge over the Menai Straits, More Especially as It Relates to the Injuries Sustained by the Roadway during the Storm of January 7, 1839," *Transactions of the Institution of Civil Engineers* 3 (1840), 357–70.

41. Bender, "Historical Sketch of the Successive Improvements in Suspension Bridges," 37.

42. R. M. Rendell, "Memoir of the Montrose Suspension Bridge," *London Journal of Arts and Sciences* 19 (1842), 367–71.

43. Bender, "Historical Sketch of the Successive Improvements in Suspension Bridges," 32–33. By contrast, James Finley pointed out the need for a stiffening truss in 1808 in his patent application.

44. Charles Ellet, "Bridge across the Potomac at Washington," *Journal of the United States' House of Representatives* 374, 23rd Congress, 1st Session (1834), 9; Sayenga, *Ellet and Roebling*, 28–29; Ellet, *Report on the Wheeling and Belmont Suspension Bridge*, 24–25; WRF, 97.

45. JAR, "Some Remarks on Suspension Bridges, and on the Comparative Merits of Cable and Chain Bridges, No. 1," 165; JAR, *Report and Plan for a Wire Suspension Bridge*, 20.

46. "Suspension Bridges, December 1847," box 7, folder 7, RFP-RU; Stephen G. Buonopane, "The Technical Writings of John A. Roebling and His Contributions to Suspension Bridge Design," in *John Roebling*, 34; W. J. M. Rankine, "Suspended Girder Bridges," *Civil Engineer and Architect's Journal* 24 (January 1, 1861), 4.

47. Kemp, "Ellet's Contribution to the Development of Suspension Bridges," 340; *Commercial Journal* (Pittsburgh), May 20, 1854, 2.

48. Lewis, *Charles Ellet, Jr.*, 133–52; *Wheeling Daily Gazette*, October 22, 1849, 2; *Wheeling Daily Gazette*, November 17, 1849, 2. Several years earlier, the *Pittsburgh Morning Post* made a tongue-in-cheek suggestion that the Wheeling Bridge ought to be built in Clay's name and

honor: "But should the project be carried out in good faith, and Mr. Clay's memory be suspended in wires across the Ohio at Wheeling, we hope our friend Roebling may get the job," they declared. John's recent accomplishments in the Iron City "shows that he 'can do the thing' to Mr. Clay's memory in the wire line," they concluded. *Pittsburgh Morning Post*, September 25, 1845, 2.

49. Karl Culman, "Der Bau der eisernen Brücken in England und Amerika," *Allgemeine Bauzeitung* 17 (1852), 208; Eli Bowen, *Rambles in the Path of the Steam-Horse* (Philadelphia: William Bromell, 1855), 360.

50. Kemp, "National Styles in Engineering," 31. See Mark M. Brown, "Nineteenth-Century Cable-Stayed Texas Bridges," in *Proceedings of the First Historic Bridges Conference* (Columbus: Ohio Historical Society, 1985), 38–46; David A. Simmons, "'Light, Aerial Structures of Modern Engineering': Early Suspension Bridges in the Ohio Valley," in Kemp, *Proceedings of an International Conference on Historic Bridges to Celebrate the 150th Anniversary of the Wheeling Suspension Bridge*, 73–86.

51. See Monroe, *The Wheeling Bridge Case*.

52. Charles M. Dupuy to Russel F. Lord, November 17, 1847, RLP-MVHS; Johnson, *Reminiscences*, 7; WRF, 127–28.

53. "Suspension Aqueducts," *American Railroad Journal and General Advertiser*, September 11, 1847, 577; Charles M. Dupuy to Russel F. Lord, October 31 and November 17, 1847, RLP-MVHS; JAR to Russel F. Lord, November 20, 1847, RLP-MVHS.

54. JAR to Russel Lord, October 20, 1847, RLP-MVHS.

55. Charles M. Dupuy to Russel F. Lord, November 17, 1847, RLP-MVHS.

56. Russel F. Lord to John Wurts, January 21, 1848, in *The President, Managers, and Company of the Delaware and Hudson Canal Company vs. the Pennsylvania Coal Company*, xxiii–xxv; Charles M. Dupuy to Russel F. Lord, April 25, 1848, RLP-MVHS; JAR to Russel F. Lord, September 15 and October 5, 1848, JAP-LHS.

57. D&HC, December 28, 1846.

58. Charles M. Dupuy to Russel F. Lord, April 25, 1848, RLP-MVHS.

59. Russel F. Lord to John Wurts, January 6, 1849, in *Delaware and Hudson Canal Company vs. the Pennsylvania Coal Company*, xxx–xxxi; *Annual Report of the Board of Managers of the Delaware and Hudson Canal Company, March 27, 1849*, in *Delaware and Hudson Canal Company vs. the Pennsylvania Coal Company*, cix. Somewhat surprisingly, none of the chaos seems to have stopped John from contemplating going to work for the Erie. Sometime during 1848, he worked up rudimentary plans for a "Rail Road Bridge over the Delaware and Hudson Canal, N.Y. & E.R.R." See JAR, "Lackawaxen Bridge and Erie RR," box 50, folder 6, RFP-RPI.

60. Russel F. Lord to John Wurts, January 6, 1849, and *Annual Report of the Board of Managers of the Delaware and Hudson Canal Company, March 26, 1850*, both in *Delaware and Hudson Canal Company vs. the Pennsylvania Coal Company*, xxxi, cxv; Johnson, *Reminiscences*, 54. The Lackawaxen cost slightly more ($81) than the Delaware ($77) on a per-foot basis. See "Suspension Aqueducts," box 6, folder 38, RFP-RU. Johnson described the boatmen who plied the D&HC, for example, as "vulgar and debased" and "lewd and depraved." "The canal was indeed a school for whatever was vile in human nature," he concluded. See Johnson, *Reminiscences*, 44–45.

61. *Honesdale Democrat*, May 14, 1849, 2. Also see "D & H Aqueduct," box 50, folder 4, RFP-RPI. John also wrote a brief description of the aqueducts for the *Railroad Journal*. See JAR, "Suspension Aqueduct on the Delaware and Hudson," *American Railroad Journal* (January 13, 1849), 21.

62. "Wire Cables and Machinery," box 7, folder 7, RFP-RU; *Independent*, October 11, 1849, 178.

63. *Annual Report of the Delaware and Hudson Canal Company*, 1850, and Russel F. Lord to John Wurts, February 6, 1850, both in *Delaware and Hudson Canal Company vs. the Pennsylvania Coal Company*, xvii–xviii.

64. "Suspension Aqueducts," box 6, folder 38, RFP-RU; JAR, "The Delaware and Hudson Aqueducts, December 28, 1847," RLP-MVHS; "Neversink Aqueduct," box 6, folder 39, RFP-RU; Malcolm A. Booth, "Roebling's Sixth Bridge, 'Neversink,'" *Journal of the Rutgers University Library* 30, no. 1 (1966), 13.

65. "Neversink Aqueduct; High Fall; October 1848," box 6, folder 39, RFP-RU; Charles M. Dupuy to Russel F. Lord, January 21, 1848, RLP-MVHS; "Aqueducts," box 6, folder 40, RFP-RU; JAR to Russel F. Lord, November 11, 1848, RLP-MVHS.

66. Minutes of the Board of Managers of the Delaware and Hudson Canal Company, December 2, 1848, D&HC; JAR to John Wurts, December 16, 1848, in "Aqueducts," box 6, folder 40, RFP-RU; JAR, "Suspension Aqueduct on the Delaware and Hudson," 21–22.

67. WRF, 128–29; JAR to Charles Swan, August 20 and September 3, 1849, in JR-CS; William Rose to Russel Lord, November 22, 1849, RLP-MVHS.

68. WRF, 128; JAR to Charles Swan, April 21, 1849, in JR-CS.

69. Sayenga, "America's First Wire Rope Factory," 3–7; JAR to James Archbald, December 23, 1847, JAP-LHS.

70. WRF, 115; see Schuyler, The Roeblings, 73–75; Steinman, The Builders of the Bridge, 135–36; Allan Nevins, Abram S. Hewitt, with Some Account of Peter Cooper (New York: Harper & Brothers, 1935), 107–8;. Clifford W. Zink and Dorothy White Hartman, Spanning the Industrial Age: The John A. Roebling's Sons Company, Trenton, New Jersey, 1848–1974 (Trenton: Roebling Community Development Corporation, 1992), 25–30. It is entirely possible that the Cooper John corresponded with was Peter's son Edward.

71. Trenton State Gazette, August 21, 1848, 2; JAR to Charles Swan, March 13 and July 14, 1849, in JR-CS; WRF, 118.

72. JAR to Charles Swan, August 20, September 3, and September 14, 1849, all in JR-CS.

73. JAR to Charles Swan, September 18, 1849, in JR-CS.

74. JAR to Charles Swan, September 28, 1849, in JR-CS; WRF, 88; Schuyler, The Roeblings, 78.

75. WRF, 123.

76. Ibid., 122–23.

77. Ibid., 123–25.

78. Ibid., 123–26.

79. Trenton State Gazette, October 10 and November 13, 1849, and December 21, 1849, 2.

80. WRF, 118–21; Trenton State Gazette, November 13, 1849, 2.

81. WRF, 122; Zink and Hartman, Spanning the Industrial Age, 35; JAR to Charles Swan, October 22, 1857, in JR-CS.

82. WRF, 126–27. Also see the report in Trenton State Gazette, December 29, 1849, 2.

83. WRF, 129.

84. Rondout Courier, January 19, 1850, 2, and April 5, 1850, 2; Johnson, Reminiscences, 28; WRF, 131.

85. William Rose to Russel F. Lord, January 17, 1851, RLP-MVHS; Russel F. Lord to John Wurts, February 6, 1850, in Delaware and Hudson Canal Company vs. the Pennsylvania Coal Company, exhibits, xxi. John was ultimately paid $45,793.92 for the two aqueducts. Unrau, Historic District Report, Historical Data Section, 55–56.

86. Peter Osborne III, "The Delaware and Hudson Canal Company's Enlargement and the Roebling Connection," Proceedings of the Canal History and Technology Symposium 3 (1984), 130.

87. Isaac N. Seymour to Russel F. Lord, September 27, 1847, RLP-MVHS.

88. Johnson, Reminiscences, 63–64.

89. Ibid.; JAR to Russel Lord, July 11, 1862, September 16, 1863, and December 5, 1863, all RLP-MVHS.

90. Lowenthal, From Coalfields to the Hudson, 239.

91. See D&HC, June 2, 1862; September 23, 1862; April 21, 1863; October 20, 1863; April 16, 1864; Johnson, Reminiscences, 56–57.

92. Unrau, Historic District Report, Historical Data Section, 83–85; "Roebling Revival on the Delaware," New York Times, May 3, 1987, 50. Unlike the Delaware Aqueduct, a vast majority of Wheeling's ironwork—especially its cables, stays, and suspenders—has been substantially redesigned and replaced. Its original elements are primarily confined to the two great towers.

93. Pike County officials briefly considered also turning the Lackawaxen Aqueduct into a bridge for commercial road traffic, but ultimately declined. See Pike County Press, December 27, 1907, 3.

94. H. C. Boynton, "Bridge Wire Tested after 75 Years," *The Iron Age*, February 9, 1928, 400. The Delaware Aqueduct has understandably attracted the most attention from historians and engineers—it was the longest, and the longest to survive—but it may be the case that John thought the Neversink Aqueduct was the more significant accomplishment. It contained the longest single span (160 feet clear) and the largest cables (9½ inches). In addition, he clearly saw it as the forerunner to his Niagara Bridge. As he wrote in the *Railroad Journal*: "I have contracted with the company, for two more aqueducts, one over the Roundout [. . .] large enough for the support of a suspension bridge over the Niagara river, at the site in contemplation below the falls." See JAR, "Suspension Aqueduct on the Delaware and Hudson," 21.

95. J. P. Merritt, *Biography of the Honorable W. H. Merritt, M.P.* (St. Catherines, ON: E. S. Leavenworth, 1875), 391.

Chapter 14

1. Abraham Lincoln, "Niagara Fall [fragment]," in *Collected Works of Abraham Lincoln*, ed. Roy P. Basler (New Brunswick, NJ: Rutgers University Press, 1953), 2:10–12; Margaret Fuller, *Summer on the Lakes, in 1843* (Boston: Charles Little & James Brown, 1844), 2–4; Mrs. Jameson, *Sketches in Canada and Rambles among the Red Men* (London: Longman, Brown, Green & Longmans, 1852), 61. Also see Elizabeth McKinsey, *Niagara Falls: Icon of the American Sublime* (Cambridge, MA: Cambridge University Press, 1985).

2. Pierre Berton, *Niagara: A History of the Falls* (Toronto: Anchor Canada, 1992), 80.

3. *Colonial Advocate*, May 27, 1824, 27; "Report of the Select Committee on the Subject of a Suspension Bridge over the River Niagara," *Appendix to the Journal, House of Assembly of Upper Canada*, session 1836, vol. 3 (Toronto: M. Reynolds, 1836), no. 135, 6–9; *Rochester Advertiser* reprinted in *Pittsburgh Morning Post*, September 25, 1845, 2.

4. Merritt, *Biography of the Honorable W. H. Merritt*, 279.

5. Charles B. Stuart, *Report on the Great Western Railway, Canada West, to the President and Directors* (Hamilton, ON: n.p., 1847), 16. Stuart was later named state engineer for New York and chief engineer of the US Navy, going on to supervise the construction of the dry docks at the Brooklyn Navy Yards.

6. Charles Ellet to William Merritt, October 12, 1845; William Merritt to Charles Ellet, October 18, 1845; Charles Stuart to Charles Ellet, October 29, 1845; and Charles Ellet to Ellie Ellet November 8, 1845, all box 3, folder 87, EP-UM; *Commercial Advertiser* (Buffalo), November 20, 1845, 2. Also see *Utica Gazette*, November 22, 1845, 2.

7. Charles Ellet to Charles Stuart, October 12, 1845, box 3, folder 86, EP-UM.

8. "Charles Ellet to George Tiffany, Esq, Chairman of the Great Western Railroad Company, and Washington Hunt, Esq, President of the Niagara Falls and Lockport Railroad Company, November 27, 1845," *Rochester Democrat*, December 16, 1845. The letter was quickly reprinted in the *American Railroad Journal*, January 17, 1846, 36–37, and the *St. Catherine's Journal*, January 29, 1846, 2, among other places. *Rochester American*, December 11, 1845, 2.

9. See D. K. Minor to JAR, January 2, 1846, in LTJR. Also see "Niagara Bridge, 1846," box 7, folder 5, and "Niagara Bridge, 1847," box 7, folder 9, both RFP-RU. Despite professing to have known Stuart "from his childhood," Minor was ignorant of Ellet and Stuart's developing relationship. He was not aware of "any connection, or friendly relation between Major S. & Mr. Ellet," he told John. See D. K. Minor to JAR, January 2, 1846, in LTJR.

10. C. B. Stuart to JAR, January 2, 1846, in LTJR.

11. D. K. Minor to JAR, January 11, 1846, in LTJR.

12. "Suspension Bridges, December 1847," box 7, folder 7, RFP-RU.

13. D. K. Minor to JAR, February 8, 1846, in LTJR; JAR to Charles B. Stuart, January 7, 1847, and Charles Ellet to Charles B. Stuart, February 13, 1847, both in *Niagara Falls International Bridge Company* (Rochester, NY: Jerome & Brother, 1847), 1–3; Washington Hunt to Charles Ellet, June 15, 1847, box 3, folder 112, and Lot Clark to Charles Ellet, June 10, 1847, box 3, folder 112, both EP-UM; Charles Stuart to Charles Ellet, July 26, 1847, box 3, folder 133, and Lot Clark to Charles Ellet, August 27, 1847, box 3, folder 133, both EP-UM; Lot Clark to Charles Ellet, September 20, 1847, box 3, folder 114, EP-UM.

14. *Niagara Mail*, October 6, 1847, 2. Also see *St. Catherine's Journal*, September 30, 1847, 2; James Dickinson to Charles Ellet, October 16, 1847, box 3, folder 115, EP-UM; *St. Catherine's Journal*, November 11, 1847, 3; Charles Ellet to Ellie Ellet, November 7, 1847, and November 8, 1847, both box 3, folder 116, EP-UM.

15. *Republic* (Buffalo), November 23, 1847, 2.

16. Charles Ellet to Mary Israel Ellet, January 24, 1848, box 3, folder 120, EP-UM.

17. "Great Suspension Bridge over the Falls at Niagara," *Mechanics Magazine*, January 22, 1848, 87–88.

18. "Niagara Suspension Bridge," *Mechanics Magazine* 54 (January 1851), 73; "Suspension Bridges, December 1847," box 7, folder 7, RFP-RU; Orrin Dunlap, "Romance of Niagara's Bridges," *Strand Magazine* 18 (November 1899), 425; *Salem Observer*, August 19, 1848, 3.

19. *Niagara Iris*, March 18, 1848, 2.

20. Ellet initially preferred the basket to be made of wood, until Hulett noted that iron would be lighter.

21. *Toronto Colonist*, March 15, 1848, 2; MVEC-M, 22; Charles Ellet to Lot Clark, March 13, 1848, in Charles Ellet, *Letters in Regard to the Niagara Falls Bridge, 1848–49* (bound volume), ELLET 65, EP-UM; Theodore G. Hulett, "The Old Niagara Car," *Publications of the Buffalo Historical Society* 25 (1921), 70–72; Theodore G. Hulett, "History of the Famous Bridges over the Niagara River" (1898), NFC, 10.

22. *North American and United States Gazette* (Philadelphia), August 4, 1848, 3, and *Baltimore Patriot*, July 31, 1848, 2. Also see *Hamilton Spectator*, August 3, 1848, 2, and *Niagara Iris*, August 2, 1848, 2.

23. MVEC-M, 6, 22.

24. *Cleveland Herald*, August 22, 1848, 2.

25. *New York Herald*, July 17, 1848, 2.

26. *New York Weekly Tribune*, July 22, 1848, 2.

27. *Rochester Democrat*, July 15, 1848, 2.

28. *Salem Register*, September 7, 1848, 3; Benson J. Lossing, *The Pictorial Field-Book of the Revolution*, 2 vols. (New York: Harper & Brothers, 1851), 1:228; Jacob Adler, ed., *The Journal of Prince Alexander Liholiho: The Voyages Made to the United States, England and France in 1849–1850* (Honolulu: University of Hawai'i Press, 1967), 113–14.

29. *Buffalo Daily Courier*, July 29, 1848, 2.

30. Lot Clark to Charles Ellet, January 11, 1848; Charles Stuart to Charles Ellet, February 22, 1848, and March 13, 1848; Charles Ellet to Lot Clark, February 27, 1848, all box 3, folders 120–22, EP-UM.

31. Charles Ellet to Lot Clark, February 27, 1848, and March 13, 1848, both in *Letters in Regard to the Niagara Falls Bridge, 1848–49*.

32. Charles Stuart to Charles Ellet, February 29, 1848, box 3, folder 121; Charles Ellet to Charles Stuart, March 20, 1848, box 3, folder 122, all EP-UM.

33. Charles Ellet to the Joint Boards of the Niagara Suspension Bridge Company, March 30, 1848; Charles Ellet to J. C. Colton, April 2, 1848; Charles Ellet to Washington Hunt, April 2, 1848, all in *Letters in Regard to the Niagara Falls Bridge, 1848–49*; Modified Contract Memo, box 3, folder 123, EP-UM.

34. *Republic* (Buffalo), November 15, 1847, 2. John's opinion was expressed in Charles M. Dupuy to Russel F. Lord, November 17, 1847, RLP-MVHS.

35. Charles Ellet to J. C. Colton, May 10, 1848; Charles Ellet to L. Spaulding, May 11, 1848; Charles Ellet to the Joint Boards of the Niagara Suspension Bridge Company, June 2, 1848, all in *Letters in Regard to the Niagara Falls Bridge, 1848–49*; Charles Ellet to Joshua Spencer, May 14, 1848, and Charles Ellet to Lot Clark, May 16, 1848, both box 3, folder 124, EP-UM.

36. *Niagara Chronicle*, June 15 and 22, 1848, 2; J. C. Colton to Charles Ellet, June 12, 1848, and Charles Ellet to Ellie Ellet, June 17, 1848, both box 3, folder 125, EP-UM; Charles Ellet to J. C. Colton, June 17, 1848, in *Letters in Regard to the Niagara Falls Bridge, 1848–49*.

37. Merritt, *Biography of the Honorable W. H. Merritt*, 333–34; Resolution of the Joint Boards of the Niagara Suspension Bridge, August 5, 1848, box 3, folder 127, EP-UM.

38. George A. Seibel, *Bridges over the Niagara Gorge: Rainbow Bridge—50 Years, 1941–1991* (Niagara, NY: Niagara Falls Bridge Commission, 1991), 10; W. O. Buchanan to Charles Ellet, April 10, 1848, in *Letters in Regard to the Niagara Falls Bridge, 1848–49*.

39. Charles Ellet to Joshua Spencer, August 8, 1848, in *Letters in Regard to the Niagara Falls Bridge, 1848–49*; Theodore G. Hulett and Jonathan Baldwin, "Niagara Falls Suspension Bridge Difficulties," broadside, box 3, folder 129, EP-UM, reprinted in *Niagara Iris*, October 28, 1848. Also see Theodore Hulett to Charles Ellet, August 7, 1848, box 3, folder 127, EP-UM.

40. Charles Ellet to Hulett and Baldwin, August 8, 1848 (telegram), and Charles Ellet to Joshua Spencer, August 8, 1848, both in *Letters in Regard to the Niagara Falls Bridge, 1848–49*; Joshua Spencer to Charles Ellet, August 21, 1848, box 3, folder 127, EP-UM.

41. Theodore Hulett to Charles Ellet, August 10, 1848, box 3, folder 127, EP-UM.

42. Theodore G. Hulett and Jonathan Baldwin, "Niagara Falls Suspension Bridge Difficulties"; Theodore Hulett to Charles Ellet, August 14, 1848, box 3, folder 127; Theodore Hulett to Charles Ellet, August 15, 1848 (telegram), box 3, folder 127; all EP-UM.

43. *Buffalo Commercial Advertiser*, August 15, 1848, 2; *St. Catherine's Journal*, August 24, 1848, 2; Theodore Hulett to Charles Ellet, August 31, 1848, box 3, folder 127, EP-UM; Charles Ellet to W. O. Buchanan, September 3, 6, and 8, 1848, all in *Letters in Regard to the Niagara Falls Bridge, 1848–49*.

44. Charles Ellet to Baldwin and Hulett, September 26, 1848, and Charles Ellet to the Joint Board of the Niagara Suspension Bridge Companies, September 27, 1848, both in *Letters in Regard to the Niagara Falls Bridge, 1848–49*; Theodore Hulett to Charles Ellet, September 30, 1848, box 3, folder 128, EP-UM. Buchanan would subsequently confess that if he had nothing to do with "old Lot Clark there would never have been any difficulty." See Theodore Hulett to Charles Ellet, October 28, 1848, box 3, folder 129, EP-UM.

45. *Niagara Chronicle*, October 5, 1848, 2; Theodore Hulett to Charles Ellet, September 30, 1848, box 3, folder 128, EP-UM; *Buffalo Daily Courier*, October 2, 1848, 2; Theodore G. Hulett and Jonathan Baldwin, "Niagara Falls Suspension Bridge Difficulties."

46. *Niagara Mail*, October 4, 1848, 2.

47. Theodore Hulett to Charles Ellet, October 2, 1848, box 3, folder 129.

48. Charles Ellet to Mary Israel Ellet, October 16, 1848, box 3, folder 129, EP-UM; Charles Ellet to Theodore Hulett, October 3 and October 15, 1848, both in *Letters in Regard to the Niagara Falls Bridge, 1848–49*.

49. Theodore Hulett to Charles Ellet, October 17, 1848, box 3, folder 129; Theodore Hulett to Charles Ellet, October 7, 1848, box 3, folder 129; Charles Ellet to Ellie Ellet, December 18, 1848, box 3, folder 131; all EP-UM.

50. Articles of Agreement between the Niagara Falls International Bridge Company and the Niagara Falls Suspension Bridge Company and Charles Ellet, December 27, 1848, box 3, folder 131, EP-UM; *Republic* (Buffalo), December 28, 1848, 2; Ellie Ellet to Mary Israel Ellet, September 12, 1848, box 3, folder 128; Ellie Ellet to Charles Ellet, January 29, 1849, box 3, folder 132; both in EP-UM.

51. Charles Ellet to Amos Tryon, August 30, 1848; Johnson to Charles Ellet, January 13, 1849; Charles Ellet to Ellie Ellet, January 16, 1849; all in *Letters in Regard to the Niagara Falls Bridge, 1848–49*; W. O. Buchanan to William Hamilton Merritt, January 18, 1849, microfilm reel C-7063, MP. Also see *St. Catherine's Journal*, September 21, 1848, 2; *Niagara Chronicle*, December 21, 1848, 2; *St. Louis Daily New Era*, October 17, 1848, 2; Charles Ellet to John Krum, October 23, 1848, box 3, folder 129, EP-UM.

52. Cincinnati Bridge Committee to Charles Ellet, December 5, 1848, box 3, folder 131; William Johnson to Charles Ellet, January 20, 1848, box 3, folder 132, EP-UM; Charles Ellet, *Letter on the Proposed Bridge across the Ohio River at Cincinnati* (Columbus: J. H. Riley, 1849); Lot Clark to J. C. Wright, March 20, 1849, box 3, folder 134; William Johnson to Charles Ellet, May 5, 1849, box 3, folder 136, both EP-UM.

53. Charles Ellet to Charles A. Withers, April 16, 1849, in *Letters in Regard to the Niagara Falls Bridge, 1848–49*.

54. Lewis, *Charles Ellet, Jr., 1810–1862*, 134.

55. Sayenga, *Ellet and Roebling*, 30–31; see *Remarks Touching the Wheeling Bridge Suite, Addressed to the Hon. G. W. Thompson* (Philadelphia: John Clark, 1852), 20.

56. See Chester G. Hearn, *Ellet's Brigade: The Strangest Outfit of Them All* (Baton Rouge: Louisiana State University Press, 2000); JAR, *Report of John A. Roebling, Civil Engineer, to the President and Board of Directors of the Covington and Cincinnati Bridge*, 51. In a strange historical twist,

during the first winter of the Civil War, Washington was marching south through Maryland when his company stopped at Tenleytown to bed down for the night. In searching for a place to sleep, Washington found himself entangled in a fence and his blanket caught in a wire splice. The splice looked familiar and yet different from the ones his father used. Eventually, Washington realized he'd seen the splice on the Wheeling Bridge during a visit in 1858, and that they were camped on Ellet's farm. He called at the house the following morning but found Ellet "had gone to the wars." See *WRF*, 98–99.

57. Lewis, *Charles Ellet, Jr.*, 107.

58. *Regenerator* (New York), April 1, 1849, 2; Stamp, *Bridging the Border*, 18.

59. Charles B. Stuart, *Lives and Works of Civil and Military Engineers of America* (New York: Van Nostrand, 1871), 257, 283.

60. JAR to James Archbald, September 12, 1848, JAP-LHS.

61. *Niagara Mail*, February 7, 1849, 2; JAR to Charles Swan, April 21, 1849, in JR-CS. Hulett and Baldwin informed Ellet of John's appointment on January 14, 1849. See Hulett and Baldwin to Charles Ellet, January 14, 1849, box 3, folder 132, EP-UM.

62. JAR, "The Great Central Railroad from Philadelphia to St. Louis," 1; JAR, *Report of John A. Roebling, Civil Engineer, to the President and Board of Directors of the Covington and Cincinnati Bridge Company*, 85–86. Simply and clearly, John affirmed Daniel Walker Howe's recent claim that the Age of Jackson was better defined by a communications revolution than by the idea of a market revolution or as a reflection of a single man (Old Hickory). See Howe, *What Hath God Wrought*.

63. Walt Whitman, "Passage to India," in *Walt Whitman: Poetry and Prose*, ed. Justin Kaplan (New York: Library of America, 1996), 531–32. Also see Raymond H. Merritt, *Engineering in American Society, 1850–1875* (Lexington: University of Kentucky Press, 1968), 110–35.

64. *Report of JAR, Civil Engineer, to the President and Board of Directors of the Covington and Cincinnati Bridge Company*, 22, 85; JAR, "The Great Central Railroad from Philadelphia to St. Louis," 1–2.

65. JAR, "The Great Central Railroad from Philadelphia to St. Louis," 8–10.

66. JAR, "Transatlantic Telegraph," *Journal of Commerce*, April 20, 1850, 1–2; Walt Whitman, "The Moral Effect of the Cable," *Brooklyn Daily Times*, August 20, 1858, 2.

67. Alonzo Jackman's "A Grand Submarine and Overland Magnetic Telegraph" (1846), reprinted in the *Telegraphic Journal and Electrical Review*, December 13, 1899, 677–78; JAR, "Transatlantic Telegraph," 1; John Steele Gordon, *A Thread across the Ocean: The Heroic Story of the Transatlantic Cable* (New York: HarperCollins, 2002), 9–11. The normally reliably supportive and forward-looking *Railroad Journal* took issue with John's plan. "We now go to Europe in ten days in steam ships. This is short time enough in all conscience; as far as our telegraphs are concerned, let us stick to dry land," they sniffed in conclusion. See *American Railroad Journal*, May 25, 1850, 326.

68. JAR, "A National University for Practical Science," *Appletons Mechanics' Magazine and Engineers' Journal* 2, no. 5 (May 1852), 117.

69. Calhoun, *The American Civil Engineer*, 45–47; JAR, "A National University for Practical Science," 117.

70. JAR, "A National University for Practical Science," 117.

71. Ibid.

72. *American Railroad Journal*, July 17, 1852, 459; Frank Griggs, "General Edward W. Serrell," *Structure Magazine* (February 2012), 34–36.

73. *Hackstaff's New Guide Book of Niagara Falls* (Niagara Falls, NY: W. E. Tunis, 1853), 28.

74. See Edward Wellman Serrell, "Lewiston and Queenston Suspension Bridge," *Appletons Mechanics' Magazine and Engineers' Journal* 2, no. 6 (1852), 137–38, 68, 216; Seibel, *Bridges over the Niagara Gorge*, 87; Stamp, *Bridging the Border*, 30. In 1864, with ice floes choking the Niagara, a decision was made to unfasten a series of guy wires that had been added to the bridge in 1853 to provide more stability during excessive windstorms. Unfortunately, no one thought to reattach the wires afterward, and the roadway was almost entirely destroyed during a gale several weeks later. Remarkably, the wreckage stayed in place—neither fully abandoned nor rebuilt—until 1899, when the entire structure was finally dismantled. See *Niagara Falls*

Gazette, February 3, 1864, 2. For the "slippers" see "July 1852 Notes," box 4, notebook 142, RFP-RPI.

Chapter 15

1. *Report of John A. Roebling, Civil Engineer, to the President and Board of Directors of the Covington and Cincinnati Bridge Company,* 23; Samuel Smiles, *The Life of George Stephenson and of His Son Robert* (New York: Harper & Bros, 1868), 431–32; JAR, "The Great Central Railroad from Philadelphia to St. Louis," 1.

2. JAR, *Report of John A. Roebling, Civil Engineer, to the Directors of the Niagara Falls International Railroad Suspension Bridge Companies* (Buffalo, NY: Jewett, Thomas, 1852), 3–4.

3. William D. Middleton, *Landmarks on the Iron Road: Two Centuries of North American Railroad Engineering* (Bloomington: Indiana University Press, 1999), 12–19; JAR, *Final Report of John A. Roebling, Civil Engineer, to the Presidents and Directors of the Niagara Falls Suspension and Niagara Falls International Bridge Companies* (Rochester, NY: Lee, Mann, 1855), 3.

4. "Beaver Meadows R.R. Bridge," box 7, folder 4, RFP-RU; D. K. Minor to JAR, October 3, 1845, in LTJAR; "R.R. Bridge over the Connecticut River," box 7, folder 5, RFP-RU; "Suspension Bridges, December 1847," box 7, folder 7, RFP-RU; "Lackawaxen Bridge and Erie Railroad," box 50, folder 6, RFP-RPI; JAR to A. B. Morton, December 12, 1846, in "R.R. Bridge over the St. Lawrence," box 7, folder 5, RFP-RU.

5. According to Robert Vogel, "In scale and general arrangement [John's Genesee Bridge] almost exactly anticipated his Niagara railroad bridge that followed four years later." See *Guide to the Roebling Collection,* 127.

6. "Suspension Bridges, 1847," box 7, folder 9, RFP-RU.

7. *Report of the Commissioners Appointed to Inquire into the Use of Iron in Railway Structures* (1849), 340; James Sutherland, "Iron Railway Bridges," in *Robert Stephenson: The Eminent Engineer,* ed. Michael R. Bailey (Aldershot, UK: Ashgate, 2003), 303. Also see John H. Proud, *The Chronicle of the Stockton and Darlington Railway to 1863* (Hartlepool, UK: North Eastern Railway Association, 1998), and Chris Lloyd, "The World's First, and Worst, Railway Suspension Bridge," *Northern Echo,* February 7, 2015.

8. The same fate also visited Marc Seguin's two-span Saône Railway Bridge (1840), the only other attempt to design, build, and operate a railroad suspension bridge in Europe in the first half of the nineteenth century. Seguin's bridge was in use for only four years before it was replaced by a stone bridge. See Henry Grattan, *Bridge Engineering* (Chicago: H. Grattan, 1911), 217; Charles Bender, "Historical Sketch of the Successive Improvements in Suspension Bridges to the Present Time," 41.

9. Robert Stephenson, "Introductory Observations on the History of the Design" and "Minutes of Evidence and Reports on the Subject of the Britannia Bridge," House of Commons Select Committee on Railway Bills, May 5, 1845, both reprinted in Edwin Clark, *The Britannia and Conway Tube Bridges,* 2 vols. (London: Day & Son, 1850), 1:13–36 and 1:46–51. Also see Nathan Rosenberg and Walter G. Vincenti, *The Britannia Bridge: The Generation and Diffusion of Technological Knowledge* (Cambridge, MA: MIT Press, 1978).

10. Stephenson, "Introductory Observations on the History of the Design," 22–23; Clark, *The Britannia and Conway Tube Bridges,* 1:41.

11. Stephenson, "Introductory Observations on the History of the Design," 25–26; Robert Stephenson, "Report of Robert Stephenson, Chief Engineer, on a Railway Bridge across the Menai Strait, to the Directors of the Chester and Holyhead Railway," *Journal of the Franklin Institute* 11 (1846), 242. Also see "Minutes of Evidence and Reports on the Subject of the Britannia Bridge," House of Commons Select Committee on Railway Bills, May 5, 1845, reprinted in Clark, *The Britannia and Conway Tube Bridges,* 1:46–51.

12. *St. Catherine's Journal,* June 4, 1846, 2; Merritt, *Biography of the Honorable W. H. Merritt,* 406; "Railway Bridge at Niagara," *American Railroad Journal,* November 5, 1853, 717; JAR to Charles B. Stuart, January 7, 1847, reprinted in Stuart, *Lives and Works,* 306–8; JAR, *Report of John A. Roebling, Civil Engineer, to the Directors of the Niagara Falls International Railroad Suspension Bridge Companies,* 3.

13. The source of the anecdote seems to be a speech Welch made to the American Society of Civil Engineers at their annual conference on May 16, 1882, thirteen years after John's death. Welch was the sitting president of the organization. In part his speech read, "We are now so familiar with the success of suspension bridges for railroads, that we can hardly realize the almost universal disbelief in that success before they were tried. The late John A. Roebling told me before his bridge was finished, that Robert Stephenson had said to him, 'If your bridge succeeds, mine is a magnificent blunder.' And yet, unexpectedly to the best engineers in the world, the suspension bridge over the Niagara answers the purpose quite as well as the tubular bridge over the St. Lawrence." See Ashbel Welch, "Engineering: Past and Present," *Transactions of the American Society of Civil Engineering Magazine* 11 (1882), 155.

14. Henry Petroski, "Britannia Bridge," in *Pushing the Limits: New Adventures in Engineering* (New York: Alfred A. Knopf, 2004), 60–70; *Journal of the Franklin Institute* 49 (April 1850), 288; *American Railroad Journal*, January 13, 1849, 22; James Sutherland, "Iron Railway Bridges," 334. As Petroski also notes, there were significant design flaws in Stephenson's bridge, not least of which was building a 1,500-foot-long enclosed tube through which one expected to run a coal-burning steam engine. As became obvious almost immediately, conditions inside the tube were awful: both suffocatingly smoky and intensely hot.

15. As the influential *Engineer* editorialized in 1860: "It is our firm opinion that we are now on the eve of the adoption of trussed railway suspension bridges for wide spans. The continued success of the Niagara Bridge, which has now borne a heavy railway and highway traffic for five years, is a strong argument in favour of the system." "Railway Bridges," *Engineer*, March 9, 1860, 158–59. For other adherents, see, for example, "Railway Bridges," *Engineer*, March 23, 1860, 192; Benjamin Baker, *Long-Span Railway Bridges* (London: E. & F. N. Spon, 1867), 52; G. B. Airy, "On the Use of the Suspension Bridge with Stiffened Roadway, for Railway and Other Bridges of Great Span," *Proceedings of the Institution of Civil Engineers* 26 (1867), 258–64.

16. Stuart, *Lives and Works of Civil and Military Engineers of America*, 270.

17. See *Scientific American*, April 26, 1851, 250; Julius W. Adams, "The New Bridge over the Kentucky River on the Line of the Louisville and Lexington Railroad," *Engineer*, June 5, 1857, 454.

18. "Grand Trunk Railway of Canada—Victoria Bridge, Montreal," *Civil Engineer and Architect's Journal* 17 (1854), 211.

19. August Köstlin, "The Vienna-Junction Railroad Bridge over the Danube Canal," *Proceedings of the Institution of Civil Engineers* 88, no. 2 (1886), 470–71; "Combined Railway and Carriage Traffic Bridge across the Hooghly," *Building News and Architectural Review*, September 12, 1862, 202.

20. Middleton, *Landmarks on the Iron Road*, 20–34; Brian Soloman, *North American Railroad Bridges* (New York: Crestline, 2016), 28–48.

21. D. Mitchell to JAR, April 16, 1852, in "Steubenville Railroad Bridge 1852–5," box 6, folder 29, RFP-RPI.

22. JAR, "Specification of the Niagara Bridge," in "Niagara Bridge Specifications, 1847," box 37, folder 9, RFP-RPI.

23. "Niagara Bridge, Specifications, 1847," box 5, folder 31, RFP-RPI; JAR, "Specification of the Niagara Bridge," in "Niagara Bridge Specifications, 1847," box 37, folder 9, RFP-RPI.

24. "Niagara Bridge Estimates, 1847," box 7, notebook 109, RFP-RPI. After failing to secure the Niagara contract, John drew up plans for an enormous pedestrian bridge right at the falls itself: a 110-foot central pier made of cast iron tubes, erected in the middle of Goat Island, flanked by two thousand-foot spans, each with a six-foot-wide walkway. John even drew up detailed plans about how to use a balloon to get the first wire across. There is no evidence anyone commissioned or even requested such a plan. It may be that John was simply casting about for ways to still "inscribe [his] name on the Rocks of Niagara Falls." See "Niagara Bridge, Estimate, 1847."

25. JAR to Lot Clark, September 5, 1848, in "Niagara Foot Bridge, 1848," box 7, notebook 110, RFP-RPI.

26. "Niagara Bridge, October 1848," box 6, folder 42, RFP-RU.

27. JAR to Lot Clark, October 13, 1848, in "Niagara Bridge, October 1848," box 6, folder 42, RFP-RU.

28. JAR to Lot Clark, November 27, 1848, in "Niagara Bridge, October 1848," box 6, folder 42, RFP-RU.

29. "Visit to Falls, April 16th–18th 1849," in "Niagara Bridge, October 1848," box 6, folder 42, RFP-RU.

30. By the end of the year, the *New York Tribune* was reporting—incorrectly, of course—that John was to "enlarge and improve" Ellet's bridge "in such a manner as to render it fit and proper for the passage of railroad cars." See *New York Tribune*, December 14, 1850, 4.

31. "JAR to the President and Directors of the Niagara Falls International Suspension Bridge Company, June 20, 1850," in "Suspension Bridges, December 1847," box 7, folder 7, RFP-RU; "Notes on Various Bridges," box 7, notebook 122, RFP-RPI; JAR to W. Hamilton Merritt and Lot Clark, May 25, 1852, in "Niagara Bridge, July 1851/June 1852," box 6, folder 43, RFP-RU; *Niagara Falls Iris*, June 26, 1852, 2.

32. JAR to the Board of Directors, June 26, 1852, in "Niagara Bridge, Wire," box 7, notebook 111, RFP-RPI.

33. *Report of John A. Roebling, Civil Engineer, to the Directors of the Niagara Falls International Railroad Suspension Bridge Companies*, 3–5.

34. Ibid., 6–9.

35. Ibid., 7, 10.

36. Ibid., 12.

37. Nikolaus Pevsner and S. Lang, "The Egyptian Revival," *Architectural Review* 119 (May 1956), 242–54; Richard G. Carrott, *The Egyptian Revival: Its Sources, Monuments, and Meaning, 1808–1858* (Berkeley: University of California Press, 1978), 47–57.

38. "Niagara Railway Suspension Bridge—Notes and Sketches," box 5, folder 33, RFP-RPI; "Niagara Bridge, October 1848," box 6, folder 42, RFP-RU; "Niagara Railroad Bridge—Notes and Sketches—Towers, ca. 1852," box 6, folder 45, RFP-RU; JAR to the Board of Directors, June 26, 1852, in "Niagara Bridge, Wire," box 7, notebook 111, RFP-RPI; "Niagara Superstructure," box 50, folder 8, and "Niagara Bridge," box 37, folder 5, both RFP-RPI.

39. A. J. Downing, *Cottage Residences* (New York: Wiley & Putnam, 1847), 11.

40. Carrott, *The Egyptian Revival*, 102–5; E. Trotman, "On the Extent to Which the Elementary Forms of Classic Architecture Are, from Their Nature and Origin, Fixed or Arbitrary," *Architectural Magazine and Journal* 1 (1834), 20; W. J. Short, "A Design for a Termination for a Railway," *Architectural Magazine* 3 (May 1836), 220–21; "Suspension Bridges," *Penny Magazine*, May 31, 1832, 84.

41. *St. Catherine's Journal*, June 16, 1853, 2.

42. See David E. Nye, *American Technological Sublime* (Cambridge, MA: MIT Press, 1994), 78; McKinsey, *Niagara Falls*, 57–65; William Irvin, *The New Niagara: Tourism, Technology, and the Landscape of Niagara Falls, 1776–1917* (University Park: Pennsylvania State University Press, 1996), 38.

43. "Notes and Monies Due, 1852–54," box 24, notebook 28, RFP-RPI; "Directory, 1854–55," box 2, notebook 18, RFP-RPI; JAR to Charles Swan, July 27, July 29, August 18, August 31, 1852, all in JR-CS; *St. Catherine's Journal*, August 12, 1852, 2; "Niagara," *Harper's New Monthly Magazine* 7, no. 39 (1853), 302.

44. *St. Catherine's Journal*, October 27, 1853, 2; JAR, *Final Report*, 16–20; WAR, "Niagara Railway Suspension Bridge—History," box 14, folder 39, RFP-RPI.

45. *St. Catherine's Journal*, June 16, 1853, 2; *Boston Morning Journal*, November 18, 1852, 2; *Lockport Journal*, December 10, 1852, 2.

46. JAR to Charles Swan, January 24, 1853, in JR-CS.

47. JAR to Charles Swan, December 9, 1853; December 21, 1853; December 29, 1853; December 30, 1853; January 6, 1854; and February 3, 1854, all JR-CS; "Will of JAR, 1867," box 8, folder 30, RFP-RU.

48. "Ledger August to October 1853," box 7, notebook 126, RFP-RPI.

49. JAR to Samuel Backus, January 27, 1854; Johanna Roebling to WAR, June 7, 1858; Ferdinand Roebling to WAR, October 13, 1858, all in SRL; Ferdinand Roebling to JAR, January 5, 1859, in "JAR, Letters Received 1827–1869," . (box 2, folder 6, RFP-RU.

50. JAR to Charles Swan, June 9, 1854, in JR-CS.
51. JAR, "Stationary Power & Inclined Planes against Locomotive Power & Steep Grades," *American Railroad Journal*, May 27, 1854, 232–34; JAR, "Hints on the New Steam Frigates for the United States," *Scientific American*, June 10, 1854, 310; JAR, "On Marine Boilers," *Scientific American*, June 17, 1854, 318.
52. *Niagara Falls Gazette*, May 24, 1854, 2; Marcus Adams, "Diary, May 20, 1854 to October 13, 1859," NFC.
53. *Niagara Mail*, March 11, 1854, 2; *Democracy* (Buffalo), October 13, 1854, 2; JAR to Charles Swan, October 12, 1854, in JR-CS; JAR, *Final Report*, 37.
54. *Wheeling Intelligencer*, May 18, 1854, 2. The *Intelligencer's* report was reprinted all over the United States, from Boston to New York to Richmond to New Orleans, and almost every place in between. Up by John, it was reprinted in the Buffalo *Democracy*, the *Niagara Falls Gazette*, and the *Niagara Mail*.
55. *Wheeling Intelligencer*, May 18, 1854, 2, and May 22, 1854, 2.
56. JAR, *Final Report*, 7.
57. JAR to Charles Swan, May 20 and 21, 1854, all in JR-CS.
58. JAR to Charles Swan, June 8, 1854, in JR-CS.
59. "Notes on Suspension Bridges," box 7, notebook 120, RFP-RPI; *Wheeling Intelligencer*, May 23, 1854, 2; JAR, *Final Report*, 7.
60. Lewis, "The Wheeling Suspension Bridge," 225–27; "Charles Ellet, Jr. and the Wheeling Suspension Bridge," 24–25. Perhaps most blatantly, Tadaki Kawada recently claimed that "since the reconstructed suspension bridge embodies the Roebling style," it must have been rebuilt by John. See Tadaki Kawada, *History of the Modern Suspension Bridge: Solving the Dilemma between Economy and Stiffness*, trans. Harukazu Ohasi, ed. Richard Scott (Reston, VA: ASCE, 2010), 94.
61. *Democracy* (Buffalo), May 25, 1854, 2.
62. *Niagara Falls Gazette*, May 31, 1854, 2.
63. John went on to borrow the piano wire analogy in his final report on the Niagara Bridge. "As another very remarkable case of great durability, under the most severe exposure," he wrote, "we may refer to the wire strings of a piano, which are kept at a high tension, and in that state exposed to an almost incalculable amount of vibration." See Roebling, *Final Report*, 30.
64. *Democracy* (Buffalo), June 8, 1854, 2; *Niagara Falls Gazette*, June 7, 14, and 21, 1854, 2. Writing in the *Railroad Record*, Edward Serrell again came to John (and the *Gazette's*) aid: "The most learned men in the world on these subjects might be cited in opposition to those who argue for the 'inherent defects of iron'—Sir I. Brunel, before a Parliamentary Committee and Royal Commission, gave it as his experience that vibrations did not impair the strength of wrought iron." See *Niagara Falls Gazette*, July 26, 1854, 2.
65. John Locke, *An Essay Concerning Human Understanding* (New York: Prometheus, 1995), 549.
66. Sanford B. Hunt, "Editorial: Cholera," *Buffalo Medical Journal* 10 (1855), 180–83; *Evening Post* (Buffalo), July 25, 1854, 2.
67. Frank H. Hamilton, "The Asiatic Cholera, as It Appeared at the Suspension Bridge, Niagara County, NY in July 1854, and Its Lessons; What We Know of the Cholera," *Transactions of the New York Academy of Medicine* 5 (1886), 22. Marcus Adams, "Diary, May 20, 1854 to October 13, 1859," NFC; *Democracy* (Buffalo), July 26, 1854, 2; *Covington Journal*, July 29, 1854, 2.
68. W. Reid Clanny, *Hyperanthraxis; Or, the Cholera of Sunderland* (London: Whittaker, Treacher & Arnott, 1832), 25; Edward H. Dixon, *Scenes in the Practice of a New York Surgeon* (New York: DeWitt & Davenport, 1855), 15; *Niagara Falls Gazette*, July 26, 1854, 2.
69. "History of the Origin, Progress, and Mortality of the Cholera Morbus," *London Medical Gazette* 9 (1849), 557.
70. Adams, "Diary, May 20, 1854 to October 13, 1859"; Hamilton, "The Asiatic Cholera, as It Appeared at the Suspension Bridge," 26–29; *Democracy* (Buffalo), July 26, 1854, 2; *Niagara Falls Gazette*, July 26, 1854, 2; *Niagara Mail*, July 26, 1854; Rosenberg, *The Cholera Years*, 7.
71. Rosenberg, *The Cholera Years*, 42–43, 137. As Charles Rosenberg observed, "That the Irish suffered severely from cholera was but additional testimony to their ignorance, their habitual filth and drunkenness."

72. Steven Johnson, *The Ghost Map: The Story of London's Most Terrifying Epidemic—and How It Changed Science, Cities, and the Modern World* (New York: Riverhead, 2006), 36–40; Hamilton, "The Asiatic Cholera, as It Appeared at the Suspension Bridge," 26.

73. Sanford B. Hunt, "Soil Drainage and Atmospheric Humidity," *Public Health Reports and Papers, Presented at the Meeting of the American Public Health Association*, 2 vols. (New York: Hurd & Houghton, 1876), 2:357–60; Marcus Adams, "Diary, May 20, 1854 to October 13, 1859."

74. Hamilton, "The Asiatic Cholera, as It Appeared at the Suspension Bridge," 32.

75. *Buffalo Evening Post*, July 28, 1854, 2; *Niagara Falls Gazette*, July 26, 1854, 2; *Niagara Mail*, July 26, 1854, 2. Later, while working in Cincinnati, John also made notes about a "mineral lemonade" he had heard about as "French treatment of cholera." The recipe was a thousand grams of water, 150 grams of simple (or raspberry) syrup, and four grams of sulfuric acid. "Makes a pleasant drink," John wrote somewhat improbably, one that "arrests the alvine evacuations, raises the pulse & the nervous system, warms the skin & gives the feeling warmth & health." See "Covington and Cincinnati Bridge, 1864," box 7, notebook 133, RFP-RPI.

76. Hamilton, "The Asiatic Cholera, as It Appeared at the Suspension Bridge," 23–26.

77. JAR to Charles Swan, July 19, 1854, JR-CS; *WRF*, 153.

78. Johnson, *The Ghost Map*, 45.

79. *Newark Advertiser*, July 31, 1869, 2.

80. JAR to Charles Swan, August 31, 1854, in JR-CS; *WRF*, 151–53; Roebling, *Final Report*, 24, 29; *Salem Observer*, November 25, 1854, 2.

81. *Niagara Falls Gazette*, January 31, 1855, 2; "Niagara Bridges, Cables, 1852," box 7, notebook 113, RFP-RPI.

82. *WRF*, 153; Marcus Adams, September 4, 1854; "Diary, May 20, 1854 to October 13, 1859"; John N. Jackson and John Burtniak, *Railways in the Niagara Peninsula: Their Development, Progress, and Community Significance* (Bellevue, ON: Mika, 1978), 39–40; *St. Catherine's Journal*, November 3, 1853, 2; Seibel, *Bridges over the Niagara Gorge*, 32, 34; Ralph Greenhill, *Spanning Niagara: The International Bridges, 1848–1962* (Niagara, NY: Niagara University, 1984), 10–12; "Ledger 1853," box 4, notebook 141, RFP-RPI.

83. *Niagara Falls Gazette*, March 7, 1855, 2.

84. JAR, "Passage of the First Locomotive over the Suspension Bridge over the Falls of Niagara," *Journal of the Franklin Institute*, April 1855, 233; "Niagara Railway Bridge—Circulars," box 6, folder 52, RFP-RU; *Niagara Falls Gazette*, 14, 1855, 2; "Niagara Bridges, Cables, 1852," box 7, notebook 113, RFP-RPI; Adams, "Diary, May 20, 1854 to October 13, 1859."

85. *Rochester Daily American*, March 9, 1855, 2.

86. Adams, "Diary, May 20, 1854 to October 13, 1859"; *Niagara Mail*, March 28, 1855, 2; *Republic* (Buffalo), March 10, 1855, 2.

87. *Western New-Yorker*, March 13, 1855, 2.

88. JAR, "Passage of the First Locomotive over the Suspension Bridge over the Falls of Niagara," 233; "Niagara Bridges, Cables, 1852," box 7, notebook 113, RFP-RPI; *Hamilton Gazette*, March 12, 1855, 2; Roebling, *Final Report*, 6; Adams, "Diary, May 20, 1854 to October 13, 1859"; *Rochester Daily Democrat*, March 12, 1855, 2.

89. *Rochester Daily Democrat*, March 12, 1855; *Salem Observer*, March 17, 1855, 2; *Niagara Falls Gazette*, March 14, 1855, 2.

90. *Morning Express* (Buffalo), March 10, 1855, 2; *Hamilton Gazette*, March 12, 1855, 2; *St. Catherine's Journal*, March 15, 1855, 2; "Railway-Engineering in the United States," *Atlantic Monthly* 2, no. 13 (1858), 641. Also see "The Niagara Suspension Bridge," *Journal of Education of Upper Canada* 8, no. 10 (October 1855), 146.

91. Roebling, *Final Report*, 5, 10–11, 36.

92. "Grand Trunk Railway of Canada—Victoria Bridge, Montreal," *Civil Engineer and Architect's Journal* 17 (1854), 211.

93. Robert Stephenson, "Report on Victoria Bridge," in *Grand Trunk Railway of Canada. Victoria Bridge: Correspondence and Reports* (London: William Clowes, 1856), 24–27.

94. Ibid.

95. Ibid.; John Rapley, *The Britannia and Other Tubular Bridges* (Charleston, SC: Tempus, 2003), 138; R. S. Buck, "The Niagara Railroad Arch," *Transactions of the American Society of Civil Engineers* 40 (1898), 126–27.

96. "Niagara Bridges, Cables, 1852," box 7, notebook 113, RFP-RPI; JAR to Charles Swan, March 20, 1855, JR-CS; *Buffalo Evening Post*, March 20, 1855, 2; *Niagara Falls Gazette*, March 21, 1855, 2; *Rochester Daily Democrat*, May 3, 1855.

97. Roebling, *Final Report*, 5–6; JAR to Charles Swan, March 20 and 23, 1855, JR-CS.

98. Roebling, *Final Report*, 4, 43.

99. "Niagara Bridges, Cables, 1852," box 7, notebook 113, RFP-RPI; JAR to Charles Swan, April 18 and 26, June 15, 1855, JR-CS; JAR, "Attempt to Sound the Niagara River," *Buffalo Democracy*, April 28, 1855, 2.

100. John Disturnell, *A Trip through the Lakes of North America* (New York: J. Disturnell, 1857), 213; John Disturnell, *The Great Lakes; Or, the Inland Seas* (New York: Charles Scribner, 1863), 152; Anthony Trollope, *North America* (New York: Harper & Brothers, 1862), 97; "The Niagara Suspension Bridge," *Journal of Education of Upper Canada* 8, no. 10 (October 1855), 146; *New York Daily Tribune*, August 21, 1855, 2; Nicholas A. Wood, *The Prince of Wales in Canada and the United States* (London: Bradbury & Evans, 1861), 236.

101. Mark Twain, "A Visit to Niagara," in *Sketches: Old and New* (Hartford, CT: American Publishing Company, 1875), 64; Charles Mackay, *Life and Liberty in America: Or, Sketches of a Tour in the United States and Canada, in 1857–8*, 2 vols. (London: Smith, Elder, 1859), 1:93; Charles C. Woodman, *Arguments in Favor of a Marine Railway around the Falls of Niagara* (Washington, DC: n.p., 1865), 1.

102. George W. Holley, *Niagara: Its History, Geology, Incidents and Poetry* (New York: Sheldon, 1872), 138; Walt Whitman, "Seeing Niagara to Advantage," in *Specimen Days and Collect* (Glasgow: Wilson & McCormick, 1883), 160; Henry James, "Niagara," in *Portraits of Places* (London: Macmillan, 1883), 365–66.

103. McKinsey, *Niagara Falls*, 253–54.

104. W. D. Howells, *Their Wedding Journey* (Boston: James R. Osgood, 1875), 134–37.

105. *Niagara Falls Gazette*, July 17, 1876; G. Linnæus Banks, ed., *Blondin: His Life and Performances* (London: Routledge, Warne, & Routledge, 1862), 33–40.

106. *Diary*, 116.

107. "The Fugitive Slave's Apostrophe to Niagara," *Boston Courier*, November 1, 1841, reprinted in Joseph Tinker Buckingham, *Personal Memoirs and Recollections of an Editorial Life*, 2 vols. (Boston: Ticknor, Reed, & Fields, 1852), 2:192–94; Eber M. Pettit, *Sketches in the History of the Underground Railroad* (Fredonia, NY: W. McKinstry & Son, 1879), 116–17; *Niagara Falls Gazette*, September 22, 1858, 2, and June 13, 1860, 2.

108. William Still, *The Underground Railroad: A Record of Facts, Authentic Narratives, Letters, &c, Narrating the Hardships, Hair-breadth Escapes and Death Struggles of the Slaves in Their Efforts for Freedom* (Philadelphia: People's Publishing, 1871), 76, 163, 222–23, 269, 323. Also see William Still, *Still's Underground Railroad Records, with a Life of the Author* (Philadelphia: William Still, 1886), 294, 490, 686.

109. Samuel Ringgold Ward, *Autobiography of a Fugitive Negro: His Anti-Slavery Labours in the United States, Canada, & England* (London: John Snow, 1855), 176–77.

110. Kate Clifford Larson, *Bound for the Promised Land: Harriet Tubman, Portrait of an American Hero* (New York: Ballantine, 2004), 94, 115; W. E. Abbott to Maria G. Porter, November 29, 1856, RL-UM; Milton C. Sernett, *North Star Country: Upstate New York and the Crusade for African American Freedom* (Syracuse, NY: Syracuse University Press, 2002), 191; William H. Siener and Thomas A. Chambers, "Harriet Tubman, the Underground Railroad and the Bridges at Niagara Falls," *Afro-Americans in New York Life and History* 36 (2012), 40.

111. Sarah H. Bradford, *Scenes in the Life of Harriet Tubman* (Auburn, NY: W. J. Moses, 1869), 32. Also see Sarah H. Bradford, *Harriet Tubman: The Moses of Her People* (New York: George Lockwood, 1897), 48.

112. Williams, *Horace Greeley*, 249–52; R. S. Burrows to JAR, December 21, 1861, box 2, folder 47, RFP-RU; George J. Ingersoll to Thomas V. Welsh, December 17, 1900, NFC.

113. "The Niagara Suspension Bridge," *Engineer*, September 23, 1859, 225.

114. *Buffalo Morning Express*, March 14, 1857, 2.

115. *Buffalo Morning Express*, March 19, 1857, 2.

116. *Buffalo Republic*, March 26, 1857, 2; *Niagara Falls Gazette*, March 25 and September 3, 1857; *Buffalo Morning Express*, March 25, 1857, 2.

117. "Iron Bridges," *Quarterly Review* (London) 104, no. 207 (July 1858), 49; *Niagara Falls Gazette*, September 22, 1858, 2; *New York Herald*, August 5, 1859, 3, and August 23, 1859, 4; *American Railway Times*, August 13, 1859, 33; *Buffalo Daily Courier*, August 19, 1859, 3. See JAR to the editor of the *Commercial Journal*, August 6, 1859, in "Niagara Correspondence," box 5, folder 30. RFP-RPI.

118. JAR, *Report of John A. Roebling, Civil Engineer, to the Presidents and Directors of the Niagara Falls Suspension and Niagara Falls International Bridge Companies on the Condition of the Niagara Railway Suspension Bridge* (Trenton, NJ: Murphy & Bechtel, 1860), 6, 20. The British engineer Peter Barlow conducted a review of John's bridge for the British Society of Civil Engineers the same year, concluding that the span was "the safest and most durable railway bridge of long-span which has been constructed." See Peter W. Barlow, "Observations on the Niagara Bridge," *Journal of the Franklin Institute* 71 (1861), 16–22, 89–93, and 160–65.

119. Barlow, "Observations on the Niagara Bridge," 7–10; Sayenga, "Cement Shoes," 20–24, 28, 30–31; 8–10, 12, 14–15; 18, 20–22, 24, 26, 28, 30.

120. In a discussion centered on this exact problem at the America Society of Civil Engineers in 1893, Gustave Bouscaren noted that in 1876 the anchorages of John's unfinished Kentucky River Bridge were unearthed and examined and "were found in a perfect state of preservation, not a spot of rust being apparent on the bars." These chains of course had never been attached to any cables and thus never been subject to the vibratory forces they would be subject to in a live bridge. They had just sat there sealed, subject to no forces at all. See "Restoration of the Cable Ends of the Covington and Cincinnati Suspension Bridge: Discussion," *Transactions of the American Society of Civil Engineers* 28 (1893), 371.

121. Sayenga, "Cement Shoes," 22–24; "Angers: La Catastrophe du Pont Basse-Chaîne," https://www.musee-du-genie-angers.fr/doc-fiche-17.pdf, accessed January 8, 2016; Peters, *Transitions in Engineering*, 169.

122. M. M. Dupuit, Mery de Contades, et al, "Rapport de la commission d'enquête pour rechercher les causes et les circonstances qui ont amené la chute du pont suspendu de la Basse-Chaîne," *Annales des Ponts et Chaussées* (1850), 394–411; WRF, 165.

123. Sayenga, "Cement Shoes," 10.

124. "Niagara Suspension Bridge," *Engineering* (London), August 5, 1881, 129; Leffert Lefferts Buck, *Report on the Renewal of Niagara Suspension Bridge* (New York: C. W. Ames, 1881), 11–12. Despite the seriousness of the rust in the anchorages, the team of engineers found no evidence of oxidation "in the main cables between the towers." In addition, "careful tests . . . proved conclusively that the wire has lost none of its original strength from the strains to which it has been subjected" and that "there is no reason to believe that bridge is now less capable of carrying the usual trains or the test load which was at first imposed upon it." See "The Niagara Railway Suspension Bridge," *Scientific American*, April 21, 1877, 249.

125. "Niagara Suspension Bridge," *Engineering* (London), August 5, 1881, 129; Buck, *Report on the Renewal of Niagara Suspension Bridge*, 34; L. L. Buck, "Replacing the Stone Towers of the Niagara Railway Suspension Bridge, with Iron Towers," *Transactions of the American Society of Civil Engineers* 17 (1887), 207; *Niagara Falls Gazette*, May 12, 1886, 2. On Buck, see Frank Griggs, "Leffert Lefferts Buck," *Structure Magazine* (December 2010).

126. "Leffert Lefferts Buck," *Engineering Record*, December 26, 1903, 819. Also see "Memoir of Leffert Lefferts Buck," *Transactions of the American Society of Civil Engineers* 73 (1911), 495.

127. Seibel, *Bridges over the Niagara Gorge*, 49–51; *Niagara Falls Gazette*, April 13, 1896, 2; WRF, 155.

128. Irwin, *The New Niagara*, 49; Stephen Buonopane, "The Roeblings and the Stayed Suspension Bridge: Its DevelopmentDevelopment and Propagation in 19th-Century United States," in *Proceeding of the Second International Congress on Construction History* (Exeter, UK: Short Run, 2006), 441–60. On the Niagara's impact, see for example R. S. Buck, "The Niagara Railroad Arch," *Transactions of the American Society of Civil Engineers* 40 (1898), 126–27; Alfred Pugsley, *The Theory of Suspension Bridges* (Bath, UK: Pittman, 1957), 4–6; Kirti Gandhi, "Roebling's Railway Suspension Bridge over Niagara Gorge," in *Fifth International Cable-Supported Bridge Operators' Conference* (London: British Engineering Association, 2006), 1–27; Andreas Kahlow, "Different Manners of Constructing in Different

Contexts: Roebling's Niagara Bridge and Gerber's Cantilever Beam," *Proceedings of the Third International Congress on Construction History* (2009), 869–78, among many others.

Chapter 16

1. "Lackawaxen Bridge, NY & Erie Railroad, 1847–1848," box 50, folder 6, RFP-RPI; "Steubenville Railroad Bridge, 1854–1855," box 6, folder 29, RFP-RPI; "RR Bridges over the Miami and Wabash on the Ohio and Mississippi RR," box 7, folder 10, RFP-RU; "Niagara Bridge," box 7, folder 5, RFP-RU; "Niagara Bridge, 1847," box 7, folder 9, RFP-RU; "Notes 1856," box 7, notebook 129, RFP-RPI.

2. Even by the close of the 1850s there were only three railroad lines operating between the North and the South. As a point of comparison, the state of Ohio housed over ten different railroad lines. Christian Wolmar, *The Great Railroad Revolution: The History of Trains in America* (New York: Public Affairs, 2012), 51–60.

3. *Testimony before the Commission of the Cincinnati Southern Railway* (1878), 90; *American Railroad Journal*, September 9, 1854, 563.

4. "The Kentucky River Bridge," *Scientific American: Supplement*, October 27, 1877, 1503.

5. The best account of the Kentucky Bridge episode is Francis E. Griggs, Jr., "John A. Roebling and the Kentucky River Bridge," in Green, *John A. Roebling*. Also see the same author's "Kentucky River High Bridge," *Journal of Bridge Engineering* 7, no. 2 (March/April 2002), 73–84, and Howard Curry's *High Bridge: A Pictorial History* (Lexington, KY: Feedback, 1984).

6. JAR to G. C. Schaefer, April 10, 1851; December 3, 1851; and April 14, 1852, and JAR to Samuel DeVeaux, February 7, 1852, all in "Letter Copy Book, 1850–1857," box 25, item 42, RFP-RPI. The two Philadelphia bridges were the Girard Avenue and Chestnut Street bridges, for both of which he drew up several handsome designs. See "Girard Ave Bridge 1851," box 51, folder 2, RFP-RPI, and "Chestnut Street Bridge 1851," box 38, folder 5, RFP-RPI. The Girard Avenue Bridge was ultimately built as a three-span timber arched Howe truss bridge that lasted less than twenty years. The construction of the Chestnut Street Bridge was postponed for a decade before Strickland Kneass designed and built a two-span cast iron structure that was greatly admired across the engineering world.

7. JAR, "Report on the Suspension Rail Road Bridge over the Kentucky River" (1852), box 7, folder 15, RFP-RU.

8. "Kentucky River Bridge Drawings, 1853–55," box 6, folder 9; "Kentucky River Bridge Estimates, 1853–55," box 6, folder 10, both RFP-RPI.

9. JAR, "Report on the Suspension Rail Road Bridge over the Kentucky River" (1852).

10. JAR to Samuel DeVeaux, February 7, 1852, "Letter Copy Book, 1850–1857," box 25, itemitem 42, RFP-RPI; *Railroad Gazette*, December 22, 1899, 887.

11. Julius Adams to the Editor of *Engineering News*, January 17, 1883, in *Engineering News and American Contract Journal*, January 20, 1883, 25.

12. *WRF*, 155–56; JAR to Julius W. Adams, June 2, 1853, in "Kentucky River Bridge Estimates, 1853–55," box 6, folder 10, RFP-RPI; "Notes 1856," box 7, notebook 129, RFP-RPI.

13. JAR to Barkley, January 1, 1853, "Kentucky River Bridge Estimates, 1853–55," box 6, folder 10, RFP-RPI.

14. JAR to Charles Swan, January 24, 1853, JR-CS; "Ledger, 1853," box 4, notebook 151, RFR-RPI; "Ledger 1853," box 4, notebook 141, RFP-RPI; *WRF*, 155–56.

15. JAR to Charles Swan, July 18, 1854, JR-CS; *Kentucky Statesman*, November 24, 1854, 3; *American Railroad Journal*, January 31, 1857, 72; *WRF*, 156.

16. *American Railroad Journal*, June 14, 1856, 377; JAR to Charles Swan, October 23, 1853; August 19, 1854; August 31, 1854; December 2, 1854, all in JR-CS; *Kentucky Statesman*, August 21, 1855, 3; *Annual Report of the President and Directors to the Stockholders of the Lexington and Danville Railroad Company* (Lexington: Kentucky Statesmen, 1855), 18–21.

17. *American Railroad Journal*, September 26, 1857, 617; *Scientific American*, September 15, 1860, 183; "Kentucky River Bridge Estimates, 1853–55," box 6, folder 10, RFP-RPI; JAR, *Report of John A. Roebling, Civil Engineer, on the Condition of the Niagara Railway Suspension Bridge*, 6; JAR to Kentucky Bridge Board President, October 16, 1858, "Kentucky River Bridge Estimates," box 6, folder 10, RFP-RPI.

18. *American Railroad Journal*, November 6, 1858, 717; JAR to Charles Swan, November 19 and 20, 1858, both in JR-CS; *WRF*, 156; A. G. Gower to JAR, December 2, 1860, box 2, folder 23, RFP-RU.

19. WAR, "Notes on the Kentucky River Suspension Bridge" (1863), box 38, folder 2, RFP-RPI; WAR to CS, August 12, 1863, box 30, folder 46, RFP-RU; JAR, "Kentucky River Bridge," box 51, folder 4, RFP-RPI.

20. *Lexington Press*, January 21, 1874, 1; Griggs, "Kentucky River High Bridge," 75; William A. Gunn, "Surveys for the Cincinnati Southern Railroad," in *Preliminary Report of the Chief Engineer*, 26; "A Historic Bridge," *Engineering Record*, July 9, 1898, 114–15; "The Kentucky River Bridge," *Scientific American: Supplement*, October 27, 1877, 1503–4; *WRF*, 156.

21. *WRF*, 156; "Iowa Land Lots," box 1, folder 16, RFP-RPI; "Ledger, 1853," box 4, notebook 151, RFR-RPI; JAR to Charles Swan, June 15, 1855, JAR-CS.

22. Dorothy Schwieder, "Iowa: The Middle Land," in *Iowa History Reader*, ed. Marvin Bergman (Iowa City: University of Iowa Press, 1996), 4; Leland L. Sage, *A History of Iowa* (Ames: Iowa State University Press, 1974), 92–93; William Fischer to Christoph Heinrich Ficke, August 27, 1851, reprinted in Zachary Michael Jack, ed., *Iowa: The Definitive Collection* (North Liberty, IA: Tall Corn, 2009), 29.

23. David Hudson, Marvin Bergman, and Loren Horton, eds., *The Biographical Dictionary of Iowa* (Iowa City: University of Iowa Press, 2008), 89–90; Sage, *A History of Iowa*, 132; Schwieder, *Iowa*, 72; Robert R. Dykstra, *Bright Radical Star: Black Freedom and White Supremacy on the Hawkeye Frontier* (Cambridge, MA: Harvard University Press, 1993), 137.

24. "Real Estate Listings, Waterloo Courier," box 1, folder 19, RFP-RPI.

25. Ellsworth quoted in Allan G. Bogue, "Farming in the Prairie Peninsular, 1830–1890," in Bergman, *Iowa History Reader*, 61–62; William Fischer to Christoph Heinrich Ficke, August 27, 1851, in Jack, *Iowa*, 30; Frances D. Gage, "Sketches on Iowa" (1854), reprinted in N. Howe Parker, *Iowa As It Is in 1856: A Gazetteer for Citizens* (Chicago: Keen & Lee, 1856), 79–80. Also see Schwieder, "Iowa," 2–3.

26. Herbert Quick, *Vandemark's Folly* (Indianapolis: Bobbs-Merrill, 1922), 111–12; Dan E. Clark, "The Westward Movement in the Upper Mississippi Valley during the Fifties," *Proceedings of the Mississippi Valley Historical Association* 7 (1913–14), 216–19; Sage, *A History of Iowa*, 108–9.

27. *WRF*, 169, 199–200. For more on Gower see Benjamin F. Shambaugh, *Iowa City: A Contribution to the Early History of Iowa* (Iowa City: State Historical Society of Iowa, 1893), 86, and "Convention Member Robert Gower," Iowa Legislature website, https://www.legis.iowa.gov/legislators/constConvenMember?pid=17200&cc=true&yr=1857, accessed February 19, 2017.

28. "Iowa Lands, 1855–61," box 2, notebook 23, RFP-RPI; *WRF*, 170; Robert P. Swierenga, "Land Speculator 'Profits' Reconsidered: Central Iowa as a Test Case," *Journal of Economic History* 26, no. 1 (1966), 27. On land warrants see Robert P. Swierenga, *Pioneers and Profits: Land Speculation on the Iowa Frontier* (Ames: Iowa State University Press, 1968), 127–28.

29. *WRF*, 161–63.

30. Ibid., 171.

31. Ibid.; John Madson, "The Running Country," *Audubon Magazine* 74 (January 1972), 8, 17.

32. *WRF*, 170–71.

33. Ibid., 163–64, 167, 170.

34. JAR to WAR, October 14, 1861, box 10, folder 7, RFP-RPI; *WRF*, 171.

35. *Covington Journal*, February 25 and April 22, 1854, 2; "Suspension-Bridge for the Ohio," *The Plough, the Loom, and the Anvil*, April 1854, 610–13; David A. Simmons, "'Light, Aerial Structures of Modern Engineering': Early Suspension Bridges in the Ohio Valley," in Kemp, *Proceedings of an International Conference on Historic Bridges to Celebrate the 150th Anniversary of the Wheeling Suspension Bridge*, 76; *Covington Journal*, March 5, September 10, and November 19, 1853, 2–3; William Ferguson, *America by River and Rail: Notes by the Way on the New World and Its People* (London: James Nisbet, 1856), 280; "Covington and Newport," *Ballou's Pictorial Drawing-Room Companion*, December 20, 1856, 392; *Cincinnati Daily Commercial*, January 17, 1854, 2.

36. *Covington Journal*, January 21, 1854, 3; *Cincinnati Daily Commercial*, January 17 and 18, 1854, 2.

37. James T. Hogane, "Licking River Bridge," *Railroad Record*, February 2, 1854, 773–74.

38. *Covington Journal*, February 11, 1854, 3. The bridge was worked on multiple times over the next few years and only finally shorn up by Washington in 1867.

39. Johnson E. Polk, *A History of Kentucky and Kentuckians* (Chicago: Lewis, 1912), 622; Anthony J. Iaciofano, "Amos Shinkle and 'The Ohio Bridge,'" MS, Covington Public Library.

40. *WRF*, 199.

41. Harry R. Stevens, *The Ohio Bridge* (Cincinnati: Ruter, 1939), 63–64; *Report of John A. Roebling, Civil Engineer, to the President and Board of Directors of the Covington and Cincinnati Bridge Company*, 20–21.

42. *Charter and By-Laws of the Covington and Cincinnati Bridge Co.* (Covington, KY: Covington Journal, 1856), 8–9.

43. *Report of John A. Roebling, Civil Engineer, to the President and Board of Directors of the Covington and Cincinnati Bridge Company*, 16–17.

44. Stevens, *The Ohio Bridge*, 65–66; *Covington Journal*, March 15 and 29, 1856, both 2; *Journal of the House of Representatives of the State of Ohio* (Columbus: Statesman Steam Press, 1856), 53:392. The rebuilt and reopened Licking River Bridge seems to have also served runaway slaves, offering a route out of Covington—a veritable bottleneck for runaways—into the much less populous and much less surveilled Newport. See for example the *Cincinnati Gazette*, August 8, 1854, 2.

45. Mischa Honeck, *We Are the Revolutionist: German-Speaking Immigrants and American Abolitionists after 1848* (Athens: University of Georgia Press, 2011), 71–81; Steven Weisenburger, *Modern Medea: A Family Story of Slavery and Child-Murder from the Old South* (New York: Hill & Wang, 1998), 6–7, 74–75.

46. *National Anti-Slavery Standard*, April 12, 1856, 3.

47. *Covington Journal*, March 29, 1856, 2; *Report of John A. Roebling, Civil Engineer, to the President and Board of Directors of the Covington and Cincinnati Bridge Company*, 17.

48. *Covington Journal*, February 2, 9, 16, and 23, 1856, 2–3.

49. *Cincinnati Gazette*, May 3, 1856, 2; *Covington Journal*, May 31, 1856, 2; *Covington Journal*, July 4, 1856, 3; Stevens, *The Ohio Bridge*, 70.

50. Isabel Lucy Bird Bishop, *The Englishwoman in America* (London: John Murray, 1856), 117–18, 125; Charles Mackay, *Life and Liberty in America* (New York: Harper & Bros., 1859), 127–28.

51. Mackay, *Life and Liberty in America*, 126; Lakier, *A Russian Looks at America*, 147–48.

52. William Hancock, *An Emigrant's Five Years in the Free States of America* (London: T. Cautley Newby, 1860), 317; Lafcadio Hearn, "Levee Life" and "Pariah People," in *Lafcadio Hearn's America: Ethnographic Sketches and Editorials*, ed. Simon J. Bronner (Lexington: University of Kentucky Press, 2002), 37, 87–89; Mackay, *Life and Liberty in America*, 123; Bishop, *The Englishwoman in America*, 118; *Daily Columbian* (Cincinnati), September 1, 1856, 2.

53. *Report of John A. Roebling, Civil Engineer, to the President and Board of Directors of the Covington and Cincinnati Bridge*, 89–90. John ended up with two quite competent stonemasons: Gebhard, "a German," and John Mulloy, "an efficient drunken fighting Irishman." See *WRF*, 198.

54. *Report of John A. Roebling, Civil Engineer, to the President and Board of Directors of the Covington and Cincinnati Bridge Company*, 30–31; *Cincinnati Daily Enquirer*, September 30, 1856, 2.

55. *Daily Columbian* (Cincinnati), September 9, 1856, 2; *Covington Journal*, September 20, 1856, 3; *Cincinnati Daily Enquirer*, October 11, 1856, 2; *Report of John A. Roebling, Civil Engineer, to the President and Board of Directors of the Covington and Cincinnati Bridge Company*, 31; William E. Worthington, Jr., "John A. Roebling and the Cincinnati Bridge," in *Proceedings of the Fifth Historic Bridge Conference* (Cincinnati, OH: American Society of Civil Engineers, 1997), 14; JAR to Charles Swan, October 19, 1856, JR-CS.

56. *Daily Columbian* (Cincinnati), September 1, 5, and 9, 1856, 2; *Covington Journal*, September 13, 1856, 2; *Cincinnati Daily Commercial*, September 12, 1856, 2.

57. *Report of John A. Roebling, Civil Engineer, to the President and Board of Directors of the Covington and Cincinnati Bridge Company*, 32–36; Phillip D. Spiess, "The Industrial Archeology of

Cincinnati, Ohio: A Guide for S. I. A. Tourists" (1978), MS, CHL; WAR, "The Cincinnati Bridge," box 14, folder 8, RFP-RPI; *Cincinnati Daily Commercial*, November 8, 1856, 2.

58. *Cincinnati Daily Commercial*, December 20, 1856, 2; *Cincinnati Daily Enquirer*, February 6, 1857, 1; *Cincinnati Daily Commercial*, February 5, 1857, 2.

59. WRF, 173; *Daily Gazette* (Cincinnati), January 29, 31, and February 13, 1857, 2.

60. Richard Kesterman, "The Burnet House: A Grand Cincinnati Hotel," *Ohio Valley History* 12, no. 4 (2012), 60–68; Hancock, *An Emigrant's Five Years in the Free States of America*, 317; JAR to Charles Swan, May 19 and 25, 1857, in JR-CS. For a description of the ball see William Prescott Smith, *The Book of the Great Railway Celebrations of 1857* (New York: D. Appleton, 1858), 216.

61. *Cincinnati Daily Times*, May 30, 1857, 2; William Prescott Smith, *The Book of the Great Railway Celebrations of 1857*, 219–21; JAR to Charles Swan, May 31, 1857, in JR-CS.

62. JAR to Charles Swan, May 25, 28, and 31, 1857, in JR-CS; *Daily Missouri Republican* (St. Louis), June 4 and 6, 1857, 2–3.

63. *Covington Journal*, June 27, 1857, 2; *Cincinnati Daily Commercial*, July 27, 1857, 2; Kenneth M. Stampp, *America in 1857: A Nation on the Brink* (New York: Oxford University Press, 1990), 210; *Cincinnati Daily Enquirer*, June 3, 1857, 2; *Cincinnati Daily Commercial*, August 26 and 27, 1857, both 2; *Pittsburgh Gazette*, August 31, 1857, 2.

64. Stampp, *America in 1857*, 208, 221–27; James L. Huston, *The Panic of 1857 and the Coming of the Civil War* (Baton Rouge: Louisiana State University Press, 1987), 1–13; George W. Van Vleck, *The Panic of 1857: An Analytical Study* (New York: Columbia University Press, 1943), 53–58.

65. Huston, *The Panic of 1857*, 14–17.

66. JAR to Charles Swan, September 28; October n.d., 9, and 11, 1857, all in JAR-CS. John's concern for his workers was threefold. He wanted to keep a core of experienced, dependable staff to manage his rope works, and he seems to have felt genuine loyalty to those core workers. "I think it advisable to give our hands a long 4th July to enjoy themselves during the dog days," he wrote the following summer. Yet he also understood the potential for labor conflict resulting from the economic collapse. "Those inflammatory german meetings, lately held in Pha, with such exclamations: *fight or Bread*—indicate what may be expected next winter in these large cities," he wrote Swan on November 1. "We must economise as much as possible, but keep a *small force* at work, if it can be done at all." See JAR to Charles Swan, November 1, 1857, and July 2, 1858, both in JAR-CS.

67. JAR to Charles Swan, September 28, 1857, in JAR-CS.

68. Huston, *The Panic of 1857*, 23; JAR to Charles Swan, October 4, 1857, in JAR-CS; Eric Foner, *Free Soil, Free Labor, Free Men: The Ideology of the Republican Party before the Civil War* (New York: Oxford University Press, 1970), 36.

69. WRF, 173–74; JAR to Charles Swan, October 22, 1857, in JAR-CS; Stampp, *America in 1857*, 224.

70. Huston, *The Panic of 1857*, 24; JAR to Charles Swan, June 11 and October 25, 1858, in JAR-CS; *Covington Journal*, April 17, 1858, 2 and 3.

71. *Annual Report of the Covington and Cincinnati Bridge Company* (Covington, KY: Munger & Croninger, 1859), 1–3, 6–10; *Covington Journal*, October 31, 1858, 2; Henry Bruce to JAR, March 11, 1859, in "Cincinnati & Covington Bridge Correspondence," box 5, folder 8, RFP-RPI; JAR to Charles Swan, May 7, 1859, in JR-CS; *Cincinnati Times*, February 11, 1860, 2; *Covington Journal*, February 18, 1860, 2; *Covington Journal*, March 10, 1860, 2.

72. Baldwin, *Pittsburgh*, 205; Elizur Wright, Jr., to Susan Clark, December 12, 1828, box 1, Elizur Wright Papers, Manuscript Division, LOC; on "cutting" incidents see *Pittsburgh Post*, August 25, 26, and 27, 1857, 2; Charles W. Dahlinger, "Old Allegheny," *Western Pennsylvania Historical Society Magazine* 1, no. 4 (1918), 205; Three Sister Bridges, HAER Report No. PA-490-A, LOC, http://cdn.loc.gov/master/pnp/habshaer/pa/pa3600/pa3659/data/pa3659data.pdf, accessed June 11, 2017; *Pittsburgh Chronicle*, August 9, 1845, 2.

73. William Roseburg, treasurer of the bridge company, was predicting profits of $25,000 per annum just five months after John had opened the bridge. William Roseburg to JAR, September 14, 1860, box 2, folder 16, RFP-RU.

74. *Engineering News*, July 9, 1881, 280; information taken from "The Bridge over the River Allegheny at Pittsburgh," *Engineering*, July 3, 1868, 1; *Scientific American*, May 31, 1879, 337; Washington Roebling, "The Allegheny Bridge," folder 1, box 14, RFP-RPI; W. G. Wilkins, "The Reconstruction of the Sixth Street Bridge at Pittsburgh, PA," *Proceedings of the Engineers' Society of Western Pennsylvania* 11, no. 5 (May 1895), 145–47. Also see "Allegheny River Suspension Bridge, Contracts," box 5, folder 3, and "Allegheny River Suspension Bridge, Costs and Estimates," box 5, folder 4, both RFP-RPI.

75. *Pittsburgh Post*, July 30, 1857, 2; *Pittsburgh Post*, August 21, 1857, 2; JAR to Charles Swan, August 23, 1857, in JR-CS; *Pittsburgh Gazette*, October 2, 1857, 2; *Pittsburgh Gazette*, October 29, 1857, 2.

76. *Pittsburgh Gazette*, August 22, 1857, 2; *Pittsburgh Gazette*, September 15, 1857, 2; Lakier, *A Russian Looks at America*, 138–39.

77. "Ledger. 1853. Kentucky Bridge. Niagara, 1856. Covington & Cincinnati Bridge," box 4, itemitem 141, RFP-RPI; *WRF*, 182; JAR to Charles Swan, April 28 and May 6, 1858, in JR-CS; *WRF*, 163; WAR to JAR, January 10, 11, and 13, 1860, box 2, folder 10, RFP-RU. Washington provided a rather austere description of his father's life in Pittsburgh. "As regards amusements," Washington claimed his father did not read novels or newspapers—which we know to be untrue—"except technical journals, never played cards or games—was very fond of conversing with the solid men of the town and had a choice visiting list among the very best families—at rare intervals he went to the theatre on interesting lectures—but he was passionately fond of the Opera, especially the light opera of the day." "He by no means abstained from going to church, but disliked ritualism of any kind, preferring the Universalist or Unitarian services when obtainable." See *WRF*, 188.

78. *Pittsburgh Evening Chronicle*, July 28, 1858, 2; JAR to Charles Swan, August 17, 1858, in JR-CS.

79. See Edgar Marquess Branch, *Men Call Me Lucky: Mark Twain and the Pennsylvania* (Oxford, OH: Friends of the Library Society, Miami University, 1985), for descriptions and firsthand accounts.

80. Mark Twain, *Life on the Mississippi* (New York: Penguin, 1986 (1883)), 152–55.

81. JAR, "Relative Value of the Different Kinds of Steam, from Different Liquids, as a Moving Power," *American Railroad Journal and Mechanics' Magazine*, July 1, 1838, 7–9; "Hints on the New Steam Frigates for the United States," *Scientific American*, June 10, 1854, 310; and "On Marine Boilers," *Scientific American*, June 17, 1854, 318.

82. The *Post* and the *Gazette* (Pittsburgh) both published JAR's "Prevention of Explosion of Steam Boilers" on June 28, 1858.

83. JAR, "Prevention of Explosion of Steam Boilers," *Pittsburgh Post*, June 28, 1858, 2.

84. William Fairbairn, *Two Lectures on the Construction of Boilers and on Boiler Explosions* (Leeds, UK: Read Newsome, 1851), 24; Louis C. Hunter, *Steamboats on Western Rivers: An Economic and Technological History* (New York: Dover, 1993 (1949)), 159; JAR, "Prevention of Explosion of Steam Boilers," *Pittsburgh Post*, June 28, 1858, 2.

85. Ibid.

86. JAR to Charles Swan, June 28, 1858, in JR-CS.

87. JAR to Charles Swan, March 17, 1859, and March 22, 1860, JR-CS; WAR to JAR, January 11, 1860, box 2, folder 11, RFP-RU; WAR, "The Allegheny Bridge," box 14, folder 1, RFP-RPI; *Scientific American*, June 18, 1870, 391; "The Bridge over the River Allegheny at Pittsburgh," *Engineering*, July 3, 1868, 1.

88. JAR to Charles Swan, May 1, May 25, and June 11, 1860, in JR-CS. Washington wrote up a short report in "Allegheny Suspension Bridge," box 26, notebook 67, RFP-RPI.

89. William Roseburg to JAR, July 4, 1860, box 2, folder 13, RFP-RU; *Pittsburgh Evening Chronicle*, May 9, 1860, 2; "The Bridge over the River Allegheny at Pittsburgh," *Engineering*, July 3, 1868, 1; *Engineering News*, July 9, 1881, 280. Earlier in the trip, the future monarch visited John's Niagara Bridge and had the duke write to express his delight in its "graceful designed and remarkable solidity," which "did honor to the ability of the eminent man who conceived and completed the work." Having heard about the visit, John wrote to bridge superintendent W. G. Swan for all the details. Swan replied with a rather tepid assessment of the occasion and the prince. The royal visitor "never looked out of the car [while traveling over the bridge] taking no more interest than a blind man in the work," reported the superintendent. "His

keepers spoke highly of the work—but the Prince had nothing to say. . . . He attended the Blondin show [however] & paid great attention. I infer he was very much more interested in this than the Falls or Bridge." Duke of Newcastle to Hamilton Merritt, September 17, 1860, and W. G. Swan to JAR, September 22, 1860, both box 2, folder 18, RFP-RU.

90. *Pittsburgh Dispatch*, June 20, 1881, 2–4; Wilkins, "The Reconstruction of the Sixth Street Bridge at Pittsburgh, PA," 145.

91. Kirti Gandhi and Andrea Seelman, "Francis Collingwood," in Green, *John A. Roebling*, 145.

92. *Pittsburgh Telegraph*, October 1, 1883, 2; *Pittsburgh Evening Chronicle*, May 9, 1860, 2; Collingwood summarized his findings in Francis Collingwood, "On Repairing the Cables of the Allegheny Suspension Bridge at Pittsburgh, PA, USA," *Proceedings of the Institution of Civil Engineers* 76 (1884), 335–45.

93. Sayenga, "Cement Shoes," 22; *Pittsburgh Telegraph*, October 1, 1883, 2; Collingwood, "On Repairing the Cables of the Allegheny Suspension Bridge at Pittsburgh, PA, USA," 335–45.

94. William Roseburg to WAR, January 29, 1889, and WAR to William Roseburg, February 1889, both in "Allegheny Suspension Bridge Co., 1872, 1889," box 14, folder 2, RFP-RPI; Wilkins, "The Reconstruction of the Sixth Street Bridge at Pittsburgh, PA," 147–48; "The New Sixth Street Bridge," *Railroad Gazette*, July 28, 1893, 560.

95. *Scientific American*, June 18, 1870, 391.

Chapter 17

1. Francis Bazley Lee, *History of Trenton, New Jersey* (Trenton, NJ: F. T. Smiley, 1895), 178; JAR to WAR, October 14, 1861, box 10, folder 7, RFP-RPI; JAR to Charles Swan, November 24, 1863, JAR-CS.

2. Wm. F. Phelps to JAR, January 9, 1860, box 2, folder 10, RFP-RU; *Trenton Daily State Gazette and Republican*, January 18, 1860, 3; Mary D. James to JAR, January 14, 1860, box 2, folder 10, RFP-RU.

3. Laura married Anton Gottlieb Methfessel—whose father had known John in Mühlhausen— the following year on July 16, 1862, at John and Johanna's Trenton home. Together they founded the Staten Island Academy. Laura died of peritonitis following childbirth on January 3, 1873, a mere thirty-three years old.

4. A. G. Gower to JAR, June 12 and July 20, 1861, "JAR, Letters Received 1827–1869," box 2, folder 33, RFP-RU; JAR to WAR, October 14, 1861, box 10, folder 7, RFP-RPI. John's pain was clearly made worse by a difficult end, as Swan informed Washington: "The dear boy must have suffered very much before death put an end to his suffering." WAR to JAR, September 29, 1861, "JAR, Letters Received 1827–1869," box 2, folder 42, RFP-RU.

5. S. A. Farrand to JAR, December 6, 1861, "JAR, Letters Received 1827–1869," box 2, folder 46, RFP-RU.

6. Keith Wilson, *Channel Tunnel Visions, 1850–1945: Dreams and Nightmares* (London: Hambledon, 1994), 4; James Chalmers, *The Channel Railway Connecting England and France* (London: E. & F. N. Spon, 1866), 1–6.

7. JAR, "Bridge across the English Channel (Drawings and Notes)," box 6, folder 15, RFP-RU.

8. Chalmers, *The Channel Railway Connecting England and France* (London: E. & F. N. Spon, 1866), 1–6; JAR, "Bridge across the English Channel (Drawings and Notes)," box 6, folder 15, RFP-RU; Wilson, *Channel Tunnel Visions, 1850–1945*, 4; "The Proposed Bridge over the English Channel," *Scientific American*, November 30, 1889, 342.

9. *WRF*, 88, 92; A. G. Gower to JAR, November 3, December 2, 1860, box 2, folder 22–24, RFP-RU; George Schaffer to JAR, November 16, 1860, box 2, folder 22, RFP-RU.

10. A. G. Gower to JAR, December 13, 1860, box 2, folder 24, RFP-RU; "The American Secession Movement," *Saturday Review* (London), December 15, 1860, 753–54.

11. "The American Secession Movement," 754; A. G. Gower to JAR, December 13, 1860, box 2, folder 24, RFP-RU.

12. *WRF*, 192. Elsewhere, Washington noted that he was "driven out of the house" by his father and "slept on the floor of the drill room the first night" before heading to Washington, DC. See WAR to James F. Rusling, February 18, 1916, in SRL.

13. *WRF*, 162–64.

14. WAR to JAR, April 9 and August 24, 1862; WAR to I. E. Boos, June 19, 1921, all in SRL; George R. Agassiz, ed., *Meade's Headquarters, 1863–1865: Letters of Colonel Theodore Lyman, from the Wilderness to Appomattox* (Boston: Atlantic Monthly, 1922), 240. For Washington's experiences in the Civil War more generally see Erica Wagner, *Chief Engineer: Washington Roebling, the Man Who Built the Brooklyn Bridge* (New York: Bloomsbury, 2017), 85–112. For Washington as a historian, see WAR, "Report of the Operations of the 5th Corps, A. P. in Genl. Grant's Campaign from Culpepper to Petersburg" (1864), WAR, Civil War Materials #2, RFP-RU. In addition, numerous historians subsequently consulted with Washington about the war in preparing historical accounts. See especially Morris Schaff, *Battle of the Wilderness* (Boston: Houghton Mifflin, 1910), and Oliver W. Norton, *The Attack and Defense of Little Round Top* (New York: Neale Publishing, 1913).

15. WAR to CS, July 31, 1861, SRL; WAR, "Life of John A. Roebling, C.E. by his eldest son Washington A. Roebling, together with some personal recollections of the latter, written partly in 1897 and in 1907," box 10, folders 31–32, RFP-RU; Wagner, *Chief Engineer*, 87, 94.

16. WAR, "Construction of Military Suspension Bridges" (1862), box 13, folder 1, RFP-RPI; Quartermaster General M. C. Meigs to Secretary of War, Edwin Stanton, November 18, 1862, in *A Compilation of the Official Records of the Union and Confederate Armies*, 3rd ser., 5 vols. (Washington, DC: Government Printing Office, 1891), 2:805; WAR to JAR, June 5, 1862, and WAR to Ferdinand Roebling, June 8, 1862, both in SRL; WAR, "Report of W. A. Roebling in Charge of Wire Suspension Bridge Equipage, to General M. C. Meigs," box 11, folder 58, RFP-RU.

17. WAR to Ferdinand Roebling, August 8, 1862, SRL; WAR, "Bridge over the Rappahannock," box 11, folder 65, RFP-RU; WAR, "Diary of the Suspension Bridge," WAR Civil War Materials #1, RFP-RU; WAR, "Life of John A. Roebling," 211–13; *Christian Banner* (Fredericksburg), July 18, 1862, 2; WAR, "Report of W. A. Roebling in Charge of Wire Suspension Bridge Equipage." One of the best sources of information on Washington's Rappahannock Bridge is "A Mystery: Roebling's 'Wire Bridge on the Rappahannock," *Mysteries and Conundrums* (blog), July 11, 2010, https://npsfrsp.wordpress.com/2010/07/11/a-mystery-roeblings-wire-bridge-on-the-rappahannock/, accessed August 25, 2017.

18. WAR to CS, July 31, 1861, and WAR to JAR, August 24, 1862, both in SRL; JAR to WAR, October 14, 1861, box 10, folder 7, RFP-RPI. John's worries about his son are palpable in his letters to Swan and other members of his circle, many of which ask directly for news of Washington or newspaper reports that mention his regiment.

19. WAR, "Report of W. A. Roebling in Charge of Wire Suspension Bridge Equipage"; WAR to JAR, December 30, 1862, in SRL.

20. WAR to JAR, January 30, 1863, in SRL; D. Rhule to JAR, January 24, 1863, "JAR, Letters Received, 1827–1865," box 3, folder 2, RFP-RU.

21. Washington told his sister Elvira that during the spring of 1863 "Gen. Comstock wanted to take him to Pittsburgh to fortify it but Ge. Warren would not let him go." Comstock served as chief engineer of both the Army of the Potomac and the Army of the Tennessee and ultimately as senior aide-de-camp to General Ulysses S. Grant. Comstock spent the early years of the war constructing pontoon bridges for the army. See Elvira Roebling to Laura Roebling, June 24, 1863, AMFC.

22. Gouverneur K. Warren to Emily C. Warren, June 24, 1863, box 1, folder 2, WP; WAR, "Life of John A. Roebling," 221; Henry J. Hunt, "The Second Day at Gettysburg," in *Battles and Leaders of the Civil War*, ed. Robert Underwood Johnson and Clarence Clough Buell, 4 vols. (New York: Century, 1884–1887), 3:307; Gouverneur Warren to Porter Farley, July 13, 1872, in Norton, *The Attack and Defense of Little Round Top*, 309; Harry W. Pfanz, *Gettysburg: The Second Day* (Chapel Hill: University of North Carolina Press, 1987), 201–40; WAR to James F. Rusling, February 18, 1916, box 9, folder 37, RFP-RU.

23. JAR to CS, July 27, 1863, June 28, August 24, and September 26, 1864, JAR-CS. John's letters during the Civil War contradict Washington's assertion that his father "was sure that Lee's army would beat ours . . . and that he would come and take Trenton, burn up his wire rope mill, his rope shop, his fine new house, and make him a beggar of the earth." See *WRF*, 192.

24. WAR to Emil Warren, June 19 and 23, July 7, 1864, and WAR to Ferdinand Roebling, August 8, 1862, all in SRL; JAR to CS, July 27, 1863, in JAR-CS.

25. WAR, "Diary of the Suspension Bridge," WAR Civil War Materials #1, RFP-RU; WAR to Emily Warren, March 27 and July 3, 1864, in SRL.
26. JAR, "Material and Immaterial. Religion" (October 1862), box 4, folder 52, RFP-RU; JAR, "The Truth of Nature (5. General Reflections)," n.d. [1863], box 4, folder 24, RFP-RU.
27. JAR, "The Condition of the US Reviewed by Higher Law" (n.d.), box 5, folder 40, RFP-RU.
28. Ibid.
29. Ibid.; JAR, "A Few Truths for the Consideration of the President of the US" (October 1861), box 4, folder 50, RFP-RU.
30. JAR, "Enquiry into the Nature and Origin of Matter" (April 1862), box 3, folder 49, and "A Few Truths for the Consideration of American Citizens" (n.d.), box 5, folder 42, both RFP-RU.
31. JAR, "The Harmonies of Creation" (April 1857), box 3, folder 48, and "The Truth of Nature," box 4, folder 14, both RFP-RU.
32. JAR, "Man in Harmony with Nature" (n.d.), box 5, folder 36, and "The Truth of Nature (5. General Reflections)," n.d. [1863], box 4, folder 24, both RFP-RU.
33. JAR, "A Few Truths for the Consideration of American Citizens" (n.d.), box 5, folder 42, and "Man in Harmony with Nature" (n.d.), box 5, folder 36, both RFP-RU.
34. Mark Holloway, *Utopian Communities in America, 1680–1880* (New York: Dover, 1966 (1951)), 140–41; *New-York Tribune*, April 9, 1846, and March 27, 1857; Horace Greeley, "Immigration," in *Essays Designed to Elucidate the Science of Political Economy* (Philadelphia: Porter & Coates, 1869), 319.
35. JAR, "An Appeal to the Philanthropist" (n.d.), box 5, folder 41, RFP-RU.
36. Ibid.
37. Ibid.
38. Donald E. Pitzer, "Introduction," in *America's Communal Utopias*, ed. Donald E. Pitzer (Chapel Hill: University of North Carolina Press, 1997), 3–14; Holloway, *Utopian Communities in America*, 135; JAR, "An Appeal to the Philanthropist."
39. JAR, "An Appeal to the Philanthropist.".
40. Chris Jennings, *Paradise Now: The Story of American Utopianism* (New York: Random House, 2016), 10; Holloway, *Utopian Communities in America*, 179; John Humphrey Noyes, *History of American Socialisms* (Philadelphia: J. B. Lippincott, 1870), 21, 133; JAR, "An Appeal to the Philanthropist."
41. WRF, 165; JAR, "The Harmonies of Creation" (March 1856), box 3, folder 47, and "The Truth of Nature" (October 1862), box 4, folder 11, both RFP-RU. As John wrote in 1863: "the human mind craves for unity . . . all music is the harmony of sound, so is poetry the harmony of speech, painting the harmony of color, architecture and sculpture the harmony of form, and truth the harmony of thought." See JAR, "Material and Immaterial. Religion," box 4, folder 52, RFP-RU.
42. JAR, "The Truth of Nature" (October 1862), box 4, folder 11, and "Enquiry into the Nature and Origin of Matter" (April 1862), box 3, folder 51, both RFP-RU.
43. John also wrote numerous small, technical essays at this time, many of which seem intended as a part of this larger project. See, for example, JAR, "Chemism and Force," "Ideas of Space and Time, Motion," "Are Metals Subject to Internal Changes?" or "Granulation Experiments," box 5, folders 16–17, 34–35, all RFP-RU.
44. JAR, "The Truth of Nature" (December 1862), box 4, folder 12, RFP-RU.
45. JAR, "Additional Notes [Reflections]" (May 1862), box 4, folder 53, and JAR, "The Truth of Nature" (December 1862), box 4, folder 12, both RFP-RU. See Walt Whitman, "Song of Myself," in *Leaves of Grass* (Philadelphia: David McKay, 1892), lines 10, 12, 82.
46. JAR, "Enquiry into the Nature and Origin of Matter" (April 1862), box 3, folder 50, and "Principle of Life" (October–November 1864), box 5, folder 28, both RFP-RU; Lawrence Sklar, *Space, Time, and Spacetime* (Berkeley: University of California Press, 1974), 182–90, 195–98.
47. JAR, "Enquiry into the Nature and Origin of Matter" (April 1862), box 3, folders 54–55, and JAR, "The Truth of Nature" (April 1863), box 4, folders 14–15, 31, both RFP-RU.
48. JAR, "A Metaphysical Essay on the Nature of Man and of Spirit" (n.d.), box 5, folder 33; "The Truth of Nature" (1863), box 4, folder 25, 31; "Introduction" (March 1863), box 4, folder 51; "The Spiritual" (December 1861–June 1862), box 5, folder 3, all RFP-RU.

49. JAR, "The Truth of Nature" (July 1862), box 4, folder 31, RFP-RU; *WRF*, 186; Adrian Desmond and James Moore, *Darwin: The Life of a Tormented Evolutionist* (New York: Norton, 1991), 239-49.

50. JAR, "The Truth of Nature" (May 1862), box, 4, folder 27; "Introduction" (March 1863), box 4, folder 51; "The Spiritual" (December 1861-June 1862), box 5, folder 3.

51. JAR, "A Metaphysical Essay on the Nature of Man and of Spirit" (n.d.), box 5, folder 33; "The Truth of Nature" (December 1862), box 4, folders 12-13 and 31; "The Harmonies of Creation" (April 1857), box 3, folder 48; "Material and Immaterial. Religion" (October 1862), box 4, folder 52, all RFP-RU.

52. JAR, "The Truth of Nature" (October 1862), box 4, folder 11; "A Metaphysical Essay on the Nature of Man and of Spirit" (n.d.), box 5, folder 33; "Material and Immaterial. Religion" (October 1862), box 4, folder 52.

53. JAR, "The Harmonies of Creation" (April 1857), box 3, folder 48; "A Metaphysical Essay on the Nature of Man and of Spirit" (n.d.), box 5, folder 33.

54. JAR, "Additional Notes" (May 1862), box 4, folder 53.

55. JAR, "The Harmonies of Creation" (April 1857), box 3, folder 48; "Material and Immaterial. Religion" (October 1862), box 4, folder 52; "The Truth of Nature" (General Reflections. 5), [1863], box 4, folder 24; "Additional Notes" (May 1862), box 4, folder 53.

56. JAR, "Material and Immaterial. Religion" (October 1862), box 4, folder 52; "A Few Truths for the Consideration of American Citizens" (n.d.), box 5, folder 42; Charles Darwin, *The Descent of Man* (New York: Penguin, 2004 (1879)), 126.

57. JAR, "The Truth of Nature," box 4, folders 13-15; "Introduction" (March 1863), box 4, folder 51; "Principle of Life" (October-November 1864), box 5, folder 28.

58. JAR, "The Truth of Nature" (1862), box 4, folder 11, 14, 28; "Additional Notes" (May 1862), box 4, folder 53; "Introduction" (March 1863), box 4, folder 51.

59. JAR, "The Harmonies of Creation" (March 1856), box 3, folder 47.

60. "Human reason is that faculty of the human mind which connects the inner with the outer world. Reason is a connecting link between the spiritual and material," John wrote in "Material and Immaterial. Religion" (October 1862), box 4, folder 52.

61. JAR, "The Truth of Nature" (1862), box 4, folders 11, 14, 28; "Additional Notes" (May 1862), box 4, folder 53.

62. William Ellery Channing, *A Discourse on the Evidences of Revealed Religion* (Boston: Cummings & Hilliard, 1821), 18; William Ellery Channing, "The Religious Principle in Human Nature," in *The Works of William E. Channing* (Boston: Unitarian Association, 1890), 931.

63. George Ripley, "Letter to the Church in Purchase Street," in *The Transcendentalists: An Anthology*, ed. Perry Miller (Cambridge, MA: Harvard University Press, 1950), 255. John classified "common sense" as one of the four branches of knowledge, along with theology, science, and philosophy. See JAR, "The Truth of Nature" (1862), box 4, folder 15.

64. JAR, "The Harmonies of Creation" (April 1857), box 3, folder 48; Richardson, *Emerson: The Mind on Fire*, 110, 185.

65. Emerson, "Nature," in *Emerson: Essays & Poems*, 9-11; Richardson, *Emerson: The Mind on Fire*, 137; JAR, "The Truth of Nature" (General Reflections. 5), (1863), box 4, folder 22; Thomas Carlyle, "The State of German Literature," in *Critical and Miscellaneous Essays*, ed. Ralph Waldo Emerson (Philadelphia: Carey & Hart, 1848), 26.

66. Czesław Miłosz, "Dostoevsky and Swedenborg," in *Emperor of the Earth: Modes of Eccentric Vision* (Berkeley: University of California Press, 1981), 121.

67. Philip F. Gura, *American Transcendentalism: A History* (New York: Hill & Wang, 2007), 93; JAR, "The Truth of Nature" (1862), box 4, folder 14; "The Harmonies of Creation" (April 1857), box 3, folder 48.

68. Hell simply doesn't exist in John's system, and neither does evil in any appreciable way. John never allowed for more than one first principle: God is good. In this manner, he was also able to sidestep the idea that God fails to prevent evil (central to David Hume and dozens of other skeptic philosophers) by denying that God was a being outside of nature. The point was moot: God does not intervene in our affairs; God is our affairs.

69. Emerson, "Swedenborg; Or, the Mystic," in *Emerson: Essays & Poems*, 662, 676; David S. Reynolds, *Walt Whitman's America: A Cultural Biography* (New York: Vintage, 1995), 265;

JAR, "Material and Immaterial. Religion" (October 1862), box 4, folder 52. John also read widely, and even wrote about Henry James, Sr. (father of William and Henry).

70. JAR, "The Truth of Nature: Introduction 5" (January 1863), box 4, folder 17.

71. JAR, "Enquiry into the Nature and Origin of Matter" (April 1862), box 3, folder 49; "Life and Creation," box 4, folder 40; "The Truth of Nature," box 4, folders 13, 22.

72. For Oken see Michael Heidelberger, *Nature from Within: Gustav Theodor Fechner and His Psychophysical Worldview* (Pittsburgh: University of Pittsburgh Press, 2004), 23-26; JAR, "The Truth of Nature" (1863), box 4, folder 23.

73. Rattermann, "Johann August Röbling: Berühmter Amerikanischer, Ingenieur und Brückenbauer," 425; Peter Kaufmann, *The Temple of Truth; Or, the Science of Ever-Progressive Knowledge* (Cincinnati: Trumand & Spofford, 1858), iii. See Karl J. R. Arndt, ed., *Teutonic Visions of Social Perfection for Emerson: A Documentary History of Peter Kaufmann's Quest for Social Perfection from George Rapp to Ralph Waldo Emerson* (Worcester, MA: Harmony Society, 1988).

74. *Massachusetts Quarterly Review* 1 (1848), 263-64; Easton, *Hegel's First American Followers*, 46-47. John visited Stallo in Cincinnati when he was living kitty-corner to Alphonso Taft (and his eight-year-old son and future US president William) on Auburn Avenue. A notebook of John's from the time includes a map and directions to Stallo's house. See "Directory: Covington & Cincinnati Bridge, 1864," box 7, notebook 133, RFP-RPI.

75. Easton, *Hegel's First American Followers*, 42.

76. JAR, "The Truth of Nature" (1862), box 4, folders 12, 30; "Introduction" (March 1863), box 4, folder 51; James Hutchinson Stirling, *The Secret of Hegel: Being the Hegelian System in Origin, Principle, Form, and Matter* (London: Longman, Green Longman, Roberts & Green, 1865), 126; Moncure Conway, "David Friedrich Strauss," *Index* 2 (1874), 158.

77. JAR, "The Truth of Nature" (1862), box 4, folder 10; "Introduction" (March 1863), box 4, folder 51; Easton, *Hegel's First American Followers*, 26; Pinkard, *Hegel*, 217.

78. JAR, "The Truth of Nature" (1862), box 4, folder 15.

79. Perhaps the most glaring contradiction in John's thought was between his abstract and social reason. Socially he thought the world made the man; metaphysically he thought divine spirit made the man. Rarely was John consistent, however.

80. See R. Laurence Moore, *In Search of White Crows: Spiritualism, Parapsychology, and American Culture* (New York: Oxford University Press, 1977), 1-16; Bret E. Carroll, *Spiritualism in Antebellum America* (Bloomington: Indiana University Press, 1997), 2; Sheridan LeFanu, "Green Tea," in *In a Glass Darkly*, ed. Robert Tracy (New York: Oxford University Press, 1993), 8.

81. JAR, "The Harmonies of Creation" (March 1856), box 3, folder 47; Desmond and Moore, *Darwin*, 314.

82. JAR, "The Truth of Nature," box 4, folder 25, 30; "Material and Immaterial Religion," box 4, folder 52.

83. The others were "One creator, one creation, and one creative law: in this law is love!" "One creator, one creation, and one creative essence, and that essence is love!" "One God, one universe, one law! This law is love and its exercise is its fulfillment!" See JAR, "The Truth of Nature," box 4, folder 10.

84. JAR, "The Truth of Nature," box 4, folder 24; "Additional Notes" (May 1862), box 4, folder 53.

85. WRF, 39-41; JAR, "The Truth of Nature" (1863), box 4, folder 23.

86. Elvira Roebling to JAR, March 14, 1860, box 2, folder 10, RFP-RU.

87. Washington claims Shinkle ran from church on the day the Covington and Cincinnati Bridge was opened, grabbed a barrel, and insisted on collecting everyone's penny toll from 11:00 a.m. to 11:00 p.m. "Not a penny got away from him," he concluded. In actual fact, the bridge company employed fourteen toll takers on opening day—seven on either end of the bridge—none of whom were Shinkle. See *Cincinnati Daily Enquirer*, December 2 and 3, 1866, both 2, and *Cincinnati Daily Commercial*, December 3, 1866, 2. Washington also claims that "with his contemptible parsimony" Shinkle was "a thorn in my father's side," although we never once hear this from John. See WRF, 199.

88. WAR to JAR, March 1, 1863, "JAR, Letters Received, 1827-1865," box 3, folder 2, RFP-RU.

89. Laura Roebling to WAR, November 14, 1858, and Johanna Roebling to WAR, November 20, 1858, both in SRL.

90. JAR to WAR, October 14, 1861, box 10, folder 7, RFP-RPI.
91. *WRF*, 185–86. All Washington's letters from Pittsburgh are reprinted in Schuyler, *The Roeblings*, 176–80.
92. *WRF*, 191.
93. Erica Wagner makes the case for the essential truth of Washington's narrative. See *Chief Engineer*, ix–xviii, 38–42.
94. WAR to Emily Warren, April 4, 1864, and JAR to WAR, March 30, 1864, both in SRL; *WRF*, 165.

Chapter 18

1. *Cincinnati Daily Commercial*, January 17, 1863, 2; *Cincinnati Daily Enquirer*, January 4, 1863, 2; *A Remonstrance against Lowering the Cincinnati and Covington Bridge* (Cincinnati: n.p., 1863); *Daily Cincinnati Gazette*, January 23 and 24, 1863, both 2.
2. Stern, "The Suspension Bridge: They Said It Couldn't Be Built," 220. By the close of the Civil War, Bruce's name was no longer included in the list of bridge officers.
3. Joseph S. Stern, Jr., "The Siege of Cincinnati," *Bulletin of the Historical and Philosophical Society of Ohio* 18, no. 3 (1960), 167; *Daily Cincinnati Gazette*, September 2, 1862, 2.
4. Lew Wallace, *Autobiography*, 2 vols. (New York: Harper & Bros, 1906), 2:609.
5. Roger C. Adams, "Panic on the Ohio: The Defense of Cincinnati, Covington, and Newport, September 1862," *Journal of Kentucky Studies* 9 (1992), 80–98; *Daily Cincinnati Gazette*, January 27, 1863, 2; *Cincinnati Daily Commercial*, January 19, 1863, 2. Also see Bert Workum, "A Confederate Threat Roused Support for Suspension Bridge," *Kentucky Press*, July 12, 1982, 4K.
6. John later even asked David if his brother Jonathan (with whom he fell out so violently on his first bridge and later accused of being an "Ellet man") was free, rather an odd request for John to make, but Jonathan was busy with other work. See D. Rhule to JAR, February 3, 1865, "JAR, Letters Received, 1827–1865," box 3, folders 2 and 14, RFP-RU.
7. JAR to CS, March 13 and April 26, 1863, both in JR-CS; D. Rhule to JAR, January 24, 1863, "JAR, Letters Received, 1827–1865," box 3, folder 2, RFP-RU; *Report of John A. Roebling, Civil Engineer, to the President and Board of Directors of the Covington and Cincinnati Bridge*, 18, 39–40.
8. *Cincinnati Daily Enquirer*, May 9, June 23, and July 13 and 14, 1863, all 2; JAR to CS, July 13, 1863, in JR-CS; *Cincinnati Daily Enquirer*, July 14, 1863, 2.
9. *Daily Cincinnati Gazette*, January 27, 1863, 2; JAR to CS, July 27, 1863, in JR-CS; Stern, "The Suspension Bridge," 221. "Skilled, educated, and intellectual" Cincinnati Germans were "daily increasing in numbers, wealth, and political importance, and constitute an influence of which the Americans themselves are afraid," wrote Isabel Bishop in 1856. They "monopolise the handicraft trades, where they find a fruitful field for their genius and industry," whereas the "Irish are here, as everywhere, hewers of wood and drawers of water; they can do nothing but dig, and seldom rise in the social scale." By 1860, 30 percent of the city's population was German. See Bishop, *The Englishwoman in America*, 119–20, and Peter M. Harsham, "A Community Portrait: Over-the-Rhine, 1860," *Cincinnati Historical Society Bulletin* 40, no. 1 (1982), 66.
10. JAR to CS, December 8, 1863, in JR-CS; JAR to WAR, March 21, 1864, in SRL; *Cincinnati Daily Enquirer*, May 10, October 4, and December 15, 1864, all 2; CS to JAR, November 22, 1864, "JAR, Letters Received, 1827–1865," box 3, folder 10, RFP-RU.
11. Johanna Roebling to WAR, May 9 and July 12, 1858, both in SRL; Johanna Roebling to Laura Roebling, January 1862, August 4, 1862, December 5, 1862, April 9, 1863, and May 27, 1863, all AMFC; Elvira Roebling to JAR, January 29, 1860, box 2, folder 10, RFP-RU; Elvira Roebling to Laura Roebling, October 26, 1864, AMFC.
12. Laura Roebling to JAR, April 1, 1860, box 2, folder 10, RFP-RU; *WRF*, 185, 191; Johanna Roebling to WAR, November 20, 1858, in SRL; Johanna Roebling to Laura Roebling, January 1862, AMFC.
13. Josephine, known as Phinie, attended school in Philadelphia but was asked to stay home in Trenton by John to help Elvira look after her mother, although "he saw that she did not do anything but help herself" and sent her back to school. Elvira seems to have been a dutiful, helpful daughter, while Phinie was more fun-loving and carefree. She also outlasted both

her sisters by over sixty years, eventually passing away in 1934. See Elvira Roebling to Laura Roebling, October 26, 1864, AMFC.

14. *WRF*, 156, 191, 201; Johanna Roebling to Laura Roebling, April 9, 1863, AMFC.

15. *WRF*, 201; JAR to CS, April 25, 1864, in JR-CS.

16. *WRF*, 201; JAR to CS, April 25, 1864, in JR-CS; Elvira Roebling to Laura Roebling, October 26, 1864, AMFC.

17. JAR to Laura Roebling, November 2, 1864, AMFC.

18. *WRF*, 201; JAR to Laura Roebling, November 2, 1864, AMFC.

19. WAR to Emily Warren, June 6, 1864, and JAR to WAR, March 21 and 30, 1864, all in SRL; JAR to WAR, October 14, 1861, box 10, folder 7, RFP-RPI; David McCullough, *The Great Bridge*, 55; JAR to WAR, November 19, 1864, box 8, folder 51, RFP-RU.

20. A. S. Gower to JAR, January 7 and February 28, 1865, and Joseph Wilcox to JAR, January 26, 1865, all in "JAR, Letters Received 1827–1869," box 3, folders 13, 15, and 19, RFP-RU.

21. [Emily Warren Roebling], "A Wife's Disabilities," *Albany Law Journal*, April 15, 1899, 342; *WRF*, 201; WAR to Ferdinand Roebling, March 29, 1865, box 22, folder 9, RFP-RU; JAR to CS, April 17, 1865, JR-CS.

22. WAR to EWR, March 16, 1865, SRL; A. S. Gower to JAR, February 13, 1865, "JAR, Letters Received 1827–1869," box 3, folder 15, RFP-RU; *WRF*, 199; JAR to WAR, March 21, 1864, in SRL.

23. *Cincinnati Daily Enquirer*, August 22, 1865, 2; *Cincinnati Daily Gazette*, August 30, 1865, 2; *Cincinnati Daily Gazette*, October 5, 1865, 2; *WRF*, 206; WAR to Ferdinand Roebling, June 29, 1865, box 22, folder 11, RFP-RU; *Cincinnati Daily Enquirer*, October 9, 1865, 2; *Cincinnati Daily Times*, October 10, 1865, 2; *Cincinnati Daily Enquirer*, December 5, 1865, 2.

24. Cincinnati Bridge notebook 106 and 135, RPI; Worthington, "John A. Roebling and the Cincinnati Bridge," 16–21; *Cincinnati Daily Commercial*, July 13, 1866, 2. The best contemporary description of the bridge and the manner of its erection is *Cincinnati Daily Commercial*, May 13, 1866, 1–2, along with *Report of John A. Roebling, Civil Engineer, to the President and Board of Directors of the Covington and Cincinnati Bridge*.

25. See "Description of the Suspension Bridge at Cincinnati," *Scientific American*, May 26, 1866, 355; *Cincinnati Daily Times*, January 18, 1866, 2; *Cincinnati Daily Enquirer*, January 19, 1866, 2; *Cincinnati Daily Commercial*, May 13, 1866, 2.

26. *Cincinnati Daily Commercial*, May 13, 1866, 2.

27. Ibid.

28. *Cincinnati Daily Commercial*, September 3, 1866, 2.

29. *Cincinnati Daily Commercial*, December 1 and 3, 1866, both 2; *Report of John A. Roebling, Civil Engineer, to the President and Board of Directors of the Covington and Cincinnati Bridge*, 3; *Daily Cincinnati Gazette*, December 3, 1866, 2; *Cincinnati Daily Times*, December 3 and 8, 1866, both 2.

30. Mayo's sermon was reprinted in the *Cincinnati Daily Gazette*, December 10, 1866, 1; *Report of John A. Roebling, Civil Engineer, to the President and Board of Directors of the Covington and Cincinnati Bridge*, 19, 87.

31. *Cincinnati Daily Gazette*, December 10, 1866, 1.

32. Ibid.; *WRF*, 41, 209. A local religious paper called the *Presbyter* published a riposte to what they mockingly called "The Gospel of Bridges." The paper was happy to contemplate the coming of Christ, "but a whole sermon made up of *bridges*, however ponderous their cables or massive and lofty their abutments," didn't seem likely "either to convert sinners, or to edify the saints." "If a man has no Christ, and no Cross, in his theology," they declared, "he is not apt to put much of them in his sermons, and much less if these be wanting in the heart." Focusing on bridges meant forgetting that man's nature is fundamentally "*carnal*" and "*sinful*." Preachers needed to remember that "men love darkness rather than light, because their deeds are evil" and that all men are "guilty and without excuse." All talk of bridges and social purpose was just a way to avoid this basic reality, concluded the humorless *Presbyter*. By contrast, the *Daily Commercial* rather enjoyed Mayo's sermon. "It is a gospel of bridges that the world needs—bridges to span the black gulf between sin and heaven . . . from darkness to light, from error to truth, from Satan to God." "The bigotry of creeds is not half so blessed a thing as the 'Gospel of Bridges,'" they concluded. See *Presbyter*, December 26, 1866, 1; *Cincinnati Daily Commercial*, December 30, 1866, 2.

33. *Cincinnati Daily Commercial*, January 2 and 6 and February 18, 1867, all 2; *Cincinnati Daily Enquirer*, January 2, 1867, 2.

34. WAR to JAR, January 29, 1867, SRL; *Cincinnati Daily Commercial*, February 6, 1867, 2; *Cincinnati Daily Times*, April 14, 1868, 2; *Cincinnati Daily Commercial*, April 15, 1868, 2. The final cost of John's Covington and Cincinnati Bridge, as calculated at the end of February 1867, was $1,480,350.55.

35. June 15, 1857, vol. 8; December 2, 1858, vol. 9; January 23, 1860, vol. 12; all TBG.

36. January 25, 1859, vol. 9; TBG.

37. *WRF*, 161, 208–10; JAR to Lucia Roebling, June 13, 1869, in "Correspondence, Letters Sent (1834–1869)," box 3, folder 46, RFP-RU; JAR, "Will," box 8, folder 30, RFP-RU; JAR, "Spiritualism Meetings: Questions and Notes, 1867–1868," box 1, folder 15, RFP-RPI.

38. Arthur Conan Doyle, *The History of Spiritualism*, 2 vols. (London: Cassell, 1926); *New York Times*, December 27, 1872, quoted in Wagner, *Chief Engineer*, 148; WAR to Ferdinand, February 28, 1966, box 22, folder 14, RFP-RU. Charles J. Colchester also conducted séances for Mary Todd Lincoln and was ultimately exposed by Noah Brooks, a journalist friend of Abraham Lincoln, as a fake, a fraud, and a blackmailer. See Noah Brooks, *Washington in Lincoln's Time* (New York: Century, 1896), 64–66.

39. Moore, *In Search of White Crows*, 1–10; Jon Butler, *Awash in a Sea of Faith: Christianizing the American People* (Cambridge, MA: Harvard University Press, 1990), 225–56. Emerson made a similar point somewhat more succinctly in 1854 when he claimed "this age is Swedenborg's." See *The Journals and Miscellaneous Notebooks of Ralph Waldo Emerson*, ed. Ralph H. Orth and Alfred R. Ferguson, 16 vols. (Cambridge, MA: Harvard University Press, 1977), 13:335.

40. R. Laurence Moore, "Spiritualism and Science: Reflections on the First Decade of the Spirit Rappings," *American Quarterly*, 24, no. 4 (1972), 478.

41. JAR, "Spiritualism Meetings: Questions and Notes, 1867–1868," box 1, folder 15, RFP-RPI; Ferdinand Roebling to WAR, November 12, 1867, box 8, folder 52, RFP-RU.

42. Spiritualism also took root throughout the family as a result. Elvira was "mesmerized" by a doctor in Philadelphia as part of her treatment for a "nervous disorder" (along with various forms of the water cure), and John's seventh child, Charles, attended séances while at RPI in 1868, having a "pleasant & useful time." See Elvira Roebling to JAR, October 30, 1868, and Charles Roebling to JAR, December 7, 1868, both in SRL.

43. JAR, "Spiritualism Meetings: Questions and Notes, 1867–1868," box 1, folder 15, RFP-RPI.

44. Ibid.; April 17, 1858, vol. 9, TBG.

45. JAR, "Spiritualism Meetings: Questions and Notes, 1867–1868," box 1, folder 15, RFP-RPI.

46. Ibid.

47. Ibid.

48. See Henry R. Stiles, "Brooklyn Ferries and Ferry Rights," in *The Civil, Political, Professional and Ecclesiastical History, and Commercial and Industrial Record of the County of Kings and the City of Brooklyn, New York from 1683 to 1884*, ed. Henry R. Stiles, 2 vols. (New York: Munsell, 1884), 1:425–46; Brian J. Cudahy, *Over and Back: The History of Ferryboats in New York Harbor* (New York: Fordham University Press, 1990), 34–37.

49. Jeremiah Johnson quoted in Henry Stiles, *A History of the City of Brooklyn, Including the Old Town and Village of Brooklyn, the Town of Bushwick, and the Village and City of Williamsburgh*, 3 vols. (Bowie, MD: Heritage, 1993 (1867–70)), 2:383–84; *New-York Evening Post*, February 18, 1802, 2. On the history of proposals to bridge (or tunnel under) the East River see Richard Haw, "Bridging the East River: The History of an Idea, 1800–1867," *Long Island Historical Journal* 20, nos. 1–2 (2008), 83–110.

50. "February 1853, Miscellaneous Notes," box 7, notebook 124, RFP-RPI; Adams's plan was front-page news in the *New-York World*, May 2, 1864; "Blackwell's Island Proposal, 1856–1857," box 16, folder 4, RFP-RPI. The best source of information about John's various East River bridge proposals is Francis E. Griggs, Jr., "John A. Roebling and His East River Bridge Proposals, 1847–1869," in Green, *John A. Roebling*, 161–210.

51. Abram Hewitt to JAR, December 27, 1861, "JAR, Letters Received 1827–1869," box 2, folder 47, RFP-RU; *Journal of Commerce*, January 22, 1857, 2.

52. *Journal of Commerce*, January 22, 1857, 2.

53. *New-York Tribune*, March 27, 1857, 2; *Harper's Weekly*, April 4, 1857, 214.

54. "Bridging the East River," *Architects' and Mechanics' Journal*, March 31, 1860, 209; April 14, 1860, 11, 13–14. Portions of John's letter to the *Architects' and Mechanics' Journal* were reprinted four years later in the *Engineer*, the leading technical journal in the United Kingdom. See *Engineer*, February 19, 1864, 107.

55. Griggs, "John A. Roebling and His East River Bridge Proposals, 1847–1869," 182–87; *WRF*, 217; McCullough, *The Great Bridge*, 112–18. John received several enquiries iabout an East River bridge during the 1860s, from a variety of sources. "I have been urged by a number of influential citizens who are going to make strenuous efforts this season and are now at it to obtain a Charter for the building of a Suspension Bridge across the east river," wrote B. J. Gilmore of Hamilton Insurance (11 Wall Street) in 1865, "and they ask me to sollicite [*sic*] you the privilege of using your name and your plans in connection therewith." John's only comment was: "2 million too little. Reserve the right to double it." B. J. Gilmore to JAR, January 5, 1865, "JAR, Letters Received 1827–1869," box 3, folder 12, RFP-RU.

56. *Brooklyn Union*, January 26 and 27, 1867, both 2; "An Act to Incorporate the New York Bridge Company" (1867), in *New-York and Brooklyn Bridge: Proceedings, 1867–1884* (Brooklyn: n.p., 1884), 499–502; C. C. Martin to JAR, February 23, 1867, in SRL; McCullough, *The Great Bridge*, 120.

57. *Report of John A. Roebling, C.E., to the President and Directors of the New York Bridge Company, on the Proposed East River Bridge* (Brooklyn: Daily Eagle Print, 1867), 3–9. The most thorough examination of the design process is Robert M. Vogel, "Designing Brooklyn Bridge," in Latimer, Hindle, and Kranzberg, *Bridge to the Future*, 3–39.

58. Vogel, "Designing Brooklyn Bridge," 10–25. On the bridge's cultural significance see Trachtenberg, *Brooklyn Bridge*; Richard Haw, *The Brooklyn Bridge: A Cultural History* (New Brunswick, NJ: Rutgers University Press, 2005); Richard Haw, *Art of the Brooklyn Bridge: A Visual History* (New York: Routledge, 2008).

59. *Report of John A. Roebling, C.E., to the President and Directors of the New York Bridge Company, on the Proposed East River Bridge*, 20–41.

60. Ibid., 41–48.

61. *WRF*, 7, 165.

62. David P. Billington, *The Tower and the Bridge: The New Art of Structural Engineering* (Princeton, NJ: Princeton University Press, 1983), 78.

63. JAR, "Steubenville Railroad, 1854–5," box 38, folder 15, and "Steubenville Railroad Bridge, 1852–55," box 6, folder 29, both RFP-RPI.

64. "Girard Avenue Bridge, 1851," box 51, folder 2, RFP-RPI; "Bayardstown Bridge, 1851," box 51, folder 1, RFP-RPI.

65. Trachtenberg, *Brooklyn Bridge*, 81; *Report of John A. Roebling, Civil Engineer, to the President and Board of Directors of the Covington and Cincinnati Bridge*, 27.

66. *Report of John A. Roebling, Civil Engineer, to the President and Board of Directors of the Covington and Cincinnati Bridge*, 22, 26–29; *WRF*, 208; John Clubbe, *Cincinnati Observed: Architecture and History* (Columbus: Ohio State University Press, 1992), 174. Also see Billington, *The Tower and the Bridge*, 80–81.

67. Trachtenberg, *Brooklyn Bridge*, 77.

68. See Vladimir Mayakovsky, *My Discovery of America*, trans. Neil Cornwell (London: Hesperus, 2005), vii, xiii, 123–32; Henry James, *The American Scene*, ed. John F. Sears (New York: Penguin, 1994 (1907)), 59–61; Montgomery Schuyler, "Brooklyn Bridge as a Monument," *Harper's Weekly*, May 26, 1883, 326.

69. Schuyler, "Brooklyn Bridge as a Monument," 326; *Report of John A. Roebling, Civil Engineer, to the President and Board of Directors of the Covington and Cincinnati Bridge*, 64; Billington, *The Tower and the Bridge*, 82.

70. *Scientific American*, September 28, 1867, 201; *New York Times*, January 5, 1868, 5; William C. Kingsley to JAR, April 16, 1868, in box 3, folder 31, RFP-RU; *New York Times*, April 16, 1868, 4.

71. Tweed's testimony is contained in *Report of the Special Committee of the Board of Aldermen Appointed to Investigate the "Ring" Frauds* (New York: Martin Brown, 1878), as are myriad references to Ingersoll. Murphy confirmed much of what Tweed had said, although somewhat

obliquely and not directly, in an interview he gave the *Brooklyn Daily Eagle*, September 19, 1877, 2; WAR to William Couper, July 26, 1907, box 9, folder 36, RFP-RU.

72. Emily W. Roebling to JAR, January 6, 1868, in SRL. Laura gave birth to her first daughter, Laura, in 1864 and her second, Emily, in 1866.

73. John A. Roebling, *Long and Short Span Railway Bridges* (New York: D. Van Nostrand, 1869); JAR, *Report of John A. Roebling, Civil Engineer, to the President and Board of Directors of the Covington and Cincinnati Bridge Company*, 24.

74. "Mr. John A. Roebling, of Trenton, U.S., has proposed to the corporation of St. Louis, M.S., to carry a wire suspension of 2,600 ft. clear span, across the Mississippi River, the bridge being made to support a wide roadway." See *Engineer* (London), February 17, 1860, 109.

75. JAR, "St. Louis Bridge Proposal, 1867–1868," box 6, folder 28; JAR, "St. Louis Bridge," box 38, folder 13, both RFP-RPI; Eads quoted in the *Cincinnati Daily Commercial*, April 14, 1868, 2.

76. *Scientific American*, March 27, 1869, 201; *WRF*, 226–27.

77. *WRF*, 220, 226–27; *New York Times*, March 14, 1869, 2; *Brooklyn Daily Eagle*, June 25, 1869, 2.

78. *New York Times*, April 2, 1869, 2; *Brooklyn Daily Eagle*, April 9 and 17, 1869, 2.

79. *Brooklyn Daily Eagle*, April 9, 1869, 2.

80. *Brooklyn Daily Eagle*, April 19 and 20, 1869, both 2.

81. *Brooklyn Daily Eagle*, April 20, 1869, 2; *Cincinnati Daily Commercial*, April 18, 1869, 2.

82. *Brooklyn Daily Eagle*, April 26 and July 26, 1869, both 2; *Niagara Falls Gazette*, April 21, 1869, 2. Washington's own copy of the photograph identifies him as the man in the stovepipe hat in the front left, but this gentleman seems too old to be Washington and maybe even too formal and impractical. One doubts Washington would wear a stovepipe at any event, much less up high on a notoriously windy bridge.

83. WAR, "East River Bridge," box 22, item 85, RFP-RPI. Washington and Emily later moved to 110 Columbia Heights but initially lived on Hicks Street. See William H. Paine, "Diary, January—July 1869," WPP.

84. WAR to JAR, June 5, 1869, in SRL; A. A. Humphreys to Henry Murphy, June 21, 1869, in *New-York and Brooklyn Bridge: Proceedings, 1867–1884*, 511–12.

85. *Brooklyn Daily Eagle*, June 29 and 30, 1869, 2 and 3; WAR to Ferdinand Roebling, June 28, 1869, box 22, folder 27, RFP-RU; William H. Paine, "Diary, January—July 1869," WPP.

86. WAR to Ferdinand Roebling, June 28, 1869, box 22, folder 27, RFP-RU; William H. Paine, "Diary, January—July 1869," WPP; *Brooklyn Daily Eagle*, June 30, 1869, 3; *WRF*, 230.

87. *Brooklyn Daily Eagle*, June 30 and July 8, 1869, both 3.

88. *Brooklyn Daily Eagle*, July 17, 1869, 3. My understanding of John's last days is taken from William H. Paine, "Diary, January—July 1869," WPP and *WRF*, 231–32. Also see JAR, "Deathbed notes, July 1869," box 6, folder 24, RFP-RU.

Epilogue

1. *New York Times*, July 26, 1869, 8; *Brooklyn Daily Eagle*, July 26, 1869, 2; *Trenton State Gazette*, July 16, 1869, 3.

2. *Brooklyn Daily Eagle*, July 26, 1869, 2; *Trenton State Gazette*, July 16, 1869, 3. Elvira was the fourth of John and Johanna's children to be married. In addition to Laura and Washington, Ferdinand had married Margaret Allison on March 14, 1867.

3. *Brooklyn Daily Eagle*, July 26, 1869, 2; *Trenton State Gazette*, December 29, 1855, 3; *Trenton State Gazette*, July 16 and October 22, 1869, both 3; JAR, "Will," box 8, folder 33, RFP-RU. John's personal estate was eventually totaled at $1,194,246.40, meaning his charitable legacies totaled about 7.5 percent of the total. See "Inventory and Appraisal of Estate, 1869," box 8, folder 32, RFP-RU.

4. *Scientific American*, August 7, 1869, 89; *Brooklyn Daily Eagle*, July 22, 1869, 2; *Harper's Weekly*, August 7, 1869, 497–98; *Der Deutsche Pionier* 1, no. 7 (September 1869), 201; *Beecher's Magazine* 3, no. 14 (February 1871), 129; *American Phrenological Journal* 49, no. 10 (October 1869), 391.

5. Wagner, *Chief Engineer*, 171–218; *Report of John A. Roebling, Civil Engineer, to the President and Board of Directors of the Covington and Cincinnati Bridge*, 6; Joseph F. Gastright, "Wilhelm Hildenbrand and the 1895 Reconstruction of the Roebling Suspension Bridge," *Northern Kentucky Heritage* 8, no. 1 (2000), 1–14. All three actors in Roebling's anchorage problem—Buck, Collingwood, and Bouscaren—discussed the issue at a meeting of the American Society of Civil Engineers in 1893. See "Restoration of the Cable Ends of the Covington and Cincinnati Suspension Bridge: Discussion," 358–71.

6. "The Death of Mrs. Roebling," *New York Times*, December 30, 1884, 3.

7. Swan received twenty thousand dollars in John's will. By far the best source of information about John A. Roebling's Sons remains Zink and Hartman, *Spanning the Industrial Age*. See "Agreement with John A. Roebling's Sons, August 1869," box 30, folder 58, RFP-RU.

8. WAR to James Rusling, January 23, 1916, in SRL; Phillip D. Spiess II, "The Industrial Archeology of Cincinnati, Ohio: A Guide for S. I. A. Tourists" (1978), MS, CHL.

9. Rattermann, "Johann August Röbling: Berühmter Amerikanischer, Ingenieur und Brückenbauer," 425, 7; JAR, "Man. Conscience," March 28, 1863, box 5, folder 23, RFP-RU.

10. JAR, "Man. Conscience," March 28, 1863, box 5, folder 23, RFP-RU.

11. *WRF*, 209–10; Worthington, "John A. Roebling and the Cincinnati Bridge," 19.

INDEX